The Bar and Beverage Book

THIRD EDITION

The Bar and Beverage Book

Costas Katsigris

Mary Porter

Chris Thomas

John Wiley & Sons, Inc.

Library of Congress Cataloging-in-Publication Data:
Katsigris, Costas.
    The bar and beverage book / Costas Katsigris, Mary Porter, Chris
Thomas.—3rd ed.
        p. cm.
    ISBN 0-471-36246-8 (alk. paper)
1.   Bartending.   I. Porter, Mary. II. Thomas, Chris. III. Title.
    TX950.7 .K37 2002
    647.95'068—dc21

                                                                                2002000780

Printed in the United States of America.

10 9 8 7 6 5 4 3

Contents

A number of wine and liquor distributors were helpful in gathering details about the history of distilling, wine and beer making, and bartending. They include: Russ Kempton, Glazer's Distributors, Dallas, Texas, who enlightened us about single-malt scotches and tequila; Ron Gray, also of Glazer's, for introducing us to the wide variety of imported beers; and Anthony J. (Tony) LaBarba, Glazer's Fine Wines consultant, who offered many industry connections for background materials. Beat A. Kotoum, of Kobrand Corporation's Dallas office, shed light on the heady topic of ports; and Robert Schafer of Classical Wines of Spain proofread early drafts of the wine-related chapters for accuracy. Todd Giesler of Boise Consumer Co-Op's Wine Department in Boise, Idaho, and Idaho Wine Merchants, Inc., helped gather wine labels to illustrate those chapters.

Nancy Gordon, a food and wine writer and editor based in Boise, Idaho, proofread some chapters and conducted some of the interviews that became between-chapter profiles; "King of Cocktails" Dale DeGroff helped with the history of bartending and advice about bar equipment. Along with DeGroff, the other folks who willingly offered advice to students about their niche of the "business" not only were delightful but, as you'll read in their "profiles," gave extremely honest and informative advice. Many thanks to (in alphabetical order): Alexandro Garcia, Sharon Goldman, Julie Hansen, Crayne Horton, George Kidder, George Majdalani, F. Paul Pacult, and Joe Takata.

The Dallas, Texas, office of the Internal Revenue Service supplied us with current regulations affecting employment taxes; the U.S. Department of Labor's Wage and Hour Division provided current regulations on wage and hour regulations for hourly and exempt employees.

Putting all this information together into textbook form was no easy task, especially with authors who have other jobs! We relied on our editors at John Wiley & Sons, Inc., to keep us in line and on task: JoAnna Turtletaub, Julie Kerr, and Tzviya Siegman. They also rounded up many of the far-flung illustrations.

As with many textbooks, early drafts of the chapters were sent to a distinguished panel of reviewers at university hospitality departments for their criticisms and suggestions. Their input truly made *The Bar and Beverage Book* a better-focused and more useful text. They are: Tim Dodd, Texas Tech University; Fred T. Faria, Johnson & Wales University; and Larry Williams, Scottsdale Community College.

Special thanks to Costas "Gus" Katsigris's colleagues at El Centro Community College: Cynthia Bozzelli-Duke, FHSV Computer Lab coordinator, and her associate Mark Moore, who patiently introduced Gus to the wonders of computers and enabled him to rewrite the drafts for this text on a personal computer. Many thanks also to Evelyn C. Katsigris, Gus's wife, who cheerfully accepted late meals, missed appointments, and unmet deadlines as Gus struggled with this rewrite.

Chris thanks Steve Zollman, her partner, whose days in the "Let 'Er Buck" room at the Pendleton Round-Up, Pendleton, Oregon, have provided, well,

Acknowledgments

In this, the third edition of *The Bar and Beverage Book*, we again relied on the contributions of many individuals and organizations in the hospitality, beverage, and associated industries. Their advice was invaluable as we updated information about social drinking patterns and changing tastes, legal matters, as well as style changes for décor and fixtures, new equipment, and business practices. We received assistance from many, and are especially grateful to the following:

Todd Brachman, Perlick Corporation, Milwaukee, Wisconsin, provided a wealth of information about draft beer systems and other components that make up the working side of the bar. Bar-King/Supreme Metal Fabricators, Inc., of Alpharetta, Georgia, supplied excellent information on underbar equipment. Bar-Maid Corporation, Garfield, New Jersey, offered information on motorized glass brushes; and Manitowoc, Inc., of Manitowoc, Wisconsin, provided all the "cold, hard facts" about icemakers. Cole-Palmer Instrument Company of Vernon Hills, Illinois, helped with operation and use of hydrometers, and their application in measuring proof of alcohol.

The Ben E. Keith Beer Company of Fort Worth, Texas, offered expertise on proper glassware and pouring techniques for the perfect draft beer, and about responsible alcohol service. We are indebted to Pat Reynolds and Beth Lawless-Pruitt. The Greater Dallas Council on Alcohol and Drug Abuse, Dallas, Texas, added more information about responsible alcohol service and consumption.

Douglas Holtz from Glasstender, Inc., of Saginaw, Michigan, provided sketches of bar layouts; and the Eagle Group of Clayton, Delaware, shared the latest storeroom shelving information. Ron Scirocco of the Gasser Chair Company, of Youngstown, Ohio, helped us examine the barstool and drew its "anatomy" for us.

The National Restaurant Association and Deloitte & Touche allowed us to use their Restaurant Industry Operations Reports to gather up-to-date budgeting data for typical restaurant operations.

Berg Company, of Madison, Wisconsin, assisted us with information on liquor control systems. Beverly T. Thomas, an inspector with the Dallas office of the U.S. Bureau of Alcohol, Tobacco, and Firearms, provided information about control states and other federal spirits laws.

you might call it research, into the whole reason behind the booming bar and beverage industry: The point is, even with a book to put out and deadlines looming . . . it's supposed to be fun.

Costas "Gus" Katsigris
Chris Thomas

CHAPTER 1

The Beverage Industry: Past and Present

The drinking of alcoholic beverages is as old as human history, and the serving of drinks for profit is as old as the concept of profit itself. In most cultures over the centuries, these beverages have been accepted as an essential part of everyday life. And yet, they also possess a magic that can sometimes take the edge off human troubles or add a special dimension to a ceremony or celebration. There has always been a dark side to alcoholic beverages, too, and that is something we will examine closely in coming chapters. The purpose of this chapter, however, is to offer a quick look at the past and the present, the good and the bad. It provides you the important background to understand the challenges the bar and beverage industry faces today.

This chapter should help you . . .

- Learn the historical importance of alcohol in religious rites, ceremonies and medical treatment; in meals, in fellowship, and in humankind's search for wisdom and truth.
- Learn about how wine, beer, and distilled spirits were created.
- Trace the history of the tavern in Europe and America and recount the role that taverns played in the American Revolution.
- Examine the impact of Prohibition on the bar industry.
- Compare and contrast types of businesses that make up today's beverage service industry.

In the last century, in the United States alone, the bar and beverage business has gone from an illegal enterprise, carried on behind the locked doors of a **speakeasy,** to one of the nation's most glamorous and profitable businesses. Together with the food service or restaurant business, the two form the country's fourth-largest industry. In fact, it is impossible to separate them.

In the 1930s, the United States was nearing the end of **Prohibition,** an unsuccessful attempt to regulate alcohol consumption by outlawing it entirely. History tells us such attempts have never worked, because people find other ways to get what they want. And from earliest times, human beings seem to have wanted alcoholic beverages. Indeed, some historians theorize that one of the reasons our nomadic forebears settled into civilized life was to raise grain and grapes to ensure supplies of what they looked upon as sacred beverages.

THE EARLIEST WINES

Perhaps 8,000 to 10,000 years ago, someone discovered that fermented fruit or grain or milk or rice tasted good, made one happy, or both. The Bible mentions wine consumption in both Old and New Testaments. When Noah settled down after the flood, he planted a vineyard ". . . and he drank of the wine and was drunken." With all its benefits and hazards, alcohol was a universal feature of early civilizations.

At least one legend claims that wine was discovered accidentally, by a neglected member of a Persian king's harem. She attempted to end her loneliness by ending her life, drinking from a jar marked "Poison." It contained grapes that had fermented. She felt so much better after drinking the liquid that she gave a cup of it to the king, who named it "the delightful poison" and welcomed her back into active harem life.

Early peoples all over the world fermented anything that would ferment— honey, grapes, grains, dates, rice, sugarcane, milk, palms, peppers, berries, sesame seeds, pomegranates. We know that grapes were cultivated as early as 6000 B.C., both in the Middle East and Asia. The Egyptians, Phoenicians, and Chinese were tending their vines at about the same time. It is believed that the ancient Greeks got their *viticulture* knowledge from the Egyptians, beginning to make wine about 2000 B.C.

The practice of aging wines was first discovered by the Greeks, in cylinders known as **amphora.** Made of clay, they were remarkably airtight. Fifteen hundred years later, the Romans tried a similar method, but their clay was more porous and didn't work as well. So they began coating their clay vessels with tar on the insides, a process known as **pitching.** Yes, it prevented air from mixing with wine, but can you imagine what the addition of tar must have done to the quality of the wine?

By 1000 B.C., grapevines were found in Sicily and Northern Africa. Within the next 500 years, they reached the Iberian Peninsula, Southern France, and even Southern Russia. Conquering Saracen (Arab) tribes in the Middle Ages brought both winemaking and distillation skills with them. In fact, the words "alcohol" and "still" are Arabic in origin.

As the Roman Empire spread, it brought grapes to Northern Europe, too. After the fall of the Roman Empire, the Catholic Church was the most prominent promoter of viticulture. Monasteries became the vanguards of wine production and knowledge, because wine was needed both in everyday life and in sacramental activities. The Portuguese are credited with shipping the first corked bottles of wine to England, but not until the year 1780.

In many cultures, people associated intoxicating beverages with wisdom. Early Persians discussed all matters of importance twice—once when they were sober and once when they were drunk.[1] Saxons in ancient England opened their council meetings by passing around a large, stone mug of beer. Greeks held their famous symposiums—philosophical discussions—during hours of after-dinner drinking. In fact, the word "symposium" means "drinking together." As the Roman historian Pliny summed it up, *In vino veritas* ("in wine there is truth").

Alcoholic beverages, often in combination with herbs, have been used for centuries as medicines and tonics. Indeed, herbs and alcohol were among the few ways of treating or preventing disease until about a century ago. But probably the most important historic use of alcoholic beverages was also the simplest: as food and drink. Bread and ale, or bread and wine, were the staples of any meal for an ordinary person, with the drink considered food. For centuries, these hearty beverages provided up to half the calories needed for a day's heavy labor. And they were considered the only liquids fit to drink, with good reason. Household water was commonly polluted. Milk could cause "milk sickness" (tuberculosis). But beer, ale, and wine were disease-free, tasty, and thirst-quenching, crucial qualities in societies that preserved food with salt, and washed it down a diet of starches.

Both wines and grapevines were imported from France to the New World in the 1700s. As U.S. Minister to France, Thomas Jefferson was one of the primary supporters of the fledgling winemaking industry, and tried (passionately but unsuccessfully) to grow his own grapes at Monticello. By the early 1900s, there were about 1,700 wineries dotting the United States, mostly small, family-owned businesses.

Wine was still considered an effete beverage until the 1800s, when Italian immigrants came to the United States with their home winemaking skills and a hospitable culture that accepted wine as a simple, everyday part of mealtimes and celebrations. Many of today's best-known California winemakers, with names like Gallo and Mondavi, are descendants of these immigrant families.

---

[1]This is soberly reported by the Greek historian Herodotus in *Persian Wars,* Book 1, Chapter 133.

WINE AND RELIGION

Early beers, ales, and wines were considered gifts from the gods, that is, miracle products with magical powers. People used them universally in religious rites, and they still do. The Israelites of the Old Testament offered libations to Jehovah. Greeks and Romans honored **Bacchus,** god of wine (see Figure 1.1). Christians used wine in the sacrament of communion. Primitive peoples used fermented beverages in their sacred rites.

Victories, weddings, and other sacred and joyous occasions were celebrated with "mellow wine" or endless supplies of ale (the word "bridal" comes from bride + ale). Camaraderie and fellowship were acknowledged with a "loving cup," passed around the table and shared by all until it was emptied.

Of all alcoholic beverages, wine has the greatest religious connection. In the book *Religion and Wine: A Cultural History of Wine-Drinking in the United States* (1996, University of Tennessee Press), the author, Robert Fuller, traces the development of winemaking from the French Huguenots, Protestants who settled along the East Coast of North America in the 1500s, to the Pilgrims in Plymouth Bay in the 1600s to the Franciscan friars and Jesuit priests who built the early missions in California during the 1700s and 1800s.

Whether these early Americans were Baptists, Methodists, or Mormons, they permitted and enjoyed limited wine consumption as part of their worship. According to Fuller, the United States did not have "grape-juice Protestants" (who decried the alcohol content of wine and replaced it in ceremonies with grape juice) until the late eighteenth century. Interestingly, this alternative was first developed by Thomas Welch, a dentist and Methodist minister. His name later became a famous trademark for juice products.

At that time, attitudes about alcohol changed as some religious groups (Fuller calls them "ascetic Christians") began to espouse the theory that the road to heaven required total self-discipline, including the denial of all earthly pleasures. It was feared by some that consuming alcohol would weaken sensibility, ethics, and moral values, and diminish self-control in an age where many churches sought greater control over their members.

On the other hand, some religious groups felt equally strongly that rituals using wine could mediate God's presence and foster greater enjoyment of what life had to offer. These included Roman Catholics, Eastern Orthodox, Episcopalians, and Lutherans. And so the rift widened.

Figure 1.1 Bacchus, the Greek and Roman god of wine. Photo courtesy of the Picture Collection, The Branch Libraries, The New York Public Library.

Since the 1800s, the relationship between alcohol and religion has been the subject of debate and ambivalence. As recently as 1990, California wine-maker Robert Mondavi designed a new label for his wines, to include a paragraph extolling the beverage's longtime role in culture and religion. In part, it read, "Wine has been with us since the beginning of civilization. It is a temperate, civilized, sacred, romantic mealtime beverage recommended in the Bible . . ." Mondavi was prohibited from using this wording by the U.S. Bureau of Alcohol, Tobacco and Firearms.

A BRIEF HISTORY OF BEER

As far back as 6000 B.C., Babylonian scribes included beer recipes in their writings, and the ancient Egyptians made note of Ramses III, the pharaoh whose annual sacrifice of about 30,000 gallons of beer appeased "thirsty gods." Before 1850, the beverage preference in the United States was **ale,** which had been popular in England. It was made like beer, but fermented more quickly, at higher temperatures than beer.

The word "beer" comes from the ancient Latin word "biber," a slang term for the beverage made by fermenting grain, with hops for flavoring. Back then, biber was considered lower-class compared to ale, which was made in similar fashion but without the addition of hops.

Just about every civilization has made some type of beer, from whatever grain or root or plant was available in abundance. African tribes made their beer from millet; in Japan, it was rice; in Europe, North and South America, the chief ingredient was barley. The brew was hearty, filling, and provided calories and nutrients to fuel manual labor. The significance of beer in the average person's diet was demonstrated at the landing of the Mayflower at Plymouth, in what is now Massachusetts. The Pilgrims were headed for Virginia, but the ship was running out of beer. So they were "hasted ashore and made to drink water that the seamen might have more beer," wrote Governor Bradford later.

Beer production and sales played colorful parts of U.S. history. The first American brewery was opened in Lower Manhattan by the Dutch West Indies Company in 1632. There is speculation that the crude streets of New Amsterdam (later, New York City) were first paved to help the horse-drawn beer wagons make better progress, since they were so often stuck in the mud!

Brewing became an aristocratic and popular business. William Penn, the Quaker leader who founded the state of Pennsylvania, Revolutionary War leaders Samuel Adams and Ethan Allen, and even George Washington, all were brewery owners. (Adams is credited with suggesting to Washington that he supply the Revolutionary Army with two quarts of beer per soldier, per day.)

By the mid-nineteenth century, brewing dynasties, that are still household names among today's beer-drinkers had begun in the United States. In

Detroit, Michigan, Bernard Stroh, from a beer-making family in Rhineland, Germany, opened his brewing company in 1850. Five years later, Frederick Miller purchased an existing facility, Best's Brewery in Milwaukee, Wisconsin. In St. Louis, Eberhard Anheuser purchased a struggling brewery in 1860. His daughter married Adolphus Busch, a German immigrant whose family supplied grains and hops, and the mighty Anheuser-Busch Company was born. A dozen years later, another German immigrant from the Rhineland, Adolph Coors, started to brew beer in Colorado.

The Germans brought with them a different brewing style that produced a lighter beer known as **lager,** which is more pale and clear in appearance than ale and has a drier flavor. Its name comes from a German word for "storage" or "storehouse," since it was routinely stored for several months in cold temperatures before serving. Making lager-style beer required ice, so it was typically brewed in winter and stored until summer, when the demand was highest. Milwaukee emerged as the nation's brewing center for the most practical reason: ice was easily available from Lake Michigan, and there were plenty of local caves to store the beer. When refrigerators and icemakers were invented, lager could be brewed anytime, anyplace.

Heat was just as important as cold to the fast-growing beer-making industry. The French chemist Louis Pasteur discovered in the 1800s that, like milk or cider, beer could be heated to sufficient temperature to kill harmful bacteria without diminishing the quality of the brew. This process of *pasteurization* allowed beer to be bottled for shipment.

DISTILLED SPIRITS IN BRIEF

The art of **distillation**—first heating, then cooling and condensing liquids to extract and concentrate their alcohol content—was known in crude form even in ancient times. The Chinese and peoples of the East Indies distilled liquids and used the resulting potions for medicinal purposes as early as 800 B.C.

About the time the Pilgrims ran out of beer at Plymouth Rock, these forms of concentrated alcohol were coming into favor in Europe. **Distilled spirits** made from fermented liquids were many times more potent than the original liquids. The first ones were called *aqua vitae* (water of life) and were used as medicines, but they were quickly assimilated into society as beverages.

Highland Scots and Irish distillers made whiskey. The French distilled wine to make brandy. A Dutch doctor's experiments produced gin, alcohol flavored with the juniper berry. In Russia and Poland, the distilled spirit was vodka. In the West Indies, rum was made from sugarcane, while in Mexico, Spaniards distilled the Indians' native drink to make mescal, the great-granddaddy of today's tequila.

With increasing supplies of spirits and their high alcohol content, excessive drinking became a national problem in several European countries. In England, cheap gin became the drink of the poor. They could—and did—

get "drunk for a penny, dead drunk for twopence," as one gin mill advertised. This particular mill, in the same advertisement, mentioned that it also provided "free straw" (a bed of hay) for sleeping it off.

Across the Atlantic, Americans welcomed the new spirits, and it wasn't long before rum became the most popular drink and New England became a leading manufacturer. George Washington put rum to political use when he ran for the Virginia legislature, giving each voter a barrel of rum, beer, wine, or hard cider. By the end of the century, whiskey was challenging rum in popularity. Washington was once again a forerunner, making his own rye from his own grain in his own stills.

However, in 1791, the new U.S. Congress enacted the first tax on whiskey production. Many of the distillers, still trying to recover financially from the Revolutionary War, did not have much money and refused to pay the taxes. By 1794, President Washington had a real problem on his hands. He mustered 12,000 troops and marched into Pennsylvania to avert the so-called Whiskey Rebellion. It ended without a shot being fired, but many angry distillers packed up and moved further west to enjoy greater freedom and avoid future confrontations. In fact, relocation to the limestone soils of Tennessee and Kentucky led some of these early distillers to a real gold mine: the cold, clear water supplies of these areas, which are still famous for their whiskey production. The spirit soon became known as "bourbon," since some of the first distillers set up shop in Bourbon County, Kentucky. As the American West was settled, whiskey—easier to store and transport than beer or wine, and much in demand—became a very popular commodity in the trade-and-barter commerce of frontier life.

Distillation gained momentum as the process was refined. **Rectification** (described more fully in Chapter 5), or distilling a liquid more than once, yielded a much cleaner and almost 100 percent pure spirits than previous efforts. Before rectification was perfected, spirits contained flavor impurities. Herbs, honey and/or flowers were added to mask them. After rectification, these items were also routinely added, but now, to enhance the flavor. Some of today's grand liqueurs are the results of these early flavor concoctions. Cognac, for instance, was a pale, acidic French wine for which there was little public demand . . . until it was concentrated in the 1600s as an *eau de vie*, French for *aqua vitae*. It became enormously popular, and still is today.

THE TAVERN: PLEASURES AND POLITICS

Pouring for profit developed hand in hand with civilization. The clay tablets of the Old Babylonian King Hammurabi refer to alehouses and high-priced, watered-down beer. A papyrus from ancient Egypt warns, "Do not get drunk in the taverns . . . for fear that people repeat words which may have gone out of your mouth without you being aware of having uttered them." Greek and Roman cities had taverns that served food as well as drink; excavations in Pompeii (a Roman city of 20,000) have uncovered the remains of 118 bars. In both Greece and Rome, some taverns offered lodging for the night, or gambling and other amusements.

After the fall of the Roman Empire, life in most of Europe became much more primitive. When next the taverns reappeared, they were alehouses along the trade routes, with a stable for the horses, a place to sleep, and sometimes a meal. In England the public house, or *pub*, developed during Saxon times as a place where people gathered for fellowship and pleasure. An evergreen bush on a pole outside meant ale was served. Each pub was identified by a sign with a picture—a Black Horse, White Swan, or Red Lion, for instance. These early "logos" were used because most people could not read.

As time went on, the tavern became a permanent institution all over Europe. There were many versions: inns, pubs, cabarets, dance halls, meeting places. Neighbors gathered at these establishments to exchange the latest news and gossip over a mug or a tankard. In cities, men of similar interests met for a round of drinks and good talk. In London's Mermaid Tavern Shakespeare, dramatist and poet Ben Jonson and other famous literary figures met regularly. Lawyers had their favorite taverns, students theirs. Members of Parliament formed political clubs, each meeting in its favorite tavern for lively discussion of strategy.

Whatever its form, the tavern was a place to enjoy life, to socialize, to exchange ideas, to be stimulated. The beverages intensified the pleasure, loosened the tongue, sparked the wit or, as Socrates once put it, "moistened the soul."

When Europeans immigrated to America, they brought the tavern with them. It was considered essential to a town's welfare to have a place providing drink, lodging, and food. In Massachusetts in the 1650s, any town without a tavern was fined! Often the tavern was built near the church so that parishioners could warm up quickly after Sunday services held in unheated meetinghouses. A new town sometimes built its tavern before its church.

As towns grew into cities, and roads were built connecting them, taverns followed the roads. In parts of Pennsylvania today, it is possible to find towns named for such early taverns—Blue Bell, Red Lion, King of Prussia. In some towns, the old tavern is still standing.

It was in the taverns that the spirit of revolution was born, fed, and translated into action. These were the rendezvous spots for rebels, where groups like the Sons of Liberty were formed and held their meetings. The Boston Tea Party was planned in Hancock Tavern, while in the Green Dragon, Paul Revere and 30 companions formed a committee to watch the movements of the British Soldiers. In Williamsburg, the Raleigh Tavern was the meeting place of the Virginia patriots, including Patrick Henry and Thomas Jefferson.

In New York's Queen's Head Tavern, a New York Tea Party was planned, and many patriot meetings were held there during the war. After the war, its owner, Samuel Fraunces, renamed it Fraunces Tavern (to shed any reference to the Queen). It was here that General George Washington said good-bye to his fellow officers in 1783. When Washington became President, Fraunces became his chief steward. Today, Fraunces Tavern is a New York City landmark.

When Americans pushed westward, taverns sprang up along the routes west. As towns appeared, the tavern was often the first building. Homes and merchants grew up around it. By the middle 1800s, the "modern" American tavern was becoming a large-scale inn for the travelers and businesspeople of a nation on the move. At the same time, drinking places without lodging were appearing. These kept the name "tavern," while the more elaborate inns adopted the term "hotel." But the hotel kept its barroom; it was often a show-place, with a handsome mahogany bar and a well-dressed bartender who might wear gold and diamonds. Certain hotel bars became famous—the Menger in San Antonio where Teddy Roosevelt recruited Rough Riders, and Planter's Hotel in St. Louis, home of the Planter's Punch.

By the turn of the century, the successors of the early taverns had taken many forms. There were glittering hotels that served the wealthy in cities and resorts. There were fashionable cabarets, such as Maxim's in Paris, where rich and famous men consorted with rich and famous courtesans, and music halls, such as the Folies Bergères. There were private clubs, cafés ranging from elegant to seedy, big-city saloons that provided free lunches with their drinks, and the corner saloons of working-class districts, where many a man drowned his sorrows in drink (see Figure 1.2). The restaurant industry also made its appearance in the nineteenth century, serving wines and other beverages to enhance the diner's pleasure.

Figure 1.2 The Tascosabar in Tascosa, Texas, circa 1908. Photo courtesy of the Library of Congress.

PROHIBITION AND ITS EFFECTS

Meanwhile, in the United States a growing number of people sought to curb the use of alcoholic beverages. At first this movement went by the name **Temperance** and its target was "ardent spirits" (distilled spirits). But its proponents soon included beer and wine and expanded their goal from temperance, or moderation, to total prohibition. In a century-long barrage of propaganda and moral fervor, the movement succeeded in convincing many Americans that drink of any kind led inevitably to sin and damnation. If you outlaw "Demon Rum," they believed, sin would disappear and Utopia would naturally emerge. Along with this belief went the notion that those engaged in making or selling alcoholic beverages were on the devil's side of this battle between Good and Evil or, as it was also dubbed, **"Dry"** and **"Wet."**

The fervor was fed by the proliferation of saloons opened by competing breweries to push their products, many of them financed by money from abroad. By the late 1800s, there was a swinging-door saloon on every corner of small-town America, as well as in the cities. These establishments often became unsavory places, because there were far too many of them to survive on sales of beer and whiskey alone, so many became places of prostitution, gambling, and other illegal goings-on.

The Prohibition movement was also an expression of religious and ethnic antagonisms, of fundamentalist middle Americans against the new German and Irish Catholic immigrants. The brewers were German and the bartenders were Irish, and both brought with them cultures that included alcohol intake as a fact of everyday life. The movement also pitted small-town and rural America against what was perceived as big-city licentiousness.

During World War I, the Dry side won its battle. The **Eighteenth Amendment,** passed during the wartime fever of patriotism and self-denial, prohibited the "manufacture, sale, transportation, and importation of intoxicating liquors" in the United States and its territories. Ratified by all but two states, Connecticut and Rhode Island, it went into effect in 1920.

Prohibition had a short and unhappy life—not quite 14 years. There was simply no way to enforce it. While legal establishments were closing their doors, illegal "speakeasies" began opening theirs to those who could whisper the right password. Legal breweries and distilleries closed down, but illegal stills made liquor by the light of the moon in secret hideouts—hence, the nickname **moonshine.** Illegal spirits also were smuggled into the country from Canada and Mexico and from "Rum Rows" offshore, bootleg supply ships that sold to small, fast boats whose entrepreneurial captains made the run to shore. Some folks just decided to make their own beer, wine, and gin at home.

Prohibition impacted the wine industry as dramatically as it did other alcoholic beverage producers. Many winery owners simply plowed their fields under and planted different crops. A few received special license to make sacramental wines, or permits to make wines strictly for home use, only up to 200 gallons per year.

Ironically, rather than decreasing drinking, Prohibition seemed almost to invite it: flouting the law became, to some, the fashionable (or, at least, enterprising) thing to do. After nine years of Prohibition, New York City had 32,000 speakeasies, about twice as many as the number of pre-Prohibition saloons! To add to the problems of enforcement, organized crime took over the bootleg business in many cities. Gangsters quickly became rich, powerful, and seemingly immune to the law. The combination of racketeering, gang warfare, and bootlegging became a major national problem. Everyone—even those who first vehemently supported it—agreed that things had gotten out of hand under Prohibition. In 1933, Congress passed the **Twenty-first Amendment,** repealing the Eighteenth.

Before Prohibition shut it down, the beverage manufacturing industry had been the fifth largest in the country. After passage of the Twenty-first Amendment, it made a quick comeback, despite stiff taxes and heavy regulation by federal and state governments. Today, alcoholic beverages are an accepted part of the American scene, and have been for some time; the sale of liquor is legal in every state and the District of Columbia. The serving of liquor in bars and restaurants is a normal part of the culture, and restaurant patrons expect to be able to buy mixed drinks, beer, and wine with their food. In fact, restaurants that don't serve liquor often have a hard time competing. But the Wet versus Dry controversy never really ended. Control of the issue was given to states, counties, towns, and precincts, resulting in a mishmash of local liquor laws that has made America into a wet-dry checkerboard. Even today, this pattern mirrors our society's longstanding mixed feelings about alcohol use.

Historically, alcohol has always had its dark side as well as its benefits, from the drunkenness in the taverns of ancient Egypt to the cheap gin consumed by the poor in eighteenth-century England to the corner saloons of small-town America 100 years ago. Today, the problems are just as critical, with drunk-driving accidents taking thousands of lives each year and some 10 percent of drinkers becoming alcohol-addicted. What is it about alcohol that can "moisten the soul," yet cause so much harm? That's what we will discuss at length in Chapter 2.

TODAY'S BEVERAGE-SERVICE INDUSTRY

Since 1990, there has been a gradual decline in alcohol consumption in all its forms—beer, wine, and spirits. Expert observers relate the drop to a change in lifestyle for many busy Americans, many of whom turned their focus on health, fitness, and job success. These people have stopped smoking, they exercise, they watch their weight and their cholesterol count, and they keep their heads clear during working hours. The "three-Martini lunch" is now a rarity, replaced by bottled waters or fruit juice or sometimes a single glass of wine. These people are moderate drinkers, limiting their consumption to the one or two drinks a day. At the same time, they are very much interested in the quality of whatever drink they choose. When they do imbibe, they tend to choose premium or superpremium liquors and wines. "Drinking less but drinking better" has become the norm.

What People Are Drinking

The health-and-fitness enthusiast is looking for lighter drinks, those perceived to have less alcohol and fewer calories. (Some of them do and some of them don't, as we shall see). Sales of spirits (high in alcohol and calories) continue to decline. "White goods" (vodka, gin, tequila, and rum) generally do better than "brown goods" (bourbon, scotch, and other whiskies) even though they all have similar alcohol contents. But according to *Beverage Digest* magazine, which tracks U.S. beverage consumption figures, Americans drank the highest amount of distilled spirits—two gallons per person, per year—back in the 1970s. Today's consumption figures are more like 1.2 or 1.3 gallons per person, per year, and have been since 1993.

Wine enjoyed its largest upsurge in popularity in the 1980s, reaching a high of 2.4 gallons per person, per year. Wine is still popular and boasts a loyal following of hobbyists and collectors, but overall consumption has leveled off at about 2 gallons per person, per year. Despite jam-packed supermarket wine section shelves and all kinds of exotic choices, the three best sellers continue to be Chardonnay, Cabernet Sauvignon, and White Zinfandel.

Beer sales look mighty impressive when compared to wine and spirits! For the last decade (also according *to Beverage Digest*) Americans have consumed more than 22 gallons of beer per person, per year. Trends during this time include the so-called light beers, which are lower in alcohol and calories than their "regular" counterparts; dry beers (crisply flavored, and touting "no aftertaste"); and nonalcoholic beers, with about two dozen brands on the market in the early 1990s. Light beers now account for about 40 percent of all beer sales in the United States.

Imported beers and beers from small, regional breweries (microbreweries) have gained substantial followings, and there's a small but lively home-brewing hobbyist market. In most major cities, you'll find at least one beer-making store where home brewers can buy equipment and supplies and get advice. For a fee, some allow you to brew on-site, let the beer age in their storage tanks, then come back and bottle your own creation yourself!

Smart restaurateurs now offer wines by the glass in addition to wines by the bottle, realizing that today's diners may not want to order a full bottle. (In Chapter 7, you'll learn more about creating a workable wine list.) Customers may also ask for a nonalcoholic drink. Offerings include mineral waters, nonalcoholic beers, soft drinks, juice drinks, and even no-alcohol mixed drinks. Some bars have invented "mocktails," alcohol-free versions of the Bloody Mary, Piña Colada, and others, mixed and served with the same care and flair as their house specialties.

This does not mean that Martinis or Gin and Tonics are obsolete, or that fewer people are patronizing bars or ordering drinks with their meals. There has been renewed interest in the traditional cocktails (Martini, Bloody Mary, Screwdriver) and "tall drinks" (Scotch and Soda or Bourbon and Soda, Gina and Tonic or Vodka and Tonic). There is also strong interest in **call brands,** the slang term for premium brands that are asked for—or, "called for"—by name. Superpremium imports, like single-malt scotches, Irish whiskeys, Cognac and Armagnac brandies, also have loyal followings. They are popular with customers who have developed a taste for and interest in "buying the best," and are willing to pay more for it. They are also interested in experimenting—trying new brands and learning more about beverages. By contrast, most brown goods customers are in the upper-age groups and are comfortable with their reliable favorites, such as Scotch and Soda or Bourbon and Water.

But be wary. By the time you read this it all may have changed! New drinks will be invented, new twists added to old favorites. Managing a bar means keeping your finger on the pulse of the market and making the changes necessary to stay ahead.

Let's look next at a few different types of beverage service. Though it is impossible to divide bars into just a few categories—there are almost as many variations as there are bars—certain kinds have distinct characteristics and styles of service, and it may be revealing to see how they differ and what they have in common.

The Beverage-Only Bar

The simplest kind of beverage enterprise is the bar that serves beverages alone, with no food service except snacks: peanuts, pretzels, cheese and crackers. This type of bar serves beer or wine or mixed drinks or any combination of the three, plus nonalcoholic beverages. It may be a neighborhood gathering place, a way station for commuters on their homeward treks, a bar at an airport or bus terminal or bowling alley.

Business at such bars typically has a predictable flow: a daily pattern of peaks and valleys, a weekly pattern of slow days and heavy days, with the heavy days related to paydays and days off. There may also be seasonal patterns. In airports and bus terminals, business is geared to daily, weekly, and seasonal travel patterns, and according to the time of day; light beverages are served mornings and afternoons, heartier drinks are ordered as the working day ends. Because only one type of product is sold, and because business is generally predictable, the operation of a beverage-only bar is relatively simple, from production to staffing and purchasing to keeping track of the beverages, money, and profits.

This type of bar also usually has a specific reason for success, perhaps its location, its reputation as a friendly place (or for pouring well-made drinks), or simply a lack of competition; maybe it has just "always been the place where everybody goes." Often such bars thrive by being the same as they always were. Customers become sentimental about them and would not tolerate change.

That said, as the mood of the country changes, many neighborhood bars are adding food to their offerings. Hotel chains such as Marriott, Radisson, and Hyatt have phased out their cocktail-only lounges in favor of food and beverage combinations. The decision is practical: some states do not allow beverage sales without food sales; other bar owners have decided it's simply more responsible to offer people food if they will be drinking. Master concessionaires, such as Host Marriott, now run more than 1,800 restaurants in 73 airports, and the trend has been to upgrade these facilities to pour more premium beverages, serve better food, partner with brewpubs, and offer entertainment for travelers awaiting their flights.

In short, beverage-only bars are definitely a minority today. Although some are highly profitable, most bars find that serving liquor alone is not enough to attract and keep customers. So the majority of bars offer something else—entertainment or food or both.

Bar/Entertainment Combinations

Bars offering entertainment range from the neighborhood bar with pool, pinball, dartboards, or giant TV screens to nightclubs with big-name entertainers and comedy clubs and ballrooms with big bands. In between are cocktail lounges and nightclubs with live entertainment—piano bars, country-and-western dancing, jazz or folk duos, or rousing rock-and-roll groups. This concept must include the decision to make room for a stage area, sound system, and dance floor. And having entertainment means hiring someone knowledgeable to book the bands or entertainers that people will want to see (negotiating contracts at a fair but affordable price) and always thinking ahead to the next fad or hottest music trend to attract the fickle public. A concept that includes regular entertainment of any kind also includes the fixed costs and additional financial risk of hiring and paying the entertainers.

In most cases, the entertainment may draw the crowd, but it is the drinks that provide the profits. If there is a **cover charge,** an admission fee per person paid at the door, at least part of it is likely to go to the entertainers. The fortunes of this type of bar will rise and fall with the popularity of its entertainers, unless the place has something else going for it.

Probably the most stable type of bar/entertainment combo is the smaller place with an attractive ambience, good drinks, and local entertainment to draw a loyal, local crowd. Its success potential is much the same as the bar-only enterprise. Larger operations featuring out-of-town entertainers have a higher but riskier profit potential. It is likely to be either feast or famine. The bar gears up for each crowd with temporary extra help, a large investment in liquor inventory, and possibly extra security personnel. Weather, holidays, location, and weeknight versus weekend crowds all heavily impact this type of business.

Casinos are another enduring combination of entertainment and beverage service. Today's casinos may be run by a huge corporation or a Native American tribal council, and may include everything from big-name stage productions and professional boxing matches to restaurants and nongambling arcades that attract families instead of adults only.

Sports bars offer a different type of entertainment. They center on the viewing of popular sporting events, such as Monday Night Football, or special events like hockey finals or the World Series. Equipped with large television screens (or plenty of smaller ones strategically placed), the sports bar often sets a fixed price or cover charge to guarantee a good profit because customer turnover is so small (see Figure 1.3). Large sports bars often serve

Figure 1.3 Some sports bars offer full-service dining. *Source:* Disney Regional Entertainment.

a menu of full-course meals, and many take reservations in advance of popular events like a professional boxing match or a Triple Crown horse race.

The **cigar bar** is another trendy addition to the beverage scene—and a profitable one, too. Men and an increasing number of women are enjoying high-priced cigars, and restaurateurs have seized the opportunity to recommend premium spirits, wines, beers, and after-dinner drinks to accompany them. The cigar boom is not legal in all venues, since smoking is prohibited in many public places by local ordinance. But the places that install heavy-duty fans and humidors and offer extensive cigar selections—plus single-malt Scotches, small-batch Bourbons, Cognacs and Ports—are filling an interesting, upscale niche. Sometimes, they are private clubs that charge membership fees.

Food and Beverage Combinations

The most common form of beverage operation is one that is linked with some kind of food service. One type is the restaurant/bar, where drinks and wine are part of the meal service, served by the same wait staff that serves the meal. The bar is often used as the waiting area for the restaurant during busy times. Drinks may be poured at a service bar out of public view or at a pickup station in a bar that serves customers while they are waiting for a table. The major portion of the sales comes from the food service. However, the beverage sales often turn the profit for the enterprise. The only added costs are for the wine and liquor, and the bartender and a minimum investment in equipment; the other necessities—service personnel and the facility itself—are built in to the restaurant operation.

Another type of food-beverage combination is the bar that offers light food in addition to drinks. In this case, the beverages and the bar atmosphere dominate, and the major sales volume comes from the bar. But the food is a nice sidelight that attracts customers and prolongs their stay. Typical menu items are appetizers: nachos, chips or crudités and dips, spiced chicken wings, stuffed potato skins.

A special variation of the food-beverage combination is the **wine bar,** which first appeared during the 1970s as Americans discovered and learned to appreciate wines. Here the customer can choose from a selection of wines by the glass or by the bottle, beginning with inexpensive house wines and going up in quality and price as far as the entrepreneur cares to go. Some wine bars offer inexpensive one-ounce "tastes" to allow guests to sample a number of wines. A full menu can be served, or fruit and cheese platters and upscale hors d'oeuvres.

There are inherent problems in running wine bars. The first is, of course, that serving only wine tends to limit the clientele to wine lovers. In some urban areas, there are enough wine enthusiasts to support a profitable enterprise; they respond to quality and expertise, and they attend and appreciate special tastings and classes and wine-centered celebrations. This enthusiasm, however, raises a second difficulty: purchasing appropriate wines requires an expertise few people have, and may require a financial investment few are willing to make.

As a result, many wine bars serve liquor and beer as well. This broadens their appeal and allows them to realize the necessary profit margin. In effect, they are simply bars that specialize in wine sales and wine knowledge. Other wine bars may broaden their offerings by serving meals, in effect becoming restaurants with an emphasis on wines. Some also sell wines at retail, offering customers discounts for volume (one case or more) purchases. This combination of on-premise service and take-home sales is not an option everywhere. Beverage laws in many areas do not allow it.

Beer aficionados also have their own version of the wine bar. At a **brewpub,** beer is brewed and served right on the premises—fresh, natural beers and ales, strong in flavor and aroma, with special seasonal offerings. Developed by small individual entrepreneurs and hobbyists, the beverage sets the theme of the restaurant. At least one shiny brew kettle is likely to be a major part of the décor, and the menu typically contains hearty, casual cuisine chosen to complement the beer. As popular as they are in many areas of the United States, brewpubs are not legal everywhere, as some states still do not allow manufacture and sale of alcoholic beverages on the same premises.

A popular type of food-beverage combination links a bar and a restaurant on an equal, semi-independent basis, with a common roof, theme, management team, and services that complement each other. The bar and restaurant areas are housed in separate portions of the building, and they may be open at slightly different hours to serve both the drop-in bar customer and the mealtime patron. The food/drink sales ratio is likely to reflect an equal status of food and drink, with bar and restaurant each doing better than it would without the other. In many cases, neither side could make a go of it alone, but together the customer attraction and income are doubled, while the overhead costs are split between them.

Hotel Beverage Operations

In hotels, the beverage operation differs in many ways from the bar or the bar-restaurant combination. There may be three or four bars under one roof, each with a different purpose and a different ambience—say a lobby bar, a cocktail lounge, a restaurant bar, a nightclub with dancing. In addition, there is room service, with a food menu that includes mixed drinks, beer, wine, and Champagne. Above all, there is banquet service, catering to conference, convention, and reception needs. Typically, the client makes beverage choices in advance of the event, which are served from portable bars by extra personnel hired for the occasion.

And in individual rooms, don't forget the **minibar.** Many hotels have installed them for the convenience of guests, an in-room refreshment center without the room service waiter. The minibar is really nothing more than a small refrigerator with an icemaker—although many have classy mock mahogany exterior cabinets—stocked with a small inventory of snacks and drinks. There are three keys to profitable minibar use, according to *Lodging* magazine. The unit must be installed so that it is easy to use and its contents are clearly visible, and a reliable system must be in place for prompt restocking of cabinets and correct billing of guests. Perhaps most important, customers must be enticed to somehow overlook the high prices of minibar goods! Its in-room convenience means the hotel can charge double, or even triple, what the same goods would cost elsewhere on the same property.

Food and Beverage Directors of large hotels say the minibar has become a necessary amenity, even though it could be argued that it does siphon some business away from the hotel's other food and beverage venues, especially room service. But overall, the minibar is not a major moneymaker for most hotels; and, interestingly, the most common minibar purchase is not alcohol of any kind, but bottled water.

Perhaps the most daunting challenge of hotel beverage service is its diversity, coupled with the up-and-down nature of demand. Since a hotel's primary clientele is its overnight guests, demand for beverages rises and falls according to the occupancy rate. This, too, is unpredictable: a hotel can be completely full for a convention and yet have very little bar trade, depending on the kind of convention it is hosting. On the other hand, a very low occupancy rate may net a lot of bar business. Again, it just depends on who the hotel guests are.

Resort and luxury hotels often have several bars and restaurants, with a variety of entertainment, food, and drink, to keep the hotel guests spending money on the premises, as well as to attract an outside clientele. On the other hand, a small commercial hotel in a big city may need only one bar with several stations to serve its lobby customers, its cocktail lounge, coffee shop, dining room, and room service.

Airline Beverage Service

Another type of beverage service that must adapt to special conditions is that on airline flights. The restrictions of space, time, weight, and equipment are formidable. (Cruise lines and passenger trains have similar storage limitations.) Of necessity, their drink menus are limited. Liquors, beers, wines, and a few types of cocktail mixes are handed out in small individual bottles or cans. The cups are nesting, plastic disposables, except in first and business class cabins. Flight attendants push a beverage cart down the aisle and, working from both ends, can garnish glasses and fill them with ice, pour beverages or hand out the individual-sized drink components, and collect the money. The process is a marvel of organization. Tight control systems follow the little bottles everywhere, since they are extraordinarily tempting to both airline employees and customers. For higher-paying passengers, drinks are free and service typically includes real glassware, a choice or wines, Champagne for breakfast, and sometimes specialty drinks.

Similarities and Differences

Grouping types of beverage service into these rather arbitrary categories does not really adequately describe the character of individual enterprises. Many establishments do not fit handily into a specific category, and those within categories can be as different as day and night.

Yet all categories have certain similarities. They all sell alcoholic beverages. They have similar staff structures, patterns of purchasing and inventory, and ways of controlling the merchandise. They all must meet certain government requirements and operate within certain government regulations. Even the prices charged for the same drinks are not wildly different from one type of place to another. Still, no two bar and beverage operations are alike, unless they are part of a chain. The successful business is one that meets the needs and desires of a certain clientele and strives to be deliberately different from others serving a similar clientele in order to stand out in the competition for customers. Other major reasons for the wide variety of bar operations are simple: the special circumstances of each operation and the personalities, desires, and budgets of their owners. But to be successful, the entrepreneur must put clientele above all else in shaping his or her enterprise.

SUMMING UP

Throughout history, alcoholic beverages have played an important role in most cultures. People drank them for many good reasons—for food and health, worship and celebration, pleasure and fellowship, wisdom and truth. As civilization developed, the inns, alehouses, and taverns were central to the growth of towns, travel, and the communication of ideas.

It was only in the past century that some began to question the propriety of alcohol use. They pointed to the problems associated with it: drunkenness and irresponsibility, illegal activity, and violent crime seemed to go hand in hand with alcohol abuse, along with decaying moral values that defied traditional religious beliefs. The pendulum of public opinion swung from acceptance to fear and disgust. First, the Temperance movement sought to shame people into giving up alcohol. Then came Prohibition, the passage of the Eighteenth Amendment to the U.S. Constitution that outlawed the manufacture and sale of alcohol except in certain, extremely limited circumstances. Prohibition lasted about 14 years (from 1920 to 1933) and created problems even more difficult to solve: a complex illegal network of bootleg home distillers, secret bars known as speakeasies, and organized crime's entrance into the lucrative business of selling people what they couldn't buy legally. Today's liquor laws still mirror some of the restrictions first created during Prohibition. Alcohol use is still controversial, but an attitude of moderation and responsibility has allowed the beverage industry to grow and flourish once again in the United States. Today's consumer is likely to drink less, but be interested in higher-quality products, even if they cost more. There are establishments that specialize in wine sales, brewing and selling beer, full-bar service, and a variety of food-and-drink combinations that often include some sort of entertainment. You can buy a drink on an airplane, in a hotel room, or in your favorite neighborhood restaurant.

POINTS TO PONDER

1. What were the most important uses of alcohol in ancient civilizations? How have things changed?

2. Why did some cultures associate alcohol use with wisdom?

3. What was the food value of alcohol in early cultures? And why did people drink alcohol when they had other beverage choices?

4. What is distillation?

5. How has alcohol been used as currency in past centuries? Give two examples.

6. Name one positive and one negative aspect of Prohibition. (Your own opinion can, and should, color your answer.)

7. What are the reasons most Americans are drinking less alcohol?

8. Why is a beverage-only bar not often seen anymore?

9. What would you have to find out before selling wines by the case in a wine bar or opening your own brewpub?

10. What are some of the challenges specific to hotel beverage service?

TERMS OF THE TRADE

ale

amphora

Bacchus

brewpub

call brands

cigar bar

cover charge

distillation

distilled spirits

Dry and Wet

Eighteenth Amendment

lager

minibar

moonshine

pitching

Prohibition

rectification

speakeasy

sports bar

Temperance

Twenty-first Amendment

wine bar

DALE DEGROFF
The King of Cocktails

Dale DeGroff came to New York City in the late 1960s. Like many aspiring actors, his first job was in the restaurant business—as a dishwasher at Howard Johnson's in Times Square. His next job, at an advertising agency, led him to work with an account called Restaurant Associates, restaurateur Joe Baum's innovative (and now-famous) group that included The Four Seasons, Charlie O's, Windows on the World, the Rainbow Room and many others.

"The ad agency team went to so many dinners and tastings with Joe," Dale recalls, "and I just fell in love with the bar business. I got my first bartending job at Charlie O's, and I was also a waiter there."

Today, Dale's résumé includes the top bars and hotels on both East and West coasts, and he is known worldwide as "The King of Cocktails." Dale has won numerous awards for his bartending skills and has been the subject of more than 40 magazine articles in the past year (2001). He writes monthly columns for Beverage Media, *BevAccess.com, and the U.K. edition of* Esquire; *he does product evaluation and menu consulting; and teaches seminars on bartending and beverage history.*

Q: What attracted you to bartending?
A: This group of advertising guys that I hung around with was so clever, so funny, so delightful, so intelligent; and their life was centered around bars. They'd have three-hour lunches, move their secretaries, forward their calls to the barroom at The Four Seasons! They worked from 6:00 A.M. to 7:00 P.M.; they worked hard and they were intense! I got to go to all these great places with them, and the life and energy of the bar just overwhelmed me.

The bartending, I think, is an offshoot of being a performer; and I was good at it. I felt right at home at the bar, and I just seemed to fit. But it took me about three years as a bartender to figure out I was doing everything wrong.

Q: How so?
A: Because the cocktail wasn't a significant part of any restaurant in the 1970s and early 1980s. That generation was drinking jug wines and smoking pot, and there was nobody moving in to fill the shoes of the older generation in the bar scene. We had one kind of single-stem glass, and every drink was made in that style of glass. The service, the flair was really on the downside; and most people in the bar business were there only until they could do something else.

Well, in that environment, I went to Joe Baum in 1986 with the idea of creating a classic 1930s supper-club cocktail menu for his new place, the Rainbow Room. It took a lot of research, but I did it and he hired me. Joe was very high-profile in the industry, and people paid attention to whatever he was doing. So as soon as I got behind that bar, it was a magnet for the press. And soon I saw these vintage drinks being prepared all over town. I was thrilled.

Q: What advice would you give to today's bar managers?
A: A good manager is just like a chef. When a dish goes out of a kitchen, there he [or she] is—he or [she] will test that sauce, look at that garnish, watch the portion size. There's got to be somebody doing the equivalent of that at the bar, and that should be the manager.

Of course you have to keep an eye on costs and portion control, but it is not necessary to always focus everything on the lowest common denominator. I see consultants who come in and suggest recipes and techniques simply because they are "bartender-proof," and that leaves no room for creativity.

If you want to grow your place in a positive direction—really try to achieve excellence in a cocktail—it's all about management's attitude toward that. If there's a manager in place who shares the enthusiasm of the bartenders, then that kind of cocktail program is possible. But it does involve a tremendous amount of training, monitoring, equipment, week-to-week maintenance of ingredients, fresh fruit, correct price points for the drinks, analysis of your audience. It's not impossible; it's just hard.

Q: What are some no-nonsense service tips you'd have for new bartenders and servers?
A: When I teach, I tell servers, "The contract is this. Those customers have rented their table for two-and-a-half or three hours. That's their property, like real estate. You need to be there when they need something, but believe me, you are an interloper. You need to get in and out; no hanging around unless they want you to. It's private property."

At the bar, the contract is totally different. It's not private property, it's public property; customers are sharing the space. And, unfortunately, a customer has the right to break the contract with unpleasantness or rudeness. So the bartender's job is to turn enemies into friends. As soon as you become rude or unpleasant back to them, you've ruined the space for all the other customers. Then nobody wants to be there.

You're an actor behind the bar, and that makes you many things to many people: a conversationalist to one guy, a good listener for another, a protector to a woman who's not happy about the advances she's getting from the guy on the next stool. It is a complex job, but it never seems to be approached that way.

I also tell bartenders, "You are going to make some mistakes if you're busy, or if you're new. It's your job to monitor what is happening at the bar. If someone hasn't touched their drink, walk over and ask, 'Is that drink a little too sweet or sour? I can fix that, no problem.'" That kind of attention is astonishing to a customer. Most people are used to bad bartenders. They will forgive a friendly bartender anything, just because he's friendly! There are so many of them who don't give you eye contact or the time of day.

Q: Are bars pressured by suppliers to use certain products?

A: Of course. But your attitude should always be, they work for you. You are providing a showcase for their products, so they should provide something for you, too, and that is support for your menus, tabletop, upcoming events. Ask them to help with your training program or print your menu for you. I want the distiller, when he [or she] comes to town, to visit my bar and talk with my staff. Everything they can provide me as a purveyor, I want. And when purveyors see your enthusiasm, they will rise to the occasion.

Q: How hard is it to deal with people who drink too much?

A: In New York we have it a little easier, because 95 percent of the people take cabs, so there's not the issue of drunk driving as in other places. But the business of withholding service to a guest is a big, big issue that bartenders need to learn. Nobody's ever happy about this issue, and they never will be. The key is to do it so you don't lose the person as a customer. I'll say, "Okay, come back tomorrow and you're welcome here. I like you too much, I wanna see you here tomorrow night." Or suggest they eat something, in a friendly way. If they feel the warmth—I call it "the embrace of the house"—they'll respond. If they don't feel it, there are a million other joints. They don't need to drink here.

Q: What are some of the marketing ideas you've used to boost business at your bars over the years?

A: I think it's very important in a restaurant environment to have a great working relationship with the chef. I've sat down with my chef, tasted things together, and created a combination menu of food and cocktails—we called them "cocktail dinners"—at the Rainbow Room and the Blackbird. They were delightful events; they were fun, they enhanced our bar business, and they sold out every time.

The other thing I did on a Monday night once a month was "celebrity bartenders." It was a slow night, so I asked professional athletes or actors to come in and tend bar with me; $2 of the price of every drink went to the charity of their choice. We'd make up drinks; ask four people in the room to each suggest an ingredient and make a drink on the spot using those ingredients! It's the kind of thing you could do on a smaller, local scale, with a local newscaster or the coach of your football team.

Q: Let's talk about bar equipment. What is necessary and what is frivolous?

A: If you're gonna have a "real" bar, you need to teach your bartenders how to use a Boston shaker. It's like the chef's knife—once you know how to use that one, all the other knives are easier. It's what every bartender should be trained on and never is. The Boston shaker is a 16-ounce glass portion and a 30-ounce metal portion that fits on top to make a seal. I have four of those at every station, because I shake all my drinks.

I think a glass chiller is a necessity. Each station should have a drainboard, and next to it a sink; a double-bin ice bin so that you can put bottles in one and one for drink use, because every health department in America says you can't use the drink ice for the bottles. You've got to have both crushed ice and cube ice. I'm a fanatic about ice! For chilling, the crushed ice works well, but for drinks, I want big, whole, hard ice cubes, like Mom makes at home. The other kinds melt too fast and weaken a good drink.

I also believe the cocktail glass should not be any bigger than 5 to 5½ ounces, no more. I mean, what is a cocktail? It's an aperitif, a shared experience before dinner. It's the beginning of your evening. It's not the end of your evening—at least, not unless you have an 11-ounce glass with 6 ounces of liquor in it! The whole sociability aspect of the cocktail is blown away by supersizing it.

It seems to me that all the modern advances that are supposed to make bars so wonderfully fast and efficient—the bar guns, the premade mixes—conspire against a good drink. Sure, it's a little harder to make a "real" drink without all the shortcuts, but not with proper training and proper management.

CHAPTER 2

Responsible Alcohol Service

The positive attributes of alcohol have always existed alongside the potential for alcohol abuse. This negative side of alcohol, too, is as old as history. Today, however, there is more far-reaching awareness of the damage alcohol can do, from the automobile accidents caused by drunk drivers to the rising incidence of alcoholism. For the beverage operator, negative aspects of alcohol raise the risks of third-party liability and result in soaring insurance costs. Sellers and servers of alcoholic beverages must now stay fully informed not just about the beverages, but the laws governing the purveyance of alcohol, which include how to deal with intoxicated customers.

The responsibility of a bar or restaurant is twofold. Of course, the bar or restaurant offers alcohol as a pleasurable addition to the dining or entertainment experience. Alcohol can have a relaxing effect on people; it creates a sense of camaraderie among friends; and wine or beer can enhance a meal by complementing the flavors of the foods being served. But just as important as encouraging their guests to enjoy their beverages, sellers and servers of alcohol are responsible for safeguarding their clientele from the unpleasant, and potentially dangerous, effects of excessive alcohol consumption.

This chapter should help you . . .

- Learn the importance of responsible alcohol service and how to spot and handle customers who may have had too much to drink.
- Understand the effects of alcohol in the human body, both positive and negative.
- Understand the impact of alcoholism in today's society.

- Become familiar with the alcohol-related laws in effect in most areas.
- Set specific alcohol service policies and train staff members.
- Become proactive on behalf of the beverage service industry to educate consumers and uphold a reputation as a responsible business.

There are many good reasons to promote responsible alcohol service. First, we can help to reduce the number of deaths and injuries in automobile accidents caused by drunk drivers, which are all the more tragic because they are preventable. In this way, we protect not only our customers, but the entire community. We also protect the reputation of our own business. A loud or belligerent drunk at the next table can permanently impact a guest's impression of a bar or restaurant, as can an employee who handles the situation badly. Finally, we protect each employee—and the establishment itself—from violating state liquor laws and, subsequently, from damaging and expensive lawsuits, which can ultimately mean the death of a business that can't recover from the financial strain or the negative publicity. Bottom line? Responsible alcohol service means protection for your business.

Before we can learn to offer responsible alcohol service, we first need to take a closer look at how alcohol impacts human health and behavior. As you'll soon see, research results on these topics are mixed . . . and somewhat controversial.

HUMAN PHYSIOLOGY AND ALCOHOL

The form of alcohol found in liquor, beer, and wine is **ethanol,** which is a form of drug; it is a tranquilizer. In moderate doses ethanol can have beneficial effects, causing relaxation, stimulation of the appetite, heightening of pleasure, and providing a sense of euphoria. In larger doses, though, it becomes toxic, a form of poison.

Alcohol is not digested by the body in the same way as foods are. Instead of entering the digestive system, it passes through the wall of the stomach or small intestine directly into the bloodstream. An alcoholic drink taken on an empty stomach empties itself into the bloodstream within about 20 minutes. If there is food in the stomach, the transfer is delayed, especially if the foods contain fats such as cheese, meat, eggs, and milk. Carbonated beverages in the digestive system, on the other hand, speed the transfer. By way of the bloodstream, alcohol travels through the body wherever there is water—to the brain, lungs, kidneys, heart, and liver—until it is broken down by the liver into carbon dioxide and water (see Figure 2.1). The liver does this at the rate of one-third to one-half ounce per hour; the rest of the alcohol continues to circulate in the bloodstream. This amount is less than that

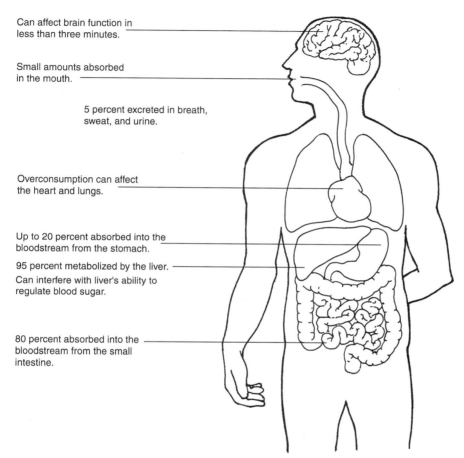

Can affect brain function in less than three minutes.

Small amounts absorbed in the mouth.

5 percent excreted in breath, sweat, and urine.

Overconsumption can affect the heart and lungs.

Up to 20 percent absorbed into the bloodstream from the stomach.

95 percent metabolized by the liver. Can interfere with liver's ability to regulate blood sugar.

80 percent absorbed into the bloodstream from the small intestine.

Figure 2.1 The path of alcohol through the human body. Reprinted with permission from Bar Code: Server Guide, Copyright ©1996 by the National Restaurant Association Educational Foundation, www.nraef.org.

contained in a typical 1.5-ounce cocktail made with an 80-proof spirit; but multiplied by several drinks it's clear that alcohol will still be circulating in the bloodstream several hours after it has been ingested. Consider that:

- The liver **metabolizes** about 90 percent of the alcohol consumed. The remaining 10 percent is eliminated through the lungs and urine.
- Alcohol reaches the brain within a few minutes of entering the bloodstream. Its effect on the brain is the key to both the pleasures and the problems inherent to the consumption of alcohol.

The first effect of alcohol is to stimulate or enliven pleasant and beneficial feelings. As drinking continues, the concentration of alcohol in both bloodstream and brain increases, diminishing both inhibitions and judgment, making the drinker more gregarious and expansive as well as less accurately perceptive of reality. As intoxication takes over brain function, the alcohol impairs motor ability, muscular coordination, reaction time, eyesight, and night vision—all normal skills that are necessary for drivers to get home safely. It does not take a great number of drinks to reach this point, and drinking coffee or other efforts to "sober up" do not have an impact on blood alcohol content, since nothing can make the liver break down the alcohol any faster. A drinker in this condition—that is, intoxicated—is unfit to drive.

Intoxication is measured by the percent of alcohol in the blood. The typical definition of intoxication is a **blood alcohol content (BAC)** of 0.10 percent, though some states have lowered the level to 0.08 percent and still others are lowering it even further, to 0.05 percent. To some extent, the size of the person affects his or her blood alcohol level: assuming the same quantity of alcohol has been consumed, the heavier the body weight, the lower the percent of blood alcohol. Consequently, women, who naturally have higher proportions of fat and lower proportions of water in their bodies than men, tend to have higher blood alcohol content than men of similar height and weight who have consumed the same amount of alcohol.

ALCOHOL AND ITS EFFECT ON HUMAN HEALTH

A 1990 editorial in the *American Journal of Public Health* stated that, after 40 years of research into diet and health issues, only two conclusions could be drawn consistently from both laboratory and clinical studies: that exercise and drinking moderate amounts of alcohol are good for humans.

Based on that statement, you might think that doctors would start prescribing a drink or two per day for their patients in the same way they prescribe regular physical activity as part of a healthy lifestyle. But it's not that simple. To determine what "moderate drinking" really is, we must look at it from a health perspective.

Generally, an alcoholic drink contains the equivalent of one-half ounce of pure (ethanol) alcohol. In a glass, this translates into:

- 12 ounces of beer, at 5 percent alcohol content
- 4 ounces of wine, at 12 percent alcohol content
- 1.25 ounces of distilled spirit, at 40 percent alcohol content ("80-Proof")
- 1 ounce of distilled spirit, at 50 percent alcohol content ("100-Proof")

Obviously, the size of glass and the size of serving can affect how strong a single drink actually is; moreover, many drinks are made with higher-proof alcohol, like 151-proof rum, or cordials and liqueurs, which range in alcohol content from 20 to 40 percent. But based on the preceding "basic list," health experts suggest that one drink for women and two drinks for men constitutes "moderation." Another piece of good news about health benefits of alcohol is that there seems to be a link between moderate drinking and a lower incidence of heart disease. This is indeed good news since heart diseases lead the list of killers in North America.

To understand heart disease, and how it is affected by alcohol, we must distinguish between "good" cholesterol, high-density lipoprotein (HDL) and "bad" cholesterol, low-density lipoprotein (LDL). To help prevent heart disease, we're supposed to increase our HDL level, because this good cholesterol cleans fatty buildup from blood vessels. It is the ethanol, the alcohol in alcoholic beverages, that raises HDL levels in the bloodstream. This does not happen immediately, but can be seen over several weeks after moderate daily alcohol intake. Long term, it may take a year to see significant HDL increases, depending on the person. Ethanol also contains a beneficial enzyme known as a **t-PA antigen.** This substance helps prevent chronic internal blood clots, and the anticlotting benefits take effect within hours of alcohol consumption.

While these findings are encouraging to those who advocate responsible drinking, the same studies emphasize the dangers of alcohol abuse, some of which conclude that a one-drink-per-day lifestyle is linked to an increase in the risk of breast cancer.

Public Policy, Public Ambivalence

Since long before Prohibition, Americans have consistently demonstrated a tortured ambivalence about drinking. The U.S. government has spent billions of dollars in an attempt to reduce problem drinking, yet many believe it should be doing more. Even with scientific studies to back them up, medical doctors seem hesitant to recommend something as controversial as alcohol to their patients, even in small amounts. They, like the general public, are finding it difficult to reduce the mountains of complex and conflicting research into simple, meaningful—and, more important—accurate advice. The controversy is ongoing. Even major organizations such as the Center for Science in the Public Interest (CSPI) and the National Council on Alcoholism (NCA)—have steered clear of supporting any study results that link alcohol consumption with good health.

Today, according to the *Journal of American Substance Abuse*, 44 percent of adult Americans are drinkers, 22 percent are former drinkers who now abstain, and 34 percent never drank. Statistically, that means there are more nondrinkers than drinkers. What does all this mean for the beverage industry?

New Guidelines. One sign of hope for the industry came in 1995, when the U.S. Department of Agriculture revised its "Dietary Guidelines for Americans," which the agency does routinely every five years, stating for the first time, that "moderate drinking may lower the risk of heart disease," and that "alcoholic beverages have been used to enhance the enjoyment of meals by many societies throughout human history." In contrast, the 1990 guidelines had stated unequivocally that "drinking has no net health benefits." Both the 1995 and 2000 guidelines balance those statements by warning that too much alcohol consumption can be harmful, raising one's risk of everything from high blood pressure to suicide. The guidelines also clearly state that alcohol should not be consumed by children or adolescents; women who are pregnant or trying to conceive; anyone taking medication of any kind; those who plan to drive; or anyone who cannot restrict their drinking to moderate levels.

Health-Related Trends and Public Perception of Alcohol

In addition to the new guidelines, three health-related trends that have been receiving considerable publicity in the past decade are having an impact on the hospitality industry:

- The so-called **French paradox**
- The **Mediterranean diet**
- The effects of alcohol on women and mothers-to-be

The French Paradox. Citizens of French and other Mediterranean cultures boast some of the lowest rates of coronary heart disease in the world, in startling contrast to America, where this disease is the number-one killer. On a recent report on the CBS television newsmagazine *60 Minutes*, two medical doctors, Dr. R. Curtis Ellison and Dr. Serge Renaud, discussed this apparent health paradox: the French subsist on a diet rich in fatty foods, which are known to be bad for the heart. So why the lower incidence of heart disease among the French? Dr. Renaud, claimed that the French custom of mealtime wine consumption—particularly of red wines—is an important factor.

Red wine contains **phenolic compounds,** part of what gives grapes their color and the acidity known as **tannins,** and these compounds are **antioxidants.** Antioxidants break down "bad" cholesterol (LDL) and help prevent clogging of arteries, as well as blood clots that can lead to strokes. **Resveratol** is another type of antioxidant, a natural component of the skins of red grapes.

The Mediterranean Diet. As everyone knows, diet plays a major role in human health; in short, what we eat determines to a great extent the kinds of illness we will or won't develop. The so-called Mediterranean diet is based on a traditional "food pyramid," which calls for daily consumption of bread, pasta, and grains, in conjunction with fruits, vegetables, legumes, and nuts.

In addition, people in that part of the world consume fish three or four times a week; poultry, eggs, and sweets a few times per week; red meat only occasionally. The "plan" also recommends an exercise regimen and moderate consumption of red wine. In the Mediterranean diet, the primary source of dietary fat is monounsaturated fat, the kind found in olive oil, cheeses, and yogurt. Americans would be wise to consider developing similar eating habits.

Alcohol and Women.   You've already learned that women metabolize alcohol differently from men. We have also discussed the relationship between alcoholic beverages and heart disease. In women, heart disease is somewhat less prevalent than in men, and when it occurs, it usually happens later in life for women. Therefore, it stands to reason that alcohol has more beneficial effects for women over age 50 than it does for those in their childbearing years.

The impact of alcohol on the female body seems to indicate that younger women in particular—those under age 40—should limit their alcohol intake, drinking only in moderation. Women who are trying to become pregnant should be aware that heavy alcohol use on the part of either the woman or her partner may impair the ability to conceive at all.

The most controversial issue for women is whether to drink while pregnant. Science indicates doing so is risky indeed. In the body of a pregnant woman, alcohol passes easily through the placenta into the body of the fetus, and drinking during pregnancy can cause a pattern of physical and mental defects in the child, known collectively as **Fetal Alcohol Syndrome (FAS)** or **Fetal Alcohol Effects (FAE).** As many as 12,000 children each year are born in the United States suffering to some degree from FAS symptoms, which include low birth weight, physical deformities, heart defects, mental retardation; or from FAE complications, which include low birth weight, mental retardation, cerebral palsy; neurobehavioral problems, and learning disorders. To counteract those alarming statistics, today, the federal government requires all types of alcoholic beverages to carry on their labels the following message:

GOVERNMENT WARNING: (1) According to the Surgeon General, women should not drink alcoholic beverages during pregnancy because of the risk of birth defects. (2) Consumption of alcoholic beverages impairs your ability to drive a car or operate machinery, and may cause health problems.

Alcoholism and Other Types of Problem Drinking

The second part of the government warning addresses the problem of drunk driving and, though less directly, the problem of **alcoholism.** Approximately 103 million people in the United States choose to drink alcohol in some form, and most do so responsibly—that is, in moderation. But it is estimated that

14 million adult Americans have alcohol abuse problems, and 1 in 7 is an *alcoholic,* defined as a person who drinks alcohol as a coping mechanism, to relieve tension or escape from problems, only to find that soon, he or she cannot control the drinking. A preoccupation with alcohol, or insistence on drinking despite worsening health problems, is often characterized by denial. The alcoholic may lie, make excuses, drink secretly, and hide alcohol.

The physiology of alcoholism in the human body is not entirely clear. It is not known precisely why one person becomes a compulsive drinker and another does not. According to the Florida Alcohol and Drug Abuse Association, three different theories are currently used by researchers to explain this destructive behavior:

- The *genetic theory* defines alcoholism as the result of a predisposed reaction to alcohol due to chromosomes, genes, or hormonal deficiencies.
- The *psychological theory* defines alcoholism as a condition in people who have a preset disposition or personality that "sets off" a reaction to alcohol.
- The *sociological theory* defines alcoholism as a learned response; that addiction happens a result of the influences of society.

Whichever theory one ascribes to, one thing is certain: alcoholism is a type of addiction and the afflicted cannot be cured without some form of treatment. Over time, alcoholism causes damage to the entire body—the liver, the heart, the digestive system, the central nervous system, the brain. The disease also causes psychological damage, in the form of depression, low self-esteem, loss of concentration, insomnia, irritability, and violent behavior, among others. Alcoholics who do not seek help for their problem can shorten their lives by 10 to 15 years. More frightening is that many alcoholics also shorten the lives of others: 40 percent of all traffic fatalities occur in alcohol-related accidents. Moreover, alcohol-related crimes in this country account for 54 percent of murders and attempted murders, 52 percent of rapes and sexual assaults, and 48 percent of robberies.

Another type of problem drinking, not classified as alcoholism but potentially just as serious, is **binge drinking.** For men, binge drinking is defined as the act of consuming five or more alcoholic beverages in a single, short time period—say, at a party. For women, four or more drinks qualify as a "binge." In a 1999 study of student drinking habits conducted by the Howard School of Public Health, 50 percent of male students and 39 percent of female students admitted they had consumed binge proportions of alcohol at least once in the previous two weeks. Caucasian students were twice as likely as those of other races to be binge drinkers; residents of fraternities or sororities were four times as likely to be binge drinkers as students with other housing arrangements. About 30 percent of the students surveyed also reported engaging in "unplanned sexual activity" as a result of their drinking. Clearly, binge drinking is a major concern on college campuses and among young adults.

As a seller and server of alcoholic beverages, you must be wary of customers who are problem drinkers. Do your best to spot them, especially those who have already had a few drinks when they arrive at your place. If they are intoxicated, it is against the law to serve them. Later in the chapter, we discuss more fully how to identify problem drinkers.

Alcohol and Nutrition

As alcoholic beverages continue to come under scrutiny in the medical world, it is important to summarize here the other roles that alcohol plays in human nutrition. Of course, Americans no longer need a stout mug of ale at lunch to give them the high-calorie boost that provided our Colonial ancestors with the energy to do their backbreaking work. Many nutrition experts today contend that alcohol should be "counted" in the diet as fat instead of calories, because of the metabolic interaction that occurs between fat and alcohol in the body.

For example, when presented with both fat and alcohol simultaneously, the body does the "logical" thing: it stores the comparatively harmless fat and rids itself of the "toxic" substance, alcohol, by burning it off as fuel. Alcohol intake may actually be promoting fat storage in the body, particularly in the central abdominal cavity. The point is, there is a medical explanation for that **beer belly,** which is noticeable even in many moderate drinkers! Recent studies have also shown that alcohol consumption slows down the body's overall fuel (fat) consumption by as much as one-third, thus causing more fat to be stored. Thus, alcoholic beverages are fattening in two ways: they add at least seven calories per gram as you drink, and they affect your body's ability to metabolize fat.

Another grim reality of recreational drinking comes as the result of overindulging. It is that awful combination of headache, nausea, stomach cramps, dehydration, and dizziness known as the **hangover.** A hangover is a chemical imbalance and a milder form of drug withdrawal. **Congeners** (from the verb "congeal," meaning to thicken or solidify) are compounds found in alcoholic beverages that contribute to the hangover. Different types of alcohol—vodka, gin, scotch—have different congeners, and some are more likely than others to produce hangover conditions at lower consumption levels.

Dehydration is a serious problem, because alcohol causes the body to lose valuable moisture everywhere, even in the brain cells. When you experience intense thirst after drinking, it's a signal that your body needs water. And as you rehydrate, the common side effects are headache and nerve pain as the brain cells swell back to their normal size.

Folk remedies for hangovers abound: aspirin, vitamins, exercise, or eating specific types of food (like the traditional Mexican tripe soup called menudo, for instance). Unfortunately, they are all virtually useless. The only thing you can do for a hangover—besides vowing never to drink that much again—is to give the body time and rest to process the excess alcohol intake and to replace the water you have lost.

Another more far-reaching side effect of drinking too much is malnutrition. The more alcohol a person drinks, the less likely he or she will be able to eat enough food to obtain adequate nutrients. Like those from pure sugar or pure fat, calories from alcohol are "empty" calories; they contain no nutritional value. When a body fills up with alcohol and so does not feel hunger, the alcohol is displacing food. Alcohol also directly interferes with the body's ability to use nutrients, making them count for less even if a person does manage to eat regular meals. The result is a dangerous spiral downward: the more you drink, the more nutrient deficiencies your body will experience.

LEGAL CONSIDERATIONS

The surge of third-party litigation, the raising of the drinking age to 21, the placement of warning labels on liquor bottles, and pressure to control media advertising of alcoholic beverages are all part of an ongoing countrywide movement against alcohol abuse. Such efforts are dubbed by some as **neoprohibition,** a throwback to the disastrous nineteenth-century movement described in Chapter 1. But those who are involved in today's movement speak of it as **neotemperance,** aimed against the *abuse* of alcohol, not consumption of alcohol entirely.

The bar and beverage industry has seen its products and practices debated on national television talk shows, in newspapers, even in the halls of Congress. A number of related issues—religious restrictions, health considerations, alcoholism, and others—tend to polarize people and create a turbulent climate for the industry. While most Americans do not support efforts to limit public access to alcohol, certain extremely vocal antialcohol groups are using the problem of drunken driving as a political agenda to push for stricter controls on alcohol sales and service.

Manufacturers and sellers of alcohol, who sometimes feel they are cast in the role of "the bad guys," worry that the concerns of both the public and private sectors will impact their profits long term. Government at all levels tends to raise the tax on alcoholic beverage sales whenever money is needed, referring to it (not entirely in jest) as a "sin tax." On the other hand, the industry itself is also very much concerned about alcohol abuse. A number of industry organizations are developing ways to fight abuse—through education, server awareness programs, and new products suitable to a new market.

If you're going to be working in this facet of the hospitality industry, you must become familiar with the specific laws that affect your job. That is the purpose of this section: to introduce and explain laws that directly affect the bar and beverage industry. Like any laws, those that apply to the sale and service of alcohol are impacted by the social and political climate, and can change accordingly. So it's important to stay up to date. The laws fall into these four categories:

- Dramshop and third-party liability laws
- Drunken driving laws
- Blood alcohol content (BAC) laws
- Drinking age laws

First, we will define and discuss each type of law. Then, we'll talk about ways the food and hospitality industries are creating and promoting responsible alcohol consumption policies.

No single federal agency or department establishes all rules and standards regarding the sale, service, or use or alcohol—nothing to compare, for instance, to the U.S. Food and Drug Administration, which sets safety and sanitation standards for foods and medicines. Consequently, alcohol-related laws may vary drastically from state to state, and even between counties or voting precincts in wet-dry areas; and they might be enforced by a police or sheriff's department, a department of transportation, an alcoholic beverage commission, or another agency. This is one more reason that the first rule of responsible alcoholic beverage service is to know your own state and local regulations.

Dramshop Laws and Third-Party Liability

In recent years, attorneys have successfully argued that bars, and restaurants that serve alcoholic beverages, should be held at least partially responsible for how the beverages affect their guests. Such laws are generally known as **dramshop laws** (from *dram*, originally meaning a small drink of liquor, plus *shop*, the place where it is sold). The thrust of these laws is that the liability for the damages—in a drunk-driving accident, for instance—should be shared by the driver who caused it and the server or alcoholic beverage licensee who provided the intoxicating drinks. This concept is known as **third-party liability.**

The earliest dramshop laws were enacted in nineteenth-century England, to protect families of so-called habitual drunkards. They penalized tavern owners if they continued to serve a patron after being notified of his or her drunkenness by his or her spouse, children, or employees. Starting in the mid-1980s, successful lawsuits resulted in millions of dollars in damages being awarded to victims of drunk drivers who had been served liquor by a third party. And even when a state does not have a specific dramshop law on the books, courts in more than 20 states have chosen to recognize these third-party liability lawsuits as legitimate "common law" causes of action. Part of their reasoning is that, since the business profits from the sale of alcohol, it should be held accountable for the "social costs" of liquor sales as well.

Whether or not bar or restaurant owners agree that they should be held responsible for their customers' drinking, the fact is that society today is doing so. It is also generally agreed that, without this "threat," licensees and servers would be less likely to establish service standards to prevent customers from becoming intoxicated, or to train their employees to recognize the problems.

Other types of legal liability related to the dramshop laws apply to alcoholic beverage service. **Criminal liability** allows the state to file a lawsuit against a licensed business, individuals employed by that business, or the social host of a private party where alcohol is served. Unlike a civil suit, the criminal suit addresses the criminal aspects of serving alcohol irresponsibly. An example would be when an intoxicated guest at a bar injures an innocent bystander (either inside the bar or after leaving the premises), and the state sues both the guest and those who served that guest alcohol. A civil suit usually includes a financial penalty; a criminal suit can mean serving jail time. Sometimes, both civil and criminal suits are filed simultaneously in separate courts, and the outcome of the criminal suit is not dependent on the outcome of the civil action. Both cases are decided independently, meaning that the defendant can be held accountable by both courts, or in one and not the other.

Administrative liability applies to any liquor license holder in a certain state. Liquor licenses are granted by state liquor control agencies (you'll learn much more about them in Chapter 16). If regulations are broken the state can mete out stiff penalties, including fines, license suspensions, and license revocations. As you might imagine, this can cause financial harm or ruin to a bar or restaurant business.

In many court cases, alcoholic beverage servers have been held responsible for **foreseeability,** that is, the reasonable anticipation that a particular course of action will likely result in harm or injury. Furthermore, the most prosperous defendant in a third-party liability suit (often the bar or restaurant owner) can be forced to pay most (or all) of the damage costs, especially if the co-defendants are unable to pay. Some attorneys choose to sue only the wealthiest of the potential defendants, even if that party is not solely—or even primarily—responsible for what happened.

The term **reasonable care** is used to describe the degree of diligence or the standards of precaution that are expected in a particular set of circumstances. Reasonable care includes, but is not limited to, what an ordinary, prudent person would do to prevent harm or injury. The flip side of reasonable care is **negligence,** which means the failure to act (that is, failure to exercise reasonable care) resulted in harm or injury to someone. In other words, a bar or restaurant has a basic duty to prevent any action that would cause injury or permit injury to occur as a result of the way it serves beverages on its premises. What does this mean to your serving staff? It means that all employees should be aware that they can be held personally liable for serving alcohol to a minor, to an already intoxicated guest, or even by letting an intoxicated guest get behind the wheel of a vehicle.

Conversely, people have also sued bars or restaurants that refused to seat them or serve them, citing the embarrassment and emotional distress it caused. Fortunately, these businesses, explaining they had good reason to believe these persons were already intoxicated, have been successfully found not liable on the grounds that they would have been negligent to serve them, then let them drive away from the premises.

With the advent of these lawsuits, the third-party liability issue caused a major crisis for insurance companies that offer coverage to the beverage-service industry. Insurance rates skyrocketed beyond the reach of many bars and restaurants, and many insurers refused outright to sell liability insurance to enterprises that served liquor on-premise. For a time in the mid 1980s, the situation threatened the entire beverage industry. Luckily, that is no longer the case. As long as its business plan and financial backing are solid, a bar can obtain insurance as easily as any other type of business.

Drunken Driving Laws

During the 1960s and 1970s, people who were convicted of drunken driving were fined from $10 to $50 and admonished by a judge. The defendant would solemnly promise not to do it again, pay the fine, and walk away, with car keys in hand. If the person had been unlucky enough to cause an accident resulting in serious injuries or even deaths, a fine of a few hundred dollars and a suspended sentence was regarded as sufficient for this "basically law-abiding citizen."

In retrospect, both the laws and the punishment seem like little more than a slap on the wrist. Today, Americans are far less tolerant of people who drive drunk. Activist groups like Mothers Against Drunk Drivers (MADD), Students Against Driving Drunk (SADD), and Remove Intoxicated Drivers (RID) have spearheaded successful national campaigns for stringent new legislation. Their efforts have changed forever the arrest, recording of charges, and penalties for an offense now commonly known as **"driving while intoxicated" (DWI)** or **"driving under the influence" (DUI)**

This national reaction to drunken driving has resulted in the implementation of:

- *Police roadblocks* to check drivers for sobriety (in effect in 37 states)
- **Per se laws** (described below) that label as person as "drunk" with blood alcohol content (BAC) of .08 (in effect in 25 states). Table 2.1 lists states' "per se levels."
- *Presumptive laws,* which allow an arresting officer's self-administered sobriety test to be the basis for proving a person guilty (in effect in 35 states)
- *Administrative per se laws,* which empower an arresting officer to immediately revoke the driver's license of a person who refuses to take, or fails to pass, an alcohol breath test (in effect in 19 states)

- Laws that prohibit drivers to have (and drink from) open containers of alcohol in their vehicles (in effect in 19 states)

Under a per se (Latin for "by itself") law, a single piece of evidence—a breath test administered to a driver, or the refusal of a driver to take such a test—is automatically presumed to indicate guilt, without regard to other possible circumstances.

The penalties for drunken driving are being raised, too. States can revoke drivers' licenses for an average of three to six months for a first offense, and one to two years for second convictions. Some 30 states now mandate jail sentences for repeat drunk-driving offenses. In New York State, for instance,

Table 2.1

State BAC Per Se Levels

States with .08 BAC per se level:	*States with .10 BAC per se level*
Alabama	Alaska
Arizona	Colorado
Arkansas	Connecticut
California	Delaware
District of Columbia	Indiana
Florida	Iowa
Georgia	Louisiana
Hawaii	Michigan
Idaho	Minnesota
Illinois	Mississippi
Kansas	Missouri
Kentucky	Montana
Maine	Nevada
Maryland	New Jersey
Nebraska	New York
New Hampshire	North Dakota
New Mexico	Ohio
North Carolina	Oklahoma
Oregon	Pennsylvania
Rhode Island	South Carolina
Texas	South Dakota
Utah	Tennessee
Vermont	West Virginia
Virginia	Wisconsin
Washington	Wyoming

All states except Massachusetts have established BAC per se levels.

Source: U.S. Department of Transportation, National Highway Traffic Safety Administration, April 2001.

a first offense brings a fine of $350 to $500; a second offense within 10 years of the first raises the fine from $500 to $5,000; and an offense that causes injury or death brings an automatic fine of $5,000 to $15,000.

Insurance companies also now penalize drunken drivers. Since 1984 in New York, for example, all insured drivers convicted of DUI can have their automobile insurance coverage cancelled; or, at least, they run the risk of it not being renewed by their carrier. This forces the individual to seek coverage by the state's "assigned risk plan," with insurance rates up to 75 percent higher than the typical premiums.

Ironically, though, given the furor over drunken driving, we probably won't see national drunken driving legislation in the United States. Although the problem is national in scope, the reality is that the most effective solutions are those administered at the state and local levels. This is not to say that Congress has not gotten involved, however. In 1981, it voted to withhold federal highway funds from states that had not raised their legal drinking age to 21 by 1986. In 1999, the same strategy was used to force states to lower the "legal" BAC level from 1.0 to .08 for motorists. And Congress has established an *Alcohol Countermeasure Incentive Grant Program* that awards federal money (ranging from $262,000 to $1.2 million) earmarked for implementing safe-driving programs and strengthening enforcement of drunken driving laws.

State laws, of course, vary. One of the more unusual penalties comes, once again, from New York. In 1999, New York City Mayor Rudolph Guiliani approved of seizing the vehicles of those arrested for drunken driving. It prompted at least one local barkeep to complain to a *New York Times* reporter, "First, Guiliani turns Times Square into Disney's living room. Now he says nobody can drink! He wants to make Manhattan a dangerous place to have a good time. Where are we, Iowa? The city that never sleeps is in a coma." Indeed, some civil liberties experts say the vehicle forfeit approach is too tough. Nevertheless, it has been adopted by other U.S. cities, including Portland, Oregon, and Anchorage, Alaska, with impressive results. While drunken driving deaths increased by 4 percent nationwide between 1994 and 1995, for example, Portland experienced a 42 percent decrease during the same time.

Others who say alcohol-related laws are becoming too stringent suggest the need for better seat belt law enforcement instead. Consider this statement, also from a *New York Times* article (April 5, 1998): "Drunken drivers kill 17,000 people per year, but the most eager supporters of the .08 BAC standard have said that such a measure would save, at most, 600 lives per year. . . . By contrast, the National Transportation Safety Board estimates that there would be about 10,000 fewer deaths per year if everyone wore seat belts, not just the two-thirds of passengers who wear them now.'

Perhaps the main reason that drunken driving has been singled out as the focus of legislation is simply that the public has chosen to distinguish between "suicidal and murderous" and "stupid and dangerous." The reasoning seems to be that if you don't wear a seat belt, you are threatening mostly yourself and your passengers, and that's "your business," while drunken drivers are a menace to all other drivers and pedestrians, making their negligence "everybody's business."

In the future, we can expect more penalties to be suggested by consumer activists and passed by lawmakers. Unfortunately, no matter what the laws, fines, penalties, or educational programs, approximately 10 percent of all drivers will continue to be problem drinkers, regardless of the cost to themselves and others. That makes it all the more important for everyone else to refuse to accept drunkenness; to learn how to recognize drunks in other vehicles and react defensively, and most of all, to drink responsibly themselves.

Blood Alcohol Content (BAC) Laws

You are considered legally intoxicated when your blood alcohol level is higher than what the law permits in your area. At this writing, the legal level of intoxication varies from state to state. Until recently, most states allowed .10— 10 percent—as the cutoff point between, shall we say, tipsy and dangerous? But other states, Oregon for one, have had a .08 BAC standard since 1983. And as just noted above, in 1999, Congress mandated that states adhere to the .08 BAC standard if they want to continue to receive federal highway improvement money. So most have adopted the .08 BAC.

The BAC figure is a percentage of the amount of alcohol in your bloodstream. For example, at a .10 BAC level, you have one drop of alcohol in every 100 drops of blood. That may not sound like much, but remember how potent alcohol is and how long it takes your system to process and eliminate it. At a BAC level of .30, you could lapse into a coma; at a BAC level of .40, you risk death.

The furious debate in the United States over BAC levels centers on the amount of alcohol absorbed by the body. Part of the conflict involves the fact that beer and wine may contain natural substances that slow the absorption of alcohol, so they have a less intoxicating effect than distilled spirits. Another issue is that the human body is as individual as the personalities that inhabit them, each has a different build, a different amount of fat, a different metabolic rate, and a different amount of food in the stomachs at the time of a BAC test. In sum, gender, age, weight, overall health, mental state, and whether a person is taking medication all affect the way bodies process alcohol. This makes it difficult, if not impossible, to draw absolute conclusions about minimum BAC standards, and hence to legislate them.

Since states began to adopt the more stringent .08 BAC level, public reaction has been mixed. Many simply are determined to spare themselves the embarrassment of blowing into a breath-test machine or standing in a police line-up, and so have decided to drink less and/or not drive if they do choose to imbibe. Others view it as a mixed blessing, but one that causes everyone to behave more responsibly. Still others see it as the continuing effort of neoprohibitionists to slowly but surely legislate morality by forbidding consumption of alcoholic beverages. After all, there have been suggestions of BAC standards as low as 0.05 or even 0.02, levels at which it would be impossible for most people to have even one drink and then drive without violating the law.

In spite of the fuss about lowering the BAC standard to .08, it may seem discouraging to its proponents that the results have not been as promising as they had hoped. In a Government Accounting Office study published in the September 1999 issue of *Restaurants USA* (the magazine of the National Restaurant Association), lowering the BAC level has not actually resulted in fewer alcohol-related fatalities. The study found that tougher alcohol law enforcement, drivers' license revocation, and zero-tolerance policies for minors who consume alcoholic beverages are the more effective methods of reducing the number and severity of alcohol-related driving accidents.

Drinking Age Laws. The mention of minors in the previous sentence brings us to the next major type of alcohol-related law. The 26th Amendment to the U.S. Constitution, the Age of Majority amendment, endows Americans who reach age 18 with nearly all the rights and privileges of adulthood. They can vote, sign contracts, marry without their parents' consent, ignore curfews, and buy tickets to X-rated movies. However, society has determined that it will be three more years before these new "adults" are responsible enough to have a drink that contains alcohol.

This reasoning stems at least partly from the controversial contention that many in this segment of the population will end up as highway fatalities if allowed to drink. Beverage industry groups have countered with statistics that show that while 16-year-old drivers have far higher rates of traffic violations and fatalities than the rest of the population, those rates decrease dramatically once the young drivers reach age 18. Other beverage industry spokespersons take the debate a step further, suggesting that the driving age be raised to either 18 or 21, to eliminate the vast majority of teen-driver-caused accidents. Of course, don't expect that kind of legislation anytime soon; after years of carpooling and chauffeuring, parents are more than willing to allow their teenagers to drive.

A diverse group of experts—sociologists, psychologists, and beverage industry representatives—have suggested that the parents of the underage drinker be the primary influence and rulemaker, not the government. One survey conducted by the University of Michigan in the mid-1990s indicated that 55 percent of eighth graders had already consumed alcohol at some time in the 30 days prior to the survey. Shockingly, one in seven claimed to have had five or more drinks in the two weeks preceding the survey.

The ongoing debate is a very personal one for anyone with children. Is it better for youngsters to learn about alcohol, and how to use it in a controlled way, in a family setting? Or is it better for parents to demand that children abstain until they are of legal drinking age? It goes without saying that teens who drink should not be allowed to drive, and that families with a history of alcohol abuse should seriously consider the message they convey to their children each and every time they take a drink. If alcohol is treated with disregard as to its risks, the message will be the wrong one, no matter who delivers it first to a child.

Beer manufacturer Anheuser-Busch has created a program called "Family Talk About Alcohol" to help teach parents how to discuss drinking with their children. Tips include:

- Always set a good example by drinking responsibly. Parents are the single most important factor in their children's decisions about alcohol.
- Talk openly with children about the law. Explain that it is illegal to purchase alcohol in any form, under the age of 21. Explain to them that the law is meant to protect people and that laws must be obeyed.
- Remind children that there are many other laws that also require people to be a certain age before they can do certain things. Tell them that the laws apply to all. It is not okay for adults to disobey them.
- Stick to the facts; avoid any scare tactics. Be truthful if you expect to continue to receive your children's trust.
- Be approachable and involved. Answer any questions your children ask about alcohol.

Parents may also want to discuss responsible drinking with other adults their children come in contact with—friends, teachers, coaches, relatives—and encourage them to reinforce the legal, responsible behavior they are trying to teach.

The benefits of helping children learn the facts about alcohol use, and abuse, not only helps in the fight against underage drinking, but underscores the importance of personal responsibility in future generations of adult consumers.

SOLUTIONS FROM A CONCERNED INDUSTRY

In light of social and legal developments, the food and hospitality industry has been at the forefront in the effort to promote responsible consumption of alcoholic beverages. The Anheuser-Busch program you just read about is only one of many examples. Obviously, training both managers and employees is a key ingredient in the success of any such commercial program. All staff members who come into contact with guests should be thoroughly trained in alcohol awareness, which is defined as the knowledge and skills to appropriately serve alcoholic beverages, monitor guest behavior, and deal decisively with any undesirable or illegal situations.

Another common sense training program, called The Bar Code, has been developed by the Educational Foundation of the National Restaurant Association. Among the facts shared with workers in this program are:

- If wine is served in an 8-ounce glass, the net result is twice as much alcohol as if served in a 4-ounce glass, and should be counted as two drinks instead of one. The use of oversized glasses is chic where wine aficionados dine, but try to limit each serving to four or five ounces.
- Since the liver can metabolize only approximately one drink per hour, consuming more than that naturally increases the amount of alcohol absorbed into the bloodstream. Alcohol will build up in the bloodstream and affect a person long after they have stopped drinking.
- A person's BAC level can continue to rise even after he or she has stopped drinking and left your establishment. The guest may appear to be acting normally, but the full impact of the alcohol may not be felt until he or she is driving home. Knowing this, a bar should never serve "doubles," drinks containing twice the amount of alcohol, or drinks containing two or more spirits (Martinis, Manhattans, Long Island Teas) at "last call."

Figure 2.2 Drinking an alcoholic beverage with food is a way to better savor both. *Source:* Disney Regional Entertainment.

Also extremely important in responsible beverage service is the practice of offering food when serving alcohol because food consumption slows the absorption of alcohol into the small intestines. Also, guests who are relaxing and enjoying their food may not drink as much or as fast (see Figure 2.2). The pace is slower when they are savoring the experience. As you monitor a guest's reactions, observe the type and amount he or she is drinking, as well as the physical size of the person, keeping in mind that women tend to become intoxicated more quickly than most men, if they drink less,.

High-Risk Factors

It is also important to be aware of a number of factors that might make someone at especially "high risk" for the negative effects of consuming alcoholic beverages. For these people, the usual BAC standard levels do not apply. It can be difficult to identify these folks, though there are guidelines to follow, again, from The Bar Code program. These are given in the following subsections.

Stress or Depression. People who are feeling intensely stressed or depressed can show strong and sudden reactions when consuming alcoholic beverages. When the human body is under duress, it self-protects by coating the stomach, to protect it from excess acid generated when the person is stressed, anxious, or depressed. Unfortunately, this protective lining can trap alcohol in the stomach and prevent it from moving on to the small intestine to be absorbed. Consequently, as the person consumes alcohol, he or she does not readily feel the effects of it and may need to drink more to induce the anticipated relaxation.

Eventually, the temporary stomach lining dissolves, and at that point, the alcohol passes quickly into the intestines and bloodstream, causing a rapid rise in BAC level.

Diets and/or Fatigue. A guest who is dieting—purposely limiting his or her calorie intake—may not have eaten, or eaten much, for quite some time. This means any alcoholic beverage consumed will be very quickly absorbed into the bloodstream. The same thing happens when an individual is tired. Fatigue also tends to affect overall judgment, thus compounding some of alcohol's side effects.

Altitude. People who live and/or work in high altitude communities—ski resorts, for instance—typically react more quickly to alcohol. It takes fewer drinks to become tipsy. This is a result of lower atmospheric pressure, and it impacts the way the human body absorbs alcohol. People accustomed to living closer to sea level, but vacationing in a high-altitude location may find that each drink seems twice as potent. This means that staff working in bars and restaurants in these locations must be more alert to clientele who are unfamiliar with this effect on their drinking.

Alcohol Tolerance. Have you ever known someone who seems to be able to drink a lot of alcohol without showing the typical signs of drunkenness? The human body and brain can build up a tolerance to alcohol. Long-term drinkers can sometimes consume large quantities without feeling or showing the effects. Conversely, inexperienced drinkers may show symptoms before they are legally intoxicated, because their bodies are unaccustomed to alcohol. It "hits" them harder, and more quickly. Bar staff need to be cognizant of these two extremes.

Medication. Whether it is over-the-counter or by prescription, anyone taking any kind of drug should be aware of the consequences of mixing it with alcoholic beverages. The fine print on the labels of these drugs warns about the danger of drinking alcohol when taking them. Some cold tablets, allergy medications, tranquilizers, blood pressure medicines, and antihistamines can depress the body's central nervous system. Drinking alcohol interferes with the body's ability to process, or break down, these medications, so they build up instead of being distributed in the system, thereby magnifying the impact of both the drug and the alcohol on the body. Certain combinations, like alcohol and tranquilizers, can even be fatal.

If you're a server and you know a guest is taking medication, monitor that person carefully to observe any behavioral changes. Curtail service to that person sooner than usual, and don't allow the guest to drive away from the premises if you feel he or she may be unsafe.

Pregnancy. Expectant mothers automatically qualify as high-risk guests. We've already discussed the tragedies of fetal alcohol syndrome (FAS) and fetal alcohol effects (FAE). Though there is no legal prohibition against serving alcohol to a pregnant woman, bar staff should be trained to watch for potential problems, and even to be able to discuss the consequences of consuming alcoholic beverages with the guest.

Watching Behavior

You've read a lot so far about keeping an eye on guests, observing their behavior, watching for signs of problems. But what exactly should you be looking for? Along with the obvious—counting the number of drinks they have ordered and monitoring how quickly they are finishing them—there's a lot to be discerned from most people's behavior about how much alcohol they can safely consume.

All of us have different ways of socializing—that's part of our personalities; and there is a difference between a guest who is loud and boisterous, and one who *becomes* loud and boisterous after having a few drinks. As a server it's important to notice the changes in a person's natural style, because the experts tell us a change in behavior is more telling than the behavior itself. It's also essential to learn that certain disabilities or physical conditions may cause a person to stumble, slur speech, or have difficulty concentrating. These are not to be confused with drunkenness; and, if you're observant enough, you'll learn the subtle differences.

Common signs of intoxication include:

- **Relaxed inhibitions.** When alcohol first enters the brain, it relaxes a person's normal sense of cautiousness and propriety. People say and do things they might not normally do or, at least, would think twice about. They become very friendly or overly affectionate to employees or other guests, or they might become brooding or quiet. They might suddenly leave a group of friends and sit elsewhere, choosing to drink alone. They might annoy other guests by making loud and candid comments or by using foul language.
- **Impaired judgment.** Emotions and judgment are influenced by alcohol. Common sense doesn't seem quite as important when you've had too much to drink. The most powerful example is, of course, the refusal to hand over their car keys, insisting that "I'm fine," and arguing with anyone who disagrees. Other signs of impaired judgment include drinking faster or

switching to a stronger drink; showing extreme emotion, by becoming angry or tearful; making irrational claims or becoming argumentative; complaining about the last drink (after having had others that were of exactly the same type and strength); or being careless with money, which includes buying drinks for total strangers or offering to buy "for the whole house."

- **Slow reaction time.** People who drink too much may report later that they felt they were moving "in slow motion." Indeed, the more alcohol they consume, the slower their reaction and/or response times. They may exhibit a loss of concentration or memory, strain to finish sentences, not make sense, or slur their words. They may also be unable to focus their eyes or to maintain eye contact with others. Often, they look and act drowsy.
- **Impaired physical condition.** Alcohol consumption almost always impairs motor skills. This condition is known as **ataxia,** the inability to control voluntary muscle movements, which affects balance and coordination. People who are experiencing ataxia spill drinks; stagger, stumble, sway, or even doze off while seated; fall down or bump into things; and seem awkward when trying to retrieve change and bills left on the table or counter.

Making a Plan

Now that you have some idea of what to look for when people overindulge in alcohol, you need to know the next step to take. Anthony Marshall, former dean of Florida International University's Hospitality Management School, believes the single best application of the dramshop laws is to prevent a drunken individual from getting into his or her vehicle. But to do that, a bar or restaurant manager must devise a system to spot those guests, determine whether they plan to drive, and be able to offer other reasonable alternatives. In an interview in *Market Watch* magazine (March–April 1997), Marshall stated that once the determination has been made that a person is unsafe to drive, access to his or her car keys must be restricted and he or she should be prevented from "sleeping it off" in his or her vehicle.

Of course, there's a lot more to it than that. It is management's responsibility to create and implement a complete responsible alcoholic beverage service program that builds awareness throughout the organization. Some beginning steps have been suggested by the National Restaurant Association's Educational Foundation, in its Bar Code program:

1. Review any existing records your operation may have about this topic.
2. Identify the special needs of your operation.
3. Develop, review, and update written policies.
4. Manage the staff to ensure a successful program.
5. Promote the responsible service of alcoholic beverages.

Let's elaborate on these steps one at a time.

Review Existing Records

First, you should carefully examine the past history of your establishment in incident reports or a current written policy, if available. Can a pattern be discerned from incidents or accidents or related factors that contribute to problems? Next, talk to employees. Ask what they have noticed; solicit their suggestions. Set up a meeting with your insurance carrier and your attorney. Ask for up-to-date information about third-party liability, and for their suggestions about good prevention programs.

When you look at past incidents that may have occurred, search for specifics: Exactly what happened and why? Was the bar or restaurant too crowded for adequate staff observation of all guests? Were the servers adequately prepared for this particular incident? Were there written policies in effect at the time to guide the staff; if so, were they inadequate or did no one bother to refer to them? Did managers and/or employees communicate well or poorly? Did they communicate at all?

You may be able to pinpoint a type of incident and even a frequency rate of occurrence. You may be able to identify the types of guests who are typically involved in problem situations at your place of business. Were they, for example, minors who were upset about not being served? Intoxicated adults? Did verbal abuse and/or physical fighting make the situation worse? Was anyone armed with a weapon? Did the people involved in the fray drive away from the establishment?

Look closely at how each incident was handled. Ask: Were certain servers involved in more problem situations than others? Did the servers use good judgment and practice the skills they'd learned in training? Were managers called when needed; how did they react? Was it necessary to call police? Was an incident report filled out completely, and is a copy of it on file? Following the incident, was additional training held for staff members to teach prevention or public relations skills?

It's also important to realize that an incident doesn't end when the guests who caused it leave your premises. Was it investigated by the local police or the alcoholic beverage commission in your area? Did your business receive unfavorable publicity in the news media? Were customer counts and sales affected that evening, or on an ongoing basis? Did your insurance rates increase as a result of the incident? Did you lose employees because of it?

The final aspect of this step is deciding what to do next. You need to assess the true readiness of your operation to handle a difficult customer, an armed customer, a suicidal customer, and a noisy and/or lewd customer who is annoying other patrons and who refuses to leave. In short, there are as many potential problems as there are customers. Ask your employees to help you think through any possible kind of tough situation, from the minor hassles to the real crises. Adapt your written policies to deal with them all. (For more on this, refer to Appendix A, which contains the Responsible Beverage

Alcohol Service General Audit from the National Restaurant Association Educational Foundation.)

Identify Special Needs

"Special needs" refers to the differences inherent in the various types of alcohol service; a bar or restaurant, for example, has very different needs from those of a sports stadium, a hotel, a casino, or a banquet/party facility. Once an audit or survey has been completed and you have pinpointed areas of your business that may require special rules or attention, consider these differences and decide how you must compensate for them.

In bars, lounges, and restaurants, most guests come to enjoy the atmosphere and camaraderie as much as the beverages. But it's the alcohol that invites the scrutiny of law enforcement agencies. Employees who interact with the customers should be polite and pleasant, not intimidating. Their goal is to encourage voluntary compliance with the laws, not to cause confrontations or be accusatory. When employees consistently exhibit a reasonable attitude and pleasant manner, they will gain the respect of all guests, as well as have an easier time dealing with the troublesome ones.

Door staff are a wise addition to many venues serving alcohol. These employees are the first to greet incoming guests—and to notice potential incoming problems. They are responsible for checking identification, so they must know how to spot increasingly sophisticated fake IDs. They should follow a specific ID-checking policy to prevent, among other legal infringements, a single form of ID being passed to multiple underage persons as individuals leave and return. No one should be "immune" from being checked for proper identification, including entertainers, their friends, or even regular guests.

The door staffers should also be able to deny entrance to anyone who appears to already be intoxicated, and even to ensure that the person who has been turned away does not get in a vehicle and drive off. Door employees can explain to the person that they will call the police if they see the person drive away; and then they should be prepared to follow through with the threat.

Servers should be alert as well as pleasant: alert to the number of drinks consumed by each guest and constantly mindful of signs of drunkenness. Having a manager walking around at all times as an additional, active observer is a necessity when the place is busy. A good manager can help servers communicate with each other, offer second opinions about questionable behavior, follow or divert suspicious guests, and generally alert employees to any potential trouble. If the facility is large and has partitioned areas, it's a good idea to consider purchasing hand-held walkie-talkies so that employees can easily contact a manager, security guard, or other employees.

The manager should be able to forecast the volume of expected business, so that he or she can schedule sufficient numbers of servers for each time period. Being understaffed during busy times is an automatic invitation for trouble, as both employees and guests suffer the frustration of long waits and inattentive service.

Banquet facilities and private event centers face unique challenges. Here are a few examples: the 20-year-old bride who insists that all her guests should have Champagne at her wedding reception; the 65-year-old retiree who insists on celebrating at his party past the point of good judgment; the business banquet spread across several different rooms at a large hotel, where guests—and crashers—can move about, into and order drinks in each room. A well-prepared manager will take preventive steps *before* each of these events is booked. The manager will explain all applicable laws to the host, verbally and also in writing, to make the host an ally of the facility, thus helping to ensure that guests will adhere to these laws. In this contract, the specific policies that govern responsible alcoholic beverage service will be spelled out, including a clause about the host's responsibilities and liabilities. The rules will be explicit; for example: You will not serve minors or intoxicated individuals; you will slow the beverage service to guests who appear to have had too much. The host should be asked if he or she would like to be personally involved if a difficult situation does arise during the event. Finally, the manager will ask the host to sign this agreement.

If minors will be attending the event, be sure to have adequate supplies of nonalcoholic beverages. Consider using two different kinds of glasses, one for those underage and one for those over 21. Groups of college students are especially challenging, because they may be of mixed age groups, making it difficult to tell who's 21 and who is not. Some facilities that cater sorority or fraternity parties, for example, have simply made it their policy not to serve alcohol at these events. Nevertheless, whenever alcohol is served, it's not unusual for a drink to be passed from adult to minor, and it is almost impossible to count drink consumption when people are moving about. This is when it is essential that all staff members be vigilant and communicate at all times, especially during shift changes.

Hotel and motel beverage directors have similar responsibilities as those of restaurant and bar managers. But hotel guests may also choose to consume alcohol in their rooms, which generates an additional challenge. When you're developing service policies for a hotel, consider:

- Whether to allow guests to take alcohol to their rooms, where staff members will not have control of the amount consumed.
- How alcoholic beverage service is requested. If it is in-room, how will your staff members know how many people will be drinking or if they are of legal drinking age?
- Minimum and maximum quantities to stock in minibars.

- Drinking to excess in the on-premise lounge or bar, assuming that the guest will be walking back to his or her room instead of driving.

And don't forget that, in hotels, housekeeping, security, and room-service employees must also be trained to note problems and to know whom to contact to report them when necessary.

Develop Written Policies

We've already discussed that for employee training purposes you should put in writing basic rules and guidelines for dealing with customers. In this section, we explain why this is necessary for a broader purpose. In case there is an incident or accident on your premises or your establishment is named as a responsible party in a lawsuit, your attorney and insurance company will use these written documents to help you out of a potentially damaging and expensive situation.

After they have undergone responsible alcoholic beverage service training, you should ask each employee to sign and date a standard form stating that he or she understands and accepts your policies and procedures. Some businesses also require employees to pass a written test before they can join the serving staff.

You should also require that a standard "incident report" form be filled out any time there is a problem. This includes when a server decides to stop serving alcoholic beverages to a guest. Why? You're covering yourself, your manager on duty, and your employee. What if this customer sobers up and calls his or her lawyer in the morning? What if the customer returns the next night, and the next, and starts harassing your wait staff? You want a record of each incident.

Your insurance company, your attorney, and local law enforcement agencies can offer advice for creating and launching your training and documentation program. They may have informational materials and/or boilerplate forms available for you to use. Ask your advisors questions such as, "If a customer—intoxicated or not—is harassing one of my servers, what are my rights; what are the server's rights? What is the best or safest way to ask such a customer to leave the premises?"

It is to your benefit in more ways than one to take advantage of the expertise of these professionals. Many insurance companies, for example, have agreed to sell liability insurance at reduced rates to enterprises that have trained all or a large percentage of their serving personnel in an insurer-approved program. Certain smaller insurance companies have formed insurance pools to spread their risks, and are now offering affordable liability-insurance rates. If you shop around, you can get the coverage you need to protect yourself from third-party liability, though the rates are likely to be *far* higher than you wish they were, so get your money's worth!

Manage the Staff

Total staff commitment to your responsible service policies is key to the success of their implementation. And it all begins during the hiring process. In a prospective worker, look for the attitude and sense of responsibility necessary to enable someone to make a quick decision in a high-energy, high-pressure situation. Is this person, simply, a responsible and levelheaded individual?

Keeping in mind that in third-party liability cases, an employer can be held responsible for employees who were not properly screened, screen each job candidate carefully for histories of violence, criminal acts, sexual harassment, drug or alcohol abuse; examine the person's work history and call past employers for references. (Think for a moment about the news stories you've read or heard about elementary school employees, for example, who have been accused of sexual impropriety with children, and whose past records were not checked. You can easily see how serious problems may arise.)

Develop a shift-change policy to ensure that incoming workers communicate with those who are ending their workdays. And, as mentioned earlier, never under-staff on days or evenings known to be busy periods. When an adequate number of servers is on the floor, each is better able to practice the essentials of customer service, which goes a long way to avoiding problems. New employees should never be serving customers without supervision. Empower more experienced employees to guide trainees through their first days on the job; give them feedback and praise for a job well done. Encourage staff to help one another during busy periods. And back up any staff member who is being harassed by a customer. If the customer is not intoxicated, you are completely within your rights to ask a troublesome customer to leave the premises, remembering that the way you do so will affect all involved—including your business. But keep in mind that if he or she is intoxicated, you may have to provide a means of transportation to avoid potential third-party liability later should the customer get into an accident after leaving your establishment.

You might want to consider implementing a salary structure that bases compensation on sales of combined food and beverage, instead of only beverages, to motivate employees to further reduce the chances that customers will drink too much on their shifts. Teach staff how to use **suggestive selling** techniques, that is, offering or recommending foods to customers who order drinks; or to *upsell*, which is suggesting drinks made with the more upscale, premium brands of liquor instead of *well brands*. Guests tend to consume the premium brands at a slower rate, presumably to enjoy the superior quality. You might want to give your wait staff permission to offer small tastes of certain food items free of charge, as an enticement to buy. In addition to being methods of encouraging responsible beverage service, all these efforts will mean higher average checks and, therefore, greater tips for your employees.

As just mentioned, always give praise for a job well done, but realize that occasionally you will have to discipline an employee. When this situation arises, you'll find that the more concise your written policies, the easier it will be to back up your critique and any necessary disciplinary action. Your polices will also make it easier to make even-handed decisions. And don't hesitate to remind your workers that if they willfully violate your state's liquor laws—say, by serving alcohol to a minor—they will be dismissed immediately.

Promote Responsible Service

If you expect your employees to support your policies, you must support them. This means that you do not ask your staff to act irresponsibly, even one time. Don't ask them to bend the rules for your friends or relatives, for so-called good customers or regular guests. Doing so will undermine any credibility you may have built with them. Instead, stress to staff that their working conditions (and probably their tips) will be at a higher level when they are serving people who are in control of themselves.

Communicate regularly with employees; this can be done in short meetings at regular intervals. At these meetings, ask them for ideas and address potential problems. Invite speakers from law enforcement agencies, your alcoholic beverage commission, or a counselor, to address, for example, the problems inherent with teen drinking, or alcoholism and related behavior. Give examples and praise those who have exhibited good judgment in handling difficult situations.

As far as publicity is concerned, many formerly popular promotions are no longer in vogue—in fact, today, some are downright illegal! Gone are the days of all-you-can-drink, two-for-one drink specials, ladies drink free, and even those so-called happy hours. Instead, the focus of promotional activities has shifted toward events, themes, holidays, and entertainment rather than on alcoholic enticements. Emphasize your food specials, however limited. Provide fun and entertainment that showcase your atmosphere.

To do this, you'll need to *know* who your customers are, both regular and infrequent. Take the time to analyze why these individuals visit your business. What makes your establishment unique? What makes it appeal to "your" crowd? You'll learn more about researching your target market and building business in Chapter 3, but for the purpose of this discussion, remember, if you promote heavy alcoholic beverage consumption, this practice could be used against you in court. Avoid advertising activity that fosters or glamorizes intoxication.

One good way to divert attention from alcohol is to plan an interesting, delicious menu that complements alcoholic beverage sales. It doesn't have to be "gourmet," just appealing and satisfying. Be sure the choices include some fatty, high-protein snacks, which help absorb alcohol. Consider offering a free or moderately priced appetizer buffet in the early evening in lieu of the two-for-one happy hour. If yours is a restaurant, consider the idea of **bundling,** offering a food and drink in combination, for example, a bottle of wine included with two dinner entrées, or a free appetizer with an alcoholic beverage. Ask your wine or spirits supplier for help with these promotions; perhaps they will be willing to give you discounts on the cost of goods or help you pay for advertising costs.

CRISIS MANAGEMENT

Smart managers plan for the possibility of injuries, legal and insurance entanglements, and bad publicity—all consequences of alcoholic beverage-related incidents. These events must be treated at least as seriously as a fire, flood or armed robbery, and they should be part of your crisis management contingency plans. The Bar Code, quoted throughout this chapter, has some suggestions for crafting a crisis management plan that will restore normalcy as soon as possible following an incident of this sort. It involves a three-pronged approach, each with a series of steps to follow.

First, you must *address immediate needs*, in this sequence:

1. Contact the manager or owner.
2. Call police, ambulance, and/or emergency services as needed.
3. Safeguard guests and employees by cleaning up spills and breakage. (Ask police about specifics in case it is a crime scene.)
4. Reassure guests while the incident is being resolved.

Second, you must *manage the crisis*:

1. Gather accurate information from as many sources as you can.
2. Contact attorneys and insurance agents.
3. Assign a trained spokesperson to handle information requests from the press or regulatory or law enforcement agencies.
4. Decide whether to temporarily close or to immediately return to normal operation.

Third, you must *assess, then repair any damages*:

1. Determine the cause of the crisis.
2. Assess damages to the property, employee wages, and the flow of business.
3. Begin repairs.
4. Launch a marketing effort to offset damages to your public image.
5. Identify and reward employees who reacted quickly to minimize damages.
6. Deal with employees' reactions—guilt, fear, anger, depression.
7. Revise policies and training procedures to prevent a recurrence.

SUMMING UP

Practicing responsible alcohol service is the only way to ensure the safety of your guests, employees, and your business. Much involved in this practice is common sense; but, in addition, you must educate yourself about alcohol and its impact on the human body, both positive and negative. For sellers of alcoholic beverages, it is important to recognize—and not minimize—the negative effects of alcohol, and to develop written policies and training programs for staff members about how to deal with uncomfortable or potentially dangerous situations.

And, as detailed earlier in the chapter, there are numerous medical, social, and legal complications you may be forced to deal with when someone drinks too much. Remember, though the liver metabolizes most of the alcohol in the body, it does not do so quickly, complicating the question of exactly when a person has crossed the line and is "legally drunk." Everything from that person's natural tolerance to his or her weight, mood, and any medications he or she is taking, coupled by the location of your establishment, can impact how "hard" alcohol "hits" them. Teach your staff members to recognize the signs and symptoms of problem drinkers, including alcoholics and binge drinkers.

Familiarize yourself with your local dramshop and third-party liability laws, drunken driving laws, blood alcohol content (BAC) laws, and the penalties for serving alcohol to minors, keeping in mind that states and counties have specific, and differing, laws, and any of several different agencies may be responsible for upholding them.

As the owner or manager of a business that serves alcohol, you should have written policies—rules and guidelines—for your establishment that cover alcoholic beverage service, intelligent management of uncomfortable or dangerous situations, and penalties for staff members who break the rules or laws. Before hiring, screen potential employees carefully for behavior problems that may be alcohol- or drug-related. Following training, require every employee to sign a statement signifying that he or she understands your policies and is willing to abide by them. Implement a crisis management plan to help all staff know how to cope with a serious incident; enlist the help of experts–attorneys, law enforcement officers, and insurance agents–to stay current with the laws.

By taking these precautions, you will create a safe, pleasant, and friendly place with a good reputation, one to which people keep coming back. You'll minimize property damage to the establishment, and reduce or eliminate conflicts between guests. Everyone benefits from well-considered and well-instituted preparedness programs.

POINTS TO PONDER

1. Why does alcohol circulate in the bloodstream several hours after it was first ingested?

2. Name three typical effects that alcohol has on most people.

3. What is the difference between neoprohibitionism and neotemperance?

4. What distinguishes alcoholic behavior from the behavior of someone who drinks occasionally?

5. What is meant by "third-party liability?" How has it affected the bar and beverage business?

6. As a waiter, how might you determine when a guest is starting to get drunk?

7. What are the responsibilities of "door staff" at a nightclub?

8. Does your school have regulations about binge drinking, on or off campus? If so, who enforces them? If not, why not?

9. What types of documentation should a restaurant or bar have on file that are directly related to the service of alcoholic beverages?

10. What are the unique challenges of in-room alcohol use in hotels?

TERMS OF THE TRADE

administrative liability	DUI (or DWI)	Mediterranean diet
alcoholism	metabolize	negligence
antioxidant	ethanol	neoprohibition
ataxia	fetal alcohol	neotemperance
beer belly	effects (FAE)	per se law
binge drinking	fetal alcohol	phenolic compounds
blood alcohol	syndrome (FAS)	reasonable care
content (BAC)	t-PA antigen	resveratol
bundling	foreseeability	suggestive selling
congener	French paradox	tannins
criminal liability	hangover	third-party liability
dramshop law	incident report	

CHAPTER 3

Creating and Maintaining a Bar Business

People are rediscovering the civilized pleasure of socializing over a good drink. As so-called suggestive selling begins to pay off, and customers' palates become more refined, more people are taking an interest in tasting, and are willing to pay for, new or better-quality beverages. And customers are coming back to the bar with a new attitude of responsibility, thanks to a combination of factors: health warnings and fitness regimens, stricter DUI laws, and changing social morés about drinking.

For the purposes of this chapter, we'll assume that you are going to open a new, or renovate an existing, bar to take advantage of this modern climate. Though this chapter discusses planning the actual physical facility in which you will serve beverages, we begin by addressing how to decide what types of customers you want to serve, what kind of physical surroundings will appeal to them, and where you will locate your enterprise to serve them.

Many ingredients go into creating just the right environment—atmosphere, décor, the efficient use of space, the bar itself. Since every bar business is different, the discussion centers on basic questions and the principles and guidelines you can follow to find the answers for your specific situation.

This chapter should help you . . .

- Develop an overall concept and tailor it to meet the needs and desires of a particular clientele.
- Study the market, choose an appropriate location, and determine financial feasibility.
- Plan atmosphere and décor suitable to a concept and its intended clientele.

- Plan efficient use of available space.
- Analyze the design and space needs of the bar itself.
- Weigh the pros and cons of hiring professional consultants or going it alone.
- List the factors to examine before investing in a specific location or building.

If you were to pick up a 10-year-old entertainment guide to almost any city in this country and compare it with a current guide, you would be astonished by the number of bars and restaurants listed in it that no longer exist, and by the number of establishments flourishing today that were not in business 10 years ago. The food and beverage industry is famous for its volatility and, often, for the magnitude of individual failure. And sometimes, it doesn't seem to make sense: Why does one bar fail while, across the street, another is a gold mine for its owners, year after year?

The reasons for successes and failures in the bar and beverage industry are often complex. Like the entertainment business, food and beverage facilities are vulnerable to bad luck, the fickleness of music and fashion trends, location, even the weather. But more often, success or failure is a consequence of management and planning. Either can be good or poor, with the consequent results.

The elements that make up good planning and management are extraordinarily interdependent, and it is a somewhat arbitrary task isolating them. In practice, they are not separate, but interact like ingredients in a cake batter. Nevertheless, for the purpose of exploring these "ingredients" of success, we'll take them one at a time, and by the end of the book you should be able to bake your own cake, so to speak. This chapter's ingredient is the physical facility.

The bar is often part of a larger operation that includes food service. Some of the discussion that follows, therefore, will apply to a total facility—you could not, for instance, plan the décor of a bar in a restaurant without considering the restaurant, too. But we will focus only on those aspects of the total facility that affect the physical setting of the beverage service.

TARGETING YOUR CLIENTELE

The starting point for designing a successful bar is to identify its target clientele—the people you want to attract and serve, who are going to pay your bills and generate your profit and give you the pleasure of making them happy. They are the focal point around which everything else revolves: the atmosphere you create—the décor, entertainment, sound, lighting, dress—and the drinks you serve, that is, the total impact. The clientele influence your location, your floor plan, the bar equipment, of the kind of staff you hire, in short, everything.

Many people dream of opening "a little place" that will be their idea of perfection, that the public will surely recognize for its excellence and flock to its doors. Well, it doesn't work that way. Everyone has his or her own idea of perfection, and it's impossible to please them all. Furthermore, people go to bars for various reasons, bringing with them differing needs and expectations. Usually, the drink is not the primary motive. After all, they can buy any beverage they want at a package store for much less money and do their drinking at home. Therefore, we must explore the different types of customers.

Types of Customers

We can divide customers into several different groups according to their reasons for choosing to drink in a public setting:

- **Diners at restaurants where drinks are served.** They come to enjoy a good meal *and* the drink, whether in the form of a cocktail, or wine, an after-dinner drink or all three. Each enhances the enjoyment of the total experience. Although the food may be the primary focus at a restaurant, people often want to drink an alcoholic beverage, too. Restaurants that do a flourishing business without alcohol are the exception rather than the rule.

- **Drop-in customers who are on their way elsewhere.** They usually want refreshment, a quick pick-me-up, or stress reliever after a day's work. In this case, the drink is the focus, one or two at most, and then the customer is on the move again. People waiting to board a plane or a train, or who are meeting someone at the bar, also belong to this group. Bars near office buildings or factories, in train or bus stations, airports, and hotel lobbies typically cater to this category of customer.

- **Meet-and-go customers.** These are individuals looking for a romantic connection, whether a date for the evening or a longer-term relationship. They go to "singles bars" or "meet bars" that are attractive to others like themselves. They stay long enough to meet someone they'd like to spend the evening with, and the two move on to a place where the food and/or the entertainment is more suitable for a leisurely evening together.

- **Entertainment-seekers looking for relaxation, stimulation, or a change of pace.** They frequent bars, lounges, clubs, and restaurants where entertainment is offered—country and western music, games, dancing. They want to meet new people or keep up with social trends. They may visit several places or spend a whole evening in only one place if the entertainment, the drinks, and the company are to their liking.

- **Sports fans.** In almost every major city, you'll now find at least one sports bar, featuring big-screen television viewing from every angle and special promotions for championship games, boxing matches, and so on. Another newer trend is the cigar bar, where guests can puff away at high-priced cigars and enjoy high-end liquors to go with them. The idea is that people want to commune with folks who share their interests, whether that means a great game or a great smoke.
- **Regular patrons of neighborhood bars or taverns.** They are interested in enjoyment and relaxation too, but their primary desire is for companionship—being with people they know and like, feeling comfortable, feeling they belong.

Most customers fall into one or more of these groups. The moods, tastes, and interests of the groups differ, and the people tend to differ in background and lifestyle as well, although some individuals cross group lines at times. A drop-in customer on a business trip may be a diner or entertainment-seeker at home, because the mood and purpose have changed. Generally, though, in spite of some crossover, these groups are not compatible. A customer from one group visiting a bar frequented by another group is prone to think of the others as "the wrong crowd" and feel uneasy and out of place. People who are turned off by the people around them do not experience the venue as having a friendly atmosphere even if the bar personnel are friendly. They won't stay long and they won't come back.

Within these broad groups, however, are many subgroups, divided loosely according to lifestyle, interests, age, income level, family status, occupation or social status, even gender. A few of the largest and most common subgroups are defined in the following subsections.

Women. As purchasers and consumers of alcoholic beverage, women exert a powerful influence, which is destined to become even greater in the years to come. At this writing, there are more than 105 million women in the United States who are of legal drinking age. They represent a huge opportunity for the hospitality industry. Today's female customer is better educated and marries later in life—or not at all. Women today also make up a large portion of the workforce, which means they have discretionary income. Moreover, there is no longer a stigma attached to women who purchase or consume alcohol, and women have become increasingly sophisticated in the brands they choose. Many women form groups to share regular, informal get-togethers—weekly or monthly—at a favorite place for dinner or drinks.

Still, for many women, "going to a bar," especially alone, can be an uncomfortable experience, so the savvy bar owner will make an effort to put them at their ease. It starts by acknowledging the customer within the first 30 seconds of her arrival in the establishment. This is a major factor in raising the female customer's comfort level. Cleanliness and unquestionable quality of ingredients also rank as very high comfort factors among female customers. For instance, surveys reveal that many women regard hanging glasses above the bar as unsanitary, particularly if smoking is allowed. Servers should always offer clean napkins with a drink, a courteous touch that women expect and appreciate.

Hispanic Customers. As the 1990s came to a close, the alcoholic beverage industry was finally beginning to appreciate the value of the Hispanic consumer. More than 30 million Americans are of Hispanic origin, and many distillers and brewers are recognizing this fact by advertising in Spanish. This is a promising start, but more needs to be done to adequately address this customer category. To build lasting relationships with this broad and diverse group, we must develop an understanding of the intricate differences that distinguish one ethnicity from the next. Many recent Hispanic immigrants to this country have not yet fully assimilated into the "melting pot." This may be because they don't feel they have to. This country boasts widespread Spanish-language media and generalized support for the various Hispanic cultures, meaning that, often, they can continue to live and work within native-language environments.

But one thing is clear: community, family, and tradition are powerful Hispanic values. In October 1997, Hispanic Marketing Coordinator for Coors Brewing Company, Paul Mediata, said in *Market Watch* magazine, "In the Anglo culture, a business relationship is developed first, then a friendship. In the Hispanic culture, it is the opposite." Words to the wise for anyone aiming to serve an Hispanic clientele.

Baby Boomers. Americans born between 1946 and 1965 are considered baby boomers, the last generation to grow up in an American society in which drinking was the norm. Members of this generation are now reaching their 50s and are in the prime of their careers. Unlike their parents, the boomers refuse to think of themselves as old or even middle-aged. According to the National Restaurant Association, this age group spends more money dining out than any other demographic category—23 percent more than the average person on restaurant dining. And though they may not be crazy about exercise, many "work out" nonetheless to stay in shape; and they continue to eat the foods they enjoy—beef, pastries, eggs—but in moderation. Boomers in general are relaxed and open about drinking, and do not hesitate to take their children with them when they dine out, and this has impacted the dining industry. Today, a whole group of casual but slightly upscale "adult fast food" eateries are designed to cater to boomer families; TGI Friday's, Applebee's, Chili's, to name just a few, appeal to these time-crunched, child-toting, beverage-savvy boomers, who enjoy relaxing over a fairly quick but well-prepared meal that features both drinks from the bar and a children's menu (see Figure 3.1).

Figure 3.1 Many bars and restaurants that serve alcohol cater to families. *Source:* Disney Regional Entertainment.

Baby boomers also tend to be partial to intense flavors in their foods and beverages, hence are willing to pay higher prices for specialty beers and premium wines and liquors. They are both knowledgeable and critical about their foods and beverages, so servers need to know a lot about the wine, beer, and cocktails available, because they will be asked!

Generation Xers. The hot demographic component for many bar and restaurant operators is also the most fickle. Generation Xers, or Gen Xers, for short, are between the ages of 21 and 30, and they comprise a fascinating amalgam of public consciousness and trendy behaviors. These are the experimental drinkers, and their tastes run the gamut, from a bargain-priced pitcher of beer to a funky New Wave Martini or Evita Martini (brandy, triple sec, red wine, orange and lemon juices), to a chilled aperitif or "shooter." Gen Xers have al-

Sidebar 3.1

SELLING HIGH-END SPIRITS

Any bar manager who runs a premium spirits program will tell you that, often, return customers bring their friends along, and inevitably share with them the information they learned on their previous visit.

Bar and restaurant owners have a love-hate relationship with high-end spirits: offering a selection of such beverages can bring both prestige and profit to the business, but it also raises the cost of inventory and requires a serious commitment to education, both for the staff and the guests. This commitment comes in the form of tastings, classes, seminars, multicourse wine dinners, publicity for public events. Suppliers and distributors are usually willing to help with these efforts, and you'd be wise to take advantage of the guest speakers and sample bottles they can provide for these occasions.

If your concept allows it, consider the benefits you may incur from selling high-end beverages. At this writing, though they account for less than 12 percent of total distilled spirit volume, they account for 26 percent of the industry's sales dollars. And that figure has grown steadily in the last five years in a market where distilled spirits as a whole have lost 6 percent of their total volume.

ready been exposed to microbrewed beers and specialty coffees, so they are adventurous enough to try new things, and are willing and able to spend money on quality spirits. As their incomes rise, so do their expectations.

Younger drinkers also appreciate and tend to expect live music, or at least a deejay who will spin up-to-the-minute music on CDs for dancing the night away. This clientele category has been well educated not to drive drunk, so they are the most likely to do the responsible thing and assign a designated driver or call a cab when they have overindulged.

Connoisseurs and Sophisticates. You'll always find a certain number of customers who are truly well-informed, who enjoy food and wine as a serious hobby or vocation, and often know more than most bartenders or servers. For these folks, it is simply not enough to offer a wide selection of wines or spirits, so some bars and restaurants have decided to specialize in a particular area, and use that as a "hook" to attract a certain, upscale clientele. They hire a sommelier, build a wine cellar, and stock an impressive selection of old-growth Bordeaux, for example. Or, like Pravda, a New York City nightspot with a Russian flair, they feature 80 different vodkas.

Making the Decision

So, who will be your customers? You may choose to cater to any one group or subgroup; you cannot expect to please them all. In fact, it is a mistake to even try; it just won't work. Part of the atmosphere of any bar is its customers, and if they don't have something in common—mood, attitude, reason for coming—the ambience will be found lacking and they won't have a good time and probably won't come back.

The experienced entrepreneur concentrates primarily on a single, definable customer group, or **market segment,** whose members will have similar reasons for visiting a bar, and shapes the entire enterprise to attract and please this group. No one group is an inherently "better" choice than another; there's a profit to be made with any type of clientele, if you can satisfy their needs.

One good way to help decide who will form your client base is to imagine your customers. How old are they? Where do they come from? How much money do they like to spend? Why do they go out? What kinds of drinks do they buy? What kind of atmosphere do they respond to? What turns them on? To answer those questions, you have to do some homework: Visit the favorite places your target clientele is flocking to now. Talk to their customers. Watch their reactions. What do they like or dislike about the place? Your goal is to learn how *they* feel, not to decide what *you* like or dislike. Study everything about the operation—the décor, drinks, layout, ambience, food, entertainment or absence of it. Talk to the bartenders. Study the bottles behind the bar, the wine list, the menu.

Conduct your research locally. Tastes and interests vary widely from locale to locale, even among the same age groups and income levels. Look at ads in local papers and read the restaurant reviews. Talk to local beverage wholesalers; they are some of the best-informed people around. They know who is buying what kind of liquor and what types of customers are drinking it; which places are raking in the money and which ones are having trouble paying their bills on time.

Planning Your Services. Once you have decided which customers you are going to target, you must decide what you are going to do for them:

- **What services will you perform for them, and how?** Will you offer drinks only, drinks and dinner, drinks and entertainment? Music? Dancing? If you serve food as well as drinks, which will you emphasize, and how will you relate the two?
- **What kind of bar do you envisage?** A stand-up bar favored by crowds or those in a hurry? Table service in a cocktail lounge? Dining-room service from a service bar? A holding area for people waiting to eat in your restaurant?
- **What kinds of drinks will you serve?** Beers, on tap or bottled? Wines? By the glass or by the bottle? For the casual light drinker or the connois-

seur? Mixed drinks? Fancy drinks? Frozen drinks? Flaming drinks? House specialties? Soft drinks? Coffee drinks? As in every other area, you need to seek answers based on what appeals to your intended clientele, not necessarily what you yourself would buy as a customer.

As you do your homework, consider the places you visit as your competition. Ask yourself how you could serve your chosen clientele better than they do? To succeed, your products and services must be distinctly different from—and better than—those of your competitors. Bars that simply copy others seldom succeed. You must position your enterprise favorably in the market in relation to the other choices customers have.

Defining Your Image. Much of what will set you apart from your competitors is your overall **image,** and it's a tough thing to define in the bar business. The mystique of some bars cannot be fully explained. Nevertheless, you must make an effort to define what will be the special character of your bar that will entice people to come to you instead of to your competitors? *Favorable uniqueness*, it is sometimes called, or image, or identity. It should be a combination of what you want to spring to customers' minds when your place is mentioned, what they anticipate before they arrive, what lingers in their memory afterward as a special pleasure, and what will keep them coming back and bringing their friends. From this description, it should be clear that image is the most intriguing and elusive element of success—and the one most worth striving for.

Some bars favor a showy or brassy image, designing places that people like to see and be seen at, where new drinks are improvised, and trends are born; others prefer the classic approach, serving cocktails in a more intimate or subdued atmosphere. In either setting, an establishment offering inventive but tradition-based drinks, executed with crispness and showmanship, will convey the image of what a bar should be.

In today's most successful bars and restaurants, uniqueness is a carefully planned total concept, not just a single distinctive element such as a special house drink or a mahogany bar with a brass rail from the 1890s. In these venues, the name of the establishment, the drinks, décor, layout, service, uniforms, and menu all fit into the total concept and reinforce it, though individual customers may remember only one element, say, the creatively written menu full of puns, the giant TV screen, the dart tournaments, the musical memorabilia, the 500 kinds of beer, or the revolving panorama of the city at night from atop a tall building. Each, however, is a symbol of the collective ambience, a crystallization of the concept.

The point is, to ensure success, you need an overall concept that can tie all the elements of your bar together. A concept should begin with an idea that can be stated simply; for example, a neighborhood bar-restaurant with a family feeling, or an upscale wine bar for wine enthusiasts, or a health-and-fitness bar-restaurant where the drinks are made with fresh juices and the food is low-fat, low-calorie, and memorably tasty. Décor, lighting, menu, and service will all be developed in keeping with the concept.

Your total concept will grow out of a thorough understanding of your chosen clientele and the careful planning you do to serve them. It will be shaped by your observations of the kinds of places your clientele favors. But it will not be a copy of these other places; its own personality, its own identity, will be the magnet that draws your target customer to your front door. Formulating this concept is a real challenge.

In certain cases, the purpose of the bar will dictate its image. Customers of a sports bar, for example, have very clear expectations about what they'll see, hear, and do when they arrive. In contrast, in a bar attached to a restaurant that takes reservations, the lines blur; of course, you'll seat people in the bar while they wait to be seated at their tables, but this should not be the only purpose of a restaurant bar. The restaurant bar should also serve as a marketing tool for the dining room, because bar customers often look in advance at the food menu and notice other customers being escorted to their seats or waiters walking by with trays full of food. It can be beautiful or intimate or trendy, and just different enough in style from the restaurant to attract its own clientele. The point is this: If you can get people to come into the bar for a drink, sooner or later, they'll stay for a meal.

The hotel bar also presents interesting image challenges. If you cater only to the travelers who are hotel guests, you'll miss out on a major source of revenue—the locals. There seem to be two kinds of hotel bars: those that have been turned into trendy gathering places for local customers, and those that are undiscovered treasures, quiet and secluded places where a more select clientele go to enjoy a good beverage selection in comfortable, if relative, solitude. If yours is a hotel-based business, you must decide which image to project, and target that clientele.

An integral part of any bar's image is the bartender. Most people view this role as being filled by someone at the pinnacle of creative salesmanship—a friendly face with an impressive repertoire. He or she knows how to mix dozens of different drinks quickly and well, yet still has time for a joke or a chat, and will remember your name, too, after you've been in a few times. Bartending is a profession steeped in nineteenth-century tradition, and reinforced by images in books, movies, and television shows that portray bartenders as kind, observant, amusing, and competent—part mixmaster, part comedian, and part psychologist. Never doubt the role that great bartenders can play in your success.

Another factor in creating an image for a hotel bar is the type of food you will serve. Simple, salty snacks—mixed nuts, pretzels, or some form of "trail mix"—are the norm in many hotel bars, but adding a small menu of, for example, delicate gourmet appetizers, crowd-pleasing nachos, mini-pizzas, or a great shrimp cocktail will add new dimensions to your customers' enjoyment and to your profit picture. Simply put, guests linger longer where there is good food.

Perhaps the best example of this was the Windows of the World restaurant atop the World Trade Center. Before falling victim to the terrorist attack on September 11, 2001, this restaurant boasted what had been dubbed the "greatest bar on Earth." Its menu was created by the husband-wife team of Michael Whiteman and Rozanne Gold. In a September 1996 issue of *Food Arts* magazine, Gold described their effort as "a new social experience." The menu did not, for instance, distinguish between appetizers and main courses. "The food is communal in nature," Gold said. "It invites people to share from a parade that represents a 'New World' view of cooking."

Gold and Whiteman developed four menu rules that can be applied to a variety of other bar-restaurant concepts:

1. Each dish should be strong enough to produce an "instant salivary response."
2. There should be no "mishmash" cooking; no multicultural foods. Everything should be true to its origin.
3. Most of the foods should be able to be eaten with forks and fingers, leaving one hand free to hold a drink.
4. The menu should encourage social interaction.

MARKET FEASIBILITY—LOCATION

The next question you need to answer is: Where will you establish your unique new beverage enterprise? You want it to be convenient to your target customers. If you are going to serve dinner as well, you want to be accessible to a residential area or to places of work or both. For people in search of entertainment or a companion for the evening, you will probably want a location in an area already known for its nightlife. To attract drop-ins, you want to place yourself on the route to wherever they are going; to attract a more regular group of people, you'll want to be near the neighborhood in which they live.

Choosing an Area

Certain areas of cities tend to be "in" places, where bars and restaurants are clustered, and where competition is intense. Still, a crowded area has its advantages. Bright lights and lots of people moving around make for a festive atmosphere. People enjoy going where they've been before—familiar places are comfortable and they know that if they can't get into one place, they'll try another, so the competitive environment benefits everybody.

On the other hand, such areas can become saturated when too many new ventures try to imitate the success of their predecessors. Therefore, if you are thinking of starting a business in such a location, take these two precautions: First, investigate the number of businesses that have opened and, especially, closed in the area during the past few years, to try to determine what kinds of places have staying power and what kinds have been overdone; second, study the competition carefully, and be very sure that you have something unique to offer. Can your businesss truly make a special contribution to the area?

The alternative is to open your enterprise in a new or isolated area. Of course, this may be risky, but it can be also rewarding if your research uncovers a market demand that is going unmet. Needless to say, however, once you have made a success in a new area, you probably will soon be joined by competitors, so think about building a following for the long term, and don't expand too quickly on the basis of an initial high demand.

In general, it's a good idea to avoid declining areas; look instead at neighborhoods that are stable or growing. That said, however, in many cities, once-neglected areas are being revived. It has become trendy and an expression of environmental conscientiousness to restore older buildings and rehabilitate dilapidated sections of town. An advantage is that many older properties are more spacious, better built, and are generally more accessible than new facilities in the suburbs. Furthermore, development money is often available for people who are willing to undertake these types of projects, especially if you agree to restore the building with historically correct details and materials.

Estimating Customer Potential

Once you have an area in mind, you need to determine whether enough of your target market—your customers—live in or frequent the area to support your concept. There are a number of resources for answering this questions. In some cities, you can get help free of charge from various state and local agencies that compile population demographics (who lives where, how much money they make, level of education, eating and spending habits, and so on) and maintain statistics about neighborhoods, urban planning, and area traffic. Chambers of Commerce have information on business growth, tourist and convention markets, and real estate development. Banks, because they loan money to restaurants and bars, can tell you a lot about the community in question; they can prevent you from opening the right facility in the wrong place, say a swinging singles bar in a retirement colony. Also talk to real estate agents; contact restaurant and club owners' associations; and pay a visit to local restaurant equipment firms—all will usually know who is opening and where, as well as who is closing and why.

In some cities, there are demographics firms that specialize in the food-service field. They can run a computerized analysis of a specific area based on census figures, giving you data on population density, age, gender, occupation, size of household, income, ethnic makeup, money spent dining out, or whatever demographic information you specify. From such figures you can determine an area's overall customer potential for your type of business.

Sizing Up the Competition

As you explore the various areas of your town to determine customer potential, you must also closely examine potential competitors. How well are the customers' needs and desires already being served? To determine this, visit all the bars and bar-restaurants in the area that serve your target customer. Count and classify them; for each one, record its location and as much as possible of the following information: number of seats, hours, price range, average check, average number of patrons per day, number of days open per week/month/year, slow days and busy days, slow and busy times of day, annual gross volume (dollar sales per year). You can gather such data by talking to people connected with each operation—bartenders, servers, managers. You can also observe. For example, count the seats: How many are empty? How many people are waiting to get in? Estimate the same information for your proposed enterprise and compare. Check the total against your study of market potential.

If all your competitiors are busy all the time, chances are good that you will be, too. But if, on the other hand, business is slow and seats are empty everywhere, you can conclude that the area is saturated and that there probably isn't room for you, no matter how delicious your food and drink or how charming your atmosphere—unless you are lucky enough to identify a void (for example, you discover there is no bar for the late-night theater crowd).

Probably the quickest and most accurate method—but also the most expensive—of learning about your competition is to hire a professional food facilities consultant or a market study specialist to conduct this kind of detailed investigation of a given area and its current competition, to determine whether there is a market in that area for your bar concept. Or, if you already have a facility but want to revamp it, a consultant's market study can help you adapt your concept to be more up to date. But be aware that using a professional, you run the risk that you'll spend a few thousand dollars for bad news—to be told that the market you are aiming for is not there—but, remember, this knowledge will save you much more money and grief in the long run. The cash you spend on a professional market study at the beginning of a project will be minor compared to your total investment in your business.

Selecting a Site

Once you are satisfied that there are enough potential customers in your chosen area, you can begin to shop for a specific site. When you do this, it is important that you attempt to see each site through the customer's eyes. Does it have good visibility? Adequate public transportation nearby? Plenty of parking? Is it easy to reach? Watch out for one-way streets, planned future construction, and heavy traffic. Keep your ear to the ground for changing circumstances; talk to other retailers in the neighborhood. If you are thinking of taking over an existing facility, find out why the last tenant left. And if you should decide to convert a failed restaurant site, plan to wipe out all vestiges of the past.

Considering Your Options. As to building type, you might choose a freestanding building, or one that's part of a complex such as a shopping mall or a unit in a strip mall with street access and good visibility. In a strip mall, the ideal location is the end unit, because it has two visible walls, front and side. Depending on your concept and target clientele, you might even consider space in an office building or along an underground walkway where there are shops and pedestrian traffic. And, as mentioned earlier, don't overlook the possibility of refurbishing an older building, whether a warehouse, a church, a school, or a gas station. Converting from a different use is usually less expensive than starting with an empty shell, and keep in mind such a building may have historic value, or image potential, to bring to your concept.

Most important, check out the licensing, zoning, and other restrictions of the area you're scouting, as even different parts of the same city may have different licensing requirements. For example, a nearby church or school may prevent your getting a license to sell alcohol in the same area, even if your business is going to be a family-themed restaurant. Simply put, zoning restrictions can make it impossible to open the kind of facility you want or to open at all in your chosen location. At the very least, cutting through the red tape involved in the permit and licensing process can delay your opening for months. In relation to all this, consider the importance of a favorable community attitude. If you discover the community is hostile to the opening of your enterprise, it might be better to start over in another area.

Determining Financial Feasibility. Finally, be aware that even the most promising site may turn out to be unprofitable if costs and operating expenses are high in relation to potential sales volume. To determine this ratio, you need to analyze the financial feasibility of your projected business for that site and market area. To begin, draft a realistic financial plan for your intended facility in terms of your profit goal. Estimate the capital needed for land and buildings, furnishings and equipment, opening expenses, plus a reserve for operating at a loss in the beginning. Next, based on your market research for your site, make a detailed projection of sales and receipts against fixed and variable expenses. These projections should represent an operating budget, which is described in Chapter 14, with detailed plans for drink menu, staff, hours open, and so on.

Estimate sales conservatively and expenses liberally. If the income does not exceed expenses by the desired profit margin, your project is not feasible for that market and location.

ATMOSPHERE AND DÉCOR

The atmosphere of your place will determine who comes to buy drinks from you, how long they stay, how much they spend, and whether they come back and bring their friends. This is simple to understand. After all, why do people go to bars? They go to have a good time. They don't go just to drink; they go to relax, to socialize, to rendezvous with old friends or meet new ones, or perhaps to be alone with a special person; they go to escape their everyday mood and scene. If you can transport them from a world of problems, deadlines, and frustrations to a world of pleasure, you have the first ingredient of success.

Successful Examples

Let's look at a few bar concepts that have thrived in recent years. Perhaps the most imitated restaurant/bar concept in America is TGI Friday's. The actual bar—which is corralled with brass rails and trimmed with stained glass—continues to be as central to the restaurant's business in the new millennium as it did in 1965, when the chain was founded in New York City. For all its years of existence, TGI Friday's has continued to serve good drinks in an atmosphere that has remained consistent: it is a bustling, friendly, and casual ambience. The chain has its own 36-page beverage manual that contains standardized directions for making more than 140 cocktails.

Another good example of a successful atmosphere is Fado's, an Irish pub in Atlanta that was, literally, designed and built in Ireland, then shipped to the United States. for assembly and decoration by a team of Irish craftspeople. Though the building's shell was already in place, most fixtures, fittings, and furniture are Irish. Its dark, floor-to-ceiling wood interior is stuffed with all things Irish, from sports memorabilia to quotes from the Green Isle's literary greats. You can get a pint (20-ounce glass) of Guinness Stout or Harp Lager, Ireland's signature brews, or sample a microbrew from the Atlanta area (the latter being Fado's way of acknowledging the local scene). The bar also offers a list of famous Irish whiskies. And, as you'd expect in a true Irish pub, conversation is the main attraction, so you won't find videogames or big-screen television sets here.

Sidebar 3.2

BLUE AGAVE CLUB

Want to know more about tequila? You can sample more than 200 different types and brands at the Blue Agave Club in Pleasanton, California. Restaurateurs Alexandro and Susi Garcia opened the 70-seat restaurant and bar in 1997 to showcase gourmet Mexican cuisine and the adaptability of Mexico's "national spirit." Tequila is part of the food menu, too: Chef Ramon Sepulveda uses it in the salad dressing, as a component of sauces, and to baste barbecued meats and flame elegant desserts.

"The idea was not only to showcase the true flavors of Mexico," explains Alexandro, "but to dispel some of the myths about tequila. People here say, 'Tequila makes me crazy,' 'Tequila gives me a headache, or a bad hangover.' Well, they need to know it's because they are not drinking the real tequila; they are drinking the more commercial, mixed spirits. Real tequila is every bit as sophisticated as wine."

Some of the larger tequila producers, says Alexandro, ship tanker trucks of product from Mexico into the United States to be blended and bottled; but, technically, tequila is the only spirit made in a single nation. So if you're interested in taste-testing tequila, the Blue Agave is the place to go, and you'll find the "tastes" are generous!

In villages of past centuries, tequila was poured into a bull's horn as measurement, and the resulting amount was about 2 ounces. Alexandro's grandfather told him long ago why the 2-ounce pour is called a *caballo*, the Spanish word for horse. "In Old

The third example is found in Puerto Rico, at the Palm Court Bar in the El San Juan Hotel and Casino. The Palm Court Bar is the epitome of sophistication, featuring hand-carved mahogany panels and columns, 250-year-old French tapestries and rose-colored Italian marble floors, all of which combine for an elegant, old world atmosphere. The bar is not big; it contains only 30 upholstered stools and 8 tables for two. Its most dramatic feature is an antique chandelier from Czechoslovakia, which shimmers with 1,000 lights and 5,000 dangling crystals.

Hudson Bar and Books, in Manhattan's West Village area, is a wonderful example of using atmosphere to blend into a neighborhood. In this case, bar owners pay homage to its avant-garde past, when writers and poets lived and worked here and sometimes visited pubs till dawn. The intellectual heritage of the West Village is evident at this establishment, with its jammed floor-to-

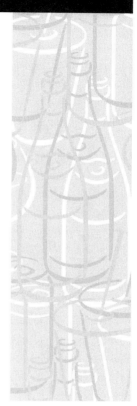

Mexico, tequila was sold on the street corners, and people were on horseback. They'd work in the fields, then ride into the small towns for a drink. But the drink was so potent that they didn't dare get *off* their horses, because they wouldn't be able to get back on! So my grandfather said you'd see groups of 10, 20, 30 men on the corner, all on horseback, drinking and talking."

Luckily, at the Blue Agave Club you can also get *caballitos* ("little horses") of 1 ounce, and also ½-ounce tastes. They also pour "flights"—tastes of several different styles of tequila–so you can compare blanco, reposado, and añejo.

Despite its availability by the shot, the most popular drinks at the Blue Agave Club are margaritas. The restaurant has been distinguished with "best margarita" honors by its patrons and local food critics. Alexandro says the secret to making the perfect margarita (there are more than 100 selections on the menu) is his proprietary sweet-and-sour recipe, which is made fresh daily. The restaurant sponsors well-attended tequila dinners and tastings, featuring tequila producers as guest speakers. Word of mouth has been the restaurant's best form of advertising.

"The customers love the idea of learning more," says Alexandro. "They sometimes comment on the prices—I mean, the high-dollar tequilas cost $45 to $75 for the 2-ounce pour—but I tell them, 'Just imagine if this was made in France! You'd be paying $200 a shot!' It's a completely natural, pure spirit with nothing artificial added in the distilling process. Showcasing it like this, in a high-end restaurant environment, has been a very good idea and a lot of fun."

ceiling bookshelves. Intimate tables line a wall opposite the fully stocked bar, and the room converges into a back area with a U-shaped couch. The effect is comfortable, dark, and literary. Beer is served in frosted glasses; each pour of wine is served in a clean wine glass; and water glasses are replenished constantly.

In Chicago's West Loop area, another good example of successful atmosphere is Drink and Eat, too!, a massive (25,000-square-foot) bar (see Figure 3.2). Larger-than-life saltshakers and lime-shaped lights grace the ceiling above its Tequila Bar; a chandelier made of Absolut Citron bottles is suspended above the Vodka Bar; and certain mixed drinks are served in buckets! There are no dark, quiet corners at Drink and Eat, too!; the bright lighting and clean, vibrant décor promotes a fun-filled environment, and the layout encourages social mingling.

In the South Beach area of Miami, Florida, you'll find an East Indian-inspired bar. Ancient artwork, scented candles, and oversized pillows are part

Figure 3.2 The tequila infusion bar at Drink and Eat, too! Chicago, Illinois. Photo courtesy of Drink and Eat, too!

of the comfortable but exotic appeal of Tankard. Moroccan tents, low tables, and grass-carpeted floors prompt guests to sit on the floor; in another room, fiber-optic stars twinkle in a faux sky; the "V.I.P. Room" features a huge hammock and ample pillow-filled romping space for up to 30 people. Tankard also has a restaurant with booths, tables, and a mahogany and copper bar.

And across the country in Seattle, Washington, the Palace Kitchen advertises itself as a "tavern with good food." Décor is simple; the central feature is an enormous, horseshoe-shaped bar giving guests a clear view of the kitchen and the employees at work (see Figure 3.3). The owner's intent is to convey the idea of a friendly, unpretentious employee dining room. You can even see the dishroom employees at work! The bar is the primary focus here, evident in the fact that it has twice as many appetizers as entrées.

Décor Requirements

Do the previous examples have anything in common? Sure they do! They prove that, indeed, "anything goes" when it comes to bar themes and décor. Whatever the specific attractions you decide on, they should be inviting from

Figure 3.3 The U-shaped bar at the Palace Kitchen in Seattle, Washington. Photo courtesy of the Palace Kitchen.

the very first moment. The atmosphere should convey a message of welcome, of festivity, of caring for customers. Some of this will come from you and your personnel, and some will come from your other customers—most customers enjoy being among likeminded people who are having a good time. But the physical surroundings are equally important. They create the first impression, set the stage, strike the keynote.

The kind of décor you choose for your facility will be the visual expression of its mood. Décor includes the furniture and its placement; the wallcoverings or decorations, floor, ceiling, lighting, and window treatment; plants and other accessories; special displays; and the front and back of the bar itself. Each element should be planned in relation to the total concept. In effect, it is the packaging of your concept; not only does it help to create mood, but it merchandises your product.

What kind of mood do you want to inspire? What does your research show your target clientele responds to? Do you want to impart a sense of spaciousness, relaxation, restfulness, a place where people come to talk to each other without shouting; or are you after a noisy, crowded, stimulating, hyped-up atmosphere? Do you want to convey elegance, opulence, luxury, or modest comfort and terrific value for the price of your food and drink?

Soft colors and rounded shapes are restful; bright colors and bold patterns are stimulating. Noise is muted by carpets, drapes, upholstered chairs, fabric-covered walls; it bounces off tile and concrete floors, plaster walls and ceilings, and glass. High ceilings give a sense of space; low ceilings make a room seem smaller and more intimate. Ceilings that are too low and rooms that are too small can make your customers feel claustrophobic. Soft lights and candlelight send messages of intimacy, romance, intrigue. Bright and/or flashing lights are appropriate to noise, crowds, action, excitement. Firelight is restful, dreamy, romantic, but be aware that fireplaces must meet local fire regulations.

Luxury can be conveyed by the use of expensive fabrics, furniture, and accessories; by museum pieces and art objects; by dramatic effects such as waterfalls, magnificent views, and murals by accomplished artists; by gleaming silver and crystal, masses of fresh flowers, ice sculptures, an elaborate list of vintage wines, tuxedoed waiters, expensive food and drinks, valet parking, and attentive service. Terrific value can be conveyed by simple, inexpensive but imaginative décor, good drinks at moderate prices, and quick, friendly service.

Investors sometimes spend a fortune on décor to compete for certain types of customers or to build a certain image in a national or international market. If this is your situation, you will probably want to hire a professional interior designer who specializes in the restaurant field. But not all décor involves spending a lot of money. It does always involve a great deal of thought and good taste. Paint, plants, posters, or art prints, for example, judiciously chosen and placed, to complement the furnishings and their groupings, the right lighting, and the right sound (or its absence) all combine to create a mood. A few inexpensive conversation pieces can add to the fun. The trick to achieving a successful décor is to keep mood and clientele constantly in mind, and pick colors, textures, shapes, furniture, and fixtures that mesh for a total, finished look.

Work toward a décor and a mood that isn't a copy of a competitor's or that's built on a passing fad. And make sure to carry out your theme in your service, drinks, uniforms, and all the small details. If you don't, you'll be sending your clientele a mixed message: crystal chandeliers say one thing; shabby restrooms with cold water only and no soap say something else.

LAYOUT AND DESIGN

Whether you are starting from scratch or remodeling, the first step is to think through your layout carefully to ensure that it jives with the essential factors—customers, services, atmosphere. To these essentials, add a fourth one: efficiency. Designers of bars face the continuous challenge of providing employees with a functional space in which to work quickly and accurately. Practical, daily bartending concerns include the ability to take orders, mix and garnish drinks, wash and dry glasses, handle cash, and restock supplies with limited effort and maximum productivity, all the while ensuring that the same bar space is clean and attractive, makes customers feel comfortable, fits in with the rest of the décor, and stimulates beverage sales. Little wonder, then, that some hard choices must be made to bring bar design in line with budgets and a confined space. Appendix A, which contains a sample Cocktail Lounge Design Questionnaire, will help in this effort.

If you'll be working with professionals—for example, an interior designer, for your look and your furnishings, and a facilities designer, for the bar equipment, plumbing, and electrical requirements, it will help you immensely if you understand what they are doing, and the best way to do this is to visit other facilities that they have designed. Also, study the trade publications that include articles about effective bar design, to keep up on trends..

Trends in Bar Design

Designers, architects, and consultants agree that bar design is highly subject to the changing lifestyles and fashions of the times. When *Top Shelf* magazine conducted a survey of "good bar designs" in the early 1990s, it found that the most popular bar décor was understated elegance. Repeatedly, guests expressed their desire for better quality and their willingness to pay for it. In hotels, for example, a redesign typically involves redoing the whole lobby, not just the bar area, in dark woods, marble, stone, and rich fabrics to achieve a feeling of intimacy and comfort.

Restaurant-based bars seek a look of casual elegance, with a trend toward "bistro" cuisine, and a design that features woods, marble-topped tables, and overstuffed chairs, all of which make the setting both comfortable yet classy. According to the *Top Shelf* surveys, people like to be in a classy environment, but are tired of the stuffy, formal eating and drinking experience. The objective is that customers feel good whether they're dressed in shorts or a business suit.

Another modern trend to watch is the **concept bar,** where the goal of the décor is to whisk patrons away to new or exotic locales. The Rainforest Cafés are one example. And there are **participatory bars,** where customers are part of the action, whether they're playing pool or video games or singing karaoke.

On the nightclub scene, design trends are tending toward lighter colors (to make the bar friendlier to women); more space for "cool-down areas" (where people can sit and talk if they prefer not to dance); and layouts that encourage eye contact and more social interaction between the dancers and nondancers (this translates to fewer "terraced" levels to negotiate within the club). Nightclub menus are also being expanded to offer more food, as part of the ongoing effort to encourage responsible alcohol consumption.

In sum, patrons are drinking less and demanding better quality and an "experience" instead of just an evening "out." So the design trend of the future is to make bars friendly and fun.

Basic Elements of Layout

Regardless where you're planning to launch your bar business, certain facets of startup must be dealt with by everyone: the amount of space available, the activities going on in that space, the number of seats, the size of the bar (large enough to hold equipment for the drink types you will offer), and the relationship of the bar area to other aspects of a larger facility such as a restaurant, hotel, or club. Other layout and design needs come into play: plumbing, refrigeration, lighting and other electrical requirements, ventilation, heating and air conditioning, health and fire regulations, local codes, and state laws and regulations such as separate smoking areas and restroom facilities for the handicapped patron. Last but not least comes profit: How can you make the most profitable use of the space available?

The final layout emerges from the decisions you make regarding all the factors, so let's discuss them one at a time to understand the impact of each.

Available Space. The amount of space available to you for your layout includes not only square footage but also the shape of the area, the position of entry and exit, and whether you'll be sharing space with dining, dancing, or live entertainment facilities.

- The *square footage* will set an outside limit on the number of customers you can serve at a time. It may also determine whether you will have seating at the bar or at tables, lounge style.
- The *shape of the room* is critical to the arrangement of the furniture and fixtures. Consider the three rooms shown in Figure 3.4: They are of the same square footage, but one is long and narrow, one is square, and one is L-shaped. Shape also affects the number and arrangement of tables, the position of the bar itself for the best visual and psychological impact, and the bar's size and shape. Shape influences the traffic flow for entry and exit and for service. And it certainly affects how you'll share space with activities like dining or dancing.
- *Entry and exit* require special attention, because the relationship between entrance and bar will influence the movement of customers into the room and the way the room fills up. Do you want your customers to move immediately into noise and conviviality? Do you want them to stop at the bar before going on to dine and dance? Or will a crowd around a bar near the entrance block access both visually and physically, leaving the room beyond it empty? If the bar is associated with a restaurant, should it have a separate entrance or be part of the restaurant? Will it serve only as a holding area for the restaurant or do you want it to be its own destination, with its own patrons?
- *Sharing space* with other activities takes careful planning. You must consider the amount of space each element requires—the bar, the activities, and the furniture and fixtures. Probably you'll want to measure everything

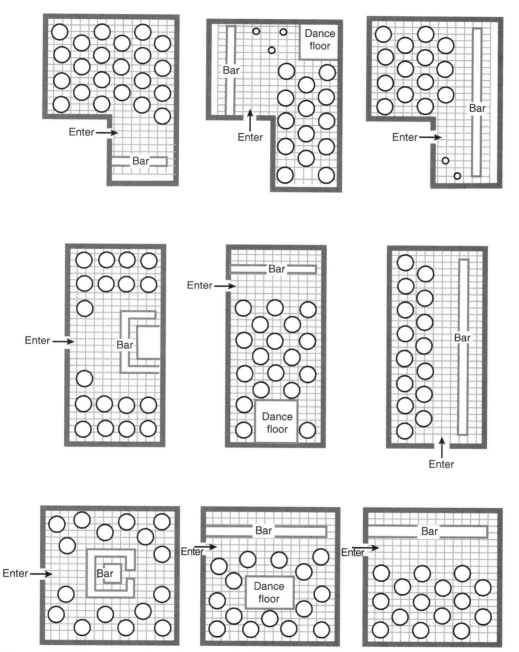

Figure 3.4 These rooms all contain the same square footage. Notice how the shape of the room affects the room arrangement.

and plot it to scale on a floorplan. It is very difficult to estimate the sizes of objects and spaces just by looking at them. An empty room usually looks smaller than it is. A room with furniture already in it is very difficult to picture accurately in a different arrangement. Most empty dance floors don't look big enough for more than three or four couples, but in action they may accommodate many more. (People may bump into each other, but that's part of the fun.) Stage areas for musicians and their instruments take up a surprising amount of space. If you plan to have live entertainment, you need to determine whether the available space is big enough to accommodate the sound, the area for the entertainers, and enough customers to support the undertaking. Is the space too big? Can you fill it? Consider how it feels to be in a half-filled room as opposed to being in a small place that is crowded with people having fun. You need to be sure that the space will function as you intend it to, while there is still time to change your plans. Set space priorities and guidelines. Then, whether you do the layout yourself or have a designer do it, there is a lower risk of problems and unwelcome surprises.

Activities and Traffic Patterns. Consider the movement of people in the room. In addition to bar service, you might need to accommodate dining, dancing or live entertainment, or the traffic of guests in a hotel lobby. You also have to factor in the coming and going of the bar patrons themselves: entry and exit; visits to restrooms, telephones, coatroom; or just milling around. For an efficient layout, the space and direction of each activity must be accounted for, so that doors, furniture, and fixtures are placed for maximum efficiency.

In particular, a good layout will establish efficient traffic patterns to and from the bar for table service, to and from the kitchen and service areas for dining service, as well as customer entry and exit; the goal is to achieve an orderly flow, instead of chaos. The bar must also have easy access to storage areas; you don't want the bartender trundling a tub of ice through a throng of customers. Figure 3.5 shows good and poor traffic patterns for the same space.

A good layout will also consider clientele, mood, and ambience. The position of the bar itself can play up or down liquor service. In a family restaurant, for example, you might place a service bar discreetly in the background, whereas in a singles cocktail lounge you might position an island bar in the middle of the room, center stage, striking the keynote of fun and festivity, like a merry-go-round at a carnival.

Furniture. Choose all furniture, and lay it out, in relation to the total bar concept. Barstools and lounge chairs should look inviting and be comfortable. Chair designers claim they can control the rate of customer turnover simply by the degree of comfort of the seat cushion!

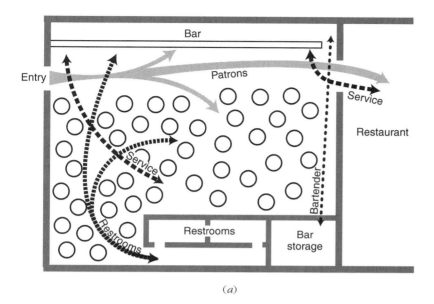

(a)

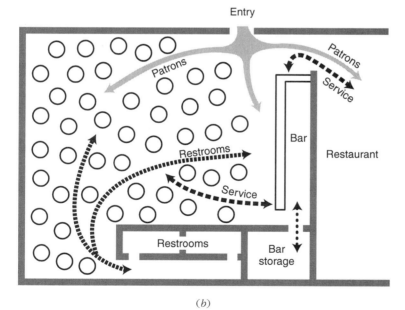

(b)

Figure 3.5 (a) A tangle of conflicting traffic patterns in a bar lounge. (b) Smoothing the flow of traffic by repositioning the entry and the bar.

Today's barstools come in all types of decorative styles, but no matter which you select, be sure to allow 24 inches of linear bar space for every stool at the bar. Looks are important, but don't overlook the other functions that stool must support. Comfort is a primary concern, which usually means a stool with a back. Upholstery that feels good, a suitable footrest height, a seat that swivels, and perhaps arms, are all options that you must decided. The "anatomy" of a bar stool is shown in Figure 3.6.

The standard barstool has a seat that is 30 inches above the floor. This allows the guest to "pull up" to a bar that is either 36 or 42 inches in height.

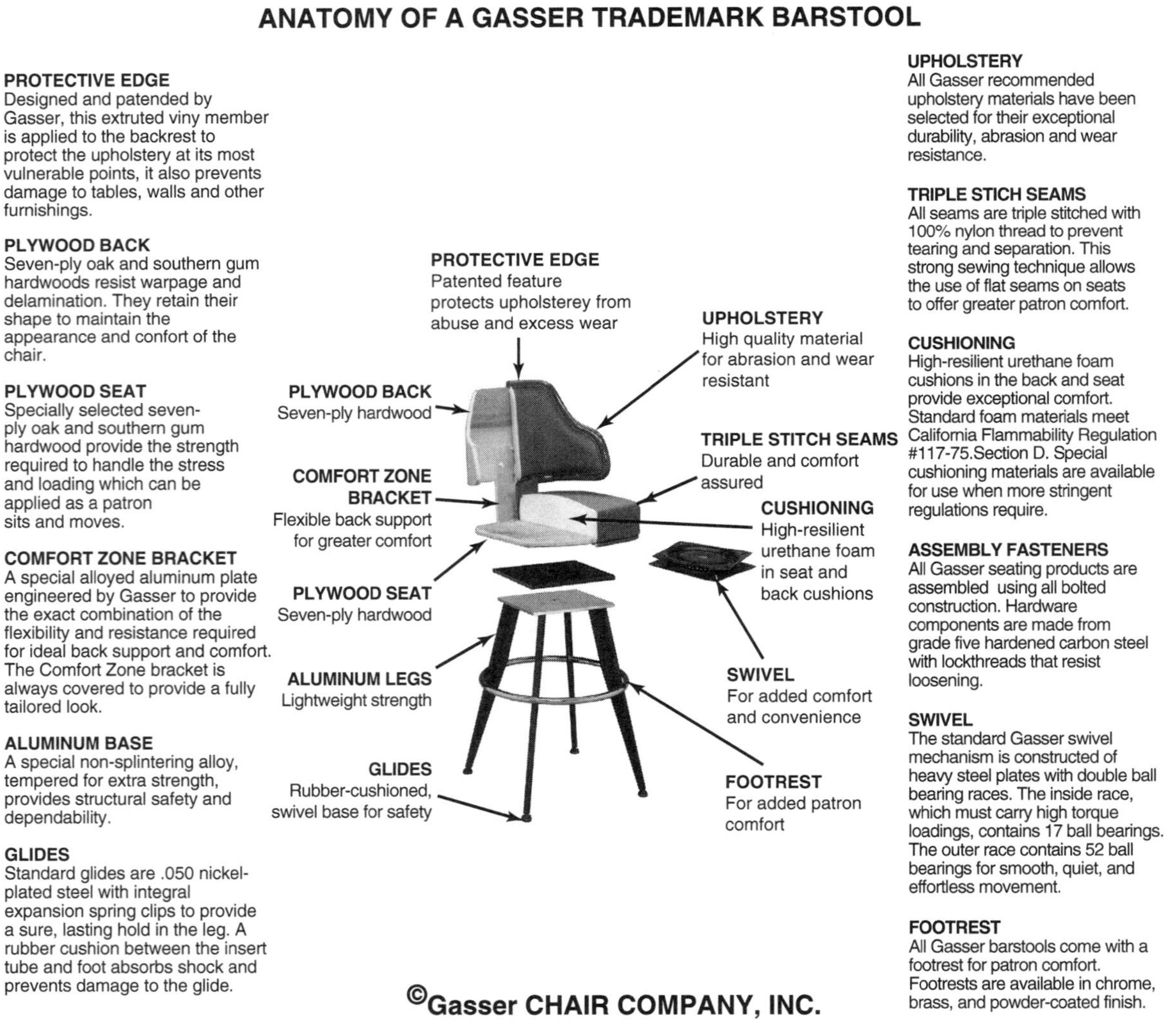

ANATOMY OF A GASSER TRADEMARK BARSTOOL

PROTECTIVE EDGE
Designed and patended by Gasser, this extruted viny member is applied to the backrest to protect the upholstery at its most vulnerable points, it also prevents damage to tables, walls and other furnishings.

PLYWOOD BACK
Seven-ply oak and southern gum hardwoods resist warpage and delamination. They retain their shape to maintain the appearance and confort of the chair.

PLYWOOD SEAT
Specially selected seven-ply oak and southern gum hardwood provide the strength required to handle the stress and loading which can be applied as a patron sits and moves.

COMFORT ZONE BRACKET
A special alloyed aluminum plate engineered by Gasser to provide the exact combination of the flexibility and resistance required for ideal back support and comfort. The Comfort Zone bracket is always covered to provide a fully tailored look.

ALUMINUM BASE
A special non-splintering alloy, tempered for extra strength, provides structural safety and dependability.

GLIDES
Standard glides are .050 nickel-plated steel with integral expansion spring clips to provide a sure, lasting hold in the leg. A rubber cushion between the insert tube and foot absorbs shock and prevents damage to the glide.

PROTECTIVE EDGE
Patented feature protects upholsterey from abuse and excess wear

PLYWOOD BACK
Seven-ply hardwood

COMFORT ZONE BRACKET
Flexible back support for greater comfort

PLYWOOD SEAT
Seven-ply hardwood

ALUMINUM LEGS
Lightweight strength

GLIDES
Rubber-cushioned, swivel base for safety

UPHOLSTERY
High quality material for abrasion and wear resistant

TRIPLE STITCH SEAMS
Durable and comfort assured

CUSHIONING
High-resilient urethane foam in seat and back cushions

SWIVEL
For added comfort and convenience

FOOTREST
For added patron comfort

UPHOLSTERY
All Gasser recommended upholstery materials have been selected for their exceptional durability, abrasion and wear resistance.

TRIPLE STICH SEAMS
All seams are triple stitched with 100% nylon thread to prevent tearing and separation. This strong sewing technique allows the use of flat seams on seats to offer greater patron comfort.

CUSHIONING
High-resilient urethane foam cushions in the back and seat provide exceptional comfort. Standard foam materials meet California Flammability Regulation #117-75.Section D. Special cushioning materials are available for use when more stringent regulations require.

ASSEMBLY FASTENERS
All Gasser seating products are assembled using all bolted construction. Hardware components are made from grade five hardened carbon steel with lockthreads that resist loosening.

SWIVEL
The standard Gasser swivel mechanism is constructed of heavy steel plates with double ball bearing races. The inside race, which must carry high torque loadings, contains 17 ball bearings. The outer race contains 52 ball bearings for smooth, quiet, and effortless movement.

FOOTREST
All Gasser barstools come with a footrest for patron comfort. Footrests are available in chrome, brass, and powder-coated finish.

©**Gasser CHAIR COMPANY, INC.**

Figure 3.6 Anatomy of a barstool from Gasser Chair Company of Youngstown, Ohio. Courtesy of Gasser Chair Company, Inc.

Though 24-inch barstools are also available, they are designed for home use beneath kitchen counters, and are too small for commercial bar use. This domestic stool is also not made sturdily enough to withstand the rigors of commercial use.

Lounge chairs should arrange well around cocktail tables. The tables themselves can be small if they are to be used only for drinks, and in a busy bar you can crowd them somewhat, adding to the conviviality. Both the size and shape of tables and chairs are important elements in layout.

Utilities, Codes, and Licensing Restrictions. When it comes to positioning the bar, plumbing is an important factor. Supply pipes and drains should not travel long distances because they are expensive to install and there is more to go wrong. If you have a kitchen, it is most efficient to coordinate plumbing for both.

Careful thought must also be given to electrical requirements in relation to layout. In addition to lighting designed for mood and décor, there are numerous special electrical needs of the underbar equipment. And if you offer live entertainment, you have to plan an electrical supply for electronic gear and a public address system. This all will affect your general layout, making you think twice, for example, about putting the bar or the musicians in the center of the room.

Heating and air-conditioning ducts and vents, smoke "eaters," and air circulators are also layout issues in the form of their output, the space they occupy, and their visual effect. A ceiling fan, for example, must have a certain visual relationship to the furniture and fixtures below it.

Local health and fire regulations often impinge on layout, especially in respect to exits and aisles. Likewise, health department requirements regarding glass washing can influence the space requirements inside the bar, as well as the plumbing and electrical requirements.

In some states and localities, requirements for liquor licensing can affect layout. Some prohibit open bars, so a restaurant must have a private club in a separate room in order to serve liquor. In other locales, food must be served in the same room where liquor is being served.

And don't forget that your layout must accommodate persons with disabilities; they must be given equal access to public or commercial buildings, according to Title III of the **Americans with Disabilities Act (ADA).** It requires wheelchair-accessible entrances, doorways, and restrooms for patrons and employees alike who may be disabled. Be aware that in some cities, building codes include these provisions, but in others, they do not, so do not assume that if you present your plans and receive a building permit, they have also been approved for ADA compliance. It is smart to have the plans checked first by an architect or contractor who is knowledgeable about the ADA. The U.S. Justice Department and Equal Employment Opportunity Commission enforce the act, and can fine building owners for noncompliance. It is less expensive to design a building that is accessible to the handicapped than to retrofit one after a complaint has been filed.

THE BAR ITSELF

Determining the size, shape, and placement of the bar itself is a twofold design problem, involving decor and function. The size and shape of the bar, its appearance, and its position in the room are typically planned by the owner, architect, or interior designer, whose primary concerns are layout and décor. The working areas, where the drinks are mixed and poured, are planned by a facilities design consultant or by an equipment dealer. Sometimes these professionals work together from the beginning, but too often a facilities designer or dealer is called in after the bar has been positioned and its dimensions set, and must do the best job possible within the allotted space.

Selecting Your Bar

When you select your bar, avoid a straight-line, rectangular model if possible, in favor of one with corners and angles. This automatically prompts guests to sit opposite each other and visit, instead of staring straight ahead at the backbar. Of course, though your imagination may be unlimited, in practice, the layout possibilities are limited by your available space and your budget. Figures 3.7 and 3.8 show two bar designs by Sue Miller of Glastender, Inc. of Saginaw, Michigan.

Today's possibilities include modular bar designs, which may cost more to purchase, but have some built-in advantages. They are already outfitted for plumbing and electrical needs and they are easy to maintain, remodel, or upgrade if necessary. The companies that design these ready-made bar units will also provide design and installation assistance.

A common mistake in bar design is to assign space for it without factoring in the projected volume of drinks that will be served and how much space and equipment will be needed to meet that volume. Only after money has been spent building the bar and buying the equipment does the owner discover its inadequacies. A poorly thought-out bar can cost more initially, limit profits, and cause daily frustration to those who work it. As we examine the bar in detail, you will see why.

Parts of the Bar

A bar is made up of three parts: the **front bar,** the **backbar,** and the **underbar.** Each has its special functions. Figure 3.9 shows these parts in profile, as though sliced through the middle, from front to back. The dimensions

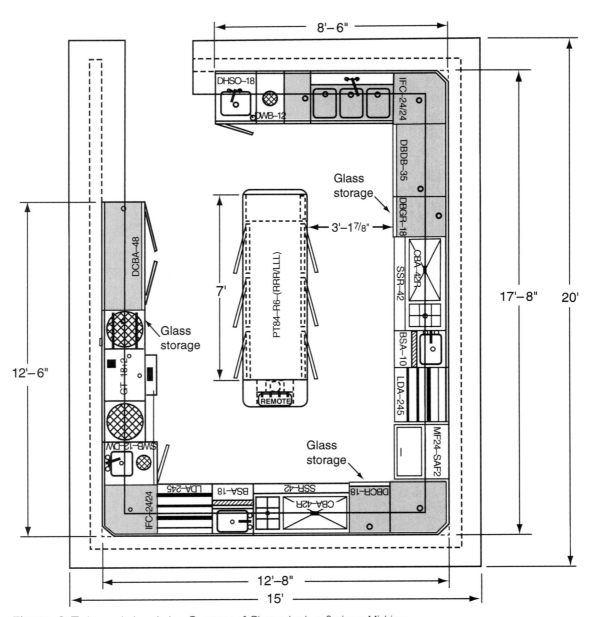

Figure 3.7 A sample bar design. Courtesy of Glastender, Inc., Saginaw, Michigan.

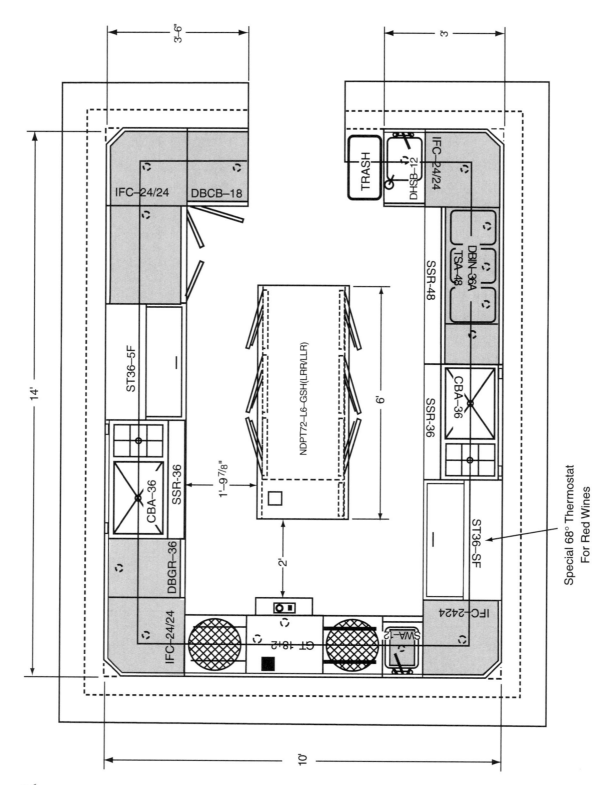

Figure 3.8 A layout for a wine and beer bar. Courtesy of Glastender, Inc., Saginaw, Michigan.

Special 68° Thermostat
For Red Wines

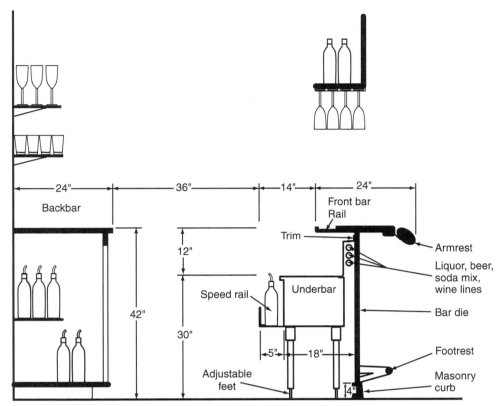

Figure 3.9 The bar in profile, showing dimensions.

given are those of a typical bar of good, workable design. The length of the bar will vary according to need.

The Front Bar. The front bar is the customer area, where they order their drinks and where the drinks are served. The bar is typically 16 to 18 inches wide, with a surface that is alcohol-proof, usually of laminated plastic. An armrest along the front edge, often padded, adds another 8 inches to its width. The last few inches of the back edge are usually recessed, and it is here that the bartender pours the drinks, to demonstrate liquor brand and pouring skill. This part of the bar is known variously as the **rail, glass rail, drip rail,** or **spill trough.**

The vertical structure supporting the front bar, known as the **bar die,** is like a wall that separates the customer from the working area. Seen in profile, it forms a T with the bar, making a kind of table on the customer side, with the other side shielding the underbar from public view. There is usually a footrest running the length of the die on the customer side, about a foot off the ground. On elegant mahogany bars of the 1800s, the footrest was a brass rail, and underneath it every few feet were brass spittoons. The Prohibitionists made the brass rail a symbol of the wickedness of drink, along with swinging saloon doors and Demon Rum.

The height of the front bar is 42 to 48 inches, because that's a good, basic working height for most bartenders. This height also makes the front bar just right for leaning against with one foot on the footrest, in the time-honored tradition of the nineteenth-century barroom. All underbar equipment is designed to fit beneath or behind a 42-inch bar.

A sit-down bar will have barstools tall enough so that customers can use the top of the bar as a table. The length of the bar will determine how many stools you'll need, since each stool is allotted a 2-foot length of bar. Barstools are designed so that their seats are high off the ground, so they typically have rungs for footrests; or the footrest of the bar is within easy reach of the feet. Even numbers of barstools make seating convenient for couples.

The elements of the front bar—the surface, die, armrest, footrest, and stools—are part of your public's perception of your establishment, so their "look" must be carefully planned in conjunction with the total décor.

The Backbar. The backbar has a dual function: as a decorative display area and as a hard-working storage space. No matter how tidy or cluttered, grand or humble, the backbar speaks volumes about a bar operation. Some people say it is the "soul" of the bar. It conveys an image of the establishment and showcases the kinds of beverages a patron can expect to be served there. It stimulates conversation, displays the wares, and can be used to post information, whether that means prices, drink specials, your logo, funny signs, neighborhood flyers, or sports pools. (It's always smart to insist that anything posted on the backbar fit in with your own décor and standards.)

The shiny splendor of bottles and glassware is usually reflected by a mirror, a tradition of the backbar. In the Old West—or at least, in old Western movies—the mirror had another function: it showed the customer at the bar whether anyone was coming up behind him, gun in hand. Today, the mirror adds depth to the room; it also gives customers a view of others at the bar and elsewhere in the room. Bartenders sometimes use it, too, to observe customers without being noticed. The typical modern bar consists primarily of mirror, bottles, and glassware. Some people feel it is just not a bar without these elements. There are functional reasons for the prominence of these elements, too: the liquor and glassware comprise the bartender's working supplies, and the backbar is a good place to display call brands as a subtle form of merchandising. **Multiple facings** are often used—three or four bottles of a known brand are displayed side by side, reinforcing its popularity. White and brown liquors are alternated for visual effect; or the backbar stock is rotated occasionally to showcase different brands. Sometimes, the bartender

Tips for Maintaining a Perfect Backbar

- Keep the labels on your bottles facing out at all times.
- Replace any bottles with torn or crooked labels.
- Group your spirits by category: Scotch with Scotch, Bourbon with Bourbon, etc. Mixing up your inventory makes it more difficult for patrons to see what you offer, and makes bartenders less productive.
- Check your inventory on a regular basis. Spirits that aren't selling don't belong on your backbar, or in your bar at all for that matter.
- If you have space, highlight special selections, like a collection of single-malt Scotches or high-end liqueurs.
- To create impact, use multiple facings of premium spirits where possible, especially if you feature a premium well. It shows your patrons that you believe in pouring the best.
- Use lighting—underlit glass shelving or bottle steps and spotlights—to highlight your backbar display and create a bit of drama.
- Be sure that signage, promotional materials, and knick-knacks that you want to keep on your backbar all fit in with your decor and your image.
- Keep it clean. Wipe down bottles, shelving, registers and other equipment at least once a week, if not daily. If you keep open bottles on your backbar, make sure pourers are clean as well. Making sure that all your pourers match also creates a clean, consistent look.

—*Mike Sherer*

Figure 3.10 Tips for maintaining a perfect backbar. *Source: Top Shelf Magazine.*

simply organizes the backbar based on what he or she will need to have handy at the busiest times. Whatever the system, the merchandising power of the backbar should never be underestimated. See Figure 3.10 for tips on maintaining a successful backbar. Fashions in backbar décor include stained glass, paneled or textured walls, murals, posters, wine racks, mood pieces, and conversation starters.

The base of the backbar is likely to be allocated as storage space, refrigerated or otherwise. Or it may house special equipment such as a glass froster, an ice machine, or a mechanical dishwasher. If specialty drinks are featured, the frozen-drink or espresso machine will probably be on the backbar. The cash register is usually there, too, in a recessed space.

Whatever its uses, the backbar must be visually pleasing from top to bottom, since customers look at it, and it must coordinate visually with the décor of the room as a whole.

The Underbar. The underbar is usually the last section of the bar to be designed, after the front of the bar has been created. It deserves the same degree of careful attention as the rest of the bar, since this is where most of the equipment and supplies for the products you are selling must be arranged compactly and efficiently, to facilitate speed of service.

Overall, your goal should be to design an underbar and backbar area that makes wise use of space, is as sanitary as possible, and is able to respond to consumer tastes and trends in drink preparation. Consider your clientele, their demographics, and their personal preferences when planning your underbar.

The area where individual bartenders work is called a **pouring station.** It must have an individual supply of liquor, ice, mixes, glasses, blender, and garnishes, all within arm's reach. Each pouring station also has an ice bin and one or more bottle racks for the most-used liquors and mixes. (You'll learn more about bar-related equipment in Chapter 4.) A supply of glasses may be placed upside down on a glass rail, on drainboards near the ice bin, on special glass shelves, in glass racks stacked beside the station, on the back-bar, in overhead racks, or in all these places, grouped according to type and size. The blender, and probably a mixer, may be placed on a recessed shelf beside the ice bin, while the garnishes are typically located on the bar top in a special condiment tray.

Most operations use an automatic dispensing system for carbonated beverages. Such a system has lines running from bulk supplies (hidden within the underbar) to a dispensing "head." The lines and head together are often called a **cobra gun,** because of the snaking lines with its head. A cobra gun is needed at each pouring station. If the bar has an automated liquor-dispensing system, the setup is similar.

Dispensing systems will vary drastically depending on the situation. The needs of a beer concession stand in an athletic stadium, for instance, are quite different from those of a bar in a fine restaurant. In the former, it may not matter that the beer lines from keg to tap are long. But in the latter it would, because line length affects the quality of the beer, and a connoisseur will notice the difference.

The number of pouring stations at your bar will depend on the volume and flow of business. The bar should be designed with enough stations to handle the peak periods, with the equipment it takes to do it. Figure 3.11 shows the plan of the hotel bar (shown in greater detail in Chapter 4, Figures 4.2 and 4.3). Notice there are three stations to serve different areas: dining room, coffee shop, and bar lounge.

Where drinks are served from the main bar for table service, the bar must always have a **pickup station,** a section of the front bar near the pouring station where serving personnel turn in and receive orders and return empty glasses. The pickup station must be separated somehow from where customers sit and order; otherwise the servers must elbow their way through the customers, in which case confusion reigns and spills occur, and your profits may end up on the jacket of a celebrity who has just dropped in for a drink, or an ice cube may find its way down someone's neck! The pickup station

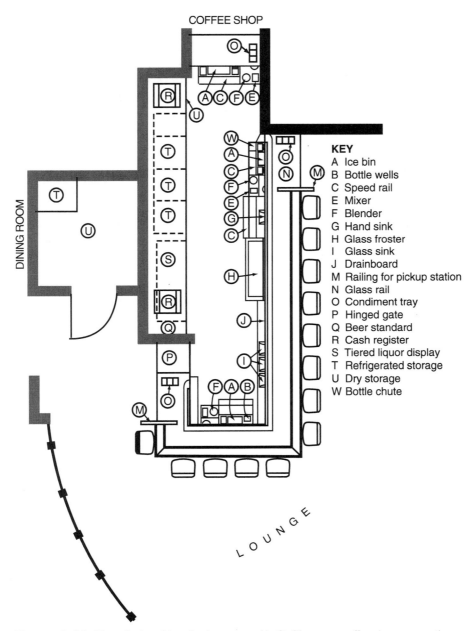

KEY

A Ice bin
B Bottle wells
C Speed rail
E Mixer
F Blender
G Hand sink
H Glass froster
I Glass sink
J Drainboard
M Railing for pickup station
N Glass rail
O Condiment tray
P Hinged gate
Q Beer standard
R Cash register
S Tiered liquor display
T Refrigerated storage
U Dry storage
W Bottle chute

Figure 3.11 Plan of a hotel bar. Station at top (A, C, O) serves coffee shop across the corridor. Right-hand station (A, C, M, O) serves cocktail lounge and bar. Station at bottom (A, B) serves bar and pickup station (M, O) for dining room to left (U). Rear portions of underbar equipment are not visible in this view. Plan courtesy Norman Ackerman, HG Rice and Company, Inc., Dallas, Texas.

should be near a pouring station and the cash register. In Figure 3.11 you can identify two of the pickup stations (top right and bottom left) by the railings (M) that set them apart from customer seating areas of the bar.

Another area of the underbar contains glasswashing equipment—a three- or four-compartment sink (I on the plan in Figure 3.11) with drainboards on both sides—or, in some cases, a mechanical dishwasher. The underbar must also have provision for waste disposal and a hand sink (G on the plan). These are typical health department requirements. Be aware that health departments are continuously scrutinizing the sanitation procedures of bars. For instance, rules may dictate where you store empty beer bottles if your operation recycles them.

Together, the underbar and backbar must provide enough storage for the day's reserve supplies of liquor, mixes, wines, beers, ice, garnishes, and such nonbeverage supplies as bar towels, cocktail napkins, picks, and stir sticks. All these must be arranged so that access to them requires a minimum of movement. Movement is time, and time, as we all know, is money.

Three feet is the customary distance between the backbar and the underbar, to accommodate the bartenders' movements and the opening of storage cabinet doors. Cabinet doors must not be so wide that they block passage when open. Storage areas must be available to each bartender without interfering with another's movements.

There are three ways to order underbar equipment. You can choose stock designs from manufacturers' catalogs or Web sites; you can have custom equipment constructed to meet specific needs or spaces; or you can use a combination of both. In most cases, a few "stock" components are ordered and a few pieces are custom-made to fit precisely in the underbar area. The equipment is installed usually by a local equipment dealer. When you design the bar, make sure to get input from an equipment dealer or manufacturer.

If you're planning on serving special drinks, you'll need to plan for the equipment they need. If you intend to have beer on tap, for instance, you must know to place the "standards" (faucets)—Q in Figure 3.11—so that they are easily accessible to the bartender (but not to the customer!); and you must have refrigerated storage space for each keg, either at the bar or in a nearby storage area with lines installed for bringing the beer to the bar. For obvious reasons, the latter arrangement is more sophisticated than having kegs at the bar, but it requires that you install custom-engineered equipment to maintain beer quality. Likewise, frozen-drink dispensers, ice cream equipment, and glass frosters have special space requirements that must be designed into the overall bar scheme.

There are plenty of design variations to choose from: Your pouring station can be a bit larger, and, as just mentioned, your beer kegs can be stored elsewhere with a system of remote lines and taps; or, if your local health department doesn't require a four-compartment bar sink, you can opt for a handy automatic glasswasher; you can also provide more room for bottle coolers if you decide to serve a wide selection of bottled beers. Whatever you choose to do, just be sure you have decided on your drink menu before you design your bar space. Give equal weight to form and function in the design process.

Hidden but essential factors in underbar and backbar design are the plumbing and electrical needs of the equipment. Faucets, icemakers, cobra guns, and dishwashers all need a water supply. Sinks, refrigerators, glass frosters, ice bins, icemakers, dishwashers, and waste disposal need proper drainage. Some equipment may need special electrical wiring.

All equipment must be installed to enable ready access for repairs. To achieve that, the entrance to the bar is sometimes made large enough to accommodate the largest piece of movable equipment, in case it has to be replaced or repaired. On the other hand, the smaller the access, the more space you have available for equipment, so usually the bar entrance is designed as a hinged section of the bar top that lifts up (P on the plan). Repairs are made in place, or replacement equipment is lifted over the bar when necessary. Sometimes one end of the bar is left open, though this leaves the liquor supply more vulnerable to tampering and makes control more difficult. Another alternative is to install a doorway in the backbar.

The Bar Floor. Think about the bartenders' comfort and safety when you plan the bar floor. They are on their feet for hours, and you want them to look fresh and feel good. The floor under their feet must have a nonporous surface, such as tile or sealed concrete, to meet sanitary code requirements. Wood and carpeting are not acceptable. A tile or concrete surface is cold, hard, and slippery when wet. And keep in mind that as an evening wears on, ice cubes, beer foam, soapy water, debris from empty glasses, and broken glass may accumulate.

There are ways to improve floor comfort and safety, but none is ideal. Slotted plastic panels allow spills to go down between the slats, to minimize hazards of slipping. But they must be taken up for cleaning, which is a nuisance, and if it isn't done often they become stale-smelling and unsanitary. They are also hard on the feet. Rubber or plastic mats minimize slippage and are easy on the feet, but they also must be cleaned frequently.

Bar Size, Shape, and Position in the Room

From the front of the front bar to the back of the backbar, the overall depth of your bar should be about 8 feet (again, refer to Figure 3.11). The minimum length of the bar should be determined from the inside, according to equipment needs. Additional length and shape will be determined from the outside, according to the number of customers you want to seat (if there are seats), the size of the room, and the overall design requirements.

The inside factors are determined mainly by the kinds of drinks served and the number of pouring stations needed to meet peak volume. The outside factors have to do with your total concept, your clientele, your décor, and the available space.

Unfortunately, the last consideration—the space available—is usually the tail that wags the dog. Often the space available is what is left over after everything else has been planned. Many times, an inadequate bar space will limit what you can serve and how much, thereby decreasing your profits. Or it may require expensive and complicated equipment solutions to problems that would be simple to solve in a larger space.

The best way to proceed is to plan your drink menu first, with your clientele in mind. Figure carefully the volume you can expect at peak periods. Size your bar to accommodate space and equipment needs for those drinks in that volume, or have a specialist do it. Don't box yourself into a bar that is too small.

If your facility is already built, and space is predetermined, it becomes even more critical to think through your bar design and equipment to make the most profitable use of the space you have. Again, your clientele and your drink menu are the logical starting points. You may, for example, have to choose between beer on tap and ice cream drinks in frosted glasses. If you know your clientele, it is much easier to make the most profitable choice.

Bars can be many different shapes—straight, curved, angled, horseshoe, round, square, or free-form. Shape, too, is a decision involving many factors: room size and shape, mood, décor, function. Unusual shapes are tricky. Most underbar equipment is factory-made in standard sizes that may not fit an irregular shape. Custom work increases cost and sometimes does not work as well in action. It can also create maintenance and repair headaches.

Usually a bar has its back to the wall; but in a large room, it may be the centerpiece or focal point, a freestanding square, round, oval, or irregular island, with stations facing in several directions and a backbar in the middle. Obviously, an island bar will have special design considerations. The backbar will be smaller and the front bar larger, and the underbar will be visible to the patrons. There may be special plumbing and electrical problems.

Whatever its shape, the bar's position in the room deserves as much consideration as its shape and size, for it may affect both. Do you want it to be seen from the street? Do you want it to set the tone of your establishment or take second place to your food service, your bowling alley, or your dance floor?

Consider the customers' reactions as they enter the room. Crossing the room to get to the bar may be inhibiting. Some people may turn around and go back out rather than cross an empty room at 4:00 P.M. or, a couple of hours later, plow through crowds of standees or thread their way through the lounge amid staring eyes. Usually, the best place for the bar is near the door where customers can head straight for it. Make these kinds of decisions before you draw up any plans.

The Bar as a Control Center

While its major function is the dispensing of drinks, the bar also functions as your control center; its where you keep records of the stock on hand, the drinks poured, and their sales value. After each serving period, the sales record is checked against money received, to verify that one equals the other. This leads to the most important piece of equipment in the bar—the cash register. It is the core of the system of controls by which management assures that its liquor is sold to the customer with little or no "evaporation" en route. In some operations, the bartender also takes in the money; in others, this is done by a cashier at a separate register.

In a large and busy bar, each bartender may have a separate register, or bartenders may share a register that has a separate drawer for each one. In any case, a register must be close to each pouring station and the pickup station so that a minimum of time and motion is lost. Since the register is usually within full view of customers, its placement also becomes a design element to be reckoned with.

Smaller, Specialized Bars

The term **service bar** refers to a bar that pours for table service only, usually in conjunction with food service. It does not serve customers directly, but deals only with filling drink orders brought by waiter staff. Usually, a single service bar station is enough to handle the volume, except in very large restaurants.

Sometimes a service bar is part of the dining room, but more often it is out of sight, in which case it is smaller and simpler in design. Instead of backbar display, it has room for bulk supplies of beer, mixes, and liquor stock, and there is no need to camouflage or hide ugly or noisy equipment. Mechanical dispensing systems are often used here in preference to hand pouring, to increase speed and reduce liquor loss; at a public bar, there may be customer resistance to such impersonal methods.

In its basics, however, a service bar is like any other bar. It has the same functions, uses the same kinds of equipment, and performs the same tasks of recording and controlling the pouring and selling of drinks. Thus, it needs the same forethought to plan as any other bar.

The same goes for the **portable bar,** a typical extension of a hotel's beverage service where banquets, meetings, receptions, conferences or conventions are being held. Portable bars give the hotel the flexibility to serve beverages on short notice anywhere on the premises, indoors or out.

The typical portable bar ranges in length from 4 to 8 feet. Larger models can accommodate two bartenders working side by side, and often can hold sealed-in cold plate units for dispensing chilled beverages. Some portable bars fold into 2-foot widths for easy storage, and most have 5-inch casters for rolling them into place, and locking brakes on the casters.

Ice bins on portable bar units should have a water drain for the inevitable melting that occurs, and a sufficient reservoir to hold this "waste water." Underbar storage should consist of removable, adjustable shelves. Speed rails (to hold liquor bottles) and storage cabinets are other desirable options. Look for a portable bar that has stainless-steel backsplash and sidesplashes, and a laminated top that cannot be stained by water or alcohol.

WORKING WITH A DESIGNER OR CONSULTANT

A wide range of expertise is available to help you plan the physical environment of your facility. Your first challenge is to sort out who you really need. Your options are described in the following subsections.

Consultants

At one end of the range is the food facilities consultant firm that will do the entire job for you, from carrying out detailed market and feasibility studies and developing a concept that will sell to your clientele through completion of the job. These professionals can choose your glassware and design your matchbook covers! Many consultant firms offer a full spectrum of design services, including architects, interior designers, graphic artists, and foodservice facilities designers who specialize in kitchens and bars. Other consultant firms have only certain of those skills within their firms, but can put together a whole design team for you by subcontracting with other specialists.

Consultants are typically used on projects for which a sizable investment has been made. The right consultant will make you money in the long run by doing the most appropriate, efficient, and profitable job. Many food facilities consultants also accept small jobs. You can find them listed in the Yellow Pages, or you can write to their professional organization, Foodservice Consultants Society International (FCSI), which offers planning, design, and management consulting services in this specialized field. Members must have 10 years of experience and must pass critical reviews of professional competence.

For bar design, the most specialized service a consultant has to offer is the design of the space inside the bar by a facilities designer. This specialist will identify the equipment you need to serve your drink menu and lay it all out for maximum efficiency and economy. Facilities designers' knowledge is different from that of interior designers and architects, especially regarding code requirements, the equipment available, and typical problems and solutions. They often work closely with interior designers and architects, however, and should be brought into the picture before the size and shape of the bar are finalized. If a facilities designer puts your bar project out for bid, you'll be given a choice of equipment from several companies. You may get a better bar for less money than if you tried to put it together yourself or had a restaurant supply house do it using only the equipment lines it carries.

Interior Designers

The interior designer who specializes in restaurants is trained in the aesthetics of this particular type of design, and an experienced interior designer will be familiar with restaurant design trends and with the commercial furniture, fabrics, and other materials available. This type of designer will typically do your space planning (layout); select your furnishings; design your floors, ceilings, walls, window treatments; and plan your lighting, coordinating the entire plan to fit your overall concept, and supervising all installations.

In choosing an interior designer, it is important to focus on the right kind of experience. Designers who have done only residential work or other types of commercial establishments may not understand the very specialized design needs of a bar or restaurant.

Choosing Design Assistance

Before choosing a designer or consultant, shop around. Find a bar or restaurant you think has been particularly well designed. It doesn't have to reflect your kind of concept or attract your kind of clientele; it simply has to be well done in terms of its own purpose and concept. Ask who designed it. Then find out what else that person has designed and visit as many of those places as possible. If they are all on target, go ahead. If not, do some more exploring until you find someone who does the kind of job you are looking for consistently well. As with any other profession, different designers will have reputations and preferences for different types of work.

Working Arrangements. Consultants and designers work on contract, an advantage to you and to them. Typically, you'll pay a retainer, a standard "starting fee" or percentage, to begin the job. Some interior designers will work on the basis of a design fee plus a commission on the furniture and materials you buy. Others will do a design on an hourly fee basis and let you carry out parts or all of it yourself.

Whatever your investment, be sure the contract spells out clearly the scope of the job, the fees to be paid, and the various stages of the project at which payment is to be made.

Smaller-Scale or Remote Projects. What if you have only a limited budget or want to open in a small town or remote area where specialists are not available to you? Specialists will go anywhere for the right money, but you will have to pay their travel expenses. You can also get help from dealers—restaurant supply houses, commercial furniture dealers, and the like. Investigate as many as you can. Some of the help will be good, as many facilities designers began their careers designing in restaurant supply houses; but some of it will be no better than you could do yourself if you planned carefully. And be aware that most, if not all, recommendations from these businesses will be limited to the brands and products they're selling.

You may find a local interior designer who is willing to work with you on an hourly basis. Or you might consult an art teacher to help you with design and color coordination. Help may also be available through manufacturers' representatives. Of course, you yourself have a talent for design. More often, though, people who have the operational know-how focus on the product, the staff, and getting the money together, and they neglect the physical ambience. However you decide to cover this base, keep in mind that in today's market, the bar-restaurant is part of the entertainment business, and the physical setting is at least half the story; where competition is keen, it may be the whole story—your identity. If you do decide to "go it alone," opt for a simple, clean look. Don't clutter it up; don't try for pseudosophistication. Today the clean line is sophisticated; it is currently one of the major design trends.

CHECKLIST OF BAR DESIGN ESSENTIALS

Whether you hire a designer or design your bar yourself, define your needs and wants clearly. The more information you can give a designer and the clearer your own goals, the better the result—and the easier the collaboration.

The following is a checklist of basics you should decide on before you meet with a consultant or designer or take the important next steps on your own:

- Target clientele
- Services to be offered
- Overall concept

- The competition
- Projected volume of business (number of seats, turnover, drinks/patrons per day, days open, annual gross income)
- Types of beverages you will serve
- Size and shape of bar area (architect's plans for an existing structure if you have them)
- Activities to take place in bar area
- Relationship of bar to dining and service areas (kitchen, storage)
- Existing décor, equipment, furniture, and fixtures you expect to keep
- Licensing, zoning, health, fire, and building code requirements
- Time limitations
- Budget limitations (This is a must before you consult anyone else, unless you are hiring a consultant just to give cost estimates for the job.)

SUMMING UP

The first step for turning a building, room, or space into a popular and profitable bar is determining your target clientele. The next step involves choosing the products and services you'll offer to this clientele, or **market segment.** The third step is to define a unifying concept with a special character or identity.

Next, you must study the market, by visiting the other bar businesses in the neighborhoods you're considering, as well as other bars with similar clientele, prices, or concepts. Choose a location on the basis of the market study and determine the feasibility of your project for that location. Only then is it time to deal with the physical facility. The goal is to make it an environment that attracts the desired clientele, gives them pleasure, and makes them want to come again.

Décor is a large factor in creating this environment. Color, light, arrangement of furniture and fixtures, efficient use of space, and the appearance of the bar itself all contribute. The bar should be designed from the inside out, beginning with the drink menu; its décor should be developed in partnership with functional needs. You will also need to accommodate disabled patrons and employees, to meet the requirements of the Americans with Disabilities Act.

The bar itself should be designed based on the types of drinks that you will serve, since some require special equipment (like blenders). The overall "look" of the backbar area is another consideration. Will it be packed with bottles and be used for storage or will it be sleek and uncluttered, with most bottles stored out of sight? Try to make the most profitable use of the limited space at and behind the bar.

Enable traffic patterns of servers and customers to flow smoothly; people shouldn't have to "cross paths" too often, for safety reasons. If entertainment is part of the concept, allow adequate room for it in the design—a dance floor, a stage, and so on. Carefully plan the locations of utilities—water, power, air vents. In large rooms, where ancillary bars (portable bars or service bars) are part of the setup, hire a designer or consultant to help with the initial plans, or try it yourself.

POINTS TO PONDER

1. Why is it so important to design the physical environment of a bar with a particular type of customer in mind?

2. In a few words, describe the colors, lighting, sound level, and types of furnishings you might use to set the mood in (a) a casual, "family" restaurant that includes liquor sales, (b) a singles bar, and (c) a cocktail lounge in a prestigious resort hotel.

3. What does the term *market segment* mean? Why is this concept important in developing a plan for a new bar?

4. What should you look for when making a detailed study of other bars in your market area?

5. Name three things you should offer, or be aware of, to make sure your bar is attractive to female customers.

6. Which of the successful bars described on pages 71–74 would be most successful in your local area? Which would not go over well in your market? Explain why.

7. In Figure 3.11, how does the overall shape of the room affect (a) arrangement of furniture and fixtures, (b) number of people accommodated, and (c) feasible activities? Can you improve the layout by changing the entry or the size, shape, or location of furniture and fixtures?

8. In designing the bar itself, why should you start with your drink menu?

9. In your particular bar, what do you think the backbar should "say" about your business?

10. What is the difference between an interior designer and a facilities designer? What are the particular skills and expertise of each? Do you need both?

TERMS OF THE TRADE

Americans with Disabilities Act (ADA)

backbar

bar die

cobra gun

concept bar

front bar

image

market segment

multiple facings

participatory bar

pickup station

portable bar

pouring station

rail (glass, drip, trough)

service bar

underbar

GEORGE MAJDALANI
Restaurant Operations Manager

After majoring in Business Information and Accounting in college, George Majdalani was trained as a bar and restaurant manager by Robert Zimmerman, former CEO of Rosewood Properties (a Texas-based company that owns upscale hotel properties). Today, he is executive operations manager for the Restaurant Life division of the M Crowd Restaurant Group. M Crowd is headquartered in Dallas, Texas, and has 19 locations and 8 different dining concepts.

Q: What does an operations manager do?

A: I have general managers, managers, chefs, and sous chefs who operate the restaurants. My main objective is to make sure that the managers and chefs are operating them the way that the owners and partners meant for each restaurant to be run—whether it's the style of the food, the service, the feel of the restaurant. I maintain that and I make sure they all focus on that. I focus on whatever the goals of each restaurant are—financial, marketing, or whatever—and I work with the chef and the general manager to achieve those goals.

Q: What have you learned about hiring people?

A: Mr. Zimmerman's theory was, "When you hire someone, always hire them with their management potential in mind. Never hire them to be an 'employee.'" So when you interview someone, ask the questions as if they were being hired for a management position. You'll have more success with them, and they'll have more success with you.

They also have to be serious about the job, and not look at it as a job, but as a career. I always look at hourly employees as managers for the future. When I go to a restaurant, I don't think, "Which one of these employees would *like* to be a manager?" I think, "Which one of them really *wants* it?" I can teach anybody this business. But I can never teach them the desire, the attitude, to be truly successful.

Q: If you're in an entry-level position, what is the best kind of experience to get? Front of the house? Back of the house? Bartending?

A: I don't believe that you have to be a dishwasher before you can become a great chef, or a busboy to become a great

manager. But I do believe that, in some way or other, a person has to understand and accept any position in the restaurant in order to grow. If you become a manager, believe me, you have to know how to mop, wash dishes, how the ovens and grills work. You may not be able to execute a dish like the chef, but when anyone doesn't show up, the staff looks up to the manager to be able to do the job. If you don't know how, you are in trouble.

Q: How do you handle liquor storage, and how do you keep it secure?

A: We store enough liquor for our approximate weekly usage at the bar; that's our par stock. Then we have a small storeroom near the bar that does not hold more than a couple of cases and other bar-related supplies. We do not mix our bar storage and restaurant or food storage. There is too much access to food storage, and with liquor, I want only the manager or bartender to have access. The bartender is held to stricter standards, I'd say, than any other employee, for obvious reasons; this person handles not only a lot of cash, but liquor, beer, and wine as well.

In terms of inventory, things that you buy per piece and sell by the piece—like a bottle of beer or wine—are much easier to keep track of. We have a proportioned pour for wines by the glass; we know we're going to get exactly four glasses from each bottle. But I must control liquor access far more carefully. There are only a few keys: for the manager who opens, the manager who closes, and the chef if he [or she] opens or closes. The owner has one and I have one. And that's it. Managers only—no employees have keys.

Q: What do you think is the hardest part of managing a beverage operation?

A: Control of the product is one thing. First, I believe you must have a computer system that does not allow the bartender or employees to verbally order and that everything being served must be recorded and charged to somebody. It's not just a trust factor; things get busy and people can't rely on their memories to ring things up later. And the second factor is, there is a lot of cash handled at a bar. As a manager, you have to keep your eyes open and make sure—if a certain bartender uses more cash than credit cards—that nothing is forgotten. Hire staff that you trust very, very much, and then create a system that supports them to be successful. If the system does not prompt their success, then they will find "ways" of making more money.

So we monitor very carefully. My philosophy is, if I see something I don't understand, I ask. There are so many ways you can interpret things, and you've got to let the staff be relaxed and comfortable—it's not that you're watching them every minute. Nobody likes to work under those conditions. But theft is a reality, and there are hints and suspicious behaviors you must be aware of. Also, random drug testing is a policy in our company.

Q: What kinds of training do you give for dealing with customers who drink too much?

A: In Texas, individual servers have to be certified to serve alcohol. The state provides a three-hour course for servers. One of the things they teach in that program is, don't serve more than three drinks to a person the first hour; don't serve more than two drinks the second hour; and don't serve more than two drinks the third hour. And they have to eat something during that time. In our restaurants, the manager is notified anytime a customer has had three drinks and orders a fourth, so that the manager can discuss it with the guest.

Q: You let the manager handle it, not the server?

A: That's right. The server just says, "I'm worried about Table 5; they've had a lot to drink, please go talk to them." It's simple. The manager observes the guests and may go up to them and say, "You are showing signs of intoxication and I can't serve you anymore." We give them their check and say, "Have a good night." And, immediately, we remove all the drinks from the table; we don't even serve a person sitting next to them at the same table, because he or she could take a sip from that drink. We do offer complimentary cab rides if a guest shows any sign of intoxication.

Q: What are the trends you're noticing at the bar?

A: Classic drinks are coming back—the Martinis, Manhattans, Cuba Libres. Lately, vodkas, gins and tequilas are "hot" on the market; also the different flavors of bottled waters and single-serving iced teas, for people who want a nonalcoholic drink.

I also think today's bartender has to know more about the food side of our business. People now like to have an appetizer with their drinks, or relax at the bar and ask for menu recommendations before they sit down to eat. Bartenders should know how to match foods and wines, more about fine dining touches, like Port and Cognac.

Q: I've noticed two things about your design: that your bar does not have a busy-looking backbar area stocked with liquor and supplies, and that the bar is the first thing you walk into when you enter the restaurant. Are there reasons for this?

A: Absolutely. We describe our concepts as "neighborhood restaurants." I don't want people to come in and eat and leave. I want 'em to have a whole package: to come in, relax with a glass of wine or even water! It's a relaxing buffer zone between the outside and the restaurant. I don't like to rush the guest.

Q: What kind of education do you think a person should have to go into bar or restaurant management?

A: Personally, I feel it is important for a person in a business environment to have a degree or some type of education from a business point of view—to understand how different industries combine and work together to be successful. My intention when I went to college was to have more than one business. I didn't know exactly what I was going to do, but I knew that I was going to be able to do more than one aspect of a business. I was not going to restrict myself to only one area!

In a bar or restaurant, we are really a type of manufacturing business. We have raw products coming in and, at a certain time of day, we have to produce a finished product. That takes more than people to do. You need equipment, service experts, chemicals, produce, and they all have to be on hand and working correctly to produce what you need to produce. So I think business sense, financial sense, is mandatory to be in this business; and second is communication, to keep yourself in check and your employees in check.

Q: In a bar/restaurant operation, how important is the bar in the overall profit mix?

A: The beverage program, as a whole, can make or break a restaurant. It has the most profit margin of any product in the restaurant. The food may keep them coming back, but it is the liquor that pays the bills. So it is important to build a good bar crowd, of people who don't necessarily stay for dinner.

For every $100 I sell, I want liquor, beer, and wine to be $35 of that, and food to be $65. That is the ideal ratio. For a fine-dining restaurant with, say, $2 million in sales per year, that means at least $700,000 running through the bar, much of it in cash. It has to be correct; it has to balance at the end of the night. So you see how important security is.

I also regularly analyze how much of each—liquor, beer, wine—is being sold. There's sometimes a good reason for a change—it's hot outside, so people are drinking more beer or frozen drinks and less wine. Other times, it points out a weakness you have to correct.

Then it is important to share this information with the staff. A good wait staff is a good sales force, and salespeople can get bored if you never give them anything new or interesting to sell. So always keep them in the loop, with training and regular meetings. And make sure they know how important the bar business is to the restaurant's overall profitability.

CHAPTER 4

Bar Equipment

Complete familiarity with the bartender's working environment—underbar, backbar, and equipment—is essential to profitable bar management. To produce the drinks ordered, of the quality desired, with the speed and efficiency needed to satisfy the customers and meet the profit goal, the right equipment must be in place. Few managers fully comprehend equipment needs, the effects of equipment on drink quality, and the limitations that equipment and space can impose on a drink menu.

The purpose of this chapter is to improve manager comprehension of this important issue, by describing the basic equipment essential to any bar, as well as the alternatives that can be used to meet a wide variety of needs.

This chapter should help you . . .

- Plan a complete pouring station.
- Choose from various methods of measuring and pouring liquors.
- Choose from various methods of pouring carbonated mixers.
- Determine the kind of ice needed for a given bar and the size of the ice machine.
- Install the required equipment for washing glasses.
- Provide for the special needs of draft-beer service.
- Determine the space needed for refrigeration, dry storage, liquor stock, and glassware.
- Assemble the hand tools and equipment needed to mix and serve drinks and prepare garnishes.
- Select glassware appropriate to the drinks to be served.
- Choose a cash register that works well for your operation.

When Abe Lincoln was selling whiskey back in the 1830s, he didn't use much equipment at all. In fact, often his customers brought their own Mason jars into Abe's general store in New Salem, Illinois, and Abe would pour whiskey out of the barrel tap into the jars.

Earlier, in colonial taverns, drinks were poured from heavy glass decanters into tumblers, mugs, and tankards. Mixed drinks were stirred with a toddy stick (an early form of **muddler**), or a loggerhead—a metal bar on a long handle, heated in the open fire and then thrust into the mug or punch bowl to stir a hot toddy or flip. Along with the beverage equipment there might have been a dice box: people would roll dice to see who would pay for the drinks.

In the saloons of the Old West, customers poured their own whiskey, neat, from the bottle set on the counter by the bartender. By the mid-1800s, hotel bars were serving mixed drinks, often with ice that was scraped, chipped, or pounded from large cakes transported from frozen lakes or rivers. By 1890, a hotel might have had its own ice machine, which could make a large block of ice in 15 hours. Mixed drinks spawned tools for mixing—barspoons, measures, shakers, seltzer bottles. The cash register was first used in a tavern in 1879. Most of today's bar equipment can be traced to post-Prohibition days. It fits handily into compact spaces, and is designed for high-speed individual service and for easy manipulation by that master of dexterity and showmanship, the bartender. Let's take a closer look at this equipment.

UNDERBAR AND BACKBAR EQUIPMENT

All underbar equipment must meet local health department requirements, which typically follow the sanitation standards set by National Sanitation Foundation International. Equipment meeting these standards carries the NSFI seal, shown in Figure 4.1. The major pieces of underbar equipment have stainless-steel surfaces. This makes them durable and easy to clean and sanitize. Stainless steel stands up to the harshest chemicals yet looks good and can be polished to an attractive sheen.

Work surfaces supporting underbar equipment are a standard 30 inches high, with a depth of 16 inches to the backsplash at the rear. Units from the same manufacturer fit side by side and give the appearance of being continuous. Each piece of equipment either stands on legs that are 6 or more inches high, for access to plumbing and ease of cleaning, or else is flush with the floor. The legs have bullet feet (tapered, to resemble bullets), again, for easy cleaning. All these features are NSF standards. The feet are adjustable to accommodate uneven flooring.

Figure 4.1 National Sanitation Foundation International seal of approval. Courtesy NSF International.

Figures 4.2 and 4.3 show the underbar and backbar of the hotel bar shown in the Chapter 3, Figure 3.11. They serve the hotel's cocktail lounge, dining room, and coffee shop from three stations. The station at center top of Figure 4.2, where you see the ice bin, bottle wells, and condiment tray, is the pouring station used to serve customers seated or standing at the front bar; it also is used as the pickup station for cocktail waitresses serving the lounge. At the bottom right in this figure, where you see a similar set up and second condiment tray is the pickup station for the dining room, seen from the waiter's side. This station also is used to serve customers seated or standing at the bar. The third station, at top left, serves the coffee shop. It is also shown from the waiter's side at bottom right in Figure 4.3.

All three stations are set up in the morning, and a single bartender works from all three, according to where the calls for drinks come in. Two bartenders are on duty for the busy late-afternoon and evening periods. Serving personnel garnish the drinks at the pickup stations; notice the condiment trays on the bar top (O in both figures). A shelf below on the server's side holds ashtrays, napkins, and other server supplies. Railings (M) set these pickup stations off from customer use. They are also return stations for used glasses; notice the waste dumps below (L).

Equipment for Mixing Drinks

Each of the stations in Figures 4.2 and 4.3 is outfitted with the following equipment:

- Ice chest, ice bin (A)
- Containers for bottles—bottle wells (B)—and speed rails (C)
- Handgun for dispensing soft-drink mixes (D)
- Mixer (E) and blender (F) on recessed shelf
- Glasses—overhead, on the backbar, on drainboards, almost anywhere there is room

The centerpiece of any pouring station is an **ice chest** or **ice bin** (A), with or without **bottle wells** (B), usually with a **speed rail** (C) attached to the front. This piece of equipment is variously known as a **cocktail station, cocktail unit, beverage center,** or colloquially, as a **jockey box.**

Figure 4.4 shows a complete **cocktail station.** Its centerpiece is a 30-inch ice chest with a sliding or removable cover. The front of the unit is a 3½-foot bottle rail (speed rail), with a shorter hand-on rail on the front. On the left of the ice chest is a double row of condiment cups, used to hold garnishes, which are chilled by the ice. Often such equipment has bottle wells rather than condiment cups; they are used to keep juices and prepared mixes cold. On the right-hand side of the unit is a blender station, essentially a recessed

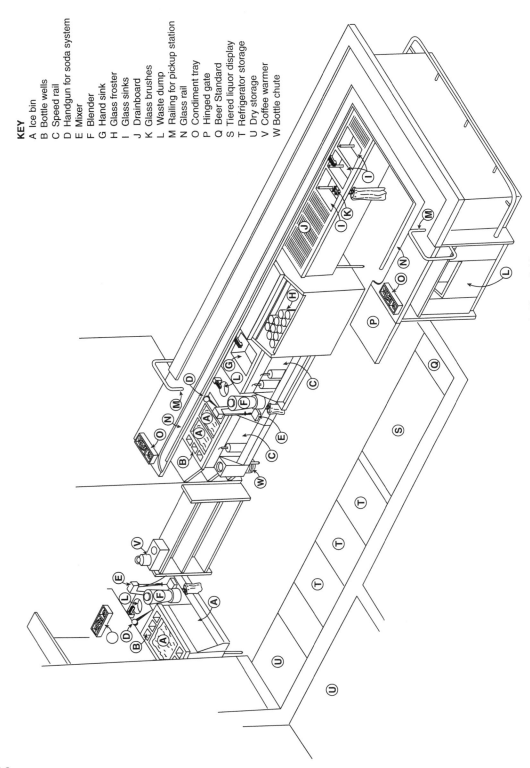

KEY

A Ice bin
B Bottle wells
C Speed rail
D Handgun for soda system
E Mixer
F Blender
G Hand sink
H Glass froster
I Glass sinks
J Drainboard
K Glass brushes
L Waste dump
M Railing for pickup station
N Glass rail
O Condiment tray
P Hinged gate
Q Beer Standard
S Tiered liquor display
T Refrigerator storage
U Dry storage
V Coffee warmer
W Bottle chute

Figure 4.2 Underbar of hotel bar in Figure 3.11.

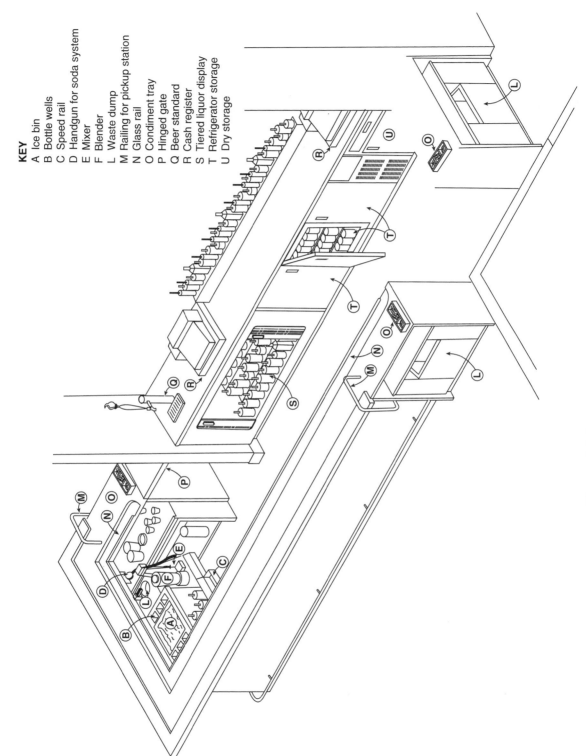

KEY
A Ice bin
B Bottle wells
C Speed rail
D Handgun for soda system
E Mixer
F Blender
L Waste dump
M Railing for pickup station
N Glass rail
O Condiment tray
P Hinged gate
Q Beer standard
R Cash register
S Tiered liquor display
T Refrigerator storage
U Dry storage

Figure 4.3 Backbar of hotel bar in Figure 3.11.

109

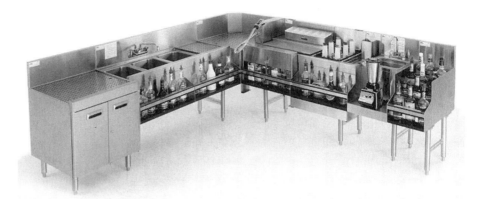

Figure 4.4 A complete cocktail station. Courtesy of Glastender, Inc.

shelf for the station's blender and mixer with a special dump sink and faucet (behind the machines). A glass shelf and a towel rack complete the unit.

Figures 4.2 and 4.3 display all these elements in slightly different configurations at the three pouring stations. In addition to bottle rails on the cocktail stations, there is a double rail on the hand sink. Not shown in any of these pictures is another type of ice chest with a divider, which enables a station to have both cubed and crushed ice.

A speed rail typically contains the most frequently poured liquors (usually scotch, bourbon, or a blended whiskey, gin, vodka, rum, tequila, and brandy). The standard variety changes with the area and clientele. The liquor supply at a bartender's station is known collectively as the **well,** and the brands used there are called **well brands, house brands** or **pouring brands.** These are the brands the house pours when a drink is ordered by type rather than by brand name. Popular **call brands** (brands customers "call for" by name), vermouths, a couple of bottles of house wines, and the current favorites in liqueurs are also set up within easy reach. Additional liquors—more call brands, liqueurs, premium brandies—are typically displayed on the backbar. Many bars have tiered liquor displays containing reserve supplies as part of the backbar itself, such as (S) in Figure 4.3.

Dispensing Beverages

At each station of the bar is the **cobra gun** that dispenses the carbonated mixes (Figure 4.5). Nicknamed the **handgun** or **six-shooter,** this instrument consists of a head with a nozzle and pushbuttons that deliver plain water and carbonated mixes (one per button) such as club soda, tonic water, soft drinks, Collins mix—whatever half-dozen you choose. Behind the scenes are bulk supplies of concentrated syrups and a tank of carbon dioxide under pressure.

Syrup lines run from each syrup supply to the underbar and through an ice-cold plate on the bottom of each ice chest, made especially to quick-chill them. The CO_2 line goes to a motor-driven carbonator under the ice chest where the CO_2 is mixed with filtered water. A carbonated-water line then runs from the carbonator through the cold plate, as does a line with plain filtered water. Finally, all the syrup and water lines run through a flexible metal hose (**flexhose**) to the head of the gun. There the syrup mixes with car-bonated water in a 5:1 ratio at the touch of the proper button; or, plain chilled, filtered water is dispensed. All this together is known as a **postmix** dispensing system be-cause the soda is mixed at the time of service.

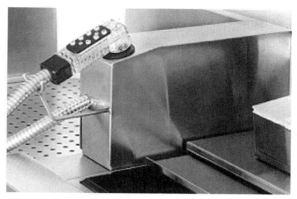

Figure 4.5 Handgun for a soda system. Courtesy of Glastender, Inc.

There are also **premix** systems, in which the complete beverage is sup-plied in bulk containers that have already been mixed at the manufacturing plant. In a premix system, a separate supply of CO_2 is needed to propel the product from the container to the dispensing head. The premix lines from the bulk supplies are run through ice or a cold plate to cool the product. A good postmix or premix drink should be cooled to between 37° to 42° Fahr-enheit in order for it to maintain good carbonation. Premix systems are sel-dom used in today's bars, except for portable bars for special-occasion use. Postmix systems are far cheaper per drink (about two-fifths the cost) and are much more compact (about one-fifth the size), hence are generally far more satisfactory.

You'll want to establish and maintain high-quality standards for your car-bonated beverages. It's a way to control their cost and to assure that the drinks made with them will be satisfactory to customers. Correctly proportioned drinks contain the right amounts of syrup, water, and carbon dioxide—and no more. Any variation will impact the taste of the drink. You should regularly taste-test each and every liquid that comes out of your cobra gun. Smell the drink, as you would a fine wine; sip a bit of it, holding it in your mouth to get the full impact of both flavor and carbonation; and breathe in and out as you taste, gently opening and closing your lips a few times.

Heat accelerates the aging process in carbonated drink syrups and mixes, and improperly sealed or stored CO_2 containers can lose their effervescence. Thus it is important that these items be stored in cool areas—ideally, at tem-peratures that don't exceed 65° Fahrenheit—and where they are protected from direct sunlight.

Neither a premix nor a postmix system comes ready-made. To assemble a postmix system, you must purchase the gun and carbonator from one man-ufacturer; the cold plate is part of the cocktail station; the syrups come from the individual drink distributors, and the CO_2 from a CO_2 supplier; these components are assembled on-site. Usually, the purchase and assembly of supplies and refills can be arranged through a single soda distributor.

A third type of soda system is the use of bottles, purchased and stored by the case. This is much more expensive than a postmix system—in portion cost, labor, time, and storage space—both at the bar and in the storeroom. Nevertheless, there are bars that use bottles by choice. Why? Because chilled, bottled soda tastes better and keeps its carbonation longer (after all, the bubbles were put in at the factory), and discriminating customers know the difference and like to see the label. Bottled mixes are a specialty item used by bars in which a top-quality drink is part of the total concept.

Automated Pouring Systems

At many bars today, you'll find pouring is all automated, not just for the soda system but also beer, wines, juices and liquor. A number of electronic dispensing systems are on the market that pour preset amounts and count each drink. Different systems measure and pour anywhere from half a dozen well brands, for instance, to a complete spectrum of mixed drinks.

Some systems use a handgun mounted on a flexhose that is similar to the gun for a soda system. Buttons on the gun activate the flow from 1.75-liter or 750-milliliter bottles mounted upside down on the walls of a remote storeroom. A preset amount of liquor is delivered, and counters keep track of each drink. A "long shot" and a "short shot" can also be poured. Another kind of dispenser is composed of a series of faucets, each activated by touching a glass to a button under the faucet. Systems like these can dispense and control perhaps three-fourths of the volume of liquor poured. Beyond the 6 or 12 brands a system controls, the call brands, liqueurs, juices, cream, and so on can always be dispensed by hand in the usual way.

In still another type of system, electronic dispensing equipment is integrated or interfaced with a computerized cash register. To operate, the bartender or server must ring up a guest check before drinks can be poured. This gives high control, but the precheck function can slow down operations in a fast, high-volume operation. Systems can be connected to a printer, for reports that detail each server or bartender's sales or output.

Automatic liquor-dispensing systems require a sizable investment and not everybody reacts favorably to them. Some bartenders are unhappy with mechanical pouring, and some customers dislike them as well; the service seems less personal, and they suspect that liquor poured out of sight is inferior to the brands they can see being poured at the bar rail. Another common problem is blocked lines. Still another is that liquors that are not ordered frequently sit in the lines for long periods of time and may acquire an "off" taste.

On the plus side, the automatic systems cut pouring costs in several ways. There is the savings that comes from using large-size bottles; the savings of speed; the savings of getting that last ounce out of the bottle that, in hand-pouring, clings to the bottle's side; the savings in labor thanks to faster pouring (it is often so much faster that you eliminate the need for an extra bartender at peak periods). One great advantage of an automatic system is the consistency of the drink served—a desirable goal that is hard to achieve with hand-pouring, even measured hand-pouring. The gun also makes for a smooth, swift operation, with less handling of glasses.

A major selling point of the automatic dispensing system is that it provides tighter liquor controls. This does not mean you automatically eliminate losses—there are still spills, mistakes, and pilferage in any bar operation. Drinks are measured and counted, but the count must still be checked daily against sales and inventory. It is far easier to spot a discrepancy with an automatic system, but the cause of it must still be removed to make this type of "policing" effective.

Each enterprise must weigh these and other savings against the cost of the equipment in relation to the volume of business being done. In a small operation, an automatic system might not be worth its high price tag. In a high-volume bar, it may be the thing that makes that volume possible and pays for itself in a couple of years or less.

Mixers and Blenders

Again referring to the illustrations of pouring stations, you see a mixer (E) on the shelf next to the cocktail unit. It is like the machine that makes your shake at McDonald's, and in this book we refer to it as a **shake mixer** or **spindle blender.** It has a shaft coming down from the top that agitates the contents of its cup. It is used for cocktails made with fruit juices, eggs, sugar, cream, or any other ingredient that does not blend readily with spirits. This mixer (Figure 4.6b) is one of today's mechanical substitutes for the hand shaker. There are countertop models that can make up to five drinks at once, or hand-held models for individual drinks. Some have three height settings to accommodate different sizes of stainless-steel mixing cups. A water source and/or drain is necessary if you're using a multiple-head spindle blender.

The machine on the shelf beside the shake mixer is a **blender** (F) of a different type, which takes the mixing process one step further. Blades in the bottom of its cup can grind, puree, and otherwise refine ingredients put into it. Some drinks that incorporate food or ice, like Banana Daiquiris or Frozen Margaritas, require such a blender (Figure 4.6a). Blenders used strictly for making drinks are called **bar mixers,** and are not to be confused with shake mixers. Many bars have both.

The commercial blender usually has two speeds, but you can purchase them with variable-speed controls, or a "pulse" function. The body of the blender has sealed seams for sanitation reasons, and it usually rests on a heavy base with rubber feet to keep it stable. A toggle switch activates the

(a)

(b)

Figure 4.6 A shake mixer (a) and spindle blender (b). *Source:* Hamilton Beach/ Proctor-Silex, Inc.

motor, which turns a set of four or six blades attached to a clutch. Look for a blender with blades that are easy to remove for cleaning. Also look for sturdy containers to do the blending in, since they'll be used a lot! Containers can be made of glass, polycarbonate, or stainless steel, with a single handle or two handles. The container top can also be a single piece (usually rubber or vinyl), or a two-piece **filler cap,** so you can add ingredients safely while the blender is in use.

Commercial bar mixers are larger than those made for home kitchens. They are identified by the capacity of their containers, from 24 ounces to 1 gallon. Their motor sizes range from one-half to three horsepower.

Bars that specialize in a particular frozen drink may have a **frozen drink dispenser.** Similar to the soft-serve ice cream machine at the Dairy Queen, it soft-freezes a large quantity of premixed drinks. Commercial machine capacities range from 8.5 quarts to 72 quarts. You pour gallons of liquid Strawberry Daiquiri or Margarita Mix or whatever into the top of the machine, and in a few moments it is frozen to a slush. To serve an individual drink, you hold a glass under the tap and move a lever.

The frozen drink dispenser pumps air into the liquid mix, increasing its volume and giving it that soft-frozen consistency. The percentage of air forced into the mix is called its **overrun.** For example, a 100 percent overrun produces exactly twice the volume of the mix that was put into the machine; thus, 16 ounces of mix with a 100-percent overrun produces a 32-ounce frozen drink; if it's a 50-percent overrun, it produces a 24-ounce drink; and so on. There are gravity-feed machines, in which the liquid mix is placed in a hopper and flows as needed into a cylinder below, where it is frozen, scraped out of the cylinder and dispensed. These are inexpensive and easy to maintain and clean. And there are more expensive pressurized machines, which use an air pump to drive mix into the freezer chamber, and then force it out through a spigot. Pressurized machines can control overrun percentages better than gravity-feed machines. With either type of machine, the hopper should be kept fairly full of drink mix for the machine to do its job well.

At the end of the day, you drain off the frozen drink contents that are left, and store them in the refrigerator for later use. Nightly cleaning of the machine is especially important, to prevent off-tasting drinks and to keep the cylinder and hoses from becoming gummy from the sweet, sticky ingredients. Regular maintenance may also include changing the blades inside the machine periodically, to keep them from becoming too dull to scrape frozen product off the sides of the freezer chamber and keep things well mixed.

Glassware

To complete the drink-mixing process, obviously, you must have glasses in which to serve the drinks. In a typical bar, there are glasses everywhere. Stemware may be stored in overhead racks, arranged according to type. Other glasses may appear upside down on drainboards, ridged shelves, or heavy plastic netting, to allow air to reach the inside of the glass. This is a typical health code requirement, to keep bacteria from growing in a damp enclosed space. Resist the temptation to put towels under netting to catch the runoff from wet glasses, as this cuts off the air, canceling the effect and making the problem worse. Unused glasses must be kept free of dust for both appearance and sanitation reasons.

You will need a way to chill glasses for straight-up cocktails, frozen drinks, and ice cream drinks. Some bars make a special promotional point of serving drinks in frosted glasses or beer in frosted mugs. For this purpose you will want to have a **glass froster,** a top-opening freezer that chills glasses at temperatures around 0° Fahrenheit (H on Figure 4.2). When the glass is removed from the freezer, it sports a refreshing coat of frost.

Glasses and mugs placed in a glass froster must be dry to begin with; otherwise a thin coat of ice will form on the glass; and when a drink is poured into it, the glass may stick to the lip of the drinker, or the ice may dilute the drink.

If you do not have a glass froster, you must have another way to chill glasses for straight-up cocktails and frozen and ice cream drinks. If you have refrigerator space, you can use it to frost a wet glass without making ice. The other alternative is to ice the glass by hand with ice cubes just before the drink is poured.

Bar Sinks and Glasswashers

Equipment for washing (both glasses and hands) is usually specified in detail in local health codes. It typically includes these items, shown in Figure 4.2:

- A three- or four-compartment sink (I)
- Drainboards (J)
- Special glasswashing brushes (K)
- Hand sink (G) with towel rack (attached to blender station)
- Waste dump (L)

A three-compartment sink with drainboards is usually a single piece of equipment (Figure 4.7) placed near a bartender station or between two stations. One compartment is for washing, one for rinsing, and one for sanitizing (killing bacteria with a chemical solution). Dimensions will vary from 60 to 96 inches in length, with a foot-long drainboard on one or both sides. Each sink compartment is 10 inches wide and about 14 inches from front to back, with a depth of 10 to 11 inches. In a four-compartment sink, the fourth compartment is usually used as a waste dump by placing netting in the bottom to catch the debris from used glasses. You'll need to decide if you want

Figure 4.7 Three-compartment sink with drainboards. Courtesy of Glastender, Inc.

each sink to have its own faucet, or if two will suffice—each one can swivel to serve two sinks. Plumbing requirements are slightly different in either case.

Glass brushes stand up to the soapy water of the wash sink. Figure 4.8 shows a motorized model: the bartender places a glass over the center brush and presses a button to make the bristles spin. With hand models, the bartender twists the glass around and between the brushes to clean the inside and rim. The glass next goes into the rinse sink, then into the sanitizing solution, and finally onto the drainboard, upside down, to air-dry. It is best to air-dry glassware, since towel drying is inefficient and can leave bits of towel fuzz on the clean glasses.

An alternative to washing glasses by hand that is gaining popularity is the automatic **glass-washer.** (Figure 4.9.) Stricter sanitation laws and labor savings are two major reasons for their increased use. This machine is a type of small dishwasher that fits neatly under the underbar or backbar. It washes and rinses glasses with tap water, provides a final high-temperature rinse to sanitize them, and blow-dries them. Wash temperatures range from 150° to 212° Fahrenheit for

Figure 4.8 Motorized glass brushes. Courtesy of Hamilton Beach/Proctor-Silex, Inc.

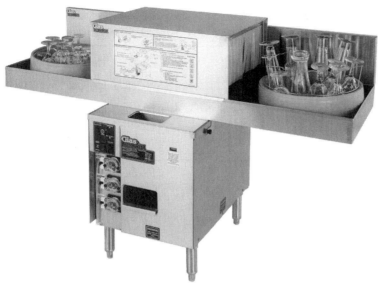

Figure 4.9 Rotary glasswasher. Courtesy of Glastender, Inc.

quick drying. An advantage of higher temperatures is that the faster the glasses dry, the less likely they are to emerge with water spots.

A full cycle of washing, rinsing, and drying takes about 20 minutes and uses about 3 gallons of water for each fill, at a water pressure of 20 pounds per square inch (psi). Some models have a variety of "cycles" for different types of glassware. You might also look for a glasswasher that provides a final rinse of cool water, which makes the glasses ready to use as soon as they are clean.

Glasswashers can easily wash up to 500 glasses per hour, giving bartenders more time to prepare drinks. There are also conveyor-type washers, capable of washing up to 1,000 glasses per hour, for use in high-volume operations.

It is usually impractical, if not downright impossible, to vent steam from glasswashers in a bar area. In these cases, bar owners opt for a sanitizing system that uses chlorine or other chemicals during the rinse cycle. Detergent suppliers sell, install, and maintain them. The sanitizing system is typically mounted under the bar, next to the dish machine. It works by injecting a preset amount of chemical solution directly into the rinse water. Some cities require periodic testing of the system, to be sure the solution is strong enough to sanitize effectively. Table 4.1 lists different guidelines for chemical concentration and rinse water temperature. A word of caution: If you put other utensils in your glasswasher, some of them, especially those made of aluminum, pewter, or silver plate, might react poorly to chemical sanitizing systems.

Table 4.1

Data Plate Specifications for the Chemical Sanitizing Rinse

Sanitizing Solution Type	Final Rinse Temperature	Concentration
Chlorine solution	min: 49°C (120°F)[a]	min: 50 ppm (as NaOCl)
Iodine solution	min: 24°C (75°F)	min: 12.5 ppm, max: 25 ppm
Quaternary ammonium solution	min: 24°C (75°F)	min: 150 ppm, max: 400 ppm

[a] For glasswashing machines that use a chlorine sanitizing solution, the maximum final rinse temperature specified by the manufacturer shall be at least 24°C (75°F).

Source: NSF International, Ann Arbor, Michigan.

You might be wondering why not just wash bar glasses in a regular, kitchen dish machine, especially if the bar is located where food is also served. Doing so has several drawbacks. Glasses have to be carried back and forth, so they are much more likely to get broken. Different kinds of dishracks are required for glasses, also to prevent breakage. The other good reason to wash them separately from other dishes is that even a trace of grease on a glass can spoil a drink or the head on a beer.

At the hotel bar pictured in Figures 4.2 and 4.3, each pickup station has a waste dump (L) on the server's side of the bar. Cocktail servers returning with dirty glasses dump the debris here. Behind the bar are removable trashcans.

A bottle chute (W on Figure 4.2) conveys empty beer and soda bottles to the basement below the bar for disposal. Empty liquor bottles are accumulated at the bar to be turned in to the storeroom in exchange for full bottles. In a bar with a storeroom below it, a bottle chute can convey the empties directly to the storeroom.

Ice and Ice Machines

A cocktail bar could not operate at all without ice, so a plentiful supply is essential. Every bar operation has an **icemaker** (ice machine); some have more than one. If the bar is large enough, the icemaker can be part of the underbar or backbar; if not, it must be installed elsewhere and the ice brought in manually.

Technology has resulted in terrific improvements for ice machines. Today, you can flip a switch on a modern icemaker and it cleans itself; or you can program the machine electronically to change its output based on daily or seasonal demands. But regardless of the technological capabilities you want, before you select an icemaker, you must decide what size and shape of ice cube to use. Why? Because there are various factors to consider: large cubes melt more slowly; smaller sizes stack better in the glass; round cubes fit the glass better at the edges; and rectangular cubes stack better than round ones, leaving fewer voids; and in a fast pour, liquor hitting a round cube can splash out of the glass. Which cube shape and size will fill your special needs? Your clientele, your drink menu, your glassware, your type of pour, and your service all go into making this determination. If you're using an ice dispenser, the cubes should also be small enough to fit into it and be dispensed easily without clogging or jamming the dispenser. If you're making a lot of blender drinks, large cubes will make your blender blades work all that much harder, and possibly compromise the consistency of the drink. Consider these factors when deciding on the type and size of ice cube to use:

- **Displacement.** Cubes should "pack" well into the glass, but not appear to. You never want a customer to think he or she is paying for a drink that's mostly ice. The shape of the cube also determines how much of its surface touches the liquid and, therefore, how quickly it works to chill the drink.
- **Clarity.** Ice should be completely clear, made with pure, sanitary drinking water that produces no "off" taste, color, or odor. (This includes not tasting or smelling like water-purifying chemicals.)
- **Density.** How "hard" or "soft" the ice is frozen determines how quickly it interacts with the drink. The cubes also should not be so soft that they stick together in the bin. Local temperature and humidity impact density, as well as where the icemaker is located in your operation, and its temperature setting.

Ice-making machines are refrigeration units. A pump inside the machine circulates water from a tank. You'll want a machine with a good filtration system, to ensure pure water and minimal buildup of chlorine and minerals found in most drinking water.

The water runs through tubing to a freezer assembly, which freezes it into a single sheet of ice. The frozen sheet is then forced through a screen (to produce ice cubes) or crushed (to produce crushed ice). Different types of screens produce different sizes and shapes of ice cubes. Each machine makes only one type and size, but in some machines you can adjust the cube size. For example, a machine will make a ¾-inch × ¾-inch cube varying from ¼ to ½ inch in thickness with a simple adjustment you can make yourself. A different grid for the same machine will give you a big 1¼-inch × 1½-inch cube, ½ to 1 inch thick. But no machine makes more than one size of cube at a time.

After the ice is crushed or cubed, it is dumped into a storage bin. When the bin fills to capacity, a sensor inside the bin stops the ice-making process until there is room to make and store more ice. Since most of the icemaker's parts come into constant contact with water, it is important that they be made of rustproof materials, with storage bins of either stainless steel or heavy-duty plastic.

In addition to cube ice there is crushed ice, cracked ice, flake ice, and shaved ice. Crushed ice can be made by running cube ice through an *ice crusher*. Another type of machine produces crushed or cracked ice from scratch instead of from ice cubes. Both machines make small random-size pieces of hard clear ice. Some drinks call for crushed or cracked ice, which is also used in making frozen drinks.

A **flake-ice machine,** or **flaker,** produces a soft, snowlike ice that is used mostly for keeping things cold. In a wine bucket, for example, flake ice will assume the shape of the bottle. If you use cubes in a bucket, they will slide to the bottom when you take the bottle out and it will be hard to replace the bottle in the ice. This more or less defeats the purpose of the bucket, except as decoration.

Flake ice is suitable only for frozen drinks, not as standard bar ice, because in an ordinary mixed drink, it melts quickly, dilutes the drink, and tends to create a water cap on the surface, which makes the drink taste weaker than it is. Shaved ice, made by a machine that shaves ice off of large blocks, is similar to flake ice; it is soft and opaque and has the same uses.

Determining Icemaker Size and Other Factors. An ice machine's size refers to the number of pounds of ice it can produce in 24 hours. Today's underbar models are so compact that even a 22-inch-wide machine can make 500 pounds of ice per day. But how much do you need? The general rule is 3 pounds of ice per guest served, but this is a very broad average. Your needs will change based on daily traffic, seasonal business, time of day, and whether you must share ice output with a kitchen or other parts of your operation. It is always smart to plan on making 20 to 25 percent more ice than you'll actually need, to allow for spillage, staff use, and the overall growth of your business. To do a basic "ice needs" calculation, try this:

1. Estimate ice usage for one full week, by multiplying the number of guests to be served that week by 3 pounds per guest.
2. Divide the result by 7 (days per week). This is the daily number of pounds of ice you will need.
3. Multiply that figure by 1.25, to add a bit of extra output.
4. If your average is not constant—say, you know that Fridays and Saturdays your place will be swamped—estimate an additional amount for those days and add it to the total. This way, you know there will be enough ice, even for your busiest days.

Where you put the machine can drastically affect its production. The warmer the air around it and the warmer the water it is fed, the less ice it will produce. Other factors to consider are the available space, the noise it makes, and the heat it generates, and whether you have to share the ice with

Sidebar 4.1

KEEPING ICE CLEAN

Although not often thought of as a food item, ice cubes are consumed by your customers, and they need to stay as clean and sanitary as anything else you serve.

Clean ice starts with a clean machine. Cleaning and sanitizing your ice machine means removing built-up mineral deposits, algae and slime from the machine's parts. According to Frank Murphy, national training director for GCS Services, this process should be completed at least every six months.

"Cleaning and sanitizing is essential to make sure the very delicate cycle of making ice is not interrupted and that every cube looks the same as every other cube," Murphy says.

Use these tips for keeping your machine and ice clean between big cleanings:

- Always have staff wash their hands before removing ice, and always have them use a plastic ice scoop.
- Keep the plastic ice scoop clean. Wash it frequently with a neutral cleaner and always rinse thoroughly.
- Do not store food and beverage items or containers in the ice bin. It is not a refrigerated storage space and shouldn't act as one.
- Clean the bin liner frequently with a neutral cleaner, rinsing thoroughly.
- Prevent corrosion on the exterior of your machine by wiping it occasionally with a clean, soft cloth. To remove oil and dirt, use a damp cloth with a neutral cleaner.
- Check the air filter on air-cooled models at least twice per month. If the filter gets clogged, use warm water and a neutral cleaner to wash it out.
- Check the condenser (if your machine has one) once a year, and clean it with a brush or a vacuum cleaner. More frequent cleaning may be required depending on the location of your ice machine.

—N.G.C.

Source: Restaurants and Institutions, Cahners Business Information, A Division of Reed Elsevier, Inc.

a kitchen. Wherever you put the icemaker, make sure it is well ventilated to ensure that it functions properly; and make sure the area meets the same sanitation standards as the bar itself.

If the incoming water supply is warm, you might consider adding an **inlet chiller** to the ice-making system. It collects cold water that would normally be drained away from the icemaker and recirculates it in a series of copper coils, to chill fresh water on its way into the icemaker to be frozen.

Inlet chillers are about the size of a household fire extinguisher. They have no moving parts and use no electricity, but their "prechill" function can save up to 30 percent on your electric costs and boost your icemaker's capacity.

In the United States, we use more ice than bread—more than 100 million tons every year! And like any other type of food or drink we ingest, it can become contaminated, retain bacteria, hence cause illness. This is why cleanliness and sanitary handling practices are critical in your manufacture, storage, and use of ice.

Icemaker Maintenance. The most important maintenance task for ice-making machines is to clean the unit's compressor and condenser coils according to the manufacturer's directions. About 80 percent of service calls can be traced to dirty coils. Keeping them free of dirt and grease allows better air circulation. The coils hold refrigerant, which is pressurized and turns from liquid to vapor and back again during the cooling process. Since the 1990s, the U.S. Environmental Protection Agency has prompted a change from old-style refrigerants (that were thought to deplete the ozone layer in Earth's atmosphere) to newer ones, called **hydrofluorocarbons (HFCs)** and **hydrochlorofluorocarbons (HCFCs).** Even these are a stopgap measure, though. They are scheduled to be phased out between the years 2015 and 2030.

What this means for bar or restaurant operators is that there are strict rules for any type of refrigeration repair. If you have an older model that still uses the chlorofluorocarbons (CFCs, or the old brand name, Freon) that have fallen out of favor, the EPA says that if the machine is leaking 35 percent or more of its refrigerant pressure per year, it must be fixed. You are required to keep records of when, and how much, refrigerant is added during servicing. (If you fail to do so, it's a violation of the federal Clean Air Act and you can be fined.) Use only repair technicians who are EPA-certified, since they know how to dispose of old refrigerant properly. And look for the Underwriters Laboratories (UL) label on any new, ozone-safe refrigerant that is added to your machine.

Other types of regular maintenance include cleaning and/or changing the water and air filters, and wiping down the inside and outside of the unit and ice storage bin, and checking for mineral buildup on switches and sensors. Some manufacturers offer an acid-based ice machine cleaning solution. Your ice machine may stop working and need to be reset if a filter is clogged or if there has been a power outage. The warmer or dirtier the environment in which the icemaker must work, the more frequent its maintenance checks should be.

Essentials for Draft-Beer Service

A draft-beer serving system consists of a *keg* or *half-keg* of beer, the **beer box** where the keg is stored, the **standard** or **tap** (faucet), the *line* between the keg and the standard, and a CO_2 tank connected to the keg with another line. The beer box, also called a **tap box,** is a refrigerator designed especially to hold a keg or half-keg of beer at the proper serving temperature of 36° to 38° Fahrenheit. Generally, it is located right below the standard, which is mounted on the bar top, so that the line between keg and standard is as short as possible. If more than one brand of draft beer is served, each brand has its own system—keg, line, and standard—either in its own beer box or sharing a box with another brand.

The supply of beer at the bar should be sufficient to last the serving period, since bringing in a new keg of beer and tapping it is a major operation. It sometimes takes several kegs to provide enough beer for a high-volume bar.

A beer system may be designed into either the front bar or the backbar. If there is not room at the bar, the beer boxes may be located in a nearby storage area with lines running into the standards. On the backbar of the hotel bar in Figure 4.3, you see the beer standard (Q), but the rest of the system is on the garage level below. The beer box consists of a large walk-in cooler; a beer line runs behind the liquor display up to the standard.

Storage Equipment

You need enough storage space at the bar to take care of all your needs for one serving period. This means liquor, mixes, bottled drinks, wines, beers, garnishes, and miscellaneous supplies like cocktail napkins and stir sticks. Generally, this storage forms the major part of the backbar, as in Figure 4.3.

The day's reserve supplies of liquor—all the unopened bottles as back-ups for those in use—are stored in dry (unrefrigerated) storage cabinets with locks, or they are displayed on the backbar. Also in dry storage are red house wines for pouring by the glass or carafe, and reserve supplies of napkins, bar towels, matches, picks, straws, stir sticks, and other nonfood, nonbeverage items.

Undercounter and backbar refrigerators (Figure 4.10) hold supplies of special mixes and juices, bottled beer, bottled mixes if used, white wines, fruits and condiments for garnishing, cream, eggs, and other perishables. They may also be used to chill glasses. It is important not to overload the cabinet, since proper airflow is key to chilling the contents properly.

From the outside, the backbar refrigerator looks just like the dry-storage cabinets. Some backbar units are half refrigerator and half dry storage. Bar-sized refrigerators are tested for sanitation and temperature control by the National Sanitation Foundation, so you should look for the NSF seal when making your selection. The refrigerator should be able to hold foods at a temperature of 40° Fahrenheit.

Referring again to Figure 4.3, you can see how this works. Backbar refrigerator cabinets (T) store supplies of perishables in one section, bottled beers and soft drinks in another section. To the right at the backbar is a dry-storage cabinet (U) for bar towels, napkins, and other supplies. Reserve supplies of liquor are stored in locked overhead cabinets above the front bar.

Figure 4.10 Backbar refrigerator. Courtesy of Glastender, Inc.

How Refrigeration Works. In basic principle, refrigerating a space means to transfer heat out of that space, extending the life of the food inside the refrigerator. The more heat you can remove from a product, the longer it can be held in usable condition. The refrigerator fights a constant battle: its door is opened and closed, to insert products that are not yet chilled, letting in outside air; and even when the door is closed, there may be tiny leaks around the rubber door seals.

The **refrigeration cycle** is the process of removing heat from a refrigerated space. The **refrigeration circuit** is the system of equipment that makes the cycle possible. Successful refrigeration is a combination of temperature reduction, humidity, and air circulation. To keep most foods at their peak, you need a refrigerator capable of cooling them to 40° Fahrenheit. (In the past, it was thought that 45° Fahrenheit was cold enough, but that is no longer the standard.)

Let's look at what happens when you open the refrigerator door of that little underbar unit. The components of the circuit are shown in Figure 4.11. First, warm air is introduced into the cooled space. The warm air rises and is drawn into an **evaporator,** a series of copper coils surrounded by metal plates called **fins.** The fins conduct heat to and from the coils.

Inside the sealed evaporator coils is liquid **refrigerant** (the HFCs and HCFCs mentioned earlier in this chapter), which becomes vapor (gas) as it winds through the coils. It is pumped by a **compressor** into another series of coils surrounded by fins, called the **condenser.** There, it turns back into a liquid. The amount of refrigerant flowing through the system is determined by a small opening between the evaporator and the condenser, known as an

expansion valve. If more cooling is needed, more refrigerant flows. Depending on the size of the refrigerator, it will have a one-half to one horsepower compressor; some larger (four-door) units rely on two three-quarter horsepower compressors. Compressors can be mounted above or below the refrigerator—bottom-mounted ones reduce interior space somewhat, and require smaller doors. You can also have remote compressors that sit elsewhere in your building and are connected to the refrigerator by copper lines so as not to take up scarce underbar space and to minimize the heat and noise generated by the compressor.

A cousin to the bar refrigerator is the horizontal bottle cooler. If you serve a lot of individual bottles or cans, it's a way to store them in chilled bins with sliding top lids. The bottle cooler has the same small refrigeration system just discussed. Like icemakers, bar refrigerators and bottle coolers require coil cleaning and periodic preventive maintenance. Servicing and recharging with new refrigerant should be done only by an EPA-certified repairperson.

Figure 4.11 Refrigerator circuit components. Courtesy of Glastender, Inc.

Wine Storage Considerations

The fictitious hotel bar we have been using as an example keeps its daily supply of wines by the bottle for dining room service in a storeroom around the corner, which includes a large cooler set at 45° to 50° Fahrenheit for the white wines. Some restaurants may store their daily wine stock at the bar, display it in wine racks as part of the room décor, or store it under lock and key in a wine cellar.

Several devices have been invented to deal with the problem of storing opened, partially empty bottles of wine. Oxygen is the enemy of wine, and leaving a bottle open for any length of time changes the taste of the remaining wine.

You'll learn more about proper wine storage in Chapter 7, but here's a quick primer on the three different approaches to store bottles for by-the-glass use:

- One is a device that replaces the wine with nitrogen as it is poured. Nitrogen is an inert gas that does not interact with the wine.
- A second device pumps air out of the bottle, leaving a vacuum. This is done by inserting a plastic nipple in the bottle, through which a small

Figure 4.12 A Vacu-Vin. Courtesy of Co-Rect Products, Inc.

pump is inserted. The air is then pumped out, and the pump is withdrawn. The nipple remains in the bottleneck, sealing off the wine. (Figure 4.12)

- A third device displaces the air with a "protective insert" made of plastic film that expands to fill the space left by the poured wine. All these methods can maintain a certain degree of wine quality for several days or even longer, but you cannot always depend on the wine being as good as it was when the bottle was first opened.

BAR TOOLS AND SMALL EQUIPMENT

Just as chefs have their favorite sets of kitchen knives that they guard zealously, so bartenders have their favorite tools. Seasoned bartenders generally agree that the simpler the tool, the better. Gimmicks take up space and may not save any time; and a good bartender doesn't waste either.

Buying high-quality tools is important because no one can afford to waste time at a busy bar hassling with poor-quality implements. Moreover, doing so can be dangerous or at least inefficient. An inexperienced bartender wielding a hand shaker with an ill-fitting lid can drench a customer!

Stainless steel is the metal of choice for small equipment and utensils, just as it is for large underbar pieces, and for the same reasons. It looks good, it's durable, and easy to clean. Most small bar equipment is used for mixing and pouring. A second group of utensils is used in preparing condiments to garnish drinks. A third group is used for serving.

Smallware for Mixing and Pouring

The indispensable tools for mixing and pouring by hand are:

- Jiggers
- Pourers
- Mixing glass
- Hand shaker
- Bar strainer
- Barspoon
- Ice scoop
- Ice tongs
- Muddler
- Fruit squeezer
- Funnel
- Glass rimmer

A **jigger** (Figure 4.13) is a small container that measures ounces or fractions of ounces of liquors used for cocktails, highballs, and other mixed drinks.

(Although these liquors are bought in bottles measured in metric terms—a liter, or 750 milliliters—they are measured in ounces when drinks are poured. One ounce of liquid equals approximately 30 milliliters.)

There are two types of jiggers. The double-ended stainless-steel jigger has a small cup on one end and a large cup on the other. It comes in several combinations of sizes, such as ½ ounce/1 ounce; ¾ ounce/1 ounce; 1 ounce/1½ ounces. The most-used combinations are probably the ¾ ounce/1½ ounces and the 1-ounce/1½ ounces, but what you need depends on the size drink you serve.

The second jigger type is made of heavy glass with a plain or elevated base. It comes in several sizes, from ⅞ ounce to 3 ounces, either with or without a line marking off another measure, as, for example, a 1-ounce glass with a line at ½ or ⅝ ounce, or a 1½-ounce glass with a line at ½, ⅝, ¾, ⅞, or 1 ounce. A glass jigger may also be used as a **shot glass** when a customer orders a straight shot.

Figure 4.13 Jiggers: two types, 13 measures all together. Courtesy of Co-Rect Products, Inc.

To measure using the steel jigger, the bartender fills the cup to the brim. To measure in the glass jigger, the bartender fills to the line. After pouring the drink, the bartender turns the jigger upside down on the drainboard so that any residual liquor drains out and one drink's flavor will not be carried over to the next. If a jigger is used for something heavy, like cream or a liqueur, it is rinsed with water before reuse.

A **pourer** (Figure 4.14) is a device that fits into the neck of a beverage bottle, constructed to reduce the rate of flow to a predictable, controllable amount. A pourer is used on every opened liquor bottle at the bar. There are three categories: slow, semifast, and fast.

Pourers are available in either stainless steel or plastic. The plastics come in different colors and can be used to color-code different types of liquor. The stainless-steel pourers are better looking and last longer, excluding the corks that fit into the bottlenecks; these wear out and must be replaced from time to time.

There are also pourers that measure the liquor poured, and cut off automatically when a preset amount is reached. They are expensive, and most bartenders don't like them, but they are a form of control not to be overlooked if they will save more money and aggravation than they cost.

Figure 4.14 A variety of metal and plastic pourers. Courtesy of Co-Rect Products, Inc.

Figure 4.15
A mixing glass. Courtesy of Co-Rect Products, Inc.

A **mixing glass** (Figure 4.15) is a heavy glass container in which drink ingredients are stirred together with ice. A typical mixing glass has a capacity of 16 to 17 ounces. It is used to make Martinis, Manhattans, and other drinks whose ingredients blend together readily. It is rinsed after each use. Mixing glasses should be heat-treated and chip-proof.

A **hand shaker** or **cocktail shaker** (Figure 4.16) is a versatile favorite of bartenders. It's a combination of a mixing glass and a stainless-steel container that fits on top of it, in which drink ingredients are shaken together with ice. The stainless-steel container is known variously as a **mixing cup, mixing steel,** or **mix can.** Ingredients and ice are measured into the mixing glass, and the cup is placed firmly on top, angled so that one edge is flush with the side of the glass. The two are held tightly together and shaken. The cup must be of heavy-gauge, high-quality stainless steel; if it loses its shape it will not fit tightly over the glass. Usually a shaker comes in a set with its own strainer. The strainer and shaker cup should have an overhang of about 1½ inches to seal properly. A shaker is used for cocktails made with fruit juices, egg, sugar, cream, or any other ingredient that does not mix readily with spirits. It is rinsed after each use.

The mixing container of the shake mixer (mentioned earlier in the section on blenders) is also called a mixing cup, steel, or can. This machine has supplanted the hand shakers at some bars. It is faster and more efficient. It can even make ice cream drinks, which is something the hand shakers can't do.

A **bar strainer** (Figure 4.17) is a round wire coil on a handle, which fits over the top of a shaker or mixing glass; it has "ears" that fit over the rim to

Figure 4.16 The shaker cup fits tightly over the mixing glass for hand shaking. Courtesy of Co-Rect Products, Inc.

Figure 4.17 Bar strainers. Courtesy of Co-Rect Products, Inc.

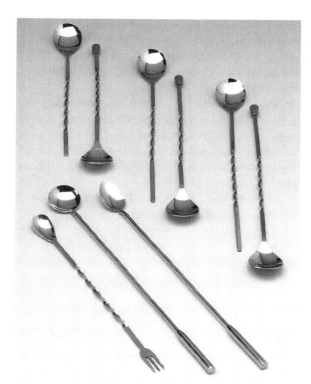

Figure 4.18 Barspoons. Courtesy of Co-Rect Products, Inc.

Figure 4.19 Ice scoops. Courtesy of Co-Rect Products, Inc.

keep it in position. The strainer keeps ice and fruit pulp from going into the glass when the drink is poured. It is used with mixing glasses and shaker and blender cups. An elongated strainer, for 19-ounce bar glasses and shakers, is a modern addition.

A **barspoon** (Figure 4.18) is a shallow spoon with a long handle, often with a bead on the end. Spoon and handle are stainless steel, typically 10 or 11 inches long. The bowl equals 1 teaspoon. Barspoons are used for stirring drinks, either in a drink glass or in a mixing glass or cup.

During Prohibition, humorist George Ade, writing nostalgically in *The Old-Time Saloon,* described the use of the barspoon in pre-Prohibition days when, he said, a good bartender would have died of shame if compelled to use a shaker: "The supreme art of the mixing process was to

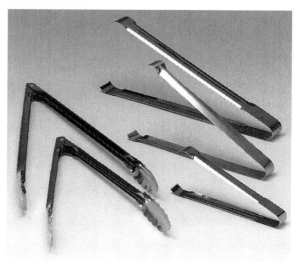

Figure 4.20 Ice tongs. Courtesy of Co-Rect Products, Inc.

Figure 4.21 Muddling sticks. Courtesy of Co-Rect Products, Inc.

place the thumb lightly on top of the long spoon and then revolve the spoon at incredible speed by twiddling the fingers . . . a knack acquired by the maestros only." Perhaps this mixing method explains the traditional bead on the end of the handle.

An **ice scoop** (Figure 4.19) is, as its name implies, an implement for scooping ice from the ice bin. It usually has a 6- or 8-ounce capacity. A standard size makes it easy to get just the right amount of ice with a single scoop. Bartenders who scoop ice out of bins directly with a glass are asking for trouble, which they will realize the first time they break or chip a glass, leaving broken glass in the ice bin and a razor-sharp rim on the glass. Use the scoop!

Ice tongs (Figure 4.20) are designed to handle one cube of ice at a time. One of the less popular bar tools, tongs are a relic from the days when all ice cubes were large. Nevertheless they are still used—in airline service, for example. They serve an important function, since ice that goes into a drink should not be touched by human hands.

A **muddler,** or **muddling stick** (Figure 4.21), is making a comeback with the renewed popularity of classic drinks like the Old-Fashioned. It's a wooden tool that looks like a little baseball bat. One end is flat for "muddling" (crushing) one substance into another, such as sugar into bitters in an Old-Fashioned. The other end is rounded and can be used to crack ice. The muddler, too, is a relic from another day; now simple syrup instead of lump sugar is used, and ice rarely needs to be cracked.

A bar-type **fruit squeezer** (Figure 4.22) is a hand-powered gadget that squeezes half a lemon or lime for a single drink, straining out pits and pulp.

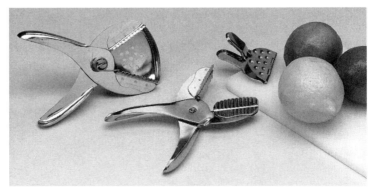

Figure 4.22 Fruit squeezers. Courtesy of Co-Rect Products, Inc.

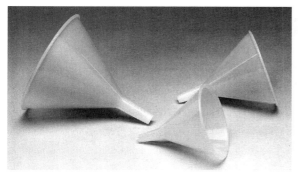

Figure 4.23 Funnels. Courtesy of Co-Rect Products, Inc.

Figure 4.24 Glass rimmer. Courtesy of Co-Rect Products, Inc.

Funnels (Figure 4.23) are needed in several sizes for pouring from large containers into small ones, such as transferring special mixes from bulk containers into plastic bottles for bar use. Some funnels have a screen at the wide end to strain out pulp.

A **glass rimmer** (Figure 4.24) is a handy gadget used to rim a glass with salt or sugar. It is made up of three trays. One contains a sponge that is saturated with lemon or lime juice, the second contains a layer of salt, and the third a layer of sugar. The glass rim is pressed on the sponge, then dipped in salt (for a Margarita or a Bloody Mary) or sugar (for a Side Car).

Tools and Equipment for Garnishing

It is usually part of the bartender's job to set up the fruits and other foods used to enhance or garnish a drink. These are typically lined up, ready to go, in a multicompartment **condiment tray.** Often the tray is mounted on some part of the underbar at the serving station. It should never be located directly above the ice bin! Many health codes define it as a potential hazard because of the likelihood of dropping foods into the ice.

An alternative to the installed condiment tray is a plastic tray on the bar top or glass rail. Such a tray may be moved around at the bartender's convenience, and can be cleaned more easily than one fixed to the underbar. If it is the servers who garnish the drinks, which is often the case, the garnishes must be on the bar top at the pickup station, as in Figures 4.2 and 4.3. A plastic condiment tray is shown in Figure 4.25.

Figure 4.25 Plastic condiment tray. Courtesy of Co-Rect Products, Inc.

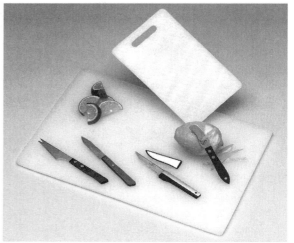

Figure 4.26 Cutting boards, bar knives, and zester. Courtesy of Co-Rect Products, Inc.

The tools for preparing condiments are few but important (Figure 4.26):

- Cutting board
- Bar knife
- Relish fork
- Peelers: zester, router, or stripper

A cutting board for the bar can be of any surface material that will not dull the knife, though rubber or plastic is usually best. Wood, however, is the most pleasant surface to work on, but most health codes rate it a health hazard because it is hard to keep bacteria-free. A small board is all you need and all you will have room for.

A **bar knife** can be any small- to medium-size stainless-steel knife, such as a paring or utility knife. It is essential that it be stainless steel; carbon steel will discolor and the color will transfer to the fruit being cut. The blade must be kept sharp, not only to do a neater, quicker job, but because it is safer because it will not slip. The one in the picture has a serrated blade, which is especially good for cutting fruit. Knife handles should be made of heavy-duty rubber or plastic for sanitary reasons.

A **relish fork** is a long (10-inch), thin, two-tined stainless-steel fork designed for reaching into narrow-necked bottles for onions and olives. The one pictured has a spring device that helps to secure the olive or onion firmly.

The **zester, router,** and **stripper** are special cutting tools for making that twist of lemon some drinks call for; they peel away the yellow part of the lemon skin, which contains the zesty oil, precluding the white underskin, which is bitter.

Tools and Equipment for Serving

The tools in this category comprise a short and somewhat miscellaneous list, but these are important items that no bar could do without:

- Bottle and can openers
- Corkscrews
- Bound serving trays
- Folios

Any type of bottle or can opener that is good quality and does the job is acceptable. Stainless steel is best; it is rust-free and easy to clean. These openers must be kept clean, an easy task to forget.

The first patent for a **corkscrew** was held by a British minister named Samuel Henshell. Today, there are many different kinds of corkscrews, or wine openers, a few of which are pictured in Figure 4.27. Each one is designed for one purpose: to extract corks from wine bottles.

The screw, or **worm,** that penetrates the cork should be made of stainless steel and be 2¼ to 2½ inches long and about ⅜ inch in diameter, with a hollow core in the middle. (A solid core would chew up the cork.) The screw should have enough spirals to take it clear through the cork. A corkscrew with an elongated spiral and a longer pitch (distance) between the twists of the screw makes for easier insertion into the cork. The screw's edges should be rounded, not sharp.

The **waiter's corkscrew** (there are three shown at bottom left in Figure 4.27) is specially designed for opening wines at tableside. It includes the

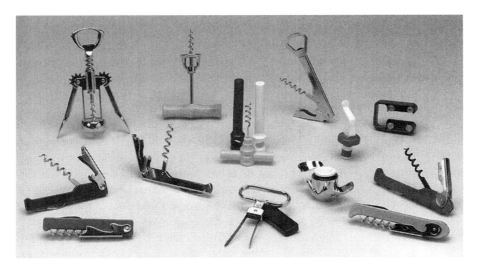

Figure 4.27 Corkscrews. Courtesy of Co-Rect Products, Inc.

Figure 4.28 Round serving trays. Courtesy of Co-Rect Products, Inc.

corkscrew itself, a small knife for cutting the seal of the bottle, and a lever for easing out the cork. Made of stainless steel, it folds like a pocketknife.

At center, the other type of corkscrew commonly used in bars has "wings" on either side that rise as the screw is twisted in. When the wings are pushed down again, this pulls out the cork. This corkscrew is fine for use at the bar, but is probably too bulky for the table server's pocket.

The device pictured at the bottom center of Figure 4.27 is nicknamed the **ah-so.** It is a simple pair of prongs that straddle the cork. You place the prongs on the side of a cork and rock them side to side until they are wedged into the neck of the bottle, between glass and cork. Then the ah-so is twisted and pulled gently, to bring the cork out whole without a puncture in the middle. People who learn how to successfully use the ah-so swear by it, but it can be slow and frustrating for those who haven't perfected the technique. For high-volume operations, you will want to invest in an uncorking machine. These are mounted on a countertop with a vise clamp and wingnut. The spiral cork is inserted into the cork, which is extracted from the bottle in a single downward stroke. Uncorking machines are between 12 and 22 inches in height. You will need *round serving trays* in two sizes: 14-inch and 16-inch (see Figure 4.28). Bar trays should have cork surfaces to keep the glasses from slipping.

GLASSWARE

The glassware you use in your bar should be considered an element of your overall décor and concept. It has a subtle but clear impact on your customer's perception of the bar's style, quality, and personality. There's a lot of tradition involved in cocktail service. When you use the proper size and shape of glass for a drink, it indicates you know your business and signals a respect for that tradition to your guest. Glassware can be a merchandising tool, stimulating sales with subtle or flamboyant variations—tall, sleek, frosted pilsner glasses for beer; oversized glasses with thin, delicate rims for certain wines; colorful, whimsical, oversized goblets for Margaritas; attractive mugs for specialty coffee. The Four Seasons Hotel and Resort in Carlsbad, California, for instance, uses a different glass for every martini recipe! And glassware isn't just used for drinks; you're likely to see gourmet appetizers like shrimp cocktail or ceviche served in eye-catching, oversized martini glasses, or fresh fruit and ice cream looking especially elegant in a large brandy snifter.

As Americans become more sophisticated about their dining preferences, glassware manufacturers try to stay one step ahead of the trends. Martini

Figure 4.29 Martini glasses.

glasses are among the trendiest, since a good martini has always been an equal combination of good spirits and great presentation. Just to give you an idea of what's available, Figure 4.29 displays one manufacturer's line of martini glasses. There are dozens more. Smart bar owners and bartenders know that drink presentation makes a pleasant experience more memorable, and bespeaks the mood and personality of the bar itself.

As microbrewed beers have become more popular, connoisseurs also have come to expect a variety of beer glasses. Heavier, lager beers are generally served in heavy glass mugs with handles; lighter pilsner beers have more carbonation, and are best showcased in a tall, narrow glass that widens at the top. For ales, including stouts and porters, a straight-sided, traditional pint glass with a wide mouth allows the guest to smell and sip. Customers who know their beers will appreciate the fact that you know how to serve them correctly.

There is an ongoing debate about wine service. Some argue that more wine would be sold if the pretense and formality of stemware were eliminated. Restaurants like Romano's Macaroni Grill, a Texas-based national restaurant chain, sets a jug of their red house wine right on each table. Guests keep track of how many times they fill their plain, glass tumblers—glasses normally filled with ice water. There are practical reasons for going this more casual route: The wait staff doesn't have to spend the time opening individual wine bottles; and tumblers stack and store more easily, in more compact space, than wine goblets. For casual dining or other informal establishments, stemware has become optional. You must determine whether you'll be gaining, or losing, wine sales if you decide to go the informal route.

Glass Terms and Types

Glasses have three characteristic features: the **bowl**, the **base** or **foot**, and the **stem** (Figure 4.30). A glass may have one, two, or all three of these features. The three major types of

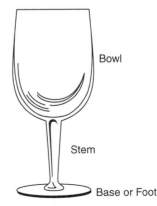

Figure 4.30 Defining glass parts.

Figure 4.31 Tumblers.

glassware—tumblers, footed ware, and stemware—are classified according to which of these features they have.

A **tumbler** is a flat-bottomed, cylindrical glass that is basically a bowl without stem or foot. Its sides may be straight, flared, or curved. Various sizes and shapes of tumbler are known by the names of the drinks they are commonly used for: Old-Fashioned, rocks glass (for cocktails served "on the rocks"), highball, Collins, cooler, zombie, pilsner (Figure 4.31). Glass jiggers and shot glasses are mini-tumblers.

Footed ware refers to a style of glass whose bowl sits directly on a base or foot. Bowl and base may have a variety of shapes. Traditional footed glasses include the brandy snifter and certain styles of beer glass (Figure 4.32). Today, footed ware is also popular for on-the-rocks drinks and highballs. In fact, any type of drink can be served in a footed glass of the right size.

Stemware includes any glass having all three features—bowl, foot, and stem. Stemware, too, comes in a variety of shapes. Wine is always served in a stemmed glass, as is a straight-up cocktail or a straight liqueur. Certain shapes and sizes of stemware are typical of specific drinks, such as wine, sour, Margarita, Champagne (Figure 4.33). Stemware, for obvious reasons, is the type of glass most easily broken, and you might as well plan for this when you place your glassware order.

Figure 4.32 Footed ware.

Figure 4.33 Stemware.

A fourth type of glass is the **mug** (Figure 4.34). You can think of a mug as a tumbler with a handle or as a tall glass cup. It is usually used for serving beer, but smaller specialty mugs are used for coffee drinks. When used to serve beer, mugs are sometimes called **steins.**

How Glass Is Made

Glass is made of very fine sand, called **silica,** that is mixed with soda, lime, and **cullet** (reused broken glass bits), and heated to temperatures of nearly 1,500° Fahrenheit. When it is in this pliable, superhot form, the molten glass is either blown into its final shape by introducing air into it, or it is pressed into a mold to shape it. Most commercial glasses are the latter, known as **pressware.** After the glass is shaped, it is put into a warm oven to cool slowly, which is called **annealing.** The slow cooling stabilizes and strengthens the glass and removes any stress points that may have developed during shaping.

After annealing, some glass goes through another step called **tempering.** The cooled glass is reheated, almost to its original high temperature, then blasted with cold air. The process "shocks" the glass and makes it more resistant to temperature extremes. If a glass is advertised as **fully tempered,** it means the entire glass underwent a tempering process; **rim tempered** means only the rim received this extra

Figure 4.34 Beer mug.

treatment. Most stemware is fully tempered; mugs or tumblers may be only rim tempered.

A curved or barrel-shaped glass is more durable than a straight-sided glass, and a short, thick stem is sturdier than a thin, delicate one. You will notice that manufacturers make glass a little thicker at possible stress points. A rolled edge at the rim of a glass, or swirled or ribbed patterns, all indicate extra thickness.

Glass Names and Sizes

In bar terminology, glasses are typically named after the drink most commonly served in them, and that drink is related to glass size. Thus, a highball glass is typically 8 to 10 ounces; a Collins glass is typically 10 to 12 ounces. In mixing a drink, the bartender relies to a certain extent on the glass size. In the making of a highball, for example, the glass is a measure of the amount of ice to be used and the amount of mix to be added. If the bartender uses the wrong size glass, the drink may be too weak or too strong. So before you purchase glassware for your bar, you must decide how strong a drink you will serve—that is, how much spirit you will use as your standard drink—1 ounce, 1¼, 1½, or whatever. Then, you can select glass sizes that will produce the drinks that look and taste right to your customers.

Tips on Glass Purchase

In selecting glasses, size is a better guide than the name of the glass, since a glass with a specific name will come in many sizes. Table 4.2 gives the range of sizes offered by one manufacturer for various types of glasses in various styles. In addition, nearly all glass types come in "giant" sizes for promotional drinks.

Buy glass sizes that you will never have to fill to the brim, to avoid spills. A wine glass to be used in meal service should be filled only halfway so the drinker can swirl the wine around and appreciate its bouquet. A brandy snifter serves the same purpose—no matter how big the glass, only 1 to 2 ounces of brandy is served, so the customer can savor the aroma.

Most bars buy only a few of the different types and sizes of glass. One type and size can work for Old-Fashioneds, rocks drinks, highballs; likewise one cocktail glass can serve for straight-up cocktails including sours, for sherry and other fortified wines. On the other hand, if you are building a connoisseur's image, you will probably want the traditionally correct glass for each type of drink, and you will want several different types of wine glasses, to serve different wines with each course of an elaborate dinner, including tall, thin Champagne flutes.

Table 4.2
Selection of Glass Sizes

Glass	Available Sizes (oz)	Recommended Size (oz)
Beer	6 to 23	10 to 12
Brandy, snifter	5½ to 34	Your choice from middle range
Brandy, straight up	2	2
Champagne	3½ to 8½	4½ or larger[a]
Cocktail	2½ to 6	4½ for 3-oz drink
Collins	10 to 12	10 to 12
Cooler	15 to 16½	15 to 16½
Cordial	¾ to 1¾	1¾, or use 2-oz brandy glass
Highball	7 to 10½	8 to 10
Hurricane	8 to 23½	Your choice for specialty drinks
Margarita	5 to 6	5 to 6
Old-fashioned	5 to 15 (double)	7
Rocks	5 to 12	5 to 7
Sherry	2 to 3	3 for 2-oz serving
Sour	4½ to 6	4½ for 3-oz drink
Whisky, straight shot	⅝ to 3	1½ to 3 depending on shot size
Wine	3 to 17½	8 to 9 for 4-oz serving; larger sizes OK
Zombie	12 to 13½	Your choice

[a] The tall thin flute is recommended over the broad shallow bowl.

How many glasses should you buy? For each type of drink, you may want two to four times as many glasses as the number of drinks you expect to serve in a rush period. Four times would be ample; two times would probably be enough for restaurant table service only. There are so many variables, you have to be your own judge, based on your clientele and rate of use.

In making your glass selection, remember that glassware is among the most fragile equipment you will be using, so consider the following: weight and durability; heat-treated glass, if you use a mechanical dishwasher; design (buy glasses that do not need special handling—flared rims break easily; rounded edges are easier to clean). And of course consider the breakage factor in figuring the quantity you need. Remember to choose existing styles and patterns, so they will continue to be available for replacements in months and years to come.

If your bar is in a trendy neighborhood or tourist area, you might also consider "take-home" glassware. In "destination cities" like New Orleans and Las Vegas, sometimes the glassware is included in the price of the drink, emblazoned with the logo of the bar or restaurant as a keepsake for visitors. Souvenir beer mugs and glasses are also popular in brewpubs.

Glassware Care

Glasses break for two main reasons: mechanical impact (when glass hits another object, causing it to crack, chip, or shatter) and thermal shock (when a quick, intense temperature change cracks or shatters the glass). Obviously, you can't prevent breakage entirely, but you can diminish it significantly by implementing a few common-sense handling practices:

- Train your staff members to never stack, or "nest," glasses one inside the other, and not to pick up multiple glasses at the same time, for example, one on each finger.
- Do not mix glasses with plates and silverware, either in bus tubs or on dishracks to be washed in a dish machine. Use separate bus tubs, and special dishracks made for glassware.
- Never use a glass for scooping ice. Always use a plastic scoop in the ice bin; metal scoops are more likely to chip a glass rim.
- Be aware of sudden temperature changes and their impact on the glass. Don't pour hot water into an ice-cold glass, or vice versa. Keep enough inventory on hand so that you're not forced to use hot glasses directly from the dishmachine. Give them time to cool off first.

Finally, keep in mind that a chipped or cracked glass is a broken glass. A crack or chip may cut a customer's lip or cause a drink to spill. Throw it out.

CASH REGISTERS

Since its invention more than a century ago by a tavern owner, the *cash register* has been a "Rock of Gibraltar" at the bar. The first version, known as "Ritty's Incorruptible Cashier," was a slow, noisy, hand-operated machine with a pot belly and a shrill bell that rang when a crank was turned to total the sale and open the cash drawer. In contrast, today's computerized register **(electronic cash register,** or **ECR)** is slim, quiet, and lightning-fast.

In some places, the bar's cash register does not always handle cash; instead, the customer pays a cashier rather than the bartender or cocktail waitress, and credit cards have become as common, if not more so, as cash. Still, the function of recording each bar sale remains at the bar, no matter how or where payment is made. This record of the type and cash value of liquor sold is the starting point of the control system by which you track your sales, your costs, and your liquor inventory to determine whether everything adds up.

Cash registers have always performed two basic functions: record sales and add and total them on a report that becomes a master record. Each register has a set of keys used to record sales in dollars and cents. Another set of keys represents sales categories—spirits, wine, beer, soft drinks, food, tax, or anything else the operation needs or wants to figure separately. There may be a third set of keys representing different bartenders or serving personnel. On some registers each of these keys controls a cash drawer, so that each person is responsible for his or her own take.

Each register prints an item-by-item record, plus the totals, category by category. This becomes your daily sales tally. It also forms the source document for all your reports to your state liquor control board. The kind of information required varies from state to state and will determine the basic key categories you need on your register.

Some registers are designed to prerecord each order on a guest check. This is known as a *precheck system*. It acts as a double control against losses when the printed order is checked against the sale, then both totals are checked against receipts at the end of the serving period.

A more elaborate register may have single keys representing specific drinks with their prices. These keys are known as **presets.** They may be code numbers or they may name the drink on the keys. Each key will print out the name of the drink and its price and make the correct extensions both on the record and on the guest check. When the Total key is pressed, the register will add up the check, figure the tax, print the total on the guest check, and record everything on the day's master record.

ECRs can also gather and tabulate sales-related data in many other useful ways. They can record the time of the sale and the server involved, along with the drink served. They can compare the liquor used in a given period with the liquor remaining in inventory. They can even function as a time clock on which employees punch in and out.

In a small enterprise, a single register at the bar may be all that is necessary, although its data-processing capability and its storage capacity (memory) will be limited. In a large system, the register at the bar feeds the data it gathers into a **central processing unit (CPU),** functioning as a **point-of-sale (POS) input terminal** for the CPU, which runs the entire system. This system is suitable for a medium-size or large enterprise having several different registers at various locations. In a chain, the registers at every bar may feed into a companywide computer network that can collect and analyze sales and inventory data from all over the country at the touch of a few computer keys.

A computerized system can also make the bar more efficient by sending drink orders electronically. An order can be transmitted from a station in the dining room to a screen at the bar so the drinks can be ready by the time the server reaches the bar. At the same time, the guest check is output by a printer at the bar for pickup with the drinks. Orders can even be transmitted to the bar from an order pad held in the server's hand. However, such devices are expensive and require a certain amount of maintenance.

Computerized register systems have many advantages. They are more accurate and more efficient, and people need far less training to operate them. A POS system also provides tighter controls over losses, and supplies data to watch and analyze operations daily, instead of weekly or monthly.

On the other hand, the more sophisticated the system, the higher its initial cost. For large operations and chains, the cost savings and the "instant" processing of vital data make a large investment well worth the money. A central computer system can also manage administrative functions, like payroll and accounting.

For a small operation, having a simple cash register and a separate computer is probably better than trying to tie it all together in one large system. Remember, what you really need to focus on at this point is the right cash register for the bar.

GENERAL EQUIPMENT GUIDELINES

We'll end this chapter with some general equipment guidelines to follow.

Look for Quality

It's very good business sense to invest in high-quality equipment for your bar. This is true across the board, from the large underbar units right down to the jiggers and pourers and the wine and cocktail glasses. There are a number of reasons why:

- **Durability.** Quality equipment will last longer and will better withstand the wear and tear of a high-speed operation. Heavy-gauge surfaces will resist dents, scratches, and warping. Heavy-duty blenders will better survive the demands of mixing frozen drinks. Quality glasses will break less easily than thin brittle ones.
- **Function.** High-quality products are less likely to break down. Breakdowns of any kind hamper service and give a poor impression of your operation. If your pourer sticks, you've got to stop and change it. If your corkscrew bends, you may crumble the cork and lose your cool as you present the wine, or the customer may refuse it. If your icemaker quits, you are in real trouble. Repairs or replacements can be frustrating, time-consuming, and costly. Quality products, moreover, usually come with guarantees.
- **Appearance.** Quality products are usually more pleasing to the eye, and are likely to maintain their good looks longer. Cheap glassware becomes scratched and loses its gleam. Cheap blender containers get dingy-looking. So do work surfaces. Since much of your equipment is seen by your cus-

tomers, it is important that it project an image of quality, cleanliness, and care.

- **Ease of care.** High-quality equipment is likely to be better designed as well as better made. This means smooth corners, no dirt-catching crevices, and dent-resistant surfaces that clean easily. All together this makes for better sanitation and better appearance.

Like everything else in life, quality cannot always be judged by price. This discussion is not to imply that you should go Cadillac all the way; you will certainly not buy lead crystal glassware unless your entire operation sustains this level of luxury. For equipment quality, examine weights or gauges of metals (the lower the gauge, the thicker the metal); at energy requirements, the horsepower of generators; insulation of ice bins and refrigerated storage; manufacturer's warranties and services. Consider the design features of each item in relation to its function, size, shape, and capacity, and in relation to needs.

Keep It Simple

The number of bar gadgets available today, both large and small, is mindboggling. They range from trick bottle openers to computerized drinkpouring systems costing many thousands of dollars. Each has its bona-fide uses, and some are highly desirable for certain operations. But the wise buyer will measure his or her purchases by these criteria:

- Does it save time or money or do a better job?
- Is it worth the time and money it saves?
- Is it maintenance-free? If not, how upsetting will it be to your operation if it malfunctions? If it needs repairs, is local service available?

It is easy to go overboard on hand tools; there's a gadget on the market for every little thing you do. It is better not to clutter up your bar with tools you seldom use. On the other hand, it is wise to have a spare of every tool that is really essential, from blenders to ice scoops. This way no time will be lost if something breaks or malfunctions. Keep the spares handy, in a place that is easily accessible in emergencies.

SUMMING UP

Bar equipment must be suited to the drink menu of an enterprise, just as kitchen equipment must appropriately service a food menu. All equipment must meet health department sanitation requirements and must be kept in top condition, with special attention to temperatures and pressures and the right conditions for proper functioning. It is easy to forget that these small details affect such things as the taste and the head on a glass of draft beer, loss of the bubbles in carbonated mixes, and the rate of production of an icemaker, but these things matter as much as the initial selection of equipment.

Typical questions bar owners must answer include: Should my bartenders pour by hand or use an automatic liquor-dispensing system? What types and how many blenders do I need (or should I buy or rent a frozen drink dispenser)? Should bartenders or barbacks wash glasses by hand or use a glasswasher? What types of ice cubes will best suit the types of drinks on the menu? What should the capacity of the ice machine be? Do I understand how a basic refrigeration system works? (This is important to know because beer and some other items require constant refrigeration.)

There are at least a dozen tools, called smallware, that make up the bartender's arsenal. These allow him or her to make garnishes, measure, pour, stir, strain and other necessities. Bottle and can openers and good corkscrews are also critical, as are cutting boards that are easy to sanitize between uses.

The right equipment, arranged for maximum efficiency and used and maintained with respect for its function, can be one of the best investments a bar owner can make. Two additional major considerations are the proper types of glassware that complement the drink menu and a POS system (the modern-day "cash register") to accurately record all sales.

POINTS TO PONDER

1. For what types of beverage service would an electronic pouring system be considered appropriate? Where would it be inappropriate? Give reasons for your answers.

2. What are the essential pieces of equipment that make up a pouring station?

3. What questions would you ask before buying an electronic cash register? What would you want it to do?

4. Why is the type of ice so important to the taste of a drink? When might you need more than one type of ice?

5. In what situation would you buy *full tempered* glasses? What about *rim tempered* glasses?

6. Why is the glass in which a drink is served important to the taste?

7. What do you consider the most valuable piece of equipment at the bar?

8. Explain the difference between a *premix* and a *postmix* soda dispensing system, and cite the advantages of each.

9. Where does the term *well brand* come from and how does it differ from a *call brand?*

10. What guidelines would you use in deciding what equipment to buy for a brand-new bar?

TERMS OF THE TRADE

ah-so

annealing

bar knife

barspoon

bar strainer

base (foot)

beer box (tap box)

blender (bar mixer)

bottle wells

bowl

call brands

central processing unit (CPU)

cocktail station (cocktail unit, beverage center)

compressor

condenser

condiment tray

cullet

detail tape

electronic cash register (ECR)

evaporator

expansion valve

filler cap

fins

flaker (flake-ice machine)

flexhose

footed ware

funnel

frozen drink dispenser

fruit squeezer

glass brushes

glass froster

glass rimmer

glasswasher

handgun (six-shooter)

hand shaker (cocktail shaker)

hydrochlorofluorocarbons (HCFCs)

hydrofluorocarbons (HFCs)

ice chest (ice bin)

ice crusher

icemaker

ice scoop

ice tongs

inlet chiller

jigger

jockey box

mixing cup (mixing steel, mix can)

mixing glass

muddler (muddling stick)

overrun

point-of-sale (POS) system

postmix system

pourer

premix system

preset keys

pressware

refrigerant

refrigeration circuit

refrigeration cycle

relish fork

router

shake mixer (spindle blender)

shot glass

silica

speed rail

standard (tap)

stein

stem

stemware

stripper

tempering (fully tempered, rim tempered)

tumbler

waiter's corkscrew

well brands (house brands, pouring brands)

worm

zester (router)

CHAPTER 5

The Beverages: Spirits

Most people know the contents of liquor bottles by linking names to tastes, but they haven't got a clue about how or from what these beverages are made. What makes them different from one another, and how can they each be used to their full advantage behind the bar? These are fundamentals questions to which every beverage manager should know the answers. This chapter explains the difference between fermented beverages and distilled spirits and examines the various kinds of spirits—how they are crafted and how they differ; why some spirits cost more than others; which ones are most intoxicating; where they come from; and all sorts of incidental information that makes for fascinating conversation. All this information is important in helping you to understand what you are buying and selling.

This chapter should help you . . .

- Distinguish between fermented and distilled beverages and identify them on your shelves.
- Define "proof" and relate it correctly to alcohol content.
- Understand the variables in distillation and their importance to the finished product.
- Become familiar with each of the spirit types commonly served from today's bar.
- Explain to customers and other audiences why scotch tastes different from bourbon, why gin tastes different from vodka, and so on.
- Define and explain such familiar but mysterious terms as bottled in bond, aged in wood, sour mash, single malt, London dry, neutral spirits, VSOP, and more.
- Serve each type of spirit correctly.
- Increase sales of after-dinner drinks.

We begin with a question: Which of the following well-known beverages are spirits: rum, brandy, Champagne, scotch, sherry, bourbon, vermouth, gin, ale, vodka? Many people incorrectly use the term **spirits** to include any type of beverage that contains alcohol. On the above list, rum, brandy, scotch, bourbon, gin, and vodka are spirits. So are the other whiskies, tequila, and all liqueurs and cordials. Champagne, sherry, and vermouth are not spirits, but wines. Ale is a beer, not a spirit. What is the difference and what difference does it make?

Beers, wines, and spirits taste different, have different alcoholic contents, are served differently and tend to have different uses. In order to provide for your customers properly, you need to know about these differences and how to handle each kind of beverage, from purchase to pouring.

TYPES OF ALCOHOLIC BEVERAGES

All beers, wines, and spirits are alcoholic beverages. An alcoholic beverage is any potable (meaning drinkable) liquid containing ethyl alcohol. It may have as little as ½ percent alcohol by volume, or as much as 95 percent. (The ½ percent was a figure chosen by the federal government at the time of the Prohibition Amendment, as it was groping to define an "intoxicating" beverage. At ½ percent, you'd have to drink 4 to 5 gallons of a beverage to become intoxicated, but the figure remains in the government's definition.)

Fermented Beverages

All alcoholic beverages begin with the fermentation of a liquid food product containing sugar. **Fermentation** is the action of yeast upon sugar in solution, which breaks down the sugar into carbon dioxide and alcohol. The carbon dioxide, a gas, escapes into the air. The alcohol, a liquid, remains behind in the original liquid, which thus becomes a *fermented beverage*.

Beers and wines are fermented beverages. Beer and ale are made from fermented grains. Wines are made from fermented grapes and other fruits. Our ancestors fermented honey, dates, rice, milk, sugarcane, molasses, palms, peppers, berries, seeds, and pomegranates, all to create alcoholic beverages. Any liquid with sugar in it could be fermented if yeast was handy to start the action. When the sugar was converted to alcohol and carbon dioxide, the result was a beverage with an alcohol content of about 4 to 14 percent, depending on the amount of sugar in the original liquid.

Distilled Spirits

If you can separate the alcohol from a fermented liquid, you have what you might think of as the essence, or the spirit, of the liquid. This is exactly what spirits are and how they are made.

The process of separation is called **distillation.** The liquid is heated in an enclosed container, called a **still,** to a temperature of at least 173° Fahrenheit (78.5° Celsius). At this temperature the alcohol changes from a liquid to a gas, which rises. Most of the water of the liquid remains behind; water does not vaporize until it reaches its boiling point of 212° Fahrenheit (100° Celsius). The gas is channeled off and cooled to condense it back into a liquid. The result is a *distilled spirit*, or simply a *spirit*. All the spirits we use today are made by this basic process, diagrammed in Figures 5.1 and 5.2.

It's not known for sure how long the distillation process has been in use, but historians credit the Chinese with distilling spirits as far back as 1000 B.C. And, although they did not use the process, the Greeks and Romans at least knew about it. If we limit our discussion to the Western (mainly European) experience, we must credit the Arabic people for introducing distillation to Europe through the Iberian Peninsula and into the area that is now Spain. Ironically, the Arabs were forbidden to drink alcohol for religious reasons—instead, they distilled perfume from flowers and used the process to produce a powdered cosmetic for eyes that they called *al kuhl* (from the word "kohl"). It's the word from which "alcohol" is derived.

In Europe in the Middle Ages, alchemists experimented with distillation in attempt to cure diseases or prolong life. These practitioners were equal parts scientist, philosopher, magician, and, some say, charlatan, who sold elixirs and potions about which great promises were made. Although their *aqua vitae* ("water of life") was not quite the miracle drug they were looking for,

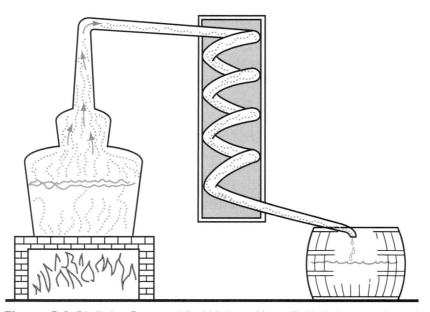

Figure 5.1 Distillation: Fermented liquid is heated in a still. Alcohol vapors rise and are carried off through a coil that passes through cold water, condensing them into a liquid spirit.

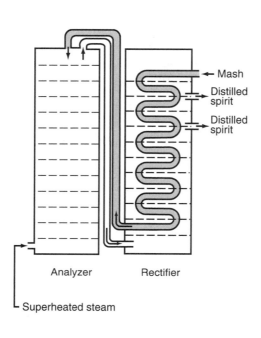

Figure 5.2 A continuous or column still. In the version shown here, fermented mash (gray) enters the *rectifier* column and flows downward through a twisting pipe surrounded by superheated steam. This hot mash is then pumped to the top of the *analyzer* column. Here it seeps down through perforated plates, meeting superheated steam entering from the bottom. This vaporizes the volatile elements of the hot mash, especially the alcohol. The vapors rise to the top and are then piped back to the bottom of the rectifier. There they rise again through perforated plates, condensing as they are cooled by the mash descending in the twisting pipe. The condensed spirits are then drawn off at their desired degree of alcohol content. Photo courtesy of Clear Creek Distillery.

it did gain respect as a medicine. When it was flavored to make it more palatable, people discovered they liked it. Soon the technique of distilling was applied to all kinds of fermented products to produce much stronger beverages.

Classifying Beverages

Which of those bottles at the bar are fermented and which are distilled? You can put the familiar names into place by examining Table 5.1.

Table 5.1

Alcoholic Beverages

Fermented		Distilled							
Beers and ales	**Wines**	**Whiskies**	**Gins**	**Vodka**	**Rum**	**Tequila**	**Brandies**	**Liqueurs**	**Others**
Lager beers	Table	Scotch	London dry				Cognac	Amaretto	Aquavit
Light beers	Reds	Irish	Hollands				Armagnac	B & B	Bitters
Ales	Whites	Bourbon					Calvados	Bailey's Irish	Neutral spirits
Porter	Rosé	Rye					Kirsch	Cream	
Stout	Aperitif	Blends					Brandy (U.S.)	Bénédictine	
Bock beer	Vermouth	Canadian					Applejack	Chartreuse	
Steam beer	Dubonnet	Light					Slivovitz	Chéri-Suisse	
	Lillet	Others					Pear William	Cointreau	
	Byrrh						Metaxa	Crèmes	
	Dessert						Pisco	Curaçao	
	Sherry[a]						Others	Drambuie	
	Port							Galliano	
	Angelica							Grand Marnier	
	Madeira							Irish Mist	
	Marsala							Kahlúa	
	Málaga							Ouzo	
	Muscatel							Peter Heering	
	Sparkling							Pernod	
	Champagne							Sabra	
	Sekt							Schnapps	
	Sparkling burgundy							Sloe gin	
	Spumante							Southern Comfort	
	Saké							Tia Maria	
								Triple sec	
								Tuaca	
								Fruit liqueurs	
								Fruit-flavored brandies	
								Others	

[a] Often served also as an aperitif.

151

The U.S. government has established **Standards of Identity** for the various classes of alcoholic beverages—that is, the types of spirits (gin, vodka, brandy, rum, tequila, the various whiskies), types of wine, and types of malt beverages (beer and ale). For example, if a bottle contains bourbon and is labeled as such, there is a Standard of Identity stating certain requirements for that type of product: what it is made of, how it is made, the type of container it is aged in, and its alcoholic content. These standards, rigidly enforced, produce a beverage having the distinctive characteristics everyone recognizes as bourbon. If the name is on the bottle, you'll know what's inside, because a federal inspector makes periodic compliance investigations at each distillery in the country. Imported products must meet similar standards in order to enter the country.

These Standards of Identity were developed after Repeal as part of the strict control system imposed on the new beverage industry to avoid the chaos of the Prohibition era. Their purpose is twofold: (1) to provide the base for assessing and collecting federal taxes, and (2) to protect the consumer. Beyond this, the standards can be helpful to you in learning to read bottle labels so you know what you are buying, and in understanding the differences between similar products. The three beverage chapters in the book draw heavily on Standards of Identity.

Alcohol Content. There are other differences between fermented and distilled beverages in addition to the way they are made. One is their alcoholic content. Beers and ales contain 2½ to 8 percent alcohol by weight (3.1 to 10 percent by volume). Table wines may be 7 to 14 percent by volume; aperitif and dessert wines 14 to 24 percent (since they have a small percentage of added spirits). Spirits usually range from 35 to 50 percent alcohol by volume, with a few liqueurs as low as 18 to 20 percent and one or two rums as high as 75½ percent. (There are even neutral spirits available at 95 percent, but they are never used as bar liquors.)

For spirits, you will see a number on the label and the word **proof.** Proof is a system of determining the alcohol content and, therefore, the relative strength of the beverage. It is also used as a base for collecting federal taxes on alcoholic beverages.

The history of the term is rather colorful. It comes from the early days of distilling, when the distiller tested ("proved") the product by mixing it with gunpowder and setting it on fire! If the liquid didn't burn, it was too weak. If it burned fiercely, it was too strong. The spirit that was "just right" for drinking (without the gunpowder) burned with a steady blue flame, and turned out to be 50 percent alcohol, more or less. The other 50 percent of the liquid was water. Thus the American proof standard was born—a "100 proof" whiskey contains 50 percent alcohol by volume. (Take the percentage of alcohol, double it, and you get the correct proof number for that spirit.)

As you might imagine, this was a less than exact science. Today, there are also very specific legal definitions of proof; for instance, a Proof Spirit is one that, at 58° Fahrenheit, weighs $^{12}/_{13}$ths of an equal measure of distilled water. At 58°, this spirit has a specific gravity of .92308. It is a mixture of about 57 percent pure alcohol and 43 percent water. An instrument called a *hydrometer* is used to measure spirit strength.

In the past, proof was indicated by the same symbol used for degrees of temperature—80°, for example. However, today, U.S. law requires that the label on a liquor bottle list both alcohol content and proof, with the alcohol percentage by volume stated first, and the proof following in parentheses with the word "proof" spelled out—for example, "Alc. 40% by vol. (80 proof)." This labeling system is not as clear-cut as it might appear, however; because other nations have adopted their own proof systems. The other common ones are the British/Canadian proof system, and the Gay-Lussac (G-L) proof system used elsewhere in Europe; the latter is simply a statement of the percentage of alcohol by volume.

To convert from one system to another, start with the G-L value (the percentage-of-alcohol figure). To convert to the American system, multiply the G-L value by 2; to convert to the British system, multiply the G-L value by 7, then divide that answer by 4. Figure 5.3 is a chart that compares the three systems of measure.

It is the alcohol in any beverage that causes the intoxicating effect as it runs through human veins. Looking at the percentage figures, one might conclude that a 90-proof gin is 10 times as intoxicating as beer. Ounce for ounce, this is true. But comparing percentages gives a statistical picture with very little meaning, since the typical serving size varies widely from one beverage to another.

Let's translate the statistics into the drinks you might be serving at the bar. A 12-ounce bottle of 4-percent beer would contain 0.48 ounces of alcohol. A 5-ounce serving of 12-percent wine would have 0.6 ounces of alcohol, or 25 percent more than the bottle of beer. A Gin-and-Tonic made with 1½ ounces of 80-proof gin would have 0.6 ounces of alcohol, the same amount as the glass of wine and 25 percent more than the beer. A Martini made with 2 ounces of the same gin and ½ ounce of 18-percent vermouth would con-

G-L System	American Proof	British/Canadian Proof
100%	200	175.2
50%	100	87.6
40%	80	70.0
10%	20	17.7

Figure 5.3 Three systems of measuring proof.

Table 5.2

Alcoholic Content of Drinks Compared

Drink	Alcoholic Content (oz)	More than Beer (%)	More than Wine (%)	More than Gin-and-Tonic (%)
12 oz of 4% beer	0.48			
5 oz of 12% wine	0.6	25		
Gin-and-Tonic with 1½ oz of 80-proof gin	0.6	25	same	
Martini with 2 oz of 80-proof gin, ½ oz of 18% vermouth	0.89	85	33	33

tain 0.89 ounces of alcohol, 33 percent more than the Gin-and-Tonic and the wine and 85 percent more than the beer. Table 5.2 condenses all this information.

Comparing these beverage types, you can see that the alcohol content has a lot to do with the size of a serving. Imagine the consequences of pouring gin in 5-ounce servings as though it were wine. So you see, it is more than tradition that dictates a certain glass for a certain type of beverage—why beer is served in tall glasses, and Martinis in small ones (it still takes almost two beers to equal the alcohol in one Martini). You can also understand why a customer who is gulping Martinis will need to be watched more closely for signs of intoxication than someone having a leisurely glass of wine or a bottle of beer with dinner.

Mixed Drinks

A **mixed drink** is a single serving of two or more beverage types mixed together, or of one beverage type mixed with a nonalcoholic mixer. The cocktail and the highball are the two most common types of mixed drinks, but there are many others—coffee drinks, Collinses, and cream drinks, for example.

Most mixed drinks are made with spirits, though a few wines are used in **wine spritzers** and as cocktail ingredients, notably the vermouths. The most common use of spirits is in mixed drinks. The rest of this chapter takes an in-depth look at spirits, those inviting and expensive bottles that are so important to your profit that you have to keep track of every ounce.

SPIRITS: AN OVERVIEW

All spirits are alike in several ways. They are all distilled from a fermented liquid. They all have a high percentage of alcohol in comparison to other alcoholic beverages—most of them are nearly half alcohol and half water (80 to 100 proof, except for some liqueurs). They are usually served before or after dinner rather than with the meal.

There are several distinct and familiar categories of spirits. The primary differences between them are flavor and body. Each type has a characteristic taste: whiskies have a whiskey taste, gins a gin taste, rums a rum taste, and so on. Within categories of spirits there are further taste variations: bourbon whiskey, for instance, tastes very different from scotch, and Irish tastes different from both. There are also taste differences between brands. And there are variations in body: full-bodied spirits and lighter ones.

While federal law regulates what is put on a liquor bottle's label, it requires almost no information about how the product was made or aged. So what are the differences and how do they impact the taste of the finished product?

There are three main factors that determine flavor and body: (1) the ingredients in the original fermented liquid, (2) the proof at which it is distilled, and (3) what is done with the spirit after distillation. To understand these factors, we need to look at the distillation process more closely.

Congeners

At lower proofs, there are more **congeners** and **fusel oils** in the spirit. Do not consider these detrimental to the quality of the product; they give some liquors (particularly whiskies and brandies) their character.

The core of the distillation process, as explained, is evaporating the alcohol by heating it until it separates itself from the fermented liquid by vaporizing. If that were the only element that vaporized at distilling temperatures, we would have 100 percent pure ethyl alcohol—a 200-proof spirit. It would be colorless and have a raw, sharp taste with no hint of its origin. The taste would be the same no matter what it was distilled from—wine, grain, molasses, whatever.

But other substances may join the alcohol as it vaporizes. One is water, as noted. In addition, there are minute amounts of other volatile substances that provide flavor, body, and aroma in the beverage. Called *congeners*, they come from ingredients in the original fermented liquid. Chemically, they have such identities as acids, other alcohols, esters, aldehydes, and trace minerals. In the product, they translate into the smoky malt taste in scotch, the full-bodied pungency of bourbon, a hint of molasses in rum, the rich aroma of fine brandy, and so on.

One congener is amyl alcohol, commonly known as fusel oil. In the dictionary, it is defined as an "oily, acrid and poisonous" mixture. But in alcohol, a very small amount of fusel oil imparts a distinctive flavor to whiskey.

Distillation Proof

By varying the distillation temperature, the length of distilling time, the type of still, and other factors, the amounts of water and congeners can be controlled. The higher the distillation proof and the less water used, the fewer the congeners and the purer the alcohol. And, since the congeners are the flavorers, the flavor is less pronounced and the body of the spirit is lighter. Conversely, the lower the distillation proof, the more distinctive and pronounced the flavor of the spirit. To experience the difference, taste a vodka and a bourbon: vodkas are distilled at 190 proof or above; bourbons are usually distilled at 110 to 130 proof.

The ideal in the world of liquor manufacture is to hit on the right combination of low distillation proof (therefore more flavor from congeners and fusel oils) and high bottled proof (not overly diluted with water).

Spirits distilled from any material at 190 proof or above show virtually no distinct characteristics. Therefore, they are known as **neutral spirits** or *neutral alcohol*, almost pure alcohol. If bottled, neutral spirits must be bottled at 80 proof or higher. These are used to make vodka and gin and to blend with spirits distilled at lower proofs.

All neutral spirits, as well as many lower-proof spirits, are distilled in *column stills* (refer back to Figure 5.2). It is also called a **Coffey still** (after its Irish creator, Aeneas Coffey, who developed the process in 1832), or a **continuous** or **patent still,** and it is the type of still used to make most spirits in this country. Cognac, malt scotch, Irish whiskey, tequila, and some rums, gins, and liqueurs are made in *pot stills* that have not changed much in design since the early days of distilling. Pot stills with copper pots are called **alambic** stills. (The ancient Moorish word for still was *al-ambiq.*) Pot stills are limited in the degree of proof they can achieve; consequently, the liquor they produce always has a lot of flavor, body, and aroma.

The column still, on the other hand, can be controlled to produce spirits at a wide range of strengths, up to about 196 proof. It consists of a tall column, or series of columns, in which the fermented liquid is heated by steam inside the still instead of heat from below. The alcohol vapors can be drawn off at various heights and redistilled in a continuous process, making it possible to separate nearly all the water and congeners from the alcohol if neutral spirits are the goal, or to produce spirits at almost any lower proof. Another advantage of the column still is that it can keep running—hence the term "continuous." With the pot still, only one batch at a time can be made, and the pot must be cleaned after every use.

Aging, Blending, and Bottling

A newly distilled spirit is raw, sharp, and biting. How is it turned into the mellow and flavorful product we sell at the bar?

Our less sophisticated ancestors drank the spirit as it came from the still. The story goes that someone noticed that a batch of spirits shipped a long distance in wooden barrels tasted better on arrival than it did when it left the still. However the discovery was made, most of today's spirits distilled at less than 190 proof are aged in wooden (usually oak) barrels for periods ranging from 1 year for some light rums to 20 or so years for choice brandies. The age on the label is the length of years the distiller kept the product in the barrel. Longer time periods do not necessarily indicate a better quality product—it's all relative. There are Cognacs that can improve for 25 years, while other spirits turn woody and bitter after only three years.

Two things happen in the barrels: (1) the spirit undergoes changes as the congeners interact with air filtering through the porous wooden casks; and (2) new congeners are absorbed from the wood itself, adding other flavoring agents. In due course, all the flavors are "married" or blended, and mellowed to the desired final taste. Aging in wood adds color as well as flavor to the spirit. Not all spirits are aged; sometimes the sharp bite of a raw but flavorful spirit is part of its appeal—gin, for example, or kirsch.

There are other means of producing or modifying flavors after distillation. One is by introducing new flavors, as is done with gin and with liqueurs. Another is by blending two or more distillates, as is done with many whiskies. A spirit taste may also be modified by filtering through charcoal, as is done in making vodka, or by other special ways of removing certain congeners.

At bottling time spirits are diluted to drinking levels of taste, usually 80 to 100 proof, by adding distilled water. This lessens the intensity of the flavor, but does not change it. When the term **cask strength** is used on a whiskey label, it means no water was added to the spirit during bottling. It does not mean that the product was never diluted, just that it was not diluted during the bottling process, and the term is a good sign the whiskey will be flavorful. Once in the bottle, a spirit does not undergo any further change. No matter how old it gets sitting on a shelf, it does not age, since it is not exposed to air or wood.

Consumers in the United States used to purchase their spirits—mostly whiskey—by filling their own jugs from a retailer's or vendor's casks. This practice kept packaging costs down, but it also enabled dishonest vendors to dilute the product. In the early 1800s, the reputation of a liquor was made by its vendor, not by the distiller who created the product. This changed in

1870 when George Carvin Brown became the first distiller to bottle, label, and market his own bourbon, known as "Old Forester." Brown put it in clear, sealed bottles that were not easily tampered with. The idea caught on, and soon other distillers began bottling, sealing, and labeling their wares instead of selling casks to retailers.

Today, all spirits produced in the United States are stored and bottled in bonded warehouses. At bottling time the bottler checks for full bottles, correct proof, accurate labeling, and purity. If everything complies with all federal standards, the federal tax is paid and the bottle is sealed with a federal revenue stamp or, more often, with a tamper-evident closure of metal or plastic.

All this does not mean that the government guarantees the quality of the product. Many people mistakenly think the phrase **"Bottled in Bond"** on a label is a guarantee of quality conferred by the government. What it really means is that a given spirit meets certain conditions: it is straight (unblended), distilled at 160 proof or less at one plant by one distiller, aged at least four years, and bottled at 100 proof in a bonded warehouse. Since all spirits are now bottled in bonded warehouses, the phrase has lost much of its meaning.

You can see that there are literally hundreds of ways in which a beverage that is roughly half alcohol and half water can be made in thousands of different varieties. Every ingredient, from the grape or grain to the water and yeast, can make a difference in taste. Distillation methods are critical. Different aging times and conditions produce different tastes. The type of wood in the barrel, and whether the barrel is new or used, charred or uncharred, has a definite effect on flavor. Blending and flavoring can produce an almost infinite number of products. All these factors explain why each brand of each spirit is unique.

Fortunately there are only a few basic spirit types, and they are easily recognizable by general taste, aroma, and character. Let's look at them in greater detail.

THE BROWN SPIRITS: WHISKEY AND SCOTCH

The first thing to note here is that you will see whiskey spelled with the "e" and without; both are correct, but signal a distinction: whiskey with an "e" is the American and Irish spelling; without the "e," most often indicates a product of Scotland or Canada. There are a couple of exceptions: Old Times and Old Forester are American whiskies that spell their name "whisky," to pay homage to their Scottish roots.

The four major whiskey-producing countries of the world are Canada, Ireland, Scotland and the United States. Ireland was the first of these four to export its whiskey. After a root-eating disease called phylloxera destroyed many French vineyards in the 1870s (and thus reduced wine and Cognac production), Scotland entered the picture and began exporting also. Scotch whisky has been the dominant product in this category ever since.

The earliest spirit makers started with whatever fermentable product was readily available. In the southern countries of Europe it was wine, already fermented and available. In northern climates such as Scotland and Ireland, grapes did not grow well, but grain did, and beer and ale were plentiful. So the first whiskey makers started with a fermented mash of grain, similar to the early stages of making beer, and distilled that. They produced a raw, biting drink called *uisgebeatha* in Scotland and *uisegebaugh* in Ireland, Celtic translations of *aqua vitae*, "water of life." Later, the last syllables were dropped and the name became *uisge*, and eventually, "whiskey," with or without the "e" depending on origin.

To get a grain product to ferment, an extra step is required to begin the whiskey-making process: the starch in the grain must be converted to sugar. This is done by adding a malt. **Malt** is sprouted grain, usually barley. It contains an enzyme called **diastase**, which changes the starch to sugars. Malt, grain, and hot water are mixed together until conversion takes place. This is the *mash*. The liquid is then fermented by adding yeast. After fermentation, it is distilled. Figure 5.4 shows the sequence of steps.

Master distillers say the quality of the water and barley, as well as the locations of their distilleries, make a difference in overall taste of the final product. (Location because it affects the flavors of the raw materials.) They also say the size of the still makes a flavor impact: the smaller the pot, the more intense the whiskey; the taller the still, the more delicate the whiskey that comes from it. As with any other handcrafted product, there are dozens of variables that are all points of individual opinion, professional pride, and heated debate!

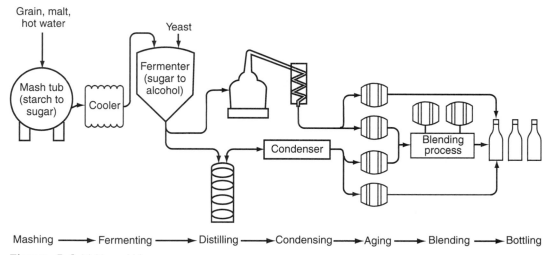

Figure 5.4 Making whiskey.

After distilling, the raw whiskey is stored in barrels (usually made of oak) for at least two years. Again, the type and age of barrel impacts the flavor. Whiskies stored in former sherry casks have a sweeter, fruity aroma; those stored in bourbon casks have a smokier aroma, sometimes reminiscent of vanilla. New barrels give off sharper, more pronounced aromas than older, well-seasoned ones. Modern-day whiskey makers have preferences about the origin of their oak—some like American, others Spanish. The length of time for barrel aging depends on the character of the raw product; some take longer to mellow than others. For this reason, a 12-year-old whiskey is not necessarily better quality than, say, a five-year-old or one whose age isn't given on the label. It all depends.

For straight whiskies, the product manufacture ends at this point. The most common straight whiskies include bourbon, rye, and corn, each containing 51 percent or more of a single grain type. But the majority of whiskies marketed in the United States (this includes imports) undergo yet another process—**blending.** Whiskies of different grains or different batches, different stills or different ages are blended together, sometimes with neutral spirits, to produce the standard of flavor and quality that represents a particular brand of whiskey. Usually the formula is a house secret, and the final blend is perfected by skilled master blenders. This person, responsible for making an appealing and consistent mix, is often referred to as a "nose," because he or she smells the whiskey's aroma but rarely actually tastes it. The alcohol content of the spirit would overpower the taste buds after only a few sips.

Whiskey belongs to the "brown goods" category whose sales have gradually declined, perhaps because its hearty flavor and dark color give the impression of a strong, high-proof drink. Yet it is a mainstay at any bar and the backbone of many traditional drinks, from Scotch and Soda or Bourbon and Branch (bourbon and water) to the Old-Fashioned and Planter's Punch. Many older customers prefer it to trendier beverages. Let's look at the many kinds of whiskey Americans drink.

Scotch. The whiskies we know as scotch are made-in-Scotland blends of malt whiskies and high-proof grain whiskies. The malt whiskies are made in pot stills, mainly from sprouted barley that has been dried over peat fires, giving it a smoky flavor that carries over into the final product. *Peat* is a natural fuel made of decomposed vegetation; its content (and, therefore, the aroma it imparts) may be moss and seaweed, or wood and heather, depending on where it was harvested. There's an ongoing debate in Europe about the peat-harvesting practices, specifically whether they are damaging the ecosystem (Figure 5.5.)

The grain whiskies are made chiefly from corn and are distilled in column stills at around 180 proof, somewhat below neutral spirits but very light in flavor. The two types of whiskies are aged separately for several years and then blended, with sometimes as many as 30 or 40 different malt and grain whiskies in a given brand.

Figure 5.5 Harvesting peat. *Source:* Picture Collection, The Branch Libraries, The New York Public Library.

Malt whiskey was born well before the fifteenth century, which is the first time Scottish records mention it. An old Scottish quip says Scotch whisky was created to reward the Scots for having to endure the cold, wet climate of their homeland. The 1600s and 1700s were marked by continuous disagreements between distillers and the government over taxation of spirits, and laws were enacted with the intent of putting the smaller (less than 200 gallons) home producers out of business. This only ensured a lively smuggling market for their product. It wasn't until 1823 that Scotland's Parliament enacted more lenient laws. About 120 years ago, a Scotsman named Andrew Usher is credited with being the first to blend malt whisky and grain whisky to reduce its pungency.

Scotch became popular in the United States during the Prohibition years, when it was smuggled into the country from Canada, the Caribbean, and ships at sea. The earliest brands were dark, peaty and strong; but after Repeal, Scotland's distillers began tailoring their products to the lighter American palate. Scotch got another boost in popularity when American soldiers returned from the world wars having acquired a taste for it.

A light-bodied scotch is not necessarily light-colored, since all scotches have caramel (burnt sugar) added to assure color uniformity. Nor does light body mean low alcohol content. All scotches are bottled at a minimum of 80 proof; most are 86 proof.

Interestingly, although the popularity of scotch has declined over the past 20 years, it has never lost its perceived prestige. The true scotch drinker will not be satisfied with anything else, except perhaps a good Cognac. Beverage marketing experts say many consumers drink scotch more for its "snob appeal" than for the taste of the beverage itself.

There are four basic types of scotch whisky:

- **Blended scotches** are blends of grain whiskies (distilled from corn or wheat) and single malt whiskies (the fine distillates of barley). They made their debut in the 1820s. Some of the more popular brand names include Chivas Regal, Cutty Sark, Dewars, and Johnny Walker.
- **Vatted malt scotches** are blends of 100-percent malt whiskies from more than one distillery. These are also called *pure malt scotches*.
- **Single-malt scotches** are unblended. They are the whisky of a single distillery, and made strictly from malted barley. These are currently the trendiest scotch drinks, often very distinctive in flavor and usually expensive. Glenlivet, Glenfiddich, and Macallan are among the most popular brand names seen in U.S. bars. (More about single malts in a moment.)
- **Single-cask, single-malt scotch** is the most "exclusive" type of scotch. Each bottle comes from a single cask, completely unblended.

Single-malt scotch has become very popular in recent years, partly because of clever marketing that capitalizes on its upscale image, and partly because Americans are drinking less, but seeking higher quality spirits. Single-malt scotch drinkers are as enthusiastic as wine buffs about finding and tasting the rare and unusual brands; they regularly pay from $7 to $8 per "shot" (1½ ounces) of scotch, and extremely rare scotches may sell for several thousand dollars per bottle. In every major city, at least one bar prides itself in having the area's largest variety of single malts; some have scotch tastings, seminars, and dinners for hobbyists. Don't overlook the opportunity to serve single malts by the "flight," like wine—that is, tastes of three different scotches for a fixed price—to promote sampling, comparison and conversation.

Liquor distributors can be of great assistance in figuring out what types of scotch to buy for your clientele. They often have sales kits and collateral material to share with your staff members.

Irish Whiskey. Irish whiskey is probably most familiar as the essential ingredient in Irish coffee. These triple-distilled whiskeys are smooth alternatives to the heavier-flavored scotches. In terms of liquor "craftsmanship," Irish whiskey is in the same league as single-malt scotches and single-barrel bourbons. It has an ancestry going back to the twelfth century, when King Henry II's troops invaded and found a well-established whiskey trade, begun by monks who settled the area in the Dark Ages.

Today's production techniques for Scotch and Irish whiskies are similar, but with some differences that definitely affect the flavor. The main difference in Irish whiskey comes from the fact that the freshly malted barley is not exposed to peat smoke when it is dried, so there is none of the smoky taste of scotch. Another difference is that it is made from several grains in addition to malted barley. A third is a triple distillation process that takes the Irish product through three separate stills (most pot-still whiskies go through two). The legal requirement in Ireland is that whiskey be aged for three years, although most is kept in wooden barrels for 5 to 8 years, and some up to 20 years. The result is a particularly smooth, mellow whiskey of medium body. This is the traditional Irish, unblended, and seldom called for in America. The more familiar Irish is blended with high-proof grain whiskey, as in making scotch, to create a lighter drink for today's market. Jameson and Old Bushmill are the familiar brand names here.

The Irish distillers have capitalized on the single-malt scotch craze by introducing single-malt Irish whiskies as "lighter" alternatives, and it has proven to be a smart move; after almost 20 years of slowly declining sales, Irish whiskies are now on the increase again. As many as 20 brands are available in the United States.

Bourbon. Bourbon is the best-known straight (unblended) American whiskey. Unlike the other "brown goods" in this category, bourbon makers prefer to think of their product as "the golden spirit," a palatable drink and versatile cocktail ingredient.

It is distilled at 160 proof or less from a fermented mash of at least 51 percent corn (most bourbons contain more) and aged at least two years in charred (burned) new oak containers. These requirements are spelled out in the federal government's Standards of Identity. Most bourbons are aged for four to six years, or for however long it takes to reach their desired mellowness. At the usual distillation proofs of 110 to 130, the whiskey produced has a strong flavor component and a full body. Also by law, bourbon does not have to be distilled in Kentucky; it can be made anywhere, as long as it is made according to the federal regulations. But if it is called "Kentucky whiskey," it must be distilled there. The same applies to "Tennessee whiskey."

The bourbon-making business is replete with legend and colorful history. In 1776, Patrick Henry helped craft and pass a "Corn Patch and Cabin Rights" law that gave settlers 400 acres of free land (in what is now Kentucky) if they would use it to build a house and grow grain. Corn was the easiest grain to grow and, as luck would have it, when combined with the mineral-free water that emerged from the area's underground springs filtered through natural limestone, it made darned good whiskey—lighter than what had been produced in the Northeast.

Bourbon was named for Bourbon County, Kentucky (which in turn, was named for the royal Bourbon family of France that had supported American colonists during the Revolutionary War). The man credited for discovering the bourbon style of whiskey-making was a Baptist preacher, Reverend Elijah Craig, in the late 1700s. He was the first to burn the insides of his oak barrels—whether intentionally or accidentally is unclear—and found that the charred wood added a beautiful, amber color and distinctive taste to his whiskey. They've been burning the insides of the barrels ever since. In those days having whiskey on hand was an ordinary part of life, and many a farmer had his own still or raised grain for his neighbor's still. Today, most bourbons are made in Kentucky, though at this writing there is no working distillery in Bourbon County.

The other historical event that sets bourbon apart from other spirits is the discovery of the **sour-mash** yeast process. In the 1820s, Dr. James C. Crow went to work at a Kentucky distillery, determined to use science to make the often rough-tasting spirit better. He found that, along with the fresh yeast, a portion of the leftovers (the "soured" mash) from a previous distilling could be added to the mash. This encourages yeast growth, inhibits bacterial contamination, and provides a certain continuity of flavor. There's nothing "sour" about the taste, either.

By the 1860s, bourbon was used as much as a medicine and anesthetic as it was a beverage. It was prescribed for at least a dozen ailments. And its quality became more consistent with George Carvin Brown's decision (in 1870) to sell his bourbon in sealed bottles. President Lincoln wondered aloud what brand of bourbon Ulysses S. Grant drank. Since General Grant was so successful leading the Union army (and quaffed quite a bit of bourbon) Lincoln thought perhaps he should send some of the same brand to his less motivated military leaders. Lincoln also taxed alcohol after the Civil War in an attempt to raise quick cash for the government, a move that inadvertently put the small guys out of business and began a steady consolidation of the industry that continued for the next century.

A hundred years later, bourbon had fallen out of favor with the public. Scotch became the drink of choice; and "white goods" (gin and vodka) also cut into its market share in the 1970s and 1980s. Today, higher-end "small-batch" and "single-barrel" bourbons are enticing customers once again, competing favorably with Cognacs. In bourbon terminology, single-barrel means just that: the bottle comes from one particular barrel. Small-batch means the bourbon is blended from a number of barrels that show the finest characteristics.

Variables in the bourbon-making process are the water, the grain (selected based on ripeness and moisture content), the yeast (a special "secret" mix known only to the distiller), the type of barrel and amount of charring, the time of year it is put into barrels (summer heat adds intensity of flavor and color, in winter the liquid "rests"), and even placement of the barrel within the storage area, called a **barrel house.** Barrels are stacked on racks a dozen high; the ones closest to the top get more heat, which intensifies their alcohol content. Barrel contents are either bottled directly, or blended first, but not until at least two years have passed.

Familiar examples of bourbons are Early Times, Jim Beam, Old Crow, Old Forester, Old Grand Dad, Old Forester, Maker's Mark, and Wild Turkey. A sour-mash whiskey similar to bourbon is Jack Daniel's, a Tennessee product. Made in Lynchburg, a town of fewer than 400 people where liquor has not been sold since Prohibition, the distillery is allowed (since 1995) to sell commemorative bottles on-site, but no one can buy and consume alcohol on the premises.

While it meets the grain requirements of bourbon, Tennessee whiskey has a special twist to its production: the distillate is filtered through maple charcoal before it is barreled for aging. This bit of regional tradition eliminates some harsher elements in the whiskey, and adds its own touch of flavor and romance. George Dickel is the only other Tennessee whiskey; there are only two legal distilleries in the state.

These flavorful whiskies are now popular mainly in the South. Today, Texas is Jack Daniels' top domestic market; Germany is its top foreign market.

Rye. A **rye whiskey** is one that is distilled at 160 proof or less from a fermented mash of at least 51 percent rye and aged in charred new oak containers at least two years. Notice this description is the same as bourbon's, except for the kind of grain.

In the early days of American whiskey-making, rye was the grain of choice. As America expanded westward, corn and other grains took the place of rye. Few people today drink straight rye whiskey, except perhaps in a Rye Manhattan. Along parts of the East Coast, blended whiskies are referred to as "rye." These are not ryes, however. Straight rye is a full-bodied spirit with the strong flavor of its parent grain, whereas most blended whiskies are lighter and less defined. Old Overholt is probably the best-known brand of straight rye whiskey.

Other Straight Whiskies. There are other straight whiskies made from 51 percent or more of wheat or malted barley or malted rye. There is corn whiskey made from 80 percent or more of corn and aged in uncharred containers. There is also something simply called "straight whiskey," which is whiskey made from a mixture of grains with no one grain predominating. And there are blended straight whiskies that are mixtures of straight whiskies of the same type—blended straight bourbon, for example.

Canadian Whiskey. Canadian whiskies are blended whiskies, light in body, delicate and mellow in flavor. In the mid-1980s, Canadian whiskey ranked as the second "most requested" spirit, after vodka; today, it ranks third, behind vodka and the liqueur category. Ten U.S. states do roughly half of the Canadian whiskey sales nationwide: Florida, Texas, and the states that border Canada.

Canadian brands provide "imported" status to consumers at less expensive prices than fine scotches. Taking a cue from their bourbon-making cousins to the south, Canadian distilleries are also marketing a variety of super-premium aged whiskies, like Crown Royal and Crown Royal Special Reserve. Seagram's V.O., Hiram Walker's Canadian Club, Lord Calvert, and MacNaughton are other well-known brands. (Ironically, the labels Canadian Mist and Harwood Canadian are bottled in the United States.)

Canadian law requires only that the whiskies be made from cereal grains and be aged at least three years, leaving the rest up to the distiller. The grains usually used are corn, rye, barley malt, and wheat, and each brand's formula is a trade secret. The whiskies are distilled at 140 to 180 proof and most are aged six years or more. Their lightness keeps them popular in the current "light"-minded market.

Blended American Whiskies. Blended American whiskies are combinations of straight whiskies or of whiskies with neutral spirits. A blend must contain at least 20 percent straight whiskey. Beyond that, the blend is wide open to whatever combinations of whiskey and neutral spirits will achieve the balance, taste, aroma, and body that characterize the particular brand. Small quantities of certain blending ingredients—sherry, prune juice, peach juice—are also allowed, up to 2½ percent. Often the neutral spirits are aged in used oak barrels to remove harshness. The process is like the blending of scotch from various straight malt whiskies and grain spirits, and the blending has a similar effect: the product is light-flavored and lighter-bodied than the original unblended whiskies, though not lower in proof.

Blended whiskies made in this country have the words "American Whiskey" on the label. Many of the U.S. whiskies we drink are blends—Seagram's 7 Crown or Schenley Reserve, for example. There is no aging requirement for blended whiskey, which means that the cheapest brands can be pretty raw, and definitely not suitable as bar whiskies.

Light Whiskey. Made-in-USA "light whiskey" came into being in order to let American distillers compete with the lighter Canadian imports, distilled at higher proofs than those allowed in the United States. Thus the federal government created a new category, effective in 1972, for whiskies distilled at above 160 proof but below 190 proof. These whiskies may be stored in used or uncharred new oak. Aging in seasoned (used) wood permits good development of the lighter flavor, without the intensity of the high-proof spirits.

There are several light whiskies on the market, but none has caught on with the drinking public. Today these whiskies are generally used in blending.

Other National Whiskies. In almost every country, you'll find someone making and selling whiskey—or at least, what they call whiskey. India, China, and Thailand are among the countries with products that occasionally make their way to the United States; and a couple of Scottish distillers have entered into joint venture agreements in India in recent years. Respectable brands from other countries include DYC from Spain, Yamakazi and Yoichi from Japan (in business since the 1920s and 1940s, respectively), and Tesetice from the Czech Republic.

Serving Whiskey

Whiskey drinks are served before, after, or between meals but are usually not offered with the meal. They may be ordered by type ("Give me a scotch . . .") or by brand name ("May I have a Dewars and water?"), except sometimes in cocktails. Common ways you'll serve them are:

Neat: Undiluted, at room temperature. Serve it in a shot glass or other small glass, with a separate glass of ice water beside it.

Straight: Same as "neat." Also called "up" or "straight up."

On the rocks: Poured over ice in a 5- to 7-ounce rocks glass. Use fresh ice, preferably made from distilled or filtered water.

With a splash: Mixed with water, preferably bottled spring water.

With soda: Mixed with club soda, or high-quality sparkling spring water.

People who know their liquor will often want it mixed with water or soda, not "straight." They know that subtler flavors may come to their attention more readily when the alcohol is diluted somewhat.

When served with soda or another mixer, a whiskey drink is served in a highball glass. Fill it first with ice, then pour in the whiskey, and fill with the mixer. Swirl it with a barspoon before serving.

The "branch" in "Bourbon and Branch," by the way, refers to clear spring water: old-timers felt bourbon was too good to mix with ordinary tap water.

THE WHITE SPIRITS

Vodka, gin, rum, and tequila are the major "white goods," so called because they are similar in color—or more accurately, lack of color—and are lighter in body and taste than "brown goods" like whiskey and brandy.

The key to the strong popularity of white goods rests on an interesting public misconception—that they are "lighter" in alcohol than brown goods. This is simply not true! When it comes to alcohol content, white goods pack just as powerful a punch as whiskies or other spirits, at 80 proof or higher. However, today's consumer, intent on a more moderate alcohol intake, often assumes that spirits lighter in color and flavor are not as "strong" as the darker, richer-tasting ones. This misconception has done wonders for the white goods producers, whose products now lead the pack in sales.

Vodka

Vodka is the top seller of all distilled spirits. Historically, its exact origin is questionable. While most purists argue over whether it was created in Poland or Russia, writings from the early eleventh century suggest that this spirit first appeared in Persia, now Iran, and was transported through Turkey and Spain to Poland. Today, however, if there's vodka at your bar, it is either of Russian or Polish origin. And the word "vodka" is derived from a Russian phrase (*zhizenniz voda*) that means "water of life." It later evolved to *wodka*, an endearment that roughly means "dear little water."

The earliest vodkas were made from grain or sometimes potatoes, distilled at fairly high proof but not aged, and so strongly flavored that they were often spiced to mask the raw grain taste. Then, in the early 1800s, it was discovered that charcoal would absorb the congeners, and modern-day vodka was born. It is clear, odorless, and, oddly enough, flavorless. Drunk neat, chilled, usually with spicy foods—caviar, smoked salmon, anchovies, at least by the upper classes—it became the rage in Russia. Peasants drank it, too. Everyone did.

In 1914, the Smirnov family was producing a million bottles a day and exporting vodka to Europe, parts of Asia and the United States. Three years later, everyone in the family of more than 100 members was wiped out by the Russian Revolution, except one: Vladimir Smirnov, who escaped to France with the family formula. He tried to reestablish the business in other European cities, but did not have sufficient funds. Eventually, he sold the rights to the vodka business to another man, who brought the formula to the United States, began distilling in 1934 as "Pierre Smirnoff & Fils," then sold the license to the Heublein corporation in 1937. Years later, a legal battle is still being waged between descendants of the Smirnov family and Heublein, which now sells the brand-name Smirnoff Vodka (half a million bottles a day in 150 countries), over the rights to the family name and product portfolio. Vodka got a slow start in the United States. Then, in 1946, the owner of the Cock 'N Bull restaurant in Hollywood put together a drink made from vodka, which wasn't selling, and ginger beer, which wasn't selling either, added half a lime, served it in a copper mug and christened it the "Moscow Mule." With skillful promotion, the drink and the spirit caught on. Vodka was "discovered" as a perfect partner for all sorts of juices and mixers, since it had virtually no taste of its own, but adds a definitive alcohol kick. Soon came the Screwdriver, the Bloody Mary, and a host of others, including the Vodka Martini, which is every bit as popular as its gin-based counterpart. In 1976, vodka sales surpassed whiskey.

Vodka is defined in the U.S. Standards of Identity as "neutral spirits so distilled, or so treated after distillation with charcoal or other materials, as to be without distinctive character, aroma, taste, or color." It can be distilled from any fermented materials, since neutral spirits from any source taste pretty much alike—which is to say, tasteless. U.S. vodkas, and the best imports, are made from grain. The final product is 80 to 100 proof, a smooth, adaptable form of alcohol that can be used in a variety of mixed drinks.

Many vodka producers in this country buy neutral spirits from distillers who specialize in them. There are two types of further processing: one is filtering through charcoal, and the other is to use such techniques as cleansing vapors that absorb the remaining congeners or centrifugal purifiers that spin them out. But not all vodkas are alike, though many people assume they are. Quality, or lack of it, is definitely perceptible, and vodka is emerging as a much more complex and sophisticated product. Some vodkas are triple- and quadruple-distilled, and the people who choose one over the other swear there are subtle differences.

In recent years, Americans have fallen in love with imported vodka. This trend emerged from a combination of factors: one, those misperceptions about it as a "light" spirit, and, two, because the "imported" product is still associated with financial success and social status. The most popular brand of vodka in the United States is Smirnoff. In addition, two imports do well at premium prices: Absolut from Sweden and Ketel-One from Poland. You may also see the Stolichnaya brand from Russia; it was once the top-selling brand in America, but the Cold War put a damper on its popularity. It has had to make a comeback in recent years. Finland has joined the upscale import market with Finlandia, number four on the list of popular imports. Truthfully, in many cases you're paying for the brand name. There are excellent values in imported vodka—less than $20 per bottle.

Ironically, the newest trend in the production of this flavorless spirit is to flavor it. Absolut has introduced a peppery vodka for spicy Bloody Marys and "Cajun Martinis"; Absolut Citron, lemon-flavored with mandarin orange and grapefruit accents; and two other flavors. Stolichnaya has countered with vanilla, strawberry, peach, cinnamon, and coffee-flavored vodkas. In the United States, there is a different Standard of Identity for flavored vodka, which requires that the name of the predominant flavor appear as part of the designation.

Figure 5.6 Inferno, a Canadian vodka infused with hot peppers. Photo courtesy of Boschler Studios.

Chile Pepper magazine reported in its April 1999 issue on a Canadian vodka, called Inferno, that has been infused with hot peppers nicknamed "9-1-1 chiles," or "Flamingo Reds," that are left in the bottle (Figure 5.6). A hot trend, indeed!

Aquavit. The Scandinavian version of vodka is often called **schnapps** (not to be confused with the liqueur of the same name), but its official names are **Aquavit** (from Norway) and **Akvavit** (from Denmark). The word schnapps is from an ancient Norwegian word meaning "to snap up or gulp" and, sure enough, the traditional way to drink this bracing spirit is ice cold, in a single gulp, sometimes followed by a swig of beer.

Aquavit is most often produced from distilling potatoes. It is distilled at 190 proof and then redistilled, like gin, with flavorings; caraway seed is the classic, but you may also find hints of cumin, fennel, dill, coriander, and orange peel. It is bottled at 86 to 90 proof, and makes an interesting substitute in some cocktail recipes that normally call for vodka. In the United States, Minnesota—with its large numbers of Scandinavian descendants—leads the nation in Aquavit consumption. Exported brands sometimes seen here include Aalborg from Denmark, and Loiten Export or Lyshold Linie from Norway. Germany makes a similar product, known as **korn** because it is made using corn, not potatoes. German korn liquor is sometimes flavored with fruit.

Sidebar 5.1

MAKE YOUR OWN FLAVORS: INFUSING SPIRITS

Some bartenders make their own signature vodka flavors, using such ingredients as horseradish, currant, mango, kiwi, cranberry, rosemary, and many others, then charge premium prices for the exclusive concoctions. Flavoring vodka or any other type of spirit is not difficult. It requires a simple **infusion,** meaning you immerse the fruit (peeled, dried, or not), herb, or vegetable in the spirit and let it marinate at room temperature in a clean container for a couple of days or a few weeks, depending on the intensity of flavor you wish to achieve. Displaying the infusions in large, clear glass containers on the backbar will add lively color to your bar setup, and will probably also spark customers' questions and interest. Just make sure the containers are always clean and well-sealed.

The possible combinations are as limitless as the list of ingredients and your liquor inventory. Consider, for instance, the Beefeaters' brand "Deli Gin," which contains sun-dried tomatoes, large olives, fresh garlic, dill, and red onions. There are also infusions made from tequila, run, gin, vodka, and some liqueurs.

Before you start making your own, however, check with your state's liquor control agency, because in some areas, these blends are regarded as "tampered" spirits, and it may be illegal to sell them.

Gin

Gin is a spirit with the distinctive, predominant flavor of the juniper berry. Juniper berries (Latin name *ginepro*) had been made into medicinal potions by monks in the fourteenth century as protection against bubonic plague, and as cures for kidney and bladder ailments and indigestion.

Gin as we know it was invented in the 1500s by a Dutch professor of medicine, Franciscus Sylvius, who made an *aqua vitae* from grain flavored with juniper berries. Dr. Sylvius also had medicinal benefits in mind, but his concoction was so potable that it swept the country as a liquor, under the name Geneva or **Genever** (from the French *genievre*, meaning juniper). It crossed the English Channel via British soldiers, who called it "Dutch courage" and shortened its name to "gin." In England, it was also sometimes known as **Hollands.**

Cheap gin was soon being made in London from almost anything—"make it in the morning and drink it at night"—and sold in hole-in-the-wall dramshops all over London. To become a distiller, all you had to do was display a "Notice of Intent" in a public place for 10 days, and then start selling. The King of England at the time—William of Orange—was from Holland, making all things Dutch suddenly fashionable. (His own gin consumption became somewhat legendary; the royal banquet hall was nicknamed "The Gin Palace.") But it wasn't just the elite who succumbed. England's desperately impoverished population drank gin on a national scale to the point of disaster—20 million gallons at its peak, in 1750.

The pattern repeated itself in the United States during Prohibition, when "bathtub gin" was made at home from alcohol, juniper, and glycerin. It, too, was a poor and sometimes lethal product, and the custom arose of mixing it with something else to kill the taste, thus popularizing the cocktail.

It took gin some years to outlive its history as a cheap road to drunkenness and degradation, but today it is a highly respected favorite. The British officer's Gin-and-Tonic (to prevent malaria) and the post-Repeal adoption of the Martini as a fashionable cocktail had a lot to do with changing gin's image.

The U.S. Standard of Identity for gin spells out the many ways in which gins are made: it is "a product obtained by original distillation from mash, or by redistillation of distilled spirits, or by mixing neutral spirits, with or over juniper berries and other aromatics, or with or over extracts derived from infusions, percolations, or maceration of such materials, and includes mixtures of gin and neutral spirits. It shall derive its main characteristic flavor from juniper berries and be bottled at not less than 80 proof. Gin produced exclusively by original distillation or by redistillation may be further designated as 'distilled.'"

Confusing? The main point is that the essential characteristic of all gins is the flavor of juniper berries. The remainder of the standard simply mentions all the various ways by which a spirit with such flavor may be produced. The juniper flavor is typically enhanced by adding undertones—flavors from other aromatics, often referred to as botanicals. These are parts of plants (leaves, roots, bark, seeds, berries and peels) that yield aromatic oils. The list includes angelica, coriander, cardamom, cassia bark, fennel, anise seed, nutmeg, caraway, lemon, and others. The precise mix and method are the secret of each producer, and these account for the subtle flavor variations from one brand of gin to another.

There are two types of gin: Dutch and English-style. Dutch gin is obtained by "original distillation from mash," and English-style gin is made by any of the other methods. The two types are quite different, and only the English-style, whether imported from England or made in America, is used in mixing drinks.

Dutch gin is a product of the Netherlands and is known as Hollands, Genever, or (rarely) Schiedam. It is made beginning with a mash of barley malt, corn, and rye, which is fermented to make a beer, which is then distilled and redistilled in pot stills at low proof, with the juniper berries and other aromatics included in the final distillation. The result is a full-bodied gin with a definite flavor of malt along with the juniper. It is a flavor that would overpower almost anything it might be mixed with. This is not a bar gin. It is drunk straight and icy cold. Bols, in a stone crock, is probably the only brand you will find in this country.

English-style gin is made in both England and the United States. It is usually called "London Dry," wherever it is made. The term "dry" means "lacking in sweetness." Some gins are labeled "Very Dry" or "Extra Dry," but they are no drier than the others.

In England, gin is made from nearly neutral grain spirits distilled in column stills at 180 to 188 proof. These are reduced to 120 proof with distilled water and then redistilled in tall pot stills with juniper berries and other aromatics either in the spirits (Figure 5.7a) or suspended above them on mesh trays so that the rising vapors pass through and around the berries (Figure 5.7b). Some gin is made by steeping the botanicals in the liquid.

American gins are made in two ways: distilling and compounding. Distilled gins are made in much the same way as the English gins, by redistilling neutral spirits with juniper berries and other aromatics. **Compound gins** are made by simply mixing high-proof spirits with extracts from juniper berries and other botanicals. Many American producers of gin buy their neutral spirits from distillers in the Midwest who specialize in these spirits. Distilled gins are allowed to use the word *distilled* on the label; compound gins are not identified as such on the label.

Gin is also made in Spain, Lithuania, the Philippines, and Africa. Gin does not need to be aged. It is stored in stainless-steel or glass-lined tanks until bottled. One type known as golden gin is aged briefly for color. **Sloe gin,** by the way, is not a gin at all; it is a liqueur made from sloe berries, which are not berries, but small wild plums.

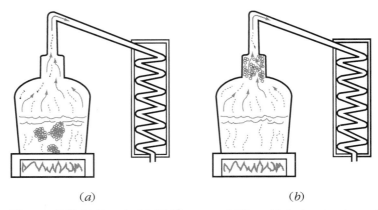

(a)   *(b)*

Figure 5.7 Making gin: (*a*) Distilling or redistilling with juniper berries and other botanicals. (*b*) Redistilling to pass vapors through juniper berries and other botanicals.

Today, as one of the "light" spirits, gin is a prominent bestseller, with imports being once again the status symbols of choice in American bars. Gin is almost never consumed "straight," except in the very dry Martini. Martini-making is practically an art form—every bartender, and every serious Martini drinker will have preferences, and opinions as strong as the gin itself! There's a definite difference between the classic, traditional gin Martini—gin, Vermouth, and a twist, garnished with stuffed olives or cocktail onions—and the trendy recipes enjoyed by younger consumers. Chocolate liqueur, cranberry juice, or maraschino cherries? Yes, they've all been Martini ingredients. And there's a new generation of flavored gins as well—lime, grapefruit, mint, pepper. Vodka is steadily outpacing gin in sales, but a good bartender will know enough about gin's colorful history to intrigue his or her customers.

Best-known gin brands are Seagram's, Gordon's, Gilbey's, Bombay Sapphire, and the British premiums Tanqueray and Beefeater. The Plymouth brand has an especially fun pedigree, being the favorite of Franklin Roosevelt and Winston Churchill, both Martini drinkers. In addition to the venerable Martini, the best-known gin-based drinks are the Gin-and-Tonic, Tom Collins, and Singapore Sling.

Rum

A good place to gaze into the future of specialty drinks is at the bar of a smart new Latin or Caribbean restaurant. These cultures represent fast-rising demographic groups in the United States, and rum is as traditional to them as scotch is to the Scottish or whiskey is to Americans.

Rum, according to its Standard of Identity, is an alcoholic distillate from the fermented juice of sugarcane—in the form of syrup, molasses, or other sugarcane by-products—produced at less than 190 proof and bottled at not less than 80 proof. It has a long and not always savory history. It was first made in the East Indies in the seventeenth century, and spread to other areas where sugarcane was grown—China, India, North Africa. The Spanish and Portuguese explorers transplanted sugarcane in the New World, when they saw that the Caribbean and South American climate was perfect for this valuable crop. A writer reported in 1660s that "the chief fuddling" (intoxicant) made on the island of Barbados was "rum-bullion, alias 'kill-devil,' and this is made from sugarcanes distilled, a hot, hellish, and terrible liquor."

No matter how harsh the taste, rum was given as payment to slaves; drunk by pirates who scourged the shores of the Spanish Main and the Caribbean islands; consumed by the British Navy, issued to the sailors with lime juice added, to prevent scurvy. (Hence the nickname "limeys" for the British.) Rum was also popular in seventeenth-century Europe and the eighteenth-century American colonies.

Rum-making became a flourishing industry in New England at this time, which marked one of the darkest periods of rum's history. For years, rum manufacturers and New England ship captains carried on a highly profitable triangular trade with Africa and the West Indies. They exchanged New England rum for slaves in Africa, and slaves for molasses in the West Indies, and turned the molasses into rum for the next go-round. British taxes and restrictions on the rum trade were as much a cause of the American Revolution as were the taxes on tea.

Little wonder that in the nineteenth century, Temperance leaders made "Demon Rum" the symbol of the evils of alcohol. The image stuck right through Prohibition when smugglers were called "rumrunners" and the offshore ships were known as "Rum Rows," though they sold as much scotch as rum. The name *rum* (or *rhum*, the spelling which still appears on French-influenced labels) may come from the name for Dutch drinking cups of the time (*roemers* or *rummers*); or it may be a derivation of the islanders' word *brum*, meaning a sugarcane drink; or a shortening of the word *rumbullion*, an antiquated term for a disturbance or uproar.

Today, rum holds a respectable place as one of the light spirits. In fact, it is at or near the top of the entire spirit list. Most people drink it mixed with Coca-Cola or club soda, although it is part of such popular cocktails as the Daiquiri, Planter's Punch, Pina Colada, and Zombie.

Rum is made from molasses or sugarcane juice and distilled at 160 proof or higher. Some distillers use pot stills, others use column stills. The spirit comes out of the still as a clear liquid, which takes on its color and much of its character from barrel aging. White (clear) rum is often not put in barrels at all, but in tanks until bottling. For aged rums, casks that once held bourbon, Cognac, wine and whiskey are redeployed as storage (see Figure 5.8). The Caribbean climate is so hot and humid that aging happens rather quickly, and some of the liquid is lost to evaporation. A few distillers ship their barrels elsewhere, to cooler climates, for long-term storage.

There are three basic types of rum, differing somewhat in flavor according to the amount of aging. These are:

- **White or Silver, aged only a year or two.** These are the lightest in color, although they have the highest alcohol content (and are sometimes referred to as **overproof**) and the least refined flavors.
- **Amber or Gold, aged at least three years.** These are sometimes colored with caramel, and take on a richer hue from more time spent in barrels. They have somewhat more flavor and are a bit mellower than the Whites and Silvers.
- **Red Label or Dark, aged six years or more.** These feature a dry, mellow, full-bodied flavor and bouquet, a deep golden color, and a slightly lower alcohol content.

It is important not to judge rum strictly by its color. Some of the clear rums are the sharpest in flavor because they haven't spent much time (or any time) in barrels; the milder and mellower ones may be the darkest in color. There are flavored rums, too, infused with lemon, coconut, or fruit juices.

Figure 5.8 Barrels of rum. Photo courtesy of Cruzan Rum Distillery, St. Croix, United States, Virgin Islands.

Much of the rum consumed in the United States is made in Puerto Rico, but Jamaican rum is also popular. The Jamaican style is full-bodied and pungent, with a dark mahogany color it owes mainly to caramel. It begins with molasses that is fermented by yeasts from the air, a process called *natural, wild*, or *spontaneous fermentation*. It is distilled at 140 to 160 proof, producing a spirit with full flavor and body. This is aged five to seven years. It is bottled usually at 80 and 87 proof, and occasionally at 151 proof, for flavoring and flaming. Myers's rum is the familiar Jamaican brand, its label proclaiming it "the Planter's Punch brand."

Demerara rum is made in Guyana along the Demerara River. Darker in color but lighter in flavor than Jamaican rum, it is bottled at 80, 86, and 151 proof. Until the Zombie cocktail was invented, the chief market for 151-proof Demerara was among lumbermen and fishermen in far northern climates, who drink it half and half with hot water as a grog to warm the bloodstream. High-proof Demerara is often used to flame drinks. You may also encounter Barbados rum or medium-bodied rums from Haiti, Martinique, and Guadeloupe that are made from sugarcane juice instead of molasses. Then there is **arrack** (or **arak**), distilled in the East Indies, Middle East, North Africa, and India from rice, molasses, coconut milk, figs, dates, or even sap from palm trees, depending on the country and the raw ingredients at hand. This broad category of small-volume liquors takes its name from an Arabic word, *araq*, meaning "juice" or "sap." Some of the results yield rum- or brandylike spirits with quite a kick.

Puerto Rico, Nicaragua, and Jamaica also make "liqueur" rums, aged up to 15 years like fine brandies. Brazil distills a sugarcane-based cousin to rum called **cachaca,** rare in the United States but sought after by rum aficionados and used in a simple, very popular South American cocktail called the caiparinha. In Mexico, rum (and any other liquor made with more than 50 percent cane-based spirits) is labeled **aguardiente,** (Spanish for "burning water"). In Mexico, as much aguardiente as tequila is consumed—which brings us to our next topic.

Tequila

Today, about three-fourths of the tequila poured in the United States goes into making the Margarita, in all its incarnations. But this Mexican spirit has its own unique history, identity, romance and flavor profile, and it's catching on big-time as a high-end product with America's liquor customers, especially those in their 20s and early 30s. Ultra-premium tequilas are commanding the same respect as single-malt scotches and single-barrel bourbons. Bars hold tequila tastings and dinners, pairing the spirit with multiple courses to show its adaptability to food. Tequila makers are creating a smoother and more refined product for the international palate and to use in cooking. There's no longer a need, as is the custom in Mexico, to "slam" or "shoot" (that is, gulp) a straight shot of tequila followed by jolts of salt and lime; gourmands say that would be wasting a truly fine product, which some even compare to Cognac.

Tequila is defined as an alcoholic distillate from a fermented mash derived principally (51 percent or more) from the Agave Tequilana Weber, commonly known as the **Blue Agave** plant. There are more than 200 strains of agave, a desert relative of lilies, but only the blue variety is used to make tequila and only if it is grown in one of five regions authorized by the Mexican government.

The agave plant has had mystical meaning to the Mexican people for centuries. It is said to be the incarnation of a goddess, Mayahuel, and the earliest spirit made from the plant—called *pulque* (PUHL-kay)—was used in celebrations and religious ceremonies to bless land, crops, and so on. Its power as an intoxicant was also well known, even to the ancient Aztecs. The agave distilling industry started to spring up around the town of Tequila in the mid-1700s (until these plantings were legally permitted by the King of Spain, all the agave had been harvested wild). The first "official," commercial agave farmers and distillers were the Don Jose Antonio Cuervo family, now the familiar Jose Cuervo brand name. Tequila was not routinely exported, however, until after World War II.

Some production details: The heart of the agave plant is called a *pina* (pineapple) because that's what it looks like. It takes about nine years to grow a pina large enough to be harvested. It weighs 50 to 200 pounds, and is harvested by hand, by workers called *juiadores*. The pinas are filled with a sweet sap that emerges as they are baked or steamed and crushed into juice. The juice is then fermented, and distilled twice at about 110 proof, producing a strongly flavored spirit with a sharp bite—a spirit light in appearance but definitely not light in taste—bottled at not less than 80 proof. It is a distinctive product of Mexico, manufactured in Mexico in compliance with Mexican regulations.

White tequila, the primary seller, is usually shipped unaged. On labels, the term for "white" may be *blanco*; it is also called "silver" (or *plata*). Gold tequila may be aged in wooden barrels or tinted with caramel to obtain its golden color. The "gold" designation refers only to color, not necessarily better quality.

In the 1970s, the Mexican government changed the rules to allow up to 49 percent of spirits other than blue agave in the mixture—that is to say, neutral spirits, or distillates of sugarcane or corn. Bad weather and increased production combined at the end of the twentieth century to severely impact the blue agave harvest (raw agave prices increased 800 percent in 1999) so perhaps it was the government's foresighted aim to keep the industry going without depleting the precious agave crop. This half-agave, half-other-sugars blend accounts for about 80 percent of Mexico's total tequila production, and is nicknamed *mixto*. Large producers send it from Mexico in tanker trucks, to be bottled in the United States.

In recent years, however, there has been a back-to-basics movement among the finer distillers, aimed at satisfying the connoisseur. They are producing small quantities of 100-percent blue agave tequila, aging it in barrels (a process called **reposado,** which means "resting") or in small barrels (termed **anejo,** or "aged.") **Reposado tequila** is aged from 2 to 11 months by Mexican law. **Anejo tequila** is aged in wood for more than one year. It is the closest thing to Cognac, but does tend to lose flavor when it has been aged more than four years. Tequila made from 100-percent agave sugars is also known as **Tequila Puro.**

Tequila's popularity is still linked chiefly to the Margarita cocktail, especially those refreshing frozen ones turned out in quantity. Some bars and restaurants have even developed Margarita menus, featuring a variety of fruity spin-offs, and cocktails made with superpremium brands. Another well-known cocktail is the Tequila Sunrise, made famous by the rock group The Eagles' song of the same name in the 1970s. Best-known brands include Jose Cuervo, Sauza, Porfidio, and Montezuma.

In the late 1990s, Anheuser-Busch began to capitalize on tequila's rising popularity by creating **Tequiza,** a hybrid that combines beer, tequila, and lime, aimed at people who currently drink Mexican beer (adding a lime wedge is customary) or nonbeer drinkers who might be willing to experiment. And, at this writing, a new generation of **tequillarias** has sprung up, in Mexico City and other urban markets, not just in Mexico, at upscale restaurants with the tequila mystique as part of their theme, in both food and drink.

Mescal

There's another Mexican-made liquor that some will insist is tequila's "poor cousin," while others will argue it is a "rare and high-end sibling." Either way, it's called **mescal** or **mezcal,** and it's the spirit made from agave plants that are not necessarily blue agave, and/or not located in the five designated tequila regions. (The plant itself is called **maguey** in some other parts of Mexico.) The center of mescal production is the state of Oaxaca.

The mescal-making process is also a bit different. The agave hearts are slow-roasted for three days, in adobe or gas ovens or in deep, stone-lined pits in the ground. This imparts a smoky flavor that is different than tequila. Then the cooked hearts are left to ferment naturally (from four or five days to a full month) before being crushed and distilled—once or twice—in clay or copper pot stills. The final product is about 80 proof.

Mescal is guaranteed by Mexican law to be 100-percent agave, which purists say indicates its overall fine quality. They call it "the Cognac of Mexico," and order it very slightly chilled in a brandy snifter. A couple of companies do export their mescal products, notably the del Maguey and Hacienda Sotol distilleries, but most of it is locally made for use within Mexico's rural communities, and flavored with herbs, bark, or fruit.

You will note that, quite often, a bottle of mescal contains a worm. Yes, a worm. It's called a **gusano,** and lives in the agave plant. Part of the lore and legend of the drink is that the worm contains some of the mythic power of the plant, and that he or she who eats the worm acquires that power. What do you think?

AFTER-DINNER DRINKS

This wide-ranging category will prove, if nothing else, how creative the world's distillers have become in satisfying just about every taste and whim. Very often, while the traditional "brown goods" and "white goods" are imbibed before meals to whet the appetite, the idea behind after-dinner drinks—brandies, liqueurs, **cordials,** digestifs—is to enjoy something smooth and satisfying that promotes good digestion of the meal. Of course, some of them are also used in cocktails. Today's restaurateurs generally agree that not enough has been done to develop the after-dinner drink market, although customers seem to enjoy the "luxury" experience of relaxing after a meal to enjoy an interesting liqueur. So the profit opportunity is huge for anyone who does it right.

This means implementing a well-executed after-dinner drink program that is both classy and consistent. A cart full of exotic, enticing liqueur bottles can be rolled tableside at just the right moment (too early if it's before dessert, too late if guests are discussing their check). A team of servers can display a silver tray full of bottles and snifters, one to hold the wares, the other to pour. Including dessert wines, brandies, and liqueurs on the dessert list or on a separate menu of their own is yet another option. Having a separate, comfortable room for guests to "retire to" for cigars and drinks is a fourth option.

You will notice that not all bars or restaurants offer extensive after-dinner drink choices. As you'll soon see, there are many to choose from. Your clientele and your budget will help you decide what to have on hand.

Brandies

Brandy began as an *eau de vie*, the French version of *aqua vitae* that in other countries became whiskey, vodka, and gin. In France, it was thought of as the spirit or soul of the wine. Italian monks and Moorish scholars began distilling, probably in the sixteenth century, and brandy was one of the first results of their efforts. The process was used even earlier in Spain to transform grapes and their juices into a more potent, but still sophisticated, spirit.

At the time, The Netherlands ruled the seas as merchants. Dutch ship captains used the powerful, distilled wine to fortify the regular table wines on their journeys and to add to drinking water stored on board, to kill parasites. They called it *brandewijn*, meaning "burned wine," which was shortened in time to brandy.

Today, most brandy drinkers are over age 30. It is perceived to be a healthy, classy spirit that fits an upscale lifestyle. U.S. Standards of Identity define brandy as the distilled product of any fruit, but what we call brandy must be made from grapes. Other fruit brandies must carry the name of the fruit. All brandies must be bottled at 80 proof or higher. Most bars use two types: a good domestic brandy in the well for mixed drinks, and premium brands, usually imported, for after-dinner service. Brandy-based cocktails include the Stinger, the Sidecar, the Brandy Alexander, and Brandy Manhattan.

American Brandies. Most brandy consumed in the United States is made in California. It is made in column stills at up to 170 proof and is aged in white-oak barrels at least two years and usually longer. Most of these brandies are blends—smooth and fruity, with a touch of sweetness—that may contain up to 2½ percent of added flavoring. There are also straight brandies having no additives except caramel coloring, and there are some premium brands that qualify as after-dinner brandies.

Christian Brothers and E&J Gallo have been duking it out for years as the two top brandy producers in the United States. Recently, they've received stiff competition from French imports, in bottles that make them look more expensive than they are. Some U.S.-based producers, including Germain Robin, St. George, and RMS, make their brandies the European way, the same as Cognac, by crushing the grapes at the peak of ripeness, not adding sugar during fermentation, and distilling in pot stills.

American brandies from other fruits—apple, apricot, blackberry, pineapple—must always include the name of the fruit on the label. They may or may not be aged. Apple brandy, also called **applejack,** was one of the earliest and favorite spirits of our New England ancestors. Today's applejack is aged in wood at least two years. It is bottled at 100 proof as a straight brandy or blended with neutral spirits and bottled at 80 proof.

Cognac and Armagnac. Of all the brandies in the world, Cognac is the most famous and prestigious. It has been called the "king of brandies," and also the "brandy of kings," and has a somewhat stuffy reputation. In recent years, an oversupply in French warehouses has driven prices down, and the government has even paid vintners to remove some of their grape acreage from Cognac production. Still, there are those who think there is no better way to end an evening than with a snifter of fine Cognac and a good cigar. Ninety-five percent of this heady spirit is exported from France.

Like Champagne, you can only call it "Cognac" if it is made in the Cognac area of France. It is made up of six specific areas, where chalky soil, humid climate, and special distillation techniques produce brandy under strict government control. Only certain kinds of white grapes may be used (primarily a variety called **ugni blanc**), and specific distillation procedures must be followed, including two distillations in traditional copper pot stills (alembics) and precise control of temperatures and quantities. The farmers sell their freshly distilled spirits to shipper-producers, who age and blend them to meet the standards of their particular brands. Cognac is aged in special oak casks at least one and a half years. Most are aged two to four years, and some even longer. Caramel may be added for uniform color.

During aging, the alcohol evaporates through the porous casks at an average of 2 percent per year. In the warehouses the escaping vapors—known as "the angels' share"—are noticeable.

A Cognac label may carry cryptic letters, special words, and varying numbers of stars. The stars may mean somewhat different things for different brands. By French law, a three-star Cognac must be at least one-and-a-half years old; most are around four. Since Cognacs are blends of brandies of various ages, no age is allowed on the label. The cryptic letters are symbols of relative age and quality, as follows:

V = very
S = superior
O = old
P = pale
E = extra or especial
F = fine
X = extra

A Cognac specified VS (very superior) is similar to a three-star Cognac. A VSOP (very superior old pale) has been aged in wood at least four and a half years, and probably 7 to 10. The designations Extra, Vieille Reserve, and Napoleon may not appear on the label unless the Cognac is at least five and a half years old. Contrary to legend, there is no Cognac around dating from Napoleon's day, though some shippers have stocks of 50 years old and more to use in blending their finest Cognacs. After a certain age Cognac does not improve, but actually loses quality.

A Cognac labeled Grande Champagne or Fine Champagne has nothing to do with the bubbly beverage. The French word "champagne" means field, and the French bubbly and the Champagne Cognac both take the name from the common word. Grande Champagne is the heart of the Cognac district, whose grapes are considered best of all. Grande Champagne on the label means that the Cognac was made from these grapes. Fine Champagne means that 50 percent or more of its grapes came from Grande Champagne and the balance came from the next-door (and next-best) area known as Petite Champagne. The best-known brands of Cognac are Remy-Martin, Courvoisier, Hennessy, Hine, and Martell.

In an effort to market their product in new ways, some Cognac producers are promoting the idea of mixing it with pineapple juice or orange juice, or adding a lemon twist and serving it in a sugar-rimmed glass. The attempt, of course, is to erase its image as an old person's drink, with a nod to the venerable Sidecar cocktail that was once so popular.

Armagnac is another French brandy familiar to Americans, with much the same upscale appeal. Like Cognac, it comes from its own restricted region—Gascony, home of "The Three Musketeers"—and is made from white grapes. There are several major differences between Armagnac and Cognac: Armagnac makers are allowed to use any of a dozen grape varietals; their product is distilled only once, not twice like Cognac; and more often in a column still than a pot still. Interestingly, these particular column stills are very small, making it a challenge to create a spirit of sufficient strength. Armagnac is also aged in oak. In the bottle, it has the same kinds of label jargon as Cognac, with the same meanings. It is permitted to have its age printed on the label.

The various Armagnacs are more different from one another than the Cognacs, and less expensive. Among the brands available in this country are de Caussade, Janneau, Chateau Laubade, and Chateau du Tariquet.

Imported Fruit Brandies. A fine apple brandy known as **Calvados** is also made in France. By law, it can only bear the Calvados name if it is made in the province of Normandy, where it was too cold to grow grapes, so the early settlers grew apples instead. Calvados begins as cider (the juice pressed out of apples) and is distilled and aged in wooden barrels. The juices of several different apple types and ages are blended to make the final mix, which is 40 to 45 percent alcohol. Calvados may be aged for many years, but most imports are aged 5 to 10 years.

The best-known nongrape brandy is **kirsch** or **kirschwasser,** made from the wild black cherry that grows in the Rhine River valley of Germany. A colorless liquid, often called a white brandy, it is made in pot stills from a mash that includes the cherry pits and skins. A low distillation proof of 100 or less allows the bitter almond flavor of the pits to be carried into the final spirit. It is bottled immediately to retain the maximum flavor and aroma of the fruit. Although production is relatively simple, the cost is high because of the large amounts of wild fruit needed. A liqueur carrying the same name is also made; it is sweetened and includes the word "liqueur" on the label.

Another fruit brandy familiar to many is **Slivovitz,** a plum brandy made in central Europe. It is distilled in the same way as kirsch but is aged in wood to a golden color. Other popular names in the world of plum brandy are Mirabelle (made from a type of yellow plum) and Questch (made from a large, mauve-colored plum variety).

A colorless, unaged brandy is made from pears in Switzerland and France. It is known here as **Pear William** and there as **Poire Williams.** You'll often see it with a preserved pear right inside the bottle, as in Figure 5.9.

Fruit-flavored brandies are not true brandies, but are sweetened liqueurs of lower proof with a brandy base. In Europe the word "flavored" is omitted from these spirits. Don't be fooled: an imported strawberry brandy is not a brandy but a liqueur of considerable sweetness. The word "flavored" is required on the labels of the comparable American products.

Other Brandies. Brandy de Jerez from Spain is making its way onto the international market, with excellent results. In Jerez, the town where brandy makers are congregated, distilling has been going on since A.D. 900. The earliest brandies were not taken seriously or consumed on their own, however; they were made to fortify sherry, for which Spain is famous. It was the Dutch traders who recognized the true worth of the Spanish brandy and prompted its export in the 1700s.

The vineyards around Jerez are used for sherry-making. For brandy, the grapes are trucked in from the La Mancha region of Spain, a hot climate that produces grapes higher in alcohol and lower in acidity than those grown in France. After distillation, the new brandy goes into sherry butts (wooden casks), and most producers use what is called a *solera* system of storage. The casks are stacked several barrels high, but each horizontal row contains brandy of about the same age. When some is taken out of a barrel—and no barrel is ever completely emptied—it is refilled with some from the next oldest "row." This constant refilling and decanting is a way of gradually blending the new with the old, for a smooth and consistent flavor.

Today in Spain, brandy is considered somewhat an "old folks' drink," but the industry is doing some marketing to bring young customers into the fold. Cardenal Mendoza and Domecq are some recognizable brand names in the United States.

Metaxa is the Greek brandy. Slightly sweetened and with herbs added, it is technically a liqueur but is generally thought of as brandy.

Pisco is a strong-flavored brandy that originated in Peru (Pisco is the name of a local tribe that created the drink from sweet, wild Muscat or Quebranta

Figure 5.9 A bottle of Poire Williams. Photo courtesy of Clear Creek Distillery.

grapes) but is now a major product of Chile and Bolivia as well. If made in Bolivia, it may be called **Singani.** It was popular in California in Gold Rush days and is still the base for a refreshing summer cocktail called the Pisco Sour.

Mexico, Armenia, and South Africa are other nations with well-established brandy businesses. Look for the brand names Pedro Domecq and Presidente (Mexico); Noyac (Armenia); and KWV or Backsberg (South Africa.)

There is one more spirit that, although it is not a brandy, is made in much the same way—in this case, by distilling the leftover skins, stems, and seeds from winemaking. The spirit is called **grappa,** and when you taste it, you'll know instantly why people either love it or hate it. Grappa used to be a cheap product, made just out of thriftiness rather than throwing anything away. It had an awful reputation and an even worse taste.

Today, there is still nothing refined about it. It has big, hot, earthy flavors and a distinctive kick of alcohol. But connoisseurs are paying $15 to $30 per shot to try it. As many as 1,000 Italian vintners make their own brand of grappa, and a few American wineries have jumped on the bandwagon, too.

The leftover grape pressings are known in Italy as *vinaccia* and elsewhere as *pomace.* The grappa's quality is determined in large measure by how fresh the batch of vinaccia is at the time of distillation. Premium grappa makers have recognized this importance, and they are also experimenting with using whole grapes (not the leftover crushed ones), using single varietals instead of blends, and aging them in wood. The grappas made from sweeter grape varietals seem to be the most flavorful. But grappa comes in a wide variety of styles, and many are sold in different types of collectable bottles—another marketing tool.

Grappa is best consumed cool, not ice cold, in shot glasses. Italian brands you may see in the United States include Nonino, Bertagnoli, Maschio, Jacopo; from California, Bonny Doon, and from Oregon, Clear Creek.

Serving Brandy. Brandy served straight is a traditional after-dinner drink, presented according to custom in a large rounded brandy glass, or snifter (Figure 5.10). The glass is cupped in the palm of the hand, to warm the brandy slightly, and rolled about to release the brandy's rich aroma, an important part of the sensual pleasure of the drink. It can also be served straight up in a 2-ounce "pony" or liqueur glass. Brandy is also served with soda or water as a highball, in coffee, and in many mixed drinks.

White brandies ordered straight should be served icy cold in a pony or liqueur glass. Their most common use, however, is in mixed drinks.

Liqueurs and Cordials

These are two words for the same thing: a distilled spirit flavored or redistilled with fruits, flowers, plants, their juices or extracts, or other natural flavoring materials, and sweetened with 2½ percent or more of sugar. To sim-

Figure 5.10 Serve brandy in a snifter.

plify things from here on, we'll use the word "liqueur." Liqueurs are natural af-ter-dinner drinks, sweet and flavorful. A few are also used as **aperitifs,** served before dinner to whet the appetite and aid digestion of the meal to come.

The makers of liqueurs are today's alchemists, with their secret formulas of herbs and spices and flowers and fruits and exotic flavorings. No longer looking for the elixir of life, they deal in flavor, color, romance, and profits. New liqueurs are constantly being developed, and both old and new are pro-moted with recipes for new drinks in the hope that something like the Moscow Mule miracle will happen again. And it does happen now and then: the oddly named Harvey Wallbanger cocktail put Galliano in every bar!

The Making of Liqueurs. Any liqueur begins as a distilled spirit—it may be brandy, whiskey, rum, neutral spirits, or others. The distinctive flavorings may be any natural substance such as fruits, seeds, spices, herbs, flowers, bark. Many of them are complex formulas containing as many as 50 ingre-dients. One (Cointreau) claims to use oranges from five different countries.

The flavorings may be combined with the spirit in different ways. One method is **steeping** (soaking) the flavorers in the spirit; this is called **mac-eration.** Another is pumping the spirit over and over flavorers suspended above it, as in a coffee pot, called **percolation.** Or the flavorers may be added when the spirit is redistilled.

The sugar may be any of several forms, including honey, maple syrup, and corn syrup. The sugar content is the main thing that distinguishes liqueurs from all other types of spirit. It varies from 2½ percent to as much as 35 per-cent by weight from one liqueur to another. A liqueur with 10 percent or less sugar may be labeled "Dry."

Color is often added to colorless spirits, as in the cases of green crème de menthe and blue curacao. Colors must be natural vegetable coloring agents or approved food dyes.

A liqueur can be consumed as a "shooter," served in a shot glass, quickly hoisted and downed as part of a celebration, or as a cocktail ingredient (an integral part of the Cosmopolitan or Margarita or Rusty Nail). It can be sipped straight (undiluted) after dinner in an elegant stemmed glass or snifter, or added to coffee, or mixed with cream to play the role of dessert. You can even try drizzling a bit of liqueur over vanilla ice cream, or into a flute of Champagne.

It's impossible to include all of their names and uses here, but we'll at-tempt to list and describe a few of the most common liqueurs—some generic types, some brand names—alphabetically. You can also consult Table 5.3.

Absinthe: Pronounced "AB-santh," this nineteenth-century French liqueur is a distillate of a variety of herbs, including aniseed and wormwood. In its past, absinthe in its strongest forms caused convulsions and hal-lucinations, so today it is strictly regulated in Europe to contain no more than 10 parts per million of *alpha thujone*, the nerve-damaging ingredient. (Absinthe of the 1800s contained as much as 260 parts per million.) It is illegal to purchase absinthe in the United States.

Amaretto: Pronounced "am-ah-RET-oh," this is a generic name for almond-flavored liqueur.

Anisette: Pronounced "ANN-ih-SET," this is the generic name for a very sweet liqueur made with anise seed, an ingredient that got its start in Switzerland as a medicinal herb. At least a dozen other herbs and fruit peels are added.

Benedictine: Pronounced "ben-ah-DIK-teen," this monk-made liqueur from France is among the world's most prestigious brands, but its formula is top secret. The monastery claims the distillation process includes five separate batches of 27 botanicals.

Chambord: Pronounced "sham-BORD," this is the brand name of a black raspberry-flavored liqueur from France.

Chartreuse: Pronounced "shar-TROOS." Like Benedictine, this brightly colored herbal liqueur's secret recipe has been handed down in a single monastery since the seventeenth century. All they'll admit is that every ingredient is natural, with no added coloring. Experts agree the two formulas (Green, 110 proof, and Yellow, 80 proof) taste like a heavenly combination of honey, flowers, and fruit, and that Chartreuse is arguably the world's best liqueur.

Cointreau: Pronounced "KWON-trow," this is the brand name of a liqueur that blends several types of citrus fruit, including bitter oranges. It's the name of the family that first produced it in the mid-1800s after visiting Curacao (see below) and discovering its orange liqueurs. Today, Cointreau is made in the United States, and in Spain.

Crème de Cacao: Pronounced "KREM dah KOH-koh," this is a generic name for a cream-based, chocolate liqueur. It may be brown or colorless.

Crème de Menthe: Pronounced "KREM dah MAW," this is the generic name for a cream-based, mint-flavored liqueur that may be green or colorless

Curacao: Pronounced "KYOOR-a-sow," this is the generic name of a liqueur made from the bitter orange peel of the fruit on Curacao, Haiti, and other Caribbean islands.

Drambuie: Pronounced "dram-BOO-ee," it is also a brand name. This amber-colored liqueur begins as scotch, with honey added for sweetness.

Frangelico: "Pronounced fran-JEL-ih-koh," this is the brand name for a sweet, hazelnut-flavored herbal liqueur made in Italy.

Galliano: Pronounced "GAL-ee-AH-noh", this is the brand name of a deep-yellow, Italian-made, herb-based liqueur.

Grand Marnier: Pronounced "GRAN marn-YAY," this is the brand name of a mixture of Cognac and Curacao that is made in the Cognac district of France.

Table 5.3

Liqueurs

Liqueur	Spirit Base	Flavor	Brand or Generic	Color	Proof
Amaretto	Neutral spirits	Almond-apricot	Generic	Amber	48–56
Anisette	Neutral spirits	Anise, licorice	Generic	Red, clear[a]	40–60
Apricot liqueur or cordial	Neutral spirits	Apricot	Generic	Orange-amber	60–70
Bailey's Irish Cream	Irish whiskey	Irish-chocolate	Brand	Pale café au lait	34
Bénédictine	Neutral spirits	Herb-spice	Brand	Dark gold	86
B & B	Neutral spirits, Cognac	Herb-spice	Brand	Dark gold	86
Blackberry liqueur or cordial	Neutral spirits or brandy	Blackberry	Generic	Red-purple	60
Chambord	Cognac	Raspberry	Brand	Raspberry	33
Chartreuse	Brandy and neutral spirits	Spicy herb	Brand	Yellow Green	80, 86 110
Chéri-Suisse	Neutral spirits	Chocolate-cherry	Brand	Red-pink	52, 60
Cherry liqueur or cordial	Neutral spirits or brandy	Cherry	Generic	Red	30–60
Cointreau	Neutral spirits	Orange	Brand	Clear	80
Cordial Médoc	Neutral spirits, Cognac, Armagnac	Brandy and fruit	Brand	Dark amber	80
Crème de bananes	Neutral spirits	Ripe banana	Generic	Yellow	50–60
Crème de cacao	Neutral spirits	Chocolate-vanilla	Generic	Clear, brown	50–60
Crème de cassis	Neutral spirits	Black currant	Generic	Red-black	30–50
Crème de Menthe	Neutral spirits	Mint	Generic	Clear, green	60
Crème de noyaux	Neutral spirits	Almond	Generic	Clear, red, cream	50–60
Crème d'Yvette	Neutral spirits	Violet, jellybean	Generic	Blue-violet	36–40
Curaçao	Neutral spirits (rum or brandy)	Orange peel	Generic	Clear, orange, blue	54–80
Drambuie	Scotch	Scotch-honey-herb	Brand	Gold	80
Forbidden Fruit	Brandy	Grapefruit	Brand	Red-brown	60–64
Galliano	Neutral spirits	Anise-vanilla, licorice	Brand	Bright yellow	80
Goldwasser	Neutral spirits	Orange-anise	Generic	Clear, gold-flecked	60–86

Name	Base	Flavor	Type	Color	Proof
Grand Marnier	Cognac	Orange peel, Cognac	Brand	Light amber	80
Irish Mist	Irish whiskey	Irish-honey-herb	Brand	Amber	80
Jeremiah Weed	Bourbon	Bourbon	Brand	Gold	100
Kahlúa	Neutral spirits	Coffee	Brand	Brown	53
Kirsch liqueur	Kirsch	Sweetened kirsch	Generic	Clear	90–100
Kümmel	Neutral spirits	Caraway	Generic	Clear	70–100
Lochan Ora	Scotch	Scotch-honey-herb	Brand	Gold	70
Mandarine	Brandy	Tangerine	Generic	Bright orange	80
Maraschino	Neutral spirits	Cherry-almond	Generic	Clear	60–80
Midori	Neutral spirits	Honeydew	Brand	Ice green	46
Ouzo	Brandy	Anise, licorice	Generic	Clear	90–98
Peach liqueur or cordial	Neutral spirits	Peach	Generic	Amber	60–80
Peppermint schnapps	Neutral spirits	Mint	Generic	Clear	40–100
Pernod	Neutral spirits	Licorice, anise	Brand	Yellow-green	90
Peter Heering	Neutral spirits, brandy	Cherry	Brand	Dark red	49
Raspberry liqueur or cordial	Neutral spirits	Raspberry jam	Generic	Red-purple	50–60
Rock and rye	Rye and neutral spirits	Rye-fruit	Generic	Gold-brown	60–70
Sabra	Neutral spirits	Chocolate-orange	Brand	Deep brown	60
Sambuca	Neutral spirits	Licorice	Generic	Clear	40–84
Schnapps, peach, etc.	Neutral spirits	Peach, other	Generic	Clear	40–60
Sloe gin	Neutral spirits	Wild plum	Generic	Red	42–60
Southern Comfort	Bourbon	Bourbon-peach	Brand	Gold	80, 100
Strawberry liqueur	Neutral spirits	Strawberry	Generic	Red	44–60
Strega	Neutral spirits	Herb-spice	Brand	Gold	80
Tia Maria	Rum	Coffee	Brand	Brown	63
Triple sec	Neutral spirits	Orange peel	Generic	Clear	60–80
Tuaca	Brandy	Eggnog-cocoa	Brand	Yellow-brown	84
Vandermint	Neutral spirits	Chocolate-mint	Brand	Dark brown	52
Vieille Cure	Neutral spirits	Herb-vanilla	Brand	Green, yellow	60
Wild Turkey liqueur	Bourbon	Bourbon	Brand	Amber	80
Yukon Jack	Canadian whisky	Light whisky	Brand	Light golden	80, 100

[a] Often referred to as white.

Kahlua: Pronounced "kuh-LOO-ah," this is the brand name of a Mexican liqueur that combines coffee and vanilla with cane spirit. It is often mixed with milk or cream.

Noisette: Pronounced "nwah-SET," this is a French brand of hazelnut-flavored liqueur.

Ouzo: Pronounced "EW-zoh," this thick, clear Greek aperitif is distilled from grapes, and flavored with aniseed, fennel, and herbs, along with *mastic* (the resin of evergreen trees).

Sambuca: Pronounced "sam-BOO-kuh," this is the generic name for a clear, plant-based liqueur with a spicy, licorice flavor. It is not unlike Ouzo, just described.

Schnapps: Pronounced "SHNOPS." In Europe, schnapps is an herb-flavored dry spirit (see Aquavit, earlier in this chapter), but in the United States today, it is a sweet liqueur, fruit or mint-flavored. Some people like it because of its relatively low alcohol content—about 48 proof.

Tia Maria: Pronounced "TEE-ah mah-REE-ah," it's the brand name of a Jamaican coffee-flavored liqueur, sweeter than Kahlua and often used for mixing.

Triple Sec: Pronounced "TRIP-ul SEK," it is the generic name for white (no color added) Curacao.

Table 5.3 also lists the base, flavor, color, and bottling proof of these and other spirits. Notice how much the proof varies. Generic types are made by more than one producer and vary in flavor and proof.

Remember, no category of beverage gets better customer response from servers' suggestions than liqueurs. And there is almost no end to the flavors, textures, price spreads, and preparation options available to the smart bar owner. It's a very trendy part of the industry—new products are released every year, as are new recipes to use existing products in new concoctions—so it's easy for a manufacturer to become the "flavor of the month." But a "flavor of the decade?" That's a true challenge.

Ciders

Cider is a drink that's so old it has become new again. **Hard cider**—the enduring term for fermented cider—dates back to the Roman Empire, and is still a staple in many British pubs. American colonists brought apple seeds, and their thirst for cider, to the New World and its popularity persisted until the late nineteenth century. At that time, other immigrants brought their beer-making skills to the United States, displacing cider because lager beer was easier and cheaper to produce.

A few producers are reviving hard cider as a beverage option, and in 1997, the U.S. government even lowered the taxes on it. Cider's alcohol content is typically 5 percent by volume—about the same as beer—but it can contain up to 14 percent. It is a nice counterpart to spicy foods, as it's not too filling and offers a crisp, complex type of refreshment that appeals to the same crowd interested in microbrewed beers. It is also piquing the curiosity of so-called New Age beverage drinkers, who like the combination of a fruit-based drink with a lower alcohol level. The U.S. Food and Drug Administration also requires hard cider to carry nutritional content labels, prompting some to feel that it is lighter and appears "healthier" than other alcoholic beverage choices. Some of the oft-marketed names on store shelves include Woodchuck, Hornsby, Ace, and Cider Jack.

Bitters

Have we finally come to the "bitter end" of this lengthy discussion on spirits? Not without a quick rundown on **bitters.** These are very unique spirits flavored with herbs, roots, bark, fruits, and so on, like the liqueurs. The difference is that they are unsweetened, so "bitter" is the right word for them.

Once used primarily as medicines or for hangover cures, there are two basic kinds of bitters: those that provide concentrated flavor and bitters for beverages. Most contain 30 or more different herbs and spices. Among the flavorers are Angostura from Trinidad (originally a malaria medicine), various orange bitters, and the lesser-known Peychaud's, a New Orleans product. They are used in minute amounts to flavor mixed drinks—Angostura in the Old-Fashioned, for example.

The best-known of the beverage bitters is Campari, a 48-proof bitter red Italian spirit. It is usually drunk with soda or tonic or in a cocktail such as the Negroni. Campari is a fashionable drink all over Europe and has become well known in this country, especially among sophisticated drinkers.

Another of the beverage bitters is Amer Picon, a 78-proof quinine-laced French bitters with a brandy base. It is said to have been what the French Foreign Legion in Algeria added to the water in their canteens. It is served with ice and water or used in cocktails.

Still another of these supposedly drinkable bitters is Fernet Branca, a 78-proof spirit, known chiefly as a hangover treatment (perhaps as a counter-irritant?). Everyone agrees the taste is terrible.

Germany's contributions to the bitters market include Jagermeister, which features a stately stag on the label and a high alcohol content; and Underberg, known primarily as a hangover cure. The latter is sold in small bottles wrapped in brown paper.

SUMMING UP

All the alcoholic beverages you serve begin in the same way: by fermenting a liquid product containing sugar to break down the sugar into alcohol and carbon dioxide. This is the basic process by which beers and wines are made.

Distilled spirits take the procedure one step further: the fermented liquid is heated in an enclosed space to vaporize the alcohol, separating it from the remaining liquid. The vapors are drawn off in a closed container and condensed as a concentrated spirit. All distilled spirits are made in this way. The sensory characteristics (taste, aroma, color, body) of each finished product come from combinations of many things: the original ingredients, the distillation proof, whether or not the spirit is aged (and for how long and in what type of container), whether it is blended or infused (and with what additional ingredients), whether and how flavorings are added, and the bottling proof.

This chapter has told you something about each bottle in your well and on your backbar, their interesting origins and histories, and how they differ from one another. Knowing all about them is an asset. It will help you in pouring, in purchasing, in answering customer questions, in preventing or dealing with intoxicated guests, and in many other ways as well. In fact, this product knowledge will give you a better understanding of the information in the chapters to follow.

POINTS TO PONDER

1. What is the difference between white spirits and "brown goods"? Give examples of each. Why are "white goods" more popular today?

2. Trace the history of the popularity of vodka in the U.S. market. How do you explain it?

3. What is a neutral spirit, and how is it used?

4. Describe how tequila is produced. How does it differ from other white spirits?

5. Why are aged whiskies and brandies considered better than younger ones, and why are they more expensive?

6. Which of the following phrases indicate superior quality in a spirit: VSOP, bottled in bond, sour mash, London Dry, aged in wood, reposado? Briefly define each phrase and explain how it applies to quality.

7. There are two different products commonly called schnapps. Describe each and explain how they differ.

8. What is the difference between a liqueur and a cordial?

9. If someone asked you for a mixed drink with very little alcohol in it, what would you suggest, and why?

10. If you were deciding on the liquor inventory for a bar, and you knew your budget wouldn't stretch to include *every* possible choice, how would you approach the challenge of what to buy?

Extra Credit

11. Would you eat the worm in the mescal bottle? Why or why not?

TERMS OF THE TRADE

absinthe

aguardiente

alambic still

Amaretto

anejo (tequila)

anisette

aperitif

Applejack

Aquavit (Akvavit)

Armagnac

arrack (arak)

barrel house

Benedictine

bitters

blending

blue agave

bottled in bond

bourbon

cachaca

Calvados

cask strength

Chambord

Chartreuse

coffey still

Cointreau

compound gin

congener

continuous
  (patent) still

cordial

crème de cacao

crème de menthe

Curacao

diastase

distillation

Drambuie

fermentation

Frangelico

fusel oil

Galliano

Genever

Grand Marnier

grappa

gusano

hard cider

Hollands

infusion

kahlua

kirsch (kirschwasser)

korn

maceration

maguey

malt

mescal (mescal)

metaxa

mixed drink

neutral spirits

Noisette

Ouzo

overproof

Pear William (Poire Williams)

peat

percolation

Pisco

proof

Reposado (tequila)

rye

sambuca

schnapps

Singani

single-malt scotch

Slivovitz

sloe gin

sour mash

spirit

Standards of Identity

steeping

still

Tequila Puro

tequillarias

Tequiza

Tia Maria

Triple Sec

ugni blanc

vatted malt (pure malt)
  scotch

wine spritzer

F. PAUL PACULT
Editor, *The Spirit Journal*
Wine and Spirits Writer

Paul Pacult (his byline is F. Paul Pacult) began his career in the wine and spirits industry like so many others—quite by accident! Working as a landscaper in the early 1970s, he was hired to beautify a new Sonoma County winery, Rodney Strong Vineyards. When the landscaping was finished, Strong asked if Pacult would be interested in staying on to help in the vineyard. He spent the next decade there, learning and participating in every facet of winemaking.

Pacult had always known he wanted to be a writer, and began penning wine-related articles for various magazines. That led to other writing jobs, relocation to New York City, and a retail manager's job at a prestigious liquor store. He also opened a wine appreciation school.

Today, Pacult writes regularly about wine and spirits for The New York Times, Wine Enthusiast *magazine, and* Delta Air Lines' Sky *magazine. He lives in the Hudson Valley area of New York, where he, his wife Sue, and brother Rick, write and publish* Spirit Journal, *with subscribers in 31 countries. They also conduct educational seminars and tastings of wines and spirits.*

Q: What made you decide to branch out and write about spirits instead of just doing wine writing?

A: Well, when *The New York Times* called and asked me to write an article about scotch for its Sunday magazine, I didn't know what to say. I didn't know a thing about scotch! But I was a good writer, and how do you turn down an offer from a paper like that?! It turned out to be 28 pages, and just fascinating to research. It got tremendous reader response—I don't think we ever imagined it would get that kind of response. And it soon became apparent to me that all of my peers were writing about wine, but nobody was really writing much about spirits. So I decided to put part of my creative thrust into that area. Spirits were still, in the late '80s, kind of impolitic. They were mostly brown, and people still had some misgivings about them.

Then I decided—since I was tasting so much product coming from all over the world to my office—to start a newsletter [and] not to accept any advertising, but to exist on subscriptions only and maintain complete objectivity. That's when *Spirit Journal* was born, and we just passed our eleventh year. We review spirits, and we have since 1991.

Q: I guess the point your career makes for students is that with the knowledge, you can take it many different directions.

A: Yes. You really need to be open and never say, "No, I can't do that." When the [New York] *Times* came to me and said, "We want you to write a 10,000-word piece on scotch whiskey,"—after I regained consciousness—I said, "I don't know a thing about it! But of course I'll do it!"

I've always been really open to opportunities, and I've never allowed myself to get into a rut. All the things I'm doing now are the sum-total of working in a winery, working in a retail store, teaching classes, learning how to cook. It's important for young men and women to have a sense of adventure, a willingness to try new things. Don't ever feel that any job is "beneath" you. You will gain something from everything, even if it doesn't end up working out.

Q: What are the trends in spirit consumption that you see today?

A: I think certain areas of spirits that were very hot in the 1990s have plateaued. Cognac—which was very quiet in the '90s—is now staging what I think is a significant comeback.

Tequila, for lots of reasons, is stagnant. The agave shortage is part myth and part reality. The industry-funded board in Mexico that tries to project trends for tequila has said that it was part disease, part frost, part El Nino. What they're not saying is that they miscalculated horribly in the early '90s as to where tequila consumption was heading, and that they were recommending steady growth but got explosive growth, particularly from 1995 to 2000. Taking that miscalculation, the agave growers in the 1990s didn't cultivate new areas. They just kept plodding along, planning for steady growth but nothing dramatic. But a few companies—mostly Cuervo—saw it coming and sewed up a lot of the agave futures through very astute contracts with growers.

One out of every four bottles of booze sold in the world is vodka, but sales have slowed and that's why you're seeing the introduction of so many flavored vodkas—they're trying to stimulate it. Gin is making a small comeback, mostly because many consumers think of vodka as bland and are looking for something a bit more challenging as their palates become more sophisticated. Gin certainly offers that, so it's on the upswing.

Brandies are all pretty static right now, not much growth. But pot-still brandy from California is really coming on strong.

Q: What about whiskey?

A: Bourbon continues to be driven by sales of Jim Beam, and Tennessee spirits sales driven by Jack Daniels. There's some minor growth in the high-end products, small-batch and single-barrel. But people are so smitten with single-malt scotch and the caché that it carries that it's making it hard for the super-premium bourbons to make inroads.

Q: What do you think makes a liquor product successful, not just a "flash in the pan"?

A: A marketer who is able to discern what direction an average consumer—not a "status" consumer, but an average consumer—will take in buying a beverage in the next one to three years. Then, to develop a product that will appeal to that person and put the money behind it to market and promote it.

I see so many brands flooding into our office at *Spirit Journal*. Sometimes they're good, sometimes they're bad, but six months later, they're off the shelves. That often happens when they are simply underfunded. Money does make a difference.

Q: What about the sexy campaign? Surely you've seen cases where you didn't think the product was good, but the ads were really a hit with younger consumers.

A: I often think, because I'm 52 years old, it's like I'm on Pluto compared to what's happening with people in their 20s! But

again, it's a good marketer who can gauge the gas tank of the industry; and that person is not the connoisseur, or even someone who is relatively savvy about beverage alcohol. The marketer must look at the person who's in his or her early 20s, fresh out of college, got his or her first or second job, and finally has a little disposable income, living away from home or newly married. This person wants to learn, and part of the learning experience is social grace. Part of that, today, means learning about wines and spirits and beers, and you have to start somewhere.

All the big hits in spirits and wine are associated with that entry-level customer. For instance, in the wine business, Sutter Home put white zinfandel on the map. Why? Because Sutter Home looked at the market and said, "What can we do to appeal to a mass audience, keep it affordable, keep it slightly sweet?" They understood that you need to get into that younger, mass audience, who is willing to be adventurous.

Q: What do you think about the state-run liquor store system?

A: I consider the control states a ripple from the tidal wave of Prohibition that is still with us today. In some sense, there is a restriction of product in control states, which is another form of Prohibition. The people who control liquor in these states, and the distributors, are extremely powerful. And they are dictating the rules—it is not a truly free and open market in those states. To me, it's absolutely appalling. In my experience, the pricing is outrageous, at least 10 to 15 percent higher than the noncontrol states. Each state in the control system is making a fortune off of liquor sales.

Q: Any advice for students about what they should study?

A: Mine was all on-the-job training, but I think one of the best ways to break into the wine or spirits industry at some level is to first take some food courses—train as a chef or an assistant chef. There is no wine or liquor school in the world that can teach you about taste and "tune you in" to the sensitivity of your palate. But cooking is where you can learn to hone and refine your sense of taste, as well as learn to match foods and beverages. All of our wonderful beverages just about always work best with food. So to understand on a sensory level what you are doing, and to learn the history behind it, is an excellent place to start.

CHAPTER 6

Wine Appreciation

The more you know about wine, it seems, the more there is to know. Any good bookstore will have dozens, if not hundreds, of books about the world's various wine regions, their histories, heroes, and wares. You can get a college degree in *enology*, the science of winemaking. There are magazines, newsletters and Web sites devoted to rating and recommending wines. Ironically, though, often both the wine buyer and purveyor in a typical bar or restaurant know little about the product. They may even feel intimidated by it. No wonder, considering there are well over 2,000 wine labels produced in Italy alone!

Buying and drinking excellent quality wines doesn't have to be such a big mystery, if you know a few of the basics and are willing to experiment a bit. That's certainly what your customers are discovering. In today's beverage service industry, wine is often ordered instead of a cocktail. It is such a potentially important and profitable part of your business that the next two chapters are devoted to wine appreciation and wine sales.

This chapter should help you . . .

- Classify wines according to type and recognize some of their distinguishing characteristics.
- Learn about different types of wine grapes and the winemaking process.
- Learn how to taste a wine so you can adequately assess its characteristics and describe them to customers.
- Familiarize yourself with the world's leading wine regions and the types of wine they produce.
- Understand how to read wine labels.

A BRIEF HISTORY OF WINE IN THE UNITED STATES

Making wine is as ancient as history itself, referred to in the Bible, in hieroglyphics, and in Greek and Roman literature. Winemaking is the process of fermenting the juices of ripe grapes. The chemical reactions in this process are as follows: Yeast converts the sugar found naturally in the fruit into alcohol and carbon dioxide. The carbon dioxide escapes into the air, leaving the juice and alcohol behind to be stored, bottled, and eventually consumed.

The quality of the fruit has a lot to do with whether the resulting wine is worth drinking. When Europeans first came to the New World, they did their best to grow grapes from cuttings they brought with them. But the grapevines did not flourish in the cold northeastern climate, so most alcoholic fruit concoctions were made from berries or apples.

In 1769, a priest named Padre Junipero Serra traveled to California from Mexico, bringing with him some European grapevine cuttings. Others followed and, by the mid-1800s, European grapes were flourishing in the temperate California climate. By the late 1800s, some California wines were winning medals in international winemaking competitions.

Of course, Prohibition slowed things down significantly. Grape growers could make small quantities of home-produced wines; sell table grapes; or make sacramental wines for churches. Some of them also sold grape juice concentrate, to which enterprising folks added their own yeast and sugar to make their own wine. But most of California's 188,000 acres of vineyards (the 1933 figure) languished from the 1930s to the 1960s. In the 1970s, wine finally became trendy again in this country, as health-conscious consumers looked for lighter drinks and California winemakers received international acclaim for some of their wares.

TYPES OF WINE

No matter where it comes from, a wine is identified by a combination of these facts: its producer, its vintage, and its varietal. The *producer* is most often a winery, but wines are also made by blending together grapes from many different small vineyards. This is common in Europe, and wine made this way is labeled with the name of the cooperative or exporter, not an individual winery. The **vintage** is the year in which the grapes were picked and the winemaking process began for that particular bottle. The **varietal** is the type of grape used. It is very common to blend different varietals in a single bottle, but unless the second grape type makes up a significant percentage of the wine, the bottle is usually labeled with the name of the predominant grape. There are laws (that vary in the United States and in other nations) about how to label these blends, depending on the percentages of the varietals used. You'll learn more about how to read a wine label later in this chapter.

There are three different types of table wines: red, white, and rosé. A table wine is simply a wine that is served at a dining table—that's the term used by the Federal Standard of Identity for wines that have an alcohol content of "not in excess of 14 percent by volume." The percentage of alcohol (usually from 10 to 14) must be stated by law on the wine label.

Here are a few very general comments about each type of wine:

- Red wines tend to be hearty, full-bodied, and nearly always dry. Their color can range from a deep crimson to purple to reddish-orange or rust, depending on the type of grape used and the age of the wine. The term "dry" in the wine business means lacking in sweetness. Dryness is one of the qualities that makes red wine a suitable accompaniment to hearty dishes like steak, game, or lasagna. Red wines are not refrigerated, but served at a slightly cool room temperature of 65 to 70° Fahrenheit—the temperature of cold tap water.

- White wines range in color from pale straw to bright yellow to gold. They are generally more delicate in flavor than reds, and they range in flavor from very dry to very sweet. Many people begin a meal with appetizers, soup or salad, and a white wine, then switch to red for a "bigger" main course. The drier whites also complement fish, veal, and pasta dishes in light sauces. The sweetest white wines are usually made as "meal enders," to be served as dessert or with desserts. White wines are always served lightly chilled.

- Rosé wines are various, attractive shades of pale red, pink, or salmon, so in recent years, it has become more common to refer to them as "blush" wines. They are made from red grapes but, in character and taste, they are lighter and more like white wines. Rosés are generally fresh and fruity, and many have a touch of sweetness. With a holiday ham or turkey or lighter-style foods, they are lovely complements. The best rosé wines of France are very dry, called Tavel, made from the Grenache grape.

Novice wine drinkers often begin with White Zinfandel or White Pinot Noir, since they provide a nice transition from soft drinks to the world of wine. For this reason, though, you'll find that wine connoisseurs sometimes turn their noses up at blush wine drinkers, considering them inexperienced or unsophisticated. To you, they are all customers, no matter what their wine-sipping preference.

Sparkling Wines

So far, the types of wine we've discussed have been so-called still wines, that is, wines that do not contain bubbles. But there are also sparkling wines, which come in red, white, and blush. Sparkling wines are often referred to as "champagne," but the French will tell you that *only* wines made in the Champagne region of France can truly be called Champagne (with a capital "C"). Indeed, most winemakers respect this designation, and although there is no law governing this, you'll find that most non-French bubbly is labeled "sparkling wine." If they are made in exactly the same way as French Champagnes, their label will also say **Methode Champenoise.** Sparkling wines are also known as **Sekt** in Germany and **Spumante** in Italy.

Champagne is the classic wine of celebration. Sparkling wines should always be served well chilled. They complement almost any food, and are also good to drink by themselves. Usually, sparkling wine is sold by the bottle, but some bars and restaurants also serve it by the glass or as an ingredient in a mixed drink, like the Mimosa (Champagne and orange juice), popular for breakfast or brunch.

You'll learn later in this chapter what puts the bubbles in sparkling wine.

Fortified Wines

There is another wine category that consists of wine that has extra alcohol or brandy added to it. This process is known as *fortifying* the wine, but the government does not allow the word "fortified" to be used on the label, lest consumers mistakenly think it is of some health benefit. The percentage of alcohol listed on the label is your first clue: anything with an alcohol content of over 14 percent has been fortified. Most fortified wines have an alcohol content of 17 to 19 percent. The legal limit is 24 percent.

Federal Standards of Identity divide fortified wines into two categories: **aperitif wines** and dessert wines. Aperitifs are also **aromatized,** meaning they are flavored with aromatic herbs and spices. Traditionally, they are sipped before dinner, to stimulate the appetite or aid digestion of the upcoming meal. The word "aperitif" comes from a Latin word meaning "to open."

The best-known aromatized wine is vermouth, which most folks probably associate with bar liquor, not wine. Dry French vermouth is put to good use in Martinis, while sweet, Italian vermouth goes into Manhattans. Vermouths and other aromatized wines, like Dubonnet and Lillet from France, can be served straight up and well chilled, or on ice, or mixed with soda and a twist of lemon. It is also popular to drink them half-and-half, mixing equal parts of dry vermouth and sweet. Sherry, another aperitif, is used more often in cooking than as a beverage nowadays.

The other group of fortified wines, the *dessert wines*, are designed to end the meal. They are rich, sweet and heavy, imbibed in small quantities like liqueurs. Dessert wines include Madeira, marsala, angelica, and muscatel. There are also "late harvest" wines, usually white, made from grapes that have been allowed to overripen on the vines almost to spoilage for maximum sugar content. These wines are not fortified, but they are included in the dessert wine category. Any dessert wine may either be served chilled or at room temperature.

Sake

There is one kind of wine served in restaurants that is not made from grapes at all. **Sake** (SOCK-ee) is a Japanese beverage made from rice. It goes through an extensive brewing process, so there is some debate about whether it is actually a beer, but our federal Standards of Identity classify it as a wine. Its alcohol content (14 to 16 percent) is definitely higher than beer, and sake is usually served warmed, from small ceramic bottles into tiny ceramic bowls for sipping. You will occasionally find sake used in cocktails; in recent years, some trendy Martinis and Margaritas have been made with sake.

THE GRAPES

It all starts with the grapes. The grape contains the natural sugar, the fruit, the liquid, the acidity that gives the wine its taste and balance; the tannins (in red wines) that provide taste and longevity. From the grape's skin comes the color of the wine. Different types of grapes exhibit different characteristics and, therefore, become different-tasting wines.

There are red grapes and white grapes. Whether the red grape is actually red or blackish or purple, it's still considered a red grape. Red wines are made when red grapes are crushed and fermented (soaked) along with their skins and stems. The color leeches out of the skin into the juice. (Rosé wines are made when the skin has limited contact with the juice, imparting only some of its color.)

It is during the fermentation process that the red wine gets its **tannin.** Yes, tannin is the same type of substance that is used to tan animal hides into leather. (It's found naturally in coffee and tea, too.) In wine, it comes from the skins and stems of the grapes, and acts as a preservative that allows red wine to age without going stale. If you've ever bitten into a grape stem, you know how bitter it can taste. Tannins impart some of this bitterness to the wine, and can taste unpleasant when the wine is young. But they mellow with age and are considered an important component of good, long-lasting red wine.

White grapes are fermented without their skins. They are lighter in color and flavor, and lack the tannins of red wines. White wines can be made from red grapes, since the juice is separated from the skin so the color does not leech into the juice. But because the tannins are missing, white wines generally do not last as long (age as well) as red wines.

Let's talk briefly about some of the most popular wine grapes. You will see these names on most wine labels today, so you should be familiar with their pronunciations and the types of wine they produce.

Red Grape Varietals

Cabernet Sauvignon (cab-er-NAY so-vin-YON) is possibly the most important grape varietal in the world. It produces the greatest red wines of Bordeaux and the best reds in both California and Australia. It is often called simply "Cabernet." Cabernet Franc (cab-er-NAY FRONK) is a close, but lower-quality relative.

The great Burgundy wines of France are made from **Pinot Noir** (pee-no NWAHR). It is also used to make some of the world's finest Champagnes, when the juice is separated from its red skin. Interesting red wines, lighter in body than Cabernets, are made from Pinot Noir in Oregon and California.

Merlot (mair-LOW) is an important red grape in Bordeaux, Italy, and California. At one time, it was used mostly to blend with Cabernets, since it is smoother and less tannic. But now you'll find just as many Merlots as Cabernets on wine store shelves, and they are a favorite red wine of American consumers because they are mellow, uncomplicated, and easy to drink.

Gamay Beaujolais (gam-AY BO-zha-lay) is the name of the light, fresh, and fruity red wine made from the Gamay grape. It was first produced in the Beaujolais region of France, but now California wineries make similar wines and call them either Gamay Beaujolais or Napa Gamay. Scientists discovered that Gamay is a clone of the Pinot Noir grape. These wines are not meant to be aged, but to drink young.

Zinfandel (ZIN-fun-dell) is a red grape grown almost exclusively in California. It was once used to make inexpensive "jug wines," but has developed its own following, and there are now some exceptional California "Zins" being bottled. Zinfandel is a very adaptable grape; it can be used to make everything from the sweet, pink, fruity White Zinfandels to thick, dark, full-flavored reds best served with steaks or hearty pastas.

The next hearty red wine producer is known as the **Syrah** (sir-AH) grape in France and California; or the **Shiraz** (shur-OZ) grape in Australia. This is "the" varietal to watch in the early twenty-first century. In California, planting of Syrah vines ranks fourth behind Cabernet Sauvignon, Merlot, and Zinfandel. In France, this intensely tannic, full-bodied wine is often blended with other grapes in such well-known wines as Hermitage and Coté Rotie.

The **Grenache** (gren-OSH) grape is sweet and red, making a lightly colored wine. You read earlier about the Tavel rosé of France; Grenache is also a major component of Rioja wines of Spain, and of California rosés.

Tempranillo (TEMP-rah-NEE-yo) is the main red wine grape of Spain, blended with Grenache to make those award-winning Rioja wines. With its softer tannins, Tempranillo has developed a kind of cult following among wine lovers. Some Spanish wineries are now bottling 100-percent Tempranillo instead of blending it. California winemakers have tried to grow this varietal, but without much success.

In Italy, the **Sangiovese** (SAN-gee-oh-VAY-zee) grape makes the well-known **Chianti** (kee-ON-tee). When blended with Cabernet, it is the base for a trendy new group of wines that have been dubbed the "super Tuscans." Sangiovese is also becoming more popular in California. In Italy's Piedmont region, the **Nebbiolo** (neb-ee-OH-loh) grape is blended with others to make **Barolo** (bah-RO-loe) and Barbaresco (BAR-bah-RESS-koe) wines. Barbera (bar-BAHR-uh) is another Italian red grape that has transplanted well in California, where it is used for blending and to make a variety of wine styles.

Finally, we have **Lambrusco** (lam-BROOS-koe), a grape grown in Northern Italy that produces a very fruity, rather sweet red wine with a fizzy characteristic (in Italian, *frizzante*). Some people think it tastes more like a soft drink than a wine, but it is popular nonetheless.

White Grape Varietals

Chardonnay (SHAR-den-NAY) is the white wine grape most Americans are familiar with. It produces mostly dry wines of strong body and distinctive flavor worldwide. It is the best-selling wine in California and is the base for all French **Chablis** (shah-BLEE) wines, as well as the famous white Burgundy wines of France. Chardonnay grapes are grown all over Europe, in Australia, and New Zealand.

In California, the grape second only to Chardonnay is **Sauvignon Blanc** (SO-vin-yon BLONK). In France, it is the predominant white grape of Bordeaux. It is used to make the dry, fruity wines of the **Graves** (GRAHVZ) district; the rich, golden **Sauternes** (saw-TURN); and the fresh, crisp Loire Valley whites called **Sancerre** (san-SAIR) and **Pouilly Fumé** (POO-ee foo-MAY). In California, some wineries call their Sauvignon Blanc wines Fumé Blanc (FOO-may BLONK).

Semillon (SEM-ee-YON) used to be a grape used primarily for blending with Chardonnay, Graves, and Sauternes wines, but it has developed a loyal following and is now bottled separately by many wineries. Semillon is known for its rich fruit flavor.

Riesling (REES-ling) is the fruity white grape used to make many of the sweeter German wines, including late harvest or dessert wines, although it can be made into a sophisticated dry wine. It is also widely grown in California.

Chenin Blanc (SHEN-in BLONK) grapes make tasty white wines, like Vouvray, in the Loire Valley region of France, some of them sparkling. Chenin Blanc is also a widely planted white grape in California, where it is made in a variety of styles ranging from dry to sweet. In South African winemaking, Chenin Blanc is called Steen.

Gewurztraminer (ge-VURTZ-tra-mee-ner) is the spicy white (actually pink) grape of the French Alsace region and parts of Germany. (*Gewurz* means spice in German.) This grape typically makes a flavorful dry white wine but, like the Riesling, can produce late-harvest sweet wines. In California, this grape produces both dry and sweet wines. It is also grown in Australia and New Zealand.

Pinot Blanc (PEE-no BLONK) is a white grape grown in Alsace, northern Italy, and California. It is an especially good grape for making sparkling wine. It also produces a varietal wine in California.

A **Muscat** (MUSK-at) grape can be either red or white, and the wines made from it are usually sweet. They are made all over the world. One made from a white Muscat—Asti Spumante (OSS-tee spoo-MON-tee)—is Italy's popular sweet sparkling wine.

Among Italy's white grapes is the Trebbiano (treb-ee-AH-no), which makes such varied wines as the light, dry Soave in northeast Italy and sparkling wines in the Po valley.

Muller-Thurgau (MYOOL-ur TUR-gau) is the most widely grown grape in Germany. It makes many soft, aromatic white wines of varying degrees of sweetness, but experts generally feel it cannot compare with the Riesling for quality.

All these grapes are listed alphabetically in Table 6.1. No one can possibly remember them all the first time around, so this is material you should return to periodically as you learn more about wines.

HOW WINES ARE MADE

All wines begin in the same way, with the grapes, the soil, the weather, and the winemaker combining to turn the same basic product into an infinite variety of forms. It is a process in which nature plays a large part.

The climate in which grapes grow is a very important influence on how they taste. Warm climates yield ripe grapes and rich wines: the riper and sweeter the grapes at harvest, the more alcoholic the wine. Australia, parts of California, and southern France, for example, have this potential. Cool climates, including Germany, northern Italy, and the Champagne region in France typically produce "greener" (less ripe) grapes and lighter wines.

Year after year in any given district, the ripeness and quality of the grapes at harvest will vary according to the weather, which means that the wines will vary in quality, too. This is why the vintage of a fine wine is important. As you've learned, vintage refers to the year the grapes were harvested and the winemaking process began.

Three factors—the grapes, the climate in a given location, and the weather in a given year—combine to determine the character of an individual wine. And each wine will be different from any other.

It's ironic that grapes grow best in gravelly soil that is considered poor for other types of crops, on well-drained land (like hillsides), in a temperate climate with enough sun and warmth to develop their sugar, and a little rain

Table 6.1
Grape Varieties

Grape	Color	Body	Sweetness	Flavor Intensity	Region/Country of Use
Barbera	red	medium to full	dry	medium to intense	California, Italy
Cabernet Sauvignon	red	medium to full	dry	medium to full	California, Bordeaux, Australia
Chardonnay	white	medium to full	dry	medium to full	California, Burgundy, Chablis, Champagne, Italy, Spain, Bulgaria, Australia, New Zealand
Chenin Blanc	white	medium	slightly sweet	medium	California, Loire
Gamay	red	light to medium	dry	delicate	Beaujolais
Gewürztraminer	white	medium	dry	spicy, full	California, Alsace, Australia, New Zealand
Grenache	red	light to medium	dry	light to medium	California, Rhône, Spain, Australia
Merlot	red	light to medium	dry	soft, delicate	California, Italy, Bordeaux
Müller-Thurgau	white	soft to medium	sweet	mild to medium	Germany
Muscat	black or white	full	medium to sweet	medium to full	Italy, Alsace, Bulgaria
Nebbiolo	red	light to medium	dry	intense	Italy
Pinot Blanc	white	light to medium	dry	light	California, Italy, Alsace, Champagne
Pinot Noir	red	medium to full	dry	medium to full	California, Burgundy, Oregon, Champagne, Australia
Riesling	white	light to medium	slightly sweet	delicate	Germany, Alsace, Australia, California, Washington, Oregon
Sangiovese	red	medium to full	dry	medium to full	Italy
Sauvignon Blanc	white	medium	dry	medium	California, Bordeaux, Loire, Chile
Sémillon	white	light to medium	dry	medium	California, Bordeaux
Silvaner	white	light	dry	light	Alsace, Germany
Syrah, Shiraz	red	medium to full	dry	intense	Rhône, Australia
Trebbiano	white	light to medium	dry	light to medium	Italy
Zinfandel	red	medium to full	dry	medium to intense	California

203

at the right times. As they mature, the grapes increase in sugar content and decrease in acidity. It takes about 100 days of sunshine from blossom to harvest before the grapes ripen to the precise balance of sugar and acid that makes the best possible wine. The moment of harvest is determined by frequent taste-testing for sugar content and by keeping an eye on the weather forecast. A heavy rain on ripe grapes can be a disaster.

The Winemaking Process

As soon as possible after picking—within 12 hours—the whole, ripened grapes begin their journey (Figure 6.1). If a white wine is being made, the grapes—no matter what their color—go through a crusher/stemmer that removes the stalks and breaks the skins. They are then pressed to extract their juices. The skins are discarded, and the juice, now called *must*, is channeled into a fermentation tank.

For a red wine or a rosé, dark-skinned grapes are crushed; then both must and skins go into a fermentation tank. It is the red or black or purple skins that yield the color, as well as much of the character, of a red wine. For a rosé, the skins are left in the fermenting must briefly (12 to 24 hours), just long enough to achieve the color desired. The must is then pumped into another tank, leaving the skins behind.

For any type of wine, before fermentation begins, special strains of yeast are added. Traditionally, winemakers depended on the wild yeasts found naturally on grape skins, but today American winemakers use laboratory-produced yeast cultures to ensure a more predictable result. The wild yeasts are killed off, either by the special yeasts or by the addition of sulfur dioxide.

In some parts of the world, when the climate or the weather has not produced enough sugar in the grapes, extra sugar—fine-grain "powdered sunshine"—is added before fermentation begins. This is called **chapitalization.**

In the fermentation tank, the yeasts feed on the sugar and break it down: one molecule of sugar yields two molecules of alcohol and two molecules of carbon dioxide. Fermentation continues for one to two weeks or even longer, until the sugar is consumed or the alcohol content becomes high enough (around 14 percent) to kill the yeast. The process stops automatically unless the winemaker intervenes. If the sugar has been completely consumed by the yeast, the wine is dry. If sugar remains, there is sweetness in the wine.

When fermentation stops, the wine is placed in large casks or vats. In the making of red wines, the skins are pressed out in the transfer. The wine pressed from the skins is rich in extracts such as tannin, which give the wine more character.

Each wine is stored until residues settle out and the wine stabilizes. Periodically the wine is drawn off the residues (the **lees**) and placed in a fresh cask to settle further. This is known as *racking*. When the wine "falls bright" (becomes clear) it is moved to other vats or casks for maturing.

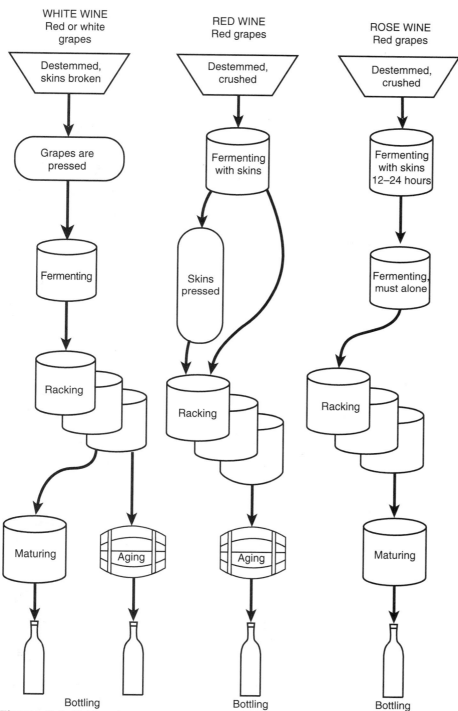

WHITE WINE
Red or white
grapes

Destemmed,
skins broken

Grapes are
pressed

Fermenting

Racking

Maturing

Aging

Bottling

RED WINE
Red grapes

Destemmed,
crushed

Fermenting
with skins

Skins
pressed

Racking

Aging

Bottling

ROSE WINE
Red grapes

Destemmed,
crushed

Fermenting
with skins
12–24 hours

Fermenting,
must alone

Racking

Maturing

Bottling

Figure 6.1 Making wines.

White wines and rosés are often matured in vats lined with plastic or glass or in stainless-steel containers. They are usually ready for bottling in a few months. Most red wines and certain whites are aged in wood casks (usually oak) for six months to two years or more. Here they undergo changes that mellow and smooth them and develop their special character. Some elements of flavor are absorbed from the wood. Some changes come from slight evaporation of the wine in the casks. Other mysterious chemistry occurs within the wine itself, contributing complexities of flavor, especially to wines that age slowly.

A winemaker's decisions about how long to age a wine and in what kind of container—tanks or wood, old or new wood (the newer the barrel, the more intense the wood character it imparts), large casks or small barrels (smaller ones yield more intense wood character)—are significant in determining the wine's quality and price.

The moment when the wine is ready for bottling is determined by taste. When tannins and acids soften and become more agreeable, the wine is moved from cask to bottle. Before bottling, the fine particles that remain in the wine are filtered out or spun out by centrifuge. The wine is then bottled and corked. The cork fits the bottle snugly, and a *capsule*—a cap of foil or plastic—is added over the cork to protect it. Many wines not intended for aging, and most fortified wines, have screw tops instead of corks.

Cork is the bark of a particular type of oak tree that grows mostly in Portugal and Spain (Figure 6.2). The bark is stripped off the trees, and the corks are stamped out of it, then cleaned. The bark grows back, but the process is so slow—nine years—that in recent years, there has been a cork shortage. Some wineries now use synthetic plastic corks, and it is generally agreed that they don't adversely affect the quality of the wine.

Some wines are ready to drink as soon as they are bottled. Others must undergo further aging in the bottle before they are drinkable. The bottles are stored on their sides in a cool dark place until the wine is ready to drink. In this position the wine keeps the cork moist so that it does not dry out, shrink, and become loose, which can ruin the wine by allowing air into the bottle. Sometimes the wine is sold before it is ready, and the buyer *lays down* or stores the wine until it is ready to drink. A vintage date identifying the year the grapes were harvested is essential to wines that mature slowly.

Most wines are blends, of different grape varieties, grapes from different vineyards, or wines of different vintages or degrees of maturity. The blending may be done at different points of the winemaking process (which is why you don't see it in Figure 6.1). Sometimes the grapes themselves are blended before crushing. Sometimes the new wines are blended during racking. Sometimes wines are blended after they mature.

Blending serves several purposes. It may be done to produce the finest wine possible; to maintain product consistency from one year to the next; to tailor a wine to a special market; to make more wine for less money; or to make the best of a bad year by combining some mediocre grapes with some better ones.

In the bottle, wine continues to change. In fact, wine is a living substance that evolves more or less quickly from youth to maturity to senility, and each wine has its own rate of maturity and its own life span.

White wines and rosés mature most quickly. Most moderately priced whites and rosés mature early and are put on the market ready to drink within a few months after harvest. They have a life span of two to five years, depending on the wine. Premium whites are not ready to drink quite as early, but they can last longer. Generally, the better the wine to begin with, the longer the life span.

Red wines mature more slowly than whites, but the rate of maturity varies greatly from one red wine to another. Light-bodied reds—for example, Beaujolais, Valpolicella, and inexpensive light Cabernets—are generally best within three years of their vintage. Fuller, richer reds can gen-

Figure 6.2 A stripped cork tree. Copyright Armstrong World Industries.

erally live many more years, thanks to the tannins and acidity that preserve them. Some of the finest wines may take 8 to 10 years or even longer to reach their peak, and may be drinkable for decades thereafter.

Most wines today list their vintage on the bottle. In addition to telling how old the wine is, it can be a clue to quality for the better wines. There are great and poor and average years for wines, depending on the weather. A great vintage year produces a wine of finer taste and longer life span than an ordinary year. But a great year in one region may be a poor year in another. A vintage date must always be evaluated in terms of the specific district and the specific wine.

Before we leave the subject of winemaking, a note on **sulfites** is in order. Sulfur dioxide exists naturally in wines in small quantities as a by-product of fermentation. It is also an invaluable tool of winemakers at every stage. It protects wine from spoilage due to contact with air, kills bacteria, inhibits "bad" yeasts while stimulating "good" yeasts, helps preserve aroma, purifies used barrels, and keeps the finished wine fresh and stable. The phrase "contains sulfites" on a wine label points out a fact that has always been true. But there are a few people—a very small percentage—who develop serious allergic reactions to sulfites. The government requires the label statement for their protection.

The Making of a Sparkling Wine

Sparkling wines and fortified wines are made by adding something to the process just described. To make a sparkling wine, yeast and sugar are added to still wine to prompt a second fermentation. This is done in closed containers, so that the carbon dioxide produced cannot escape, and thus becomes part of the wine. In the aforementioned French Champagne method (Methode Champenoise—pronounced "meth-ODE SHAMP-en-WAZ") the closed containers are the heavy glass bottles in which the still wine was first bottled. It is a long and complicated process involving handling each bottle many times, removing sediment bottle by bottle, and other refinements. All this makes the Champagne very expensive and very good. A wine made in America using the Champagne method may legally be called Champagne. It may mention the Champagne process on the label or it may say "Fermented in this bottle."

Two other methods have been developed to shortcut the more time-consuming process. In the **Charmat** (shar-MOT) or **bulk process,** refermentation is carried out in large, closed pressurized tanks and the wine is then bottled under pressure. Such wines can be very modestly priced, but they do not begin to approach the quality of those made by the Champagne method. For one thing, they lose their bubbles quickly. In the United States, the label must refer to this type of wine as a "sparkling wine" rather than Champagne. The label may contain the words "champagne style" or "champagne type," or may call it "American (or New York State, California, etc.) champagne-bulk process."

Figure 6.3 A French Champagne label. Label courtesy of Weygandt Metzler Importing, Ltd.

The other alternate method referments the still wine in bottles but then transfers it under pressure to other bottles, filtering it in the transfer. This produces a moderately priced product of a quality that may satisfy popular tastes, but not wine buffs. Sparkling wines made in this way are labeled "fermented in the bottle." Figure 6.3 shows a French Champagne label.

TASTING WINES

Wine is an extremely complex beverage. It fascinates some people and bewilders others. No matter what your level of wine understanding or appreciation, you can only read so much about the subject. The only way to truly learn more is to taste the stuff! Drinking wine and tasting wine are two distinctly different pursuits, and tasting comes first. Tasting can help you to understand your own preferences and why a good wine is good, and this can give you pleasure and confidence. But more important for the restaurateur or bar owner is what that confidence and understanding can do to increase business. It can help you to buy the most suitable wines for your clientele; to develop a wine list; and most of all, to train your serving staff about the wines on your list so that they can describe and sell them to your customers. So let's learn some wine-tasting basics.

When you taste a wine, pour it in a thin, clear glass with a stem. Hold the glass by the foot or the stem, never by the bowl, which would convey the heat of your hand to the wine. Whenever you taste wines, use the same size glass and the same amount of wine so you can make valid comparisons. Comparison tastings—of the same varietal by different producers, or the same varietal from different years—are terrific ways to learn more about the subtle differences between wines.

Tasting a wine really begins with appraising its appearance. Pour a small amount and hold it up to the light, or look at it against a white background, like a white tablecloth. The wine should be clear and bright. A wine that looks cloudy or hazy has a problem. Don't buy it and don't serve it. Note that sediment in a bottle of aging wine is not a problem; this will settle out when the bottle is left to sit a while.

Next, focus on the wine's color. Color will tell you if the wine is light, medium, or full-bodied. Many white wines have a pale, straw color. Young whites, especially those from cooler climates, may have a tinge of green. Wines from warmer climates and sweet dessert wines are often a beautiful golden hue. White wines darken, turning brownish as they age, so any tinge of brown or amber may signal a problem.

Red wines range from purple in a young wine to reddish-brown in a mature wine. Too much rust or amber color is a warning signal that the wine may have been stored incorrectly or not sealed properly. Oxidation—oxygen coming into contact with the wine—can cause this discoloration, a sign of spoilage.

Rosé wines are pink to pale orange; too pink or too orange is not good, and again, any touch of amber is a warning.

The next step is to smell the wine, and to do that most effectively, you must learn to swirl it around inside the wineglass. The best way for a novice to manage this is to keep the glass on the table, hold the bottom of the stem between your fingers, and move the base of the glass around in a small, clockwise circle, which will cause the wine inside the bowl to move in a circular manner, too. You don't have to swirl too hard to get the wine moving around. When you are confident doing this with the glass still sitting on the table, you can pick up the glass and try swirling it.

Why swirl? Swirling allows some of the alcohol in the wine to vaporize. As it rises, it brings with it the scent of the wine. If you doubt this, sniff two glasses of the same wine—one sitting still and one just after you've swirled it. The scent will be more intense from the swirled wine. Some people put one hand over the bowl of the wineglass as they swirl, to hold the aroma inside until they sniff.

Aroma is the term used if the scent is fruity or flowery; it will give you some important clues about the grapes and winemaking methods used. The scent of a more complex and mature wine is called its *bouquet*. Bouquet may include aroma, but aroma does not include bouquet, an important distinction in learning to describe wines.

When sniffing the wine, don't be shy. Put your nose right inside the glass so that the bridge of your nose touches the far side of the glass, and inhale. Try to describe the fragrance to yourself. A wine's bouquet reflects the changes that have slowly taken place inside the bottle. The bouquet of a good mature wine is a significant part of the pleasure it gives.

There are also "off" odors to check for: vinegar, sulfur, or an inappropriate smell of sherry or Madeira in an ordinary table wine. Such wines should not be served.

Finally, you taste the wine. Take a small sip and roll it over your tongue. Hold it in your mouth for 10 seconds or so. The key to the taste of the wine is on your tongue; your taste buds are arranged so that they detect certain flavors on certain parts areas (see Figure 6.4). As you taste the wine, you will perceive its sweetness first, then its sourness or acidity, and any bitterness at the back of your mouth, as you swallow the wine.

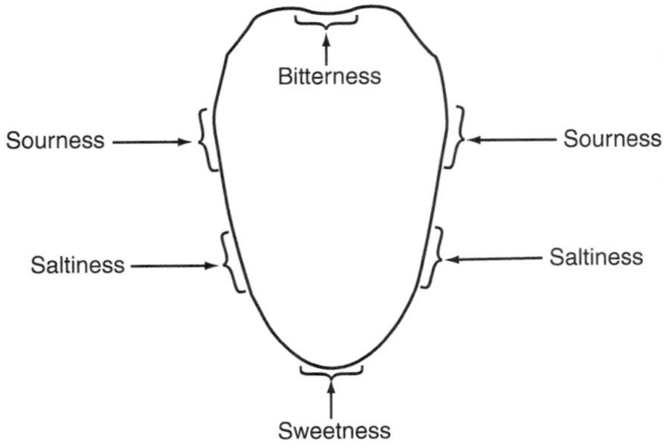

These tastes represent four components of the wine's *structure,* a term used to describe the nature of a wine apart from its scent and flavors. The components that make up structure are:

Figure 6.4 The taste buds on the human tongue.

- **Sugar.** Sweetness is sensed as the wine first enters your mouth.

- **Acid.** This is perceived mainly on the sides of your tongue as a tartness or sharpness.
- **Tannin.** A bitterness or astringency sensed on the rear of the tongue, tannin puckers the mouth, as strong tea does. It is found mainly in red wines.
- **Alcohol.** Alcohol has a sweet flavor that enhances any other sweetness. It makes a wine seem round and full, though in high quantities it can cause a slight burning sensation in the mouth.

The way in which these four components relate to each other determines the **balance** of a given wine. Balance is the dynamic of the structure, that is, the way the components relate. Ideally, the richness created by the sweetness-plus-alcohol will counterbalance the harshness of the tannin-plus-acid, creating an impression of harmony. To the degree that this occurs in a wine, we say that the wine is balanced. More than any other factor, balance is the determinant of wine quality.

When you first taste a wine, what exactly are you trying to find? Here are some of the common terms and characteristics:

- **Body.** The feel of the wine in the mouth, body comes from the amount of alcohol, sugar, glycerin (a soluble substance formed during fermentation), and extracts from the grapes, such as tannin. A wine is referred to as "light" or "light-bodied" if it is low in one or more of the body components. A "full-bodied" wine is typically high in body components. It will cling to the sides of the glass if you swish it around. (The glycerin content causes small streams of wine to run down the sides of the glass after you swirl; aficionados refer to these streams as the "legs" of the wine.) When you taste a full-bodied wine, it has a texture all its own, filling your mouth in a sensuous way.
- **Degree of sweetness.** If the grape sugar has been entirely consumed during fermentation, and none has been added, a wine will be totally lacking in sweetness, or *dry*. This is an important characteristic for your servers to know about each wine on your list, since the most often-asked questions involve wine dryness. Generally, a dry wine or one with only a little sweetness is preferred with the meal, while a sweet wine is an appropriate "beginning" with lighter appetizers or as a finish to a meal. Many Americans brought up on carbonated soft drinks prefer a wine with some sweetness.
- **Flavor intensity.** This refers to whether a wine is light and delicate in flavor, or full and concentrated, or somewhere in between. Again, your servers should have this information for each wine on your list. It is important in matching wines with food.
- **Tartness, acidity.** A sharp, acid taste, like green fruit. In a balanced wine, tartness is a crucial quality: it gives life to the wine.
- **Softness.** The opposite of tartness. The term is also used for an overaged wine when its tannin is gone.

- **Astringency.** A taste the beginner may mistake for dryness or acidity; astringency puckers the mouth. You'll find it in young red wines, not quite ready to drink. It comes from the tannin derived from the grape skins and will disappear as the wine matures and mellows.
- **Mellowness.** The opposite of astringency; softened with age, ripe.
- **Finish.** Finish is the aftertaste. A good wine should have a pleasant aftertaste in keeping with the wine itself.
- **Character.** Positive, distinctive taste characteristics that show the wine is truly representative of the grape varietal(s) from which it was made.

As to taste preferences, the customer is always right. There are no longer rigid rules about what kind or color of wine to drink with what type of food. In the end, taste is a personal matter. The Romans sometimes mixed their wines with seawater. Who's to say they were right or wrong?

Many customers, however, know nothing about wines, are intimidated by a wine list, and may not order wine at all unless they are encouraged by a friendly server who knows just how each wine on the list tastes and which wine goes well with which food. We will have more to say on this subject in Chapter 7.

HOW WINES ARE NAMED

The bewildering variety of table wines on the market is enough to inhibit any novice, whether it is a restaurateur introducing wines for the first time or a customer struggling to make a selection from a long wine list. The picture may become simpler when we examine why wines are named as they are.

Every label must carry a name to identify the product inside the bottle. In this country, wines are named three ways: (1) by the predominant variety of grape used (varietal); (2) by broad general type (generic); or (3) by brand name. Imported wines may also be named by these methods, but a fourth method is more common: place of origin.

Varietal Names

A varietal wine is one in which a single grape variety predominates. The name of the grape is the name of the wine, and that grape gives the wine its predominant flavor and aroma. Well-known examples are Cabernet Sauvignon, Chardonnay, Chenin Blanc, and Zinfandel. In the United States, to be named for a particular grape, the wine must contain at least 75 percent of that grape. Within the European Economic Community the minimum is 85 percent, and some countries or districts have raised that requirement to 100 percent. In France, the figure has been 100 percent for some time. Figure 6.5 shows labels of two varietal wines from California.

Figure 6.5 Two varietal wine labels from California: a Chardonnay and a White Zinfandel. Labels courtesy Berringer Blass Wine Estates, Napa, California.

Varietals are very popular in this country, and they are well worth exploring for your wine list. The names, once learned, are quickly recognized; and the better-known varietals almost sell themselves. Varietals range in price from moderate to high, depending to some extent on the wine quality. Taste them before buying, because they can vary greatly from one producer to another and one vintage to another. (Of course, this is true of all wines.) The name and fame of the grape alone do not guarantee the quality of the wine.

Generic Names

A *generic* wine is an American wine of a broad general style or type, such as Burgundy or Chablis. Their names are borrowed from European wines that come from well-known wine districts, but their resemblance to these European wines is slight to nonexistent. Federal law requires all American generics (the law refers to them as *semi-generics*) to include a place of origin on the label (such as California, Washington State, Napa Valley, or even America). The idea is to distinguish them clearly from the grapes of European wines whose names they have borrowed. Figure 6.6 shows labels of two generic wines.

The best of the generics are pleasant, uncomplicated, affordable wines that restaurants can serve as house wines. There is nothing about a generic name to indicate the character or quality of the wine. If you are exploring generics to serve at your bar or restaurant, the only way to determine reliable character and quality is by taste.

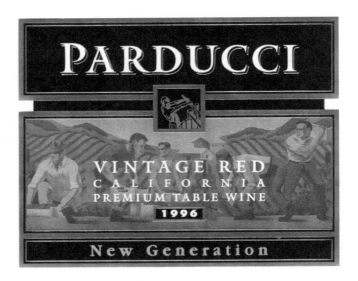

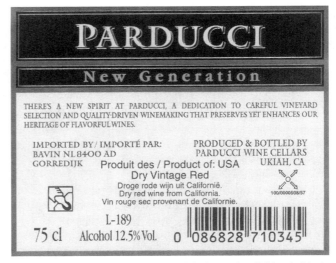

Figure 6.6 Generic wine labels: an American Merlot and a California Merlot. Labels courtesy of Carmela Vineyards and Adler Fels/Newland.

Generics frequently come in large-size bottles—1½ to 3 liters or even 4 liters—and are sometimes called *jug wines*. Nowadays these wines often come in bag-in-a-box form, in a sturdy cardboard box lined with a heavy plastic bag that holds 10 to 15 gallons of wine. The wine is dispensed through a spigot in the side of the box, and the bag shrinks as wine is removed, so the wine remaining in the bag is unspoiled by contact with air.

Many wineries have begun to use the names Red Table Wine and White Table Wine instead of the old generic names. These are inexpensive blends like the generics, and can be used as house wines if they pass your own taste test.

Generics used to be much more popular than they are today. As Americans have learned more about wine, they have come to recognize varietal names, and in general, only a few inexpensive wines continue to use the generic names.

Brand Names

A brand name wine may be anything from an inexpensive blend to a very fine wine with a prestigious pedigree. A brand name, also called a *proprietary* name (in France, a **monopole**) is one that belongs exclusively to a vineyard or a shipper who produces and/or bottles the wine and takes responsibility for its quality.

A brand name distinguishes a wine from others of the same class or type. It is a means of building an identity in the mind of a customer who is used to choosing liquors and beers by brand, is confused by the profusion of wines from which to choose, and would rather pick one and stay with it, like a favorite beer. Brand names are also used in California for some high-quality wines when the winemakers deliberately choose not to meet the 75-percent varietal requirement. They feel they can make a better wine with more skillful blending of the dominant grape with others. Examples of these are Opus One, Dominus, and Sterling Reserve. Blended wines are sometimes known as Meritage wines.

A brand name alone does not tell you anything about the wine. The reputation of the producer and the taste of the wine are better keys to choice. An example of a brand name wine, Spain's famous Tinto Pesquera, is shown in Figure 6.7.

Figure 6.7 This popular Spanish wine emphasizes a brand name. Label courtesy of Classical Wines of Spain.

Figure 6.8 Wines known by place of origin. Note the Denominación de Origen designation. Label courtesy of Classical Wines of Spain.

Place-of-Origin Names

Many imported wines use their place of origin as the name on their label. The place of origin is usually a rigidly controlled area that produces superior wines of a certain character because of its special soil, climate, grapes, and production methods. Wines from such an area must meet stringent government regulations and standards of that nation in order to use the name. The defined area may be large (a district, a region) or small (a commune, a parish, a village, a vineyard). Generally the smaller the subdivision, the more rigorous the standards and the more famous the wine.

Along with the area name on the label is a phrase meaning "controlled name of origin." It may be "Appellation Controlee" in France, "Denominazione di Origine Controllata" (DOC for short) in Italy. Other countries have similar requirements for using the name of a particular place of origin. A typical label is shown in Figure 6.8.

Generally, a wine from a controlled area has a certain claim to quality, and the best wine-growing areas have the strongest claim. But the name is not a guarantee, and all wines from the same area are not the same. Picking the right wines from the right places is a job for an expert. Ultimately, a good producer is the only assurance of quality.

In recent decades in the United States, a system called Approved Viticultural Appellations (AVA) has been in force. Through this system the names of unique vineyard areas (for instance, Napa Valley, Russian River Valley, Sonoma County) are officially defined and their use is controlled. New AVAs are continually being approved. These geographic names are generally coupled with a varietal name, and there is no indication on the wine label as to whether a geographic name is an approved AVA or not.

WINES FROM AROUND THE WORLD

Although American wines outsell imports in this country by a wide margin, in some areas, especially major metropolitan centers and on the East Coast, imported wines are extremely popular. Those who know wine best will generally drink and enjoy wines from all over the world. No wine list in an upscale restaurant can be considered complete without wines from France, Italy, Germany, and Spain, as well as American wines.

American Wines

California is by far the leading producer of wine in the United States. California's best wines come from its cooler regions, such as coastal valleys where the ocean breezes moderate an otherwise hot climate. The most famous areas include the Napa and Sonoma Valleys, Mendocino, Monterey, and the South Central Coast areas of Santa Barbara and San Luis Obispo. Fine wines also hail from mountainous areas, such as the Sierra foothills and the Santa Cruz Mountains. In the hot, inland San Joaquin Valley, huge quantities of ordinary wine are produced.

Most California wines are labeled as varietals. Chardonnay is the most popular white wine; its style ranges from simple and fruity to rich and exotic, and its price ranges from only a few dollars a bottle to four and five times as much. Sauvignon Blanc (sometimes called Fumé Blanc), with a characteristic herbaceous flavor, is the next most popular.

Cabernet Sauvignon is California's premium red, especially when produced carefully to make rich, authoritative wines that reward several years' aging. Merlot, similar to Cabernet but softer and less tannic, is gaining in popularity, as are grapes native to France's Rhone Valley—Syrah, Mourvedre, Grenache—although wines from these grapes are so far produced in California in small quantities. Pinot Noir, a temperamental grape that has teased winemakers all over the world, has found a suitable home in the coolest areas of the state.

The quintessential California wine is Zinfandel, a versatile red wine made from a grape seldom found in other countries. It is made in a variety of styles. One style emphasizes the fresh, fruity character of a young wine. Another is modeled on the style of the Cabernet wines, with increased body and complexity. The third—and still the most popular version—is the "blush" wine called White Zinfandel. Though White Zinfandel has outshone the other styles, red Zinfandel is gaining in popularity.

After California, New York is the leading wine-producing state. Its best wines are made from classic grapes such as Chardonnay and Riesling in the northerly Finger Lakes or Lake Erie areas. Upstate New York and the Niagara peninsula in Ontario, Canada, provide suitable climates for Riesling, Chardonnay, and Gewurztraminer wines (the Ontario area is known for its version of Eiswein), while Long Island has been very successful with Chardonnay, Cabernet, and Merlot.

Oregon has had enormous success growing Pinot Noir because its coastal valleys are cooler than California's. Chardonnay, Riesling, and Pinot Gris are Oregon's main whites.

Washington State is becoming recognized as one of America's best growing areas for Cabernet Sauvignon, Merlot, and Sauvignon Blanc. Although it is even more northerly than Oregon, the climate is not necessarily cooler because the vineyards are located inland, far from the cooling breezes of the ocean.

Numerous other states have made very creditable wines, including all the mid-Atlantic states, Idaho, Ohio, and Texas. These wines are generally in small production, however, and seldom become well-known enough to land themselves on restaurant wine lists, except in their own home state or region.

Wines from France

Fine French wines lead the world in prestige, and no wine list in any up-scale restaurant or fashionable hotel would be complete without these choices. Patrons who know wines may expect to see several well-known French wines at very high prices on the wine list, even if they do not order any of them, along with several at lower prices that they would be glad to buy. The label on the bottle will carry the name of a well-known vineyard or commune or district or shipper, a vintage date, and the phrase "Appellation Controlee," indicating all government requirements have been met. Rarely will a French wine be identified by the name of the grape. However, as you will see, the same outstanding wine grapes are used all over the world to produce quality wines.

In France, the major wine producing regions are Bordeaux, Burgundy, the Rhone Valley (Côtes du Rhône), the Loire Valley, Champagne, and Alsace.

The wines of the Bordeaux region have been famous since Roman times, and they are just as famous today. Bordeaux wines come in the high-shouldered bottle shown in Figure 6.9a. A wine spoken of as "a Bordeaux" means a red wine from Bordeaux; it is also referred to by the British term **claret.**

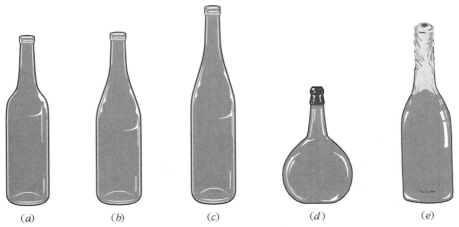

(a) (b) (c) (d) (e)

Figure 6.9 Traditional bottle shapes: (a) Bordeaux, (b) Burgundy, (c) Rhine, Mosel, Alsace, (d) Bocksbeutel (German Franken, Chile, Portugal), (e) Champagne and other sparkling wines (heavy, with a wired cork).

Bordeaux produces a range of wines, from connoisseurs' dreams to every-day table wines, from more than 50 distinct regions within the Bordeaux area.

Nearly all red Bordeaux is made by blending grapes—mainly Cabernet Sauvignon, Merlot, and Cabernet Franc. The style of the wine depends on the blend, which varies from one producer to another. There are two distinct production areas, divided by the Gironde River. On one side, in the Medoc and Graves districts, Cabernet is the main grape. On the other side of the river, in Pomerol and St. Emilion and numerous satellite zones, Merlot and Cabernet Franc tend to dominate the grape blend.

Most prestigious are the Bordeaux wines named for the chateau (vineyard) that produces them. The best wine from each vintage is usually bottled at the vineyard and carries the phrase "Mis en bouteille au chateau" (literally, "placed in the bottle at the vineyard"), or "Mise du chateau." The rest of a vintage may be sold to a shipper (negociant) who blends wines from various vineyards to sell under the shipper's label or under a registered brand name (monopole).

At the top of the Bordeaux quality pyramid are the **classified growths,** chateau wines that were recognized as the leaders as long ago as 1855, when an official classification of French wines was ordered by Napoleon III. Such chateau wines as Lafite-Rothschild, Latour, Margaux, Mouton-Rothschild, and Haut-Brion are known as the "first growths" and are the most prestigious. There are 65 classified growths in the Medoc and Graves, ranging from first growths to fifth growths. In St. Emilion, 74 chateaux are classified as Premiers Grand Crus Classes or Grand Crus Classes, but they are little known because most are too small to produce much.

There are also plenty of Bordeaux reds, either generic or brand name (monopole), blended from wines produced anywhere in the large Bordeaux zone or from vineyards in a specific commune—St. Julien, St. Estephe, and others. Some of these wines are outstanding.

In addition to the reds for which it is famous, Bordeaux produces white wines from the Semillon and Sauvignon grapes. Those from the Graves district are fresh, dry, full-bodied, and fruity. Those from the Sauternes district to the south, though made from the same grapes, are very different; they are extraordinarily sweet and rich. These qualities come from the warm climate and especially from the method of harvesting. The grapes are left on the vines until they are overripe and develop a special mold, *Botrytis cinerea*, known as "noble rot" (*pourriture noble* in French, *Edelfaule* in German). This mold dries the grapes, concentrating their sugar and flavor. Each bunch is individually selected at its peak of desirability; a vineyard may be hand-picked in this way as many as eight times. The wines from Sauternes are served at the end of a meal, either with dessert or as dessert. Of them all, Chateau d' Yquem is the ultimate in fame and fortune.

Burgundy wines also belong on a fine wine list. The French wines referred to as Burgundy are the classical reds made from the Pinot Noir grape in the

Cote d' Or region. Like the Bordeaux, they are wines of great character and long life. They are shipped in the Burgundy bottle shown in Figure 6.9b.

Burgundy vineyards are also classified for quality; the magic phrase here is **Grand Cru** (great growth). Of the Grand Cru vineyards, the most famous are Romanee-Conti, Clos de Vougeot, and Chambertin, followed by certain hyphenated Chambertins and Musigny.

Knowing what sort of wine lies beneath the label of a Burgundy wine is a far more complicated business than it is for a Bordeaux wine. In Bordeaux, each vineyard (chateau) is owned by a single family or corporation; but in Burgundy a single vineyard may be owned by many individuals, each with a few acres or perhaps just a few rows of vines. Each vineyard is an Appellation Controlee, and each owner/grower is therefore entitled to make an individual wine with the name of the vineyard on the label. Thus there may be great variation in quality depending on the skill of the grower, and conceivably as many as 5 to 50 different wines of the same name and vintage could come from a single vineyard. Likewise the phrase "Mis en bouteille au domaine" ("bottled at the vineyard") does not guarantee quality or consistency, since there is no uniformity among growers' products even when they *are* bottled at the vineyard.

For this reason it has become the practice for Burgundy shippers to buy wines from several growers in a vineyard and make a wine carrying the vineyard label on which they stake their own reputation.

What a shipper's wine offers is consistency, but often at the expense of individual vineyard character. Many shippers make wines that tend to taste almost like each other, in the shipper's "house style," regardless of the commune from which the grapes come. Thus they play a valuable role in providing readily available, fairly predictable, decent wine—just not the very best. The best Burgundies come from individual growers and are made in miniscule quantities, and knowing one's way around among them is one of the most challenging tasks any wine expert can face.

The district of Beaujolais is also part of the Burgundy region, but it produces a very different wine from the classical Burgundy. The wine called Beaujolais, made from the Gamay grape, is a fresh, light red with a short life span of two to three years. It too is shipped in the Burgundy-shaped bottle shown in Figure 6.9b. Unlike most red wines, it is often served at a cool cellar temperature. The best Beaujolais is identified on its label as "Cru Beaujolais," along with the appellation of the commune it comes from. Next in rank is the Appellation Beaujolais-Villages.

The arrival of Nouveau Beaujolais (or Beaujolais Noveau) in America on the third Thursday of every November is one of wine's charming celebratory traditions. The young wine, barely two months old, is the first wine of the new harvest; it is meant to be uncorked and consumed immediately. Always served chilled, it is grapey, refreshing, and fun. It has a very short life span, of only about four months.

Although Burgundy is probably best known for its red wines, the whites, made from the Chardonnay grape, can be magnificent, among the best white wines in the world. One of the reasons Chardonnay has become so desirable all over the world is the success of the Burgundian prototype.

The term "white Burgundy" encompasses several rather different wines, even though all are made from Chardonnay grapes. The vineyard of Montrachet and its neighbors are one group, Macon wines are another, and Chablis wines are a third.

Montrachet is a small vineyard that produces a white wine of great prestige and excellence. The vineyard is so famous that its neighbors have hyphenated its name to theirs. Other well-known white Burgundies from this region are Meursault and Corton-Charlemagne. It is said Charlemagne himself planted this latter vineyard. As with the red Burgundies, there are many small growers in these vineyards, and a reliable producer/shipper rather than estate bottling is often the key to quality.

Of the white wines of the Macon region, the best known in this country is **Pouilly-Fuissé** (POO-ee fweh-SAY). Other Macon wines with a district or village appellation are also imported and are often better values.

Chablis is a Burgundy region that produces an entirely different white wine from the others, though made from the same Chardonnay grape. In fact it is seldom called a white Burgundy; it is simply called Chablis. It is pale, greenish, light, and very dry, with a taste described as flinty; it is most definitely different from the typical, sweet American "chablis." There are several classifications: Grand Cru, **Premier Cru,** and Chablis, in descending order. Quality varies greatly from one vintage to another because of the weather. This cool northern climate does not often give the grapes a chance to ripen fully, resulting in a light, crisp personality in the wines.

Red wines from the Rhone valley—the Côtes du Rhône district—have recently become very interesting to Americans, especially that adventurous group that likes to try something new and different (Figure 6.10). These wines are far from "new." The best-known Chateauneuf-du-Pape vineyard is said to have been planted in the fourteenth century by Pope Clement V, the first of the French popes who moved the papacy temporarily from Rome to Avignon, hence the name, which means Chateau of the Pope. But these wines are different in several ways. They are made from blends of many different, mostly unfamiliar grapes; a single bottle of Chateauneuf-du-Pape may contain as many as 13 grape varieties. They are big, deep-red, full-bodied, alcoholic wines that must be aged many years before they are ready to drink. And they have a richness that derives from the grapes ripening in the long hot growing season of southern France.

Other fine Rhone reds, such as Hermitage and Cote Rotie, are similar in style and pedigree. The district is also the home of Tavel, a fresh, dry but fruity rosé wine.

Another group of white wines comes from the Loire valley. The best known are Pouilly-Fumé (POO-ee fyoo-MAY), often confused with Pouilly-Fuissé but very different; plus Sancerre, and Vouvray. Sancerre and Pouilly-Fumé both

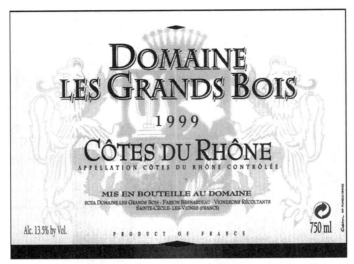

Figure 6.10 Wines from the Côtes du Rhône region have become popular. Label courtesy of Weygandt Metzler Importing, Ltd.

come from the Sauvignon Blanc grape so popular in the United States today. Although this is also the grape of white Bordeaux, these Loire wines have a crisper, fruitier style. Vouvray is made in several styles, from bone-dry and fruity to sweet to sparkling.

Rosé d' Anjou is also from the Loire valley. One of the most popular rosés until the advent of White Zinfandel, it is made primarily from Gamay grapes. It has a charming pink color and a touch of sweetness.

The Champagne district of France produces the sparkling white wine that bears its name. All French Champagnes are blends of wines from several vineyards and carry the name of the shipper/producer rather than a vineyard label. They are made from both white and dark grapes unless they are labeled *Blanc de Blancs,* literally, "white from whites." A French Champagne carries a vintage date only if it is from an exceptionally good year.

A Champagne label indicates its degree of sweetness. The French terms may confuse the novice. They range from:

- Brut or Nature (the driest)
- Extra Sec (extra dry, meaning it contains a small amount of added sugar)
- Sec (dry, which actually indicates slight sweetness)
- Demi-Sec (semi-dry, which actually is quite sweet)
- Doux (very sweet; this style is seldom made so this label designation is seldom used).

These French terms should appear on a wine-list entry, and servers should be familiar with them. Most of today's Champagnes are Brut or Extra Dry.

Figure 6.11 A Gewurztraminer wine from the Alsace region. Label courtesy of Weygandt Metzler Importing, Ltd.

Nearly every Champagne house, besides making a nonvintage Champagne, also makes vintage-dated Champagnes (in good years only) and a super-premium wine that is tremendously prestigious, not to mention expensive. Dom Perignon and Cristal are two of the best known.

The wine region of Alsace lies across the Rhine from Germany, and grows many of the same grape varietals. Because of the district's cool climate, most of the wines are white. Chief among the grapes are Riesling (full-bodied, fruity, and slightly sweet) and Gewurztraminer (spicy and full-flavored). Unlike the wines of the rest of France, most of the Alsatian wines are varietals.

Alsace wines are big, firm, flavorful, and dry. They are unlike any other wines in the world, and they have a small but loyal following of fans. Because they are not especially stylish, they are also excellent values (Figure 6.11). You'll find them in the distinctive tall, slender green bottle required by law. It is similar to the bottle shape for German wines and looks more German than French.

Wines from Germany

The wine regions of Germany lie in cool, northerly climates, not at all friendly to the growing of red grapes. Nearly all the winemaking effort of the entire country is dedicated to white wines. Grapes such as Riesling and Silvaner, which flourish in cool climates, form the backbone of Germany's production, along with Muller-Thurgau, a hybrid of the two developed by the Germans

Figure 6.12 A Riesling from Germany. Label courtesy of Classical Wines of Spain.

to suit their climate. But all the great wines derive from the noble Riesling (Figure 6.12).

The prototype of German wines for the past 50 years has been fruity but acidic wines, light in body and low in alcohol (about 9 to 10 percent), which combine a pleasant sweetness with a naturally high level of crispness. Today there is a movement in Germany toward dry and somewhat dry wines. (On the label, *trocken* means dry; *halb-trocken* means off-dry.) These have been slow to make headway in the American market, where we still expect German wines to be at least slightly sweet. Germany's range of quality extends from ordinary, inexpensive wines to some of the greatest white wines in the world. Unfortunately, the best-selling wines outside Germany are often at the lower end of the scale.

Germany has a rigorous system of quality classification and control. There are three basic quality categories:

- *Tafelwein* (table wine), the most ordinary wine. It has to have sugar added for fermentation to make up for the inadequate ripeness of the grapes. It is seldom exported.

- *Qualitatswein* (QbA), translated as "Quality wine from a designated region." This may mean a single vineyard, a group of vineyards, or a group of villages. These wines have also had sugar added for fermentation.
- *Qualitatswein mit Pradikat* (QmP), translated as "Quality wine with special attributes." The major attribute is the ripeness of the grape.

There are five subcategories (pradikats) arranged in ascending order according to the ripeness of the grapes at harvest:

- **Kabinett.** This wine is made from grapes ripened in the ordinary manner, but sweet enough to ferment without adding sugar.
- **Spatlese.** This wine is made from fully ripened grapes late-picked after the official harvest date.
- **Auslese.** This wine is made from particularly ripe grapes picked selectively in bunches at any time during the harvest. Auslese wines can be very sweet (dessert-style), or only somewhat sweet.
- **Beerenauslese.** This wine is made from perfectly ripened grapes chosen one by one.
- **Trockenbeerenauslese.** This wine is made from individually selected over-ripe grapes that have shriveled with the "noble rot" that, as you've learned, the Germans call *Edelfaule*. The term *trocken* (dry) refers to the fact that the grapes have dried, not that the wine is dry.

A special category of wine is Eiswein, a very rare and expensive wine made from grapes that have actually been allowed to freeze on the vine, concentrating their sweetness and richness. The QmP wines ascend in order in quality, availability, prestige, and price. Kabinetts are typically light and fruity. Spatleses have more body and sweetness. Ausleses are richer, fuller, and usually sweeter than Spatleses. Beerenausleses are very rich, top-quality wines. A Trockenbeerenauslese is the ultimate in a rich, luscious wine—the German equivalent of a French Sauternes.

There are 11 wine regions in Germany, all of them surrounding rivers that moderate the climate. The wines we know as Mosel come from the vineyards lining the Mosel River and its tributaries, the Saar and the Ruwer. Because ripeness is a particular challenge in the Mosel region, the style of the wine is characteristically light, delicate, and fresh, with lemony fruit flavor and high natural acidity.

Several of Germany's wine regions are named for the Rhine River: Rheingau, Rheinhessen, and Rheinpfalz. The most famous is the Rheingau, Germany's smallest region, which is crammed with top vineyards. Its wines are riper and fuller than Mosels, yet steely and firm. Among the famous vineyards here are Schloss Johannisberger and Schloss Vollrads.

The wines from the Rhine and Mosel valleys together account for most U.S. imports of German wines. You can tell them apart at a glance by the color of the bottle—brown for Rhine and green for Mosel. Both bottles have a typical tall tapered shape, like a stretched-out Burgundy bottle, as seen in Figure 6.9c. A green Bocksbeutel (Figure 6.9d) is used for wines from the Franken region.

Wines from Italy

Italy vies with France as the largest producer of wine in the world, but its wines are considerably less well known in America and often represent excellent values. Most Italian wines come from native Italian grapes that are not grown anywhere else in the world. Italy also makes plenty of wines from well-known grapes such as Chardonnay and Cabernet, and these wines are often varietally labeled. The style and character of Italy's wines vary tremendously from one region to another, depending on climate, grape variety, and local custom.

Part of the problem with Italian wines "catching on" in the United States is that the labels can be difficult to read. Knowing three label designations may be helpful in determining overall quality:

- *Riserva* means reserve, and in Italy, it legally means that the winery has aged the wine longer than the standard minimums. It sometimes means the wine has a slightly greater alcohol content than nonreserve wines of the same type.
- *Classico* means the wine comes directly from a particular wine-producing region. If it's a Chianti Classico, for instance, it comes straight from Chianti, not a neighboring area.
- *Classico Superiore* means both of the above, that the wine is from that "classico" part of the region *and* that it has a higher alcohol content.

Most of Italy's quality wine production is governed by an appellation system called Denominazione di Origine Controllata, or DOC. This system recognizes and defines more than 200 types of Italian wine from specific geographic areas. However, unlike France's appellation system, which actually classifies individual vineyards, Italy's laws do not classify wines by quality.

A high level of DOC status is DOCG, where the G stands for *garantita* (guaranteed), because every wine must pass an official taste test before being sold. The DOCG system builds in incentives and risks that encourage producers to make quality wine. There are currently six DOCG wines: Barolo, Barbaresco, Chianti, Brunello di Montalcino, Vino Nobile di Montepulciano, and a white wine, Albana di Romagna.

Some of Italy's best wines, however, exist outside the framework of DOC, often because their producers have chosen not to participate in the system. They are technically merely *vini da tavola* (table wines), but their high price tags are a clue that these are serious wines, not to be taken lightly.

Of the many wine regions in Italy, three are of particular importance to American restaurateurs. They are: Piedmont and Veneto in northern Italy, and Tuscany farther south.

In northwest Italy, Piedmont borders on France and produces two of Italy's greatest reds, Barolo and Barbaresco. These wines come from the native Nebbiolo grape. They are big, robust reds of great distinction, Barbaresco being somewhat more delicate than Barolo. In this part of Italy, it is common to label wines with individual vineyard names in addition to the name of the wine itself.

Piedmont is also home to Asti Spumante, a delicious sparkling white wine made by the Charmat (bulk) method from Muscat grapes. It captures the fruity freshness of the grapes and is sweet, making it more appropriate with dessert than other sparkling wines.

In northeastern Italy, Veneto is famous for the trio of wines from Verona: Soave, a white; Bardolino, a light red; and Valpolicella, a medium-bodied red. They are all made from blends of local native Italian grapes.

Along with its two neighboring regions, Friuli and Trentino, the Veneto also makes many varietally labeled Cabernets and Chardonnays. Because the weather is relatively cool, and Italians prefer their wines slightly on the acidic side, to accompany food better, these will usually be lighter than their counterparts from other parts of the world. Pinot Grigio is a popular white wine from these areas.

Tuscany is Italy's other great red wine region. It is the home of Chianti, a DOCG wine that has been improving its quality and image since the mid-1970s. Chianti is a blend of four grapes, predominantly Sangiovese, a native grape grown throughout central Italy. Once known as a rough young wine in a cute, straw-covered bottle, it is now taken more seriously in the wine community, and is aged in a Bordeaux-shaped bottle. Chianti Riserva, for example, is aged at least three years. The best Chianti is from the Chianti Classico district, often identified by a black rooster on the neck of the bottle.

Another DOCG wine from Tuscany is the red Brunello di Montalcino, made from a type of Sangiovese called Brunello. It is considered Italy's most expensive red.

Many producers in Tuscany are now making premium-quality reds and whites that are not DOC, in the manner mentioned earlier. These wines are often made with Cabernet and Chardonnay, using the most sophisticated winemaking techniques. As a result, they are richer and fuller than the Cabernets and Chardonnays from the northeast, and considerably more expensive. You will often find enough information for two labels on an imported wine. In Figure 6.13, the winery's information about the product, and details about the U.S. firm that imports it are shown.

Of the many wines made in other Italian wine districts, Orvieto, Verdicchio, and Frascati (all made from native grape varieties) are popular in the United States. All three are light, crisp whites. There are also good white varietals made from Verdicchio, Pinot Bianco (Pinot Blanc), and Pinot Grigio

Brand name

Name of wine

DOCG (controlled name of origin)

Bottled on the producer's premises

Importer

Contents

Country of origin

Wine type

Alcohol content

Figure 6.13 A typical Italian wine label. Label courtesy of Classical Wines of Spain.

grapes. A varietal of a different sort is Lambrusco, an off-dry grapey red with a hint of sparkle. It is not considered a fine wine, but it is easy to drink, and is among the best-selling Italian wines in America.

Wines from Spain

Spain has its own wine appellation system. In it, there are more than 50 Denominacion de Origen, or DOs. Wineries in Spain are called *bodegas* (bo-DAY-guss), so you'll see that word as part of the name on some labels (Figure 6.14). There are three other clues to the overall quality of a Spanish wine: Ordinary table wines are called Crianza (kree-ON-zah); a little bit better-quality wines (usually aged longer) are called Reserva (reserve); and the top-of-the-line wines, selected only in the best growing years, are labeled Gran Reserva.

Figure 6.14 A Spanish wine label. Label courtesy of Classical Wines of Spain.

The most famous red Spanish wine is Rioja (ree-OH-hah), a smooth and elegant wine, most often a blend of the Tempranillo and Grenache grapes (called *Garnacha* in Spain). With flavors reminiscent of Cabernet and Pinot Noir, Tempranillo has become popular enough with wine aficionados that some Spanish wineries also now bottle 100 percent Tempranillo. Although prices have been on the rise, Rioja continues to deliver exceptional quality for a low price. There is also white Rioja.

From the same grapes, Ribera del Duero (rih-BEAR-ah dell DWAIR-oh) is similar to Rioja, but "bigger" and more intensely flavored. The Tempranillo is sometimes blended with Cabernet Sauvignon grapes for this hearty wine.

Near Barcelona, the Penedes region is becoming increasingly important as a source of red and white table wines, sometimes made from world-class grapes like Cabernet and Chardonnay. Its Methode Champenoise sparkling wines, called *Cava* (KAH-vuh), are extremely good values. The names Codorniu and Freixenet are found on many a moderately priced American wine list. And in the Navarra region (where they run with the bulls at Pamplona!), there are some excellent varietals made, as well as a rosé wine known as Rosado.

Spain is the original home of sherry, a fortified wine made for centuries in the Jerez district using time-honored methods and strict controls that yield a connoisseur's product. Its style ranges from crisp and lean to rich and sweet depending on production methods. It is one of the world's top aperitif wines.

Wine from Other Countries

Australia is a booming producer of relatively inexpensive, good quality table wines. Its native Shiraz grape (known elsewhere in the world as Syrah) makes wonderful, full-bodied reds. The three southernmost states of Australia—South Australia, Victoria, and New South Wales—have the coolest climates, and are responsible for most of the country's wine output. The grape harvest occurs in March instead of in the fall, since the seasons are opposite in that hemisphere.

For an Australian wine to be labeled a particular varietal, it must contain at least 80 percent of that grape type. If it's a blend, the percentages of each grape used must be listed on the label.

New Zealand, with a climate considerably cooler than its neighbor Australia, releases some impressive, crisp Sauvignon Blancs and Chardonnays for export. The Pinot Noir production is also causing wine aficionados to take notice.

Portugal has its own appellation system, called Indicacao da Proveniencia Regulamentada (IPR; Indication of Regulated Provenance). Portugal is famous for the great fortified wines, Port and Madeira. For years, the only others to cross the ocean for sale in the United States were a few brand-name rosés, pleasant but undistinguished. More recently this has changed, and you'll find some great values for by-the-glass pouring. The reds labeled Vinho Verde are particular bargains; the designation Quinta on a wine label means the same as a chateau or domain in France.

In South America, the nations of Chile and Argentina are becoming recognized as important wine producers. Chile grows the same varietals as the United States, including Sauvignon Blanc, Chardonnay, Cabernet Sauvignon, and Merlot. Some excellent bargain-priced varietals are imported to this country from Chile. Argentina is the world's fifth largest wine producer. The Argentinian wines that have received the most acclaim are reds made from the Malbec grape, which was transplanted long ago from Bordeaux, and Cabernet Sauvignon.

Wines from many other countries make it onto ethnic wine lists or onto shelves of wine merchants. They may be from South Africa, Switzerland, Austria, Greece, Yugoslavia, Romania, Bulgaria, or other nations. If you're curious about them, first-hand knowledge is as close as the bottle and the corkscrew.

In the following chapter, you'll continue your quest for wine knowledge, by learning to make a profitable wine list and to correctly serve wine to your guests for their enjoyment.

SUMMING UP

The art and science of winemaking is thousands of years old, yet many people, even those who enjoy drinking wines, are relatively unfamiliar with the wide range of products available.

No matter where they are made, wine labels all identify the producer, the year in which the grapes were picked (the vintage) and the type of grapes used (the varietal). The percentage of alcohol must also be included on the label.

Wines can be red, white, or rosé (blush) in color; and they can be still (not bubbly) or sparkling (bubbly).

This chapter introduced you to the major grape varietals used around the world and to the winemaking process. Grapes are picked, crushed, and fermented. Yeast is added to the crushed grapes, and as it feeds on the sugar in the grapes, it creates alcohol and carbon dioxide. When fermentation stops, the wine is stored until it stabilizes and settles; then the storage process continues in stainless-steel or oak casks, depending on the type of wine and the desired results. In sparkling wine or Champagne, the carbon dioxide is captured in the wine bottle instead of being released into the air, making the wine naturally bubbly.

Tasting wine involves much more than sipping it. You should look at a wine, swirl it around inside the glass, and smell it. The swirling motion allows a bit of the alcohol to dissipate, making the smell more intense.

Wines are named for their grape varietal (Chardonnay or Sauvignon Blanc); or they are given a generic name (like Meritage or Table Wine) that signifies a blend of several different types of grapes; or they are labeled with the name of a prestigious producer (Opus One or Tinto Pesquera); or, in some countries, their place of origin is used on the label (like Condrieu or Chateau Margaux). It might be a town or the winery name.

Wine labels may seem difficult to understand, but they are not so mysterious after you learn the basics and taste enough to notice a few of their distinguishing characteristics.

POINTS TO PONDER

1. What are the four basic factors that go into making any type of wine? (Extra credit or discussion questions: Which of these four factors do you think is the most important, and why? Which is least important, and why?)

2. What does a wine's vintage tell you? Is the vintage date related to the quality of the wine; if so, how?

3. What do the skins of the grape have to do with the final wine product?

4. How does Champagne production differ from still wine production?

5. Why do winemakers sometimes blend different types of grapes?

6. Why do you swirl a wine before tasting it?

7. List two things that you can learn from the color of a wine.

8. Name and briefly describe four of the characteristics of wine that you are examining when you taste it.

9. What is the difference between generic chablis and French Chablis?

10. What information should you be able to learn from most wine labels, no matter what their country of origin?

TERMS OF THE TRADE

aperitif wine	glycerin	Riesling
aroma	Grand Cru	sake
aromatized	Graves	Sancerre
balance	Grenache	Sangiovese
Barolo	Lambrusco	Sauternes
Chablis	lees	Sauvignon Blanc
chapitalization	legs	Sekt
Chardonnay	Merlot	Semillon
Charmat bulk process	Methode Champenoise	Shiraz
Chenin Blanc	monopole	Spumante
Chianti	Muller-Thurgau	sulfites
claret	Muscat	Syrah
classified growth	Nebbiolo	tannins
dessert wine	Pinot Blanc	Tempranillo
enology	Pinot Noir	varietal
Fumé Blanc	Pouilly Fuissé	vintage
Gamay Beaujolais	Pouilly Fumé	Zinfandel
Gewurztraminer	Premier Cru	

CHAPTER 7

Wine Sales and Service

Now that you've been introduced to the complexities of wine, you can understand how it might become a lucrative part of your business. But that can happen only if you know what to sell and how to sell it. You've already learned that most people expect wine to taste good, to complement their food choices, and to be a good value. The key to creating a successful wine sales program is to understand your designated clientele and market.

In this chapter, you'll learn how to . . .

- Create a wine list (select and price the wines you want to sell).
- Train your service staff to recommend and serve wines.
- Increase your wine sales.
- Open and store wine properly.

CREATING A WINE LIST

Before you begin to create a wine list, you first should ask yourself, "Do I *need* a wine list at all for my establishment?" Many inexpensive and midscale bars and restaurants serve only a few house wines by the glass or carafe and make a very good profit in this uncomplicated and inexpensive way. Usually, they offer just two or three wines—a white, a blush, and a red—with familiar names and general appeal. This simple selection, typically offered along with an assortment of beer and soft drinks, is very appropriate for certain types of casual dining situations.

If you are going to sell wine by the bottle, your first consideration is your type of clientele. This will dictate the overall character of your list. You can keep it short, simple, and inexpensive; make it extensive, expensive, and loaded with prestigious choices; or settle somewhere in between.

The second consideration is your food menu. If you serve fine French cuisine, clearly you will want to choose well-known French wines. If you have a steak house, you will concentrate on red wines, with a few hearty whites for people who don't care for red wine, and perhaps a rosé for people who want a compromise. If you serve Italian food, you will want wines from Italy, in addition to some familiar American names. If you specialize in seafood, you will feature white wines, with perhaps one or two light reds to go with salmon, maybe a Beaujolais from France or a Pinot Noir from Oregon.

The third guideline is price compatibility. Your wine choices should suit not only your food menu, but also your menu prices. The average customer does not want to pay more for the wine than for the dinner check. In practice, the best sales result when the wine costs approximately one-fourth of the typical total check. You should also stock a selection of wines in several price ranges. Wine expert Kevin Zraly, who teaches classes in New York City and was the founder of New York's former Windows on the World Wine School, suggests a list that is 60 percent midpriced wines, 20 percent inexpensive, and 20 percent high-dollar.

Another point to consider is availability. Are you going to invest in a large stock that "sits on cash" in the cellar until it is sold or can you get regular selections in small quantities from your supplier? You don't want to print a list that will soon be full of wines you can no longer obtain.

If you are just beginning to offer wine as part of your service, it is better to start with a short list of readily available wines, including a sparkling wine—say, 15 to 20 brands altogether—and to buy frequently, a little at a time, until you find out what sells. A long wine list doesn't necessarily generate more sales than a short one, since it can be intimidating to many customers. Remember: It is easy to add to your list but difficult to get rid of a wine that customers don't seem to care for. A limited, moderately priced wine list usually assures favorable sales and regular inventory turnover.

Speaking of inventory, your final consideration—and a major one—is storage. No matter how small your selection, you must have a separate room (ideally, a cellar) to stock cases of it, depending on your needs. Fine wine should never be stored in your kitchen, where the average temperature is too hot. Wine stored this way can develop leaky corks and go bad or age too quickly. Wines served too warm are a turnoff to most customers, and the more knowledgeable ones may even mention it or send back their glass.

If you want a wine list to go with an expensive menu and a knowledgeable clientele, it is essential to find an expert to help you develop your list and advise you on purchasing. Critical factors to consider are the cellar space needed and the capital that must be invested. If space and funds are limited, wines that mature early and are good right now are the best choice. Pricing for this type of list may not be so closely tied to menu pricing, since wine enthusiasts are more likely to tolerate, and even expect, a higher markup.

Taste the wines you are considering for your list; ask your serving personnel to taste them, too. It will greatly increase their interest in selling wines if they have been in on the selection. Most suppliers will arrange comparative tastings, at least of moderately priced wines. But beware of imposing your own tastes on your customers. You might hold a wine tasting for a group of your regular customers to see which wines are well liked.

Matching Wine with Food

Andrea Immer, one of the world's nine master sommeliers, and author and longtime beverage director, calls wine "a love letter to food." Why? Acidity that is a natural characteristic of wine primes the customer's taste buds for food. In cooking, this is why so many chefs use acidic ingredients—mustard, lemon, tomato, vinegar. They enhance other flavors and work well to increase our enjoyment of food.

Food and wine consumed together should "marry" well. That is, the two should be in balance; neither should dominate the other. Each should bring out different flavors in the other, and the combination should taste better than either one alone, thus multiplying the total enjoyment. The wrong combination can diminish the food or the wine or both.

Table 7.1 lists traditional guidelines for serving wine with food. Overall, they are sound, but it is hard to apply them in individual situations, because today's menu items often blend so many different spices, flavors, and ethnic styles that rules are hard to make and harder to follow. Furthermore, one dry white wine or one hearty red may differ widely from another. Which one will provide the balance needed?

The only way to determine how to match a wine to a given menu item is to taste the two together. If possible, from the beginning, plan your wine list with your menu in mind. You can sit down with your wine expert and taste each item on your menu with wines that the expert suggests. Include your kitchen staff and servers, too. Involvement is contagious; and keep in mind that they are part of your "sales team," whether they are behind the scenes or interacting with the customers.

Table 7.1

Which Wine with Which Food? Starting Points

Menu Item	Wine Suggestion[a]
Appetizer	Champagne, dry white wine, dry sherry
Salad	No wine
Fish or seafood	Dry or medium-dry white
Beef	Hearty red
Lamb	Hearty red
Veal	Light red or full-bodied white
Ham or pork	Dry or medium-dry white or rosé
Turkey, duck, chicken	Full-bodied white or light red
Game (venison, pheasant, wild duck)	Hearty red
Lasagna, spaghetti, pizza	Hearty red
Cheeses, full-flavored	Hearty red,[b] sweet white (with roquefort)
Cheeses, mild	Sherry, port, madeira, mild table wines of any type
Desserts, pastries, fruits, mousses	Semisweet sparkling wine, sweet white table wine

[a] The diner's choice takes precedence. If more than one wine is to be served, the general rules are white before red, light before hearty, and dry before sweet.

[b] Some experts disagree.

If you already have a wine list, you can pick the best matches from what you have, adding new wines if you discover you need to. You can simplify the whole wine sales process by matching wines with foods in advance, and putting this information right on your menu.

Presenting Wine Selections

The wine list is a silent salesperson for your wine, just as your menu is for your food. There are several formats for presenting your wine list. The chalkboard is the simplest; it is typically used in wine bars, especially for wine by the glass. It has a nice air of continental informality and gives the impression that the proprietor gives daily personal attention to the wine menu. The advantage of the chalkboard for the proprietor is that he or she does not have to make long-range commitments in print. You can take full advantage of your wine suppliers' sales and discounts, and "feature" these wines on your board.

The **table tent** has similar advantages. It is appropriate in informal restaurants serving only a few wines. It can also be used to promote specials or new offerings.

A more formal list—a more permanent, printed one—is given to one person at the table, usually the host, since wine by the bottle is typically ordered for the whole party. Such a list comes in two common formats: a printed card (or *carte*), similar to a menu, or pages folded inside a nice-looking cover. The latter format has several advantages: you can change the inside pages easily as your offerings change, reusing the more expensive cover. This type of list is often easier for the diner to handle than a single, oversized card. And depending on your state laws, your wine supplier may provide you with the permanent cover or even pay for the printing of the inner pages. If not, today's computers and printers make it easy to print your own lists, changing them as often as you need to or to highlight daily specials or food/wine pairings.

Expensive restaurants, especially those featuring fine wines, often use a multipage wine list inside an embossed cover, typically designed to coordinate with the establishment's overall décor. Sometimes each wine is listed on a single page, with a copy of the wine label attached to the page. The page is then inserted into a plastic sleeve. These sleeves can be pricey, but they are attractive and enable quick changes as your inventory does.

There are advantages to pricing wines by the glass on your wine list as well as by the bottle. Often, one customer or a couple would rather buy one or two glasses of wine than a full bottle they might not finish. Wine by the glass is also a good option for people eating together but who prefer different wines. Perhaps most important, by-the-glass sales can prompt people to experiment, to try new and perhaps more expensive wines than they'd usually buy. If they like it, they will buy it again, perhaps by the bottle. Wines by the glass can also be very profitable, which we will discuss in a moment.

What your wine list says about your wines should be clear and honest and useful. It should include key information relevant to making a choice, such as the place of origin and the vintage year. You can arrange your wine list in a number of different ways, but most good lists group the wines according to type: reds, whites, rosés, sparkling wines, dessert wines. If you offer wines from different countries, you might list them by country and then by "color" or varietal. Another alternative is to list the wines within their subcategories, from the sweetest to the driest, or vice versa. Customers and servers will find this handy. One line on the menu can instantly inform anyone who reads it.

Each wine should have a brief description of its chief characteristics—dry, slightly sweet, or truly sweet; delicate or medium or intense in flavor; light-bodied or full or medium in body. And there's no reason the wording should be pretentious. Your wine list should show imagination and enthusiasm; it should make the whole subject of wine simple and inviting, not formidable and exclusive.

Hire a writer with some wine knowledge, research the wine publications and experts' descriptions, or ask your suppliers to help create wording that will make the wines sound as good as they taste: "delightfully fresh and fruity," "a memorable bouquet," and so on. Perhaps most helpful, mention what food each wine complements. If you are catering to connoisseurs, give all the essential information that will establish the wine's pedigree. Your wine expert will help you with this.

A **bin number** for each wine should precede its name on the list. No, you don't have to actually store your wine in bins! But numbering the wines serves three important purposes. It makes it easier to organize and inventory them in your storage area, and easier for servers to find them. It also spares the customer embarrassment if the wine is unfamiliar to them or hard to pronounce. Figure 7.1 is a nicely developed wine list, chosen, annotated, numbered, and priced with the customer in mind.

Pricing Wines

A few words here about what to charge for wine. At this time, the standard markup in the industry for bars and restaurants is "2.5," which means you can charge two-and-a-half times what the bottle cost you to purchase from the supplier. For example, you would charge $15 for a bottle that cost you $6. Some establishments—country clubs, private clubs, fancy restaurants—get away with charging three times the wholesale cost, or even a bit more. That $6 bottle of wine would cost $18 or $20 at such places.

Within these guidelines, there are notable exceptions. For fine wines that wholesale at more than $35 per bottle, a triple markup is also normal. For rare wines, the sky's the limit. A connoisseur will sometimes pay dearly for the privilege of drinking something he or she cannot get elsewhere. In these cases, your supplier can suggest suitable prices.

For wines sold by the glass, the simplest way to price is to take the price you are charging for the bottle on your wine list and divide it by four, since you'll pour four glasses from each bottle. However, some bar owners and restaurateurs feel it is only fair to charge a bit more for the general hassle of offering individual glasses. Their aim is to pay for the bottle with the sale of the first glass. The other three glasses are pure profit. Of course, wine sales improve tremendously when prices are reasonable. There should always be a few by-the-glass selections under $5. The whole idea is to prompt the guest to try it.

Before you print your list, check everything carefully and be sure all items on it are spelled correctly. Your computer's spell-checking program is virtually worthless in the world of wine. When you're in doubt, look at the labels! If your list contains misspellings, your credibility is shot, especially with knowledgeable customers.

THE ROLE OF THE SERVER

Even a great wine list does not sell a great deal of wine by itself. No matter what their level of wine knowledge, most people depend on their server for some guidance. Many customers worry about choosing the wrong wine, mispronouncing the name, showing their ignorance, and wasting their money on something they might not enjoy, so rather than agonize over it, they simply avoid it.

WHITES

BIN #		BOTTLE
101	**Adler Fels Sauvignon Blanc** Assertive citric flavors make this a great accompaniment for most foods	22.00
102	**DeLoach Chardonnay** Dry, with soft fruit flavors and a lingering finish	24.00
103	**Penfold's Chardonnay** Light and fruity, with tropical undertones and a flowery bouquet	26.00
104	**Dr. Burklin/Wolf Estate Riesling** Ripe apple flavors; a white with depth and a strong finish	28.00
105	**R.H. Phillips Viognier** Smell this wine! Fresh, vibrant bouquet and strong fruit flavors set it apart	24.00
106	**Clerget Pouilly Fuisse** A classic French-style Chardonnay: austere and rich	33.00
107	**Cavit Pinot Grigio** Fresh, light and palate-pleasing, a "summer-style" white.	20.00

BLUSH WINES

BIN #		BOTTLE
201	**Sutter Home White Zinfandel** Fruity, pretty salmon color, perfect with lighter dishes.	15.00
202	**Bonny Doon Vin Gris ("Pink Wine")** A dry, food-style Rosé with a whimsical finish.	20.00

RED WINES

BIN #		BOTTLE
301	**Hess Select Cabernet Sauvignon** Rich flavors with cedar overtones; classic Napa style.	22.00
302	**Newland Merlot** A subtle red wine with finesse; layers of flavor.	35.00

RED WINES (continued)

BIN #		BOTTLE
303	**Ravenswood Vintner's Blend Zinfandel** Good body and nice raspberry flavors; strong finish.	26.00
304	**Saintsbury Pinot Noir "Garnet"** Soft, earthy flavors; great choice for wild game or fish.	30.00
305	**Chateau Bel Air (Haut Medoc)** A classic French Claret; soft, rich and flavorful.	30.00
306	**Georges du Boeuf Beaujolais Villages** Light, fruity, good-natured and all-purpose red.	20.00
307	**Rosemount Shiraz** Full-bodied but soft red from Australia.	24.00
308	**Lorinon Crianza Rioja** Spain's classic Tempranillo grape; spicy and earthy.	22.00
309	**Antinori Chianti** An Italian standard; peppery and tangy, lingering finish.	25.00

SPARKLING WINES

BIN #		BOTTLE
401	**Cristalino Brut Cava NV** Spain's Methode Champenoise sparkler, bright and fun.	18.00
402	**Korbel Brut NV** California's most popular sparkling wine.	22.00
403	**Moet & Chandon White Star** An elegant, semi-dry French Champagne	35.00

HOUSE WINES

By the glass		By the bottle
	Leaping Lizard (Sonoma, CA)	
$5	Chardonnay, Merlot, Cabernet	$18

Figure 7.1 A wine list for a moderately priced restaurant.

If, instead, customers felt they could comfortably discuss the choices with their server, they might be interested in trying a bottle or, at least, a glass. Unfortunately, most servers have their own concerns. Often, they, too, are intimidated by the wine list, or don't feel comfortable opening the bottle at the table, or wonder if they'll know how to answer guests' questions. It all sounds a little like a first date, doesn't it? But for the proprietor, if these concerns go unaddressed, countless opportunities to increase wine sales—and servers' tips—will go unmet.

The solution is to educate your serving staff about each wine on your list, beginning during the hiring process: include questions about wine knowledge in your employment interviews. And develop a well-organized and ongoing wine sales training program for your staff. It will enable them to answer customer questions; build their own enthusiasm for selling wine; assist in team-building efforts; and give them a sense of professionalism. When they realize that wine knowledge and sales techniques can increase their tips by $5 to $25 or more per shift, they will be eager to know more.

A good training program is carefully planned, scheduled regularly in short sessions (15 or 20 minutes a week), and consistently carried out. It must include tastings and retastings of every wine, and comparisons of one wine with another. Taste training should include learning to describe each wine in terms of color, degree of sweetness, body, flavor intensity, and other aspects of tasting discussed in Chapter 6. Most wine suppliers are happy to provide wine samples and the instruction, as long as they are given adequate advance notice. You should be involved, too, whether as instructor or as one of the trainees.

Your training sessions should also deal with the region of origin of each wine; the meaning of the information on the wine label, especially vintage date and specific quality category; and the name and characteristics of the grapes from which the wine is made. Talk about what menu items the wine goes well with—serve sample-sized food portions at the training session. Keep each lesson simple, focused on no more than two or three wines and a few key points. There is much to be learned, and too much at a time is discouraging.

The other thing that wine lessons should cover occasionally is the very practical business of wine etiquette—opening bottles, what to do if a cork breaks, what to say if a customer rejects a wine, and so on. Allow the servers to role-play and practice.

One restaurateur quizzes his staff about what they've learned in their wine sessions and rewards correct answers with scratch-off lottery tickets. The tickets cost him only $1 apiece, but they add a dimension of fun to the learning process.

Increasing Wine Sales

Take wine education one step farther by adding sales techniques. Any kind of special occasion—birthday, retirement, engagement, anniversary—calls for the server to suggest a sparkling wine or Champagne. An attentive server who notices the wine levels in customers' glasses, continues to refill them, mentions promptly that the bottle is empty and says, "Would you care for another bottle, or glass?" is giving good service and probably boosting sales as well. Selecting a couple of "featured wines" and mentioning them to just-seated guests will implant a sales suggestion. ("Featured" doesn't mean lowering prices, just that the wines are of special focus.) If guests decline dessert, your servers should be trained to ask, "Well, then, how about a dessert wine or nice glass of port?" Consider splitting the staff into teams and running a contest to boost wine sales, with a specific percentage and time frame in mind. Ask the wait staff to brainstorm with you for new wine sales ideas.

Many people in the wine business feel the potential for wine sales is only beginning to be realized. One segment of this growing market is the "drinking-less-but-drinking-better" customer. Many of them are interested in exploring wines, expanding their knowledge about them, and sampling good food/wine matches. They are candidates for food-and-wine dinners, during which foods and wines are matched for each course, at a fixed price. These may focus on the food and wine of a particular region, celebrate a special occasion, introduce wines from all over the world, or offer several samples of wines from a specific winery. Not only can such events be very profitable, they build customer interest in wine that can pay off in future sales.

These customers may also be intrigued by special wine tastings, which enhance your reputation as a place to enjoy wines. Your suppliers will often help organize a tasting event if there's a visiting winemaker in town, who can preside and instruct. Invite your own customers and entice the general public by contacting your local newspaper and radio stations a couple of weeks in advance of the event. Again, give a theme to the tasting: regional wines, varietal wines, wines from Australia, wines for the holidays. Serve light foods—baguettes, crackers, fruit and cheese—in conjunction with the tasting, with a delicious food-and-wine match as a finale. A "taste" of wine is 1 to 3 ounces per guest per taste, so you should be able to serve 8 to 10 people per 750-ml bottle.

Wine by the glass also appeals to this customer group, so they can sample a variety of wines in an evening. Systems that preserve wine in the opened bottle, which we'll discuss later in this chapter, make this possible for almost any wine. Above all else, the best way to expand wine sales to all kinds of customers is to develop your sales personnel. When you train them to know the wines on your list and the foods they accompany, you increase their enjoyment, their professionalism, their enthusiasm, and their value to you as employees, and ultimately, your profit margin.

SERVING WINES

There are few aspects of the gastronomic experience that are as steeped in tradition as wine service. Part of the pomp and circumstance is necessary to present certain wines at their physical best; other parts are strictly showmanship, done for fun, or out of respect for tradition. One thing is sure in the bar and restaurant business: Whether it is an inexpensive wine at the bar or the finest wine in the finest restaurant, customers generally expect and appreciate proper wine service.

Wineglasses

One of the "policy decisions" you must make as a bar owner or restaurateur is whether to bring the wineglass to the customer already poured or place an empty glass in front of the customer and pour as he or she watches. When brought already poured to the guest, the glass should hold 6 or 7 ounces of wine. The customer may feel cheated if the glass contains less than that, because it looks less than full. Ironically, by pouring in the presence of the guest, it is traditional to pour a little less—perhaps 5 ounces—since it is assumed the customer will want to swirl the wine in the glass.

The basic all-purpose wineglass has an 8- or 9-ounce **bowl,** and is made of clear glass with a long, thin stem and a base; but if wine service is going to be a priority in your business, you will probably want to invest in glasses with slightly larger (12-ounce) bowls. Even bigger ones are available—20- to 24-ounce bowls—but these are showy, expensive, and can be awkward to drink from. The reason for a larger glass is *not* to pour more wine per serving, but to allow for better swirling inside the bowl.

You should also consider having three different, but very basic, types of wineglasses: for reds, whites, and sparklers. Figure 7.2 shows the difference.

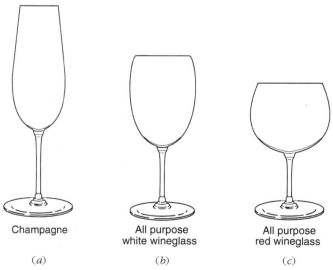

Champagne   All purpose   All purpose
                   white wineglass   red wineglass

(*a*)   (*b*)   (*c*)

Figure 7.2 Three types of wineglasses: (*a*) sparkling wineglass, (*b*) white wineglass, and (*c*) red wineglass. Courtesy of The Culinary Institute of America.

Glasses for reds have larger, more rounded bowls to allow for better swirling and sniffing of the wine. Glasses for whites are narrower at the top, which helps "hold in" their more delicate bouquets. Rosé wines are also usually served in white wineglasses. Tall, thin glasses (called **flutes**) are appropriate for Champagnes. Their very narrow opening keeps them colder longer and helps keep the bubbles from dissipating. (The wide, flat Champagne goblets that used to be so popular at weddings are no longer in vogue, and haven't been for a long time. If you inherited some, use them for dessert dishes, not for wine service.)

In addition to the three basic wineglass designs, there are many specialty glasses for different types of wine. Dessert wines are served in small after-dinner glasses, larger than a liqueur glass but much smaller than an ordinary wineglass, and generally without a stem. The glass is 4 to 6 ounces, but the serving size is half that. Ports and sherries are served in simple, straight-sided glasses—again, a 4- to 6-ounce size, for a 2- to 3-ounce serving (see Figure 7.3).

Port   Sherry
(a)   (b)

Figure 7.3 A port glass (a) and a sherry glass (b). Courtesy of The Culinary Institute of America.

Serving Wine at a Table

Proper table setting for wine service is important, both for etiquette and efficiency of service. To begin, your glassware should be kept sparkling clean, and staff should hold it by the stem and set it down before the customer in a manner that dignifies it as the graceful drink it is. The wineglass belongs to the right of the water glass, as shown in Figure 7.4. If setting tables with wineglasses in advance doesn't fit your image and your clientele, your servers should place them in the correct position when the wine is brought to the

(a)   (b)   (c)

Figure 7.4 Table setting with wineglasses. (a) One wine: a single, all-purpose glass. (b) Two wines: the white wine glass at the bottom, to be served first. (c) Three wines: an aperitif (white) at bottom right, a white above it for the fish course, a red at left for the entrée. If more than three wines are to be served, each additional glass is set in place at time of service. Empty glasses are removed. The extra glass at each setting is for water.

table. If more than one wine is to be served—for instance, at a formal multicourse banquet—the wineglasses are arranged in order of service with the first wine at the right; and each glass is removed at the end of the course the wine accompanied. Though, as just stated, a wineglass should generally be handled by its stem, a more informal way of carrying them is to hold them upside down by the base, with the stems between the fingers. You can carry as many as four in one hand this way. In either case, the server should never touch the bowl. In formal service, the glasses are brought to the table on a tray held at waist level.

Serving Temperatures

Wine must be served at the right temperature: 45° to 55° for white wines and rosés, 65° to 70° Fahrenheit (18° to 21° Celsius) for reds. Wines served by the glass or carafe should be prechilled to the proper temperatures. White wines by the bottle should be kept in a cool place and chilled as ordered. This takes 10 to 20 minutes in a **wine chiller.** The most efficient procedure is to put some crushed ice in the bottom of the chiller, put the bottle in, surround it with crushed ice, and add a little water (and some table salt for faster melting if you wish). If you do not have crushed ice, use a layer of cubes in the bottom of the chiller, put the bottle in, fill the chiller two-thirds full with cubes, and add cold water. Bring the wine to the table in the chiller.

Figure 7.5 shows one of the latest styles in chillers for the table. Some chillers have a separate ice compartment, thus avoiding the problem of pouring from a wet and dripping bottle. For truly elegant service, a fine Champagne or sweet white wine is often served from a tall silver wine chiller placed beside the host's chair.

It is rare, but not unheard of, for wine to be ordered on the rocks, generally for refreshing wine coolers or wine spritzers. In these cases, the wine may still be served in a wineglass. Fill the glass one-third full with ice and pour the wine over the ice to within about half an inch of the top.

If you offer a white wine that sells at a steady, predictable rate, you can keep one or two days' supply in the refrigerator. But no wine should be kept chilled for more than a week. And no wine should be put into a freezer. Overly quick chilling may cause it to **throw sediment,** which means precipitate solids that are in solution. These solids are tiny crystals that drift to the bottom of the bottle and stick to the surface of the cork. The crystals are completely harmless, but some people—aghast that there's something crunchy in their wine—assume it is shards of glass and, understandably, will refuse to drink it. You can try to explain and reassure them, but the customer is within his or her right to refuse a bottle that contains sediment. (We'll discuss the decanting process for older wines that also contain sediment later in this chapter.)

Red wines should never be served over 70° Fahrenheit. A fine, expensive red wine should be served at 65° to 68° Fahrenheit; younger wines, like the

Figure 7.5 A table wine chiller. Courtesy of Co-Rect Products, Inc.

fruity Beaujolais, can be served a few degrees colder. Sometimes a bit of chilling takes the harsh edge off a thin or rough wine. Sparkling wines should be served well chilled. Sweet white wines should also be very cold, except for certain German wines, which should not go below 55° Fahrenheit (12.7° Celsius).

The process of opening a bottle of red wine and allowing it to "breathe" a few minutes before pouring is the subject of much wine-snob-related humor. **Breathing** means **aeration,** the act of exposing the wine to air. Red wines do change slightly when exposed to air, and some people feel that giving the wine a minute or two after opening allows these delicate chemical changes to rid the wine of any aroma of mustiness it may have developed in storage. In fact, the wine gets plenty of air as it is poured and while it sits in the wide-mouthed red wineglass, so an extra "breathing" ritual is not necessary.

Presenting the Wine

The ceremony of wine service is one part efficiency and one part showmanship. Seasoned wine drinkers expect a ritual, each of whose steps has a practical reason. These steps are shown in Figure 7.6.

With the glasses in place on the table, the server stands near the host (at the right of the host whenever possible) with the bottle of wine. If the bottle is in a chiller, the server removes it from the chiller and wipes it off with a clean napkin. Your servers should have a clean, white **service napkin** (or **serviette,** French for napkin) or towel on hand whenever they serve wine. The napkin serves several purposes, as you'll soon see. The other item servers should bring to the table is an additional wineglass. You'll learn why in a moment.

Holding the body of the bottle from underneath, with the label toward the host the server shows the bottle to the host for his or her approval (Figure 7.6a). (Of course, before he or she even got to the table, he or she looked carefully at the label to be sure that, indeed, it is the wine the customer ordered. Now it's time to open the bottle. The most practical opener is the flat jackknife type, known as a **waiter's friend,** or waiter's corkscrew, which fits easily into the pocket. Using the blade of the small knife on one side of the opener, the server cuts through the capsule, the piece of foil that covers the neck of the bottle (Figure 7.6b). The server doesn't remove the entire capsule, just the top part, using the ridge near the lip of the bottle as a guide (Figure 7.6c). Note: Some wineries now skip the capsule and use a little circle of plastic or wax instead to seal the top of the cork. If that's the case, there is no need to remove it; leave it in place and let the corkscrew go right through it.

If there's mold around the top of the cork, the server should just wipe the cork and the lip of the bottle with his or her napkin; the mold won't hurt

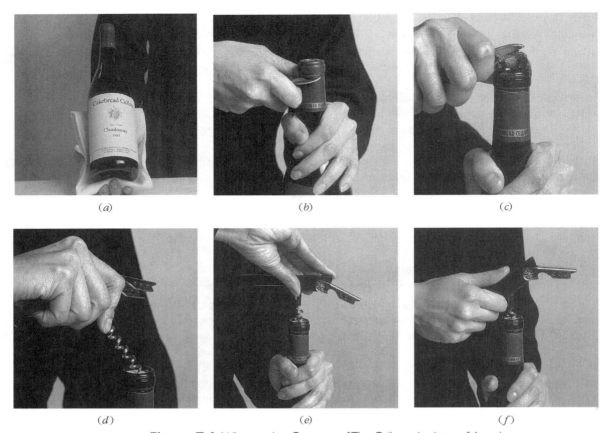

(a)   (b)   (c)

(d)   (e)   (f)

Figure 7.6 Wine service. Courtesy of The Culinary Institute of America.

the wine. The server then closes the blade, extends the lever at the other end of the corkscrew, and pulls down the corkscrew to form a T. He or she then inserts the corkscrew with the point slightly off center (Figure 7.6d) so that the screw (also called an **augur** or **worm**) is directly over the middle of the cork. Keeping the augur completely vertical, the server turns it clockwise until all of it has disappeared into the cork up to the shaft (Figure 7.6e).

Next the server moves the prongs of the lever into position on the rim of the bottle (Figure 7.6f) and holds the lever firmly in place with his or her thumb. The lever is designed to catch the lip of the bottle, but the server really does need to hold it or it may slip. The server holds the bottle and lever together with a firm, steady pressure and slowly raises the opposite end of the opener (Figure 7.6g). This will bring the cork out of the bottle (Figure 7.6h and 7.6i). The steady pressure on the lever is most important. Without it, a stubborn cork could cause the lip of the bottle to break.

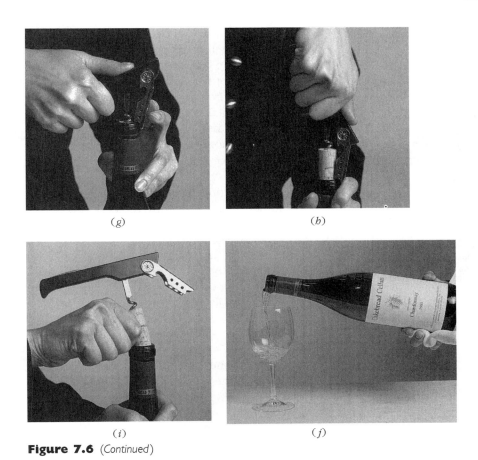

(g)

(h)

(i)

(j)

Figure 7.6 (*Continued*)

Now that you know how the wine-serving process is supposed to go, let's address potential problems that may occur during the procedure:

- **What if the cork just won't budge?** To dislodge it, the server may need to twist the whole corkscrew back and forth, which should help to loosen a cork with a tight seal.
- **What if the cork breaks?** The server removes the top half of the cork, then gently places the screw back inside the bottle and removes the rest of the cork just like the first half. Working gently prevents pushing the other half of the cork down into the bottle. Some waiters prefer to handle a broken cork away from the table. They apologize, take the bottle away, extract the cork, and bring it back. This should be handled as discreetly as possible, remedying the problem and returning quickly with their wine.
- **What if the server pushes the cork into the bottle?** It certainly won't hurt the wine, but it's not good form and wine shouldn't be served that way unless the customers insist that it's okay. Most bars and restaurants

Figure 7.7 Wine service tools (counterclockwise from top right): basket or cradle, candle used for decanting wine, wine chiller, decanting funnel, thermometer, sparkling wine pliers, cork retriever, sparkling wine cap or preserver, cork retriever, tastevin, thermometer. Courtesy of The Culinary Institute of America.

should have a **cork retriever** on hand (Figure 7.7) Its long wires are designed to be inserted into the bottle to grab the cork and tighten around it. The idea is to turn the floating cork upright and use the wires to pull it out of the bottle. It takes some practice, but works very well. Again, servers should not do this in front of the guests! They take the bottle away with an apology, promising to have it back promptly.

Most of the time, the cork will come out with no problem. After removing the cork, the server should wipe the lip of the bottle inside and out with a clean corner of the napkin, remove the augur from the cork, and set the cork down on the table near the host. There is usually no need to "present" the cork for an elaborate inspection. Once in a while, a knowledgeable guest will touch the cork or pick it up, mostly to see if it is damp on one side. This indicates the wine has been properly stored, on its side, so the cork stayed moist and expanded enough to keep a good seal on the bottle. Wine lore suggests sniffing the cork to see if the wine has gone bad, but today's experts agree that won't tell you much of anything—except how cork smells. Wine has to be looked at and tasted to determine its quality and condition. The tradition of presenting the cork can be traced to the first half of the twentieth century, when enterprising con artists tried to make money off great European wineries. The empty bottles with their prestigious labels were reused—refilled with inferior products and recorked. One way of ensuring the wine was not "counterfeit" was to check for an original cork, which was always stamped with the winery name or logo.

The next step in the wine presentation process is to pour about an ounce of wine into the host's glass for tasting and approval (Figure 7.6j). If a bit of cork falls into this glass, the server uses the spare glass he or she brought to the table to pour another taste for the host, removing the wine with the cork in it when he or she leaves the table. To prevent drips, the server twists his or her wrist slightly as the pour is ended and raises the neck of the bottle.

When the host has approved the wine, the server pours wine for the other guests first, serving the host last. It is permissible to move counterclockwise around the table, serving from the right if possible. Etiquette suggests pouring ladies' glasses first, then gentlemen, then the host—whether the host is male or female. Each glass should be poured not more than half full. The best way to hold the bottle is by the middle of the body, not by the neck. When everyone is served, the wine should be placed on the table near the

Sidebar 7.1

OTHER TYPES OF CORKSCREWS

There's more than one way to do just about anything, and opening wine is no exception. There are several other devices for getting corks out of wine bottles, shown previously in Chapter 4, Figure 4.27.

If you can get the hang of it, the **ah-so** works pretty well and is gaining in popularity among waiters. It has a handle and two long, straight prongs that fit on either side of a cork. You gently rock the prongs back and forth to push them into the bottle, along the sides of the cork, then twist the handle while pulling the prongs and cork out of the bottle together. People who learn to use the ah-so really like it, but others say using it makes it more likely they'll push a cork into the bottle or that it's tricky to get the feel of it. **Screw-pulls** or **lever-pulls** are very easy to use. You just position the screw over the cork and start twisting the handle. All you do is continue to twist: the screw goes into the cork and pulls it right out. For long, delicate corks from older wine bottles, the screw-pull works very well. However, many professionals consider this type of opener appropriate only for home use. You don't see them often in bars or restaurants.

Wing corkscrews are probably the least desirable for professional use. They are too large and bulky to carry in a pocket or apron. As you twist the augur into the cork, two metal "wings" at the top of the opener rise with each twist. Push the levers back down, and the cork is supposed to ease out of the bottle. The trouble is, you can't always tell how far the augur has penetrated the cork. All too often, you pull up half of a very chewed-up cork and must retrieve the other half.

host or returned to the chiller if it is being served cold. The server takes the capsule, the spare glass, and the napkin when leaving the table.

As the meal progresses, the server should keep an eye on the wineglasses, replenishing them as they are emptied. When white wine is gone, it is customary to put the bottle upside down in the chiller to signal the host that it is empty. Suggestive selling would include a polite question to the host: "May I bring you another bottle?"

Serving Champagne

Champagne and other sparkling wines, because the wine is under great pressure (about 90 pounds per square inch) and the bottle is sealed with a special mushroom-shaped cork, have to be opened and served in a special man-

Figure 7.8 Champagne service. Courtesy of The Culinary Institute of America.

ner. Champagne is always served well chilled, partly to dull the pressure a bit. The warmer the wine, the more it will fizz and the more quickly it will lose its effervescence. It is important to handle these bottles gently so as not to agitate the wine. Shaking it up only makes it messier to open, which looks fun in the movies but wastes half the bottle and flattens the rest of the wine.

Figure 7.8 shows how to open a Champagne bottle. Present the bottle for the host's approval (Figure 7.8a). Remove the foil capsule that covers the top of the bottle and you will find a wire hood called a **cage.** You can remove the foil with the blade on your corkscrew or just do it with your hands. Keep one thumb on the top of the cork (Figure 7.8b) while you untwist the wire fastener that holds the cage on. You can remove the cage (Figure 7.8c), or just loosen it.

You do not need a corkscrew to open a Champagne bottle. Keep one hand on the cork. (Some people cover this hand loosely with a clean towel or napkin—your choice—to prevent the cork from hitting anything if it pops out with force.) With the other hand, hold the bottle at about a 45° angle, pointing it away from the guests (or anything breakable). The reason you tilt the bottle is to give the wine inside as much airspace as possible. This eases pressure and prevents the wine "exploding" from the bottle.

Hold the cork steady, and slowly twist the bottle in one direction only, about a quarter turn at a time (Figure 7.8d). Don't pull on the cork; just hold it firmly and rotate the bottle. The pressure inside the bottle, plus the twisting motion, will ease the cork out gently. It should make a nice "thunk," not an enormous pop-and-spray!

When the cork comes out, hold it close to the bottle and keep the bottle at an angle for at least five seconds before pouring (Figure 7.8e). This equalizes the pressure, letting gas escape without taking the Champagne along with it. No gush, no fizz. But just in case, have a towel and an empty Champagne flute with you. If you happen to have a wild bottle, pour some immediately and it will stop gushing.

You serve Champagne like other wines, by setting the cork near the host and pouring a taste for the host first. Bubbly is poured in two motions. The first one brings mostly frothy effervescence (Figure 7.8f). Let the bubbles settle; the second pour should slowly fill the glass about two-thirds full (Figure 7.8g). When everyone is served, the bottle goes back into the chiller to conserve the bubbles.

We've already mentioned that sparkling wine should be served to a discerning clientele in a tall, thin tulip-shaped flute, to better conserve the effervescence and aroma. Do not chill these glasses in advance. The condensation dilutes the Champagne and dissipates the bubbles more quickly.

Decanting Wines

To **decant** a wine means to pour it out of the bottle and into another container. This is done so that sediment that may have formed inside the bottle stays in the bottle and so that the wine poured for guests is clear and not clouded by the sediment.

Which wines need decanting? Generally, reds that are 10 years or older; rare, older white wines; and vintage-dated ports. The latter almost always contain sediment—the older the port, the more sediment it has "thrown." Occasionally, a "big" young red wine is also decanted, not because of sediment, but to aerate it by pouring it into a beautiful crystal carafe (decanter) and letting it sit a while before serving.

In case you haven't seen it done, there's a bit of romance and tradition involved in the decanting process. Here's how to do it: First, handle the bottle to be decanted very gently. You want the sediment all in one place in the bottle and keep it from mixing with the wine. You can do this in two ways: by standing the bottle up for a day or two before opening it, so the sediment all falls to the bottom, or by keeping the bottle on its side, just as it was stored, so the sediment settles on one side of the bottle. (If you remember to store the wine with the label face up, the sediment will fall to the back of the bottle. This is best, because the customer can see the label when it's time to decant and serve.)

Sometimes the bottle is carried to the table in a special decanting cradle or wine basket, as shown in Figure 7.7. These keep the wine in an almost horizontal position. The wine is not removed from the cradle or basket; you present, open, and decant it while it's still on its side.

You'll need a decanter (a clear glass container in which to put the wine) and a lighted candle. (Figure 7.9a). Place the candle just behind the shoulder of the bottle. This bit of extra light is used to see the wine clearly as it passes through the neck. Open the bottle, then pour the wine slowly and steadily in a single motion without stopping, until the candlelight shows sediment approaching the neck of the bottle (Figure 7.9b). The remainder of the wine—only a small amount—is not served, and the clear wine is served from the decanter. Leave both decanter and bottle with the guests, so they can still look at the label.

Since only a small proportion of wines served will require decanting, only the **sommelier** (wine steward) or one or two experienced servers need this special training. However, your entire serving staff should at least be familiar with the process and the reason for it, as well as the other routines of wine service.

"Bad" Wine

It's bound to happen; sooner or later, someone will refuse a bottle of wine, claiming even before they taste it, that it has an off odor or color; or they may send it back and not want to pay for it because they tasted it and do not like it. You might as well have a policy in advance to deal with this rare instance. It is customary to replace the bottle of wine with the customer's choice: another bottle of the same wine or a different wine altogether, in a similar price range.

(a)

(b)

Figure 7.9 Decanting wine. Flame is behind bottle, not touching it. Courtesy of The Culinary Institute of America.

Here's the tough part: the fact that the customer doesn't happen to like a wine doesn't make it a "bad" wine. Wine that contains sediment or crystals is not bad, although you may have to explain to some customers that the sediment is a perfectly natural, and harmless, by-product of the wine. In the world of wine service, "bad" usually means that the wine is:

- **Oxidized.** Oxygen has gotten into the bottle and the wine has become musty or even vinegary. Oxidized wine looks like air has gotten to it. The color appears dull or brownish, and sometimes the wine smells like dried apples or prunes instead of fresh grapes. This is different from wine that is "old." It is going bad or has already gone bad.

- **Corked.** The cork has chemicals on it and they have gotten into the wine. This imparts a moldy, unpleasant taste to the wine that some people describe as "wet cardboard" or "wet newspaper."
- **Maderized.** This term is not heard as often, but it refers to the fact that a wine smells overly sweet, like a Madeira (hence the name) or Port, when it is not supposed to. Wine that has been exposed to heat or otherwise improperly stored can become maderized.

In these cases, the wine can taste "just a little bit off," or be absolutely terrible. If the customer is insistent, you might as well offer to replace the bottle. If the customer mentions a possible problem but isn't quite sure, the bar or restaurant owner, manager, or wine steward should be summoned to taste to make the decision.

WINE STORAGE

We've already talked about not storing wine in a kitchen or other warm area. Unless it is sake, the Japanese rice wine, you don't want to serve it warm. And high temperatures can prompt wine to mature faster or cause the problems you just read about. The idea is to keep the wine at a steady, somewhat cool temperature, and away from sunlight or ultraviolet light, which also ages it more quickly.

Depending on your storage capacity and the size and value of your wine inventory (rare wines versus jug wines), it might be sufficient to store the wine in the cardboard case it comes in. If you're not stacking cases very high on top of each other, you can lay them on their sides. Otherwise, you can store them with the bottles upside down. This keeps the corks moist and well sealed. Use a thick marking pen to label each case with the bin number, and try to keep them stored in numerical order so they'll be easy for servers to find quickly.

Unless your establishment is an elegant fine-dining place or a wine bar known for its wide and exotic selection, you won't have the need for long-term, temperature- and humidity-controlled wine cellar capacity. (If you do have these special storage needs, by all means you should consult with a wine expert before building or equipping such a space.) More likely, your goal is to turn over your inventory regularly and not tie up thousands of dollars of capital in a back room.

Do you want customers to be able to see your wine investment? If so, you might think of ways to incorporate wine storage into your décor, say a floor-to-ceiling wine rack along one wall, with a sturdy, attractive, and movable ladder for fetching bottles near the top; or a wine cellar that is also a private dining area for special parties and tastings.

You could have a room specially insulated and air conditioned by a contractor who has experience building such spaces. Commercially made wine storage cabinets are also available, from those with capacities that hold a dozen bottles to those that look like rooms themselves, with separate temperature and humidity controls, as in cigar humidors. Bar and restaurant supply houses sometimes sell them; there are also a number of well-known wine accessory companies with Web sites and mail order catalogs from which you can order. These cabinets come with lots of attractive options, including locking doors, movable shelves, decorative finishes, and so on. Just be sure to check with professionals about your electrical capacity and venting requirements before you buy.

By-the-Glass Storage

The more wines you serve by the glass, the greater your need for individual bottle storage. The idea is to keep oxygen out of the bottle between pours, even when it is partially empty.

For just a few bottles, it is easy to purchase rubber stoppers that have a one-way valve on the top. Place the stopper on the bottle, then use a hand-pump vacuum sealer to get the air out. The vacuum sealer is made of plastic and fits on top of the stopper. You pump the sealer up and down a few times, until it starts to resist your hand pressure. This means the oxygen has been removed from the bottle and that it is sealed until you remove the stopper again. You can buy these at kitchen stores, department stores, in wine shops, or by mail order. They allow you to keep wine for two or three days after opening with no loss of quality.

Wine specialty catalogs also sell cans of inert gas that can be used in a similar fashion. No need for a stopper here; just insert the tiny nozzle into the opened wine bottle, squirt it for one second, and immediately reseal the bottle with its original cork. The gas displaces any oxygen in the bottle. For more expensive wines by the glass, the inert gas is a little more effective than the vacuum sealer method. Wines resealed this way can last up to a week.

If you are going to offer a wide variety of wines by the glass, you can purchase wine cabinets. These are sometimes known by the name of one of the well-known models, as a Cruvinet (KROO-vin-AY). The wine bottles stay inside the cabinet and you dispense each one from an individual hose or spigot. As each glass is dispensed, the bottle is filled with inert gas to keep the rest of the wine fresh. Some of these cabinets are very attractive and can be incorporated into backbar décor.

WINE LIST FOLLOW-UP

A book of this scope cannot hope to treat wines in any depth. By the same token, a restaurant or bar that is just beginning to add wine service should not attempt to handle wines for connoisseurs. But by all means serve wines!

Wine by the glass or carafe is easy to sell and can be very profitable. A modest wine list of two or three wines of each type can also be very successful if the wines are of general appeal, the list is informative, the servers are well informed and helpful, and the whole effort is well organized.

The most important effort you can make to boost your profit and satisfy your customers is to commit to regularly researching and revising your wine sales program. It is not difficult to track wine sales, but you've got to keep up with it. Find out how much wine is sold per person: divide the total number of customers by the total number of bottles sold. This includes bottles used for by-the-glass sales. For the number of glasses sold, take this total and divide it again, by 4 (since, as you now know, there are four glasses in the average 750-ml wine bottle).

Track wine sales by "color" or type: Do you sell more red, or white, and by how much? More Californian or European wines? Perhaps you need to adjust your list accordingly. Ask servers or bartenders to make a note of any wines the customers request that you do not have; you may see a pattern. Inventory the wines regularly, to see what sells the most and what just sits around. Close out the slow-moving wines by putting them "on special" or selling them by the glass.

Finally, keep track of the wines by price. What is the average price of a bottle sold in a given time period? If your customers seem to order mostly the bargains, you'll want to expand that part of the list and stock fewer of the high-dollar bottles.

SUMMING UP

Any bar or restaurant business should decide whether to serve wine and how extensive to make its selection based on its clientele, its food menu, and the price range of the food, taking into consideration how much space is available for storing wines at correct (cool) temperatures.

If you do serve wine, there are a number of good ways to publicize the fact. The wine list can be as formal as a leather-bound book or as casual as a chalkboard of daily by-the-glass selections posted outside your establishment. Again, it depends on your concept and atmosphere. Wines sell better when the list contains a brief description of each and, perhaps, a suggestion of which foods it complements. For pricing wines, there are standard markups in the industry, but rare or prestigious vintages warrant a higher profit margin.

Most customers will depend on their servers to be able to make a wine recommendation, so be sure your staff members are well trained. Schedule regular training that includes tasting, comparisons, and discussion. Enlist the help of your suppliers. Every server should also know how to correctly open a wine bottle and what to do if a cork breaks, if there is sediment in the wine, or if a customer sends back a "bad" bottle.

There is a growing customer base of wine-knowledgeable people. Impress them with correct wine name spellings, proper glassware, and table service that follows the rules of wine etiquette.

POINTS TO PONDER

1. After you have decided you need a wine list, what are the five major points to consider when determining what and how much to buy?

2. Why would you assign bin numbers to each wine on a wine list?

3. What kinds of information should be included on a wine list to help sell the wines besides their names?

4. List five topics you should include when you have wine-training sessions for your servers.

5. What is the single most important piece of information a server must have about wines that will result in greater sales?

6. Why do you need different types of glasses to serve different types of wines?

7. What do you do when you've broken a cork as you open a bottle of wine for guests?

8. What is the purpose of the cage on a Champagne bottle?

9. How do you decide when to decant a wine?

10. How do you determine how much wine your bar sells per customer, both by the bottle and by the glass?

TERMS OF THE TRADE

aeration	corked	table tent
ah-so	decanting	throw sediment
augur	flute	waiter's friend
bin number	maderized	wine chiller
bowl	oxidized (oxidation)	wing corkscrew
breathing	screw-pull (lever-pull)	worm
cage	service napkin (serviette)	
cork retriever	sommelier	

CRAYNE HORTON

Founder and Vice President of Sales
Fish Brewing Company
Olympia, Washington

Crayne Horton was a political science professor at a branch campus of Heidelberg College . . . in Japan! An avid home brewer for many years, he was finally pleased enough with his product to brew his own craft beer for sale when he moved back to the United States in 1992. He had, in his words, "absolutely zero business experience" when he wrote his business plan, put together a stock offering, and raised $200,000 to open a small brewpub, called The Fish Bowl, in Olympia, Washington.

More capital was raised to expand the business to include an 8,000-barrel brewery. Today, the brewpub is still in business, and Fish Tale Ales are sold in six western states, with output that has grown 20 percent annually. The company is known for its organically brewed beers and a passionate commitment to environmental causes (at the time of this writing, Fish Brewing donates money from each keg or case sold to eight different Pacific Northwest charities, most dedicated to protecting endangered fish species and their habitat. In 2001, Fish Brewing Company purchased Leavenworth Brewery, another craft brewer in Washington State.

Q: What has the last decade been like in the craft and regional beer business?

A: It's been tough. Since 1996, all the major regional brewers added capacity—some by making large stock offerings—and this additional output created an oversupply. And there was also a bunch of ill will in the industry, with the craft brewers fighting against the major domestic brewers. It was a very public feud, and it made us all look mean-spirited. A lot of quickly made, poorly made, beer hit the market and suddenly the craft beer "fad" wore off. The growth that had been a predictable 40 percent per year went to 18 percent, to 3 percent, to flat. Lots of breweries went out of business, and mine

almost didn't survive either. But today, the market appears to be growing again, at the rate of about 5 percent per year.

The next new fad, which is just starting now, is microdistilling of spirits. *American Brewer* magazine just changed its name to *American Brewer and Distiller*. It will be a smaller revolution, though, because the federal licensing for distillers is much more rigorous than for breweries. It'll keep a lot more people out.

Q: What is the hardest thing about this business?

A: The most challenging thing is that there are still too many competitors for the amount of business. It's too easy to get into the microbeer business—there are no real barriers to entry—and it's seen by a lot of people as a fun, charming, romantic way to make a living. Instead, it's a lot of hard, sweaty labor with very low profit margins. [The] Budweisers and Millers are successful because of volume, so at low volumes and relatively low margins, there's no money to be made. And the amount of capital investment to get quality equipment is huge. For a small brewpub, with a 10- to 15-barrel capacity, there are bargains now because so many have gone out of business, so you can purchase it used at $30,000 to $40,000. But new equipment is very expensive—a single, brand-new 2,000-gallon tank is going to cost you $15,000. Stainless steel is not cheap.

Q: What about the regulations? What is it like to deal with the different agencies, from local health departments to the Federal Bureau of Alcohol, Tobacco, and Firearms (BATF)?

A: The health department has almost no jurisdiction; we don't see them. The BATF is almost nonexistent except as a tax collector. They don't have the personnel. The closest office to us is in Cincinnati. If you pay your taxes and send in the appropriate paperwork on time, you might never see them unless you're newly in business and they come to do an initial inspection. Of course, every label you produce has to pass BATF approval, and you can do that by mail. It's a procedure that must be followed very carefully, for every brand, every size of package, and it must be done well in advance because it can be a slow process.

The real problem is that each state you do business in has its own liquor laws, and none of them are the same. In some, we pay a lot of excise tax; others have different tax structures based on the strength of the alcohol product. Some have their own label-approval processes; others just accept the BATF approval. Some allow you to print alcohol amounts by volume on the label; others want it by weight; some won't let you print it at all! It is a huge management process that takes a lot of hours.

Q: What is it like working with distributors?

A: It's extremely frustrating. We have all Northwest distribution and good name brand recognition, but you're not a large part of the dollars for any of these people. Their profit margins on your products are much better than on any of their domestic beers, but still, there has been a dramatic consolidation among distributors over the last five years, so you have fewer choices of who you want to sell your product in a given market.

In my experience, distributors don't "sell" product; they take orders and deliver product. You have to sell it yourself and make sure there is follow-through. You can hire a "rep" [representative] in a given market, and that's a lot more effective; they really keep an eye on the distributor and work with them.

There are some distributors who are really honorable, with quality salespeople who are well trained, out there representing your product. But some of them are just totally unscrupulous, with their hands out or trying to skirt the local laws by giving away product, for instance, or installing draft systems at their cost. In every market, there are players of both ilk, and it takes a while to figure out which one you're dealing with.

Q: What role does your brewpub play in your overall business?

A: The pub is very profitable, and draft beer is where you make your money. The margins for bottled beer are even smaller than on draft.

We've changed the food service in the Fish Bowl every year we've been open. We used to do just smoked salmon and cream cheese, and little appetizer platters, from behind the bar. For a while, we owned a restaurant in the same building and managed that. We bought food from another restaurant for a while, and finally we installed a small kitchen of

our own. Now, we're doing great little panini sandwiches and a good, rich seafood soup. We have two rooms that each seat 40 or 50. It's a small output for a kitchen, but our pub is probably 30 percent of our overall sales for the company.

Q: Do you have advice for newcomers to the brewing business?

A: I would honestly discourage newcomers to the business at this point. There are so many good quality beers being made in the world [that] you have to ask yourself, "Does the world *need* another pale ale?" No! I just don't think so. There are so many good choices now. The ones that are still in business have survived and are probably making good product. I just don't see the need, from the consumer's standpoint. If you've got money to burn and just think it'd be fun, that's great. But just realize you're not going to make any money at it.

Q: What about the service area of the business?

A: Really knowledgeable beer servers are rare. I think it does help to have bartending experience. But anyone who wants to know more about beer as a server should know that any supplier or manufacturer is so happy to put information in their hands that they can share with customers. A good bartender or good server, really, is the one who sells the beer.

We have some specialty beers—Poseidon Imperial Stout and Leviathan Barleywine—that are aged six months or more in wine barrels. It's just like wine, 10 to 12 percent alcohol, lays down for a year, and is bottled in Champagne bottles or 3-liter jeroboams. These are on the wine lists of some wonderful restaurants, and Poseidon was just named one of the "Top Ten Cult Beers" in the United States. People chase these things down, and there's so much expert information to be had—it's much like wine in that way.

I do beer dinners, exactly like wine dinners, pairing foods and beers and working with chefs. So, for servers, food knowledge is a prerequisite. When you think about it, the basic domestic beer from a major commercial brewery is a simply a beverage, whereas wine, or craft beer, is an extension of food. It is food itself! If you have food knowledge, so much the better.

Q: Is there anything else you think hospitality students should concentrate on?

A: Yes, without a doubt, customer service. That is what makes or breaks a bar or restaurant. Be gracious, and don't act like you're doing someone a favor to wait on them.

CHAPTER 8

Beer

America is a beer-drinking nation. Though it is true that we're showing great and growing interest in wines, of all the alcoholic beverages, beer has the largest and most loyal following in this country. According to *Beverage Digest* magazine, we consume more than 22 gallons of beer per person per year, compared to 2 gallons of wine and fewer than 2 gallons of distilled spirits. Moreover, beer is the fourth most popular beverage overall in the United States, after the "big three": soft drinks, coffee, and milk. And of the three types of alcoholic beverage, beer has the lowest percentage of alcohol and the highest nutritional value as a food—although food value is seldom the reason it is drunk.

After a century of consuming the lagers produced by brewery giants, a new trend is emerging among the beer-drinking public who frequent both the neighborhood taverns and fashionable restaurants in this country: customers are ordering beers in a wider range of flavors, with bolder tastes and deeper character. And, as in other facets of the beverage business, they're looking for quality, for an interesting experience, for a more distinctive style; and, for the most part, they're willing to pay more for this experience. In 1999, bar and restaurant beer sales alone totaled $370 billion. Beer bought in supermarkets and convenience stores raises that amount significantly higher.

This is, of course, exciting news for bar owners, but the question is, how do you capitalize on this market? Developing a plan for selling and serving beer is not as simple as it may seem initially. As with wine, to give the customers what they want, you've got to learn a great deal more about the broad topic of beer, including lagers, ales, porters, stouts, microbrews, and so on. You'll have to know how it's made and stored and the right way to serve it. Do you know, for example, whether beer has a lifespan? And how do you decide which ones to stock? This chapter answers these questions and more, and explains how to sell beer successfully. You will become familiar with beer's unique serving requirements so that you'll be able to serve your guests a perfect glass of beer, from either the tap or the bottle.

This chapter should help you . . .

- Recognize and describe the various types and styles of beer.
- Learn how beer is made and the role of each of its ingredients.
- Understand the perishable nature of draft beer, as well as the space and care it requires.
- Learn how to take proper care of a draft-beer system and why each step is important.
- Learn the proper care of canned and bottled beer.
- Correctly choose and care for beer glasses.
- Sell beer profitably in a bar or restaurant setting.

A BRIEF HISTORY OF BEER

Human beings may have been making grain into beer even before they were baking it into bread. But whichever came first, beer and bread together comprised the principal items of the ordinary family diet for centuries. Noah took beer onto the Ark. The Egyptians were the first to record their brewing process; they made beer from corn, and passed their techniques on to the Greeks.

Primitive peoples derived much of their body fuel from the carbohydrates and alcohol in beer. Columbus found Indians making a beer from corn and sap of the black birch tree. The English and Dutch colonists could not have survived without beer, and made their own. George Washington had his private brewhouse; Sam Adams and William Penn both operated commercial breweries. The soldiers of Washington's army each received a quart of beer a day. It was often safer to drink beer than water, and it offered nutrients and carbohydrates.

But it wasn't until the nineteenth century that the brewing industry in this country began in earnest, when German immigrants brought European know-how and beer-drinking customs to the United States. The art of brewing beer had made a major leap forward as a result of Pasteur's experiments with yeasts. Not only did he unravel the mysteries of fermentation, he developed the technique of sterilizing through pasteurization. The process was used to stabilize beer 22 years before it was applied to milk. Before that time, beer could not be stored safely for long periods of time before showing signs of spoilage.

By the late nineteenth century, beer was sharing the limelight with bourbon in the old-time saloons. It was the excesses of both the beverage industry and the individual drinker during this time that brought about Prohibition.

Today, America is undergoing a beer renaissance of sorts, that recaptures the period in European history when local breweries were valued community businesses, and the corner tavern was the favorite gathering place for news, dinner, entertainment, and spirited political debate. Whether shared with friends, good food, and/or good conversation, Americans today are not only drinking beer more responsibly, they are learning (and caring) more about what they are drinking. A growing population is experimenting with home-brewing, and buying, sampling, and cooking with beers.

The Players, Big and Small

Though the giant commercial breweries still hold a lion's share of the beer market in this country, as shown in Figure 8.1, the microbrewery aspect of the industry is booming. A **microbrewery** (sometimes referred to as a **craft brewery**) is defined as one that produces fewer than 15,000 barrels of beer per year. (A **barrel,** in the beer business, contains 31 gallons.) In 1980, there were fewer than 40 breweries operating in the United States; today, there are more than 400, most of them microbreweries. In almost every good-sized town, there's at least one **brewpub,** a combination restaurant and brewery that sells the majority of its own beer on-site, with food. (If a brewpub's off-site sales exceed 50 percent of its total sales, it is classified as a microbrewery.)

As of December 31, 2000, there were 1,456 microbreweries, brewpubs, and regional specialty breweries in the United States, broken down as follows:

Regional Specialty Breweries	43
Microbreweries	423
Brewpubs	990
Total	1,456

U.S. Market Shares by Segment in 2000

Large Brewers + Traditional Regional Brewers	86.8%
Imports	10.2%
Domestic Specialty or "Craft" Brewers	3.0%

Figure 8.1 Breweries in the United States. *Source:* Institute for Brewing Studies, Boulder, Colorado.

Next up the volume ranking is the *regional brewery,* which can produce from 15,000 to 500,000 barrels per year. "Regional," in this case, refers only to its overall output, not its area of distribution. Some regional breweries are hired as **contract brewers,** to make and market other private-label brands for brewpubs. The regional brewery becomes known as a *regional specialty brewery* when, although its output is fairly large, the brewery's primary or largest-selling product is a specialty beer that is generally considered a microbrew.

Finally there's the **macrobrewery,** the large national or international beer-manufacturing conglomerate with multiple locations and an impressive output of more than 500,000 barrels annually. (The largest, Anheuser-Busch, makes more than 91 million barrels a year!) Statistics are tracked for each category of brewing by the Institute for Brewing Studies, a national trade association of brewers based in Boulder, Colorado.

As you can see, the national beer industry has become as complex and sophisticated as its consumers, who by the way are also increasingly interested in international products. Following in the footsteps of many other industries, brewing has "gone global." For many years, Heineken, Carlsberg, and Guinness were the world's only truly international beers, actively marketing and distributing outside their home countries. Now, the big American breweries and others—Bass PLC in England, Interbrew in Belgium, South African Breweries Ltd.—are looking outside their native borders for interesting new beers to acquire for their portfolios. Since 1995, Anheuser-Busch has been forging partnerships in India, England, Spain, Brazil, and China. The company has even purchased a brewery, and become a major stockholder, in Tsingtao, China's leading brewery. The other two leading American brewers—Miller and Coors—have also gained footholds in international markets. Miller has acquired partial ownership of several Chinese breweries; to date, Coors has zeroed in on Spain and South Korea. At the time of this writing, Miller is ranked third in terms of worldwide sales; Coors is twelfth.

Still, these American giants earn only a fraction of their income from overseas sales. Their international business is in its infancy compared to Heineken, which is sold in more than 170 markets worldwide, with international sales accounting for 90 percent of its total volume, or to Guinness, with 84 percent of its sales outside of Ireland.

The interest in the Chinese market is understandable, with its 1.2 billion thirsty consumers. Industry experts say that within a few years, China will overtake the United States as the world's largest beer market, so every forward-thinking brewery is vying for the Chinese beer-drinker's loyalty. Other recent "hot spots" for market expansion are Vietnam, Taiwan, and India.

The Domestic Beer Market

Meanwhile, back at home, the business has also undergone enormous changes in the past few decades. Consolidation has concentrated market share among a few large companies, making them larger still. In 1985, the "big three"—

Anheuser-Busch, Miller, and Coors—accounted for 65 percent of all beer sales in this country. Today, after swallowing up smaller breweries, that figure is more like 80 percent. In 1999, the Stroh's brewery sold its formulas and brand names to Pabst and Miller. And it has long been rumored that Pabst, the fourth largest brewer, may be sold. At the same time, the foreign and multinational breweries continue to eye the lucrative American beer market.

As far as specific brands, Bud Light has been a remarkable success story. In the last five years of the twentieth century, Bud Light sales increased by double-digits to reach 394 million cases (a case contains 2.25 gallons) in 1999. Bud Light may soon outsell its "parent" beer, Budweiser.

In the imported beer market, after 20 years in the United States, Corona Extra from Mexico overtook Heineken in 1997 to become the top-selling import. Since 1996, Corona Extra sales have grown an average of about 12 million cases per year. This boom has paved the way for increased sales for other Mexican brands (Tecate, Dos Equis, and others) and reflects in part the growing Hispanic population in this country. (You'll learn more later in this chapter about the imported beers available from a variety of nations, and how to sell them.)

Meanwhile, the flagship brewers strive to maintain market shares for their primary brands—the full-calorie brews—with advertising strategies that position them as reliable standards that beer drinkers have come to know and love. Recently, for example, Anheuser-Busch ads called Budweiser "a classic American Lager since 1876," and Miller Brewing Company ads shouted that "It's Time for a Good Old Macro-Brew!" Such campaigns are meant to rally the domestic premium beer patrons, by appealing to the rather patriotic notions of consistency and authenticity, while sometimes giving a friendly jab to the upstart imports and microbrews.

Beer advertising also seem to imply that brewers believe there is no better way to get a customer excited about its product than to show people having a good time while they are drinking it. To reinforce their fun and lively brand images, the macrobreweries align themselves closely with big events (called **event marketing**) in sports, comedy, music, and other forms of entertainment. In particular, these breweries have a longstanding connection sporting events, especially football and baseball. Event marketing can also be implemented by individual bars and restaurants, thanks to breweries that make and distribute support material (banners, table tents, posters). Local distributors, too, are often willing to sponsor event-related promotional campaigns in their markets.

When it comes to the sale of so-called light beers, the lower-calorie versions of major brews, which you'll learn more about later in this chapter, the marketing focus is on lifestyle and health. You'll see ads that tout these beers as "less filling," compared to the heavier microbrews and imports. Ironically, the healthy image of light beer may encourage people to drink more of it—two lights instead of a single, regular beer—which negates its lower-calorie advantage. The latest marketing campaigns also focus on flavor, promising that the person who chooses a light alternative doesn't have to bypass taste and quality, in an effort to attract more upscale beer drinkers.

Two other terms you'll hear in conjunction with beer sales are on-premise and off-premise. **On-premise sale** means beer that is sold and consumed on the same site. When you buy a beer at a bar or restaurant, it is an on-premise sale. When you buy beer at a grocery or convenience store to drink someplace else, that is an **off-premise sale.**

BEER-MAKING BASICS

Actually, the term "beer" refers generically to ales, lagers, pilsners, and stouts—all beverages made from water, malted grain (usually barley), hops, and yeast. In fact, the U.S. Standard of Identity uses the term "malt beverage" rather than beer, defining it as "a beverage made by the alcoholic fermentation . . . in potable brewing water, of malted barley with hops," with or without various commonly used ingredients, such as malted or unmated cereals and carbon dioxide. Federal regulations also define beer's minimum alcohol content as one-half of 1 percent by volume. Maximum content is not defined; this is a matter for state law, which varies from one state to another. It may seem ironic that, while federal regulations require alcohol content to be shown on a wine label, they *prohibit* this information from appearing on beer labels, except where state laws require it. That is why some brewers make the same beer in different "strengths," to meet different state requirements.

In the United States, a beer's alcoholic content is usually quoted as a percentage by weight; in Canada, it is shown as a percentage by volume. Therefore, a 3.2-percent beer and a 5-percent beer cannot be compared unless they are both expressed in the same terms. For example, a 4-percent beer by weight is 5-percent alcohol by volume, while a 4-percent beer by volume is 3.2-percent alcohol by weight. These differences are small and probably would not affect taste, but you would be able to taste the difference between a 3.2-percent beer and a 5-percent beer by weight (4 and 6.25 percent by volume).

The alcohol content of beers is roughly one-third to one-half that of wine; but when average servings of the two beverages are compared, the content is not very different, as you can see by referring back to Table 5.2.

Raw Ingredients

Depending on the type or style of beer being made, the brewer will use different strains of yeast, and somewhat different methods of fermentation. In spite of these differences, which you will learn about in this chapter, the basics of production are the same for both beers and ales. First, let's look at each of the raw ingredients in beer: water, malt, hops, and yeast. In the United States, there is often a fifth ingredient, another cereal in addition to the malt, called a **malt adjunct** or **grain adjunct.** Variations in the character of each ingredient are important to the final product.

Water. Beer is nine-tenths water, so water quality is a huge factor in beer production. Coors emphasizes its use of "Rocky Mountain spring water," for instance; and this is not just advertising hype, it is essential to the taste of Coors. Some waters are suitable for ale but not for beer, and vice versa. Standard American tap water, for instance, is treated with chlorine or fluoride, hence is not suitable for brewing without being boiled or filtered first. Hard water doesn't work to make certain styles of beer, so brewers must know the characteristics of their water supply in advance.

The term *pH* is used to describe the amount of acidity in water, expressed on a scale of 1 to 14. A low number indicates high acidity; 7 is "neutral"; and numbers higher than 7 indicate low acidity. The best brewing conditions for beer include water at a pH level of 5.0 to 5.8. Lower pH levels are good for beer of lighter colors.

The minerals in water, of course, also contribute to the taste of the beer. Many brewers modify their water—adding mineral salts, for instance—to produce a successful, standardized product.

Malt. **Malt** is actually barley that has been placed in water, allowed to begin to sprout, and then dried to stop germination. Except for a few beer malts made from wheat, all are barley malts. The sprouted grain creates enzymes that break down the grain's starch molecules into simpler, sugar molecules; these, in turn, break down into alcohol and carbon dioxide when attacked by the yeast. The drying process is called **kilning** because it takes place in a kiln.

After drying, the malt is roasted, which gives the final brew much of its "character," which can be likened to another grain product—bread. If you toast the bread at a low temperature for a short time, it looks and tastes different than if you burn it. Malt is made in every possible gradient, from barely toasted to burnt. The lightest malts give beer a golden color and lightly sweet flavor; higher roasting temperatures allow malt to take on rich, dark colors, and such flavors as caramel, coffee, chocolate, and, yes, even toast.

Most brewers buy their malt in the form of dried or roasted malt or even malt extract; many of the cheaper beers use malt extract. Anheuser-Busch, Coors, and some small regional breweries malt their own barley.

The malt and the adjuncts provide the sugars to be fermented. In addition to flavor and color, they contribute the body of the beer and the type of **head** (foam) on top when it's poured. The body of the beer contains its nutrients: carbohydrates, proteins, and traces of the vitamins riboflavin, niacin, and thiamine.

Hops. Hops look like tiny pinecones waiting to open, and they grow on tall, thin vines. The hops that give beer its characteristic suggestion of bitterness are the blossoms of the female hop vine. The best are Bohemian hops, imported from Czechoslovakia, but high-quality hops are also grown in the Pacific Northwest, and their names—like Willamette and Cascade— reflect their heritage. California's Sonoma Valley was a prime hop-growing region until winemaking became popular in the 1950s. The blossoms are picked, dried, and refrigerated until used. In brewing, they may also add aroma, depending on how and when they are added.

Yeast. Yeast causes fermentation, converting sugar into alcohol. There are two categories of **brewer's yeast**—*ale yeast* and *lager yeast*—and many individual variations within each category. The yeast may impart flavor to the beer. In a bottle-conditioned beer (about which you'll learn more later), yeast is added just before the beer is sealed in bottles, allowing it to continue to "grow." The freshness and ripe flavors make this a favorite type of beer, but it does look oddly cloudy when first poured into a glass.

The brewer's yeast is the special laboratory product of each brewer, and its behavior (it is constantly active) is closely watched. Erratic behavior or stray yeast from the air getting into the brew could cause a disaster, requiring shutdown of a brewery, followed by cleaning and sterilizing the equipment and starting all over again.

Adjuncts and Additives. The most commonly used adjuncts are rice and corn, and they are very prevalent in American brewing. They give beer a lighter color and milder flavor, and cost less to use than barley malt. Rice imparts the lightest color to the beer. In general, the higher the proportion of barley to adjunct, the more flavor and body in the beer and the better the head.

Superpremium beers typically use a higher proportion of barley malt: Anheuser-Busch's Michelob, for example, uses 95 percent barley malt and 5 percent rice, while its premium beer, Budweiser, uses 65 percent barley malt and 35 percent rice. In some European countries, like Germany, Switzerland, and Norway, adjuncts are prohibited by law. Their beers are made entirely with barley malt.

Another type of ingredient has become more common in recent years. **Additives** are used to stabilize beer foam, prevent cloudiness, facilitate conversion of starch to sugar, prolong shelf life, and/or adjust color. All additives must be substances approved by the U.S. Food and Drug Administration. Many brewers, however, continue to produce beers without additives, relying on good ingredients, good production methods, and their own experience to prevent the problems the additives are intended to solve.

The Beer-Making Process

Now that we've got the raw ingredients, it's time to learn how to use them to make beer. It is a four-step process: (1) mashing, (2) brewing, (3) fermenting, and (4) **lagering,** or storing (maturing, aging, conditioning). The first three steps are very similar to the first stages of making whiskey. Figure 8.2 diagrams the whole sequence.

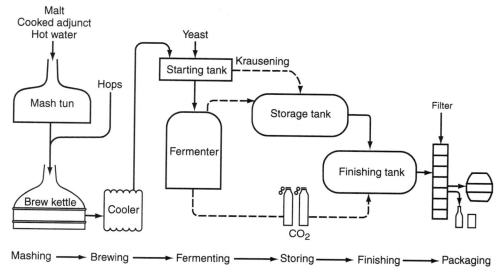

Figure 8.2 Making beers and ales. Broken arrows show alternate ways of carbonating.

Mashing, the first step, converts starches into sugars. The barley malt is ground into grist, which is fed into a container called a **mash tun** along with hot water. Adjuncts (usually corn or rice) are precooked and added to the mash tun. Everything is mixed and cooked together at low temperatures (up to 169° Fahrenheit or 76° Celsius) for one to six hours. During the process, the malt enzymes are activated and turn starches to sugars. Then the grain residue is strained out and the remaining liquid—now called **wort**—is conveyed to the brew kettle.

Brewing, the second step, is the process of boiling the wort with hops. It extracts that distinctive hops bitterness that makes beer taste like beer. In huge copper or stainless-steel brew kettles, the wort-plus-hops is kept at a rolling boil for one to two and a half hours. The boiling also sterilizes the wort, and draws out the natural antiseptic elements in the hops that protect beer from spoilage.

After brewing, the hops are strained out and the wort is cooled. At this point, the techniques vary according to whether a lager beer or ale is being made. For ales, the wort is cooled to a range of 50° to 70° Fahrenheit (10° to 21° Celsius). For lager beers, it is chilled to a range of 37° to 49° Fahrenheit (3° to 10° Celsius).

The third step, *fermenting,* or converting the sugars into alcohol and carbon dioxide, begins when yeast is added. If a lager beer is being made, the yeast settles to the bottom of the fermentation tank, and the action proceeds from the bottom. In beer-making terminology, lager is referred to as **bottom fermented.** The yeasts for ales are different strains that work at warmer temperatures—they rise to the surface and work from the top. Ale, therefore, is referred to as **top fermented.** The usual fermentation period is a week or more, depending on the type of beer being made. During fermentation, the carbon dioxide given off may be collected and stored under pressure, to be added again at a later stage.

Carbon dioxide creates the effervescence in beer. As a beer can or bottle is opened, or beer is poured from a tap, the bubbles essentially bounce against the glass and break up, creating the beer's foamy head. These bubbles are relatively large, and they also cause what some people describe as a full or gassy feeling from drinking beer or soft drinks. In the late 1960s, Guinness brewers began using nitrogen in addition to carbon dioxide. Nitrogen is an inert gas, colorless and odorless, which creates smaller bubbles and, therefore, less "gassiness" in the beer. **Nitrogenated beer** is known for its smoother, creamier consistency. The nitrogen is forced out of the beer just before pouring, by a special restrictor disk in the tap.

Lagering (from the German word *lagern,* "to be stored"), the fourth step, means storing or conditioning; this step matures or ripens the beer, mellowing its flavor. Some further slow fermentation may also take place and impurities may settle out. Lagering of beer takes place at near-freezing temperatures and may last several weeks or several months. Ales are ripened, too, for a much shorter time at warmer temperatures. Both beer and ale are matured in stainless-steel or glass-lined tanks. They are commonly called **barrels,** but are nothing like the wooden casks in which spirits are aged. A wooden barrel would spoil the beer taste. (Anheuser-Busch uses beechwood chips in its lagering tanks to clarify the beer, but since these are specially cooked and sterilized, they impart no taste.)

During lagering, some beers are given a small additional amount of newly fermenting wort, to add zest and carbonation by prompting a little further fermentation. This process is called **krausening** (from the German word *krausen,* referring to froth that forms in fermenting wort at a certain stage), and is sometimes referred to as *natural carbonation.* If the beer is not krausened, it may be carbonated instead by adding the stored carbon dioxide at the end of the lagering period. Of the three major types of alcoholic beverages, beer alone retains the carbonation of its fermentation as an essential characteristic—that distinctive head of foam in the glass.

Beer Packaging

After storage, the beer is filtered and then kegged, bottled, or canned.

Kegs, or half-barrels containing 15½ gallons, provide bar supplies of **draft beer,** beer drawn from a tap into the glass (the British spell it *draught*). You'll learn more later in this chapter about the care and correct use of beer kegs.

Bottles now come in a variety of sizes. The 12-ounce glass bottle accounts for the bulk of packaged beer sales, but there are also 16-, 20-, and 40-ounce sizes, some with wider mouths. Consumer research shows that female customers like the wider-mouth bottles, finding them easier to drink from. Early in 2000, Miller became the first brewery to sell beer in plastic bottles. After a year of test-marketing, they released 16- and 20-ounce plastic sizes, convenient for places where glass containers are often forbidden (like beaches, swimming pools, and stadiums). They are resealable, and one-seventh the weight of a comparably sized glass bottle.

Cans are another option for individual servings. The standard-size aluminum can is 12-ounce, but some beers sell well in the oversized 25-ounce "oil can." The recent blitz of beer-packaging options means that bar managers and bartenders must do careful research to decide what to stock. Your decision will depend on your storage space and what size, style, or shape of container your customers like best. The recycling program in your area may also impact your decision, because a bar creates a lot of solid waste with cans and bottles.

Pasteurizing. Most canned and bottled beers are stabilized by pasteurizing, that is, exposing them in the container to temperatures of 140° to 150° Fahrenheit (60° to 66° degrees Celsius) for 20 minutes to an hour. This heating process kills bacteria and any remaining yeast cells. Draft beers may be flash-pasteurized with steam, but most are not pasteurized at all. This is why they taste better. It is also why they are packaged in metal kegs that will withstand increased pressure that may come from slight continuing fermentation, and why they are kept refrigerated constantly from brewery to bar. The constant cold temperature is essential to maintain the quality of an unpasteurized beer. A beer that has been warmed and cooled again is known as a **bruised beer;** it suffers a loss in quality.

Some canned and bottled beers are not pasteurized. Instead the beer is passed through ultrafine filters that remove yeast cells and other impurities. Thus it retains many of the characteristics of draft beers and may be labeled and advertised as draft beer. Coors products are the best-known examples of unpasteurized beers. They are made under hospital-clean conditions, and not only kegs, but cans and bottles are shipped and stored under refrigeration. They are supposed to be kept cold every step of the way until they are consumed—bar managers please take note! Many people, including some delivery personnel, are not aware of this and store bottles and cans at room temperature. Unpasteurized beer should not be accepted on delivery if it is not cold.

Under federal regulations, pasteurized beers in cans or bottles may refer in advertising to "draft flavor" or "on-tap taste" only if the label states clearly that they have been pasteurized; they may not be called "draft beer." The difference is subtle, and though most consumers probably are not aware of these label nuances, anyone running a bar should be.

TYPES OF BEER

There are at least 5,000 breweries in the world, producing some 15,000 brands of beer, but they are categorized into two basic types: lagers (bottom fermented) and ales (top fermented). Within these two broad categories are many different styles. We'll discuss the major ones here.

Lager Beers

As you've already learned, *lagern* is German for "to store" or "to stock." It refers in this case to the long period of time during which the beverage is stored as it undergoes its slow second fermentation. This process produces a beer with thinner body and dry, subtle flavors. Before the invention of refrigeration, lager beers were very unstable in warm weather. German brewers did not make them in the summer, and stored their beer in the caves of the Bavarian Alps. They noticed that, after some months in cold storage, the beer gained a permanent stability because the yeast had sunk to the bottom. The major kinds of lager are the pilsner-style beer, light beer, malt liquor, bock beer, and steam beer.

Pilsner (also spelled Pilsener and sometimes shortened to Pils) is named after the village of Pilsen, in what is now the Czech Republic. The name may or may not appear on the label of the beer, but this is the brew that we typically think of as "beer" in the United States, the lively, mild, dry, light-bodied, amber-colored, thirst-quenching liquid. It benefits from the use of extremely soft water and has a noticeable hops aroma and flavor.

Pilsner-style beers (which today, bear little resemblance to what was actually brewed in Pilsen) are by far the biggest sellers in the United States. They include Budweiser, Miller's High Life, Busch, Coors, and Michelob. Generally, they contain 3.2 to 4.5 percent alcohol by weight (4 to 5 percent by volume).

Light beers are variants of the Pilsner style, and now account for about 40 percent of overall U.S. beer sales. Practically dismissed as a fad when Miller acquired the rights to the name "Lite" in 1972, today three of the four top-selling brews in America are low-calorie products. How low? These beers typically contain 100 calories or less per 12-ounce serving, compared to 135 to 170 calories for regular beer, and have one-third to one-half less alcohol—3.2 percent by weight, or 4 percent by volume. There are even a few "extra lights," with alcohol content of 2.3 percent by weight (2.8 percent by volume).

Fewer calories and less alcohol mean a higher proportion of water, and the brewer's challenge is to be sure their beers are still flavorful. As popular as light beer is, the style will always be controversial, as "serious" beer makers and drinkers scoff at these "watered-down" options.

Malt liquors are lager beers with higher alcohol content than pilsners (generally 5.5 to 6 percent or more by weight) frequently produced by adding extra enzymes to increase fermentation. The name of this beer style is misleading: it is neither very malty nor is it a liquor. It has a small share of the market and tends to be chosen for its modest price and alcohol content. Colt 45 is today's leading seller.

Bock beers are traditionally strong, usually dark lagers with a high alcohol content and a full, malty, sweet flavor. They are mainly German beers, but some small U.S. brewers produce their own bocks. Bock is one of the few types of beers that improves with age. You'll often see a goat on traditional bock labels; it is the zodiac symbol for Capricorn, a spring astrological sign.

In addition to ordinary bocks there are **double bocks;** the goal of their brewers seems to be the strongest, richest beer it is possible to produce, with alcohol content in the neighborhood of 6 to 10.5 percent by weight (7.5 to 13.2 percent by volume). The Bavarian bocks and double bocks (*doppelbocks*) are traditionally served as "warming beers" in stone mugs at a temperature of 48° to 50° Fahrenheit (9° to 10° Celsius).

Bock beer is among the **seasonal beers.** Centuries ago, German brewers adapted their styles to create different beers for different times of year, depending on what might fit a particular holiday or type of weather. The tradition makes sense, and so has been adapted by brewers in other countries. Fruit beers, for example, are usually made during the months in which the particular fruit is harvested. Bock beer is generally brewed in the fall, to be consumed in the spring. In spring, they'd make *Oktoberfest* beer, which is aged one to six months, with a slightly higher alcohol content (5.3 to 5.9 percent by volume) than regular beer. Aged through the summer, it is ready to consume at fall harvest celebrations. *Vienna lager* is a crisp, medium-bodied beer that is also considered seasonal. There are *Marzeubiers* ("March beers") and *Maibocks* ("May bocks"). Once in a while, you'll see an *eisbock*, made by freezing the beer during the brewing process, then removing the ice crystals. This makes a highly concentrated, highly alcoholic (11 percent by volume) beer.

Steam beer is a truly American invention; it's the only kind of beer not borrowed from Europe. Its method of production developed in California during the Gold Rush days, when ice was hard to come by. It combines the bottom fermentation of lager beer with the higher-fermenting temperatures of ale. It makes a beer with a lively head and the body and taste of ale, but the same alcohol content as regular beer—4 percent by weight, 5 percent by volume. The name has nothing to do with brewing, but comes from the "steam" released when the barrels are tapped. San Francisco's Anchor Steam brewery makes the most famous steam beers; German steam beers are called *dampfbiers.*

Ales

Ales have a characteristic fruity flavor that derives from the quicker, warmer top-fermentation process, at 60° to 77° Fahrenheit (15.5° to 25° Celsius). Most styles of ales also have more body and more hops flavor and tartness than lagers, and some have more alcohol. In fact, some states have a law requiring that any beer with more than 4 percent alcohol by weight must be labeled as ale even if it is not a true ale (which rather confuses things). Ales are best enjoyed without being thoroughly chilled. They were made warm, and made to be consumed at room temperature or with only a very light chill.

American ales are descended from the ales of the British colonists. Today, there are several styles, generally mild reflections of colonial brews, classified as mild, pale, Scotch ale and brown ale. (The term "pale" applied to an ale means translucent, rather than light in color.) A few U.S. brewers make a hearty and hoppy India pale ale, a superpremium style borrowed from the British. The best known of the British ales is called **bitter;** a copper-colored pale ale high in flavor and low in alcohol, drunk by the pint and an integral part of every British pub.

Americans have inherited two other British-style ales: porter and stout. **Porter,** a dark, bittersweet brew, is no longer found in England but is made in the United States as a specialty brew. Its dark brown color and distinctive bitterness comes from the use of roasted, unmalted barley. America's oldest existing brewery—Yuengling's in Pottsville, Pennsylvania—makes a "Celebrated Pottsville Porter," among other specialties, and several other small craft brewers have developed their own porters.

Stout is the successor to porter in England; it is a "stouter" porter, fuller-flavored, aromatic, almost black in color, and more alcoholic. Also made with roasted, unmalted barley, it ranges from 3 to 7.5 percent alcohol. Guinness, imported from Ireland, is the most famous bitter stout.

There are three basic types of stout: sweet, dry, and imperial. The latter was originally brewed in England and exported to Russia for the czars. Stout has experienced a popularity surge in recent years, a natural extension of consumer interest in specialty products—from beer and wine to breads, cheeses, coffees, and so on. Beer experts suggest linking it to different types of cuisine. It can be overwhelming on its own, but with a good steak or even a rich chocolate dessert, a pint of stout can be wonderful. Later in this chapter, you'll learn about using stouts and other strong brews to make "mixed pints."

There are also *seasonal ales,* big brews to take on winter's chill. Complex brews with sharp aromas, rich flavors, and lots of character, they may contain hints of allspice, coriander, and cinnamon to temper their higher alcohol content, and have names like Christmas Ale or Winter Ale.

Hybrids

There are some types of beer that can be made using either the lager or ale process. One of them is *wheat beer,* also known as white beer (in German, *weisenbier* or *hefeweizen;* the term *hefe* means it contains yeast). These are first cousins to the other ales when they are top-fermenting brews; there are some made lager-style. Their distinguishing feature is a high percentage of wheat in the malt (up to 50 percent) with the balance being malted barley, and a slightly cloudy appearance when poured, because the yeast sediment was not filtered out, to better preserve its subtle flavors.

Lambic beer is one of the best-known wheats; dry and tart, it is used as the base for adding fruit to make refreshing summer beers laced with peaches, cherries, apricots, raspberries, or honey. Also spelled *Lambiek*, the name comes from a Belgian town of Lembeek, where it has been made since the 1500s. The United States imports wheat beers from Belgium (called *Wit beer*) and Germany and produces many microbrewed, fruit-flavored versions of its own. The European imports sometimes use strains of yeast that impart spicy or fruity flavors, and are **wild fermented,** that is, exposed for long time periods to natural yeasts in the air.

Blonde beers—both lagers and ales—are so named because of their light color. The term is used somewhat loosely, but it has been around since the mid-1800s when, after years of dark, cloudy beers, the first clear, golden lager was created in Pilsen. Blonde beers are light to medium-bodied, and contain less alcohol and less hop bitterness than true pilsners and ales. They are all malt products, made only with barley and very little wheat. They're viewed as "starter beers" by beer aficionados, but they have a nice side benefit: very low alcohol content (2.5 percent by volume) and about 86 calories per bottle, less than so-called light beers. Whether their current popularity is just a fad remains to be seen.

Nonalcoholic Beer

Nonalcoholic beer is in a class by itself. It cannot be labeled "beer" because of the federal regulations; it must be labeled a "nonalcoholic malt beverage containing less than 0.5 percent alcohol." At first, this type of beverage was targeted toward the health-and-fitness enthusiast and the nondrinking driver, but today's market approach is to emphasize flavor and satisfaction as well. Currently, there are about two dozen no-alcohol beers, ranging from the Swiss imports Moussy and Kaliber to Sharp's (made by Miller) and O'Doul's (from Anheuser-Busch).

These "beers" are made either by removing the alcohol after brewing or by stopping the fermentation process before alcohol forms. An added attraction for many customers is their low-calorie count, which is about half as high as regular beer and a third less than light beer. Though sales have risen, sales of these "beers" still comprise only a tiny percentage of the beer market. But at least one expert compares this healthy niche market to that of decaffeinated coffee: there'll always be a demand for it, so it will always be around.

INDUSTRY TRENDS

The bland, light-bodied lagers of today's giant brewing companies may still dominate the beer market, but there is a persistent and growing interest in specialty beers and imported beers from a very active international brewing scene. Let's take a moment to look at both.

We've already established that today's consumer is willing to experiment with new and different products, is willing to pay a higher price for them, and may well be more sophisticated than the prototypical beer drinker of years past. This is fueling the trend toward increasing availability of what are termed *craft beers,* made by people who consider brewing as much an art form as a science. In contrast to the standard American beers and many of the imports, these "hand-crafted" brands are typically rich, hearty, colorful, aromatic brews that range from European-style beers to specialties developed by the individual brewer. While the national giants are locked into their own rigid formulas and images, most craft brewers have tried to capitalize on the trend by introducing their own, fuller-flavored products or by purchasing or contracting with smaller breweries to sell their specialty beers. This hot competition is likely to increase.

Microbrewing is not without its risks: one in four microbreweries and one in five brewpubs fails. The main reasons are lack of distribution; they really are small, including their output, and lack of a big enough advertising budget to make their presence well known. But for those who are dedicated to experimentation and creative freedom in the beer business, this route is worth a try. There are now about 1,000 brewpubs in the United States, and another 400-plus microbreweries. Add to that about 40 regional specialty breweries, and you've got a niche market worth more than $3 billion in sales.

Craft beers are especially popular in the bar and restaurant industry because they command higher prices than a regular beer or even the super-premium varieties. Profit can be as much as 200 percent on bottled beers and 300 percent on draft beers.

Brewpubs

The restaurant-brewery combination known as the brewpub is a special segment of the microbrewery industry. The first ones appeared in the 1980s; by 1990, they numbered still fewer than 100. Today, however, there are approximately 1,300, according to the Institute of Brewing Studies.

Since a brewpub's market is its own local customers, it is not locked into a rigid product, nor does it have the costs and hassles of packaging, transporting, and competing for space and visibility on retail shelves. Thus, their profit potential is exceptional. The pub can rotate its offerings and brew special seasonal and holiday beers. What has happened in the past decade is the metamorphosis from the casual tavern atmosphere to more of a full-service restaurant. By law, most brewpubs have to derive 50 percent or more of their sales from food. The food used to be simple, hearty fare—for example, sausage and sauerkraut, nachos, and hamburgers. If you weren't a beer drinker, you probably didn't choose a brewpub for dinner.

Today's brewpub is primarily a mainstream, full-service restaurant, often with a chef, full kitchen and service staffs, and a menu of upscale cuisine. Good food shares the spotlight equally with the brewmaster's wares. The industry has learned that great beer is not strong enough on its own to build a loyal following; the food, too, has to be top quality or customers will spend their money elsewhere. In addition, the brewmaster and chef must work in tandem, to match the types and styles of beer with the foods that are offered (Figure 8.3).

Along with great potential, brewpubs face unique business challenges. To begin with, they are part restaurant and part small manufacturing plant. Storage space for grain, yeast, and hops is needed, as well as room for lagering and bottling. There are bulky tanks to clean and heavy barrels to move around. The environment must be absolutely sanitary along every step of the brewing process, to eliminate bacteria that will spoil the beer. And because 10 gallons of water are required for every gallon of beer brewed, provisions must

Figure 8.3 A Denver brewpub. Photo courtesy of the Denver Metro Convention & Visitors Bureau. Photo by Richard Grant.

be made for disposal or recycling of water and used grains. The latter can be used as livestock feed, but someone has to store it and haul it away.

To all this, add the licenses and bonds that must be obtained, the inspections that must be undergone, and the fees that must be paid, even more than for a restaurant. Brewpubs must be licensed with the U.S. Bureau of Alcohol, Tobacco and Firearms (BATF). Their owners must be bonded, and they must pay a yearly $500 occupational tax. Each state's alcoholic beverage authorities has a separate set of regulations and licenses, and counties or cities have health- and safety-related rules that must be followed.

Beer Bars

You don't have to brew it yourself to be able to offer customers an interesting assortment of lagers and ales. A certain percentage of beer drinkers are similar to the consumers of fine wines and spirits who want to be offered a wide selection of products, and one way to reach them is at the *beer bar*, which specializes in a huge, ever-changing and ever-expanding list of beers. There is little brand loyalty among customers who like to experiment, so they can sample beers by the taste or by the glass at the beer bar to find new favorites.

The obvious challenges for the beer bar include storage space and maintaining freshness and quality. Some beer bars have a "13-day pledge"; that is, all kegs will be disposed of 13 days after being tapped, to ensure freshness. Here are some examples of beer bar sales strategies:

- A New Orleans beer bar stocks 350 different beers, 42 of them on tap. (Those that are available on tap are not available in bottles.) A beer menu is updated every month; walls are decorated with dozens of neon beer signs.
- In Albany, New York, a beer bar that once boasted 750 brands has pared down its inventory to include 350, with 25 on tap.
- Beer lovers in Boston can find 480 microbrews and 110 beers on tap in the same bar. Small inventories, daily deliveries, and a full-time cellarmaster, who rotates stock, ensure product freshness.
- In Long Beach, California a so-called mega-tap bar takes draft beer to a new extreme, featuring 250 tap handles and 180 different beers. It requires more than five miles of nylon tubing to connect its 400-barrel inventory from keg to tap.

These types of bars are considered "destinations"; that is, you go there specifically to taste and experiment and enjoy the wide variety and knowledgeable servers and bartenders.

Sidebar 8.1

MAY I SEE YOUR PASSPORT, PLEASE?

Encouraging trial is a key to keeping a large selection of beer turning quickly to ensure freshness. A number of on-premise accounts have found that rewarding customers for sampling is an effective method for generating trial.

At Hubb's in Florida and Washington, customers can make the Hubb's Wall of Fame for trying 99 different beers in 90 days. Members of the Wall of Fame receive a liter mug, T-shirt and discounts on future purchases. If they do it three times they get a Hubb's jacket. The fifth time they get their name engraved on a plaque on the back of a bar stool. "We have 3,000 people working on it," says Hubb's owner Fran Ungar, noting that one customer has done it 100 times. "It gives them a chance to try different beers."

At Mahar's in Albany, New York, customers receive a passport listing the more than 1,950 beers the bar has stocked since the program began in the early 1990s. "The beer tour keeps things moving. We have 12,000 members signed up. The program goes on forever," says owner Jim Mahar. Customers who consume 50 different beers receive a T-shirt; at 125 beers they get an engraved mug and discounts on future purchases, and at 200 different beers they can select a case of beer to take home. Five customers have tried more than 1,900 beers, and new and seasonal beers sell the instant they are placed in Mahar's cooler.

Though the passports issued at Mahar's do have the look of the real thing, Mahar does not recommend trying what one customer did: "We have one customer who told me for fun he has given our passport at customs while crossing borders."

—R.L.

Source: Market Watch, July/August 1996.

Private-Label Beers

Although the beer market is a crowded one, there's no reason you can't have your own beer with your own label to serve at your bar or restaurant. And you don't even have to brew it yourself! *Contract brewing* enables you to hire an established brewery or microbrewery to make and label beer for you. It's a relatively new phenomenon; TGI Friday's was among the first to try it, offering a TGI Friday's Premium Amber on its menu.

The first step in creating a private label is to decide what type of beer is acceptable to your customers. This is no time for experimentation; you want something reliable, that's going to sell well, and that complements your food menu. You should also be able to estimate fairly accurately how much beer you'll need. Then, find a local or regional brewery (customers seem to think there's something more "genuine" about a local company doing the beer-making) and approach them about making a private-label product. You may have to get your beer wholesaler or distributor involved, since your state's liquor laws may require that you get beer only from them. Usually, though, they are happy to pick up the beer and deliver it from the brewery to you.

Any new bottling requires federal (BATF) approval of the label (the brewery can advise you or handle this paperwork) and you must choose a style of bottle and size of label that are compatible with the bottling equipment. Or you can choose to buy kegs from the brewery, which is faster and less expensive than bottles.

Mixing Beers

For many consumers, the thought of a big, dark, somewhat bitter brew is just not appetizing, especially when they are not accustomed to drinking or appreciating them. So bartenders have found interesting ways to present what is called the **mixed pint**—a blend of one beer with another or even with some other type of drink—to create a unique flavor. Mixing beers is a skill and a balancing act, much like successfully mixing a cocktail. You'll find the different brews and other liquids each have different densities, or specific gravity. They will layer one on top of another, creating a fun and dramatic appearance. The layers remain intact when the glass is sitting still; when it is tilted, the heaviest liquid slices along the angle of the glass in such a way that both liquids can be consumed together. Some possibilities include:

• Black and Tan: A blend of Guinness Stout and Bass Ale
• Half and Half: A bitter ale draught and a pilsner.
• Black Velvet: A stout mixed with Champagne.
• Black Velveteen: A stout mixed with hard cider.
• Shandy Gaff: Draught beer and ginger ale.
• Rock 'n' Bock: Rolling Rock beer and Shiner Double Bock.
• Snake Bite: Harper's Lager and hard cider.
• Purple Death: Bass Ale, Chambord, and hard cider.
• Black Death: Guinness Stout and hard cider.
• Bloody Bastard: Bass Ale, Bloody Mary mix and horseradish, with a peeled shrimp as garnish.
• Bloody Russian: A Bloody Bastard with Russian vodka added.

When you learn to make these, or create your own combinations, their names alone will spark some interesting conversations at your bar!

Draft Beer

In the past decade, draft beer has undergone a remarkable revival—a combination of new brands, microbreweries, packaging innovations, mandatory bottle deposit legislation in some states, and good old-fashioned merchandising efforts in taverns and restaurants.

Draft beer comes straight from the keg and is dispensed into a glass through a tap. While most bars still serve more bottled beer—people like to see the label, and want other people to see the label and admire their taste in beer—draft beer has a much greater markup, ounce for ounce, than bottled or canned beer.

Variety, selection, and freshness are the buzzwords bartenders use to push the draft beer. They say that the most flavorful brews are best served fresh and unpasteurized. Bars that have a greater number of beers on tap sell more beer, overall. The latest trend is to serve it straight from the keg it was brewed in, when it is called **cask conditioned** beer. Cask conditioning is a secondary fermentation of the beer by adding some yeast and priming wort to the wooden cask. The beer is served directly from the cask (called a **firkin**) that sits on the bar and is hand-pumped. But most often, draft beer is stored in stainless-steel kegs. In just a moment, you'll learn how kegs work and how to take care of them properly.

IMPORTED BEER

Selling imported beer is another important trend in the bar industry. Currently accounting for only 10 percent of total sales in the United States, the import market may seem relatively small, but the category is experiencing explosive growth. Lured by fatter profit margins than most domestic beer brands, bars and restaurants have welcomed the onslaught of new foreign beers. Today, collectively, they sell about 18 million barrels of imported beer. As long as the U.S. dollar is strong and consumers seem interested in new brands, sales of imports will continue to grow at a faster rate than for domestic beer.

At this writing, 6 of the top 10 imported beers are lagers. Here's a quick tour of the international powerhouses driving import sales in this country.

Mexico

Corona Extra bumped Heineken out of its number 1 imported beer spot in 1997, and is now the number 10 brand in overall U.S. consumption, with 2.5 percent of the total beer-drinking market. Without question, the Hispanic consumer has been a key factor in driving Corona beer sales. But the beer is just as popular with people in their 20s and 30s of other races—young, adventurous, liberal professionals. To combat Corona's image as a hot-weather beverage, recent ad campaigns targeted skiing enthusiasts.

There are two giant brewing empires in Mexico—Grupo Modelo, which exports the Corona, Negro Modelo and Pacifico brands, and Femsa Cerveza, which exports Tecate and Dos Equis. In 1998, Femsa Cerveza introduced another brand to the American market. Sol resembles Corona in taste, color, and its clear, longneck bottle.

Belgium

This tiny nation is the home of 150 breweries, which produce nearly 450 different beers. Beer is a serious pursuit here, and many of the best breweries are operated by religious orders. Although the industry lacks the marketing strength that is required to deeply penetrate the competitive American market, Belgian beer does have a following in the United States, primarily because of American microbreweries that have paid homage to it with their own versions of Belgian-style brews. We've already discussed Belgian Wit, or "white" beers, named for their pale color.

Abbey beer is a Belgian tradition dating back to A.D. 800, when the emperor Charlemagne ordered monasteries in his realm to open their doors and provide hospitality to travelers; beer-making was part of the ritual. Today, six Trappist abbeys in Belgium and the Netherlands, as well as some smaller sects, still produce beer. The style of beer labeled Abbey Dobble or Abbey Dubbel has a rich, malty flavor and an 8.5 percent alcohol content by volume. Belgian Farmhouse beers are lighter and hoppier, and have a 7.5 percent alcohol content by volume. You'll often see Belgian beer in Champagne-sized bottles, sealed with a cork, with a price of $8 or more per bottle.

Great Britain

In the United States, British beer sales are largely driven by on-premise keg sales. The British beers have not kept pace with imports from other countries, some say because of the American perception that English beer is served without being chilled. Bass Ale, the leading English import, holds less than 2 percent of the total market share for imports. It is ironic that, in the United States, Bass is brewed at the Guinness Brewing Company's importing operation in Stamford, Connecticut, the same folks who produce the Irish beer, Guinness Stout.

Germany

German beers enjoy an excellent reputation among American consumers, partly because of that nation's historical mastery of brewing as an art form, partly because of its well-known celebratory beer culture, and partly because of the intrinsic quality of the country's beers. In short, American drinkers associate Germany with beer. Many know at least a little about the *Reicheits-gebot*, the beer purity law that has been in existence there since the sixteenth century. Most German brewers adhere to it today, and so do many American microbreweries. (The law dispenses with all the "fancy stuff," and limits the brewing ingredients to the basics: water, malt, hops, and yeast.)

Consumer research indicates Americans are more likely to try a new German product than some other type of import—again, a nod to the perception of high quality. German beers come in a wide variety of styles and colors, and serving them in beer steins, or pairing them with hearty, traditional German foods, are good ways to show them off. The two leading German beer imports are Beck's and St. Pauli Girl. In 1999, Beck's ranked number 5 among imports to the United States.

Ireland

Irish beer has become closely identified with specialty or craft beers, and drinkers seem to categorize it differently from either German or English counterparts. People claim to like the creamy texture and lack of bitterness in Irish imports like Guinness Stout and Harp Lager. Other Irish-style beers include George Killian's Irish Red, which is made in the United States, and McNally's Irish Ale, made in Canada.

Guinness currently holds the number 10 spot on the top 10 list of imported beers, with about 2 percent of on-premise sales. Its marketers are making a concerted effort to appeal to the younger drinkers, who may assume that Guinness is a big, sour, "chewy" beer made to be consumed without chilling. A recent campaign positioned it as a drink "to refresh the spirit." The idea is to make it a best-seller on more than just St. Patrick's Day.

The Far East

You might not associate Asia with beer, but brews from half a dozen Asian countries are being poured and enjoyed with the foods of their native lands in many ethnic restaurants in the United States. Perhaps you'll recognize one or more of their names: Sapporo (Japan), Tsingtao (China), Singha (Thailand), San Miguel (The Phillipines), OB (South Korea), and Hue Lager (Vietnam). They are listed in order of their sales success; at this time, Sapporo is, by far, the leader. Its rise to prominence is due in large part to its availability in sushi bars, which have also grown more popular in the last decade.

Most Asian imports have not made the jump from ethnic restaurants and grocery stores to the bar scene, but a couple of Japanese brewing companies have partnered with North American beer makers to make their products more readily available in the United States. Today, Kirin is brewed by Anheuser-Busch, and Miller brews Asahi.

You learned earlier in this chapter that China is the hot new beer market, and its native beer, Tsingtao, seemed unstoppable in the 1990s. It comprises 70 percent of the beer exported from China. Named for the city in which it is brewed, Tsingtao has been made since German colonists opened a brewery there in 1903. But even as an exporting powerhouse, within its own borders it holds a market share of less than 3 percent. China's restrictive government has not allowed Tsingtao to capitalize on its popularity elsewhere. (At home, its keenest competitors are Asahi and Kirin from Japan and Foster's from Australia.) Anheuser-Busch bought 5 percent of Tsingtao, but has held back any further involvement. In fact, at the time of this writing, it is planning to produce Budweiser in China—with a different brewer. Pabst of Milwaukee, Wisconsin, and Beck's of Germany are now also making beer in China, for Chinese consumers.

Eastern Europe

Two countries have made news headlines in the beer world in recent years. First is the Czech Republic. This is a beer-obsessed nation—Czechs each drink 42 gallons of beer annually—and its lagers are considered among the worlds' best. Foreign companies have indicated more than casual interest in acquiring these brewing rights; for instance, Pilsner-Urquell is now owned by South African Brewers, which is the world's third-largest beer producer.

Ironically, while Czech beer shows great promise as an import, the country's domestic breweries are rarely profitable because of government-imposed price controls. The average Czech citizen pays only about 50 cents per pint at the bar, a fraction of what it would cost in the West.

Russia, with its rich history of vodka making and exporting, is a relative newcomer to brewing beer. However, consumption has risen sharply, and the biggest Russian breweries—all owned by Western European breweries—are investing heavily in new plants and equipment to keep up with the demand.

Why do Russians drink beer? It was very hard to find in past decades, and what was available was not especially well made. Today's Russian consumer is younger and better educated, and thinks of beer as a relatively healthy drink. After all, 25,000 of his or her comrades die each year from alcohol poisoning—an unfortunate side effect of impure, bootlegged vodka. Beer, on the other hand, is not profitable enough for bootleggers to bother making in any quantity. Some feel Russia is the last untapped (pardon the pun) beer market in the world. Beer festivals in Moscow and St. Petersburg attract

Sidebar 8.2

MARKETING IMPORTED BEERS

In 1985, *Market Watch* magazine questioned John Kucich, a beverage professional, about the viability of imports in the United States. What he said then still applies; that is, for every successful import, too many fail because they do not take the time "to do a few very basic things right." He also pointed out that building a brand name (for beer or anything else) is a long-term process. The United States is a melting pot, and the best thing about American consumers is their willingness to try a new thing; however, it is also a fickle market. Just because someone will try a new product does not mean he or she ends up a loyal customer. Kucich advises patience in developing a market, reinvesting in the business, and in building relationships with suppliers. He recommends taking a five-point strategy toward building brand loyalty:

1. **Determine your position.** This is the most important element of the overall strategy: brands must address a significant desire of a large consumer base. Who will want to buy the beer and why?

2. **Execute programs.** A brand will go nowhere without well-executed programs that communicate its position. The most obvious way to do this is through advertising, but it is also the most expensive. The special event (remember event marketing?) can be used very effectively to position a brand.

3. **Develop supplier relations.** A foreign brewer who wants to export to the United States should take an active interest in the American market and develop a partnership, of sorts, with his or her importer. Make every effort to help the supplier learn all they can about the imported beer consumer. Discuss issues about packaging, production and quality control.

4. **Understand distribution.** The "three-tier" method of selling products is truly the strength of the beer business. Strong local wholesalers (distributors) give small companies a real advantage, a "presence" in the local marketplace so that importers will take them seriously. However, it is the importer's job to learn and understand each local market as well as its wholesaler does. To maximize an imported beer's chances for success, the importer must be willing to adjust plans to fit the wholesaler's needs.

5. **Manage pricing strategies.** This is the most volatile issue between brewers, importers and wholesalers. The long-term growth of a brand requires a stable price, and that price should reflect the increased costs associated with importing. Discounting too heavily actually damages the brand in the eyes of the U.S. consumer, since imported beer relies heavily on its upscale image. A bargain basement price simply does not "fit" the beer's image.

millions of fans, who feel some loyalty to purchase beers that are locally made instead of more expensive imports.

STORING AND CARING FOR BEER

Beer has the shortest shelf life of any alcoholic beverage. Even pasteurization does not give it indefinite shelf life. All beers should be kept cool and used promptly. Beers kept too long will lose both flavor and aroma.

Although canned and bottled beers are either pasteurized or specially filtered, they also have a limited shelf life, and should be used within three to four months of the date of packaging. Some brewers mark each package with a **pull date,** the date you should pull it off your shelves if you haven't served it yet. Others code their containers with the date of brewing. Your supplier can tell you which system applies to the beers you are buying. To avoid serving over-age beers, rotate your stock, using the oldest first and putting new supplies behind existing stock.

Beer in aluminum cans is most often used for off-premise sales. They are an acceptable option only if your establishment is casual enough. They are easy to stack, and not breakable. Canned beer gets colder more quickly than bottled beer, but it also loses its chill quicker. Cans will stay fresh when stored between 40° and 70° Fahrenheit (4° to 21° Celsius). Warmer temperatures will destroy flavor and aroma.

Bottled beer storage temperatures are the same as for canned beer. Light will also cause deterioration, and direct sunlight will bring about change in a matter of minutes. This is the reason many beers are bottled in brown or green glass; even so, keep canned or bottled beers away from light and heat in all cases. Unlike wine, beer bottles should be stored upright, to avoid contact of the beer with the bottle cap.

If beer gets cold enough to freeze it is likely to precipitate its solids and form flakes that will not dissolve when thawed. Beer kept too cold for a long time may "gush" and spew out when opened. The same thing happens when bottles or cans are handled roughly.

Draft beer in kegs has the most stringent temperature requirements. It must be kept cold from brewer to distributor to storeroom to bar, preferably at 36° to 38° Fahrenheit (2° to 3° Celsius). Since it has not been pasteurized in the way that bottled beers have been, it is much more susceptible to deterioration and may begin fermenting again if it is exposed to heat. Even at ideal temperatures, kegs have a life cycle. They start aging as soon as they are tapped, and last up to 45 days after that.

Kegs come in two sizes for bar and restaurant use: the half-barrel (15.5 gallons) and the quarter-barrel (7.75 gallons). For extremely specialized beers, like some microbrews that won't be enormous sellers, there is even a one-sixth barrel available. Buying in these small quantities will cost you more,

Sidebar 8.3

TIPS FROM THE EXPERTS: DELIVERING THE BEST

Whether you stock 6 beers or 600, the experts offer these tips to on- and off-premise retailers to make sure the lagers and ales you serve are fresh and the best quality possible:

- Jim Koch of the Boston Beer Co. suggests avoiding the urge to stock up: "Buy no more than one month's supply."
- To keep the beer in his bar fresh, Jim Mahar of Mahar's in Albany, New York, works with a local supplier who holds both a wholesale and retail license, allowing the bar to buy half-case and single six-packs of some slower-moving beers. "I'm able to order more often and rotate beer stock," Mahar says.
- Don't keep old beer on your shelves. Send old product back to the distributor, throw it out, or find some other method to get rid of it. "We give it away to friends or I take it home," says Dean Leto of Country Food & Liquors in Mokena, Illinois.
- Keep an eye on slower-moving brands and be ready to offer special pricing to deplete stock before it is out of date. "You have to be ready to knock the price down to move it. Otherwise you have to take the hit on it and dump it," says Tom Greguska of Discount Liquor in Milwaukee, Wisconsin.
- For bars setting up multiple tap selections, working with proven vendors to install the draft lines and supply gas to propel the beer, and to come in regularly to clean the lines, is critical, according to Ken O'Callahan, a Guinness Import Co. draft specialist in Chicago. "Once you get below 40° Fahrenheit you don't get the proper gas breakout. The gas stays in the beer so the customer gets filled up. It can lead to a bitter taste and creates a small head on the beer," O'Callahan says.
- Judy Ashworth of Lyon's Brewery in Dublin, California, says proper handling and dispensing of draft beer is critical. "It's like you're dealing with a quart of milk," Ashworth says. To insure a fresh, consistent flavor, Lyon's uses nitrogen gas to propel draft beer.
- Location has a great deal to do with success. Ashworth advises, "If someone goes into the multiple tap business they need to be in a location with the traffic to support it."
- Train your staff to know more than the basics about beer. "If someone has the least bit of interest they'll be like a sponge," says Dave Gausepohl of The Party Source in Bellevue, Kentucky.
- Have staff incentives for selling certain beer styles or brands. "We offer incentives. We have contests for T-shirts, gift certificates, and bottles of beer and wine," says Mark Kadish of the Sunset Grill & Tap.

Source: Market Watch, July/August 1996.

Figure 8.4 A self-contained beer system. Dark lines carry beer from keg to tap. Light lines carry carbon dioxide from cylinder to keg. Cylinder is outside refrigerator at room temperature. Courtesy of Glastender, Inc.

meaning you'll have to charge more for the beer, but the low-volume keg should guarantee beer of higher quality.

Much of the quality of a good glass of draft beer lies in the proper use and care of the *beer system.* A beer system includes one or more kegs of beer, a cylinder of carbon dioxide (CO_2 cylinder) with a *pressure gauge,* a tap (faucet), heavy-duty lines (nylon or vinyl hoses) running from the CO_2 cylinder to the keg and from the keg to the tap, and a refrigerated **beer box** or remote cooler to store the keg. Figure 8.4 shows the beer system.

The carbon dioxide gas in the CO_2 cylinder is under pressure of 1,000 pounds per square inch (psi) at room temperature. It has a pressure regulator that reduces the pressure of the gas between cylinder and keg to 12 to 15 psi, depending on the brand of beer. The carbon dioxide under pressure has two functions: it maintains the carbonation of the beer, and it moves the beer through the line to the tap when the tap is opened. The cylinder should be kept at room temperature. It should not be in the beer box with the keg of beer.

A pressure gauge indicates the pressure in the keg. When beer is sitting in the keg at a temperature of 38° Fahrenheit (2° Celsius), its natural pressure is 12 to 15 psi. When a similar amount of gauge pressure is applied to the keg, it is enough to keep the natural carbonation in the beer and let it flow freely through the lines to the tap. If pressure is too low (less than the natural pressure of the beer), the beer will lose carbonation and taste flat and stale. If pressure is too high, the beer will absorb too much carbonation from the CO_2 and it will foam too much upon pouring or will squirt wildly from the tap. The correct pressure, constantly maintained, will keep the beer in the keg lively and tasty.

A common mistake that decreases profitability at the bar is the unnecessary spillage that comes with drawing draft beer. For some reason, people think it is necessary to open the spigot for a couple of seconds and let the foam spill out before putting a glass under the tap. If the taps are properly pressure-regulated, there is no need to do this. And do not ever partially open a spigot—that automatically creates more foam!

The CO_2 and beer lines are connected to the beer keg by couplings that fit into valves in the keg. Connecting the lines to the kegs is called **tapping.** There are two principal types of connections. In one system the CO_2-line coupling fits into a valve in the top of the keg and the beer-line coupling fits into a valve at the bottom (Figure 8.5a). In the other system, a single coupling with two branches connects both CO_2 and beer lines through a valve in the top of the keg. Carbon dioxide pressure forces the beer to rise through a long hollow rod reaching up from the bottom of the keg to the beer line (Figure 8.5b).

In either system, kegs may be connected in series, giving high-volume operations a continuous supply of beer without having to change kegs frequently (Figure 8.6). The latest innovation is a totally stainless-steel draft system—storage keg, lines, and taps—which is more sanitary and less susceptible to buildups in the lines.

Your beer supplier will determine which tapping system is best for you and will supply the couplings that go with the type of kegs being delivered. Usually you must buy your carbon dioxide cylinders from a different supplier. If you are serving more than one kind of draft beer, each beer type must have its own carbon dioxide supply, since the pressure required may be different.

Underbar beer dispensers take up a lot of room, and changing kegs at the bar can be disruptive. The hotel bar described in Chapter 3 stores its beer in its own walk-in cooler in the garage below the bar. With this type of remote system, the beer is piped up to the faucets at the bar. The beer lines are kept

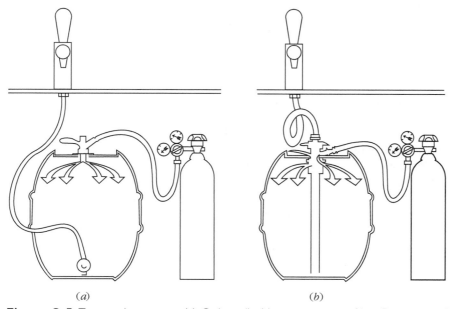

(a)   (b)

Figure 8.5 Two tapping systems. (a) Carbon dioxide enters at top of keg. Pressure sends beer up through line connected to keg at bottom. Keg must be tilted toward connection. (b) Carbon dioxide enters at top of keg. Pressure sends beer up through internal rod and into beer line. Both lines are attached to keg at top with single tapping device.

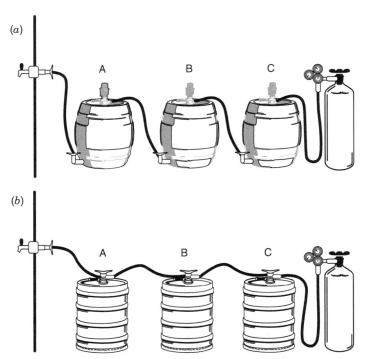

(a)

A   B   C

(b)

A   B   C

Figure 8.6 Kegs in series. Beer is drawn from keg nearest tap (A). Carbon dioxide enters Keg C, pushing beer flow from keg to keg. When fresh supplies are added, partly empty keg must be placed near the CO_2 cylinder.

cold by a special separate coolant line, and all lines are heavily insulated from the cooler to the faucets. Of course, the best configuration would be to locate the cooler directly behind the bar, so draft lines could be run through the wall and wouldn't have to snake very far from keg to tap. The longer the draft lines, the more expensive it is to install and maintain the system. Electricity costs are a big component of bar utilities, to keep the beer at a steady, cold temperature.

A remote beer supply should not share a walk-in cooler with food storage, since frequent opening and closing the door will make it impossible to keep the beer at a constant temperature. For the same reason, kegs in an underbar beer system should have their own special refrigerated storage space.

The beer box or cooler should be maintained at a constant temperature between 36° and 38° Fahrenheit (2° to 3° Celsius). Beer allowed to warm over 45° Fahrenheit (7° Celsius) may become cloudy or turn sour. Beer allowed to chill below freezing may become unsalable; the water content of the beer freezes and separates from the alcohol. If allowed to thaw slowly at its normal temperature of 36° to 38° Fahrenheit (2° to 3° Celsius), it can sometimes be blended back together by gently rotating the kegs. (This is best done by your distributor.) But if the beer is cloudy after thawing and rotation, it is beyond salvaging.

To care for your beer properly, you have to care for the whole beer system. The thermometer and the pressure gauge should be your allies, but if they are inaccurate, they can be your enemies. Check them frequently. If the arrow on the pressure gauge moves up or down from the pressure at which you set the regulator, either the regulator or the gauge is not doing its job properly. Check the thermometer by placing another thermometer in the cooler.

Clean beer lines are essential to good beer taste. Dirty lines can cause pressure imbalances, but also an eventual buildup of yeast and bacteria that will affect the beer's flavor. The beer may appear flat or cloudy and have an off-taste or odor that renders it unsalable. Beer lines should be thoroughly sanitized on a regular basis, usually once a week or at least once every two weeks. Your distributor may do this as part of the regular service in areas where it is allowed by law, or you may do it yourself, or you can hire a professional beer-line cleaner. Since cleanliness is so vital to beer quality, the hired professional is often the best choice. As a rule of thumb, the more sophisticated the beer system, the more technical the line-cleaning system process becomes.

Short and medium-length beer lines can usually be cleaned by nonprofessionals with simple, manually operated sterilizing equipment and special coil-cleaning compounds containing trisodium phosphate (TSP). Remote beer systems with long lines are cleaned with the same coil-cleaning compound, but an electric pump must be used for best results. Generally this type of equipment is operated only by professionals.

Never let your beer lines dry out! They should be kept full of beer at all times. If a line is left empty before a new keg is tapped, it will dry out, leaving dried beer residue and foam in the line, like a dirty beer glass. This will cause a bad taste and is very unsanitary. In an emergency, you can fill the beer line with water until a fresh keg is available. Then, when the new keg is tapped, you must draw off all traces of water with the beer from the new keg.

Another housekeeping tip is to flush the drains below your beer taps with a pitcher of hot water and sanitizer when closing the bar for the night. Sometimes yeasts and bacteria can become active in the pipes overnight, clogging drains.

Since your distributor is the person you are going to call if your beer begins to taste funny, he or she may well give you a list of troubleshooting suggestions, such as those listed in Table 8.1. If you can figure out what is wrong, you will be able to give the distributor a clue, so the trouble can be taken care of faster. We suggest you copy this table and post it at the bar. It also makes a good training guide.

Table 8.1

Troubleshooting Draft-Beer Problems

Trouble	Causes
Flat beer	Greasy glasses
	Beer drawn too soon before serving
	Pressure: too low, leaky pressure line, sluggish regulator, pressure shut off overnight
	Obstruction in lines
	Loose connections (tap or vent)
	Long exposure to air instead of carbon dioxide pressure
	Precooler or coils too cold
Wild beer	Beer drawn improperly
	Too much pressure: faulty pressure valve or creeping gauge
	Beer too warm in keg or lines
	Lines: too long, poorly insulated, kinked or twisted
	Faucets in bad condition
Cloudy beer	Beer too warm at some time (storeroom or delivery)
	Beer frozen at some time
	Beer too cold
	Defective valves at keg
	Old beer (was stock properly rotated?)
	Lines: dirty, hot spots, poor condition
Bad taste	Keg too warm: 50°F and over at some time can cause secondary fermentation and sour beer
	Glasses: not beer-clean, not wet
	Dirty lines, dirty faucets
	Failure to clean beer lines
	Bad air in lines, oily air, greasy kitchen air
	Unsanitary conditions at bar
Unstable head	Beer drawn incorrectly (tilt of glass)
	Glasses not beer-clean
	Too short a collar
	Flat beer causes (see above)

SERVING BEER

Serving a perfect glass of beer depends on three things: the condition of the glass, the way the beer is poured, and the temperature of the beer. But first, you have to let the customer know what's available.

Beer service requires thoughtful planning: deciding what your customers will buy, and stocking enough of it to meet their needs; then keeping it fresh and finding ways to market it so that you can sell it at its peak of flavor. The popularity of craft beer has made the job more complex. How many micro-brews should you stock? Kegs, bottles, or cans? Where will you store them all? And how will you let your customers know what is available?

The Beer List

Like a wine list, this is one option that showcases your beer selection and allows you to make it part of the personality of your bar or eatery. Whether it's a chalkboard rundown of what has been freshly brewed by your local microbrewery, or a printed list, people can't order what they don't know is available. Casual pubs and restaurants may print beer recommendations on the food menu with each of the entrees. The Hudson Club in Chicago lists its beers with descriptions, and groups them based on type of fermentation. It also offers **flights,** just like wine-tasting, of several, smaller samples of different beers instead of a full glass of one beer. A flight can be organized by country of origin, color or style of beer.

Remember, a bigger list is not necessarily a better list. It's expensive for you to add every brew that any distributor tries to sell you. Instead, ask yourself these questions:

- What do my customers want to see on a beer list?
- Which beers will boost my sales and increase customer satisfaction?
- How many selections can I safely afford to stock and serve based on my budget and available space?
- How extensive do I want the training program for my wait staff and bartenders to be?
- When does a beer list cross the line from informative to ridiculous? (In other words, how much information is enough—not too much?) A snobby list will turn customers off.

Customers take variety for granted when they pick up a beer list. Sheer size of the list does not please them as it used to; in fact, it may overwhelm some people. But if you have a beer list, it should have a "point of view." It should represent major beer styles as well as novelties, and contain something interesting for the "hopheads" as well as mainstream beer drinkers.

When creating a beer list, start slowly. Carefully select seasonal offerings, and don't overbuy. Start with a case or two, and gauge customers' interest. The goal is to rotate from 20 to 25 percent of your inventory every 30 days, to keep things interesting and keep your stock fresh. Keep in close contact with your beer distributors (wholesalers) and let them know you are interested in sampling new brews as they become available.

Matching Beer with Food

Above all, your beer list should be part of your overall image, and complement whatever types of food you are serving. Figure 8.7 is a basic rundown of beer and food matching, but the combinations are almost limitless.

In the last decade, there's been a renewed interest in beer as a gourmet commodity. Books like *Famous Chefs Cook with Beer* (W. Scott Griffiths and Chris Stephen Finch, Doubleday, 1996) and *Cooking with Beer: Taste-Tempting Recipes and Creative Ideas for Matching Beer and Food* (Lucy Saunders, Time-Life Books, 1996) can be used to create your menu and beer list in tandem. Beer is an interesting complement to food. Curried Thai dishes are wonderful with dry, hoppy India pale ales; the buttery flavors of traditional French cuisine marry well with ales that contain more malt and less hops. In the course of a multicourse meal, you would serve the least hoppy to the most

The Quick Beer & Food Reference Guide

Food	Best Matching Beer(s)
Meat-based barbecues	Domestic Porter; English Pale Ale
Spicy Mexican, Southwestern-USA, Thai, Chinese, East Indian	Mexican gold and amber Lagers; dry hoppy domestic Lager; domestic chili beer
Pizza with sweet tomato sauce base	Malty, dry beers like domestic Lager and Brown Ale
Fresh Fish entrees	Domestic Wheat Beer or dry Lager; dry imported Pilsener
Chicken entrees	Domestic or imported Lager
Smoked salmon, turkey	Malty domestic Amber or Ale; domestic/imported dry Porter
Beef, lamb, game	English Pale Ale; full, fruity domestic dark Ale or Amber
Fruit Desserts	Domestic Lambic; Belgium fruit flavored lambics
Sweet desserts (chocolate, cream)	Belgian Trappist dark Ales; English Imperial Stout; domestic Double Bock; Scotch Ale

Figure 8.7 The quick beer and food reference guide.

hoppy beers, in the same manner you'd pour less tannic wines with lighter courses like appetizers or salads, then "bigger," more tannic wines with entrees. And opposites attract: light, cold, clean-tasting beers go well with complex, spicy foods. If the food is complicated, keep the beer flavors simple.

At the Bar

There are several ways to market beer for customers sitting at the bar itself. The tap handle has become an art form as well as a miniature advertisement for the beer in its keg. Many brands now offer customized tap handles that look unique and prompt customers to take a second look; they feature colorful labels, or are molded to look like, for example, a bowl of fruit for a fruit-flavored beer, or a sailboat for a refreshing summer brew.

Brewers (and their distributors) clamor for a spot on that tap line, so they may provide the tap handle free of charge. If you'd rather have your taps look uniform, you can also buy many different styles of tap handle that reflect your décor, but you're passing up a good marketing opportunity if you don't use the "branded" tap handles. The backbar is also a great place to display your bottled beers.

And, finally, the use of coasters—miniature versions of the beer labels on which people set their glasses—remind them subtly about what they are drinking. Remember to use them! Some brewpubs, like Harrison Hollow in Boise, Idaho, employ coasters as décor. Hundreds of them are tacked to the walls in neat rows, enhancing the colorful, casual atmosphere.

Clean Glasses. This is important! Have you ever had a beer that tasted flat or looked filmy? Chances are it was because of the glass it was poured into. A "beer-clean" glass is completely grease-free, film-free, and lint-free. Beer is incredibly susceptible to any type of grease, oil, fat, or foreign substance, visible or invisible, on the glass. It will spoil the foamy head on the beer, cause an immediate loss of overall carbonation, and perhaps an off-taste or an off-odor as well. A beer-clean glass, on the other hand, will support the original head and, as the glass is emptied, will leave the foam in rings on the sides of the glass. The taste will stay fresh and zesty all the way down to the bottom.

The ideal way to achieve the beer-clean glass is to use a special glass-washer at the bar in which nothing but glasses are washed using a special fat-free washing agent. If you do not have a glasswasher you can produce a beer-clean glass by very carefully following the steps shown in Figure 8.8 and described here:

1. Using a special fat-free washing agent and hot water in the wash sink (a), submerge the whole glass and thoroughly brush the inside and rim with a glass brush designed for this purpose. Empty the glass of all wash water.

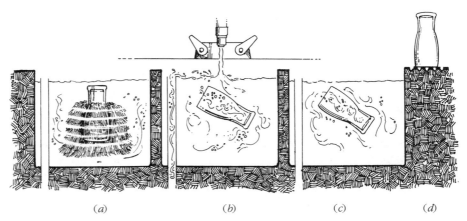

(a)   *(b)*   *(c)*   *(d)*

Figure 8.8 How to wash a glass "beer-clean."

2. In the rinse sink (b), in clean hot water (running water if possible), immerse the glass bottom end first, to be sure you fill it completely. Swish it around or rotate it, then empty.

3. In the sanitizing sink (c), repeat the rinsing procedure.

4. Turn the glass upside down on a clean rack or corrugated drainboard (d), and let it air-dry, inside and out. Do not place the glass on a towel or rubber mat or any flat surface; and do not dry it with a towel.

The bartender who polishes glasses until they sparkle isn't around any more, if they ever existed outside of books. There is a good reason for not polishing glasses: bar towels and fingers can transmit grease, lint, chemicals, and bacteria to the glass.

Pouring Beer. The second key to a perfect glass of beer is the way you pour it. A good, foamy head on a beer is a thing of beauty to a thirsty customer. The head is a collar of firm, dense foam reaching slightly above the top of the glass. It is the beer's natural way of releasing excess carbon dioxide. The head is a total of $3/4$ to 1 inch thick. If the head is scant, the beer looks flat and lifeless, even when it isn't. If the head is too thick, the customer may feel cheated, and rightly so. The more foam, the less beer in the glass!

The size of the head depends on two things: the angle at which you hold the glass while pouring and how long you hold the angle. Figure 8.9 shows you how. Rinse a beer-clean glass with fresh cold water and follow these steps:

1. Start by holding the glass upright (not angled), directly under (and about 1 inch below) the tap. Let the beer pour down into the middle of the glass, keeping the tap wide open (a).

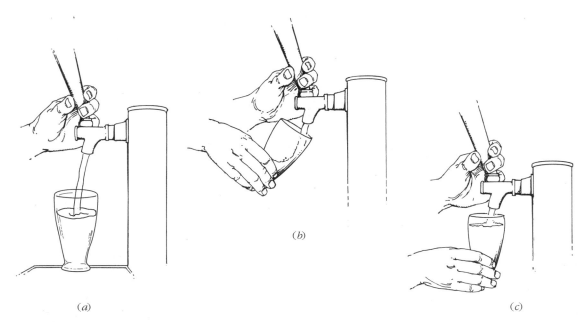

(a)   (b)   (c)

Figure 8.9 Pouring beer from a tap.

2. When the glass is about half full, tilt it to a 45° angle and let the rest of the beer hit the side of the glass as it pours out of the tap. The foam that built in the first part of the "pour" is controlled during this second part. A tilted glass and steady stream of beer down the side stops the beer from foaming excessively (b).

3. When the head has risen a little higher than the rim of the glass (c), close the tap.

Notice that the draw is a single motion from beginning to end, not little spurts of opening and closing the tap. Some bartenders prefer to fill the glass three-quarters full, then let it settle for a moment and put the head on last. That does require that you open and close the tap two times. A few practice draws will establish for you the angle of the glass and the time you should hold the angle to produce the head you want.

Sales representatives are fond of pointing out that your profit is in your head. But customer taste is your real criterion, and customers don't come back for little glasses that were mostly foam. In serving beer from a can or bottle you can produce a good head with the same tilting procedure, except that you place the glass upright and tilt the can or bottle instead, as shown in Figure 8.10. You should open the can or bottle in the customer's presence, to show you are serving what the customer ordered, and proceed thusly:

1. Pour the beer straight into the center of the wet glass with the can or bottle at a steep angle (a) so that the beer gurgles out.

(a)   (b)   (c)

Figure 8.10 How to serve beer from a can or bottle.

2. When it creates a fine-textured head of some substance, lower the angle (b) and fill the glass slowly until the foam rises to just above the lip.
3. Wipe the container and set it beside the glass on a coaster or napkin (c).

Temperature is the third key to a perfect glass of beer. A beer that tastes "right" to the typical American customer is served at 40° Fahrenheit (4° Celsius). Ales may be served at 45° Fahrenheit (7° Celsius). Guinness and bock beers are usually chilled only lightly, and other imports may have different serving temperatures. The glass the beer is served in has a big impact on its temperature.

Types of Beer Glassware. The beer glass is part of the drinking experience, and just like fine wines, certain beer styles call for certain types of glassware. The tall, thin pint glasses for stouts, ales, and porters have been in use for many years for a reason: they help capture the full character of the beer. The traditional 20-ounce pint glass is called a **nonik** or a **tulip pint.** There are also tall, thin pilsner or footed pilsner glasses.

The all-around beer glass most often seen in American restaurants is called an **hourglass,** and is available in sizes from 10 to 16 ounces. Beer mugs or steins can hold up to 16 ounces, but are also available in smaller sizes. It is smart to stock two different glass sizes, and price them accordingly. Not everyone wants a full pint.

Also consider the thickness of the glass. If beer is served in a thin glass at room temperature, its temperature will rise 2°. If served in a heavy glass such as a thick mug, it may rise as much as 5°. Thus a 40° beer served in a mug at room temperature may be 45° by the time it hits the customer's mouth. That is one reason that frosted glasses or mugs for beer are in fashion, especially in warm climates. To some extent, the freezer-frosted glasses are a merchandising gimmick: they spark interest and underscore beer's cooling, thirst-quenching character, and they do keep the beer cold longer. But some people don't like them. If they make the beer too cold, the taste buds will perceive less flavor. Refrigerated glasses may be an alternative. Your beer distributor should have suggestions for what types of glasses to use, from German steins to Trappist ale goblets, and whether to chill them before serving. Making the correct choices will impress knowledgeable beer customers, and intrigue those who want to learn more.

Training Options. Making sure beer is presented properly is one of the biggest challenges for a bar owner. Learning about beer in America was easy 25 years ago, when almost everything was a lager. Today, customers expect their servers to tell them things like: Where is this beer from? Is it "hoppy" or "malty?" How "strong" is it? What is the difference between an ale and a lager? And the true test: What would you recommend?

The macrobreweries have entered the new "beer information age" in grand style. Anheuser-Busch began its mobile Budweiser Beer School in 1996, and has a traveling exhibit called "Bud World." The latter uses three tractor-trailers, joined together to create three 40-person classrooms. A 35-minute class earns participants a "Certified Beer Master" certificate.

Miller Brewing Company distributes a video called "The Beer Facts," a brief discussion of beer history, ale, and lager styles, and a rundown of ingredients and the brewing process. The video also gives tips on keeping tap lines clean, serving beer, and proper cleaning of glassware.

Pete's Wicked Ales has a touring seminar package appropriately called "Pete's Wicked Tour," for both customers and bar and restaurant staffers. Peter Slosberg of Pete's has developed a handy beer judging chart called the "Landscape of Beers." The Boston Beer Company, brewers of the Samuel Adams brand, has published a guide on how to hold a beer dinner; and an on-premise tasting program known as "Table Talk" to acquaint servers with the craft beer market. LaBatt USA has a 5,200-square-foot "Beer Academy" in Manchester, New Hampshire, complete with three theme bars—European, Mexican, and sports—and a range of courses from a few hours to several days.

SUMMING UP

Beer rounds out the trio of alcoholic beverages found at every bar. Its four ingredients—malted grain, hops, water, and yeast—produce a lively, refreshing carbonated beverage that is as unique as the brewers that combine them. The two main types of beer are bottom-fermented lagers and top-fermenting ales, and within each of these categories is a variety of styles. Nonalcoholic beers have also joined the beverage scene, although they are not technically beers.

Beer is a product with a short life span and a need for special care. For certain clienteles, draft beer is a big attraction, worth the space it takes, the added cost of constant refrigeration, and the care required in keeping it at its best. Employees should be well trained in the care of the beer system, the washing of glasses, and the pouring of the beer in order to serve a consistent, top-quality product.

Until recently, most beer drinkers stuck with a single brand, but people have begun to experiment. Superpremium beers, light beers, imports, and specialty beers like microbrews are growing in popularity. Some bars and restaurants are using beer lists and beer tastings as promotional devices, hiring breweries to make their own private-label brands, cooking with beers, and wisely matching their beer selections to their food menus. Changing trends in beer preferences offer good merchandising opportunities.

POINTS TO PONDER

1. In which types of beverage operation do you think draft beer would be essential? In which types of operation would it be out of place?

2. What makes light beer "light?" How do you account for its popularity?

3. What does beer have in common with Champagne and soft drinks? How do the care and service of beer resemble the care and service of these beverages?

4. Explain which conditions you would want if you were installing a remote beer system because you didn't have room to put it at the bar.

5. Your customers have been complaining that their beer "tastes flat." What might the possible causes be? How would you analyze and correct this problem?

6. Who determines whether or not the alcohol content of a beer appears on the label? How does this differ from the labeling of wines and spirits?

7. In what way is each of the following related to beer quality in the glass: Temperature? Pressure? Care of the beer lines? Age? The glass itself?

8. Describe three current trends in beer consumption, and comment on their significance to a bar or restaurant.

9. List three ways you can increase beer sales in a restaurant.

10. How is the alcohol taken out of nonalcoholic beer? Why should a bar stock this type of product?

TERMS OF THE TRADE

Abbey beer

additives

barrel

beer box

beer system

bitter (ale)

blonde beer

bock beer

bottom-fermented

brewer's yeast

brewpub

bruised beer

cask conditioned

CO$_2$ cylinder

contract brewery

craft brewery

double bock

draft beer

eisbock

event marketing

firkin

flight

head

hops

hourglass

keg

kilning

krausening

lagering

Lambic beer

macrobrewery

malt

malt adjunct
 (grain adjunct)

malt liquor

mash tun

microbrewery

mixed pint

nitrogenated

nonik (tulip pint)

off-premise sale

on-premise sale

Pilsner (Pilsener)

porter

pull date

steam beer

stout

tapping

top-fermented

wild fermented

wort

CHAPTER 9

Sanitation and Bar Setup

Setting up the bar means organizing it for smooth operation each day. This entails two things: organization, or creating the correct routine for the setup, which is a management responsibility; and the actual set-up tasks, which are performed by bar personnel. The manager should see to it that every bartender and barback is trained to clearly understand the set-up routines and carry them out with precision and care. The correct procedures for closing the bar—at the end of the day or the end of a work shift—are equally important.

This chapter stresses the importance of organization and sanitation while detailing every aspect of opening and closing routines. It will be useful for you in ensuring quality and establishing sanitation standards, for training employees, for giving meaningful follow-up and feedback, and for substituting at the bar in emergencies. The manager also has ultimate responsibility for correcting sanitation issues, no matter who is careless.

This chapter should help you . . .

- Set, teach, and maintain sanitation standards and routines.
- Set up and maintain bar stock.
- Arrange liquor supplies for efficient pouring.
- Determine the mixes, garnishes, condiments, and accessories needed, and train employees in preparing and setting them up.
- Train employees to handle glasses and ice properly.
- Set up and close the cash register and train employees to do so.
- Coach employees in behind-the-bar behavior.
- Close down the bar correctly, and train employees in closing procedures.

Usually, your bartender sets up the bar. You will have scheduled his or her shift to begin half an hour or so before you open your doors so that everything will be ready. But exactly what does it take to "be ready?" There is nothing very complicated about it; it involves a series of routines, a few rules, and good organization. Good organization is the ingredient you supply, by clearly communicating the way you want things done and the way you have trained your employees. If you have things organized, the day will flow smoothly. If something is overlooked, if things are left undone, customers will have to wait for their drinks and your bartenders will be playing catch-up all evening.

The essentials of setting up are few. Everything must be superclean. The day's supplies of everything you need must be on hand and in position. Most bars have a diagram of liquor and mixer locations for a work station (Figure 9.1). The list also includes beer, wine, ice, glasses, garnishes, condiments, utensils, bar towels, napkins, snack foods, ashtrays and matches, money in the register. That's it! Now, let's take a closer look at how to get it all ready.

SANITATION

Cleanliness is essential for two equally important reasons: customer appeal and customer health. Your local health department comes into the picture, too, as guardian of customer health. If you don't meet the health department standards, you can be fined or even lose your permit to operate. But most health regulations establish only minimum standards for cleanliness and safety, so your goal should be to exceed them.

A superclean bar is attractive; it has sparkling glassware, gleaming countertops, clean ashtrays, and fresh-looking garnishes, and everything neatly arranged. The underbar should be in the same condition, with shiny-clean stainless steel, bottles all in order, ice bins full to the brim with fresh ice. Remember, it is *all* visible to customers, if not directly, then in the mirror. Even though the underbar functions as the "kitchen area" of the bar, in a real kitchen, the chef can make a mess and clean up later, since he or she is working behind the scenes. The bartender has no such luxury. Train your bartenders to start clean and work clean.

Bacterial Hazards

A bar does not present nearly as many potential health hazards as a commercial kitchen. There are very few things you serve from the bar that are potential vehicles for illness or disease. In fact, in most cases, alcohol kills bacteria. But there are a few items that may harbor unhealthful types of bacteria, which your employees should know about and guard against. They

Work Station With Soda Gun

Front Counter Top

DRINK RAIL	Gun	DRINK RAIL	
Laminated work counter	TOM CR GR OJ	Ice storage (Jockey box)	Drain board

(PC)(SYR)(LJ)(SS)(GD)(SWV)(DYV)(V)(B)(G)(S)(TEQ)(BR)(R)

Definition of Abbreviations

Bottled Mixes in the Speed Rack		Bottle Juices		Well Alcohol	
PC	Pina colada	TOM	Tomato	TEQ	Tequila
GD	Grenadine	CR	Cranberry	TS	Triple sec
LJ	Lime juice	GR	Grapefruit	B	Bourbon
S/S	Sweet & sour	OJ	Orange	G	Gin
SWV	Sweet vermouth			V	Vodka
DYV	Dry vermouth			SC	Scotch
SYR	Simple syrup			BR	Brandy
				R	Rum

Figure 9.1 A diagram of a well-organized workstation.

should also be aware of the nature and habits of bacteria, in order to understand why it is important to treat cleanliness very seriously.

Bacteria that cause disease in humans have two characteristics that are of peculiar importance to food and beverage enterprises. One, they multiply at room and body temperatures; and two, they multiply very quickly. They do this by splitting in half. If conditions are right, they can double themselves every 20 minutes or so. This means a single bacterium can become 4,000 bacteria in four hours! To do this, it needs three things: moisture, warmth, and food.

Fortunately, few foods at the bar make good nourishment for bacteria. Potentially hazardous foods include:

Dairy products: eggs, milk, and cream
Meat products: beef, pork, fish, poultry, stock
Sauces, especially those that need to be heated or refrigerated
Hors d'oeuvres or appetizers that contain any of the above items

A single episode of food-borne illness can be devastating to your reputation as a business that serves the public. There are 400 to 500 outbreaks of disease, either through ingesting contaminated food or drinking water, every year. (Health officials believe far more go unreported.) The way to avoid such disasters in your business is to keep your hot foods hot and your cold foods cold. The danger range for bacterial growth is 40° to 140° Fahrenheit (7° to

60° Celsius), as shown in Figure 9.2. Bring your hot foods *hot* from the kitchen and keep them above 140° Fahrenheit (60° Celsius) until they are served. Holding equipment for maintaining foods at this temperature should be set at 165° to 180° Fahrenheit (74° to 82° Celsius). Keep your hazard-prone cold foods at 40° Fahrenheit (4° Celsius) until they are about to be served. Check your refrigerator temperatures daily and keep them at this temperature.

Preventing the Spread of Bacteria. The most likely situation is that germs brought in by people will be transmitted to other people. Your health department may require your employees to get routine doctors' examinations to help prevent their bringing in chronic diseases. But everyone all the time carries bacteria and viruses of various sorts in the nose, mouth, and throat, and on the hands, skin, and hair, so of course it's impossible to prevent all occurrences. We all know how colds, flu, and other viruses can be spread when people sneeze or cough, sending the virus catapulting into the open air where it can be breathed in by others. Germs can also be transmitted more directly, by touching; or indirectly, on glasses, towels, or napkins.

To fight all this "undercover" bacterial action, not only must all bar equipment be kept superclean, but scrupulous personal cleanliness is necessary. Each staff member must have clean hands, clean nails, clean clothing, and clean hair at all times. Each employee must wash his or her hands as a matter of course before beginning work, before handling equipment and supplies, after using the bathroom, after blowing the nose or covering a sneeze, after smoking, and as necessary during the workday. Many health codes require a separate hand sink at the bar for this purpose. Soap and hot water and thoroughness are essentials. Effective hand washing for handling foods and beverages takes a minimum of 20 seconds and includes a prerinse, use of soap, and a complete final rinse and dry. Paper towels from a dispenser—not cloth towels—are used for hand drying. The U.S. Food and Drug Administration also recommends a thorough scrubbing of the fingernails with a nail brush.

The consequences of lax hand washing in foodservice are making news headlines in numerous communities. Poor personal hygiene is the second cause of all food-borne illness, topped only by improper holding temperatures of food, and is responsible for as many as 30 percent of disease outbreaks, according to the U. S. Centers for Disease Control (CDC). A number of companies now market high-tech hand-washing and monitoring systems. Their noncontact "touchless" equipment (so that the employee can't spread germs by touching the faucets, soap, or towel dispenser) automatically delivers hot water, soap, and a sanitizing solution, and even has the capability to track hand-washing data and download it to a computer. There are also machines that sanitize hands with infrared or ozone technology—all you do is stick them in, past the wrist. Though technology has made some very useful advances in sanitation, none will replace your own vigilant training and monitoring of employees, to create a sanitation culture where safety is always

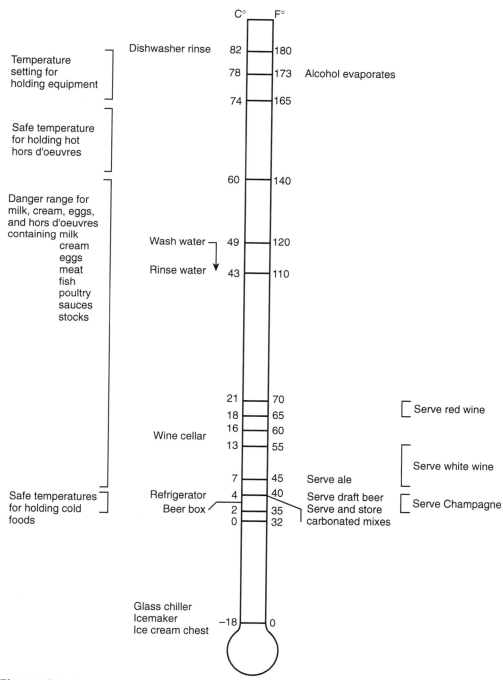

Figure 9.2 Bar temperatures.

a top priority, without exceptions. You should insist that employees stay home if they have colds or other illnesses. A cut, sore, or lesion of any kind should be securely covered. If a cut occurs on the job, it must be bandaged immediately and covered with a plastic glove. Any food, liquid, or ice on which blood is spilled must be discarded, and any glassware or equipment must be washed and sanitized using whatever sanitizer your local health department requires. There should be no hand contact with ice. If your employees use plastic gloves in any aspect of serving, these gloves should be disposables that can be changed and tossed frequently (glove surfaces can harbor bacteria as readily as the hands themselves).

Spills should be wiped up promptly. Warm and moist, they can be ideal breeding grounds for bacteria. Used bar towels should be relegated to the laundry, never just rinsed in the bar sinks for reuse. Towels are among the worst offenders in spreading disease. A common habit among service personnel is to carry a towel on the shoulder or tucked in the belt. Doing so isn't sanitary and shouldn't be allowed.

Washing and Handling Glassware and Utensils. Glassware and utensils should be washed as soon as possible after use; dirty glasses are breeding grounds. The same method that produces a beer-clean glass (see Chapter 8) produces a bacteria-free glass. You don't need a dish machine if you use your triple sink correctly. The water in the wash sink should be 120° Fahrenheit (49° Celsius); do not let it cool below 110° Fahrenheit (43.3° Celsius). It is important to use the right amount of detergent. The package instructions will indicate a certain amount of detergent per gallon of water, so to measure correctly, you must know how many gallons your sink holds. The nonfat detergent you use for your beer-clean glasses is suitable for all the others. Brushing the glass thoroughly is particularly important, paying special attention to the rim for traces of lipstick, as well as the invisible residues of use. The rinse water in your middle sink should be 110° Fahrenheit (43.3° Celsius). It should be changed often; or the faucet can run slowly and the overflow drain can take away sudsy or cloudy water.

The third sink is for sanitizing, the most important of the three steps, for it kills bacteria and makes the glasses truly clean. Very often, your health department will recommend or specify a particular sanitizing compound. Again, follow the package instructions carefully to mix the right amount per gallon of water. Use too much and it may linger on the glass; use too little and it won't do the job. Water temperature should be at least 75° Fahrenheit (24° Celsius) but not over 120° Fahrenheit (49° Celsius) to produce the right chemical reaction. Glasses should be submerged for 60 seconds, and the solution should be changed if it starts to look cloudy.

All glasses should be air-dried by inverting them onto a deeply corrugated drainboard, a wire rack, or thick plastic netting made for the purpose. These surfaces should, of course, also be clean. Air-drying avoids recontamination by fingers and towels. The rack, netting, or corrugated surface allows air to circulate inside the glass as well as outside, removing the moisture that germs love, if any have survived the rigors of the thorough washing routine.

As part of their initial training, all your service personnel should be coached about how to handle glassware. The fingers should never touch the inside of a glass, even if it's empty, no matter whether it is clean or dirty. Fingers stay off the rim, and in fact should not touch the outside of the glass anywhere below the rim where a person's lips may touch it while taking a drink. Likewise, the insides of mixing glasses and cups and plastic containers, the bowls of spoons, and the "business end" of any utensil should not be touched. Anything that touches food or drink should be untouched by human hands—and this includes the actual food or drink, and ice as well.

NSF International says that sanitation should be a way of life. If this is to be true in your enterprise, your own attitude, plus the training you give, must set the tone.

LIQUOR SUPPLIES

One of the first things the bartender does in setting up is to replenish the supplies of liquor used the day before. Each bar should have a standard brand-by-brand list of liquors, beers, and wines that should be in stock at the bar to begin the working day, with specified quantities of each brand. This is known as **par stock.** The primary purpose of par stock is to ensure an adequate working supply, one day at a time. In setting up the bar, the bartender checks the bottles in stock against the list and adds from the storeroom whatever is needed to bring the stock "up to par." Figure 9.3 is a typical par stock form.

Getting the liquor from the storeroom typically involves filling out a requisition slip or some other form to record what is being withdrawn, signed by the person withdrawing it. In a small enterprise, only the manager and perhaps one other person—the assistant manager or head bartender—have access to the storeroom. In a large operation, there is a storeroom staff and no one else is allowed in. A requisition slip requesting the liquor is presented to the person in charge, who issues the liquor and signs the slip. In this way, the amount is recorded as the liquor leaves the storeroom and responsibility is pinpointed for issuing it. It now becomes the responsibility of the person withdrawing it, who has also signed the slip. Requisitioning and issuing processes are described in greater detail in Chapter 13.

Next, the beverages must be arranged for efficient use. Bottled beer, white wine, and sparkling wine must be chilled; the stock in the refrigerator must be rotated to bring forward the cold bottles from the day before. The speed rail at each station must be checked to be sure there is a starting supply in every bottle, and reserves must be set up (with pourers in place) for those that are almost empty. The arrangement of bottles in the well must also be

Bar Par Level Form
Bar Name
Address

Effective as of (date): _____   Bar Outlet: _____

Page _____ of _____ (total pages)

Item Number	Item Name	Size	Bar	Par	Item Number	Item Name	Size	Bar	Par

Figure 9.3 An example of a bar par level form.

checked and arranged in a standard order, with the most-used liquors in front of the ice bin. Having everyone adhere to an arrangement ensures that every bartender knows where every bottle is and can reach it with speed and accuracy. If one is out of place, another will be, too, and the guest may end up with tequila in a Vodka Martini.

Pourers should be checked daily. If corks on stainless-steel pourers are wearing loose, now is the time to replace them. All pourers should be positioned at right angles to the label, and the bottles should all face the same way, so the bartender can use each one quickly without having to check the direction of the pour.

Setup is also the time to check the draft beer system to prepare for the first draw of the day. If the beer lines in your system are not properly cooled all the way to the faucet, there may be some warm beer in the dispensing head that will foam when the faucet is opened. Draw beer until a clear, solid stream of beer is present in the line, with no water or excessive foam; then it is ready to go.

MIXES

The supply of mixes must be checked and replenished, and any you make up fresh must be prepared. It is advisable to have a list of quantities needed daily—essentially, "par stock" for mixes—based on records of past sales. Amounts may vary according to the day of the week, with some quantities rising on weekends. Fresh-made mixes are one thing you don't want an oversupply of, since they won't stay fresh indefinitely. More about that in a moment.

Water Safety and Potability

One of the "mixes" you'll use the most of is the one you probably take for granted—water. Americans drink nearly 2 gallons of water per person per day, and yet there are serious water quality problems in many cities and towns. Because you will use water to make ice, to mix drinks, to brew coffee, to serve on its own, and to wash glasses and dishes, you should be keenly aware of the water quality in your area.

In the United States, the Environmental Protection Agency (EPA) is responsible for setting, implementing, and monitoring water quality standards. Its critics say there are hundreds of toxic substances that have been found in random samples of drinking water, and they decry the minimal standards water suppliers are required to meet. How safe is your drinking water? It depends on where you live and when you check it. Water quality varies from city to city, by season, and even from day to day within a single water system. Common problems that might affect the water a bar business uses include odd taste, color, or turbidity (cloudiness), possibly caused by a substance like chlorine or fluoride that your city uses to treat water. The most common water-borne parasites include *Cryptosporidium* and *Giardia Lamblia,* which both cause flulike symptoms—diarrhea, vomiting, and so on.

With that in mind, you might want to consider filtering your tap water. There are a number of commercial filters available, depending on what you're filtering out. You can get systems that kill viruses, remove particles or heavy metals, counteract taste or odor problems, absorb chemicals, and so on. For commercial use, the **micron rating** of a water filter is an important consideration. It refers to the size of particles the filter can remove—a lower micron rating means greater filtration. To remove the parasites mentioned above, NSF International requires a **submicron rated filter** that removes at least half-micron sized particles (that's 1/50,000 of an inch). Compare that to a system designed to filter only chlorine, which has a rating of 5 to 10 microns. NSF International also recommends a submicron filter that carries a 99-percent particle reduction rating; an ordinary water filter has an 85-percent rating.

NSF International is an objective third-party organization that tests equipment for safety and sanitation standards, so look for its certification on any system you are considering. The specific standards it must meet are Standard 42, which means the filter complies with taste and odor guidelines, and Standard 53, which means the filter complies with health guidelines, including reduction of *Giardia* and *Cryptosporidium.*

To keep a water filtration system in top shape, you've got to replace the filter cartridges at least every six months or as instructed by the manufacturer. Cartridges are rated by the number of gallons that can pass through them before they need to be replaced—say, 9,000 gallons. Use only the brand of cartridge intended for the system, or you will void any warranty that was part of the sale.

Carbonated Mixes. The indispensable carbonated mixes are club soda, tonic water, ginger ale, cola, and 7UP. In addition, you may use Collins mix, diet drinks, root beer, Sprite, and Dr Pepper, depending on your part of the country, your type of operation, and the preferences of your clientele.

There are two criteria for setting up carbonated beverages: an *adequate supply* and a *cold supply.* A carbonated beverage at room temperature will lose all its bubbles as soon as you pour it, filling the glass with fizz and then leaving a flat and scanty drink. It is critical to have your mixes as cold as possible.

There are three kinds of carbonated mixers: bottled, premix, and postmix. As explained in Chapter 4, both premix and postmix come in bulk containers and are chilled and carbonated automatically at the time they are dispensed. Setting up these systems consists simply of having the right number of containers—at least one in reserve for each mix—and checking the pressure gauge on each CO_2 cylinder. This gauge should read 60 psi, which is the amount of pressure needed to carbonate the beverage and deliver it to the dispenser. If the indicator gives a different reading, pressure should be adjusted accordingly.

If you use bottled mixes, the small bottles are the only way to go. They stay fresh since they are used up more quickly, but they must be thoroughly chilled and opened only as needed. If an opened bottle sits more than half an hour, it should be discarded: your next customer wants a sparkling drink. A 12-ounce bottle will make three highballs.

So-called microsodas were the late 1990s contribution to the world of trendy beverages, the soft drink industry's answer to craft beers or hard ciders. In a market dominated by colas, you might keep your eyes open for interesting, premium noncolas. The National Soft Drink Association estimates there are 450 different soft drinks, many of them "microbrewed" with nostalgic ingredients like herbs, roots, and spices, or spiked with caffeine or nutrients. Their image is upscale, and their packaging usually reflects this. They may make a unique offering for the nondrinker or serve as a base for your own cocktail creation.

Juices and Juice-Based Mixes. Fruit juice, spirits, and ice have combined to provide refreshment for years. Whether it's a thick, spicy Bloody Mary in the winter or a cold, frozen Margarita made in the blender at poolside during the summer, fruit-based drinks are easy to like and easy to sell.

Fruit juices are some of your most popular mixes. Aside from the most common—orange, lime, lemon, tomato, and grapefruit—cranberry juice cocktail is becoming more popular in drinks like the classy Cosmopolitan. You may also need to stock vegetable (V-8) juice, pineapple, and sweet-sour mixes, depending on your type of bar, the drink menu, clientele, and regional preferences. Let's use cranberry juice cocktail as an example of how versatile a single mix can be, by listing a few drinks in which it is featured. We already mentioned the Cosmopolitan (made with vodka, triple sec, lime juice, and a lemon twist):

Metropolitan: a Cosmopolitan with currant-flavored vodka
Bay Breeze: with rum and pineapple juice
Sea Breeze: with rum, grapefruit juice, and lime wedge
Cape Codder: with vodka and a lime wedge
Woo-Woo: with peach schnapps
Sex on the Beach: with peach schnapps and orange juice
Madras: with vodka and orange juice

Just about any of the juices commonly found at the bar are at least as adaptable. How you prepare your juices depends a lot on your location and the time of year; access to (and cost of) fresh fruits varies in many places. Orange juice may be bought fresh in cartons, frozen in concentrated form, and canned. Canned orange juice, even the best of it, tastes unmistakably canned. Frozen, unsweetened orange juice concentrate is the most consistent in flavor, keeps for months unopened in the freezer, and is quickly prepared.

Some proprietors find that drinks made with fresh orange juice squeezed to order are a great house specialty even when they carry the high price tag of a labor-intensive product. You can buy oranges and squeeze your own juice, but the taste will vary depending on the season and the types of fruit available. The juice should be strained through a coarse strainer to exclude pith and seeds, but a little fine pulp gives authenticity. Florida and Texas oranges give the most juice.

Grapefruit juice comes in cans or as frozen concentrate, as well as fresh in the grapefruit itself. Each form has the same advantages and drawbacks as the comparable form of orange juice, except that there may be less flavor variation in fresh grapefruit juice.

Tomato, V-8, and pineapple juices come only in cans; cranberry juice, in bottles, cans, or as a frozen concentrate. Lemon and lime juices may be freshly squeezed in quantity and kept in glass or plastic containers. Lemon and lime granules are also available, both sweetened and unsweetened. They leave much to be desired. Frozen, concentrated, unsweetened lemon and lime juices make the best drinks.

The "granddaddy" of bottled fruit juices is probably Rose's Lime Juice, although it is not a juice per se, but a syrup made of lime juice and sugar. Rose's is named for a Scotsman, Lauchlin Rose, who developed and patented a process in the 1860s to preserve fresh fruit juices by stopping the fermentation process. (Somewhat ironic, when most of Europe was trying to *get* things to ferment, to make liquor.) Rose's fortunes were made when the Merchant Shipping Act of 1867 was passed by the British Parliament, requiring all British military ships to carry lime juice onboard for a daily ration. It contained a dose of vitamin C, which prevented scurvy. Today, Rose's Lime Juice sports virtually the same label it did back then. Most bartenders agree there is no substitute for this sweet but pungent combination of lime and sugar.

A sweet-sour mix of fresh lemon juice and sugar can be made ahead of time. Sweet-sour mixes can also be bought bottled, as frozen concentrate, or in powdered form. Some have a foaming agent (called frothee) that simulates egg white. Some mixes are better than others, so give them a try in small quantities first.

There are several mixes for specific drinks: Bloody Mary, Daiquiri, Margarita, Mai Tai, Pina Colada. All you do is add the liquor. Of these, the frozen concentrates are likely to be best. And you can always make a mix a little bit better by "customizing" it to your own taste. To a Bloody Mary mix, for example, you might add your own splash of lemon or lime juice, cumin, horseradish, olive juice, roasted garlic or spicy salsa.

All the juices and mixes keep for at least a day or two. Some keep a week or more—cranberry, tomato, and pineap-

---

BLOODY MARY MIX

2 46-oz cans tomato juice

2 6-oz cans Bullshot

2 lemons (from 135–165 count batch), juice only

½ cup Worcestershire sauce

5 dashes Tabasco sauce

2 Tbsp celery salt

2 Tbsp coarsely ground black pepper

ple, for example. But as soon as they are opened, canned juices should be transferred to glass or plastic containers. All should be refrigerated until just before you open your doors. Although they are not subject to bacterial contamination, they will lose their flavor at room temperature and they will melt the ice in the drink too fast, diluting its fresh tart flavor. A new batch of juice should never be added to an old batch. It is a good idea to tape the date of preparation on the container.

Setting up juices and mixes is a matter of checking supplies, tasting leftover supplies for freshness, making new batches as necessary, and arranging them in place for efficiency and speed. If you have a frozen drink machine, making a recipe for the day ahead is part of setting up. But don't forget to first use anything left from the day before.

Other Liquids for Mixing. Another mix you will find convenient to have in constant supply is **simple syrup.** This is a labor-saving substitute for sugar in other forms, as it blends more quickly than regular or superfine sugar or the traditional lump of sugar muddled with bitters in an Old-Fashioned. To make simple syrup, you use equal parts by volume of sugar and water and boil one minute, or blend 30 seconds, or shake until thoroughly mixed. For 1 teaspoon of sugar in a recipe use ½ ounce of simple syrup (1 tablespoon). Keep it in a bottle or plastic container. It is safe at room temperature.

There are a few other, common nonalcoholic liquid ingredients. Technically, Rose's Lime Juice is in this category. Others are grenadine, beef bouillon, and cream of coconut. Grenadine is sweet, red syrup flavored with pomegranates, used as much for color and sweetness as for its special flavor. Beef bouillon is an ingredient of the Bullshot and is best purchased in single-serving cans. Cream of coconut comes in cans or bottles and is used in tropical drinks. Passion fruit syrup is a bottled mix of tropical juices, sugars, and additives.

Less common are **orgeat** (pronounced OR-zhat), a sweet almond-flavored syrup made from barley; **falernum,** a slightly alcoholic (6 percent) sweet syrup with an almond-ginger-lime flavor and a milky color; and orange flower water, a flavoring extract. All these syrups are okay to store at room temperature.

Milk and cream are often called for in drink recipes. Cream is usually half and half, but may be heavy cream for a well-to-do clientele. Whipped cream is especially popular as a topping for dessert/coffee drinks. Milk and cream must be kept refrigerated, both for health reasons and because they quickly turn sour at room temperature. Cream substitutes are sometimes used, but the drink is not as good and the substitutes spoil easily. Keep them cold in the refrigerator, too. Cream whipped ahead with a little fine sugar will hold well. Consistency should be just short of stiff for most drinks. Whipped cream is also available in aerosol cans. It must be kept below 40° Fahrenheit (4.4° Celsius). If coffee drinks are on your menu, the customers won't want to wait until you brew a pot of coffee to deliver their drink. However, coffee held for longer than an hour changes flavor and will spoil the finest recipe. Fresh coffee is essential, and in today's market, there are people as knowledgeable and particular about their coffee as their liquor, wine, or beer.

Bottled Water. Bottled water continues to be popular with American consumers. Brand-name water first became a sign of chic in the mid-1970s, when Perrier advertised heavily and made itself a socially acceptable nondrink alternative for partygoers. Then, the workout craze began, and people took their water bottles to the gym with them. Today, bottled water has the additional market appeal of "purity," which appeals to the health concerns of consumers. Peruse the names and labels in any supermarket water section and they conjure up alpine landscapes and fresh-looking springs. Currently, the strongest growth in this market is in the "convenience" or single-serving size, for fitting in a gym bag, lunchbox, or backpack. U.S. consumption of bottled water topped 17 gallons per person in 2000. The point is, bottled water is yet another item with great profit potential at the bar. For the slimmed-down, pumped-up generation, it is seen as a healthy alternative to soft drinks. For the restaurateur or bar owner, it is a way to make money on a product that used to be given away, with a profit margin similar to that of coffee, wine, and beer (see Figure 9.4).

There are two kinds of bottled waters—still and sparkling—and it's smart to offer both. You can offer liter-sized bottles for groups or serving-sized bottles for individuals. Either way, they should be kept in the refrigerator and

Revenue Growth Potential Worksheet

500 glasses **(Number of glasses of tap water an operator serves each day)**

× 10% **(Convert 10% of these to bottled water sales)**

= 50 bottles **(Number of servings of bottled water per day)**

$2 × 50 bottles **(Multiply by selling price per serving of bottled spring water)**

= $100 **(Added daily revenue)**

× 7 **(7 days, or weekly revenue from one unit)**

= $700 **(one unit)**

× 52 **(× 52 weeks = yearly revenue from one unit)**

= $36,400 **(one unit)**

Figure 9.4 Revenue growth potential worksheet for bottled water. *Source: Restaurant Hospitality,* May 1999, p. 102.

Sidebar 9.1

BOTTLED WATER "MOCKTAILS"

Perrier from France was the first bottled water product to break in to the American market. The company even created nonalcoholic drink recipes to complement its sparkling water. They seem like a refreshing change of pace, but are probably not drinks that people will ask for by name.

KIWI COOLER

METHOD: BLEND

1 kiwi fruit, peeled and sliced

2 Tbsp coconut cream

Juice of one lime

6.5 oz Perrier, chilled

GARNISH: KIWI SLICE

SUNDOWN SPRITZER

METHOD: BUILD

1 cup white grape juice

6.5 oz Perrier, chilled

GARNISH: MINT SPRIG

LE FRENCH OPEN

METHOD: BUILD

4 parts Perrier

2 parts orange juice

2 parts grapefruit juice

2 parts strawberry syrup

GARNISH: FRESH STRAWBERRY

served chilled, in the opened bottle with an empty glass. A wedge of lime or lemon may be added if the customer wishes, but never add ice unless the customer requests it. Most customers are annoyed if they purchase an expensive glass of mineral water and then have it diluted with the local tap water of your ice cubes. This is why you chill an adequate stock of mineral water in advance, making ice cubes unnecessary. It also makes sense to serve "designer" water in a different type of glass than regular tap water—perhaps a stemmed glass. This lessens the chance that a server will come around and refill the half-empty glass with tap water.

What exactly is in the bottle? The world's two major bottled water exporters, France and Italy, produce it in an untreated state. It is truly "ground water," collected from protected underground sources that have not come in contact with animals, people, or the pathogens they might carry. American-made bottled water is often "surface water," but what is labeled "spring water" must (according to the U.S. Food and Drug Administration) originate underground and flow naturally to the surface. Same goes for "artesian" and "well" water. But much of the U.S.-bottled water is simply, as it states on the label, "purified drinking water"; no special attributes. The FDA also says bottled water must be calorie-free and contain no added sweeteners or chemicals; flavors, extracts, or essences may be added if they compose less than 1 percent of the weight of the final product, hence, a few of the fruit-flavored sparkling waters.

While environmentalists worry about what is *in* bottled water, dentists worry about what is *not* in it. They feel children who drink strictly bottled water may not be getting the fluoride (from their municipal treated water systems) that can protect against tooth decay; and adults also need it to prevent receding gums. Fluoride is added to about 60 percent of the nation's water systems, although its use has been somewhat controversial for the last 30 years. Dentists have even released a couple of brands of bottled water that contain fluoride. The debate has not slowed America's thirst for this convenient form of H_2O.

GARNISHES AND CONDIMENTS

Garnishes sell drinks. Heads turn when people see a pair of orange "eyeglasses" hanging from a tropical cocktail, or the steam (from dry ice) rising from a pitcher of Long Island Iced Tea. Even lemonade rises a few notches in sophistication with a triple garnish of orange, lemon, and lime slices. And everybody remembers the drink they had on vacation that was served with a little paper umbrella. There are exotic cocktail olives, stuffed with almonds or bleu cheese; pickled green beans, onions, and asparagus spears; fresh shrimp; skewers of golden kumquats . . . the list of potential garnishes is as long as the bartender's imagination.

Each garnish—tasteful, goofy, or outrageous—has a niche in every style of bar operation. They all contribute something: a flavor, a texture, a contrast, eye appeal. You should view them (as does the TGI Friday's organization) as a drink ingredient and part of the unique appeal of that particular cocktail.

Fruit Garnishes

Fruits are among the most popular garnishes, and preparing them for bar use is one of the most important parts of setting up. The standard items include lemon wedges and lemon twists, lime wedges, orange and lemon slices, cherries, olives, and cocktail onions (not a fruit, but used like a fruit in some cocktails). Other fruits and vegetables sometimes used for eye and taste appeal are pineapple spears or chunks, cucumber spears, celery sticks, fresh mint, stick cinnamon for hot drinks, and anything of your own inspiration.

Preparing Citrus Fruits. Lemon wedges are used for appearance and for squeezing juice into individual drinks. Lemon twists are used for the tart, unique flavor of the rind; they are rubbed along the rim of the glass and twisted to squeeze the oil into the drink. Whole lemons are also squeezed for fresh lemon juice in quantity.

All citrus fruits should be washed thoroughly before cutting, and so should the hands. For cutting, use a sharp knife and cut on a cutting board, not in midair. Always cut down and away from yourself, keeping the fingers and thumb of your other hand curled out of the way (Figure 9.5). The best lemons are medium in size, with medium-thick skin (too thick is wasteful; too thin is hard to work with and not as nice to look at). A good size of lemon is 165 **count,** which means 165 lemons to the case. You can increase juice yield of lemons by soaking them in warm water and rolling them back and forth on a hard surface while exerting pressure with the flat of the hand.

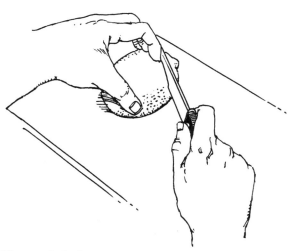

Figure 9.5 Cutting technique for fruit. Hold fruit firmly on board by placing fingers on top as shown, fingertips curled under slightly, thumb well back. Cut down toward board. Knuckles can guide knife.

To cut lemon wedges (Figure 9.6), first cut a small piece off each end—just skin, not pulp (a). Cut the lemon in half lengthwise (b) and, with cut side down, cut each half lengthwise into wedges of the size you want (c). An alternate way of cutting wedges is to cut the lemon in half lengthwise, then, with the cut side down, slice each half crosswise into half-inch slices (d). These smaller wedges fit nicely into the hand squeezer or are easy to squeeze between the fingers. If you want a wedge that will hook onto the rim of the glass, make a cut lengthwise down the middle of the half-lemon before slicing.

To make lemon **twists** use a zester or stripper. These tools strip off just the yellow part of the skin, the zest. Cut pieces about 1½ inches long. To produce twists without a special tool (Figure 9.7), first cut off both ends of

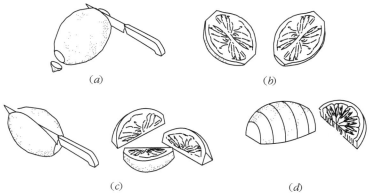

(a)   (b)

(c)   (d)

Figure 9.6 How to cut lemon wedges.

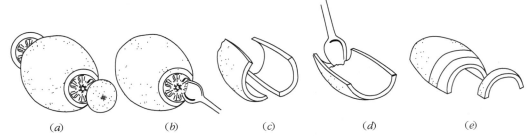

(a)   *(b)*   *(c)*   *(d)*   *(e)*

Figure 9.7 How to cut twists.

the lemon (a), then scoop out the pulp with a barspoon (b), saving it for juice if you want it. Then cut through the rind (c) and lay it flat. Scrape away the white pith (d), and discard it, leaving about ⅛-inch thickness of yellow skin. Slice this in half-inch wide strips (e).

If you want lemon **wheels** for garnishes (Figure 9.8), simply cut crosswise slices beginning at one end of the lemon (a). Discard end pieces having only skin or pith on one side. Slices should be thin, yet thick enough to stand up on the edge of the glass. Make slits halfway across slices for this purpose (b).

The best limes are deep-green, seedless, and on the small to medium side (54 count, since the cases are smaller than lemon or orange cases). That said, the bar manager is often at the mercy of the market, taking what is seasonally available. The ideal size lime will make eight neat wedges (Figure 9.9). First you cut off the tips, then cut the lime crosswise (a). Then put the cut sides down (b) and cut each half into four equal wedges (c). Lime wheels are made the same way as lemon wheels.

Orange slices are made by slicing the orange crosswise as you do the lemon. Make slices ¼-inch thick; if they are any thinner, they don't handle well and tend to dry out. Orange slices can be used whole, as wheels, or quartered and impaled on a pick (called "flagged") with or without a cherry as in Figure 9.10 (a) and (b). The best-looking oranges are the California varieties; the navel oranges are ideal because they have no seeds. A case count of 80 gives you a good size.

All citrus garnishes should be kept moist. They keep best if you can form each fruit back together again, but often there are too many pieces. Covering them with a damp bar towel helps to retain moisture and appearance. So does refrigeration: you can bring them out in small batches. Often you can prolong life by spraying them with 7UP. Twists dry out especially quickly and should not be made too far ahead.

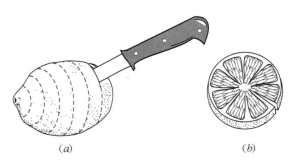

(a)   *(b)*

Figure 9.8 How to cut wheels.

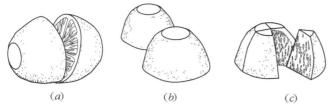

Figure 9.9 One way to cut lime wedges.

Other Garnishes

Cherries, olives, onions, and pineapple chunks come in jars or cans and need no special preparation. Cherries used as garnish are maraschino cherries, pitted, both with and without stems, depending on the drink. Cocktail olives are small, pitted green olives of the manzanilla type. They are available plain or stuffed with anchovies, nuts, pimientos, or bleu cheese. They are often used on picks as flags (as in Figure 9.10c). But because your customers may not like your choice, it is best to go with the traditional empty olive they expect. Cocktail onions are little onions pickled in brine.

Pineapple chunks can be purchased canned, but when in season, it makes a lovely, fresh tropical garnish. To prepare these, cut an untrimmed pineapple into half-inch slices, as seen in Figure 9.11 (a). Trim the skin from each slice, and cut it in half (b). Cut out the hard center core of the slice (c), and then cut the fully trimmed slice into wedges (d). You can use these on a cocktail pick with a bright cherry to contrast their pale yellow color.

Canned garnishes are removed from their juices, set up in glasses, cups, or a condiment tray, and kept moist until time to serve. The damp-towel covering is good for them, too.

Other fresh-cut garnishes such as fresh pineapple spears, cucumber sticks, and celery sticks should be cut to size and shape with an eye to appearance in the drink. They too are kept chilled and moist. For added crispness,

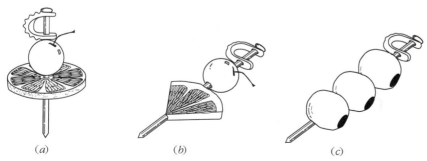

Figure 9.10 Garnishes on picks.

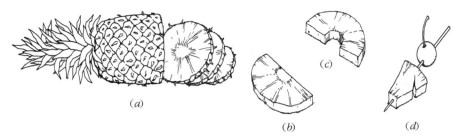

Figure 9.11 How to cut pineapple garnishes.

celery and cucumbers can be kept in ice water in the refrigerator until needed. Just before serving time, all perishable garnishes are set up on the bar in an arrangement that is both efficient and attractive, often in a condiment tray such as the one shown in Figure 4.25. If the bartender does the garnishing, everything should be within easy reach; there should be a separate setup for each station. If servers garnish the drinks, the garnishes should be at the pickup station. Each set of garnishes must have a supply of picks, for spearing the garnishes to go into the glass. If you don't want picks in your drinks, have tongs handy for placing the garnish. Don't allow fingers for this ceremony, as that is both unsanitary and unsightly.

Condiments for Flavor

The term *condiments* is used for those garnishes prepared for eye appeal in a bar setting. In more general terms, the word applies to a spicy or pungent food used to add a special flavor or enhance the total flavor of a drink or dish. These, too, are part of the well-stocked bar, and they include Tabasco and Worcestershire sauces, bitters, salt, sugar and spices.

Tabasco is liquid hot pepper, an integral part of most Bloody Marys. Other brands are available, but Tabasco is the one your customers traditionally expect in their drinks. It is dispensed drop by drop, from the dispenser that comes with the bottle.

Bar bitters are actually nonbeverage spirits (undrinkable by themselves). They are like liqueurs without sugar, made by distilling or infusing alcohol with secret formulas of bitter herbs, spices, and other flavoring agents, and you'll use them in everything from cocktails to sparkling mineral water as an aperitif. They were originally created as a medicine to calm upset stomachs. Today, Italy makes the most brands of bitters, known there as *amaro*. The best-known Italian bitters are Campari and Fernet Branca.

You will need two kinds at the bar: Angostura bitters from Trinidad (a venerable brand originally made in Venezuela as a malaria medicine) and orange bitters. A truly "bitter" bitters formula from New Orleans, Peychaud's, is also called for in some drinks. Bitters are dispensed by the **dash,** which is the equivalent of one-sixth of a teaspoon. The dispenser built into the neck of the bottle is called a **dasher.** If you want only a drop, you can hold the bottle level and tap it with one finger.

Worcestershire sauce is a sharp, savory nonalcoholic kitchen condiment that found its way to the bar to season some versions of the Bloody Mary. It comes with a handy built-in dasher/pourer: turn it horizontally, and it is a dasher; turn it vertically, and you can pour from the bottle.

You will need salt at the bar in two forms: ordinary table salt and **coarse salt,** called kosher salt or Margarita salt (probably at a higher price). You'll use table salt in Bloody Mary mixes; coarse salt is for **rimming** (applying to the wet rim of) glasses, for drinks like the Margarita or Salty Dog.

You should stock sugar at the bar in several forms. Simple syrup blends best in drinks. Superfine sugar, often called **bar sugar,** is the best granulated type, but you can use ordinary sugar if you mix longer. Sugar cubes are not altogether obsolete; they are used in bars that make Old-Fashioneds in the traditional manner, soaking the sugar cube that's part of the recipe with a couple of dashes of bitters. They are also an excellent means of making flambéed drinks: soak a cube in 151-proof rum and set it aflame. Even honey figures in some recipes. You have to decide how far you want to go, how much room you have to store "extras" at the bar, and whether you can keep them well organized enough so you can find them when you need them. Certain ground spices should be on hand: nutmeg, cinnamon, pepper, celery salt. And everything at each station, no matter how small or how seldom used, must be in its appointed place.

ICE

Shortly before opening time, the ice bin at each station must be filled with fresh ice, with clean ice scoops ready in the bins. Some precautions are essential to keep the ice in the bins clean and fresh. All your service people should observe them:

- Never touch ice with the hands. Use a scoop.
- Never use a glass as a scoop. This is a common practice because it is fast, but it is very dangerous. You can easily chip the glass or break it outright; then you will have glass mingled with your ice. You won't find it, but some customer will. As soon as a glass breaks, empty the ice bin and wash it out.
- Never put anything in the ice bin to cool—no wine bottles, no warm glasses. These may transmit dirt and germs. The sudden temperature change may also damage the warm glass.
- Do not position condiment trays over an ice bin; something may drop in.

- Never reuse ice, even if you wash it. Throw out all ice from used glasses. Start each drink with fresh ice in a fresh glass, even if it is the same kind of drink for the same person.
- Do not use your ice scoops for anything but ice. Keep them in the bins.

SERVICE ACCESSORIES

Near the condiments at each station are placed the accessories to garnishing: the cocktail picks, straws, sip sticks, stir sticks, and the cocktail napkins. You will have chosen them all carefully as you planned your drink menu and your garnishes, so that the visual impression of each drink served carries out the total image of your enterprise.

Picks may be either the colored plastic kind, sword-shaped, or round wooden toothpicks. They are used to spear the olive, onion, or the cherry-plus-orange, and both spear and garnish go into the glass. Some establishments fill up the pick with three olives or onions, adding flare and an impression of generosity.

Straws are useful in two lengths: the 5-inch length for drinks in stemmed or rocks glasses and the 8-inch length for highballs and Collins-size drinks. Straws are essential for sipping frozen drinks, while in highballs and rocks drinks, customers use them as stirrers.

You may prefer to use plastic stir sticks for highballs. These can be custom-made as souvenirs of your place for patrons to take home. Sip sticks are somewhere between straws and stir sticks; they are hollow but firmer than a straw and smaller in diameter, and usually only one is used per drink. Some places also use these for coffee drinks.

Figure 9.12 Serving accessories set up for quick service. Courtesy of Co-Rect Products, Inc.

The final essential is a supply of cocktail napkins, stacked with the folded edge toward the bartender or server for easy pickup, or arranged into a fan shape so they don't stick together. These napkins should be two-ply; anything thinner disintegrates in no time. There should be a good stack at each station and plenty in reserve (Figure 9.12).

Where smoking is permitted, a good supply of sparkling clean ashtrays should be stacked. Bartenders or servers should keep them emptied, frequently replacing the used ashtray with a clean one. (It is no longer considered proper etiquette to stand there and wipe the used ashtray clean at bar or table; this should not be done in view of the guest.) Smoking tends to make people thirsty. Often, the emptying of an ashtray will trigger a request for a second drink or another glass of wine. Where there are ashtrays, there must be plenty of matches available, with the bar's name, logo, and address and phone number on them. "Plenty," because they will go home with customers. You'll be amazed, even if few people smoke, how many will take the free matchbooks.

Any snacks you serve are placed on the bar or on tables just before you open. These can be part of your image, or they may be subtle thirst promotion: small bowls of savory mixtures of peanuts, pretzels, popcorn, cheese crackers. Some places opt to set up an old-fashioned popcorn maker, where customers can fill their own bowls.

All the essentials for table service must be clean and in readiness at the pickup station. These include, all in good supply: drink trays, folios for check presentation, guest checks for servers, drink or appetizer menus and wine lists, wine chillers, bottle openers, bar towels (or white table napkins), cocktail napkins, beer coasters, matches and ashtrays.

OPENING THE CASH REGISTER

Most bar operations work with a standard amount of starting cash for the cash register, called the **bank.** The purpose of the bank is to have ample change in coins and small bills—primarily ones and fives. The amount of the bank will vary according to the sales volume and the policy of the bar.

When the bar is closed, the bank is put into the safe, usually in a cashbox or a locked cash-register drawer. In opening the register, the first task is to count the bank to make sure there is adequate change, in the correct amount to start the day. In some systems, the person closing the bar the night before has left a **bank count slip** (Figure 9.13) listing the amounts of the various coins and bills. The opening bartender checks the opening count against this slip. If everything checks out, the money goes into the register drawer, ready for business.

If the register uses a paper tape, the next step is to check to see that there is an ample supply for the day and that the printing on the tape is clear; that is, it's dark enough to be read easily. A clear tape is essential to the record-keeping of the bar. Next, the register is cleared to make sure no transactions have been recorded since the last shift. The next step is to ring up a "No Sales" transaction to obtain the first transaction number on the tape. This number must be recorded on the cashier's checkout slip (discussed later). This is a control procedure that gives management an audit trail when reconciling the register and the money at the end of the shift.

The person opening the bar should make sure that the usual materials are available at the register: pencils, pens, paper clips, rubber bands, stapler, payout vouchers, credit card forms, guest checks.

Mise en Place

There is a fine tradition in the restaurant industry expressed in the French phrase ***mise en place***: "Everything in its place." It means that the setting up is complete and everything is in position ready to go, right down to the last olive! The first customer has only to cross the threshold to set it all in motion.

Bank Count Slip

Total in drawer: $ _300.00_

Bills: $ _250.00_		Coins: _50.00_		

$1 Ones	$ _100.00_	Pennies $ _3.00_	
$5 Fives	$ _30.00_	Nickels $ _6.00_	
$10 Tens	$ _60.00_	Dimes $ _20.00_	
$20 Twenties	$ _60.00_	Quarters $ _20.00_	
		Halves $ _1.00_	

Name _C. Smith_

Date _7/4/01_

Shift: 11–3   3–7   (7–close)
(Circle one)

This form is to be used by cashier turning in the bank after sales have been accounted for. This slip should be left with the bank.

Figure 9.13 Bank count slip.

Perfect *mise en place* is the result of good planning and organization. It brings a moment of equilibrium between preparation and action that is important to start off the action right. Not only is everything ready, but the bartender *knows* it. The resulting confidence influences all the action that follows—the readiness is psychological as well as physical. A relaxed, confident bartender is a better host, makes fewer mistakes, and can cope with emergencies far better than one who wasn't quite ready for that first customer and is still trying to catch up. A bartender who takes pride in *mise en place* is a real pro, and one to cherish.

Part of *mise en place* is creating and adhering to a specific system for things like the underbar workstation. Overall, good *mise en place* is all the things you have learned about in this chapter, plus a few more:

- Glasses of all the necessary kinds and sizes are clean and in place in the numbers needed.
- Bar implements are clean and in place at every station. This means jiggers, mixing glasses and cups, shakers, barspoons, strainers, squeezers, openers, zesters, scoops, and tongs.

Sidebar 9.2

REPLACING BAR TANKS

To replace a carbonated mix tank, follow these steps:

1. Remove the incoming air hose and the outgoing syrup hose from the tank.
2. Replace the empty tank with a full tank.
3. Dip both hose fittings in hot water. This removes any syrup residue and ensures a clean connection.
4. Refit both hoses on the replacement tank.

To change a CO_2 (carbon dioxide) tank, follow these steps:

1. Turn the handle on top of the CO_2 tank to the Off setting.
2. Remove the regulator from the used tank.
3. Replace the empty tank with a full tank.

4. Use a new washer to attach the regulator to the new tank.
5. Tighten the regulator fitting as tightly as possible, using an open-ended wrench.
6. Turn the handle on top of the new tank to the On setting.
7. Take these additional precautions:
  - Don't lay CO_2 tanks flat on their sides.
  - Don't drop the tank—it could shatter.
  - Do not refrigerate or store CO_2 tanks in coolers.
  - Keep carbonated bottled mixes on hand in case your system malfunctions.
  - Keep the phone number of the service company handy.
  - Never attempt to take a carbonated drink system apart yourself. The system is usually leased to you, and if you damage it, you are responsible for paying to fix it.

- Equipment, including blenders, mixers, and ice crushers, is clean and in working order. The dispensing gun (or cobra head) and its system of hoses for dispensing liquids is used extensively (Figure 4.5). Remove the tip of the nozzle and clean it in hot water to remove syrup deposits from soft drinks. The syrup and CO_2 canisters for carbonated drinks should also be checked, and replaced if necessary. Figure 9.14 shows the line system of a typical cobra gun.
- A supply of guest checks and credit card slips are in place; the credit card machine is in position and operating correctly.
- Coffee is made, if it's part of your menu.
- Money is in the cash register, counted and ready to go.

Figure 9.15 is a suggested checklist for a complete *mise en place.* Such a list can be very useful in keeping procedures standardized and for orienting substitute bartenders and new personnel.

BEHIND-THE-BAR BEHAVIOR

We've already discussed the fact that your bartender is the key person who conveys the image of your enterprise. You may have special requirements in personality, dress, and behavior if you are after a certain image. But some basic rules apply across the board.

Prompt, friendly and courteous service is the overriding requirement. Greeting a new person immediately conveys a sense of welcome and belonging. Remembering a loyal customer's favorite drink makes that person feel appreciated. One warning applies here, however: if a regular customer comes in with a new companion, it is best not to give away that "regular" status. A genuine smile for everyone is a great sales asset—and a safe one.

If uniforms are not required, dress should be conservatively appropriate to the general atmosphere. Blue jeans and T-shirts are out of place behind a hotel bar, just as a tuxedo would be at a truck stop. White shirt, dark pants, and conservative tie are safe dress anywhere. A bartender should never outdress the clientele. It goes without saying that clothes should be as neat and clean as the personal cleanliness you require.

Bartenders should not drink while working. Smoking, eating, and chewing gum are distasteful to many customers and should be confined to breaks away from the bar.

The legendary bartender you "tell your troubles to" does not belong in most bars nowadays. It is best for bar personnel not to get too involved in conversations, for simple reasons: they might neglect other customers or be seen as playing favorites. This is especially true of personal conversations, in particular remarks about the bar, the boss, the other help, and the other customers. It makes a bad impression all around. It is also inappropriate to butt into an ongoing conversation, whether it be about football, politics, men, women, or religion; and it's disastrous for the bartender to get involved in an argument—even if he or she is asked to "settle a bet." For you, it's always a bad bet.

Discretion is an absolute must. The bartender's lips should be sealed when a customer reappears after having too much to drink the night before, or brings in a different date, or brags about something the bartender knows isn't true. If a phone call comes for a customer, his

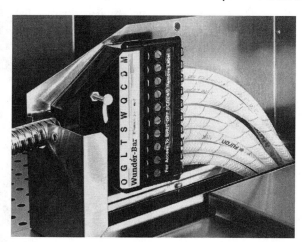

Figure 9.14 The series of hoses for a dispensing gun. Courtesy of Glastender, Inc.

CHECKLIST FOR SETTING UP THE BAR

Liquor: Bring stock up to par. Turn in empties.

Well: Check supplies. Set up reserves. Check pourers. Line up bottles.

Bottled drinks: Replenish and rotate beers, wines, wine coolers, mixers, bottled waters in cooler. Check cooler temperature (40°F/4°C).

Draft beer: Check supply. Drain off excess foam, taste beer. Check pressure. Check beer-box temperature (36°–38°F/2–3°C).

Soda system: Clean the (Cobra head) gun. Check soda supplies. Check CO_2 pressure.

Glasses: Wash used glasses. Check supplies. Arrange in order.

Implements: Check and set up blenders, mixers, mixing glasses, shakers, jiggers, barspoons, strainers, squeezers, openers, scoops, tongs.

Juices and mixes: Taste leftovers for acceptability. Prepare fresh juices, mixes; refrigerate. Prepare frozen drink mix; start machine. Check and replenish bottled-mix supplies. Make simple syrup.

Ice: Check and clean bins. Fill with ice. Be sure there is a clean scoop in each bin.

Garnishes: Prepare and set up lemon wheels, wedges, twists, lime wheels, wedges, orange wheels, flags, cherries, olives, onions, cucumber sticks, celery sticks, special garnishes.

Condiments: Set up salt and sugar for rimming, bar and cube sugar, bitters, Tabasco, Worcestershire, pepper, nutmeg, cinnamon, celery salt.

Serving accessories: Set up picks, straws, stir sticks, sip sticks, cocktail napkins, bar towels, coasters, bottle openers, wine carafes and chillers, ashtrays, matches, serving trays, folios.

Cash register: Count bank and set up register. Check register tape. Check and set up cashier supplies: guest checks, credit card forms, payout vouchers, pencils, pens, paper clips, rubber bands, stapler and staples.

Coffee: Make fresh. Set out sugar and cream, stirrers.

Snacks: Set out in clean containers.

Figure 9.15 Checklist for setting up.

or her presence should not be acknowledged without checking with that customer first.

Courtesy goes beyond the initial greeting. It extends to keeping one's cool under duress. There will always be that contentious customer who challenges everything—the drinks, the prices, the change you've carefully counted back. Only the cool, calm bartender can handle this one. (And be sure the change is right every time!) The list of tips that follows is a compilation of common sense and experience from real-life bartenders.

- Don't transfer your own stress to your customers.
- Don't underestimate the economic power of fun. A bartender can positively affect how people enjoy themselves.
- Smile when you're not sure what to do or how to respond to a comment. A frown or deadpan expression is more easily misinterpreted.
- Put the "house" first. Never forget that the bar is a business. Run an honest till—don't steal or put up with others who do.
- Work smart, not hard. Learn how to do things in the least possible number of steps, with the least amount of motion.
- After closing the bar, just go home. Checking out the competition is fine once in a while, but having time at home saves money, preserves brain cells, and gives you a chance to enjoy the peace and quiet.
- Drink-making is an art. Every drink that you serve should reflect your artistry and pride of workmanship.
- Treat everyone as a guest, and remember that there are no "first class" and "second class" guests. To the bartender, everyone is equal.
- Keep your bar clean. Otherwise, it reflects poorly on the cleanliness level of the overall establishment.
- Don't fret about tips. Make good drinks, give great service, and the tips will follow.
- Remember, every night is a new show. Appearance and demeanor should reflect this. Set professional standards and live by them.

If a customer begins to have too many drinks, or shows clear signs of intoxication, the bartender or server has no choice but to stop serving alcohol and to suggest coffee, a soft drink, or food—compliments of the house, if necessary. If there is trouble, it is up to you as the manager to take over as discreetly and tactfully as possible, and to arrange for a safe ride home for the guest. This might require enlisting the help of a sober friend, calling a taxi, or even getting a hotel room for the night. Your reputation is on the line, and possibly your license too, and third-party liability may be just around the corner if that customer gets into the driver's seat.

At this point in your studies, you may find it useful to review the material on alcohol-related laws and server training in Chapters 2 and 12.

CLOSING THE BAR

After standing on your feet for six or eight hours, maybe more, the prospect of cleaning up the bar is not thrilling. But clean you must. A good way to start is to put away any wines that have been on temporary display. They must be locked safely away. Next, you should put away all the perishables, such as cream and juices. These go into the refrigerator. Juices should be in covered plastic containers. If you have any opened cans of Bullshot, Coco-Lopez, or other mixes, empty them into glass or clear plastic containers, label the contents, and refrigerate them.

Along with the juices, look after the cut-up fruits. Generally, cut limes will last for 24 hours. Place them in a jar with a lid, add some 7UP or Collins mix to keep them moist, put the lid on the jar, and place it in the refrigerator. Cut-up oranges do not keep well, and it really does not pay to keep them. Whole fruits go into the refrigerator. Olives and onions should be put back into their jars, submerged in their original brine, with the lid of the jar closed. The same goes for cherries: be sure they are covered with syrup, otherwise they will dry out and wrinkle. Anything that came from a can should be transferred to a clean, see-through plastic container with a lid. Everything goes into the refrigerator, where the cold, moist air will preserve the quality of the product and help assure the health of your patrons.

Next to be put away are the bar snacks: pretzels, chips, peanuts, crackers, popcorn. Empty all leftovers into the trash. Never put anything touched by customers' hands back into a container with fresh items, unless each one is individually wrapped. This is a health precaution to protect your clientele. Close all lids tightly to keep everything fresh.

At this point wash all the glasses and put them on the drainboard to air-dry. Wash all tools and equipment: blender and mixer cups, utensils. Leave them up-ended on the drainboard to air-dry.

If you have a frozen drink machine, drain the contents into a plastic container and store them in the refrigerator. Turn off the machine and clean it out according to the manufacturer's instructions.

The next step is to remove and soak all the pourers from the liquor bottles. This will prevent the sugars found in most spirits from building up and slowing the flow.

While the pourers are soaking, clean the soda gun and the ring that holds it. Remove the nozzle parts and wash, rinse, and sanitize them. Wipe down the flexhose with a damp cloth. After the pourers have soaked for about 10 minutes, dry them and replace them on the bottles at the standard angle. Bottles get sticky with use, so wipe each one down with a damp cloth to remove any spills, and put them in back in their correct places on the pouring line.

When all the supplies have been put away, the glasses washed, and the liquor bottles taken care of, it is time to clean out the ice bin. First, scoop out all the ice into the nearest compartment of the bar sink. Then, run hot water into the bin to melt all the remaining ice and wash down any debris left in the bin. Most of this debris will be trapped at the drain. With a towel, remove this and shake it off the towel into the trash. With a clean towel, scour the walls and bottom of the bin. If your bin has an old-style cold plate at the bottom (part of your dispensing system), pay particular attention to cleaning thoroughly under and around it. This is a great place for gunk to collect, which can make your bins smell stale and affect the taste of your ice, as well as being unsanitary.

After cleaning the ice bin, proceed to the bar top. Remove everything and wipe down the surface with a damp cloth. A bar with a top of brass or other metal should be polished at this time. Empty the ashtrays, making sure all cigarettes are out before you dump them into the trash. Wipe the ashtrays clean. Replenish the supply of matches, ready for a new day.

Now that everything has been washed, it is time to empty the sinks and scour them with a mild abrasive and very fine steel wool. It is also a good time to rinse the drains below the beer faucets with a pitcher of hot water and some sanitizer, to keep them from clogging overnight. It is also a good time to check the CO_2 pressure on each beer system.

After the sinks have been cleaned, the bar floor must be swept and mopped. There are nonskid floor mats to be removed and hosed down outside at least every other day. Emptying the trash is the next closing ritual. Hose down the receptacles and give each one a new plastic trash liner.

Up to this point, the cleanup has dealt with the sanitation and safety needs of the bar. The next step is to get the supplies replenished for tomorrow's business. If the storeroom is closed at this hour, the stock can't actually be brought to the bar, but the accumulated empties (you have been storing them on a certain shelf of the backbar) can be counted and listed, and a requisition form can be completed for their replacement. Beer and wine supplies should be checked along with spirits, and necessary replacements added to the list.

Supplies of bottled mixes, fruits, and condiments should also be counted, and necessary replacements should be listed. The syrup supplies should be checked, too, as well as the pressure at the CO_2 cylinder.

The entire closing-down procedure is designed to do two things:

- Ensure that the sanitary practices essential to successful operation are carried out.
- Ensure that, if anything happens to the person who opens up tomorrow, the bar is ready to go with very little effort by a substitute. This is crucial: to be able to open at a moment's notice if you must.

In some enterprises, closing the bar also includes closing down the register. This will differ from bar to bar, but here is a typical order of procedure:

1. If tickets/checks are used, be sure that all have been rung up.
2. If a tape is to be used for checking out the register, remove it, sign it, and date it.
3. Read the register, and record the readings on the cashier's checkout slip (Figure 9.16). This step, of course, will depend on the system used.
4. Remove the cash drawer with the cash and all supporting papers such as credit card charges, checks, payout vouchers.

Cashier's Checkout Slip

Date _____   Opening transaction # _____

Shift _____ 11–3 _____ 3–7 _____ 7–2 _____   (Circle appropriate shift)

Cashier _____   Checked by _____

Beginning bank   _____

Bills   _____

Coins   _____

Checks   _____   Number of checks _____

Charges: _____

Amer Express   _____

Visa/MasterCard   _____

Other   _____

House credit   _____

Payouts   _____   (Itemize below)

TOTAL   _____

Less bank   _____

CASH   _____   (Include payouts and charges)

Total sales   _____   (From register tape)

OVER / SHORT   _____   (Circle one)

Overring/Underring   _____   Transaction # _____   Amount _____

ACTUAL OVER/SHORT _____   Guest check # _____

Server _____

ANALYSIS OF PAYOUTS

Name	Amount	Name	Amount

Figure 9.16 Cashier's checkout slip. Record additional overrings or underrings on back of slip.

5. Reconcile the total register sales with the actual cash, plus house-credit slips, credit card slips, checks, and payout vouchers. Record everything on the cashier's checkout slip.

6. Count out the bank and place this money in the cash-register drawer or cashbox. Write on a new bank count slip (refer back to Figure 9.13) the amounts of the various coins and bills. This procedure is a continuous activity. It helps the person who opens the next shift to check the bank.

7. Turn the money over to the manager, or lock it in the safe.

8. Leave the empty register drawer open. In case of a break-in, if the drawer is empty and open, it won't be pried open and ruined.

Now the closing process is almost complete. Check your refrigerators to be sure they are running and cold, and that all their doors are tightly closed. Check your sinks to be sure they are clean. Make sure your coffeemaker is turned off. Check to see that no lit cigarette butts, including your own, are left on the bar or anywhere else. Lock everything that should be locked; turn off the lights; check the thermostat if you're supposed to turn the room temperature up or down for the evening; check to see that the Exit lights are on. Now you can go home.

SUMMING UP

The bar is the heart of every beverage service, and its smooth operation affects sales and profits in many ways. It influences the quality of the drinks, the quality of the service, the number of drinks that can be poured, and the number of people needed to serve them. Only if everything is in order at the start of business can the bar run smoothly and bartenders remain calm and serve customers with efficiency and good humor.

Safety and sanitation are critical in bar operations. This means everything from proper hand washing to storage of perishable foods at correct temperatures to handling of glassware to minimize skin contact with it. City and state health codes set only minimum standards; your goal should be to exceed them.

Bar setup procedures commonly include making any mixes from scratch; preparing garnishes; chilling mixers and bottled waters; filling ice bins; replenishing supplies of accessories (straws, napkins, coasters); organizing the bar tools and equipment; checking the draft beer and carbonated soft drink canisters. The French term *mise en place*—"everything in its place"—is what you are striving to achieve.

The financial part of the setup means making sure there is an accurate count, and an adequate supply, of cash in the register, and guest checks for the servers. At the end of the day, of course, it's time to count the money and reconcile it with the starting count, as well as to thoroughly clean everything to get it ready for the next day's business.

Good management plays an important role in efficient bar setup: by setting the standards and procedures and requiring they be observed; by thoroughly training employees in the routines and clearly explaining what is expected; and by frequent follow-up on employee performance.

POINTS TO PONDER

1. What is wrong with tucking a towel in your belt or hanging it over your shoulder?

2. Why is it better to air-dry glasses than to polish them with a clean towel?

3. How do you determine what par stock should be?

4. What are the danger-zone temperatures for foods susceptible to bacterial growth? What kinds of bacteria are most prevalent and troublesome?

5. What is the proper way to wash hands if you are handling food or drink as a bartender or server?

6. How do you make simple syrup? Why would you use it for mixing a drink?

7. What is the correct way to serve bottled water?

8. What is *mise en place*, and why is it important to bar operation?

9. What should the bartender do if a customer shows clear signs of intoxication?

10. Give two reasons why the cash register is balanced at night as part of the closing process.

TERMS OF THE TRADE

bank	dasher	par stock
bank count slip	falernum	rimming
bar sugar	*Giardia Lamblia*	simple syrup
coarse salt	micron rating	submicron rated filter
count	*mise en place*	twist
Cryptosporidium	mocktail	wheel
dash	orgeat	

GEORGE KIDDER
Imperial Club Bartender

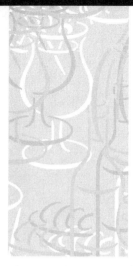

George Kidder is a lifelong bartender. "The Great Kidder," as he is affectionately known in the Eastern Idaho farming community of Ashton, got his first job at age 21, working as a barback for his father, who was also a bartender. At the time of this writing, George is 71, and celebrating 50 years behind the bar. He says he didn't plan to make a career of it, but has "always been able to make a good living this way."

George says he has tended almost every bar in Fremont County, Idaho. It is an unusual career choice in a rural area known for its conservative political climate; the majority of residents are members of the Church of Jesus Christ of Latter-Day Saints (Mormons), who don't approve of drinking. At the moment, he works at the Imperial Club, locally nicknamed "The Imp."

In addition to bartending, George has a second career—as a cowboy poet of regional note. He performs at local fairs, poetry gatherings, and is often asked to deliver the eulogies of customers and friends.

Q: What's the hardest thing about tending bar in a small town?
A: When you have to be the bouncer, too! I have a bunch of steel and plastic in my left hip socket as the result of one of the bar fights.

Q: Wow! What happened?
A: I tried to break up a barroom brawl, and after a while, they all ended up in a big pile. Guess who was at the bottom? Y'know that little knob on your hipbone? Well, mine busted off. They couldn't pin it back, so they took it out; had to cut the bone off and stick a prosthesis thing in there.

Luckily, bartending ain't near as tough as it used to be. Years ago, this town was pretty wild. A lot of loggers and miners around here. Some nights, we'd have four or five fights goin' on in one night. Now, you might have one in a month.

Q: Do you call the cops? What's the official procedure?
A: You call 'em if there's time, yeah. If not, you do it yourself.

Q: Do you keep a baseball bat behind the bar, or what?
A: (smiles broadly) Oh, we've got all kinds of accoutrements back here, yep.

Q: Do you have any advice for newcomers to the business?
A: First, stay sober on the job. Some places, you're not allowed to drink, but other places you are—and that can be a problem. Keep a smile on your face, and agree with everything the customers say, whether you really agree or not. In a small town, everybody that comes in the door is a friend . . . because they're a customer! Of course, you do occasionally have opinions about things. But a good bartender is noncommittal.

Q: Is there any fallout from selling alcohol in such a conservative and religious area?
A: Oh, we've got some pretty good Mormons who come in and drink. And some pretty good Catholics, and some pretty good Methodists, and all the rest of 'em. They don't drop their church-going tendencies, they just relax them a little bit when they come in here. It's the companionship they're looking for.

Of course, some come in lookin' for fights. But most come in just to be sociable. There are some who can be a little belligerent.

Q: What kinds of character traits do you think a bartender ought to have?

A: Patience is first. You've got to keep your cool if you can, because people are just gonna rub you raw sometimes. You know that to begin with, so patience should be your top priority. Then I'd say personality; and dependability and honesty, if you're gonna keep your job.

Q: Is your well or backbar set up differently from most bars, because you like it a certain way?

A: Not really. Most bars have it described the way it's supposed to be set up. It just makes sense: the bottles you pour from the most, you set in front; those you don't pour too much of, you set in back. I have six bottles in the well. The backbar has a wooden panel that I can pull down and lock, and that's where I store most of the bottles. You can serve beer in Idaho at 7 A.M., but most people in the morning just come in for coffee. The backbar stays locked until 10 A.M., when you can serve booze.

Over the years, you figure out an easy way to make just about any drink. And we have what we call a "bible" back there behind the bar, a book with our recipes and a lot of our own notes in it. It's always there.

Q: Do you have an automatic glasswasher?

A: (laughs) You're lookin' at him! Some places have a power brush, but I do it all by hand. We used to have one in the old Derby Club, but I don't think they work very well. The power brush requires the extra steps of turning it on, then turning it off. By the time you do that, you could have had 'em all done.

Q: What are the best things about your job?

A: I guess the companionship, the sociability of it. I was gonna quit when I started my cowboy poetry, but then I found out that some of my best material comes right out of this bar, the quips and quotes and profound things that people say. "The Sloppy Bartender," "The Lady Bartender," "The Honky-Tonk Angel"—all those poems I wrote based on people here at the "Imp."

The other advantage to bartending is, you can always find a job. Working as a bartender has saved my bacon when it came time to start payin' child support and alimony and all that stuff! One job wasn't near enough!

Q: Does your bar have a policy about serving food?

A: Some of them do, but not this particular place. We do put out popcorn or pretzels, and we have pepperoni sticks and beef sticks for sale.

Q: Are there any trends here in Ashton? What are the "hot" drinks now?

A: Frozen Margaritas. Geez, I hate 'em! I make 'em in a blender, don't have a Margarita machine. It takes longer, so it's a hassle and they aren't worth that much more money, either.

Q: What's the oddest thing anybody's ever asked you to fix?

A: I don't dare tell you. But I will say that all those drinks— the ones called Skip and Go Naked, Sex on the Beach—they ain't new drinks! They're just some of the old drinks from years ago that have new names to make people blush.

Q: Well, what's your favorite kind of drink to mix?

A: Whiskey and water, because that's what I like to drink— but only when I'm not on the job!

CHAPTER 10

Mixology One

The term **mixology** is typically defined as the art or skill of mixing drinks containing alcohol. It includes the techniques of the bartender, which do indeed require skill and sometimes art, along with the knowledge to back up the skill. The bartender must know the drinks by name, their ingredients, their mixing methods, and the way they are served. The bar manager must know even more, as the person responsible for setting the house standards for the drinks—drink size, glass size, types of ingredients (premix or fresh), proportions—as well as developing drink menus and specialty drinks. A manager may not have a bartender's dexterity, nor know as many different drink recipes, but it is the manager who makes decisions about how drinks are to be made and marketed, and who trains the bartenders in the ways of the house.

This chapter and the next are aimed at giving managers a thorough understanding of three topics: the structure of a good drink, the structure and essential ingredients of each different type of drink, and the basic methods of mixing drinks. Illustrated step-by-step instructions will help you understand each method and will serve as good training tools.

This chapter should help you . . .

- Know what makes a "good drink" good.
- Understand the relationship between glass size and amounts of liquor, ice, and mix, and apply this knowledge in designing drinks.
- Decide on the method, equipment, ingredients, and garnish to be used for each drink you serve.
- Know how ingredients are measured and choose an appropriate method of measurement.

- Know how to use premixes and shortcuts appropriately.
- Explain and demonstrate the "build" method of drink mixing.
- Make highballs, juice drinks, liquor-on-ice drinks, Collinses (with mix), coolers, coffee drinks, pousse-cafés, and other build-in-glass drinks.

The biggest mixed drink on record was a rum punch made in eighteenth-century West Indies. The ingredients included 1,200 bottles of rum, 1,200 bottles of Malaga wine, 400 quarts of boiling water, 600 pounds of the best cane sugar, 200 powdered nutmegs, and the juice of 2,600 lemons. It was made in a marble basin built in a garden especially for the occasion and was served by a 12-year-old boy who moved about the basin in a mahogany boat serving 600 guests, who "gradually drank up the ocean upon which he floated," according to an observer. Did they drink it all—four bottles of rum-plus-wine per person? Maybe the bottles were small, or perhaps some of it evaporated in the West Indian sun. Or perhaps there was a collective hangover as big as the recipe.

Today's mixology doesn't typically include big recipes but, rather, single drinks made to the customer's order. It is a skill dating from the nineteenth-century days of the grand hotel and the fashionable cocktail bar. Before that there were a few mixed drinks, mostly hot, dating from colonial days: flips, toddies, slings, and a colonial brew called Whistle-Belly Vengeance, made by simmering a concoction of sour beer, molasses, and "Injun bread."

The mixed drink as we know it was developed to cater to the wealthy city dwellers and patrons of fashionable resorts that opened up with the building of the railroads. (Ordinary folk in taverns and saloons drank straight liquor or beer.) One of the essentials, ice, was just becoming available. It came in huge blocks that were chopped or whacked into drink-size lumps, or shaved for finer ice.

The origin of the word **cocktail** for a mixed drink is cloaked in mystery. There are about a dozen good stories about its history. The most persistent fixes its birth in 1779 at a rural New York tavern, Betsy Flanagan's Inn, where American Revolutionary soldiers and their French allies mixed their gin and vermouth together as a token of brotherhood, stirring their concoction with the tail feathers of Flanagan's rooster. Another version has the Americans raiding the British Army's commissary and stealing several roosters, and their favorite innkeeper (Betsy) stirred their drinks in celebration with the cocks' tail feathers. The accompanying toast—"Here's to the divine liquor which is as delicious to the palate as cocks' tails are beautiful to the eye!"—was shortened by a toasting Frenchman to "Vive le Cocktail!"

In his book *The Cocktail: The Influence of Spirits in the American Psyche* (Picador USA, 1995), author Joseph Lanza observes that cocktails became appealing in the twentieth century precisely when drinking them became a crime. Prohibition brought a new mystique to the same old drinks. A new breed of bartender developed to man the speakeasies, and later, the elegant bars of the first half of the 1900s. He (it was almost always a man) was splendidly dressed, wearing diamonds and gold, and could pour with such flourish that one contemporary proclaimed, "Such dexterity and sleight-of-hand is seldom seen off the conjurer's stage." It was these artists who began the mixed drink as we know it today. They were the first true mixologists.

Their skills fell out of fashion in the 1950s and 1960s, but by the 1970s, the disco culture helped bring people out of their homes and back onto the club scene. The trend continued in the cash-flushed 1980s, and by the 1990s, the cocktail was "back," thanks to a combination of ready availability of high-quality ingredients and consumers with more adventurous and "gourmet" tastes.

Today, more information is available than ever before about the art of mixology: entire bookstore shelves are devoted to the topic, as are specialty sections of stores, and articles in lifestyle and cooking magazines. There are also exclusive clubs and lounges that cater to the sophisticated customer by serving upscale appetizers and superpremium beverages and cigars. Another unique attribute of the twenty-first century is that, so far, the cocktail culture seems to cross generational lines. Bartenders report that generation Xers are every bit as fascinated with mixed drinks as their baby boomer parents. And today's customer doesn't stick to just one or two favorites; they are more likely to experiment and sample other things. Chefs and bartenders work together to pair foods and drinks on trendy menus, or to match malt scotches or small-batch bourbons with foods, just like wines. It is an exciting time to be part of the industry.

Moderation and good sense are also part of the trend. The so-called Happy Hour may include bargain prices on drinks, but it is no longer an excuse to gulp or guzzle alcoholic beverages. Smart establishments market the cocktail hour as a way to wind down from the pressures of the workday, offering a substantial snack and a drink that is too good to be "slammed" down but, instead, should be sipped and savored.

ABOUT MIXED DRINKS

The term **mixed drink** includes any drink in which one alcoholic beverage is mixed with another or others or with one or more nonalcoholic ingredients. This includes cocktails, highballs, tall drinks, frozen drinks, coffee drinks, and almost every other bar product—except a glass of beer or wine or a straight shot of whiskey or brandy.

Structure and Components of a Mixed Drink

Mixed drinks of all kinds have certain characteristics in common. One of these is a **structure** that is loosely typical of all drinks. Each drink has (1) a major alcoholic ingredient, or **base,** usually a spirit, which determines its character and usually its predominant flavor; add to this (2) one or more complementary ingredients, which modify or enhance that flavor. A Manhattan, for example, has whiskey as the major ingredient and sweet vermouth as the modifier or enhancer, while a highball has a carbonated mixer or water as the modifier. A drink may also have (3) one or more minor ingredients that add a flavor or color accent, and (4) a garnish. Thus, a Manhattan sometimes has a dash of bitters or a drop of oil from a lemon twist added for a flavor accent, and a stemmed maraschino cherry is its standard garnish.

The major ingredient is the **base** of the drink. The modifiers and flavor accents make each drink different from all others having the same base. Some highly flavored mixes manage to reverse flavor roles with the major ingredients, as in a Bloody Mary or a Cuba Libre. These types of drinks are often ordered by people who don't really like the taste of the spirit and expect the mix to cover it up. In this case, from the drinker's perspective, the mix is the major flavor ingredient and the liquor gives it the desired kick. But from behind the bar, the spirit is still considered the major ingredient of a cocktail.

Most drinks contain one jigger of the major ingredient, and the jigger size is a policy decision of the management—a basic cost-control factor, for obvious reasons. If the modifier is another liquor, it is typically a smaller amount—anywhere from one-half to one-eighth the amount, compared to the major ingredient—from half a jigger to the splash of vermouth in a Dry Martini. Even when several modifiers are added, the major ingredient typically comprises at least half the liquor in any drink. Accent ingredients are nearly always added in drops or dashes.

Many drinks have standard garnishes that customers expect and want. In many cases, they've become as much a part of the drink as the liquid ingredients. Change the garnish on one of these, and you have to change the name of the drink as well. Adding an onion to a Martini instead of an olive makes the drink a Gibson.

Some drinks have no prescribed garnish, but the showmanship of "dressing them up" is appreciated by guests in many different bar settings. It would be a grave mistake, however, to garnish such sacred standards as a Scotch and Soda, or indeed any drink that has been ordered by call brand, unless there is a standard garnish. Patrons who order such drinks usually want the unadulterated taste of the liquor itself.

Developing Drink Recipes

A successful mixed drink is based on carefully calculated relationships of ingredients and, further, on the relationship between the glass, the ice, and the drink ingredients. You should make these calculations when you plan your drink menu and before you buy your glasses and choose your size of ice cubes. If you write down specific calculations for each drink you serve, you will have a set of standardized recipes for your bar. The idea is to train your bartenders to follow the recipes consistently, so customers are served a consistent product no matter who is tending bar.

For each drink you establish the following:

- The amount of major ingredient to be poured (1 ounce, 1¼ ounces, 1½ ounces, ⅞ ounce) or whatever. In metrics, it's 25 ml, 30 ml, 37 ml, 45 ml, and so on. This standard amount becomes your jigger size.
- The other ingredients and their proportions to the major ingredient.
- The size of glass to be used.
- The amount of ice in the glass.
- The garnish and its arrangement.

The ice in the glass is a key ingredient in the taste of any drink made with a carbonated mix or fruit juice. While its primary function is to chill the drink, it also controls the proportion of liquor to mix by taking the place of liquor in the glass. The ice goes into the glass before the mix, and the more ice, the less mix.

Suppose, for example, you want a highball to have 3 ounces of mix to 1 ounce of liquor in an 8-ounce glass. You put enough ice in the glass to take the place of 3 ounces of liquid, which will bring the finished drink up to a volume of 7 ounces, about half an inch below the rim. An 8-ounce glass filled three-quarters full with small rectangular cubes will displace 3 to 4 ounces of liquid. (Different sizes and shapes of cubes will make a difference; with large, square cubes, you have to fill the glass fuller with ice because the cubes have big spaces between them.) If you want a strong proportion of mix in relation to liquor, you use less ice or a larger glass. If you want a stronger liquor taste, use more ice or a smaller glass.

Taste Complexity. In addition to the list of ingredients, you should consider two things when creating a drink: its taste complexity, which means the overall sophistication (or lack) of the drink, and the degree of difficulty it will take to make the drink. Evaluate each drink you're thinking about pouring, based on these criteria:

Taste Complexity Categories

Commonplace: These drinks are simple, are ordered frequently, and are well received, though rarely "remembered" as anything exceptional.

Tasty but artless: These drinks are for those who rarely order a cocktail; they generally enjoy wine or beer instead.

Inspiring: A truly classic cocktail. These drinks are sophisticated and expertly mixed and will prove enticing to most guests. They can be served with pride.

Challenging and complex: This is the type of drink that may require some explanation before presenting it to the guest, to prepare his or her taste buds for the experience.

Mixing Difficulty Categories

Elementary: Mixing drinks in this category is about as difficult as preparing a glass of ice water.

Basic: These drinks are simple enough to be made well by anyone with a genuine interest or a little bartending experience.

Moderate: These are drinks that can be made fairly easily, but require some skill.

Difficult: Not the typical cocktails; these require extra steps in preparation.

Advanced: In addition to being difficult, this category of drink complexity is compounded by a hard-to-find ingredient or a more challenging step in preparation.

Measuring. The only way to pour a drink that follows a recipe is to measure every ingredient. There are various ways of measuring liquor. There is the metered pour, in which at least the major ingredients are measured and dispensed through a handgun or through pourers that shut off at the proper measure. A second way is for the bartender to pour into a measured jigger of your chosen size—with lines along its side, like a tiny measuring cup—and to stop pouring at a certain line.

A third way is to **free-pour.** Free-pouring is a subjective form of measurement that involves turning the bottle—with its pourer cap in place—upside down for full-force flow while the bartender counts silently. There's a little bit of a trick to it. To pour an ounce, you count "one-twenty-three" or "ten-twenty-thirty." "One-two-three" will give you $7/8$ of an ounce. "One-two-three-four" will yield $1\frac{1}{4}$ ounces, and so on. Each person develops an individual way of counting that ensures the greatest accuracy for that person.

Free-pouring takes practice, experience, confidence, and good reliable pourers. It is the showiest but, usually, the least accurate way to pour since it is likely to vary from person to person and from day to day. Even the best bartender should check his or her pour every few days to see if it is still on target. If the free-pour is accurate and consistent, it can have the advantages of speed and showmanship. But few bartenders can rival the accuracy and consistency of an objectively measured drink.

The typical manager tends to think of measured pour in terms of achieving the full value of each bottle in sales, and that is certainly a major reason for measuring. But perhaps the best reason to measure is to ensure the best drink, consistently, every time. After all, it is the proportions of the ingredients to one another that make a drink what it should be. If you pour an extra quarter-ounce of gin in a Martini but only the usual amount of vermouth, that Martini is going to taste drier than usual. Perhaps the customer won't like that as well. Or perhaps that customer thinks you made a great drink. That's terrific—until he or she returns and orders another Martini based on that standard and is disappointed.

So measurement is important to keep the proportions right. We measure liquors in terms of jiggers or sometimes ounces. We measure ice in terms of how full to fill the glass. We measure condiments by drops or dashes, and

Table 10.1

Bar Measures

dash = $\frac{1}{6}$ teaspoon or 10 drops

teaspoon (tsp) = $\frac{1}{6}$ ounce (oz, fluid ounce) or 5 milliliters (ml)

barspoon = 1 teaspoon

standard jigger = $1\frac{1}{2}$ ounces or 45 milliliters (or whatever amount you set as your basic drink)

pony = 1 ounce or 30 milliliters

scoop (of ice) = approximately 1 cup

splash (of syrup, lemon juice, etc.) = $\frac{1}{4}$ ounce

wineglass = 4 ounces or 120 milliliters

1 fluid ounce = 30 milliliters

1 ounce by weight = 28 grams

pinch = whatever you can get between your fingers and thumb

sugar by teaspoonfuls. Table 10.1 gives you the standard measurements and their relationships.

Mixing Methods. The way you want a particular drink made in your bar is another aspect of mixology related to quality and consistency, as well as to speed and service. Many drinks are always made the same way; for others you have a choice. There are four basic mixing methods: build, stir, shake, and blend.

- To **build** a drink is to mix it step by step in the glass in which it will be served, adding ingredients one at a time. You typically build highballs, fruit juice drinks, tall drinks, hot drinks, and drinks in which ingredients are "floated" one on another.
- To **stir** a drink is to mix the ingredients together by stirring them with ice in a mixing glass and then straining the mixture into a chilled serving glass. You stir a cocktail made of two or more spirits, or spirits plus wine— ingredients that blend together easily. The purpose of stirring is to mix and cool the ingredients quickly with a minimum of dilution.
- To **shake** a drink is to mix it by shaking it by hand in a shaker or using a mechanical mixer (shake mixer). You shake a drink if it contains an ingredient that does not readily mix with spirits, such as sugar, cream, egg, and sometimes fruit juice.
- To **blend** a drink is to mix it in an electric blender. You can blend any drink you would shake, and you *must* blend any drink that incorporates solid food or ice, such as a strawberry Daiquiri or a frozen Margarita. Some bars use a blender in place of a shaker or mixer, but it is not nearly as fast and easy as a mechanical mixer and doesn't make as good a drink as the hand shaker.

Before the days of electrical mixing equipment, all drinks were built in the glass, stirred, or shaken in a hand shaker. In some establishments today, where the pace is leisurely and the emphasis is on excellence, they are still mixed by hand from scratch—using no premixed ingredients, shortcuts, or substitutes. This kind of bar may have a blender, but it is used only for the newer drinks that can't be made without it, and the shake mixer is never used. There is no question that the drinks are better.

At the other end of the spectrum is the high-speed, high-volume operation. This is the bar at the airport or the fairground or the baseball stadium, where the staff blends or shakes everything mechanically and stirs only in the serving glass if the drink is stirred at all. The use of premixed products, shortcuts, and substitutes is absolutely necessary for speed and economy, and the drink selection is often limited. The drinks are not perfect, but they have the right ingredients, they are cold, they are fast, and they are what the customer expects.

Between the two extremes are many enterprises that use some elements of both, with the majority near the simplified, mechanized end of the scale. Most bars have eliminated the mixing glass and hand shaker altogether and use at least some premixed products. There are valid reasons—speed, volume, cost, suitability to the enterprise and the clientele. Many types of customers are not connoisseurs of premium drink quality and don't appreciate premium prices.

But as a bar manager you need to know both ends of the scale—how to make drinks from scratch, as well as all the shortcut options. You need to understand what, if anything, you are compromising if you decide to use a shortcut. Only then can you tailor your drink menu to your type of enterprise and your clientele, choose your equipment and supplies, and train your personnel accordingly.

To this end, in describing how to make the various types of drinks, this text will often give you both the original method of mixing (which is what most bartender manuals provide, although three-fourths of today's bars don't use it) and the "speed method" most commonly used today. It will enable you to understand each drink type and see how the shortcuts fit into it, so you can work out what best suits your goals.

Common Mixology Terms

Like any other type of recipe, drink recipes use some jargon that you should become familiar with; they are useful terms, sort-of "bartender's shorthand." Here are the most common ones:

Add: Combine into the drink or container. "Build" is the more correct term.
Blend: To blend (as defined above) and pour unstrained.
Broken ice: Large cubes, chopped down to about one-third their original size.

Dry: For a Martini, this means the proportion of vermouth is very small compared to the proportion of gin—a teaspoon of vermouth, say, to 3 ounces of gin (the teaspoon may be called a "splash" of vermouth).

Frosted: A glass chilled in the freezer, or by filling with crushed ice, so that a cool mist forms on the outside of the glass.

Garnish: To decorate or attach to the rim of a glass.

Ignite: To set on fire.

Long: A total of five measures or more of fluid.

Neat: A liquor poured as is, undiluted, not mixed with anything.

Pour: To add to the glass without straining, unless specified.

Rim: To coat the edge (rim) of the glass by moistening it and then dipping it into something like salt or sugar.

Short: Less than five measures of fluid in total.

Smooth: A mixture that, when blended with ice, achieves the thick consistency of a milkshake.

Spiral: A long, coiled, almost pith-free length of citrus peel.

Straight up: Undiluted; no ice or water added.

Strain: To filter out ice and other solids, leaving them behind when you pour out liquid. If the drink has been stirred, a bar strainer is used for this purpose.

Twist: A piece of citrus peel, about 1.5 to 2.5 inches (3 to 6 cm) in length, held over a drink and twisted to release a drop or two of oil from the fruit peel into the drink. The twist itself is usually dropped into the drink after releasing its oil.

DRINK FAMILIES

Mixed drinks are a lot like people: they have a structure, but within that structure are countless variations. Pick up any bartender's manual, and unless you know your way around, you will find it mind-boggling; one of them has 4,000 drink recipes, and the New York Bartenders Union lists 10,000. To confuse the issue even further, new drinks are appearing all the time, proliferated by distillers, magazine writers, bartenders, and beverage managers!

Fortunately for the manager planning the drink menu, and for the bartender learning dozens or even hundreds of drinks, these drinks evolved in families—again, like human beings. The number of families is fairly small, and if you know the "family characteristics" you have some basic knowledge about every family member. There are two keys to family character: the ingredients and the method of mixing the drink. A third element often comes into play, which is the size and type of glass. Whether the "glass determines character," or "character determines glass" is an interesting point to ponder.

In the rest of this chapter and in the next one, we will look at different drink families, with their characteristic ingredients and the mixing method that applies to each. Table 10.2 summarizes the drink families.

Table 10.2

Drink Families

Drink Type	Ingredients[a]	Method	Glass
Buck	Liquor, lemon, ginger ale, cube ice	Build	Highball
Coffee	Liquor, (sugar), coffee, (whipped cream), (brandy float)	Build	Mug or wine glass
Collins	Liquor, lemon, sugar, soda, ice (cube or crushed), cherry	Shake/Build	Collins
Cooler	Liquor or wine, carbonated mix, (sweet, sour), (bitters), cube ice	Build	Collins
Cream	Cream, liquor, liqueur (or 2 liqueurs)	Shake	Cocktail or champagne
Daisy	Liquor, lemon, grenadine, crushed ice, (soda), fruit garnish	Shake	Mug, tankard, tall glass
Eggnog	Liquor, sugar, egg, milk, nutmeg	Shake	Mug
Fizz	Liquor, lemon, sugar, soda, cube ice	Shake/Build	Highball or wine
Flip	Liquor or fortified wine, sugar, egg, nutmeg	Shake	Wine
Flip, hot	Liquor, sugar, egg, hot milk, nutmeg	Shake	Mug
Frozen drink	Liquor, crushed ice, (any others)	Blend	8–12 oz, chilled
Highball	Liquor, carbonated mix or water, cube ice	Build	Highball
Hot Buttered Rum	Rum, sugar, hot water, butter, spices	Build	Mug
Hot lemonade	Liquor, sugar, lemon, hot water	Build	Mug
Hot toddy	Liquor, sugar, hot water	Build	Mug
Ice cream drink	Liquor, ice cream, (any others)	Shake-Mix or Blend	8–12 oz chilled
Juice drink	Liquor, juice, cube ice	Build	Highball
Liquor on rocks	Liquor, cube ice	Build	Rocks
Martini/Manhattan	Liquor, vermouth, garnish, (cube ice)	Stir	Cocktails (rocks)
Milk punch	Liquor, sugar, milk, cube ice, nutmeg	Shake	Collins
Milk punch, hot	Liquor, sugar, hot milk, nutmeg	Build	Mug
Mint Julep	Bourbon, mint, sugar, crushed ice	Build	Tall glass or mug
Mist	Liquor, crushed ice	Build	Rocks
Old-Fashioned	Bourbon (or other), sugar, bitters, cherry, orange, cube ice	Build	Old-fashioned

(continued)

Table 10.2 (Continued)
Drink Families

Drink Type	Ingredients[a]	Method	Glass
Pousse-café	Liqueurs, (cream), (brandy), floated	Build	Straight-sided cordial
Rickey	Liquor, lime, soda, cube ice	Build	Highball
Shooter	Liquors, (juice flavorers), straight up	Shake	Shot, rocks
Shot	One liquor straight up	Build	Shot
Sling	Liquor, liqueur, lemon or lime juice, soda, garnish, cube ice	Shake/Build	Highball or collins
Sling, hot	Liquor, sugar, lemon, hot water	Build	Mug
Smash (rocks)	Liquor, mint, sugar, cube ice	Build	Rocks
Smash (tall)	Liquor, mint, sugar, soda, cube ice	Build	Highball or collins
Sour	Liquor, lemon or lime juice, sugar	Shake	Sour or cocktail
Spritzer	Half wine/half soda, cube ice, twist	Build	Highball or wine
Sweet-sour cocktail	Liquor, lemon or lime juice, sweetener, (cube ice)	Shake	Cocktail (rocks)
Swizzle	Liquor, sweet, sour, (soda), (bitters), crushed ice	Build	Highball or specialty
Tom and Jerry	Rum, whisky, or brandy, egg-sugar-spice batter, hot milk or water, nutmeg	Build	Mug
Two-liquor	Base liquor, liqueur, cube ice	Build	Rocks
Tropical	Liquor (usually rum), fruit juices, liqueurs, syrups, ice, fruits, (mint), (flowers)	Shake	Specialty

[a] Ingredients in parentheses are optional.

The Highball Family

A **highball** is a mixture of a spirit and a carbonated mixer or water, served with ice in a highball glass. It is said to have gotten its name from the railroad signal for "full speed ahead" used in the late 1800s—a ball raised high on a pole. Legend has it that a St. Louis saloonkeeper invented the drink when his regular customers, mostly railroad engineers, asked him to "lighten up" their drinks so they wouldn't get in trouble on the job. The resulting whiskey-and-water combination, served in a tall glass, was probably speedy and satisfying enough, and has since become a classic combination.

In the original method of building a highball, you would use a small bottle of mixer and go through all the steps as they are given (Figure 10.1). In

HOW TO BUILD A HIGHBALL

Ingredients
Liquor
Carbonated mix or plain water
Cube ice
Garnish, varying with the drink,
    sometimes none

Glass
Highball (6 to 10 ounces)

Mixing Method
Build

Equipment and Accessories
Jigger (standard house size)
Barspoon
Ice scoop
Fruit squeezer (for some drinks)
Stir stick or straws
Pick (sometimes)
Cocktail napkin

step 1: Using the ice scoop, fill the glass with the required amount of ice and place it on the rail.

step 2: Add 1 jigger of the liquor ordered.

step 3: Fill the glass with mix to within ½ to 1 inch of the rim.

step 4: Stir with two or three strokes of the barspoon.

step 5: Add the garnish, if any, and a stir stick or straw. Serve on a cocktail napkin.

Figure 10.1 How to build a highball.

the speed method, you add the mixer from a handgun, and your stirring would probably be limited to a couple of swirls with the stir stick, counting on the customer to finish the job.

Now let us look more closely at the whole procedure. First, the sequence. Some people argue in favor of reversing steps 2 and 3, using an ice-mix-liquor sequence. The rationale for this sequence is that if you pour the wrong mix by mistake, you have wasted only the mix, not the liquor. If you use this sequence, you must leave room for the liquor when you pour the mix, the exact depth depending on width and shape of the glass.

The rationale for pouring the liquor first is that most mixes, being heavier than liquor, will filter down through the liquor and you will probably need to stir less, which means less loss of sparkle from the carbonated mix. Also it is more natural to "think" the drink this way: ice, liquor, mixer. Another point: If you free-pour, you are more likely to pour a consistent amount of spirit if you are not looking at how much room there is left for it.

A point to note about working with carbonated mixes comes up in step 4. Notice that you stir with the barspoon very briefly, just long enough to spread the liquor around in the mix. Like beer or Champagne, carbonated liquids should always be handled gently. A lot of stirring dissipates the bubbles. Vigorous stirring melts the ice, too, diluting the drink. The customer can use the straw or stir stick if he or she wants it mixed more.

The finished drink should always be the same size; that is, it should always reach an imaginary line half an inch (or some other distance you set) below the rim of the glass. Each drink will then be the same as the one before it and will have the same proportions and the same taste. A glass should never be full to the brim, to avoid spillage. As to what is the "right" glass size, jigger size, and amount of ice, that is up to you. Highball glasses should be no less than 6 ounces, no more than 10. An 8-ounce glass is a good all-around choice. It will make an excellent highball using 1 to 1½ ounces of base liquor. Any smaller glass is likely to look stingy and certainly won't work well for anything stronger than a 1-ounce drink.

Now let's look at some of the highballs most in demand. In this book we use an abbreviated recipe format, which is all you need. We give you the method, glass, ingredients, and garnish. Anything in parentheses is optional. You do not have to follow our choice of glass size, but it will give you a proportion of glass-to-ice to ingredients that you can adapt to your needs. You can use these prototypes for all similar drinks.

Any liquor called for with soda or water is prepared like a Scotch and Soda. A garnish may be added if the customer wishes—usually a twist of lemon. Many highballs, like the Gin and Tonic, are served with a garnish of

SCOTCH AND SODA

BUILD

8-oz glass

¾ glass cube ice

1 jigger of scotch

Soda to fill

GIN AND TONIC

BUILD

8-oz glass

¾ glass cube ice

1 jigger of gin

Tonic to fill

Wedge of lime, squeezed

lemon or lime—a wheel on the side of the glass or a wedge with juice squeezed in and the squeezed hull added to the drink.

In making the Gin and Tonic and similar drinks, allow a bit more room for the garnish when pouring the mix—say, an extra $\frac{1}{4}$ inch of glass rim. Squeeze the lime wedge with the hand squeezer (original method) directly into the glass. Then drop the squeezed wedge, minus seeds, into the drink. Use your two or three strokes of the barspoon at this point. In the speed method, you would probably squeeze the lime by hand or dispense with it altogether. When using a garnish whose flavor is added to the drink, standardize the garnish size so that your drinks will always have the same taste.

The procedures given in these two recipes apply to any liquor-mixer combination, for example, Rum and Coke, Brandy and Coke, Campari and Soda, Bourbon and 7UP, Vodka and Bitter Lemon, Rye and Ginger. Some combinations have special names:

> *Seven and Seven:* Seagram's 7-Crown whiskey and 7UP
> *Presbyterian:* Customer's choice of liquor with half ginger ale and half club soda
> *Cuba Libre:* Rum and cola with squeezed lime wedge
> *Mamie Taylor:* Scotch and ginger ale with a lemon twist or squeeze of lime
> *Moscow Mule:* Vodka and ginger beer with squeezed lime half, served in an 8-ounce copper mug
> Fruit-Juice Drinks

Fruit-juice drinks are first cousins to the highball family. In fact, many people consider them highballs, since they are made in a similar way in the same type of glass. The major difference is that fruit juice takes the place of the carbonated mix as the body of the drink. Figure 10.2 tells the story.

The original method and the speed method are identical here in most cases. One notable exception occurs in making a Bloody Mary: in the original method it is made from scratch, ingredient by ingredient, and is sometimes shaken; whereas in the speed method, a prepared mix is poured from a bottle and stirred in the glass. We'll discuss it shortly.

Two points are worth noting in the basic method:

- In step 1, the amount of ice is often less than in the highball, to give a higher proportion of juice. The added juice is enough to retain the full flavor to the last drop even though the melting ice dilutes the drink somewhat.
- In step 4, the stirring is vigorous, since juice and liquor do not blend as readily as mixer and liquor, and there are no bubbles to worry about.

Juice drinks are very popular, and there are many of them. Most have special, sort of "cutesy" names. The only real trick in making them is to recall

HOW TO BUILD A JUICE DRINK

Ingredients
Liquor
Fruit juice (sometime premix)
Accent ingredients (sometimes)
Cube ice
Garnish (sometimes)

Glass
Highball (6 to 10 ounces)

Mixing Method
Build

Equipment and Accessories
Jigger (standard house size)
Barspoon
Ice scoop
Fruit squeezer (sometimes)
Stir stick or straws
Pick (sometimes)
Cocktail napkin

step 1: Using the ice scoop, fill the glass with the required amount of ice and place it on the rail.

step 2: Add 1 jigger of the liquor ordered.

step 3: Fill the glass with juice to within ½ to 1 inch of the rim.

step 4: Stir vigorously with the barspoon.

step 5: Add the garnish, if any, and a stir stick or straw. Serve on a cocktail napkin.

Figure 10.2 How to build a juice drink.

SCREWDRIVER
BUILD
8- or 10-oz glass
½ glass cube ice
1 jigger vodka
Orange juice to fill

CAPE CODDER
BUILD
8- or 10-oz glass
½ glass cube ice
1 jigger vodka
Cranberry juice to fill
Lime wedge

which name goes with which juice and which liquor. Here are some variations of the Screwdriver:

Left-handed Screwdriver: Gin and orange juice
Kentucky Screwdriver or Yellow Jacket: Bourbon and orange juice
Bocce Ball: Amaretto and orange juice
Persuader: Half amaretto, half brandy with orange juice
Cobra or Hammer or Sloe Screw: Sloe gin and orange juice
Southern Screwdriver or Comfortable Screw: Southern Comfort and orange juice
Fuzzy Navel: Peach schnapps and orange juice
Golden Screw: Galliano and orange juice
Madras: Vodka and half cranberry, half orange juice

Then there is a whole series of Screwdrivers with "national names," using the appropriate nation's liquor: Mexican Screwdriver (tequila and orange juice), Italian (Galliano), French (brandy), Greek (ouzo), Cuban (rum), Irish (Irish whiskey), Scotch Driver (scotch), Canadian Driver (Canadian whiskey).

In other drinks, the liquor is the same as in the Screwdriver but the juice changes:

Seabreeze: Vodka, cranberry juice, grapefruit juice
Greyhound: Vodka and grapefruit juice
Salty Dog: Greyhound served in a salt-rimmed glass (usually a Collins glass, and sometimes made with gin)

Rimming a glass with salt is the first step in making a Salty Dog. To rim the glass, use the rimmer described in Chapter 4. If you don't have a rimmer, run a cut lemon or lime evenly around the rim (half a lemon will give you a firm, even surface). Dip the rim in a shallow dish of salt; then build the drink as usual, taking care to keep the rim intact. A crisp, even rim enhances the drink, but if the lemon is applied unevenly, the rim will be uneven. Too much salt will spoil the taste of the drink.

Another series of drinks takes off from the Screwdriver by adding another ingredient as an accent and traveling under a fanciful name that is sometimes better than the drink, for example, the Harvey Wallbanger and Tequila Sunrise. Legend has it that "Harvey the Wallbanger" was a surfer's nickname. Depending on who tells the story, Harvey either won a surfing contest and celebrated with this drink, or lost a surfing contest and drowned his sorrows in it. Either way, he had too many, and "bounced from wall to wall" as he staggered out of the bar.

In both these drinks, when you pour the orange juice you leave more at the top for the last ingredient, and you do your stirring *before* you add it.

The Galliano, poured carefully with a circular motion, will float on top of the Harvey Wallbanger. The grenadine in the Tequila Sunrise will sink to the bottom, since it is heavier than everything else. Some Sunrise aficionados believe a true Sunrise should have the red color rising from the bottom. To create effect, you can pour the grenadine first and disperse it with a splash of soda, then add the ice, the tequila, and the orange juice, and forget the stirring.

A number of other drinks are variations of these two. Made with tequila, a Harvey Wallbanger becomes a Freddy Fudpucker or a Charley Goodleg (or Goodlay). Made from rum it is a Jonkanov or Joe Canoe. If you keep the vodka but change the juice from orange to grapefruit, you have Henrietta Wallbanger. Or use half orange juice and half heavy cream and you have Jenny Wallbanger.

Variations on the Tequila Sunrise include Russian Sunrise, with vodka replacing tequila, and Tijuana Sunrise, using a dash of Angostura bitters instead of the grenadine.

Perhaps the most distinctive, classic fruit juice drink is the Bloody Mary; it is robust, loaded with taste, and even nutritious. There are many versions, but the essentials are vodka and tomato juice with accents of lemon or lime and spices. There are many different stories of its origin, but the name is generally believed to be a reference to Mary Tudor, the English Queen who was infamous for her savage persecution of Protestants. (On a lighter note, another version has it that comedian George Jessel was mixing himself a heterogeneous early-morning pick-me-up in a Palm Springs bar when along came a woman named Mary, upon whom he spilled the drink.)

Whatever its origin, the secret to the Bloody Mary is the mix, whether it begins with tomato juice, V-8 Juice, or Clamato. The next step includes the modifiers, which, again, vary radically, from Worcestershire to Tabasco sauces to horseradish, pureed salsa, A.1 steak sauce, and so on. Spices include celery salt or garlic salt, coarse ground pepper, and chili powder. There are as many Bloody Mary versions as there are bartenders.

The Bloody Mary has a host of close relatives that are, once again, made by substituting another liquor for the vodka or changing the mixer. They include:

Red Snapper: Standard Bloody Mary made with gin
Bloody Maria: Substitutes tequila for vodka
Danish Mary: Aquavit takes the place of vodka
Virgin Mary: Everything but the liquor, also called a Bloody Shame
Bleeding Clam or Clamdigger: 1 jigger clam juice added
Bloody Bull: Substitute beef bouillon for one-half the tomato juice
Bullshot: Substitute beef bouillon for all the tomato juice

HARVEY WALLBANGER

BUILD

8- or 10-oz glass
½ glass cube ice
1 jigger vodka
Orange juice to fill
Top with ½ jigger Galliano

TEQUILA SUNRISE

BUILD

8- or 10-oz glass
½ glass cube ice
1 jigger tequila
Orange juice to fill
Top with ½ jigger Grenadine

BLOODY MARY (FROM SCRATCH)

BUILD

8- or 10-oz glass

½ glass cube ice

1 jigger vodka

3 oz tomato juice

Juice of ½ fresh lemon (½ oz)

2–3 dashes Worcestershire

2 drops Tabasco

Salt, pepper

Lemon wheel

BLOODY MARY (SPEED)

BUILD

8- or 10-oz glass

½ glass cube ice

1 jigger vodka

Bloody Mary mix to fill

Serve with celery stick "stirrer"

Sometimes the Bloody Mary glass is dressed up with a rim of celery salt, and sometimes the glass is special—a tulip shape or a balloon wine glass. And the garnishes are many: favorite alternates to the lemon slice include a lime wedge, cooked and peeled shrimp, cherry tomato, or stuffed Spanish olives on cocktail picks. Stirrer options include the celery stick, marinated asparagus spear, or cucumber spear.

You can have some fun with the Bloody Mary and all its incarnations by offering upscale presentations like a rolling cart to mix them tableside at Sunday brunch; or a buffet-style setup, where an attendant pours the choice of liquor into an iced glass, then the customer completes the drink to his or her taste from a table of mixes and condiments.

Any of the highballs or juice drinks we have discussed can become "tall" drinks if the customer specifies. To mix these, you use a larger glass such as a Collins or Zombie glass, and increase the amounts of everything in the same proportions—except for the liquor, which remains the same. What this customer wants is a long, cool drink that is not as strong as a highball.

Many fruit-juice drinks are easily dressed up to become house specialties, using a specialty or larger size glass and garnishing imaginatively, for promotional purposes and at a slightly higher price.

Liquor on Ice

Another type of drink built in the glass consists of a liquor served over ice; nothing else is added. In today's drink market, liquor on ice gets a lot of attention; it is the method often used for serving single-malt scotches, small-batch bourbons, and a few of the super-premium whiskeys. These types of drinks appeal to the image-conscious consumer and, although they're no substitute for an after-dinner brandy, they are making inroads. Such drinks are typically served in a rocks or old-fashioned glass, usually of 5 to 7 ounces. Strictly speaking, they are not "mixed" drinks, but they are generally thought of as being related to the highball family. Often they contain more liquor—typically 1½ jiggers.

For example, to build a Scotch on the Rocks or a Scotch Mist, the method is so simple it needs no explanation; you do not even stir the drink. But a few comments may be useful. A glass ¾ full of cube ice will leave plenty of room for the liquor without any danger of spilling. It will also make the glass look more full than if you fill it totally with ice. Do

---

SCOTCH ON THE ROCKS

BUILD

Old-fashioned glass

¾ glass cube ice

1 to 1½ jiggers scotch

SCOTCH MIST

BUILD

Old-fashioned glass

Full glass cracked or crushed ice

1 to 1½ jiggers scotch

Lemon twist

not worry if the ice stands higher in the glass than the drink does. People who order this type of drink do not expect a glass filled with liquor.

If your rocks drinks look too scant, you might try a different combination of glass size and ice cube. A 5-ounce footed glass with small cubes is often a good choice. Large square cubes do not fit well in small glasses; they leave spaces too large for the liquor to fill. Some establishments increase the jigger size for spirits served alone on the rocks.

Any kind of spirit can be served either on the rocks or as a "mist." Those most commonly requested are whiskies, brandy, and a few liqueurs ordered as after-dinner drinks, such as peach schnapps or other fruit liqueurs, Drambuie, and coffee liqueurs. If these are served over crushed ice in a cocktail glass or snifter instead of a rocks glass, they are known as **frappes.**

If you do not have crushed ice or an ice crusher, you can wrap enough cubes for a mist or frappe in a towel and crack them with a mallet. You can also crack the wrapped ice by hitting the whole towelful on a hard surface such as a stainless-steel countertop.

Just a note: Wines, especially white wines and the aperitif wines, are rarely ordered on the rocks, but sometimes it happens. In this case, they will be served in 4- to 6-ounce portions poured over cube ice in an 8- or 9-ounce wine glass.

Two-Liquor Drinks on Ice

Short, sweet drinks on the rocks appeal especially to younger drinkers, and make good drinks to sip after dinner. They are too sweet to be true aperitifs, though people do order such drinks as a Black Russian or Stinger before dinner.

Two-liquor drinks typically combine a jigger of a major spirit (whiskey, gin, rum, brandy, vodka, tequila) with a smaller amount of a flavorful liqueur such as coffee, mint, chocolate, almond, anise, licorice. Proportions vary from 3:1 to 1:1, depending on the drink and the house recipe. Even with 3:1, the liqueur flavor often takes over the drink. Equal parts make a very sweet drink, though this varies with the particular liqueur.

Since the two liquors blend easily, these drinks are built in the glass and are among the easiest and fastest to make. Together, the two liquors usually add up to a 2- to 3-ounce drink. Anything less would be noticeably scant in the glass. Figure 10.3 shows the method. Notice that in steps 2 and 3 you add the base liquor first and the liqueur after. This is because the liqueur, having a higher sugar content, is heavier and will head for the bottom of the glass, filtering through the liquor and making it easier to blend the two.

Few of these drinks call for a garnish (see step 5). If there is one, it is usually a lemon twist. Step 6 is necessary as the

BLACK RUSSIAN
BUILD
Rocks glass
Full glass cube ice
1 jigger vodka
½ jigger Kahlua

STINGER
BUILD
Rocks glass
Full glass cube ice
1 jigger brandy
½ jigger white Crème de Menthe

HOW TO BUILD A TWO-LIQUOR DRINK

Ingredients
A base liquor
A liqueur
Cube ice
Garnish

Glass
Rocks (5 to 7 ounces)

Mixing Method
Build

Equipment and Accessories
Jigger
Barspoon
Ice scoop
Stir stick or straws
Cocktail napkin

step 1: Using the ice scoop, fill the glass with ice to within ½ inch of rim and place on rail.

step 2: Add the base liquor.

step 3: Add the liqueur.

step 4: Stir with the barspoon.

step 5: Add the garnish, if any, and a stir stick or straw. Serve on a cocktail napkin.

step 6: Rinse the jigger.

Figure 10.3 How to build a two-liquor drink.

liqueur, because of its sugar content, clings to the sides of the jigger and will flavor the next drink.

Two typical two-liquor drinks are the Black Russian and the Stinger, both of which have many variations and spin-offs. The Black Russian spawns the following:

White Russian: A Black Russian with a cream float (another version is made in a blender with ice cream)
Black Magic: A Black Russian with lemon juice and a twist
Black Jamaican: Rum substituted for vodka
Black Watch: Scotch substituted for vodka, with a twist
Brave Bull: Tequila substituted for vodka
Dirty Mother: Brandy substituted for vodka
Siberian: A Black Russian with a brandy float

In similar fashion, there are many variations on the Stinger:

Cossack or White Spider: Vodka substituted for brandy
Irish Stinger: Green crème de menthe substituted for white
International Stinger: A Stinger with Cognac as the brandy
Greek Stinger: A Stinger with Metaxa as the brandy
White Way: Gin substituted for brandy
Smoothy: Bourbon substituted for brandy
Galliano Stinger: Galliano substituted for crème de menthe

Other popular two-liquor drinks include:

Rusty Nail or Knucklehead: Scotch and Drambuie
Godfather: Scotch or bourbon and Amaretto (the bourbon version is also called The Boss)
Godmother: Vodka and Amaretto
Spanish Fly: Tequila and Amaretto

All of these two-liquor drinks may also be served straight up in a cocktail glass, in which case they are stirred with ice in a mixing glass and strained into a chilled glass, in the manner we explore in the next chapter.

Collinses, Rickeys, Bucks, Coolers, Spritzers

Several other drink families are also built in the glass. Some of them take off from the highball and juice drinks by adding other characteristic ingredients. The best known of these is the Collins family.

Family Characteristics

Ingredients: Liquor, lemon juice, sugar (or sweet-sour mix), soda, cube ice, maraschino cherry garnish, optional orange slice. Today the lemon juice, sugar, and soda are typically combined in the *Collins mix*.
Glass: Collins (12 to 14 ounces)
Mixing method (speed version): Build with Collins mix.

The basic steps are those for making a highball. (We discuss making a Collins from scratch in the next chapter.) In the Collins family, the "first name" of the drink changes with the liquor: Tom Collins for gin, John Collins for bourbon, Mike Collins for Irish whiskey, Sack for applejack, Pierre for Cognac, Pedro for rum. There are as many other Collinses as there are spirits—vodka, scotch, rye, tequila, and so on.

Rickeys are cousins to the Collinses. They use lime instead of lemon and are a shorter, drier drink—that is, they are served in a smaller glass and have little or no sugar.

Family Characteristics

Ingredients: Liquor, fresh lime, soda, cube ice
Glass: Highball or old-fashioned
Mixing method (speed version): Build with Collins mix.

The basic steps are like those for making a highball, but starting off with half a fresh lime squeezed over ice. Do not use Rose's lime juice because it is much sweeter than regular, unsweetened juice, which is essential to the drink.

A Rickey may be made with any liquor or liqueur. A liqueur makes a sweeter drink, cutting the extreme dryness of the lime. Rickeys made with nonsweet spirits may have a small amount of simple syrup or even grenadine added. Change the soda of the Rickey to ginger ale and the lime to lemon, and you have a *Buck*. It is made like a highball, usually in a highball glass. It is not as dry as a Rickey because the ginger ale is sweet. Today's buck usually goes by another name, such as:

> *Mamie Taylor:* Made with scotch, with lemon wedge or lime juice
> *Mamie's Sister or Fog Horn:* Made with gin
> *Mamie's Southern Sister:* Made with bourbon
> *Susie Taylor:* Made with rum

The original *cooler* was typically a long drink made with liquor and soda or ginger ale, and served over ice in a Collins glass decorated with a long spiral of lemon peel curling around inside the glass from bottom to top. One of the best-

---

WINE COOLER

BUILD

8- or 10-oz glass

¾ glass cube or crushed ice

Half fill with red wine

7UP to fill

Twist or flag

SPRITZER

BUILD

8- or 10-oz glass

¾ glass cube or crushed ice

Half fill with white wine

Club soda to fill

Twist, lemon slice, or lime wedge

known coolers was the Horse's Neck with a Kick, which consisted of 2 ounces of liquor with ginger ale and the long lemon spiral. A plain Horse's Neck was a Prohibition drink without the liquor.

Today the term **wine cooler** brings to mind the familiar sweet combination of bottled wine plus fruit juice. But there is also a mixed-to-order wine cooler that is half wine and half soda, iced, and served in a Collins or highball glass. If it is made with white wine, it is called a **spritzer**.

Another similar drink is the Vermouth Cassis, which couples 1½ to 2 ounces of dry vermouth with crème de cassis in a 4:1 to 6:1 ratio over cube ice, with soda to fill, and a twist or slice of lemon. A different but related drink is Kir (pronounced keer), a glass of chilled white wine with ½ ounce or less of cassis, no soda and sometimes no ice. Kir Royale is a variation of Kir, with chilled Champagne in place of white wine, served without ice in a flute or tulip champagne glass.

Some Old-Fashioned Drinks

Some mixed drinks have been around since colonial times. Many others originated in the era of the grand hotel bars of the late 1800s, or during Prohibition, when new ways were devised to mask the awful taste of homemade gin. Some described here you may never encounter directly, but they may have potential as specialty drinks, dressed up with modern techniques, intriguing names, and the romance of the past.

Two venerable drinks are still very much alive: the Old-Fashioned and the Mint Julep. In structure, they are simply liquor-over-ice-drinks that are sweetened, accented, and garnished. However, both involve more mixing than many other cocktails.

Ironically, the Old-Fashioned is a cocktail that is never served in a cocktail glass. It is always built in the glass, like a highball, but it isn't a highball because it contains little or no mixer. This drink is such a classic that its traditional glass bears its name—a sturdy, all-business tumbler of 5 to 7 ounces, just the right size to make the drink without adding more than a splash or two of water.

Family Characteristics
Ingredients: Liquor, sugar, bitters, water, fruit cherry, orange, cube ice
Glass: Old-fashioned
Mixing method: Build

OLD-FASHIONED (TRADITIONAL)

BUILD

Old-fashioned glass
1 lump sugar
Splash of soda or water onto sugar
1–3 dashes Angostura bitters
  Crush sugar with muddler; stir till dissolved
Full glass cube ice
Up to 2 oz whiskey
  Stir briskly
Cherry, orange slice, lemon twist (optional)

OLD-FASHIONED (CURRENT)

BUILD

Old-fashioned glass
Full glass cube ice
Up to 2 oz whiskey
1–2 teaspoons simple syrup
1–3 dashes Angostura bitters
  Stir briskly
(Soda or water to fill)
Lemon twist (optional)

This drink came out of Old Kentucky, and is full of tradition—the glass, the garnishes, and the tender loving care with which it is made. You certainly won't find this drink at a speed bar. Even less elaborate versions take several minutes to make. Older customers prefer it as it used to be; they want the rich taste of sweetened bourbon accented with bitters and fruit. If the undiluted drink does not fill the glass, use smaller cubes, more liquor, or a smaller glass. Today's younger customer with a taste for lighter drinks often prefers it made with soda or water added. The customer should be queried as to preference.

An Old-Fashioned can be made with any whiskey or with other liquors—brandy, applejack, rum, even gin—but unless the customer orders one of these, make it with bourbon in the South, a blended whiskey in the East, and probably brandy in Wisconsin. Simple syrup really makes a better drink than lump sugar, unless you are emphasizing ritual for the customer. Stir it very well in any case, and garnish it handsomely. If you want to "gild the lily," you can add a dash of Curacao or sweet vermouth, or even a bit of the juice from the maraschino-cherry bottle. If you add these, use less sugar accordingly. You can change the bitters (such as orange bitters with rum or gin) or you can float a teaspoonful of 151-proof rum on a Rum Old-Fashioned. You can elaborate on the fruit garnishes—pineapple is often used.

Someone in Old New Orleans elaborated on the Old-Fashioned to create the Sazarac by coating the inside of the glass with absinthe. Today, a substitute such as pernod is used instead, since absinthe is illegal in this country. You roll a splash of it around inside the glass until it is well coated, discard what is left, and proceed to make an Old-Fashioned using Peychaud bitters, often with straight rye as the liquor. The Sazarac is served in New Orleans as prebrunch refreshment.

The Mint Julep, another southern U.S. tradition, seems to have always represented the southern elegance and leisure, and it's a must-have on the day the Kentucky Derby horse race is run every year. The word "julep" is a modern adaptation of ancient words meaning "rosewater." There are said to be at least 32 different recipes for this classic, but they all have certain things in common:

Family Characteristics
Ingredients: Liquor (traditionally bourbon), fresh mint, sugar, and crushed or shaved ice
Glass: 12- to 16-oz chilled glass or silver mug
Mixing method: Build (ritual methods stir first, then build)

If the customer specifies, you can make a Mint Julep with rye, rum, gin, brandy, or Southern Comfort, but the classic version is made with 100-proof, bottled-in-bond bourbon.

MINT JULEP

BUILD

16-oz glass, chilled

10–12 fresh mint leaves, bruised gently

1 tsp bar sugar with splash of soda (or 1½ tsp simple syrup)

Muddle sugar and mint

Add ½ glass ice

1 jigger bourbon

Stir up and down until well mixed

Fill glass with ice

Add another jigger bourbon

Stir contents up and down until glass/mug is completely "frosted"

Insert straws

Garnish with mint sprigs, perhaps dipped in bar sugar or with fruit

Why else would you go to all this trouble? It makes a good premium-price specialty drink for some enterprises.

A Smash is a cross between a Mint Julep and an Old-Fashioned. It is made with Julep ingredients by the Old-Fashioned method, in an old-fashioned glass. You muddle a cube of sugar and some mint with a splash of water, add cube ice and a jigger of liquor, and garnish with mint sprigs. Or you can make a Smash as a long drink in a tall glass by adding club soda.

Another old-timer is the Swizzle, a sweet-sour, liquor-and-soda drink served over crushed ice in a tall glass with a swizzle stick. A swizzle stick is a special stirrer (now rarely seen) with multiple tentacles at the bottom that are whirled about by rolling the top of the stick between the palms of the hands until the drink froths and the outside of the glass frosts. The handy old Caribbean recipe for such drinks is "one of sour, two of sweet, three of strong, and four of weak." The "sour" in a Swizzle is lemon or lime. The "sweet" may be sugar, simple syrup, a flavored syrup, or a liqueur. The "strong" can be any spirit, and the "weak" is, in this case, melted ice or sometimes soda. Often a dash of bitters is added for accent. Fruit or mint garnishes are in order. This would make an interesting specialty drink if you can find some old-fashioned swizzle sticks.

New drink trends are often the result of improving on venerable recipes—by venerable bartenders! As long as you're stocking fresh mint leaves to make juleps, you might try the "Alberto I," a specialty of La Caravelle, a New York City restaurant. It is named for its creator, Alabeto Alonso (nicknamed "Alberto"), who has been the bartender for 38 years.

ALBERTO I
SHAKE
10- to 12-oz stemmed glass
10 fresh mint leaves
Juice of one lime
(*Muddle mint and lime in shaker*)
2 oz vodka
1½ tsp bar sugar
½ oz Champagne
Do not strain; float Champagne after mix is poured.

Pousse-Cafés

"Coffee-pusher" is the literal translation of the term **pousse-café.** In France, it is a sweet liqueur drunk with or after coffee at the end of a meal. In America, the drink first gained popularity in 1840s New Orleans as a show of bartending skills. It has taken on a very complex and elaborate personality, and you need a very steady hand to pour ribbons of different colored liquids into a liqueur or pony glass, layered so that each remains separate in a bright, beautiful rainbow. An added attraction is to make brandy the last ingredient, then flame it when served.

In his *Ultimate Cocktail Book* (Foley Publishing, 1990), author Raymond Foley presents a list of 56 ingredients, any of which can be used in making a pousse-café.

Family Characteristics
Ingredients: Liqueurs of different densities, sometimes nonalcoholic syrups, brandy, cream or all these things

---

POUSSE-CAFÉ

BUILD

Straight-sided liqueur glass

⅙ Grenadine (red)

⅙ white Crème de Menthe

⅙ apricot brandy (orange)

⅙ Chartreuse (green)

⅙ brandy (amber)

ANGEL'S KISS

BUILD

Straight-sided liqueur glass

¼ dark crème de cacao (brown)

¼ Crème d'Yvette (violet)

¼ brandy (amber)

¼ cream (white)

Glass: Straight-sided liqueur or brandy glass
Mixing method: Build (float)

Since so many different liqueur combinations can be used for a pousse-café, there is no one formula. The secret of layering is to choose liqueurs of differing density, and "float" them in sequence from heaviest to lightest. Density depends a good deal on the sugar content of a liqueur, but because there is no indication of sugar content on the bottle, we can only infer it from the alcohol content, or proof. In general, the lower the proof, the higher the sugar content and the density. Thus a 36-proof crème de cassis is usually heavier than a 50-proof triple sec, which is usually heavier than a Curacao at 60 proof. At the top of the scale is green Chartreuse at 110 proof. Grenadine (which has no alcohol) is often used as a pousse-café base, while brandy (which has no sugar) is often used as the top layer. Cream will also float atop most liqueurs.

But proof is not an infallible guide. Nor is the generic name of a liqueur; products of different manufacturers often have different densities. The best system is to work out your own recipes, by trial and error if necessary, and to use the same brands of liqueurs every time. Tables that specify are available from liqueur manufacturers; ask your suppliers. (A partial list is given in Table 10.3.) For best results, Foley says, use products that have at least five units of difference in terms of their specific gravities, and start with the product that has the highest specific gravity.

Table 10.3

Density of Various Liqueurs

No.	Proof	Product	Specific Gravity	Color
1	40	Crème de Cassis	1.1833	Purple
2	25	Grenadine	1.1720	Red
3	54	Crème de Cacao	1.1561	Brown
11	56	Crème de Banana	1.1233	Yellow
12	54	Chocolate Mint Liqueur	1.1230	Brown
13	48	Blue Curacao	1.1215	Blue
16	60	Crème de Menthe—White	1.1088	White
17	60	Crème de Menthe—Green	1.1088	Green
44	70	Apricot Brandy	1.10548	Tawny
45	70	Peach Brandy	1.0547	Tawny
54	60	Sloe Gin	1.0241	Red
55	70	Ginger Brandy	0.9979	Light Brown
56	90	Kirschwasser	0.9410	Clear

The pousse-café is mainly a drink for show rather than taste, the object being to create a handsome sequence of colors and to show off the bartender's prowess. The technique is to pour each layer gently over the back of a spoon, into or over the glass, so that the liqueur spreads evenly on the layer below (Figure 10.4). If you hold the tip of the spoon against the side of the glass, the liqueur will run slowly down the side and onto the layer below.

Like the Old-Fashioned, this is no drink for a speed bar. Because of the time and skill required, and the cost of the specialty liqueurs, a pousse-café commands a good price, even though there may be only 1 ounce of liqueur in it altogether. The pousse-café is never stirred. Instead, the customer drinks the rainbow of colors layer by layer, as neatly as possible. Since the ingredients are chosen for color and density rather than for complementary tastes, some sequences of flavor can be rather odd. Keep this in mind as you develop your own pousse-café specialty.

Figure 10.4 How to build a pousse-café.

Coffee Drinks and Other Hot Ones

Mixed drinks are not limited to the chilled glass, as bartenders in ski lodges and other cold-weather establishments know well. Many of the mixed drinks in the early American colonies were warmer-uppers heated in the tankard by thrusting a red hot poker or loggerhead into the liquid. Today's hot drinks are not limited to cold climes: coffee drinks are served just about anywhere.

Many dinner restaurants have developed specialty coffee drinks that double as dessert and coffee, with the added benefit of ending the meal on a note of excitement or sophistication. Since these drinks are usually high-profit items, they are to the restaurateur's advantage in every way.

No doubt people have been spiking their coffee with spirits for generations and finding it delicious. It's what you do to dramatize it that makes it memorable. The Buena Vista Café in San Francisco started an Irish Coffee craze some 50 years ago when they put Irish whiskey, coffee, and sugar in a goblet and floated whipped cream on top. People came from all over and fought their way through the crowds for a glass mug of it—and they still do. Another way of adding drama is to flame a brandy float or a liquor-soaked sugar cube as the coffee is served. Tony's Restaurant in Houston made Café Diablo into a dramatic tableside brewing ceremony involving a long flaming spiral of orange peel that can be seen all over the dining room.

The basic hot coffee drink is very simple. Figure 10.5 shows you how to make it. For a hot drink, the decision about what to serve it in is especially important. The customer must be able to pick up the drink without it being too hot to grasp firmly. This means a cup, mug, or stemmed glass is preferable. Stemware should be made of tempered glass, which is better able to withstand heat without cracking. If your glass is not heat-treated, preheat it by rinsing in hot tap water. Thin glass is better than thick, since it heats more evenly and quickly.

For garnishes, you can sprinkle nutmeg, cinnamon, shaved chocolate, or finely chopped nuts on top of the whipped cream, whatever is appropriate to the drink. A cinnamon stick can substitute for the stir stick or spoon in a shallow cup. Make a decaffeinated version by putting an individual portion of instant decaf coffee in the cup along with the sugar in step 1 and filling the cup with hot water in step 3. Some other variations include sweet liqueurs in place of sugar, or a liqueur float in place of whipped cream. Or you can float a little additional high-proof spirit and serve it flaming; or soak a sugar lump in spirit, put it on a spoon across the cup and flame it, dropping it into the drink when the flame dies. Here are some cream-topped hot coffee drinks:

Irish Coffee: Made with Irish whiskey.
Café Royale: With bourbon or brandy; another version is made with half Metaxa and half Galliano.
Dutch Coffee: With Vandermint, and no sugar.
Mexican Coffee: With tequila, sweetened with Kahlua.
Café Calypso or Jamaican Coffee: With rum and brown sugar. A "deluxe" version substitutes dark crème de cacao for sugar, and a "supreme" version uses Tia Maria in place of sugar.
Café Pucci: With half Trinidad rum and half Amaretto.
Kioki (or Keoke) Coffee: With brandy and coffee liqueur for sugar; another version includes Irish whiskey.
Royal Street Coffee: With Amaretto, Kahlua, nutmeg, and no sugar.

Of course, the coffee doesn't have to be hot to make a good drink. There are a few interesting summer drinks that include coffee.

Most coffee drinks are simple, so simple that slip-ups and inferior ingredients are very noticeable. In any of these drinks, the quality of the coffee is a major factor. Make sure it is fresh, preferably made within the hour. There are also at least a dozen coffee-flavored liqueurs and spirits to experiment with. Two other popular coffee specialties are Cappuccino and Café Diablo. Each of these has a number of versions, depending on who is making it.

Cappuccino is an American elaboration of an ancient version of coffee-with-milk drunk by the Capuchin monks in Italy. (The word comes from the Italian term for the pointed

MOCHA RUM COOLER

SHAKE

Collins glass
8 oz black coffee
3 oz dark rum
1½ oz Crème de Cacao
Garnish (optional) ¼ cup rum-raisin ice cream

Ingredients
Hot coffee
Liquor
Sweetener
Whipped cream topping (or brandy
   float)

Glass
Coffee cup, mug, or preheated
steam glass

Mixing Method
Build

Equipment and Accessories
Jigger
Barspoon
Coffee spoon or stir stick
Straws
Cocktail napkin

step 1: Add 1 spoonful
sugar or other sweetener
to cup, mug, or glass.

step 2: Add 1 jigger of
the appropriate liquor.

step 3: Fill with hot
coffee to within 1 inch
of the rim.

step 4: Stir well with
barspoon until sugar
is dissolved.

step 5: Swirl whipped
cream on top (or float
brandy).

step 6: Add garnish if
any, stirrer, and straws.
Serve on a saucer or
cocktail napkin.

Figure 10.5 How to build a hot coffee drink.

hoods on their robes.) There are plenty of nonalcoholic cappuccinos served in today's trendy coffee bars, but the modern alcoholic drink is made with espresso and contains rum, brandy, creme de cacao, cream, and probably Galliano, all mixed together with the espresso and topped with whipped cream.

Café Diablo is a highly spiced brew. It is made with brandy as a base liquor, and includes Grand Marnier or Cointreau, orange peel or grated rind, and various sweet spices such as cinnamon, cloves, allspice, and sometimes coriander, along with the coffee, of course. It may also include an anise-flavored liqueur, additional sugar, and even chocolate syrup in some versions. It can be built in the cup, stirring all the liquors and flavor accents together first, then adding hot coffee and flaming additional brandy on top; or it can be flamed while mixing several servings tableside, then served in small cups with whipped-cream topping. Either way, it is an unforgettable drink, worthy of a high price tag.

In New Orleans, the famous Commander's Palace restaurant serves a house specialty called Café Brulot Diabolique. It's a showstopper, with orange and lemon peels, whole cloves, and cinnamon sticks adorning a brew of brandy and orange liqueur, which is ignited, tableside, in a silver bowl. The mixture is mixed with chicory-laced coffee and ladled into demitasse cups for serving.

Many hot drinks can be traced to the centuries when they supplied the only central heating available. One, a Hot Toddy, is made by mixing a jigger of liquor with sugar and hot water in a mug or old-fashioned glass. If the liquor is rum, you may call the drink Grog. If you use dark rum and add butter and spices, you call it a Hot Buttered Rum. This drink is best if you premix the butter, sugar, and spices (cinnamon, nutmeg, cloves, salt) in quantity and stir in a teaspoonful per drink. Or use a packaged premix. In any case, serve with a cinnamon stick for stirring.

You can also add spices to any toddy and still call it a Hot Toddy, or a Hot Sangaree. Add an egg to a Toddy, use hot milk instead of water, and it becomes a Hot Flip or an Eggnog, or a Hot Milk Punch. Sprinkle nutmeg on the top. Add lemon juice to a Toddy and it becomes a Hot Lemonade or a Hot Sling or a Hot Scotch, Gin, Rum, Rye, or whatever.

Feel free to make your own hot concoctions, which may or may not contain coffee. The Peppermint Patty blends peppermint schnapps with hot cocoa; the Mounds Bar mixes cocoa with rum. Mix hot cocoa with butterscotch-flavored schnapps and you've got a drink called Butterfingers. Just about any flavorful spirit makes a good base, with the exception of vodka, which is not distinctive enough. Build your drink in a glass or mug, one ingredient at a time. Make it festive and make sure it smells good—aroma is an important sales tool.

There is one more hot drink that makes a good specialty for the Christmas season: the Tom and Jerry. It was invented by Jerry Thomas, bartender extraordinaire of the last century, who also invented the original Martini and something called the Blue Blazer. The Tom and Jerry involves premixing a bowl of batter made of eggs, sugar, spices (allspice, cinnamon, cloves), and a little Jamaican rum (there are also packaged mixes and premade batters on the market). You put a ladleful of batter in a mug, add bourbon or brandy, and hot milk or water, and stir vigorously until everything foams. Dust it with nutmeg and serve it warm.

As for Jerry Thomas's Blue Blazer, you usually find some version of his recipe in every bartending manual, but who has ever seen one made? You put whiskey in one silver mug and hot water in another, set fire to the whiskey and fling it with unerring accuracy into the hot water. Then you toss the flaming beverage back and forth between the two mugs to make a long streak of flame. "The novice in making this beverage should he careful not to scald himself," wrote Thomas in his 1862 treatise on mixing drinks. Now *that's* an understatement . . .

SUMMING UP

A *mixed drink* is any drink in which one alcoholic beverage is mixed with other ingredients. From that jumping-off point, you can mix almost anything to create a new drink recipe. But it is important to understand the way a drink is structured: with a base (liquor), other complementary flavors to modify or enhance the base, minor ingredients (for color or a hint of additional flavor), and a garnish.

Drinks of similar structure and ingredients are known as *drink families.* Being aware of these "family relationships" makes it easy to learn a great many drinks using just a few fundamentals. It also makes it possible to recognize a drink type from a list of its ingredients and to make it even when no instructions are given. Beyond that, a grasp of drink types and ingredient relationships makes it easy to invent drinks by substituting or adding appropriate ingredients to familiar drinks.

When creating a mixed drink, take into account its taste complexity and the degree of mixing difficulty it requires. Drinks built in the glass are the simplest and fastest kinds to make, and in this chapter, you learned about the basic mixing techniques for highballs and juice drinks, two-liquor drinks, pousse-cafés and coffee drinks. The next chapter presents drinks made by other methods that require mixing equipment beyond the barspoon and the handgun.

POINTS TO PONDER

1. What is meant by the following phrases: drink structure, drink families, free-pouring, building a drink?

2. How do you measure the following drink ingredients: liquor, ice, mix?

3. Why is it necessary always to use the same type and size of glass to make a given drink?

4. What are the advantages and disadvantages of free-pouring?

5. Explain why using premixed ingredients enables you to build certain drinks (such as the Collins) in the glass instead of shaking them.

6. What are the keys to making a good highball with a carbonated mixer?

7. Try your hand at devising a variation of a current drink by substituting or adding another ingredient. Explain why you chose this combination of ingredients.

8. Choose a drink from each family and write down the recipe from memory, including the glass type and size.

9. What is the difference between a wine spritzer and a wine cooler?

10. Why does the specific gravity of a liqueur make a difference when using it in a pousse-café?

TERMS OF THE TRADE

base	long	spiral
blend	mixed drink	stir
broken ice	mixology	straight up
build	pour	strain
cocktail	pousse-café	tall
drink structure	rim (rimming)	twist
frappe	shake	wine cooler
free-pouring	short	wine spritzer
highball	smooth	

CHAPTER 11

Mixology Two

To continue our discussion of mixology, this chapter presents the remaining methods of mixing drinks, including the original method of shaking by hand and the current methods of blending and mechanical mixing that make frozen drinks and ice cream drinks possible. The chapter also explores additional drink families, as well as current methods and techniques for preparing and filling drink orders quickly and properly. The chapter then moves on to explain how the manager can use all this knowledge to plan drink menus and create specialty drinks—a most profitable endeavor these days.

This chapter should help you . . .

- Explain and demonstrate the stir, shake-by-hand, blend, and shake-mix methods of drink mixing.
- Explain and demonstrate how to make frozen and ice cream drinks.
- Understand how to prepare cocktails, sours, Collinses (from scratch), slings, fizzes, tropical and cream drinks.
- Learn to fill drink orders efficiently and train others to do so.
- Write drink orders on guest checks.
- Develop a suitable drink menu for a limited-menu bar.
- Create specialty drinks.

Picking up the historical note on which we ended the last chapter, we find that Jerry Thomas of Blue Blazer fame was also a key figure in developing the art of mixology in general. When he wrote his first drink-making manual in 1862, the word "cocktail" referred to "composite beverages" that were generally bottled to take on picnics or hunting trips. As the world's most prestigious bartender of the day, Thomas's zeal and expertise turned the cocktail into a fashionable and desirable bar drink. He became known as "the Professor," out of respect for his dedicated research and experiments in mixology.

Which brings us to those contemporary "composite beverages," many of them cocktails, that are not built in the glass but are stirred, shaken, blended, or mechanically mixed with the shake machine. These drinks, too, can be grouped into families, with common ingredients and mixing methods as the family ties. These drinks are important to be familiar with because they are making a big comeback among younger people, who may have only read about the glamour of the 1950s nightclub scene or seen it in the movies, but who are developing a taste for "venerable" cocktails like **Manhattans** and **Martinis.**

THE MARTINI: A BRIEF HISTORY

The city of Martinez, California, hosts an annual Martini Festival to celebrate its heritage as the "birthplace of the Martini." Jerry Thomas ("the Professor") is said to have worked his magic and created it there. Of course, there are other equally colorful claims. The British say the Martini is their invention, named after a renowned rifle—the Martini & Henry—for its accuracy and its "kick." The Italians take issue with both of these stories. The Italian vermouth maker Martini & Rossi says the drink was so named because it was first made with Martini & Rossi brand vermouth—and plenty of it. The controversy about whether this cocktail was named for a town, a gun, or a vintner will never be settled. And no matter, for it has long since been dwarfed by another controversy that has been brewing since there *were* Martinis, that is, "How should a Martini truly be made?"

From the moment in the early 1800s when gin and vermouth were first blended, the Martini has been a very special drink. It was the Martini that prompted many Americans to sample a mixed drink instead of drinking whiskey straight. It was the Martini that many women enjoyed when social drinking standards relaxed in social and business circles that were previously "for men only."

In the White House, President Franklin Roosevelt enjoyed his Martinis (4 parts gin, 1 part vermouth) nightly before dinner. John F. Kennedy, while still a U.S. senator, singled out the cocktail as a symbol of wealth or special privilege, and created the phrase "Martini lunch" to disparage business-related dining—especially at taxpayers' expense. Later, President Jimmy Carter made headlines by proposing tax reform that would end the "three-Martini lunch" wheeling and dealing of Congresspeople and bureaucrats. But the cocktail's popularity did not wane.

By 1979, *The Perfect Martini Book* by Robert Herzbrum (Harcourt, Brace, Jovanovich, 1979) listed the ingredients for 286 different variations! Today, the Martini is the mutant of the drink world. Drinks called "Martinis" have sake and a cucumber in them; or cranberry juice, crème de cacao, and a chocolate kiss for garnish!

The size of the Martini has also changed. Traditionalists remember a 4-ounce drink served in a 5-ounce cocktail glass. But today, the Martini—like almost everything else—has been supersized, often served in 10-ounce glassware. And with it comes more than olives. Today's recipes may include tomatoes, carrots, even oysters! There are also fruit Martinis. In an issue dated October 4, 2000, *The New York Times* mentioned the Apple Martini, which includes pureed apples, Calvados, vodka, and apple cider; the Georgia Peach is a Martini made with vodka and peach nectar, served in a 10-ounce glass. The dwindling use of vermouth and the substitution of vodka for gin addresses the younger-palate preference for sweeter drinks, with the bite of alcohol softened by mixers or flavors.

So . . . the classic cocktail is making an impressive comeback, but only by being wildly adaptable. If this megatrend intrigues you, how about experimenting with these Martini adaptations?

- Silver tequila, vodka, and Cognac, or gin with a dash of scotch, are new Martini-making ideas. Why limit yourself to just gin and vodka?
- Departing from the "dry" days of the 1950s and 1960s, today's bartenders sometimes prefer to use more vermouth, to "soften" the taste of the liquor. Vermouth is the classic modifier, but there are also interesting results to be had by using dry sherry, sweet vermouth, or Dubonnet with a dash of Angostura bitters. Also consider using Port, Madeira, or even sake!
- A splash of liqueur will add a blast of flavor and an attractive color to the Martini. Recommendations include Frangelica, Godiva, Curacao, Chambord, Grand Marnier, Amaretto, B&B, and black Sambuca.
- Using infused liquors can garner delicious results, from lemon-flavored gin to chili-pepper-flavored tequila. There are also cherry-infused rums and pineapple-infused vodkas.
- A sophisticated, attractive garnish adds much to a good drink. For Martinis, some of the more unique options include olives stuffed with bleu cheese or prosciutto, or wrapped with anchovies; fresh strawberries, pickled green tomatoes, chunks of lobster meat or peeled, cooked shrimp.
- The better the liquor, the better the Martini. Today's customer appreciates the top quality, superpremium brands and will pay more for them.
- Try presenting your guests with chilled cocktail glasses and a tray of all the condiments and ingredients to build their own "perfect" Martini. Pre-

measure the liquor, of course, in a small carafe nestled into a bowl of ice; put vermouth in another carafe.

THE MARTINI/MANHATTAN FAMILY

It is hard to decide whether to call this group of drinks one family or two. Though today's Martinis and Manhattans are distinctly different from one another, in their second-generation variations and refinements, lines cross and distinctions blur. Unlike the Martini, however, the lineage of the Manhattan is not in dispute: it was introduced at New York's Manhattan Club by Winston Churchill's mother.

At any rate, the basic characteristics of both branches of this drink family are very much the same:

Family Characteristics
Ingredients: Liquor, vermouth (in a 4:1 to 8:1 ratio), garnish
Glass: Stemmed cocktail, chilled
Mixing method: Stir

As to differences, in a Martini, the liquor is gin, the vermouth is dry, and the garnish is an olive or a lemon twist. In a Manhattan, the liquor is whiskey, the vermouth is sweet, and the garnish is a cherry. The mixing method spelled out in Figure 11.1 is for a **straight-up** drink, that is, one served in a chilled stemmed cocktail glass with no ice in the drink itself. Nowadays, Martinis and Manhattans and all their relatives are served more often on the rocks than they are straight up. We'll talk about that shortly.

There are several things to consider carefully in the mixing of these two drinks. The first is the chilled glass. The cold glass is absolutely essential to the quality of the drink, since there is no ice in the drink itself. You handle the chilled glass by the stem so that the heat of your fingers does not warm it or leave fingerprints on the frosty bowl. If you do not have a chilled glass to start with, you must chill one. You do this by filling it with ice before you begin step 1. The cocktail glass chills while you are completing steps 2 through 4. Then you pick up the glass by the stem, empty the ice into your waste dump, and proceed with step 5.

The purpose of the stirring in step 4 is twofold: to mix the vermouth and liquor without producing a cloudy drink and to chill them quickly without unduly diluting the mixture. If you vigorously stir or shake a drink containing vermouth, the clarity of the drink will be lost. If you stir too long, melting ice weakens the drink's flavor. So you stir just long enough to blend and chill these two easily blended ingredients and to add about an ounce of water—no more. Note that "ice" means cube ice; crushed ice would dilute the drink too quickly. In step 5 you use the strainer to keep the ice out of the glass.

THE STIR METHOD: HOW TO MAKE A MARTINI OR MANHATTAN

Ingredients
Liquor, 4 to 8 parts
Vermouth, 1 part
Garnish

Glass
Stemmed cocktail glass, chilled

Mixing Method
Stir

Equipment and Accessories
16-ounce mixing glass with strainer
Jiggers
Barspoon
Ice scoop
Tongs, pick, or condiment fork
Cocktail napkin

step 1: Place a chilled cocktail glass on the rail, handling it by the stem.

step 2: With the scoop, fill the mixing glass ⅓ full of cube ice.

step 3: Measure liquor and vermouth and add to the mixing glass.

step 4: Stir briskly in one direction 8 to 12 times.

step 5: Strain the liquid into the cocktail glass.

step 6: Add the garnish, using tongs, pick, or a condiment fork. Serve on a cocktail napkin.

Figure 11.1 The stir method: How to make a Martini or Manhattan.

MARTINI
Chilled 4-oz cocktail glass
6 parts gin
1 part dry (French) vermouth
Olive or lemon twist

MANHATTAN
Chilled 4-oz cocktail glass
6 parts whiskey
1 part sweet (Italian) vermouth
Maraschino cherry

In the "parent" drink recipe you'll see a 6:1 ratio for both drinks. In terms of amounts, it is commonly 1¼ ounces of liquor and ¼ ounce of vermouth. Allowing for a small amount of melted ice and the space taken up by the garnish, you will need a 4- to 4½-ounce glass.

A 6:1 drink is fairly dry. The accepted standard used to be 4:1, but today's trend has been toward drier drinks. If a customer asks for a *dry* Martini, you can decrease the vermouth in the recipe or increase the gin, depending on house policy. For a *very dry* Martini, use only a dash of vermouth or none at all. Bartenders develop their own forms of showmanship about this: they may use an eyedropper or atomizer, or pass the glass over the vermouth bottle with great flourish, or face in the general direction of France and salute!

If you use equal parts of dry and sweet vermouth in either a Martini or a Manhattan, it becomes a Perfect Martini or a Perfect Manhattan. The garnish usually becomes a lemon twist in each case. If you change the olive to a cocktail onion in the original Martini, you have made a Gibson. A Martini is always made with gin unless the customer specifies another liquor. Vodka is the most common alternative, and this is sometimes called a Vodkatini. Then there is the Rum Martini; and if you add a dash of bitters or a little lime juice and sweeten it with grenadine and Curacao it becomes the El Presidente. There's a Tequila Martini, or Tequini; or, if it is made with Sauza Gold tequila, you may call it a Cold Gold. There's a Silver Bullet, which keeps the gin but substitutes scotch for the vermouth or uses both scotch and vermouth, floating the scotch. There are at least 20 or 30 other variations of the Martini—each one substitutes ingredients, varies proportions, or adds flavor accents to the original recipe. You should be familiar with any that may be regional favorites in your area. Or try introducing them as "house specialties."

A Few Words about Manhattans

As the popularity of bourbon has surged, there has been an equivalent renewal of interest in the classic whiskey cocktail known as the Manhattan. The drink is smooth, aromatic, and satisfying. Unlike the Martini—which many will agree is an "acquired taste"—the Manhattan possesses an almost universal appeal, with the sophistication (but not the snobbery) of the Martini.

Like any traditional drink, the Manhattan has many variations. For instance:

Dry Manhattan: Substitute dry vermouth for sweet vermouth, and a lemon twist for the maraschino cherry.

Perfect Manhattan: Use half dry and half sweet vermouth, and garnish with a lemon twist.

Sweet Manhattan: Add a dash of the maraschino cherry juice to the classic recipe.

Rob Roy: Use Scotch whiskey, sweet vermouth, and a dash of bitters.
Latin Manhattan (or Little Princess): Use rum instead of whiskey.
Quebec Manhattan: Use Canadian whiskey instead of bourbon.
Raspberry Manhattan: Add a splash of Chambord.
Italian Manhattan: Add a splash of Amaretto.
Spanish Manhattan: Add a splash of sherry.
Paddy: Made with Irish whiskey.

A Manhattan can be made with other liquors too. Irish whiskey makes a Paddy. If you use rum you may call it a Little Princess, or if you use equal parts of rum and sweet vermouth, you'll be making a Poker. If you make a Manhattan with Southern Comfort as the whiskey, use dry vermouth to cut the sweetness of the liquor.

All these versions of both the Martini and Manhattan are made in the same way, stirred in the mixing glass and strained into the chilled cocktail glass. Straight-up cocktails made with other fortified wines (such as sherry or Dubonnet) are made the same way.

As noted earlier, all these drinks may also be served on the rocks. In this case, you have a choice of mixing methods. You can make a drink as you do the straight-up cocktail, simply straining the contents of the mixing glass into a rocks glass three-quarters full of cube ice. Or you can build the drink in the rocks glass as you do the two-liquor drinks on ice. The latter method, described in Chapter 10, is the easiest and fastest and, by far, the most common. If you build in the glass, it is wise to pour the vermouth first. Then, if the mingling of the ingredients is less than perfect, the customer tastes the liquor first.

If volume warrants, Martinis and Manhattans can be premixed in quantity. Just follow these steps:

1. Fill a large small-necked funnel with ice cubes and put it into the neck of a quart container.
2. Pour 4 ounces of the appropriate vermouth and a 750-ml bottle of the appropriate liquor over the ice into the quart container.
3. Stir with a long-handled barspoon.
4. Keep chilled in the refrigerator until used.
5. To serve, measure out 3½ ounces per drink into a chilled cocktail glass.

SOURS AND OTHER SWEET-SOUR COCKTAILS

The idea of combining sweet and sour flavors with liquors has been around a long time. It is no accident that several of the drinks in the sweet-sour cocktail family originated in tropical climates, where lemons and limes grow in profusion.

Family Characteristics

Ingredients: Liquor, lemon or lime juice, and a sweetener, "sweet, sour, and strong"

Glass: Sour or cocktail, chilled

Mixing method: Shake (or blend, or shake-mix)

The subgroup of drinks known as **sours** use lemon rather than lime, have a standard garnish of cherry and orange, and are traditionally served in a sour glass of about 4½ ounces, whatever size and shape accommodates the garnish attractively. Sometimes a sour is made with egg white or a mix containing frothee, giving the drink an appetizing fizz topping.

The other cocktails in this family, such as the Daiquiri or the Gimlet, are served in a standard cocktail glass of 4 to 4½ ounces. Some use lime in preference to lemon; some use a sweet liqueur or syrup in place of sugar. Most have no standard garnish. Any of these drinks may also be served over ice in a rocks glass if so ordered. Some of them are also made in a frozen version or a fruit version; more on that later.

Mixing Sours

Their contents—citrus juices and sugar—demand that these drinks be shaken or blended or mechanically mixed, whether you make them from scratch or use a sweet-sour mix. Neither the sugar nor the fruit juices can be smoothly combined with the liquor by stirring.

The Shake Method. The cocktail shaker was a symbol of the joyous return to legal drinking after Prohibition. The shaking of a drink was a ceremony of skill that whetted the customer's appetite while commanding admiration. When mechanical mixers were invented, it was quickly discovered that they made a smooth drink a great deal faster than the hand shaker. Today, most bars use shake mixers and blenders, and those that use hand shakers do so for reasons of tradition or showmanship. Ironically, there are bartenders who do not even know how to shake a drink by hand.

Figure 11.2 shows the making of a sour using the hand shaker. You will notice that the first three steps are essentially the same as the stir method. It is step 4 that is the heart of the matter, so let's look at this technique more closely.

The cup of the shaker fits tightly over the glass, since a certain amount of flex in the metal makes for a good fit. It should be put on at an angle with one side of the cup running along the side of the glass. This makes it easier to separate again. (Sometimes shaking creates a vacuum, and the cup adheres to the glass.) Shake vigorously, using long strokes that send the contents from one end to the other. Some people shake up and down; others shake back and forth over the shoulder.

THE SHAKE METHOD: HOW TO MAKE A SOUR IN A HAND SHAKER

Ingredients

Liquor
Lemon juice
Sugar or simple syrup } or sweet-sour mix
Egg white (optional)
Cherry/orange garnish

Glass

Sour glass (4½ ounces), chilled

Mixing Method

Shake

Equipment and Accessories

Shaker: mixing glass with stainless-steel cup
Strainer
Jiggers
Barspoon
Ice scoop
Tongs or pick
Cocktail napkin

step 1: Place a chilled sour glass on the rail, handling it by the stem.

step 2: Fill the mixing glass ⅓ to ½ full of cube ice.

step 3: Measure liquor, lemon juice, and sugar (or mix) and add to the mixing glass.

step 4: Place the cup over the glass and shake 10 times.

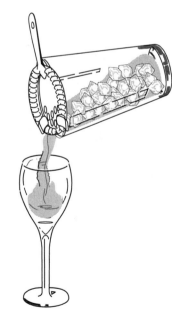

step 5: Remove the cup and strain the drink into the chilled glass.

step 6: Add the garnish, using tongs or a pick. Serve on a cocktail napkin.

Figure 11.2 The shake method: How to make a sour in a hand shaker.

THE SHAKE-MIX METHOD: HOW TO MAKE A SOUR IN A SHAKE MIXER

Ingredients
Liquor
Lemon juice
Sugar or simple syrup } or
Egg white (optional) } sweet-sour
Cherry/orange garnish } mix

Glass
Sour glass (4½ ounces), chilled

Mixing Method
Shake-Mix

Equipment and Accessories
Shake mixer
Strainer
Jiggers
Barspoon
Ice scoop
Tongs or pick
Cocktail napkin

step 1: Place a chilled sour glass on the rail, handling it by the stem.

step 2: Fill the mixer can ¼ full of cube ice.

step 3: Measure liquor, lemon juice, and sugar (or mix) and add to the mixer can.

step 4: Place the mixer can on the mixer and mix for 10 seconds.

step 5: Remove the can and strain the drink into the chilled glass.

step 6: Add the garnish, using tongs or a pick. Serve on a cocktail napkin.

step 7: Wash the mixer can and invert it on the drainboard.

Figure 11.3 The shake-mix method: How to make a sour in a shake mixer.

If you have trouble separating the glass from the cup, don't yield to the temptation of banging the cup on the rail. You can easily break the glass this way. You may also dent the cup. Instead, hit the cup with the heel of your hand halfway between the point where the cup touches the glass and the point where it is farthest away from the glass.

Washing, step 7, is necessary because sugar and fruit juices may cling to the sides of the containers after shaking.

The Shake-Mix Method. If you use the shake mixer to "shake" your cocktail, you substitute the mixer can for the mixing glass and proceed as shown in Figure 11.3. As you can see, the procedures are very similar, but there are some noteworthy differences. Notice that in step 2, you use only one-fourth can of ice. That is because the mixer can is bigger than the mixing glass. You need only enough ice to chill the drink. In step 4, you substitute the mixer can for the hand shaker. To estimate 10 seconds, count "one-hundred-one, one-hundred-two," and so on up to "one-hundred-ten."

The Blend Method

To make the same drink using a blender, substitute the blender cup for the shaker glass or mixer can. The mixing method is like that for the shake mixer, as you can see in Figure 11.4. Set the blender speed on high, but do not blend longer than the specified time. You do not want to incorporate bits of ice into the drink; you only want the ice to chill it. Blending too long will turn it into frozen slush.

A Whiskey Sour is usually made with bourbon or a blended whiskey. A sour can be made with any other liquor, such as gin, brandy, scotch, rum, tequila, vodka. For speed production, you can substitute a jigger of sweet-sour mix for the lemon juice and sugar, but at considerable sacrifice in quality. In the other direction, a special touch would be to add a teaspoon of egg white before blending the ingredients.

The Daiquiri dates back to the Spanish-American War and was named for the Daiquiri iron mines in Cuba. The story goes that the one of the mine's chief engineers, an American, developed the cooling, thirst-quenching drink using rum from the nearby Bacardi rum plant to replace the malaria-tainted local water. The Daiquiri is the prototype for a number of other drinks made with different spirits. Most similar is the Bacardi; it is essentially a Daiquiri made with Bacardi rum, with a dash of grenadine replacing half the sugar.

Change the liquor, substitute a liqueur or a syrup for the sugar, and you find these family members, some familiar, some passé but still occasionally called for:

WHISKEY SOUR
SHAKE, SHAKE-MIX, OR BLEND
4½-oz sour glass, chilled
1 jigger whiskey
Juice from ½ lemon
1 tsp sugar or ½ oz simple syrup
Lemon or orange slice, cherry

DAIQUIRI
SHAKE, SHAKE-MIX, OR BLEND
4½-oz cocktail glass, chilled
1 jigger light rum
1 jigger lime juice
1 tsp sugar, or ½ oz simple syrup

THE BLEND METHOD: HOW TO MAKE A SOUR IN A BLENDER

Ingredients

Liquor
Lemon juice
Sugar or simple syrup
Egg white (optional)
Cherry/orange garnish

} or sweet-sour mix

Glass

Sour glass (4½ ounces), chilled

Mixing Method

Blend

Equipment and Accessories

Blender
Strainer
Jiggers
Barspoon
Ice scoop
Tongs or pick
Cocktail napkin

step 1: Place a chilled sour glass on the rail, handling it by the stem.

step 2: Fill the blender ¼ full of cube ice.

step 3: Measure liquor, lemon juice, and sugar (or mix) and add to the blender cup.

step 4: Place the blender cup on the electric blender and blend for 10 seconds.

step 5: Remove the cup and strain the drink into the chilled glass.

step 6: Add the garnish, using tongs or a pick. Serve on a cocktail napkin.

step 7: Wash the blender cup and invert it on the drainboard.

Figure 11.4 The blend method: How to make a sour in a blender.

Ward 8: A Bourbon Sour with grenadine added.

Side Car: Brandy or Cognac, lemon juice, Cointreau, with a sugared rim (a drink invented by a World War I captain who rode to his favorite Paris bistro on a motorcycle with a sidecar).

Between the Sheets: Half brandy and half rum, lemon or lime juice, triple sec (a variation of the Side Car).

Jack Rose: Apple brandy, lemon or lime juice, grenadine.

Clover Club: Gin, lemon or lime juice, grenadine, egg white.

Tequila Rose: Tequila, lime juice, grenadine.

Pink Lady (yesterday's version): Gin, apple brandy, lemon or lime juice, grenadine, egg white. (The modern Pink Lady adds cream and often omits the juice and the brandy.)

Gimlet: Gin, Rose's lime juice (sweet) or fresh lime juice and sugar. (The Gimlet is said to have been the creation of the British in colonial India. If you use Rose's Lime Juice, as nearly everyone does, you can stir it instead of blending or shaking.)

Scarlett O'Hara: Southern Comfort, cranberry juice, lime juice. In this dry version, the liqueur provides the sweetness. (A sweeter version uses Southern Comfort, grenadine, and lime juice—a totally different drink, no doubt invented by a bartender who had no cranberry on hand.)

Make another very popular version of the Daiquiri by adding fresh fruit. You can blend in half a crushed banana for a Banana Daiquiri, garnishing it with a banana slice. Or blend in crushed fresh or frozen strawberries for a Strawberry Daiquiri, using a whole fresh strawberry as a garnish. Fruit Daiquiris are often made as frozen drinks, a type of drink we will examine shortly.

You can serve any sour on the rocks in a rocks glass. You shake or blend or shake-mix it in the same way you make a straight-up sour and then pour it over ice in a rocks glass.

The Margarita

One of the most popular drinks of the sour family is the **Margarita.** It can be classified as a shake or blend method drink, and there are endless variations on its three simple ingredients: tequila, a flavorful liqueur, and citrus juice. Fruits—whatever is fresh and local; peaches, berries, melon, mango, pineapple, and even prickly pear cactus—are commonly used. The liqueurs range from triple sec to Cointreau to Grand Marnier, and you can use either fresh lime or Rose's lime juice, depending on desired sweetness. Some bartenders add a tablespoon of simple syrup to the mix. Servers should also ask the all-important question when taking drink orders: "Frozen or on the rocks?" Many love their Margaritas as sort-of adult snow cones; others insist that this dilutes the drink, and want it served with just a bit of ice. Customers also have strong preferences for rimming the Margarita glass; the tradition is salt, with a nod to "Los Tres Amigos" (the three friends): tequila, lime and salt. But many folks don't like to sip a sweetish drink through salt, and prefer an un-rimmed glass. Its refreshing nature makes the Margarita a popular summer drink, but you'll sell them year-round.

Sour-Related Drinks

You can start with the ingredients of the sour and make several other drink types by adding another basic ingredient. This gives us another set of drink families: Collins, Fizz, Sling, Daisy. Like the cocktail, these drinks originated in the Victorian era and have changed to keep pace with the times.

The **Collins** is simply a sour with soda added, served over ice in a tall glass. We noted in Chapter 10 that today's Collins is usually just a blend of liquor and mix, built in the glass. But if you break down the drink to its components, you can see there are other ways of making it—from scratch with fresh ingredients or with a sweet-sour mix and soda. You can also see by looking at its structure that you can make other new drinks by changing or adding an ingredient or two.

Figure 11.5 shows a Collins from scratch using a hand shaker and freshly squeezed lemon juice. The essential point to grasp here is that the drink is made by combining two methods: first shake, to mix together liquor, sugar, and fruit juice; then build, to incorporate the soda without losing its bubbles.

You can also make a Collins from scratch using a blender or a shake mixer, as in Figures 11.2 and 11.4, adjusting the ice measurement in step 2. You can make this substitution in any drink you can shake by hand. Thus, when a recipe says "shake," you have your choice of three methods.

If you substitute sweet-sour mix for the lemon and sugar in Figure 11.5, you will still make the drink the same way, though you will no longer be making a Collins from scratch.

A number of drinks take off from the Collins-with-soda by substituting or adding other ingredients:

> *French 75:* a Tom Collins (gin) with Champagne in place of soda.
> *French 95:* a John Collins (bourbon) with Champagne in place of soda.
> *French 125:* a Brandy Collins with Champagne in place of soda.
> *Skip and Go Naked (or Strip and Go Naked):* a Vodka Collins or Tom Collins with beer instead of or in addition to soda.

A **Fizz,** in its bare essentials, is like a Collins except that it is a shorter drink, served in a highball glass or a stem glass of highball size. At one point in cocktail history, a Fizz was designed to be gulped down like an Alka-Seltzer, and for the same reasons. To make it as bubbly as possible, it was shaken long and hard with ice, the soda was added under pressure

HOW TO MAKE A COLLINS FROM SCRATCH

Ingredients
Liquor
Lemon
Sugar
Cube ice
Cherry, optional orange slice

Glass
Collins (10 to 12 ounces)

Mixing Method
Shake/Build

Equipment and Accessories
Shaker (for blender or shaker mixer)
Strainer
Jigger
Barspoon
Ice scoop
Fruit squeezer
Long straws
Pick
Cocktail napkin

step 1: Fill Collins glass 3/4 full of cube ice and place on rail.

step 2: Fill mixing glass 1/3 to 1/2 full of cube ice. Measure and add liquor, sugar, and lemon.

step 3: Shake the contents 10 times.

step 4: Strain shaker contents into Collins glass.

step 5: Add soda to within 1/2 to 1 inch of rim. Stir gently (2 or 3 strokes).

step 6: Garnish, add long straws, and serve on a cocktail napkin.

Figure 11.5 How to make a Collins from scratch.

from a seltzer bottle, and the drink was served foaming in a small glass without ice.

Today, because of our modern use of ice, a simple Fizz is more like a short Collins or a cross between a sour and a highball. However, some of the elaborations on the basic Fizz make it a good deal more than a simple drink. Here is today's basic Fizz:

Family Characteristics

Ingredients: Liquor, lemon, sugar, soda, cube ice.
Glass: Highball or 8-ounce stem glass.
Mixing method: Shake/build.

To make a Fizz, follow the Collins-from-scratch method. The liquor can be any type—gin is the most common, but rum, scotch, brandy, or sloe gin are called for now and then. The Gin Fizz is the one most frequently elaborated on; others include:

Silver Fizz: A Gin Fizz with an egg white. If you add grenadine, it becomes a Bird of Paradise Fizz.
Golden Fizz: A Gin Fizz with an egg yolk.
Royal Fizz: A Gin Fizz with a whole egg and sometimes cream.
New Orleans Fizz or Ramos Fizz: A Gin Fizz made with both lemon and lime, with added egg white, cream, and a few dashes of orange flower water, served in a tall glass.

These more elaborate Gin Fizzes have undergone further transformation by being made with ice cream, which introduces new methods we'll discuss soon.

Other Fizzes include the Morning Glory Fizz, made with scotch and a little pernod, and the Sloe Gin Fizz. If you add cream to the Sloe Gin Fizz, you have a Slow Ride Fizz.

A Sling is like a Collins to which something more is added—a liqueur or a special flavor or garnish. It is usually made by the Collins-from-scratch method and is served in a Collins glass with fruit garnishes. The most famous Sling—and probably the one made most often today—is the Singapore Sling.

Notice that this drink is just like a Tom Collins except that it uses cherry liqueur (sweet) in place of sugar and has a different garnish. The Sling as a "species" has terrific potential for creating your own specialty drinks.

A *Daisy* is nothing more than a sour made with grenadine as the sweet, served in a larger glass over crushed ice and garnished lavishly with fruit. Sometimes it is served in a silver mug and stirred until the mug frosts, like a julep.

SINGAPORE SLING

SHAKE/BUILD

12-oz glass

¾ glass cube ice

1 jigger gin

½ jigger cherry-flavored brandy

½ jigger lemon juice

Soda to fill

Lemon or lime slice

SHOOTERS AND SHOTS

This group of drinks is only loosely considered a "family," as it is defined not so much by its pattern of ingredients as by the size of the drink, its purpose, and the manner in which it is consumed. These are small, straight-up drinks, served in a shot glass, and their purpose is frankly pleasure and conviviality. Shooters and shots are generally gulped rather quickly, in the company of friends. Creative bartenders are always coming up with new concoctions for this drink category, as they provide a good way to give a customer a taste of liquor without ordering a "whole" drink. Most contain no more than ¾ ounce of liquor—except the drinks made specifically to be shared. More about those in a moment. First, the basic shooter characteristics:

Family Characteristics
Ingredients: Any of the following: liquors, liqueurs, fruit juice, soda, cola, sour mix, coffee, cream, and almost anything else—even black pepper with straight vodka, or Tabasco with cinnamon schnapps.
Glass: Shot or small rocks.
Method: Most are shaken briefly by hand with ice; a few are layered in the style of a pousse-café.

The shaker is used for two reasons: to mix and to chill. A few vigorous shakes are enough; you don't want to dilute the drink. For a layered shooter, the order of pouring is critical for visual effect (review the information about pousse-cafés), but the layered shooter is consumed in a gulp or two like any other shooter, not sipped.

Shooter recipes vary from year to year, from bar to bar, and from one part of the country to another. Here, for example, are three versions of the very popular Sex on the Beach:

Original: Chambord or raspberry liqueur, Midori, pineapple juice.
New York style: Peach schnapps, vodka, orange and cranberry juices.
Bennigan's: Vodka, Midori, Chambord, pineapple juice.

Other popular shooters include:

Alabama Slammer: Southern Comfort, Amaretto, orange juice, grenadine. Another version adds sloe gin and vodka.
No Name: Grenadine, Kahlua, Bailey's
Orgasm: Kahlua, Bailey's, Amaretto, cream. If you add vodka, it's called a Screaming Orgasm.

KAMIKAZE

SHAKE

Shot glass
½ oz vodka
¼ oz Rose's lime juice
Splash triple sec
Shake briefly in hand shaker with ice; strain

B-52

BUILD

Shot or pony glass
¼ oz Kahlua
¼ oz Bailey's Irish Cream
¼ oz Grand Marnier
Layer ingredients in order given

Russian Quaalude: Stolichnaya, Frangelico, Bailey's.
Watermelon: Southern Comfort, Creme de Noya, vodka, pineapple and/or orange juice) grenadine.
Woo Woo: Peach schnapps, vodka, cranberry juice

In the late 1990s, the trend in many types of food and drink was to "up-size" or "supersize" the portion, and the shooter was not immune. Upsizing has evolved in some bars into sales of the **Fish Bowl,** a 32-ounce clear bowl filled with liquor that is designed to serve at least four persons. One popular variation, called the Shark Bowl, is a mixture of vodka, triple sec, rum, gin, tequila, and a dash of grenadine, with fruit juices (orange, pineapple, and cranberry) and 7UP. A bubblegum "shark" swims on top! The drink is made to be sipped by as many people as can get a straw into it, at a cost of $12 to $18.

Today's cocktails are, for the most part, drier, lighter, and include more different kinds of flavors than their turn-of-the-last-century predecessors. And, remember, that additional splash, dash, or float of a juice or liqueur can be the "master stroke" that propels a drink to fame. Two such derivatives of the Kamikaze have become very popular in the 2000s: the Cosmopolitan, and the Kazoo. The latter is a signature cocktail of the Axis restaurant in Seattle, Washington.

Another enterprising Seattle, Washington, bar called Cutter's Bayhouse infuses its own vodkas to create its Cosmopolitans, steeping them for five to seven days with a variety of additions, including strawberries, vanilla or coffee beans, and Lifesavers candies.

The cocktail known as the Metropolitan substitutes either Stolichnaya Limonaya or Absolut Kurant to the recipe, with a lime wedge as garnish. Both Cosmopolitans and Metropolitans are more likely to be sipped than "slammed," as true shooters.

Although shooters are relatively new on the American scene, you can find their antecedents and counterparts in the use of straight spirits downed quickly for toasts, such as vodka in Russia, Dutch gin in Holland, and aquavit in the Scandinavian countries. These, however, are straight **shots** of liquor, not mixed drinks. Another related drink is a straight shot of a spirit (such as whiskey) ordered with a **chaser**—something to drink immediately after the alcohol, such as beer or water. This is a jigger-size drink served in a shot glass. If no chaser is ordered, a glass of ice water is usually served anyway.

A confusing aspect of shooter recipes is that drinks by the same name and with the same ingredients are often ordered on the rocks or as highballs, to be sipped and savored. In this style of drink, the total liquor content may be at least

---

COSMOPOLITAN

STIR

5- to 6-oz cocktail glass, chilled

1½ oz Absolut Citron (citrus-flavored vodka)

½ oz Cointreau

½ oz Rose's lime juice

½ oz cranberry juice

Twist of lemon or orange peel garnish

THE AXIS KAZOO

SHAKE

5- to 6-oz cocktail glass, chilled

One Golden Delicious apple, sliced and marinated in apple juice

1½ oz Absolut Kurant vodka

½ oz Cointreau

1 oz cranberry juice

1 oz sweet and sour mix

Muddle all ingredients in shaker with ice

Apple slice garnish

twice the ¾-ounce limit suggested for shooters, but it will be diluted by longer mixing and melting ice, and consumed over a longer period of time. The person taking the order (for a Kamikaze, for example) should be careful to ask whether the customer wants a shooter, a rocks drink, or a highball. If it is a shooter, the server should monitor consumption and behavior carefully, keeping in mind that it is illegal everywhere to serve anyone "clearly" or "visibly" intoxicated.

Many shooter recipes given today in books and magazines call for 2 ounces of liquor; and there are undoubtedly bars that pour shooters this size. But the prudent bar operation standardizes its shooter recipes on the safe side, and trains its personnel to carefully monitor consumption.

In spite of the shooter vogue, you may see these drinks dwindling in popularity, along with the general decline of alcoholic beverage sales. They are characteristic of the old neighborhood bar where the primary focus is on drinking. This species of bar has, for the most part, been edged out by new values. The American obsession with health, the neoprohibitionist movement, the crusade against drunk driving, and proprietors' fear of liability have combined to prompt a change of emphasis, which now links drinking with dining; drinking for its own sake simply is no longer fashionable. So it is important to have food available—and offer it—to customers who order these types of drinks. Eating and drinking are best when done together.

TROPICAL DRINKS

The collective term **tropical drinks** as used in the bar trade comprises a loose collection of drinks originating in the resorts of the tropics, or in restaurants with a tropical ambience. The family characteristics are diffuse: there are no indispensable ingredients that tie them all together. Generally, they have various kinds of rum as their base and make lavish use of fruit juices, liqueurs, syrups, and flower and fruit garnishes. They are showy, often expensive to make, and thus command a high price tag. Cheaper and easier versions of some can be made using bottled mixes.

Family Characteristics
Ingredients: Rum (occasionally brandy, and once in a while gin), fruit juices, liqueurs, syrups, coconut milk, fruit garnishes, flowers, fresh mint.
Glass: Anything from a cocktail glass to a whole coconut or pineapple.
Mixing method: Shake (or blend, or shake-mix).

MAI TAI (FROM SCRATCH)

SHAKE, BLEND, SHAKE-MIX

12-oz glass
¾ glass cube or crushed ice
1 jigger light rum
1 jigger dark rum
1 lime (juice and peel)
½ oz orange Curacao
½ oz orgeat
Pineapple stick, cherry, mint sprig

PINA COLADA (FROM SCRATCH)

BLEND

12-oz glass
¾ glass cube or crushed ice
1 jigger light rum
1 jigger cream of coconut or coconut milk
1–2 jiggers pineapple juice or crushed pineapple
Cherry, pineapple, lime

Among the fruit juices are pineapple, papaya, coconut milk, and such other exotics as kiwi and mango, in addition to the usual lemon, lime, and orange. Among the syrups, grenadine, orgeat, falernum, and passion fruit are popular. The liqueurs frequently called for are fruit-flavored brandies, cherry liqueur, Curacao, and pernod or some other absinthe substitute. Among the garnishes are pineapple cubes, coconut, mint leaves, the usual oranges, limes, and cherries, and orchids, if available.

Both these drinks can also be made from prepared mixes, and usually are. The Mai Tai, like many other tropical drinks, was created by Trader Vic in the 1940s, and is still going strong. In Hawaii, where orchids grow on trees, your bountiful glass of Mai Tai will be topped with at least one.

Pineapple used in the Pina Colada can be either fresh or canned. If you use the crushed fruit, be sure to blend at high speed until smooth. A variation of the Pina Colada is the Chi Chi, which substitutes vodka for rum.

Other classic tropical drinks are the Planter's Punch, the Scorpion, and the Zombie. It is said that buckets of Planter's Punch were carried to workers in the sugarcane fields. Another story says the drink was a specialty of the famous Planter's Hotel in St. Louis. Both stories could be true. These three drinks are typically finished off with a float of 151-proof rum, so that the customer's first sip is the "sting" of the scorpion, the "punch" of the planter, or the "kick" of the zombie. The Zombie made its fame with the kick, the name, the challenge of "only one to a customer," and in some cases the recipe— some include four or five kinds of rum.

The Brazilian rum called cachaca, mentioned in Chapter 5, is the base for a very simple, popular South American drink that is catching on big in North America now, too: the Caipirinha.

CAIPIRINHA

SHAKE

6- to 8-oz Old-Fashioned glass

½ lime cut in four wedges

   Muddle lime in bottom of glass

2 oz cachaca

¾ oz simple syrup

CREAM DRINKS

Cream drinks are smooth, sweet, after-dinner drinks made with cream and usually served straight up in a cocktail or Champagne glass.

Family Characteristics
Ingredients: Cream, one or more liqueurs or a liquor-liqueur combination.
Glass: Cocktail or Champagne, chilled.
Mixing method: Shake (or blend or shake-mix).

The proportions of the ingredients vary from one house to another. Some use equal parts (from ½ ounce to 1 ounce of each), some use up to 2 ounces of cream and smaller amounts of the other ingredients, some use more of the predominant flavor or the major liquor if there is one. The total ingredients should add up to about 3 ounces—any more and you might have to use a larger glass. Light cream or half-and-half is typically used, but heavy cream makes a better drink. The cream must be very fresh. Whether you blend, shake, or shake-mix a cream drink, you follow the steps given for a sweet-sour cocktail. You may want to serve it with a pair of short straws. After mixing you must wash and rinse both your jigger and your glass or cup, because the cream and liqueurs cling to the sides.

Two familiar cream drinks are the Brandy Alexander and the Grasshopper. You can make an Alexander with any base liquor, substituting it for the brandy in the recipe. Apparently, the earliest was the Gin Alexander, invented to disguise the awful bathtub gin of Prohibition days. Light crème de cacao is used when the base liquor is a light color, such as vodka, rum, or tequila. Dark crème de cacao is used with brandy and whiskies. A vodka-based Alexander is sometimes called a Russian Bear or a White Elephant. An Alexander made with rum is a Panama.

The original cream concoctions spawned a whole menagerie of "animal" drinks:

Pink Squirrel:	Light crème de cacao, Crème de Noyaux, cream
Brown Squirrel:	Dark crème de cacao, Amaretto, cream
Blue-Tailed Fly:	Light crème de cacao, blue Curacao, cream
White Monkey or Banshee:	Light crème de cacao, crème de banana, cream
Purple Bunny:	Light crème de cacao, cherry-flavored brandy, cream

In addition to the critters, we have:

Golden Cadillac: Light crème de cacao, Galliano, cream
White Cadillac: Light crème de cacao, Cointreau, cream
Velvet Hammer: Vodka or Cointreau, light crème de cacao, cream
Cucumber: Green crème de menthe, cream. Another version adds brandy or gin as the base ingredient.
White Russian: Vodka, Kahlua, cream (a Black Russian with cream)
Golden Dream: Galliano, triple sec, orange juice, cream
Pink Lady: Gin, grenadine, cream

Any of the cream drinks may be served on the rocks if the customer requests it. A cream drink on the rocks must be blended or shaken as for a straight-up drink, then strained over cube ice in a rocks glass. Sometimes it is built in the glass without stirring over cube ice in a rocks glass. Sometimes it is built in the glass without stirring, with the cream as a float. This makes a very different drink.

Another spin-off of the after-dinner cream drinks is to add a mixer and make them into a highball-sized drink. Thus, the Colorado Bulldog starts off

---

BRANDY ALEXANDER

SHAKE, BLEND OR SHAKE-MIX

Cocktail or Champagne glass
¾ oz brandy
³/₄ oz dark crème de cacao
I oz cream

GRASSHOPPER

SHAKE, BLEND OR SHAKE-MIX

Cocktail or Champagne glass
¾ oz green Crème de Menthe
¾ oz light crème de cacao
I oz cream

RUM MILK PUNCH

SHAKE, BLEND, MIX

12-oz glass

¾ glass cube ice

1 jigger rum

1 tsp sugar

4 oz milk

Sprinkle of nutmeg

EGGNOG

SHAKE, BLEND, MIX

12-oz glass

1 egg

1 jigger brandy

1 tsp sugar

4 oz milk

Sprinkle of nutmeg

AGGRAVATION

BUILD

8-oz glass

¾ glass cube ice

1 jigger scotch

½ jigger Kahlua

Milk to fill

SMITH & KERNS

BUILD

8-oz glass

¾ glass cube ice

1 jigger dark crème de cacao

Milk to ¾ full

Soda to fill

as a vodka-Kahlua-cream drink, shaken and poured over ice in a highball glass; then the glass is filled with Coke. It's a shake/build method.

OTHER DAIRY DRINKS

In addition to cream, other dairy products are sometimes used in mixed drinks. These are usually long drinks rather than cocktails—pick-me-ups or nightcaps rather than appetizers or desserts. They are simply too filling to precede or follow a meal.

It is hard to say whether the current crop of milk drinks is a logical extension of the popular cream drinks or a modern version of old colonial libations. There seem to be some of each type.

Today's **milk punches** are clearly descendants of the older punch drinks, using milk in place of water and served either iced or hot, as the season—or the customer—dictates.

Family Characteristics
Ingredients: Liquor, sugar, milk, cube ice, nutmeg.
Glass: Collins.
Mixing method: Shake (or blend or shake-mix).

Liquors most commonly called for are brandy, whiskey, rum, and gin. Make your basic milk punch with brandy, add an egg, and you have an eggnog. You don't use ice in the eggnog glass. The egg will add volume, and the drink does not demand the ice-cold temperatures of most. Do shake it with ice, however. You can add half a jigger of brandy to Rum Punch, if you wish, to pep it up.

Some drinks of the highball family use milk or cream as a mixer, such as the Aggravation and the Smith & Kerns. Another milk drink is Scotch and Milk. It is served over ice in a highball glass like any scotch highball. You can also substitute milk for cream in cream drinks if a calorie-conscious customer requests it.

An additional egg drink is the **Flip,** a cold, straight-up drink of sweetened liquor or fortified wine that is shaken with egg and topped with nutmeg. This is the descendant of the Colonial Flip, which was drunk piping hot, either simmered over the fire or heated with a hot poker from the fireplace.

Ice Cream Drinks

An ice cream drink is any drink made with ice cream. Many of the ice cream drinks are variants of cream drinks, with ice cream simply replacing the cream. Others are made by adding ice cream to another drink, such as a Fizz. Figure 11.6 tells the whole story, including the family characteristics and the step-by-step mixing method.

In addition to the equipment listed, you will need a special freezer chest at the serving station for storing the ice cream, and your health department will probably require you to have a special well with running water and an overflow drain into which to put your ice cream scoops between uses. An alternative to all this is to dispense your ice cream from a soft-serve machine. Two ice cream drinks that may make the extra effort worthwhile are the Grasshopper Blend and the Ramos Fizz—a short one and a long one.

In both drinks, ice cream replaces the cream of the original recipe. Other popular ice cream drinks include the following, in which vanilla ice cream replaces cream: Brandy Alexander, Velvet Hammer, White Russian, Pink Lady, Golden Dream. Other Fizzes, such as the Royal Fizz and Silver Fizz, are sometimes made with ice cream.

The specialty coffee craze opens up other hot sales possibilities for cold coffee drinks. People already often drink their mochas, lattés, and cappuccinos "iced." Blend one with Tia Maria and Chambord, and substitute two scoops of vanilla ice cream for the steamed milk of a regular latté, and you have a raspberry-flavored coffee cocktail.

Ice cream drinks make good house specialties. You can invent your own: not only do you have many drinks to start from, but just as many flavors of ice cream to experiment with. Remember the rum raisin ice cream that topped the Mocha Rum Cooler? Consider exotic flavors, pretty garnishes, and special glasses for your frosty creations. And speaking of frosty . . .

GRASSHOPPER
BLEND OR SHAKE-MIX
8-oz stem glass, chilled
1 scoop vanilla ice cream
½ jigger green Crème de Menthe
½ jigger white crème de cacao
Straws

RAMOS FIZZ
BLEND/BUILD, SHAKE-MIX
12-oz glass, chilled
3 scoops vanilla ice cream
1 jigger gin
1 oz lemon juice
½ oz lime juice (or sweet-and-sour frothee mix)
1 egg white
1 tsp sugar
3–4 dashes orange flower water
Soda to fill
Straws

FROZEN DRINKS

It is almost impossible to be unhappy sipping a frozen specialty cocktail. The smooth, icy libation stimulates the same pleasure center in the brain as an ice cream cone. As a group, frozen drinks are extremely versatile—and they are moneymakers, especially in warm climates. You can mix them easily as individual drinks or make them by the batch in special cocktail freezers. You

HOW TO MAKE AN ICE CREAM DRINK

Ingredients
Liquor
Ice cream
Optional ingredients
Optional garnish

Glass
8- or 12-oz chilled

Mixing Method
Blend or Shake-Mix

Equipment and Accessories
Blender or shake mixer
Ice cream scoop, #20 or #24
Jigger
Barspoon
Straws
Cocktail napkin

step 1: Place prechilled glass on the rail.

step 2: Scoop ice cream into blender or mixer cup.

step 3: Add the liquor and other ingredients.

step 4: Blend or mix until ice cream has liquefied.

step 5: Pour the entire contents into the glass. Use barspoon to scrape cup.

step 6: Add garnish and straw and serve on a cocktail napkin.

Figure 11.6 How to make an ice cream drink.

can rent or buy portable "Margarita machines" that freeze premeasured amounts of perfectly smooth, slushy ice, and dispense it on demand.

The method is simple and straightforward: you simply blend crushed ice along with the ingredients of the drink until everything is homogeneous and the ice has refrozen to the consistency of slush (see Figure 11.7 for details). The flavors can vary, depending on fresh fruit, juices and packaged drink mixes—which can be combined with crushed ice, ice cream, frozen yogurt or sorbet.

Several points are critical in making a successful frozen drink:

- In step 3, the right amount of ice is important. Too little, and you have a drink without body. Too much, and you have a drink without taste.
- In step 4, it takes quite a long time to reach the right consistency— several times as long as blending any other drink. Listen closely! When you no longer hear the bits of ice hitting the blender cup, it is ready to serve.
- In step 5, use the barspoon to scrape everything out of the cup.

The various sours make the best frozen drinks because of their tangy flavors. Remember when mixing ingredients, a bland drink will be even *more* bland when frozen. Many frozen drinks are sweet-and-sour drinks with fruit added, such the Frozen Strawberry Daiquiri and the Frozen Peach Margarita, two classics.

The recipes for those two drinks require fresh fruit, although you can substitute frozen strawberries in the **Daiquiri,** omitting the simple syrup since they are usually already sweetened. For the Peach Margarita, you can use fresh peaches in season, blending the puree in advance with simple syrup and a dash of lemon juice. In winter, just puree frozen peaches without the added sugar.

Frozen tropical drinks seem to "blend" well (pardon the pun) with Mexican, Asian, and Caribbean cuisine. Make them hip; fun and casual and people will order them year-round. The best-sellers today feature premium spirits, true fruit flavors, and elaborate presentations—even party-sized for multiple sippers, like the Fish Bowl! At Café Odyssey in Minneapolis, Minnesota, a customer favorite is the Mystical Fogger, which is essentially a Daiquiri with a chunk of dry ice. For maximum showmanship, the server blows a foghorn and shouts, "Iffy!" the Swahili word for "Cheers!"

What layering does for a pousse-café, "swirling" does to a frozen drink. If you prepare two drinks of different colors in different blenders, you can pour them into the same glass and lightly swirl them to alternate—but not mix—the two hues for complementary tastes and colors.

FROZEN STRAWBERRY DAIQUIRI
BLEND
8- to 10-oz stem glass, chilled
1 jigger rum
1 tsp lemon juice
2 tsp simple syrup
1 jigger pureed strawberries (or six fresh berries, cut up)
Crushed ice to submerge liquids
Whole berry garnish

FROZEN PEACH MARGARITA
BLEND
8- to 10-oz stem glass, chilled
1 jigger tequila
½ jigger peach liqueur
1½ jiggers pureed peaches
Crushed ice to submerge liquids
Fresh peach wedge (in season)

HOW TO MAKE A FROZEN DRINK

Ingredients
Liquor
Optional ingredients
Optional garnish
Crushed ice

Glass
8- or 12-oz stem glass

Mixing Method
Blend

Equipment and Accessories
Heavy-duty commercial blender
Jigger
Barspoon
Ice scoop
Short straws
Cocktail napkin

step 1: Place prechilled glass on the rail, holding it by the stem.

step 2: Pour cocktail ingredients into blender cup.

step 3: Using the scoop, add crushed ice to come just above liquor level.

step 4: Blend on high speed until mixture blends and refreezes to a slush.

step 5: Heap contents of the cup into the glass. Scrape cup with barspoon.

step 6: Garnish, add straw, and serve on a cocktail napkin.

Figure 11.7 How to make a frozen drink.

FILLING DRINK ORDERS

Most drinks are made to order drink by drink, but the orders seldom come in one drink at a time. Here are a few tips on handling orders, aimed at these objectives:

Speed: Keeping up with the orders.
Quality: Getting the drink to the customer at its peak of perfection.
Accuracy: Delivering the right drink to the right customer.

First, deal with one set of orders, that is, one server's guest check or one party of bar customers. Set up all the glasses at once; it will help you remember what was ordered. Group them according to the base liquor, setting them up in the same sequence as the liquor bottles in the well. (Have your servers "call" drinks—state their names to you—in this order, too.) In this way, a good bartender can handle a fairly long list without taking time to refer back to the written ticket.

If there is more than one drink of the same kind that is not built in the glass, make them together. Put extra ice in the mixing glass or the blender or mixer cup, multiply each ingredient by the number of drinks, and proceed as for a single drink. Divide the finished product among the glasses you have set out for these drinks, but not all at once. Fill each glass half full the first time around; then add a little more to each glass in another round or two until you complete all these drinks evenly.

Make drinks in the following sequence:

1. Start frozen drinks and ice cream drinks (they will be made in their machines while the rest are being poured).
2. Pour straight liquor drinks (straight shots, liquor on rocks).
3. Fix juice drinks and sours.
4. Prepare cream drinks and hot drinks.
5. Mix highballs with carbonated mixers.
6. Pour draft beer.

This sequence allows you to make first those drinks that keep best and to make last those that don't hold well. Some places have the server call drinks in this sequence instead of in the well order.

When writing an order on a guest check, use a standard set of abbreviations for drinks, liquors, brand names, mixes, and special garnishes. Table 11.1 gives you some suggestions. Abbreviations vary from one bar to another. You can adapt these to your needs or work out your own. Then be sure that everyone on both sides of the bar knows and uses them correctly.

In writing a drink order, a slash is used to separate the items in the instructions. For example, a very dry vodka Martini on the rocks with a twist

Table 11.1
Guest-Check Abbreviations

Liquors, etc.		*Drinks*		*Call Brands*	
Liquors					
Bourbon	B	Bourbon and Water	B/W	Absolut	ABS
Brandy	Br	Black Russian	BRUS	Beefeater	BEEF
Gin	G	Brandy Alexander	BR ALEX	Canadian Club	CC
Rum	R	Bacardi	BAC	Chivas Regal	CHIVAS
Scotch	S or SC	Banana Daiquiri	BAN DAQ	Courvoisier	COUR
Tequila	TEQ	Bloody Mary	MARY	Cuervo Gold	C GOLD
Vodka	V	Daiquiri	DAQ	Cutty Sark	CUTTY
		Fuzzy Navel	FUZ	Dewars White Label	WHITE or WL
Mixes		Godfather	GOD	Drambuie	DRAM
Coke	C	Gibson	GIB	Early Times	ET
Ginger ale	G	Gimlet	GIM	Glenlivet	LIVET
7UP	7	Grasshopper	GRASS	Grand Marnier	MARNIER
Soda	S	Irish Coffee	IRISH C	Hennessy	HENN
Sprite	SP	Harvey Wallbanger	BANGER	J & B	JB
Tonic	T	John Collins	JOHN	Jack Daniels	JD
Water	W	Kamikaze	KAM	Jim Beam	BEAM
		Manhattan	MAN	Johnny Walker Black	BLACKS
Garnishes		Margarita	MARG	Johnny Walker Red	REDS
Lime	LI	Martini	MT	Old Fitzgerald	FITZ
Olive	OL	Old-Fashioned	OF	Old Grand-Dad	DAD
Onion	ON	Ramos Fizz	RAMOS	Remy-Martin	REMY
Twist	TW or ~	Rob Roy	R ROY	Seagrams 7 Crown	7
		Rusty Nail	R NAIL	Seagrams V.O.	VO
Special instructions		Screwdriver	DRIVER	Sloe gin	SLG
Double	DBL	Scotch and Water	SC/W	Smirnoff	SMIRN
Dry	X	Tequila Sunrise	SUNRISE	Southern Comfort	SO C
Extra dry	XX	Tom Collins	TOM	Stolichnaya	STOLI
On the rocks	R	Virgin Mary	V MARY	Tanqueray	TANQ
Straight up	Up or a	Vodka Martini	V MT	Wild Turkey	WILD
Frozen	Z	Whisky Sour	WS		

is written: V MT/XX/R/TW. This **shorthand** may seem like Greek when you're first getting used to it, but soon you will find it indispensable.

When the server takes a table order, the best way to get the right drink to the right person is to pick out one seat as number 1—say, the one closest to the bar. Then each seat is numbered in order around the table. Each drink is written on the check following the number of the customer's seat. Figure 11.8 is an example of a guest check for a party of six.

RESTAURANT & BAR

GUEST CHECK

Server CC	Table No. 12	Guests 6	Date 12-23-01	
1 1	V / MT / R / TW			4.75
2	XX / TANQ / MT / R / O11			5.50
3	7 / 7			4.75
4	Chivas / W			5.00
5	Br / Man / R			4.75
6 6	MARG/ Z / C GOLD			5.95
7				
8				
9				
10				
11				
12				
13				
14				

THANK YOU

FOOD	—————
BEVERAGE	30.70
SUB TOTAL	
TAX	—————
TOTAL	30.70

Figure 11.8 Guest check using typical abbreviations. Seat numbers are in the left column.

DEVELOPING DRINK MENUS AND SPECIALTY DRINKS

Once you have a thorough knowledge of drinks and the ways they are made, you will understand why planning the drink menu—that is, the range and types of drinks you will serve—is one of the most important things you do. The drinks you serve will determine the sizes of glassware, the number and type of ice machines, the refrigerator and freezer space, the small equipment and utensils, the space on the backbar. They will also determine the skill level you require of your bartenders and servers. And, of course, they will determine the kinds of liquor and supplies you buy and the number of items you must keep in inventory.

The Unlimited Bar Concept

If your menu concept is an **unlimited bar,** that is, one that serves the full spectrum of drinks, you must be able to produce those drinks. This means having the equipment that produces both cube and crushed ice, glassware that will accommodate everything from the after-dinner liqueur to the Zombie, a freezer or soft-serve machine for ice cream, a means of chilling cocktail glasses, all the necessary small equipment, an ample draft-beer setup, and 100 or more different beverages in your inventory. In addition, you must have skilled and knowledgeable bartenders, as well as servers who know how to take and transmit orders.

There are many types of enterprises where the versatility of the unlimited bar is part of the bar's image. Even though the customer may order the same drink time after time (often without knowing what is in it or how much it costs), the assurance that that drink is available at that bar is important. It is also possible for a whole party of people to order widely different types of drinks to suit their individual tastes. The unlimited bar is essential to the expensive restaurant, where excellence in everything is the image.

The Limited Drink Menu

Many restaurant-bars today are using printed drink menus. You may find them in restaurants where drinks are secondary to food or in the trendy neighborhood bar-and-grills. They usually feature specialty drinks, along with old favorites, with descriptions that raise the thirst level as they list the ingredients. Or there may be a list of special drinks chalked on a blackboard at the bar. These drink menus are proving to be good sales stimulators. At the same time, by focusing attention on a limited selection, they can avoid some of the costs of a full-spectrum bar.

For example, a well-designed specialty menu can reduce the extensive liquor inventory required in an unlimited bar. If you offer an attractive selection of 15 or 20 drinks—all carefully planned to be based on a few liquors, liqueurs, and mixes—you can cut the number of items in your inventory by half, at least. You should still be prepared to serve the standard highballs, Martinis, and Bloody Marys, and you will still carry a small selection of the popular call brands, but your customers will order up to 90 percent of their drinks from your printed menu.

The limited drink menu applies the philosophy of the limited food menu: instead of offering everything anyone might want, you specialize, in the same way that you develop a successful food menu. You combine a few basic ingredients using a skillful mix-and-match technique, in the same way that an Italian restaurant offers a long list of entrées by mixing and matching pastas and sauces.

The limited drink menu also shares some other advantages of the limited food menu. Properly developed, it can mean that less equipment is needed at the bar, as well as less space for the smaller inventory, and thus less investment overall. It can mean that fewer skills and less experience are required of the bartenders, so you do not need to pay higher-skill wages. Your own training of personnel to prepare your own selection of drinks can produce that sought-after consistency of product. Also, you can choose the base ingredients with an eye to keeping down costs: vodka and rum are cheaper than the whiskies, and they mix well with a variety of flavor additions. And buying larger quantities of fewer items may give you better quantity discounts.

For a limited menu to be successful, the first requirement is that it must reflect the tastes of your customers. If you are already in business, you have data on your most popular drink types. Include the favorites and go on from there to make new drinks by changing or adding flavors and flavor accents. If yours is a new enterprise, find out what your target population is drinking in other places. Be sure to include house wines and a selection of popular beers—something for everybody.

Creating Signature Drinks

A number of the drinks mentioned in this chapter and the last are the specialties of particular bartenders, bars, or restaurants. So let's take a moment to briefly discuss what makes a drink a **"signature"** cocktail, with marketability and "staying power"?

The signature cocktail must have a flavor that appeals to a variety of palates, and it should convey the spirit or theme of the bar or restaurant in which it was created. A bit of mystique—whether it's a funny story, an upscale image, or a top-secret recipe—never hurts. It is absolutely critical to keep the taste and quality of this drink consistent.

The key is to take the "right" ingredients and make them your own. Since bartenders are experimenting all the time, it's up to you to cleverly substitute interesting new ingredients in tasty new ways, and vary the presentation just enough to be unique.

In case you haven't noticed, even the most famous bars have only one or two "signature" drinks. In New Orleans, it's the Hurricane at Pat O'Brien's, and the Brandy Milk Punch at Dickie Brennan's Steakhouse. Don't overwhelm your guests with a barrage of new drinks. It'll scare them away. Introduce them seasonally, or one every month, to see what sells and what has potential. Here are a few additional pointers about developing specialty drinks:

- **Cater to your clientele and their preferences.** Observe the basic drink structure discussed in Chapter 10. A successful drink has a base liquor, plus one or more flavor modifiers or flavor accents. The base liquor should be at least 50 percent of the liquor in the drink.

- **Do not treat this as a contest to challenge your customers' taste buds.** Choose flavor combinations that are compatible—mixing orange juice and chocolate probably won't work! Work with popular flavors. Try adding a trendy flavor as a float atop a familiar drink, or be the first to make an old drink with a new product—if you have a clientele this would appeal to.
- **Consider your equipment, glassware, and space.** If you want to feature frozen drinks, you must have an ample supply of crushed or flake ice and plenty of blenders, or enough demand for a single specialty to invest in a frozen drink machine. If you want ice cream drinks, you must have ice cream equipment at the bar.
- **Consider your bartenders' skill level.** If you want to serve pousse-cafés, be sure your personnel can make them.
- **Keep the drinks fairly simple so they can be made quickly.** Consider including **mocktails,** nonalcoholic specialty drinks. Dress them up handsomely and offer them free of charge to designated drivers.
- **Plan attractive visual effects, dream up catchy names, and blend it all into your image.**

Promoting Your Wares

Making a commitment to creating specialty drinks means you'll also need to promote them. A successful promotion should be consistent with your bar's "personality" or concept and its clientele. A classy after-work business crowd may not appreciate your rum drinks served in pineapple "bowls" with paper umbrellas in them, but they'd probably go for an upscale scotch selection and knowledgeable servers who can make recommendations about it.

You are doing two things with a promotion: either generating repeat business or generating more sales from existing customers. It is a long-term process, not a week-long endeavor, and it may require spending a little of your hard-earned money to print collateral material: table tents, individual drink menus, or a list of drinks on your regular dining menu. A chalkboard list is another method that gives guests the impression they're trying something up-to-the-minute. Listing after-dinner drinks in a separate dessert menu is a good idea, as seen on the sample menu in Figure 11.9. A dessert menu is also the perfect place for touting coffee drinks.

The printed menu must catch the customer's eye and whet the appetite and create a thirst. It should spell out the ingredients in each drink, since your specialties will be new to the customer, and the names you give them won't mean anything. (They may also be interested to read what their old favorites are made of.) Depending on your clientele and your budget, you might want to illustrate your menu with inviting photos or sketches of your drinks. The point is, make the menu interesting to browse through; like your food menu, it is a promotion piece.

Coffee Specialties

ROYAL STREET COFFEE . . . . . . Freshly brewed coffee   **$3.50**
blended with Amaretto and Kahlua, topped with heavy
whipped cream and sprinkled with nutmeg.

DUTCH TREAT . . . . Freshly brewed coffee,   **$3.50**
Tia Maria and Vandermint, topped with heavy whipped cream
and sprinkled with chocolate.

IRISH COFFEE . . . . Freshly brewed coffee   **$3.50**
blended with Irish whiskey and simple syrup, topped with
heavy whipped cream.

IRISH FRIAR . . . . Freshly brewed coffee   **$3.50**
blended with Bailey's Irish cream and Frangelio, topped with
heavy whipped cream and topped with clove.

MOUNT OLYMPUS . . . . Freshly brewed coffee   **$3.50**
blended with Metaxa Brandy and Kahlua, topped with heavy
whipped cream and laced with Amaretto.

KIOKI COFFEE . . . . Freshly brewed coffee   **$3.50**
blended with Brandy and Creme de Cacao and topped with
heavy whipped cream.

Figure 11.9 Dessert menu with a list of dessert drinks.

One national chain of Mexican restaurants cut its inventory down to 35 liquors and 9 mixes, plus 4 wines and 4 beers with careful market research and planning. That's about one-third of the average unlimited bar. Its four-color printed menu offers 20 mixed drinks—frozen drinks, cocktails, and slings, some new, some old. The line-up may seem unsophisticated, but it satisfies the tastes of its youngish, blue-collar clientele. All the drinks are made from the same few base liquors, liqueurs, and made-to-order bottled mixes. This makes it possible to hire persons with little or no previous bartending experience, train them thoroughly to mix each drink on the menu, and serve the customer the same drink in Denver as in Tallahassee at an attractive price.

SUMMING UP

There are many interesting and historical tidbits associated with the development of the world's most popular drinks, and these—Manhattans, Martinis, Cuba Libres, and others—are making a comeback in bars today. The younger generation enjoys the lore and drama, if you will, of bygone times and nightclubs that movies have painted as chic and glamorous.

If the drinks aren't good, though, they won't return. Behind the scenes, the systematic development of drinks and a drink menu provides you with performance standards and products of consistent quality, and makes training easier for bartenders and cocktail servers. Standardizing also facilitates accurately pricing drinks, controlling costs, and cutting losses, all of which enhance the profit picture. These factors are discussed in the upcoming chapters.

In this chapter, you learned about making (from scratch) the members of a number of drink families—Martinis, Manhattans, Sours and Collinses, plus shooters, tropical drinks, dairy and ice cream drinks, and frozen drinks.

Most bars have a common form of "shorthand," abbreviations used to write orders, and a system to "call" the drinks (place the order) at the bar. Planning a drink menu makes it much easier to order liquor, with fewer overhead costs and less storage space required. In short, not every bar has to be able to make every drink known to man. That said, a thorough knowledge of drinks opens the door to fun and invention for you, your bartenders and servers. A few unique specialty drinks to complement your food menu are excellent merchandising devices.

POINTS TO PONDER

1. Why is it important to make a Martini or Manhattan in a chilled glass?

2. Why are some drinks known as "sours"?

3. Why is the hand shaker used when there are blenders and mixers to do the job?

4. Explain the reasons for preparing a multidrink order in the sequence this chapter recommends.

5. What is the difference between a Collins and a Fizz?

6. Why is it important for a server to use standard drink notations ("bar shorthand") on guest checks?

7. From memory, write down the standard recipe for a Martini as given in this chapter.

8. What are the family characteristics of tropical drinks?

9. In your area, what is a shooter? Give two examples, including how they are made and the amount of liquor they contain.

10. Develop a sample menu of about a dozen drinks. Use vodka, tequila, rum, up to four liqueurs, fruit juices, and your choice of condiments and garnishes. Write a description of each drink designed to interest your customers.

TERMS OF THE TRADE

bar shorthand	Flip	shot
chaser	Manhattan	signature drink
Collins	Margarita	sour
cream drink	Martini	straight up
Daiquiri	Milk Punch	tropical drink
Fish Bowl	mocktail	unlimited bar
Fizz	shooter	

JOSEPH TAKATA

Beverage Director, Hilton Hawaiian Village Beach Resort & Spa

You could say that Joseph "Joe" Takata just fell into his career in the bartending and hospitality industry. Although he was an education major at the University of Hawaii, Joe found his calling through various hospitality industry jobs. Over the past 30 years, Joe has worked in a wide variety of bar businesses, including stand-alone restaurants, dance clubs, showrooms, and large resorts like the Hilton Hawaiian Village Beach Resort & Spa.

Joe is currently the Director of Beverage for one of Hilton Hotels Corporation's largest hotels in the world, the Hilton Hawaiian Village Beach Resort & Spa. The Hilton Hawaiian Village spans 22 acres and offers 2,998 rooms. Joe oversees 8 bars and manages a staff of 37 servers and 49 bartenders and barbacks.

Q: What does a beverage manager do?

A: The role and responsibilities of a beverage manager depend on the type of operation. For example, in a freestanding restaurant, the manager is in charge of the bar, and often serves as the most senior bartender. The manager is also in charge of staffing and ordering supplies. The same position in a nightclub atmosphere would include these responsibilities; in addition, the manager would coordinate advertising and promotions. In a hotel or resort setting, the manager also coordinates all of the supply orders and works with the Human Resources Department for staffing needs.

Q: What is the most difficult part of the job?

A: The most difficult challenge of being a beverage manager or working in any large organization is communication. Communication is probably the hardest lesson to learn and the most challenging skill to perfect. In any career, you work with a wide variety of personalities. It helps greatly if you have a positive attitude. You cannot get hung up on doing things a certain way, by micromanaging or by having the attitude that "I'm the boss!" You must learn to be flexible. You expect this of your employees, and so you too must be flexible and work as a team.

Q: Are your operations manuals and drink recipes standardized?

A: All our recipe and operations manuals are written down. Our measured pour is an ounce, and we also use a jigger. In the past, we also have used mechanical pouring systems. The greatest concern with mechanical systems is the required ongoing maintenance, ensuring no leaks and that the system lines are clean. Sometimes you can have a pinhole leak that will spray a fine mist of alcohol, which evaporates, and you may never even notice the leak until your bottom-line costs and inventory don't match up.

Q: What kinds of precautions do you take to prevent theft?

A: To prevent theft, we keep all liquor and wine bottles under lock and key when the bars and restaurants are closed. All ordering goes through a central purchasing office and all supplies are stored in one central, secured area. Each bar has a par stock that is issued, and we put our own sticker on each bottle that goes out of the storage area. The sticker serves as a quality check to ensure that someone is not bringing in their own bottle of wine, selling it, and pocketing the money. The sticker system helps to validate your costs at the end of the month. These simple steps help to control inventory and monitor costs, something that is essential to being a good beverage manager.

Q: When there is a problem, how is it handled?

A: If a theft occurs, there are policies in place to investigate, and the investigation would be coordinated by the manager and a representative from the Human Resources Department. Theft can be grounds for immediate termination.

Q: What is your typical day like?

A: There is usually something new each day. It's always an adventure! I usually start my day at 9:00 A.M. with a site inspection, surveying all of the outlets to make sure everything is secure, equipment is in proper working condition, and needed supplies are on hand. Prior to a bar opening, we have a 10- to 15-minute meeting before each shift. We also have a monthly food and beverage meeting to share restaurants and bars revenue status, promotions, and so on. After my site inspection, I answer voice-mails and e-mails. Since I am a beverage manager in a resort setting, our department also provides staff for banquet events. I thoroughly review the event orders and identify what assistance is needed from our department. Then I review the prior day's labor costs and revenue generated to see if we are meeting our goals. Afterward, I return to the frontline to check on the status of the bars and check how my staff is doing. Quality customer service is paramount.

Q: Do your menus and drink recipes reflect anything unusual because your clientele is so international?

A: Customers visiting our Hawaii resort expect the standard tropical drinks such as Mai Tais, Blue Hawaiis, Pina Coladas, and the like, but we also take special requests.

Q: What kind of training or previous experience do you require for new hires?

A: Required staff experience depends on the role they will be expected to fill. For example, if it's a fast-paced restaurant or bar, we need seasoned staff who can keep the pace. If the pace is slower and the requests are straightforward (like soft drinks or beer), then I will hire someone with less or no experience if they have a positive attitude and a desire to learn. In the Hawaii resort market, good bartender jobs are few and far between. I've worked in Hawaii for 25 years and I've seen people start off as a barback just to get a chance at the coveted bartender job.

Q: What are some of the most unusual situations you've had to cater to?

A: The most unusual work situation I've experienced occurred in a prior position where we were asked to close all of the fast-food outlets and bars to make everything kosher for Passover. All of the products, even the glassware, were cleaned or we purchased brand new items that were then blessed by the Rabbi.

Q: What would you suggest for hospitality students to get real work experience?

A: Students should get a wide variety of experience by working as a barback, bartender, and host or hostess. You really need to be Jack [or Jill] of all trades. Then, when you're ready to move up to a manager position, you will have a much better understanding of your staff and how you can better support them to ensure a cohesive team that will better serve your customer. You can never say "That's not my job, I'm the manager!" You have to be trained in all areas and open to rolling up your sleeves and pitching in! In any career, flexibility in skill and attitude will lead you down the path of success.

CHAPTER 12

The Staff

The people who deal with your customers represent your enterprise to the public. They sell your wares and help create the ambience that keeps customers coming back. That's the upside. The downside is that employees are also among your highest costs and cause most of your headaches. High turnover, poor performance, and unreliability are frequent complaints among employers.

Let's face it, this is an industry fraught with "people problems." Most of the employees are hourly; their shifts are irregular; pay is variable; there are few opportunities for advancement and many temptations along the way. Fortunately, there are effective ways to approach these concerns, to train and nurture and reward loyal people. This chapter suggests points where such attention pays off.

This chapter should help you . . .

- Identify jobs that must be filled and write job descriptions for them.
- Recruit, interview, and select appropriate employees.
- Develop effective training programs.
- Schedule personnel to meet daily needs.
- Supervise employees effectively, and to avoid legal pitfalls.
- Meet federal and state compensation and record-keeping requirements.
- Figure wage and overtime amounts for various methods of payment.
- Understand the laws about tips and tip reporting.
- Decide which employee benefits to offer.

Never underestimate the importance of your employees. You can't be everywhere, and it's often up to them to make customers feel welcome and important. They can help guests relax and celebrate, or prompt them to vow never to set foot in this place again! They can please customers with their friendly style and efficiency, or turn them off with inattention, carelessness, bad manners, or dishonesty.

Employees affect your profits in many other ways. They are important links in any cost-control system. They are your best merchandising agents. To your customers, they represent you and your philosophy.

So how do you go about finding the right people and putting them all together to function in a smooth operation? The kinds of employees you'll need depend a lot on your type of operation. First, we'll look at the whole spectrum of positions, and then consider how to figure your own staffing needs.

STAFF POSITIONS

The staff needs of bars are unique to each establishment, and there is probably no bar that has all the positions we describe. At one extreme is the small owner-operated bar in which the owner is manager, bartender, and everything else. At the other end of the spectrum is the beverage service of a large hotel or restaurant chain. The organization charts in Figure 12.1 show typical positions and their relationships in two types of beverage operation.

The duties and responsibilities of the job described may vary greatly. In a small operation, a single individual may handle the functions of three or four jobs, while only very large operations need a full-time beverage manager. Even the job of bartender or cocktail waitress varies from one bar to another.

The Bartender

The central figure in any beverage operation is the **bartender,** an amalgam of salesperson, entertainer, mixologist, and psychologist (Figure 12.2). Of course, the bartender's primary function is to mix and serve drinks for patrons at the bar and/or to pour drinks for table customers served by waiters or waitresses. Some say that is the easy part of the job. Less obvious, but not less important, are the roles of custodian and caretaker. These responsibilities include recording each drink sale, washing glassware and utensils, maintaining a clean and orderly bar, stocking the bar before opening, and closing the bar. In many operations, the bartender also acts as cashier. The bartender is typically a host and a promoter whose combination of skill and style translates into public relations benefits that build goodwill and good business.

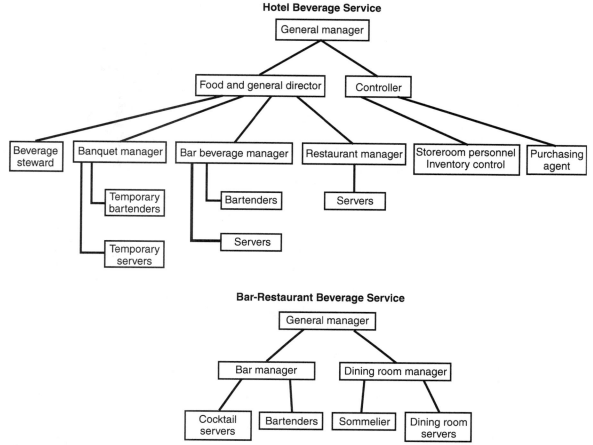

Figure 12.1 Organization charts for two different types of beverage service.

Bartending is as wide-ranging a job as you can get in the food service business, and it's never as simple—or as glamorous—as it seems. The bartender is the person who notices when things are getting crowded and crazy, and uses eye contact and a smile to buy time when newcomers or singles approach the bar; the person whose wit, wisdom, and approachability make him or her the center of conversation and the purveyor of advice as well as drink concoctions; the person who can hold court behind a sleek bar at the ritziest private party or unclog the men's room toilet in a pinch.

Bartending requires certain skills and aptitudes—not the least of which are patience, adaptability, and a good attitude. The bartender must know the recipes for whatever drinks the house serves (from dozens to hundreds, depending on the bar) and the techniques for mixing them, and be able to work quickly and accurately. To this end, the job requires dexterity and a

ANATOMY OF A BARTENDER

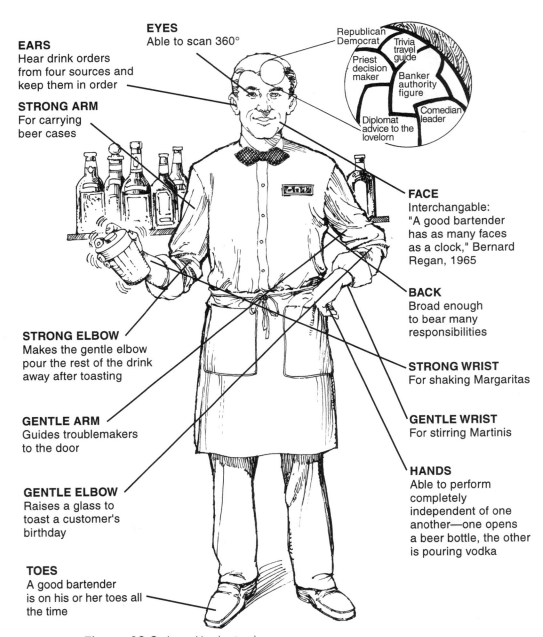

EYES
Able to scan 360°

Republican
Democrat
Trivia travel guide
Priest decision maker
Banker authority figure
Diplomat advice to the lovelorn
Comedian leader

EARS
Hear drink orders from four sources and keep them in order

STRONG ARM
For carrying beer cases

FACE
Interchangable:
"A good bartender has as many faces as a clock," Bernard Regan, 1965

BACK
Broad enough to bear many responsibilities

STRONG ELBOW
Makes the gentle elbow pour the rest of the drink away after toasting

STRONG WRIST
For shaking Margaritas

GENTLE ARM
Guides troublemakers to the door

GENTLE WRIST
For stirring Martinis

HANDS
Able to perform completely independent of one another—one opens a beer bottle, the other is pouring vodka

GENTLE ELBOW
Raises a glass to toast a customer's birthday

TOES
A good bartender is on his or her toes all the time

Figure 12.2 A working bartender.

good short-term memory. In a high-volume bar (often referred to as a *speed bar*), the ability to work quickly and under pressure is essential. A pleasing appearance and a pleasant personality are essential in any bar, though less so in a service bar out of customer sight. Honesty is the most important quality of all and—many bar owners insist—the hardest to find.

When you're looking for candidates for a bartender job, consider these points:

- **Gender makes no difference.** A good bartender is a good bartender, male or female. A good bartender can handle any situation in any bar at any time. For a long time, the bar was a man's world, but no longer. In fact, some club owners feel that women bring a different temperament to bartending—that they have the ability to diffuse tense situations without becoming aggressive—and find them more willing to learn, practice, take notes, and ask questions.
- **The bartender is a good host.** The ideal person can get along with all the other groups of employees—front of the house (servers, hostesses, etc.), the kitchen staff, management, and every guest who walks through the door. He or she can make people feel welcome; serve as an ice-breaker to introduce a new staff member or customers to others; apologize for slow service or a mishap; and generally keep "the party" running smoothly.
- **The bartender is a diplomat.** Since this person is observant, a good bartender knows when to talk or joke around and when to be silent; knows when to gently but firmly refuse to serve more to someone who has had too much to drink; and knows the difference between someone who's being a nuisance and someone who's just trying to be friendly. The bartender's attitude in these situations is a major component of the bar's tone and atmosphere.
- **The bartender is an authority figure.** The man or woman behind the bar should be able to take control of the entire business, prioritize when things get busy, or step in to solve problems, at the drop of a hat. When the manager is gone, it is typically the bartender who is next in command. A smart manager respects the bartender's judgment, allowing him or her to make those decisions that directly impact the bar operation. Leadership and the ability to make on-the-spot decisions are key attributes.
- **The bartender is a role model.** As a representative of the bar or restaurant, the bartender's style and personality should reflect the type of business it is. But the rest of the staff should also be able to look up to the person who runs the bar. Ethics and honesty start at the top, and this is one of your most important positions to fill. Since bartenders handle so much cash, there is a built-in temptation to steal. You want an employee who wouldn't even consider it, and will model that behavior to others.
- **The bartender knows how to mix a drink.** Ironically, this is not at the top of the priority list when most owners are asked what their prerequi-

sites are for hiring a bartender. Some prefer to hire fairly inexperienced people and train them to do things "their way." Others hire only those individuals who have had formal training at a bartending school. Still others promote from within their ranks—that's the norm in most national chains. But as master bartender Dale DeGroff (profiled on page 22) puts it, "A bartender must know at least as much as the customers about the products he [or she] serves. And there are some very sophisticated customers out there."

Warning Signs. Now that we've discussed what good bartenders should do and be, let's focus for a moment on what they should *not* do. In the February 1998 issue of *Restaurant Hospitality Magazine*, author Robert Plotkin listed some undesirable traits of bartenders. We paraphrase them here:

- **They maintain a "me first" perspective.** They're not willing to help others accomplish an objective that doesn't happen to be part of their direct responsibility.
- **They disregard specified serving portions.** They have the misconception that pouring "stiff" drinks (containing more alcohol than necessary) results in bigger tips. This practice is also disastrous for your bottom line.
- **They serve inferior products.** The overall quality of your ingredients—from liquors and mixers to garnishes—is critically important. A good bartender won't take shortcuts and won't settle for poor-quality merchandise to save a buck.
- **They lack short-term memory.** It's important to remember people's names, and even more important to remember what they're drinking when they want a refill in the same evening.
- **Their priorities are scattered.** It's great to be friendly, but if your glasses are going unwashed and your drink orders pile up while you're conversing with a regular customer, you're neglecting your bartending duties.
- **They give preferential treatment.** Of course you appreciate your "regulars," and develop relationships with them. But a good bartender can do this without treating other guests like second-class citizens. And no customer should get free drinks or stiffer or heavier drinks than others just because he or she is a regular.
- **They are unimaginative order-takers.** Complacency kills the natural liveliness of a bar. Good bartenders make things happen by doing a little marketing at the point-of-sale; talking up the nightly special; suggesting something to a customer who's unsure what to order.
- **They let their professional demeanor slip.** Bartenders must maintain their composure and control their emotions, no matter how intense or busy the atmosphere around them. Their anger and frustration should never be aimed at either the guests or fellow staff members.

Sidebar 12.1

ALL I REALLY NEED TO KNOW I LEARNED BARTENDING

Everything I really need to know about how to exist in this world, personal or business, I learned Bartending. This knowledge was shared with me by owners, managers, salesmen, waitresses, waiters, bartenders and customers. Most of these teachers were successful in life's everyday challenges. These tips you cannot spend, they are the tips you keep for life:

Give everyone a fair shot.
If you haven't anything nice to say, don't say it.
Use the BEST premium products and you'll be the BEST.
Serve.
Be the solution to the problem, not part of the problem.
Don't drink and drive; don't let others.
Respect salesmen, you're one.
Don't take sides. You'll make two enemies.
Be NEAT.
Wear a clean shirt every day.
Don't cheat or steal.
Smile!
Keep your hands and fingernails clean.
Use Mr., Sir, or Ms. when talking to strangers.
Don't be a part of a rumor.
Keep your space clean.
Don't waste.
Be on time.
Help others when they're busy.
Don't use the easy way. Use the right way.
Don't give up. Follow your dream.

Courtesy of *Bartender Magazine.*

The Barback

In a small operation, one bartender may perform all the tasks just listed. In larger operations, there may be several bartenders and one or more helpers, known as **barbacks.** These are often bartenders-in-training, whose job is to assist the bartender. In larger operations, the situation calls for a *head bartender* who has overall responsibility for the bar function and acts as supervisor for the other bar personnel. The head bartender may also participate in hiring and training new bar employees and in teaching cocktail servers how to describe drinks to customers, how to transmit orders, how to garnish drinks, and how to use the special vocabulary of the bar.

A barback typically relieves the bartender of all chores except pouring the drinks and handling the customers and the cash register. Among the barback's duties are setting up the bar; preparing garnishes and special mixes and syrups; filling ice bins; washing glassware and utensils; maintaining supplies of towels, napkins, picks, straws, stir sticks, matches; keeping bar surfaces and ashtrays clean; washing fixtures; and mopping floors. The barback is also a runner or "gofer," going for liquors, beers, wines, and other supplies as needed by the bartender. Often a barback is an apprentice bartender and may serve beer or mix simple drinks under the bartender's supervision.

The Servers

Beverage service at tables, whether in a cocktail lounge or in a dining room, is handled by waiters or waitresses, a group we refer to collectively as *servers*. Servers record the customers' drink orders, transmit them to the bartender, pick up the drinks, serve the customers, present the tab, and collect payment. They also keep the serving areas clean and return empty glasses to the bar. In heavy-volume bar lounges, servers may also help prepare drinks by putting ice in glasses and adding garnishes. Sometimes they use the cash register systems to ring up their own tabs; in other places, the bartender does this. Like the bartender, the server is also a host and a promoter.

A few basics requirements for table servers include a pleasant personality, a neat and attractive appearance, poise, and a mind for detail. Serving personnel must be able to deal with both customers and bartenders pleasantly and efficiently. Being alert and observant is also key, whether it is deciding whether a customer has had too much to drink or spying a chipped or soiled glass before it gets to the table. But make no mistake, this is a sales job, one that is not appropriate for the insecure or uncommunicative person.

Bar and restaurant owners worldwide debate ideas for how to maximize the server's ability to sell the customer any type of drink, from a single dry Martini to a fine bottle of Bordeaux. Two critical points here:

- The server must actually *offer* cocktails, wine, or beer to every table. As elementary as it sounds, failure to ask for the sale is the principal reason a sale is not made. (And remember, there are numerous opportunities during every guest's visit when a selling suggestion is appropriate. A good training program should help servers learn these important cues.)
- The server must make it known to the customers that they are happy to *assist* them in selecting a beverage. Again, training gives your servers these skills, which builds their confidence and improves your business.

At the very least, good bar service requires basic knowledge of a broad array of drinks and some variations, so the server can pin down the customers' exact preferences: Does he want his Martini with an olive or a lemon twist? Will her sour be straight up or on the rocks? The best cocktail server's drink knowledge is almost as extensive as a bartender's. They may even mix drinks to allow the bartender to take a break.

In many restaurants, waiters and waitresses serve both food and drinks, including wine by the bottle, with the meal. Servers must be able to open a wine bottle properly, carry out the rituals of wine service, and answer questions about wines, specialty drinks, and recipes.

Like bartenders, most servers are actively involved in whatever control system management uses to keep track of beverages. Whether you call them orders, checks, or drink tabs, they literally "keep tabs" on what has been ordered, and allow the payments to be recorded on the cash register. Quick, accurate, and honest carrying out of check routines is an essential part of the server's job.

The Wine Steward or Sommelier

Finer restaurants that feature elegant service may have a special employee who handles the ordering and serving of wine. The **wine steward** (also called **cellarmaster,** *winemaster* or *wine waiter,* all terms applying to both sexes), presents the wine list at the table, makes recommendations, discusses wines with customers, and takes care of serving the wines. On busy evenings, this is a huge help to the rest of the wait staff.

The image of the stuffy, tuxedo-clad wine steward is changing, replaced by smartly dressed men and women whose goal is to make the wine buying and tasting experience approachable and pleasurable, not intimidating. A new generation of young, college-educated wine lovers has breathed new life into this profession in recent years. Some have spent time working in vineyards or for wine importers or distributors. Others have learned as apprentices or as serious hobbyists who decided to impart their love of the history and complexity of wine to others. They enjoy discovering wines from unexpected places, searching for new favorites from "undiscovered" vineyards, and seeking out good values to pass on to guests.

Those who are true connoisseurs of wines and wine service merit the title **sommelier** (SUM-el-yay or SOHM-ee-yay). This is the French word for "wine steward," but it has come to be associated with excellence in this field. Sommeliers are usually found in upscale restaurants featuring expensive wines, extensive wine lists, and cellars containing thousands of bottles. This is not an endeavor to be taken lightly, but a full-time profession that requires ongoing education and a passion for the wine industry. It is attracting a growing number of people. The Sommelier Society of America doubled its membership in the last five years before 2000. Career sommeliers can study for the prestigious Master Sommelier Diploma, awarded by the Guild of Sommeliers of London, England. Including both salary and tips, sought-after wine experts can make from $50,000 to $100,000 a year.

The traditional symbols associated with the sommelier are a tasting cup called a **tastevin** (TAT-van or TASS-tah-van) that hangs from their neck on a cord or ribbon, a cellar key, and, sometimes, a leather apron. Sometimes a more modest enterprise may use these trappings and bestow the title of "sommelier," "cellarmaster" or even "wine director" on its most wine-knowledgeable employee to help create an upscale image. Although not everyone with these titles has an expert's level of wine knowledge, they must at least be thoroughly familiar with their own wine lists and competent in helping guests to select wines appropriate to the food they order.

When selecting a person for this position, remember that you are looking for someone who can do more than pamper guests during a dining experience. A well-qualified wine steward can help you:

- Create a wine list that fits your atmosphere and menu.
- Deal with suppliers and importers and do the wine ordering.
- Negotiate "exclusive" deals to carry certain wines that no one else in your market has.
- Control and keep inventory of the cellar or wine storage area.
- Make purchasing decisions to maximize profits (in some cases, this includes buying wines to store for future years' lists).
- Train your servers and other staff members about wine appreciation.
- Orchestrate and help publicize tastings, wine dinners, seminars, and other wine-related events for your business.

So you see, there's a lot more than wine appreciation involved in wine service, and you must expect a lot from anyone you select to specifically order and sell your wines. An interesting new position that has emerged in the "beverage expert" category is the *beer sommelier,* for pubs or restaurants that specialize in exotic brews. The Four Points Sheraton Hotel in Los Angeles, for instance, pours 50 beers from at least 10 countries in its fine dining restaurant, called the Palm Grill. Beer sommelier Carlos Solis supervises tableside beer service, arranges beer seminars, tastings, and dinners. The menu includes beer recommendations for foods. If you can't decide on a single brew, you can order six of them, a three-ounce taste of each, for $9. Little wonder that half of the dining room's beverage profit now comes from beer sales. Customers enjoy the knowledgeable service and the attention to detail.

Security Positions

Certain types of bars and nightspots that have no need for sommeliers may instead have a need for crowd control. This may come in the form of a doorman or door person. This person is expected to keep order if there are long lines to get in; to ask for customers' identification (and firmly but politely enforce a dress code or refuse to admit underage people); or to collect a **cover charge** at the front door. The cover charge is a fee for admittance to the bar, sometimes given to, or split with, the band if there's live music.

Door people may perform small but significant acts of courtesy: they open doors for customers, walk unescorted female patrons to their vehicles, call for taxis, keep the lobby area looking tidy. They may also be required to keep an overall headcount of incoming patrons, or to fill out incident reports when customers get angry when they're turned away at the front door.

Security may also include hiring one or more **bouncers,** generally fit (or somewhat tough-looking) men whose job it is to protect both bar patrons and employees from unruly behavior. Although the very word "bouncer" comes from ancient words that mean "to thump or strike," you want your bouncers to provide a sense of safety and order, not throw their weight around like all-star wrestlers. Legally, a bouncer has no more authority than a private citizen so, as your employee, you must make the rules for this person very clear. Exactly what are they supposed to do with disruptive customers? Do they ask them to quiet down or to leave the bar? At what point can they physically eject them from the bar? How do you handle patrons who start a fight? At what point should police be called?

The bouncer should be impartial and professional, with the same "people skills" and ethics as any of your other staff members, and your hiring process should include a background check of these job candidates. Some bar owners have noticed that dressing their bouncers well—not in jeans and T-shirts—adds credibility to their image. Drinking on duty is strictly forbidden in this, and most other, bar jobs.

The bouncer is on the lookout for disruptive conduct, but he should never use unnecessary or excessive force to eject a patron. You might ask the local police department to come in and talk with your security staff, to share advice about how to diffuse tense situations and when to call police.

Beverage Management Positions

High-volume establishments, large hotels, private clubs, and restaurants with extensive wine cellars may have a person in charge of all wine and liquor purchasing, storage, receiving, requisitioning, and inventory control. This person must know a great deal about wines and spirits, the wine and spirits market, and the entire beverage operation. It is a position of considerable responsibility, and the official job title is typically **beverage steward.**

In very large operations, the beverage steward may work for the *beverage manager* or *beverage director.* This is often a senior management position, part of the team that runs a corporate operation—a hotel, large nightclub, high-volume restaurant, or an entire hotel or restaurant chain. The beverage director is in charge of hiring, training, and supervising all beverage-related personnel; purchasing all beverages and beverage equipment; establishing and maintaining inventory and control systems; setting standards and making policy on matters relating to beverage operation.

The more sophisticated the corporation, the greater mark a good beverage director can leave on it. At the 3,000-room Hotel Bellagio in Las Vegas, Nevada, Tony Abu Gamin is considered one of the best. At the time of this writing, he supervises 22 bars, with 170 bartenders, and 60 apprentices. Abu Gamin has virtually declared war on the bar gun (or cobra gun), insisting instead that freshly squeezed juices be used in all drinks. He is passionate about using only fresh, hand-cut garnishes and chilled glassware. Order an in-room cocktail when you stay at the Bellagio, and it will be shaken right there in the room—not at a bar elsewhere and then delivered 10 or 20 minutes later. These may seem like small items, but this kind of attention to detail may be the reason that, in its first year of business, the Bellagio did a record $50 million in bar sales!

A beverage director is either part of, or reports to, top management. In some large organizations, responsibility for food and beverage service is combined into one position, called the *food and beverage director.*

Such positions require several years of industry experience, preferably first-hand experience in each area of responsibility. A beverage director must also have management training and/or experience. It's a very public position, so he or she must have the appearance, personality, poise, and wardrobe that are generally associated with management positions. This will ensure credibility in their dealings with other management personnel, within or outside the company.

Even in a big hotel with multiple food and beverage outlets, each individual bar or restaurant usually has a *manager* who is in charge of all aspects of its operation. In a small business, the owner is often the manager. If not, the manager is a surrogate, or stand-in, for the owner, running the show on the owner's behalf, whether the owner is an individual or a corporation. The owner sets the goals, establishes policies, and gives the manager the authority and responsibility for carrying them out. Within this framework, the manager must make any and all decisions necessary to running a profitable operation.

It takes a lot of savvy to run a bar, and not everyone can do it well. From the January 2000 issue of *Restaurant Hospitality* magazine, here's a list of qualities you'll find in the best bar managers:

- **Business training.** Well-grounded in working knowledge of how business operates, their role in the business, and how each aspect of the business works together cohesively.
- **Market knowledge.** No business operates in a vacuum. A good manager knows his or her market well, what the competition is doing, and how to respond to competitive activity.

- **Desire to lead.** An effective manager is a leader. He or she easily grasps what has to be done, sees how it can be done, believes it can be done, and can energize the staff to get it done.
- **Maturity and stability.** It can be stressful working in a service industry with a young, socially active staff, a variety of guests, and a fiercely competitive business environment. The best manager can gracefully withstand the countless distractions and temptations.
- **Financial wisdom.** The best managers spend the business' money as it if were their own, with prudence and an eye for value.
- **Street smarts.** If a manager exerts too much control, the customers or staff members won't stick around. If a manager exerts too little, the place runs out of control. A good manager knows how to walk the fine line between the two.
- **Legal knowledge.** Running a bar involves some familiarity with liquor laws, health and safety codes, fire regulations, fair employment practices, and more. And that's just to stay in compliance! A good manager makes these topics into a continuing self-education program.

A manager's overall responsibilities may include hiring and firing; training, scheduling, and supervising personnel; forecasting and budgeting; purchasing beverages and related supplies or requisitioning them from a corporate commissary; maintaining records; carrying out control systems (the manager typically has the only key to the storeroom); handling cash and payroll; maintaining quality; promoting the enterprise and the merchandise. All this must be done in a way that meets or exceeds the owner's profit goals. (We'll discuss many of these activities in greater detail in later chapters.)

Day to day, a good manager keeps everything running smoothly. This means settling staff problems, dealing with difficult customers, coping with emergencies, and often pitching in to do someone else's job. Interestingly, at this time, there is a lawsuit pending by managers of a large, casual dining chain. The suit claims that the restaurants are chronically understaffed, requiring the managers to do many hourly labor duties, like cleaning and washing dishes; thus they're working far longer hours than their salaries compensate them for. But that should give you a sense of the wide range of duties managers find themselves tackling. Their typical day is crowded with major and minor decisions, because every day is different and things are always happening that have never happened before.

A manager should be well trained in every aspect of the enterprise and experienced enough at all jobs to substitute in any one of them, and be able to relate to the people who do these jobs daily. He or she must be the kind of person who can make decisions easily and deal effectively with all kinds of people, both patrons and staff. Essential personal qualities are a good memory, a cool head, a positive attitude, sensitivity to people, leadership ability, self-confidence, and honesty.

It shouldn't surprise you that a 1997 National Restaurant Association study pinpointed some interesting differences in what motivates managers versus what motivates other lower-level employees on the job. The results look like this:

Ten Top Motivators

Manager	Employee
1. Salary	**1.** Interesting work
2. Bonuses	**2.** Involvement in decisions
3. Vacation	**3.** Feedback
4. Retirement benefits	**4.** Training
5. Other benefits or "perks"	**5.** Respect
6. Interesting work	**6.** Salary
7. Involvement in decisions	**7.** Bonuses
8. Feedback	**8.** Vacation
9. Training	**9.** Retirement benefits
10. Respect	**10.** Other benefits or "perks"

Isn't it interesting that the managers chose money-related items as their top five motivators, while issues of communication and feeling valued ranked highest with other employees? It says a lot about how to entice both groups to do their best possible jobs.

DETERMINING STAFF NEEDS

The type and size of the enterprise and the projected volume of business will immediately put certain limits on the kinds of jobs you need to fill. Nearly every enterprise has bartenders; a bar lounge also requires cocktail servers. You may or may not need security personnel or a sommelier. The numbers of bartenders, serving personnel, and people in charge depend on the projected volume of business and the days and hours of operation.

Every business needs a manager. Will you do it yourself or hire someone to do it for you? In a chain of hotels or restaurants, there will be a clear chain of command: a food and beverage director at the top, with unit managers in each individual facility. In a restaurant, it is often one person who manages both the food and the beverage side of the operation.

Many employers "guesstimate" staff needs, run an all-purpose ad in the daily newspaper, rely on intuition, and hire the first warm bodies who seem to have a promising personality and a bit of job experience. Sometimes this approach works. More often it results in friction, high turnover, and an operation that is not successful in converting first-time visitors to loyal customers.

Careful planning and hiring can reduce the occurrence of these problems. The goal of planning is to put the right worker into the right job at the right time. The more detailed your plans before you hire your first employee, the more effective (and less costly) your hiring process.

The first step in planning is to define each job in your enterprise—literally, write them down, as a job description. This will determine the qualifications a person needs in order to do that job. You must also decide whether each job is a full-time or part-time job. How many people will you need, and exactly when will you need them? Only then are you ready to begin hiring.

Developing Job Descriptions

You've already learned a bit about what is expected of each major bar-related job. You can adapt those job descriptions in the previous section to the needs of your enterprise, by adding more detail. For example, will your bartenders be working a service bar or public bar? Free pour, measured pour, or metered gun? How many drinks per hour minimum? What kind of person will maintain your image? This kind of information belongs in the *job description,* a written "blueprint" of what is required in each job.

To create job descriptions, you might take a hint from large organizations and perform a **job analysis.** There are a couple of steps to it. First, the **task analysis** lists each small task performed as part of a particular job: its purpose, how it is done, what equipment and skills are required to do it. Then, the **job specifications** are written. This is another list, of the knowledge, skills, or abilities a person must have to perform the tasks. Together, these lists are combined in writing—yes, it's important that they be written—to make up the job description.

The same technique can profitably be used in any size operation. A side benefit: examining each job in such detail often reveals things you hadn't thought of before. Is it too much work for one person, or not enough work to fill a shift? Are there ways to combine or divide jobs; are there gaps in coverage; do responsibilities overlap? Should you hire skilled people or train them on the job?

The next step is to list the qualifications for each job. Think about:

- Skills and aptitudes
- Physical characteristics
- Health requirements
- Mental ability and attitude
- Age requirements

The latter is because state laws prohibit underage persons from handling liquor, even if they do not drink or sell it.

The final step is to combine the data from your job analysis with your list of personal requirements to write a concise job description. You'll see examples as Figures 12.3 and 12.4. In addition to duties, tasks, and qualifica-

Bartender Job Description

Description:

Bartenders work behind the bars and in back-of-the-house areas. They prepare and sell drinks to Cocktail Hostesses and customers. They prep their work area with several functions, measure and prepare drinks according to recipe, and make cash register transactions.

Bartenders must handle credit card tabs, note spills and overrings, and address the cash register immediately after preparing an order. They accept tips, but do not allow tips to remain on the bar or do not exchange tips or change with cash register monies prior to the end of their shift. Bartenders perform cleanup and register checkout functions at the end of their shift. They also stock products and supplies.

They perform "silent selling" and "upselling" techniques and inform customers of club activities and promotions. They serve customers by using "experience time" goals and create an upbeat, friendly environment in their work area. They must function as a team member with Barbacks, other Bartenders, and Cocktail Hostesses. They must learn and use alcohol management techniques and advise the management staff of intoxicated or unruly customers.

Due to the high level of customer interaction, the Bartender must perform all duties with great emphasis on cleanliness, personability, professionalism, and service. Bartenders are strongly encouraged to work up individual "Showtimes"—complete with costumes—to be performed throughout the evening with the Programmer.

Functions:

Prepare cocktails per recipe and serve per specifications.
Prep, clean, and stock work area—before, during, and after shift.
Accept credit cards, cash, and coupons for products.
Perform cash register functions, and checkout accurately.
Perform "silent selling" and "upselling" functions.
Monitor customers for intoxication, rowdiness, or need for drinks.
Have "Showtime" mentality.

Supervisors:

Bar Manager.
Management Staff.

Figure 12.3 Bartender job description developed after analyzing individual tasks.

Barback Job Description

Description:

Barbacks work behind the bar areas and in back-of-the-house areas. Barbacks support the work of Bartenders by performing tasks of fruit cutting, juice making, filling of ice bins, removal of trash, and preparation of "specialty" cocktails. They have several opening and closing duties involving product stocking and cleanliness, and assist in keeping their work area clean through operating hours.

Barbacks do not accept tips or money from customers and do not handle transactions or register functions. They assist in the preparation of the Liquor Requisition form and advise the Bar Manager of needed supplies and products.

Barbacks only prepare frozen cocktails. They wash glassware and utensils, and supply the Bartenders with needed liquor, beer, and supplies. Because of the extensive customer contact, Barbacks must work with courtesy, energy, and speed. Barbacks are strongly encouraged to work up individual "Showtime" routines—complete with costumes—to be performed throughout the evening with the Programmer.

Functions:

Set-up the bars for operation.
Clean and mop the bars during operation and at the end of operation.
Stock glassware and product.
Change out condiments and juices for the Bartenders.
Prepare club "specialty" cocktails.
Monitor customers for intoxication, rowdiness, or need for drinks.
Have "Showtime" mentality.

Supervisors:

Bar Manager.
Management Staff.
(Directed by Bartenders during operating hours.)

Uniform:

Black work shoes or coaching shoes, black pants, white button-down oxford shirt (long sleeve), blue apron, blue bowtie, name tag, three club buttons, one button of choice, pen, lighter, and a smile.

Grooming:

"All-American scrubbed-up" look for hair. Clean and neat hair, nails, and skin. For men, no beards or earrings.

Figure 12.4 Barback job description developed after analyzing individual tasks.

tions, it should include (1) the scope of the job, (2) workstation or area, (3) title of supervisor, and (4) positions supervised, if any.

The job description gives you a solid outline of points to cover during your employment interviews. It also informs the applicant of all aspects of the job so that he or she understands it fully before agreeing to take it. Used consistently, it will ensure that all your employees have the same idea of what you expect from them.

Planning a Staff Schedule

It is impossible to staff a beverage operation without planning a detailed schedule. This means matching the days and hours of business and the peaks and valleys of customer demand with work shifts that make sense to employees and to your budget. A chart for each day of the week you are open (Figure 12.5), showing each hour of the day you must staff, is an indispensable planning tool. On it, you can plot the highs and lows of customer demand along with personnel needed to handle the volume at each hour of the day.

Many would-be employees are looking for a full-time job with full shifts. Regular part-time jobs (fewer full shifts or several shorter shifts) are attractive to students, moonlighters, and others who do not depend entirely on your wages for their living, and they can help you deal with peak demand periods.

Eight-hour shifts should include scheduled breaks for meals and short rest periods. Breaks should be scheduled during periods of low volume if possible; if not, your schedule must include someone who can take over the job during the break. An experienced server, for example, can tend bar for 15 minutes; or breaks can be staggered where there are several bartenders.

Personnel on full shifts may have periods of time when there is little to do. You may be able to schedule tasks from other jobs during such periods, such as purchasing or restocking, training new employees, developing promotional materials, answering the phone. (If yours is a state in which employees are unionized, check with the union shop steward or the local union office to see if this is allowed.) Another way to handle peak volume without idle time at both ends is to stagger shifts.

A manager's work hours must be scheduled like everyone else's. The day is past when managers will work 80 hours a week, unless they are owners too. Someone must be in charge in the manager's absence—an assistant manager or head bartender, for example—and the detail of such duties and extent of responsibilities must be carefully worked out on a job description.

In figuring the number of bar employees needed, you may find the following approximate figures useful:

- A good cocktail server can handle 40 customers or 10 tables of 4.
- A good restaurant server can handle beverage orders for four or five lunch or dinner tables, along with food service.
- A bartender can pour 60 to 150 drinks an hour depending on dexterity, experience, types of drinks, method of pour, and efficiency of bar design.

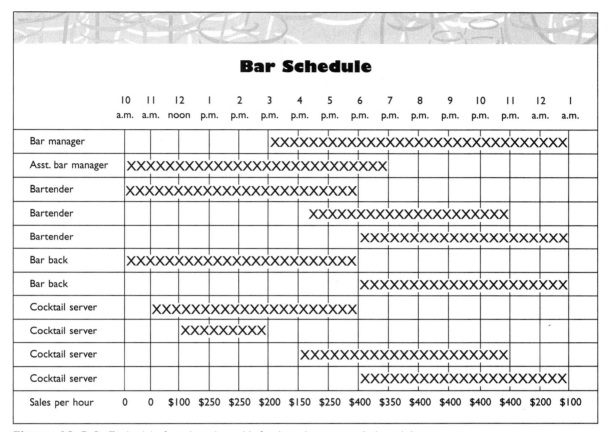

Bar Schedule

	10 a.m.	11 a.m.	12 noon	1 p.m.	2 p.m.	3 p.m.	4 p.m.	5 p.m.	6 p.m.	7 p.m.	8 p.m.	9 p.m.	10 p.m.	11 p.m.	12 a.m.	1 a.m.
Bar manager						XXX	XXX	XXX	XXX	XXX	XXX	XXX	XXX	XXX	XXX	
Asst. bar manager	XXX	XXX	XXX	XXX	XXX	XXX	XXX	XXX	XXX							
Bartender	XXX	XXX	XXX	XXX	XXX	XXX	XXX									
Bartender							XXX	XXX	XXX	XXX	XXX	XXX	XXX			
Bartender									XXX	XXX	XXX	XXX	XXX	XXX	XXX	
Bar back	XXX	XXX	XXX	XXX	XXX	XXX	XXX									
Bar back									XXX	XXX	XXX	XXX	XXX	XXX	XXX	
Cocktail server			XXX	XXX	XXX	XXX	XXX	XXX								
Cocktail server				XXX	XXX											
Cocktail server							XXX	XXX	XXX	XXX	XXX	XXX				
Cocktail server									XXX	XXX	XXX	XXX	XXX	XXX	XXX	
Sales per hour	0	0	$100	$250	$250	$200	$150	$250	$400	$350	$400	$400	$400	$400	$200	$100

Figure 12.5 Staff schedule for a busy bar with food service on a typical weekday.

Job descriptions and a tentative schedule form a sound, well-organized basis for recruiting and selecting the right people for the right jobs. For a small operation, it may seem like a lot of paperwork, expensive in time and effort. But whether or not it is formalized in writing, the same careful planning and analysis should take place. In hiring for a large enterprise, the written process is essential.

FINDING THE RIGHT PEOPLE

Where in the world do you find people who want to spend hour after hour on their feet, working under pressure to satisfy a demanding and unpredictable public? And if you find them, will they have the necessary pleasant personalities and service skills and will they be honest, and dependable—that is, will they meet the requirements you so carefully spelled out in your job descriptions?

To hear some bar and restaurant owners talk, you would think it is impossible to find good people to work in their establishments. They would have you believe that the only people available are drifters without career goals, or those doing part-time work while they're going to college, or those trying to "make it" as something else—and that they'll leave for "better" jobs as soon as you get them trained.

Though it is true that the bar and restaurant industry attracts people in these life situations, it is equally true that there are many honest and personable individuals who find bar and restaurant work attractive. The hours fit their schedules and other commitments; they like people, and they like ending the day with a pocketful of tip money; or they're learning every facet of the business so they can someday open their own bar.

The 1997 National Restaurant Association survey mentioned earlier also pinpointed four major "career types" in foodservice and related hospitality fields. They are:

- **Careerists.** People who like the business and want to remain in it. The survey reports that only 18 percent of current foodservice workers are in this category, although they make the best prospective employees.
- **Undecideds.** People who avoid career issues by having a series of jobs, rather than a career.
- **Pass-throughs.** People who have goals in occupations other than foodservice, but are here for the moment.
- **The misplaced.** People who are ill-suited for their foodservice jobs but, ironically, plan to remain in them. A full 25 percent of current foodservice workers are in this category.

The same survey reports that the retail and health-care fields are our chief competitors for employees, so you might want to look at the pay and benefits those industries offer workers in your market.

For some people, the positive aspects of the jobs you offer will outweigh the hard work, pressures, and difficult customers. They truly enjoy the exhilaration of working under pressure, the challenge of pleasing customers, and the camaraderie of bar or restaurant work that make it fun. The hours of work are attractive to many, including students, people seeking a second job, husbands or wives who take turns working in order to care for families, people who want only part-time work. On-the-job training may be attractive for persons looking for their first job. Money is certainly a drawing card, especially if tips are involved.

Recruiting Applicants

How do you reach these people? And can you reach them selectively so that you won't be overwhelmed with unsuitable applicants? There are several likely sources. Here are just a few:

- Many experienced managers say friends of present employees are among the best sources. If you and your present employees are happy with each other, they are likely to bring in others like themselves, and they are not going to risk your displeasure by suggesting someone unsuitable. They may want to bring relatives, too, although hiring members of the same family has definite drawbacks. If there is friction or disagreement, it is multiplied. If you lose one, you lose the others as well, and have more positions to refill. In many places, it is a stated policy not to hire members of the same family.
- State employment agencies often have a reservoir of potential applicants, since anyone applying for unemployment insurance must register there. If their employment counselors are familiar with your needs, they can often do a good job of screening applicants for suitability and sending them on to you, and there is no fee.
- Private employment agencies may supply prescreened managerial candidates. These agencies charge a fee, and for high-level personnel it is usually the employer who pays it. The right person is probably worth it. You won't find service-level personnel listed with such agencies because for service jobs, the fee is charged to the applicant.
- Schools offering hospitality and related courses may be a source of students who are interested in the field and have some training and experience. Some schools have apprenticeship or internship programs that might dovetail nicely with your needs.
- Bartender schools often look for placements for their graduates.
- Unions can usually furnish applicants for bartender and server positions if you meet union requirements.
- Placement offices in nearby colleges may be a source of suitable part-time help.

As you go about your business, look at other service industries and you'll surely notice the kinds of people you'd like to have working for you. Talk with them about it. You may find that the friendly lady at the dry cleaners or the polite young man bagging your groceries might be interested in your kinds of jobs, especially if the pay is better.

Keep in touch with former employees who left on good terms. After a year or so, their circumstances may have changed, and they might welcome the opportunity to come back. You never know until you ask.

When advertising for workers, pick the places where your kind of person might be shopping for jobs. Selective advertising can draw the types of applicants you are looking for without flooding your office with unsuitable types. Run your ad in the kind of paper your prospects read—that may be the weekly paper of the local college or the campus weekly.

Be sure the ad includes the essential qualifications for each job—legal age, skill level, and appearance—but avoid anything that might suggest discrimination on the basis of race, sex, age, national origin, or religion. (And note, it's not age discrimination if you must hire someone over the legal drinking age because they'll be handling or serving alcohol.) Describe the qualifications for the job in a way that intrigues the reader, and play up the advantages. Craft an eye-catching headline for your newspaper ad (Figure 12.6) and:

- Try placing ads in other sections of the paper, not just the classified pages. How about the local news section or the food or lifestyle sections?
- Daytime radio can reach people thinking of entering the labor force who haven't yet reached the point of combing through the ads.
- Check out the Internet job posting sites in your area. There is often no fee to list jobs on these sites.

The Interviewing Process

If the recruiting has been done well, a good interviewer with a good job description in hand has a good chance of selecting the right person to fit the job. At this point an additional tool is needed: an application form.

A written application is a necessary prelude to the interview. It provides a concise summary of the necessary data about the job candidate and gives the interviewer ideas for further questioning. In addition, the way the applicant fills out his or her paperwork provides valuable clues to personality traits and habits that are relevant to the job. Did he or she follow instructions? Write clearly? Spell things correctly? Leave questions unanswered? Take forever to finish? How will these characteristics relate to the job you are filling?

The basic application includes three categories of information: personal data, employment history, and references. Again, it is important to avoid asking for information that could be used to discriminate on the basis of race, sex, age, religion, or national origin. The United States has more attorneys per capita than any other nation, and Americans keep them busy with all manner of employment-related lawsuits. Figure 12.7 is a list of taboo topics in job interviews; for your own protection, familiarize yourself with them. Such questions may be violations of various federal laws. It is also illegal to discriminate against the handicapped, although inability to perform some aspect of a job is a legitimate reason for not hiring. Questions about police records should be handled carefully. Federal law allows you to ask whether a person has been convicted of a felony, but you cannot refuse employment on the basis of conviction unless the crime is pertinent to the duties of the job. For instance, you wouldn't want a convicted embezzler to be your cashier.

Two items of personal data are crucial in complying with state and federal laws. One is that anyone who will handle liquor on the job must meet the national minimum age requirement of 21. The second is that anyone you hire must have documents proving identity and eligibility to work in the United States (in other words, he or she cannot be an illegal alien). It is against the law to hire anyone from another country without valid U.S. immigration documents that allow them to work. Questions on proof of age and legal status should appear on your application form.

Bartenders . . . Join us at the Ultimate Bar and Grille

The Ultimate Bar and Grille has immediate openings for:
Day-Time Bartender

Full-time shifts from 10:30am to 7:00pm (including every other weekend off). Responsibilities includes the preparation of all alcoholic beverages such as highballs and cocktails as well as bar set-up. Knowledge of wines helpful. 1- to 2-years previous experience required as well as the possession of a current Beverage Commission server certification. We offer an excellent compensation package including employer-paid health insurance. If interested you can apply:

In person Monday-Friday 10am to 4pm
Email your resume to ubargrille@domainname.com and complete our electronic application form at our web site at www.ubargrille.com

THE ULTIMATE BAR AND GRILLE
5 South Central Ave.
City, State Zip

The Opportunity you are looking for is at . . .
THE ULTIMATE POUR LOUNGE

The Ultimate Pour Lounge offers the most exciting and rewarding bartending/managing experience. Our facilities include four full-service bars with stools as well as several service bars and a showroom lounge.

Immediate Opportunities Available
Bartenders   Cocktail Servers   Assistant Beverage Managers
Barbacks   Cashiers   Security

Each position offers competitive salary/wages and Benefits Program as well as the opportunity to be part of this city's Most Exciting Bar Experience.

APPLY
In person Monday-Friday 10am to 4pm
Email your resume to pourlounge@domain.com and complete our electronic application at our web site www.pourlounge.com

THE ULTIMATE POUR LOUNGE
111 Main Street
City, State Zip

Figure 12.6 Recruiting ads for bartenders and servers. Which one would you respond to?

Don't Ask	Why/Exceptions
Age/Date of Birth	There's no reason to ask about age unless you can prove that the job requires the person to be a certain age (for example, to qualify for licensing or for driving a car to make calls). You may ask, "Are you eligible to obtain a driver's license?"
Gender	The only job this counts for is restroom attendant. Don't think of men as the sales staff and women as the service agents. There are lots of men who are great service people and plenty of women who are very successful salespeople.
Language spoken	In a bilingual community it may be important for you to have bilingual staff. But where English is the community's single language, you may not eliminate an applicant because of a slight noninterfering accent. You may, however, require that applicants demonstrate ability to communicate effectively.
Parents' name/Maiden name	May reveal nationality or marital status.
Homeowner or renter	By asking this, you might be perceived to be discriminating against low-income people, who cannot afford to buy houses.
Number of children—child care	This is confidential information; you have no right to this information prior to hiring the person.
Club memberships	May reveal religious affiliation or ethnic background.
Emergency contact information	You have no right to this information prior to hiring the person.
Recent photo—height/weight	May reveal national origin, race, or physical disability.
Health status/Physical exam	May reveal physical disability. Physical disability must not be discussed until after hiring. You may ask if the candidate is able to lift a certain amount of weight, or sit or stand for long periods of time, if this is a requirement of the job.
Eye/Hair color	May reveal national origin or race of the applicant.
Arrest records	Don't ask. You may ask whether the person is eligible to be bonded, since this might be a requirement for some of your positions.
Citizenship/Place of birth	May reveal national origin of the applicant.

Figure 12.7 Taboo topics during a job interview. *Source: Outfront Magazine,* Fall 2000.

Figure 12.8 is a copy of **form I-9,** the federal Employment Eligibility Verification form that lists the correct documents used to establish identity and eligibility to work in the United States. A detailed "Handbook for Employers" further explaining these requirements and employers' obligations is available from any U.S. Immigration and Naturalization Service office. It is well worth your study as you plan your hiring program.

Be organized about the way you collect the incoming written applications for any job. Legally, you are required (by the U.S. Civil Rights Act) to keep applications on file for six months after a job is filled or an applicant is rejected; yet another federal law, the Age Discrimination Act, requires that applications be kept for a full year. Protect yourself; don't toss them.

What *can* you discuss in the personal interview? Ask the applicant about his or her skills, previous work experience, reasons for applying for this particular position. Managers of small operations often find themselves too busy to sit and talk with applicants, relying instead on intuition or even hiring based strictly on the written application. Yet it is in the oral interview where the applicant's personality and potential can best be assessed. The way a person responds to questions will tell you whether he or she is friendly, open, intelligent, alert—and interested enough to ask *you* a few questions as well! Nonverbal clues are also important. The way the person sits, stands, moves, gestures, and speaks can indicate capacity for speed and dexterity, as well as confidence and poise. And, of course, a personal interview is essential in judging appearance and ability to relate to others.

The interview should have two phases. First, you as an interviewer should explain clearly the job being offered, using the job description as a basis for discussion. As a result, both you and the applicant should be able to judge whether he or she has the required skills—or the capacity to develop them quickly enough—to fill your needs.

The other phase of the interview should amplify the data on the application. Are there gaps in past employment? If so, why, and are the reasons good ones? What did this person like or dislike about previous jobs, and are there parallels in your job? If there are no former employers listed as references, why not? Would there by any transportation problems, any conflicts of schedule (such as school classes or spouse's schedule), any difficulties with basic skills required for the job (such as handwriting or math)? Is there any history of frequent or chronic illness?

The Hiring Process

The 10 points in Figure 12.9 are a good framework to use when you have narrowed the field to several promising candidates. Go ahead and call former employers, whether they are on the applicant's reference list or not, especially if the job requires handling money. Though most people are honest, it is the ones who are not that you want to avoid hiring. At one time,

Please read instructions carefully before completing this form. The instructions must be available during completion of this form. **ANTI-DISCRIMINATION NOTICE:** It is illegal to discriminate against work eligible individuals. Employers CANNOT specify which document(s) they will accept from an employee. The refusal to hire an individual because of a future expiration date may also constitute illegal discrimination.

Section 1. Employee Information and Verification. To be completed and signed by employee at the time employment begins.

Print Name: Last	First	Middle Initial	Maiden Name

Address (Street Name and Number)	Apt. #	Date of Birth (month/day/year)

City	State	Zip Code	Social Security #

I am aware that federal law provides for imprisonment and/or fines for false statements or use of false documents in connection with the completion of this form.

I attest, under penalty of perjury, that I am (check one of the following):
- [ ] A citizen or national of the United States
- [ ] A Lawful Permanent Resident (Alien # A_____)
- [ ] An alien authorized to work until ___/___/___
  (Alien # or Admission #) _____

Employee's Signature	Date (month/day/year)

Preparer and/or Translator Certification. (To be completed and signed if Section 1 is prepared by a person other than the employee.) I attest, under penalty of perjury, that I have assisted in the completion of this form and that to the best of my knowledge the information is true and correct.

Preparer's/Translator's Signature	Print Name

Address (Street Name and Number, City, State, Zip Code)	Date (month/day/year)

Section 2. Employer Review and Verification. To be completed and signed by employer. Examine one document from List A OR examine one document from List B and one from List C, as listed on the reverse of this form, and record the title, number and expiration date, if any, of the document(s)

List A	OR	List B	AND	List C
Document title: _____		_____		_____
Issuing authority: _____		_____		_____
Document #: _____		_____		_____
Expiration Date (if any): ___/___/___		___/___/___		___/___/___
Document #: _____				
Expiration Date (if any): ___/___/___				

CERTIFICATION - I attest, under penalty of perjury, that I have examined the document(s) presented by the above-named employee, that the above-listed document(s) appear to be genuine and to relate to the employee named, that the employee began employment on (month/day/year) ___/___/___ and that to the best of my knowledge the employee is eligible to work in the United States. (State employment agencies may omit the date the employee began employment.)

Signature of Employer or Authorized Representative	Print Name	Title

Business or Organization Name	Address (Street Name and Number, City, State, Zip Code)	Date (month/day/year)

Section 3. Updating and Reverification. To be completed and signed by employer.

A. New Name (if applicable)	B. Date of rehire (month/day/year) (if applicable)

C. If employee's previous grant of work authorization has expired, provide the information below for the document that establishes current employment eligibility.

Document Title: _____ Document #: _____ Expiration Date (if any): ___/___/___

I attest, under penalty of perjury, that to the best of my knowledge, this employee is eligible to work in the United States, and if the employee presented document(s), the document(s) I have examined appear to be genuine and to relate to the individual.

Signature of Employer or Authorized Representative	Date (month/day/year)

Figure 12.8 Form I-9: Employment Eligibility Verification. The back of form contains instructions for its use. *Source:* U.S. Department of Justice, Immigration, and Naturalization Service.

Ten-Point Hiring Process

Develop a standard operating procedure for the hiring process, just as you have for other tasks. This will help to ensure that you don't skip any important steps or leave yourself open to litigation from a disappointed applicant.

1. Collect all applications that come in response to your advertising or recruiting for a specific job.
2. Screen for those applicants who meet your advertised criteria. File rejected applications for later notification.
3. Set up interviews with all applicants who meet the requirements stated in your advertising/recruiting materials.
4. At the interview, have the applicant sign a form authorizing previous employers to release information about the applicant's employment with them.
5. Mail or fax the reference check authorization to each applicant's previous employers, or to those of the last 10 years of work experience.
6. Conduct appropriate nonbiased preemployment tests, or arrange for outside testing. Be sure to treat all applicants for the position the same— consistency is everything when using testing.
7. Using information from the applicants' resumés, reference checks, preemployment testing, and your interviews, select the top three candidates. Rank them in order of preference.
8. Offer the position to the number one candidate. Don't eliminate the other two until the top candidate accepts the position in writing.
9. Notify all applicants (not just those you interviewed) in writing that the position has been filled.
10. Mark the applications of all rejected applicants to be discarded after the required retention period.

Figure 12.9 Ten-point hiring process. *Source: Outfront Magazine,* Fall 2000.

some employers used a lie detector or polygraph test to screen applicants, but this is now illegal for most types of job. Most former employers won't or can't say anything negative about a former employee because of fear of litigation, but you can still glean factual information, such as employment dates.

You can also require that they take a drug test to screen for illegal drug use. Many employers feel it is worth the money spent on the lab fee for this test. You may also request a basic medical examination, but both drug tests and health exams are somewhat controversial. Since AIDS and drug use cannot be passed on to customers in a typical on-the-job setting, are such tests actually discriminatory? That's what some people assert. But what about hepatitis, which is contagious and could be disastrous in any sort of public-contact job? You might want to contact your state health department to find out if there is a norm for foodservice and related businesses in your area. If you do require a health exam, it should establish that nothing is physically wrong with the individual that would be a hazard on the job. This could spare you the need to pay workers' compensation in case of an accident.

Finally, you must check the applicant's proof of age (usually a driver's license with date of birth, photo, and signature) and citizenship or work eligibility documents, as listed on the federal I-9 form.

You may not always find the perfect person for every job, and you are the only one who can judge when a compromise is in order and when to go on looking. In any case, if you have done a thorough job of interviewing and checking, you know just what kind of person you are hiring and you have minimized your risks.

As part of the final hiring process you must complete an I-9 form for each new employee within three business days. Both you and your new employee must sign this form. It is up to you to get these forms from the Immigration and Naturalization Service (INS). You must keep a completed I-9 form for each employee in your files for at least three years (or for one year after termination of employment) and be prepared to show these to an INS inspector. If you have hired someone whose documents do not prove eligibility, or if you have failed to keep I-9s on file as required, you will be subject to a fine for each employee concerned. INS inspectors may check your files at any time after giving three days' notice. Food and beverage establishments are the category of operations most frequently fined for failure to comply with I-9 requirements.

MANAGING PERSONNEL FOR SUCCESS

Hiring is only the first step in the management of people. The manager is also responsible for explaining jobs and assigning responsibilities, for making sure that people carry out the jobs assigned, and for taking disciplinary action when they do not. It seems like a simple and clear-cut assignment, but it is not.

Good personnel management is crucial to running a profitable operation. For one thing, the traditionally high turnover rate in this industry means high labor costs, as you constantly hire and train new workers, whose productivity is naturally lower when they are unfamiliar with the job. Even more important, high turnover and employee dissatisfaction are bound to affect the quality of customer service. When the quality of service drops, customers go elsewhere.

Let's look at some of the things large enterprises are doing today to improve the management of people. The same principles will apply in smaller operations.

Orientation and Skills Training

The first part of the manager's personnel responsibility—explaining jobs and assigning responsibilities—begins right after employees are hired. Think about it. Every person must learn exactly what is expected of them: to whom they must report, whom they are supposed to work with or supervise, how to use the equipment and follow the house routines, what the menu includes, how to report work hours, whether tips are shared and with whom, and much more. It is quite a lot for a new person to absorb. Yet many a manager puts a new employee right to work, counting only on a bit of coaching as mistakes are made and questions asked. Often the coaching is left to another employee, who may resent the extra burden and who may not be the world's best teacher.

So there are at least four good reasons for taking the time and effort to give employees a basic, all-inclusive orientation session before they start work:

- They will be able to work faster and with less confusion.
- They will feel more confident in their jobs, and this will be reflected in their attitude toward work and in the way they relate to your customers.
- They will more easily establish good relationships with coworkers.
- They will be more likely to stay if you see to it that they have a good experience from day one.

Some enterprises also develop a written orientation manual to give to new employees. Certainly it is a sound idea to have all the rules and information on paper, so there is no possibility of misunderstanding or leaving something out. Make it modular, in notebook form, so that pages can be added or replaced as rules are added or changed. A completed form similar to Figure 12.10 is the absolute minimum of written information for a new employee. In addition to job duties, you can put information in the manual about vacation days, sick days, payroll, benefits, and other similar topics.

However, handing a new employee a sheet of paper or a manual is not enough. It's a good start, but you can't cover everything on paper, and there is no guarantee that he or she will understand it, remember it, or even read it. Everything should be discussed step by step on a one-to-one basis. To make sure the employee understands, ask to have the information repeated back to you. Then go over it again if necessary. It is important to gear the training to what the employee can absorb. Experts recommend teaching one task at a time, one step at a time, over a period of several days.

A formula for job instruction training developed during World War II to train people quickly in industry proved so successful it has been used widely ever since. It applies a four-step method of instruction to each task:

1. **Explain the task.** Tell the employee about the task itself, its importance, and its place in the job and the operation as a whole.

TO OUR NEW EMPLOYEE:

Welcome!
We are glad you are joining us and we hope you will enjoy working here.

Your hours are: _____ Punch in and out on clock beside kitchen door.

Your days of work are: _____

Your pay rate is: _____ (1½ regular rate after 40 hours)

Payday is: _____

Your supervisor is: _____

You supervise: _____

You work with: _____

Dress: Conservative blue blouse, navy blue skirt or slacks, closed-toe shoes

Meals: You may buy your meals here at our discounted price.
        You must eat on your own time.

Breaks: _____

Rules: Wash your hands as soon as you come to work. Make this a habit!
        No smoking or drinking on the job.
        Hair, nails, and clothing must be neat and clean.
        Do not serve a minor any alcoholic beverage.
        Do not serve an intoxicated person any alcoholic beverage.

Your duties are:

A menu, drink list, and wine list are attached. Please study these. You will receive further personal orientation. Meantime, do not hesitate to ask questions.

Figure 12.10 Sample information handout for a new employee.

2. **Demonstrate the task.** Show, explain, step by step. Emphasize key points, techniques, standards. Repeat the demonstration until the employee is ready to try it.
3. **Have the employee perform the task.** Encourage and correct. Repeat until both you and the employee are comfortable with the performance.
4. **Follow up.** Once the new employee is on the job, supervise as needed. Check frequently; coach and correct. Taper off as performance meets stan-

dards consistently. Check periodically to see that the employee is following standard procedures.

If you do not have the time or the personnel to do a proper job of training, then you might do better to hire skilled workers and pay the extra wages. One way or another, you will have to pay for trained personnel. Many managers feel it is easier to train "from scratch" than to retrain someone accustomed to a different way of doing things.

Sales Training

The other great reason for training is to impart better sales and customer relations skills, which are also critical to your bottom line. This type of training is ongoing—it can be done in short weekly staff meetings or as monthly seminars, but it should definitely be scheduled on a regular basis. Your servers and bartenders sell not only your beverages, but your entire enterprise. They can turn your guests on or off at the very first contact. It is your job as owner or manager to teach and reinforce social skills—the value of a smile and eye contact, of enthusiasm, of courteous attention and prompt, accurate service—as well as grace under pressure. Teach them what to do or say when a customer wants to send something back; when a cork crumbles in a wine bottle; when an order has been botched and must be rectified; when someone walks out without paying.

This kind of training is a combination of:

- **Product knowledge.** Let employees taste new menu additions. Ask them to help you pick wines or beers that complement the foods you serve. Ask distributors and suppliers to share wine information and sales tips. Tape record these meetings so those who could not attend can still listen.
- **Sales skills.** Denver sales trainer and restaurateur Jim Sullivan says there are "right words" that can help trigger just about any type of sale; and that there are five opportunities in any bar/restaurant setting to suggest a beverage sale. If you don't know them, you can bet your staff doesn't either. Invest in professional training that is designed specifically to increase your sales—and their tips.
- **Guest psychology.** This is certainly part of sales skills, but it also includes how to deal diplomatically with problem customers: people who are loud or belligerent, who've had too much to drink, who are making improper advances to staffers or other customers. It also includes safety training: being robbed, or harassed, or being faced with any type of emergency situation. Your local police department may be willing to help you with this type of training.
- **Rules, etiquette and technique.** There are procedures that every bar adheres to because they help things run more smoothly and professionally. These vary from place to place, but they typically include: the way drinks

are ordered by the server (in a sequence, to help the bartender keep the orders straight); use of a tray to carry things; wiping sides of glasses before they are delivered; types of garnishes used for each drink. If you have preferences about these issues, you must regularly share these with your staff.

Training in Beverage Laws

This type of training is essential and should be taught immediately to serving personnel. Beverage laws are complex, and sometimes antiquated, but they begin with the basic assumptions that consuming alcohol—and therefore, selling alcohol—are privileges, not rights. If the privileges are abused, they can be taken away.

There are three more general ideas on which beverage laws are based:

- Alcohol may be served only during the days and hours established by law in your area.
- It is against state law everywhere to serve alcohol to anyone under 21.
- It is against the law to serve alcohol to anyone who is clearly intoxicated.

Legal serving hours vary from one locale to another. Make sure that new employees know the legal hours in your area and that you expect them to observe these hours without exception.

The drinking age in every state is 21. At the time the order is taken, if there is any doubt at all about a customer's age, the server should ask for proof of age, such as a driver's license, passport, birth certificate, or special ID card issued by state or local government authorities. Some proof-of-age documents are easy to fake and even easier to borrow from a friend, so they must be examined closely. Your local law enforcement agencies can probably show examples of fake IDs, and explain ways to spot the forgeries. Many state laws specify "a document with a signature, description, or picture." If the picture, description, and signature fit the individual, you as the seller are usually (though not everywhere) presumed innocent in case of trouble. The law sometimes contains a key word for your protection: you may not "knowingly" sell to anyone under legal age. You are also entitled to refuse to serve anyone you suspect is underage. And be aware: If your establishment serves an underage person, it does not matter that this young customer has broken the law by misrepresenting his or her age. Instead, it is usually you, the seller, who is held responsible.

The other people you may not sell to, as you learned in Chapter 2, are those who have had too much to drink. It is all too easy for a busy or inexperienced employee intent on increasing check averages and tips to forget this. Not only is it against the law, it puts you at risk of third-party liability. The best you can do is to reduce the chances that someone will become intoxicated at your place of business. A number of good training programs have been developed to teach bar managers and servers how to tell when people are drinking too much and what to do about it. In these courses, you can expect to learn how to:

- Keep track of numbers of drinks served each customer.
- Recognize behaviors that may indicate increasing intoxication.
- Understand drink equivalencies (just how strong different drinks are).
- Observe guests' body type and size to determine how many drinks are "too many."
- Encourage alternatives to alcohol (snacks, a cup of coffee, dinner).
- Tactfully but firmly refuse to serve the person who can't handle any more ("I'm sorry, but I'm not allowed to bring you another drink").

Suggestions are given to safely arrange for transportation home: a sober companion or taxi service; getting a room at a nearby hotel rather than driving; calling police as a last resort. A growing number of state and local liquor control boards now require bars to have their serving personnel trained and certified in a course or seminar approved by that agency. Some boards develop their own course or adapt an existing one to their state's requirements. Among the existing programs are:

TIPS (Training for Intervention Procedures by Servers of Alcohol): TIPS was developed by Health Communications Inc. under Morris E. Chafetz, founder of the National Institute on Alcohol Abuse and Alcoholism. In a six-hour course using videotapes, written materials, and role-playing, servers are trained to recognize the onset of intoxication and to handle the inebriated customer. They are certified for three years upon passing a written exam. TIPS instructors have been trained in a two-day course and have passed a trainer certification exam.

Responsible Beverage Service: Server Awareness Course: This course was developed by the Responsible Hospitality Institute. The institute sends its own trainers to you, for two three-hour sessions; then servers are certified by written exam. This organization also offers a separate program for owners and manager.

TAM (Techniques of Alcohol Management): TAM is a creation of the National Licensed Beverage Association. This one-day seminar is tailored to the laws and requirements of each state.

The Bar Code (formerly known as SERVSAFE): Compiled by the Education Foundation of the National Restaurant Association, the Bar Code provides manuals for managers, a study guide for servers, a videotape, and test materials.

Serving Alcohol with Care (usually known as CARE): CARE was developed by the Educational Institute of the American Hotel/Motel Association; it provides a 28-minute videotape, a leader's guide, and server manual for developing your own seminar.

An excellent source of further information is the Responsible Beverage Service Council, a professional organization devoted to in-depth planning and promotion of beverage service training programs and related activities. Individual communities are also developing programs suited to their own special needs and standards.

A staff of trained and certified serving personnel can reduce the cost of your liability insurance, as well as the risk that one of your guests will be involved in a drunk-driving incident. It can also earn you the goodwill of customers, who will appreciate a caring approach to the problem and a skillful avoidance of unpleasant incidents.

No matter what kind of training you do, it is usually more useful to present it as education or career development than as "penance." Make it interesting, meaningful, and not too lengthy. If you require employees to attend, be sure that they are paid for these hours. Servers dislike a "hard sell" as much as customers do, but some repetition and review will pay off. You must communicate to your employees what you expect them to get from the training, and how you expect them to use it.

Some bars designate one person as the primary trainer for any new hire. The trainer should be an experienced employee with a positive attitude and a belief in your overall philosophy. You might set up a training system so that the first two weeks on the job, a newcomer works as a barback before "graduating" to bartender; or that he or she passes a test that combines written questions with a behind-the-bar demonstration of skills. Test on an ongoing basis, not just at the beginning of the job.

The cost of training is high, but the cost of *not* training may be higher in the long run. You may find that the chief benefit of training is giving your staff a sense of professionalism that keeps morale high and keeps good employees on the job.

HANDLING PEOPLE SUCCESSFULLY

It may be a new century, but some things never change—beverage managers and bar operators still wrestle with the topics of how to find and keep good employees. Competition for them is intense, and we've already discussed the high cost (both in budget and morale) that turnover creates. In addition, getting employees to perform their duties to the required standards, day in and day out, is a real challenge. So the smart business today gives its managers and supervisors special training directed to understanding the "human factors" that turn workers on or off. Among the most essential factors are:

- The Manager's attitude toward the employees and their work
- Good communications
- Methods of maintaining performance standards
- Teamwork

The manager's attitude is probably *the* most influential factor in employee performance. Nothing is more devastating to an enterprise than a manager's negative attitude toward the workers; and nothing is more constructive than a positive attitude. If you as a manager look down on the people you supervise and the work they do, you create resentment and anger. If, on the other hand, you respect each employee as a person and recognize each job as important to the business, then you cannot help but establish valid person-to-person relationships. You are encouraging the employees to feel good, about themselves and about you. If you expect the best of people, they will generally give their best. If they think you consider them capable and hardworking, they will try hard to maintain the image. This has been proven time and again.

Corollaries of these positive attitudes are fairness and concern for individuals. Employees respect a boss who treats them fairly, does not show favoritism, and listens to their point of view even when disagreeing with it. Concern for individuals does not mean relaxing standards or becoming involved in employees' personal lives; it simply means appreciating them as human beings and being aware of human needs and feelings.

A second factor in maintaining good employee performance is good communications. There are many pitfalls in the sending and receiving of verbal instructions. The speaker may not say what he or she meant, or may use unfamiliar terms or words that have more than one meaning. The employee may not grasp the meaning because his or her anger, embarrassment, or defensiveness gets in the way. Either person, or both, may be busy, distracted, and "on the run" when the direction or instruction is given. So it pays to be sure your messages are sent clearly and received and understood clearly.

With all of this in mind, you might look at employee turnover as a symptom instead of a problem. Writing in *The Consultant* magazine (second quarter issue, 2000) Bill Main suggests that managers find out why employees leave by conducting exit interviews with them, including the few simple questions listed in Figure 12.11.

Main also feels managers can make a huge morale difference simply by paying attention to their workers. He has devised an easy technique he calls the "30-Second Boost." He suggests spending at least 30 seconds each day chatting with every employee about something other than work—a hobby or vacation; what's going on at school; how are their kids? Main even suggests keeping a small daily checklist with every worker's name on it, to be sure nobody on that shift is left out. You'll see a sample "Boost Sheet" in Figure 12.12.

A fourth important aspect of communication is to make sure that employees are told in advance of all changes affecting them and their jobs, along with an explanation of the reason for the change, if you can give one. They will appreciate your concern and be more ready to adapt.

Another vital aspect of good communication is to be receptive to what employees have to say. Often, they know more than you do about their jobs and can come up with good suggestions. Some organizations ask that employees evaluate their managers, not just vice versa. (Figure 12.13 is a sam-

Employee Exit Interview

Name _____   Date _____

1. The type of work I was assigned was enjoyable.
   ❏ strongly agree   ❏ agree   ❏ disagree   ❏ strongly disagree

2. My job was important to the company's success.
   ❏ strongly agree   ❏ agree   ❏ disagree   ❏ strongly disagree

3. Wages are about average compared to other local restaurants.
   ❏ strongly agree   ❏ agree   ❏ disagree   ❏ strongly disagree

4. My fellow employees were cooperative.
   ❏ strongly agree   ❏ agree   ❏ disagree   ❏ strongly disagree

5. I was given adequate training for the job.
   ❏ strongly agree   ❏ agree   ❏ disagree   ❏ strongly disagree

6. Working conditions are about average for the restaurant business.
   ❏ strongly agree   ❏ agree   ❏ disagree   ❏ strongly disagree

7. My supervisor handled his/her job well.
   ❏ strongly agree   ❏ agree   ❏ disagree   ❏ strongly disagree

8. The company was well-organized, scheduled, and controlled.
   ❏ strongly agree   ❏ agree   ❏ disagree   ❏ strongly disagree

9. My specific work responsibilities were clear.
   ❏ strongly agree   ❏ agree   ❏ disagree   ❏ strongly disagree

10. My abilities were well utilized.
    ❏ strongly agree   ❏ agree   ❏ disagree   ❏ strongly disagree

Figure 12.11 Employee exit interview. © Bill Main & Associates. All rights reserved.

ple form for this type of evaluation.) These kinds of efforts can point out trends or legitimate complaints that owners or managers were not aware of. Be appreciative of your workers' ideas *and* their criticisms. They give you free and valuable feedback about your performance and the morale of your staff. In trying to remedy problems you may uncover, never promise anything unless you can and will deliver.

One-On-One Notes

Crew Member _____   Date _____

What is your greatest frustration about your job?

What new skill would you like to learn?

What needs to be fixed, changed or eliminated?

Boost Sheet

Employee	Position	Sign-in	
Kitchen			
Sal M.	Prep	8:00 am	☑
Ted J.	Wash	9:45 am	☑
Kevin L.	Line	10:30 am	☐
Dining Room/Bar			
Rhonda R.	Server	10:30 am	☐
Darren A.	Bus	9:45 am	☑
Mary W.	Host	11:15 am	☐
Administrative			
Carol R.	Books	9:00 am	☐
Char D.	Cashier	7:30 am	☑

Figure 12.12 Boost sheet.

Be vigilant in maintaining the standards you have set, yet considerate in how you point out lapses and shortcomings. Never lecture or berate an employee in front of customers or coworkers. If workers leave things undone, don't do their work for them and then fume about it; insist that they do it. If a problem recurs, ask the employee for a solution, or work one out together; then follow through.

Manager Evaluation by Employee

Date _____

Manager's Name _____   **Return By** _____

Please answer the following questions to the best of your ability. A ⑤ is the highest score, and a ① is the lowest score.

1. How would you rate this person's grooming? ⑤④③②①

2. How would you rate this person's ability to communicate? ⑤④③②①

3. Does this person instill a sense of teamwork among those s/he supervises? ⑤④③②①

4. Does this person have good training skills? ⑤④③②①

5. How would you rate this person's ability to train the management staff? ⑤④③②①

6. Do you feel you can approach this person about subjects that trouble you? ⑤④③②①

7. Does this person respond in an adult manner to criticism and suggestions? ⑤④③②①

8. How willing is this person to help out in areas where s/he sees the need? ⑤④③②①

9. Does this person deal fairly with everyone? ⑤④③②①

10. Does this person show good judgment & common sense in emergencies? ⑤④③②①

11. How well does this person follow through? ⑤④③②①

12. Does this person leave his/her problems at the back door and concentrate on job performance? ⑤④③②①

13. How well does this person adhere to company policy? ⑤④③②①

14. Does this person help you to be the best employee you can be? ⑤④③②①

15. How well do you like working with this person? ⑤④③②①

16. In what one, single area should this person improve to increase his/her overall performance?

17. What one word would you use to describe this person?

18. What single thing does this manager do that makes your job easier?

19. What single thing does this manager do that makes your job harder?

20. Comments:

Figure 12.13 Manager evaluation by employee.

Give positive feedback; too often the boss's remarks are all critical. Express your appreciation for jobs well done. And make sure your own performance meets the same high standards you set for others. Your employees are watching you.

The truly effective manager of people builds a spirit of teamwork among the personnel. It begins with the hiring process—selecting people who will get along together. It continues with the careful training of each employee, to integrate new people to the operation successfully. It is nurtured by a positive attitude toward the workers and their work, a spirit of respect and concern for individuals. People who work together in a positive atmosphere usually develop a feeling of belonging together, even if they have little else in common. The manager who can build a team can hardly lose. And every manager needs a team to win.

LABOR AND EMPLOYMENT LAWS

There is a growing realization among all types of employers that the work relationship is fraught with potential legal risks, from minor misunderstandings between workers that are settled informally to million-dollar court judgments for alleged errors, injuries, pay disputes, and discrimination. Generally, front-line managers and supervisors receive little or no training about how to handle disputed issues or what the consequences of a careless remark or simple decision might be. On the other hand, some employers are so concerned about the risk of a lawsuit that they refuse to make difficult decisions, resulting in reduced productivity, sagging morale, and inadequate communication with their workforce.

Increasingly, when allegations are serious, an individual manager or supervisor is named in a complaint or lawsuit right along with the company. So today's manager cannot be too careful when faced with a touchy situation. Managers should be trained to spot potential problems and to act in ways that reduce their employers' exposure to legal action. BNA Communications, Inc. of Rockville, Maryland, a company that conducts corporate training for managers, has created these "10 Rules for Workplace Liability."

Rule 1: Watch What You Say.
- **Don't make threats.** Occasionally, managers in the course of a day's business will make a casual comment that seems threatening to an employee, who is trying to take advantage of those rights that are protected by law. The supervisor's ignorance of this employee's sensitivity may lead to litigation.
- **Don't make promises.** At times, especially during tense situations, supervisors make promises to appease employees or to reward someone for outstanding performance. These promises, although not made

in writing, can create legally enforceable expectations that can later hurt the organization.

- **Don't denigrate.** Never make any comment, on or off the job, that can be considered demeaning to a person's age, gender, race, religion, national origin, or type of disability. Such statements are not only illegal, they can be used as evidence of unlawful motivation in case of discharge, causing the employer to be liable for back pay, punitive damages, and other costs. Look at all employees as having valuable contributions to make.

- **Don't ask improper questions.** An example: By inquiring about an applicant's medical condition in a preemployment interview, you may be violating the Americans with Disabilities Act. By asking questions of one class of applicants that would not be asked of another class, you could be creating evidence of discrimination, in violation of Title VII of the Civil Rights Act. An example: By asking women about child care arrangements, and not men, you could be perceived as discriminating against the women. If you insist that a "green card" is the only sufficient proof of a person's U.S. citizenship or right to work, when other forms of identification are also accepted, you are violating the Immigration Reform and Control Act.

Rule 2: Keep Accurate Records of Hours Worked. There are work-related situations in which supervisors carelessly break the law when they ask employees to perform chores after hours without recording it. Another problem arises when employees who are eligible for overtime pay (one and a half times their regular pay rate) are not paid this higher rate for all hours worked over the standard 40-hour workweek. "Swapping" overtime in one week for time off the next week is also illegal. (Record-keeping is discussed in greater detail later in this chapter.)

Rule 3: Be Sensitive to Implications of Sexual Harassment. Supervisors must understand that their words can be taken out of context and, more important, can be used against them in jury trials. Avoid using sexually oriented phrases, even in jest, as an attempt to create social relationships. Further, condoning pornographic material in the workplace can result in a charge of "Environmental Sexual Harassment."

Rule 4: Document Everything. It's not paranoia, it's smart business practice. A supervisor's memory of a discussion or incident may be hazy, especially in the absence of related documentation. Statistics show that, in court, juries typically will believe an employee over his or her supervisor.

Rule 5: Be Consistent. In an attempt to "be nice," supervisors may in fact open their companies up to lawsuit potential for using different behavior or standards with different employees. An employee with a disability, for instance, can claim that he or she was treated differently on the basis of that characteristic, even if your intention was to make their duties less strenuous! And the Equal Pay Act prohibits employers from paying individuals differently based on their genders for doing the same jobs.

Rule 6: Be Safety Conscious. The Occupational Safety and Health Act (OSHA) requires employers to document all work-related injuries that require medical attention other than minimal first aid or that result in a restriction of work assignments. Supervisors must also be aware that pushing for increases in productivity does not result in sacrificing safety rules or not taking precautions. Employees will notice.

Rule 7: Seek Outside Help When Unusual Circumstances Arise. When a supervisor encounters any difficult or questionable situation that may involve an employment law, they should seek professional advice immediately. This may be the company's Human Resources department, an attorney, or a trade group like the National Restaurant Association or American Hotel/Motel Association. Managers are not expected to know the intricacies of employment law, and even though a logical solution may be evident, it may not necessarily be the correct legal solution to a problem with potential repercussions.

Rule 8: Consider All Implications of Any Special Request. A simple request for leave—a longer period of time off work—can trigger obligations under a number of laws, including Title VII, which requires accommodation of certain religious requests; the Americans with Disabilities Act, which spells out the rights of persons with disabilities; and the Family and Medical Leave Act, which allows employees to take leave (even on an intermittent basis) to care for the medical needs of a spouse, child, or parent.

Rule 9: Take Seriously All Situations in Which Termination Is Implicated or Threatened. When employees threaten to quit, take them seriously and immediately report this to your own superior or your company's Human Resources department. If they are not given the opportunity to consult higher-ups about this decision before they actually quit, they could later argue that they were "forced" to quit, thereby entitling them to full back wages.

Rule 10: Be Aware of the Laws. New and veteran supervisors share one dangerous trait: they often believe that a "common-sense" approach to managing employees shields them from legal liability when employment disputes arise. Unfortunately, few are aware of the complexity and changing nature of labor and employment laws. Take advantage of every opportunity to familiarize yourself with these laws, and to gain a fuller understanding of how they might impact your daily decisions as a manager. Seminars are offered at trade shows and conventions, by local and national trade groups (like restaurant associations), or by business groups. Applying this knowledge on the job will save you and your organization time, money, and aggravation.

An Overview of Labor and Employment Laws

The following offers a brief summary of the major federal labor and employment laws, those most frequently implicated in court actions. Remember, these are only the U.S. federal laws; many states have passed their own similar, legislation about these topics that, in some cases, is more restrictive. These capsules are no substitute for legal advice, which should always be sought from an attorney familiar with employment issues.

Americans with Disabilities Act (ADA): This prohibits discrimination against disabled job applicants in privately owned companies with 15 or more employees. Employers are required to make "reasonable accommodations" to allow an otherwise qualified disabled person to be able to work, unless making the accommodations would cause "undue hardship" to the employer. The Equal Employment Opportunity Commission (EEOC) is responsible for enforcing this act. The ADA also covers accessibility in the overall design of your building.

Age Discrimination in Employment Act of 1967: This law states that companies with more than 20 employees may not discriminate against workers, or job applicants, who are over 40 years of age. The EEOC is also responsible for enforcing this act.

Equal Pay Act of 1963: This act requires equal pay for jobs that are substantially equal in skill, effort, and responsibility, and thus are performed under similar working conditions in the same workplace. It is primarily designed to prevent sex discrimination in payment of wages, salaries, and other forms of compensation. It applies to private employers and all government employers too. The EEOC enforces this act.

Immigration Reform and Control Act: This act prohibits discrimination against people for their national origin, citizenship, or intended citizenship, and it applies to any company with four or more employees (unless the company is already covered under Title VII of the Civil Rights Act of 1964; see next paragraph). Termination of employment is also covered by the act, which is enforced by the Office of Special Counsel, U.S. Department of Labor.

Title VII, Civil Rights Act of 1964: This says employers may not discriminate against applicants or workers on the basis of their race, skin color, national origin, or gender. Title VII is a far-reaching act, which applies to all companies and all forms of government. Unlawful discrimination includes overt or "disparate" treatment, "disparate impact" treatment, sexual or racial harassment, and retaliation. The EEOC enforces this act.

Title VII, Sexual Harassment: This act applies not only to supervisors and managers, but to employees—if their supervisor knows of their actions and does nothing to stop them. This type of harassment includes unwelcome sexual advances, requests for sexual favors, and other verbal or physical conduct of a sexual nature. In the case of a bar or restaurant, the act also includes sexual harassment of your employees by guests, if management is made aware of such activities and does not attempt to stop them. Sexual harassment is a tough call, since many people have different standards. To help, the EEOC, which enforces this act, has clarified a few points:

- When submission to such contact is made a term or condition of an individual's employment, either explicitly or implicitly.
- When submission to, or repetition of, such contact is used as a basis for employment decisions that affect an individual.
- When such contact has the purpose or effect of reasonably interfering with an individual's work performance, or whether it creates a work environment for this person that is intimidating, hostile, or offensive.

National Labor Relations Act: This act gives employees the right to form, join, or assist labor unions, to bargain collectively through representatives of their own choosing. (It is also known as the Wagner Act, passed in the 1930s, which was amended by the Taft-Hartley Act in the 1940s.) The act prohibits employers from interfering with, restraining, or coercing employees as they exercise their collective bargaining rights. Companies cannot donate to unions or interfere with their operation; they can't discriminate against people for being union members; they can't encourage or discourage union membership; they can't refuse to negotiate in collective bargaining; and they can't fire or penalize a worker for using the act to file complaints against their employer. This act also covers unfair behavior on the part of unions. A union cannot coerce or restrain a worker in exercising his or her rights; cannot discriminate against employees who don't join the union; and cannot refuse to negotiate in collective bargaining. This is a far-reaching act with many implications for large employers and chain operators. The National Labor Relations Board (NLRB), a division of the U.S. Department of Labor, enforces the act.

Fair Labor Standards Act: This is covered in detail in the next section, "Compensation and Benefits."

Family and Medical Leave Act of 1993: Any company with more than 50 workers must permit them to take leave (up to 12 weeks, unpaid) for family medical reasons. These might include care of a newborn or newly adopted child or to care for themselves or a family member during a serious illness. The act requires that, although the employer does not have to pay the workers' salary during their leave, they must maintain insurance coverage and hold their job for them until they return. The act also specifies the number of hours and years an employee must work to become eligible for this coverage. The U.S. Labor Department enforces it.

Employee Polygraph Protection Act: Private employers cannot administer or require polygraph (lie detector) tests, either to job seekers or current employees, except under certain circumstances. For instance, employees or applicants who have direct access to controlled substances as part of their jobs can be tested; prospective security guards can be tested; and employees can be tested if they are part of an investigation into workplace theft or other incidents that have caused an "economic loss" for the employer. This act is also enforced by the U.S. Department of Labor.

Occupational Safety and Health Act: Commonly known as OSHA, this act prohibits employers who are "engaged in interstate commerce" from requiring their workers to perform tasks in unsafe places or unsafe manners. At this time, new ergonomic standards are being discussed to include common ailments of the computer generation, like carpal tunnel syndrome, tendonitis, and back strain. The act also requires employers to keep various types of records about on-the-job safety and accidents, and prohibits them from retaliating against workers who bring health or safety related claims against them. It is enforced by the Occupational Safety and Health Administration, an arm of the U.S. Department of Labor.

COMPENSATION AND BENEFITS

An employer may pay the members of a staff in several different ways, some of whom will receive additional income in tips. The compensation picture is often made more complex by overtime pay, bonuses, commissions, incentive pay, and perquisites, while wage and hour laws, both federal and state, have many provisions that come into play when payroll is figured. Every employer must know the requirements well. Let us look first at the usual ways in which various positions are compensated.

Methods of Compensation and Rates of Pay

Bar personnel are usually paid by one of two methods: straight-time hourly wages or a fixed salary. Tips add substantially to the earnings of bartenders and cocktail servers, while a supervisor or beverage director may receive a monthly bonus.

Table 12.1 shows (in general terms) the typical methods of compensation for beverage-related positions. As usual, no one formula applies to all enterprises, and wages and salaries vary widely from one enterprise to another and from one locality to another.

Rate of pay is related in a general way to sales volume, number of employees, and number of seats; in other words, the bigger and busier a place is, the better the base pay (but not in direct proportion). To a lesser degree

Table 12.1

How Bar Personnel Are Paid

Position	Base Pay	Supplemental Pay
Barback	Hourly wage	
Cocktail server	Hourly wage	Tips (customer-paid)
Bartender, public	Hourly wage or weekly salary	Tips (customer-paid)
Bartender, service	Hourly wage or weekly salary	
Unit manager	Salary, weekly/monthly	Periodic bonus (employer-paid)
Beverage director (corporate)	Annual salary	Periodic bonus (employer-paid)

pay is related to type of ownership, with sole proprietors generally paying less than partnerships and corporations. Other differences in pay may come from local and regional differences in prevailing wages and cost of living, local labor supply and demand, and union activity.

Federal laws require every employer to give equal pay for equal work without regard to age, sex, race, national origin, creed, or skin color.

Federal Minimum Wage Requirements

In determining compensation, federal and state minimum-wage laws provide a base. When it was first created in 1938, the federal minimum wage was 25 cents an hour! The federal Fair Labor Standards Act (FLSA) that sets the minimum wage was last amended in 1996, and the hourly rate is now $5.15. (At this writing, Congress is debating the possibility of raising it to $6.15 per hour in two annual 50-cent increments.)

Paying the minimum wage to employees applies to any food/beverage enterprise grossing $500,000 a year. A few states have decided the federal amount is not enough, and more than a dozen have passed their own minimum wage laws. Washington and Oregon currently have the highest, at $6.50 per hour.

A special provision of the act concerns wages of tipped employees, who are defined as persons receiving at least $30 per month in tips. The employer may consider the tips part of that person's salary, and pay him or her a smaller hourly rate of $2.13, allowing for a **tip credit** of $3.02. However, if an individual's tips plus wages amount to less than the minimum wage ($5.15 per hour) in any workweek, the employer must make up the difference. It is the employer's responsibility to advise employees of the tip-credit provisions of the act.

Suppose, for example, a waitress working a 40-hour week makes $85.20 in wages at $2.13 per hour and $150 for the week in tips, an average of $3.75 per hour in tips. Her tip average is well above the employer's tip credit of

$3.02 per hour. (Remember, these amounts are calculated using year 2000 figures, which may change slightly over the years.) The next week, however, a spell of bad weather means less business. This waitress makes only $100 (or $2.50 an hour) in tips. Her employer must make up the additional 52 cents per hour to bring her total pay for the week up to the minimum wage of $5.15.

In 1990, the act was amended to add a lower, **subminimum wage** for employees under age 20 during their first 90 days on the job. At this writing, it is $4.25 per hour. But employers are prohibited from getting rid of full-time employees or cutting their hours to hire lower-paid newcomers. The subminimum wage may also apply to full-time students in the workplace, some apprentice and trainee jobs, and individuals whose productivity is limited by a physical or mental disability. The idea was to encourage employment of youth and disabled persons, but the use of the subminimum wage in these situations is decided by the U.S. Department of Labor on a case-by-case basis. The Labor Department has free publications that explain the subminimum wage and how it can be used.

Defining the Workweek

The FLSA also requires that minimum wage be computed on the basis of a **workweek,** whether the employee is paid weekly, biweekly, monthly, or at some other interval. A workweek is defined as a fixed and regularly recurring period of 168 hours—7 consecutive 24-hour periods, beginning any day of the week at any hour of the day. For computing minimum wages and overtime payments, each workweek stands alone; that is, you can't average two or more weeks of different working hours to make your calculations.

Employees must be paid for all hours that they work in any workweek, including breaks or rest periods of 5 to 20 minutes that occur within their work times. You do not have to pay employees for a meal period or lunch break, but you do have to pay them for short coffee breaks or rest periods. And, if "lunch" involves performing any work-related duties while they eat, you must pay them for that time, too.

Tip Pooling

The FLSA specifies that all tips belong to employees. The employer cannot claim any part of the tip money for the business. However, the employer may require **tip pooling.** This is when servers or bartenders **"tip out,"** or share a percentage of their tips with barbacks, busboys, and other service people who have direct guest contact—that is, they're part of the "team," but don't generally get tipped. The tip-pooling requirement cannot apply to an employee until his or her tips have satisfied the employer's $3.02 tip credit. In other words, the tipped employee does not pay into a tip pool until after he or she has made enough in tips to bring their total hourly pay up to the minimum wage for the week.

In some cases—say, for large parties—there's a policy at many bars or restaurants of adding a compulsory service charge (of 15 or 20 percent) to the bill. Interestingly, this charge is not considered a tip. Instead, it is defined by the act as part of the employer's gross receipts. In this case, the employer must pay at least the full minimum wage to service personnel, and must pay applicable sales taxes on the full amount of the service charge.

Other Charges

Most bars, as part of their ambience, specify uniforms for both bartenders and servers, and some employers charge uniform costs to employees. The FLSA says such charges must not reduce an employee's wages below the minimum wage. The employer must also reimburse employees the costs of laundering uniforms (as necessary business expenses for the employer) if such cost reduces employee wages below the minimum wage level.

Employers also cannot deduct from paychecks such occurrences as breakage of glassware or a shortage in the day's cash register receipts, if the deductions drop the total wages below the minimum wage rate or if they reduce overtime pay that is legitimately due to the employee. So you see why it is important for both workers and their supervisors to keep accurate, written records of all these factors: to ensure that everybody gets paid fairly and that no one feels cheated.

For all its technical complexity, there are some standard workplace issues that the FLSA does not address and does not require. These include: vacation, holiday, severance or sick pay; meal or rest periods; bonus pay for working holidays, nights, or weekends; pay raises or fringe benefits; or immediate payment of final wages to anyone who is fired. The act doesn't even require that fired employees receive a reason for being terminated. It also does not limit the hours in a day, or days in a week, an employee can work if he or she is over age 16.

Supervisors as Exempt Employees

The FLSA exempts supervisors, managers, administrators, and executives from minimum wage requirements. They are called **exempt employees,** while those covered by the act are called **nonexempt employees.** Managers are considered exempt if:

- Their primary duty is to manage a company or department.
- They "regularly and customarily" direct the work of two or more other employees.

- They have the authority to hire and fire or have major input into the hiring and firing of other workers.
- They regularly exercise discretionary power in daily work activities.
- Any nonsupervisory duties that they are responsible for take up less than 40 percent of their work time
- They are paid at least $250 per week (the latest federal figure, admittedly old—from 1993).

All six of these requirements must be met for the employee to be considered supervisory or managerial. If they are not met, the employee is eligible to receive overtime pay. And that brings us to the next topic.

Calculating Regular and Overtime Pay

The Fair Labor Standards Act requires that employees receive overtime pay for any time over 40 hours worked in one workweek. The act further specifies that the rate of overtime pay must be at least one and a half times the employee's regular rate.

The **regular rate** for figuring overtime is always an hourly rate. No matter whether the employee's rate of pay is tied to the hour, the shift, the week, the month, or a percentage of sales, pay for a given week is translated into an hourly rate by dividing the week's pay by the number of hours worked that week. A week's pay includes all remuneration: wages or salary, commissions, attendance bonuses, production bonuses, shift differentials, and tips credited as part of a worker's wages (the *tip credit*).

Let's see how employers use the regular hourly rate to calculate the correct amount of overtime pay for different methods of payment.

The Hourly Employee. To figure overtime for an hourly employee, begin with his or her regular hourly rate and simply multiply it by 1.5. For example, an employee's hourly wage is $8.00 and she works 48 hours in one workweek; the calculation would be as follows:

Regular rate: $8.00   40 hours @ $8.00 = $320.00
Overtime rate: $8.00 × 1.5 = $12.00   8 hours @ $12.00 =   96.00
                                   Week's gross pay: $416.00

Another way to figure this is the following:

Regular rate: $8.00   48 hours @ $8.00 = $384.00
Overtime Premium: $8 × 0.5 = $4.00   8 hours @ $4.00 =   32.00
                                   Week's gross pay: = $416.00

The Salaried Employee Paid Monthly. The regular rate is computed by multiplying the monthly rate by 12 (months) and dividing by 52 (weeks per year) to find the weekly salary. This is divided by the number of hours worked to find the hourly rate. For this example let's assume an employee's monthly salary is $2,500 and that he works a standard 40 hours a week. But in one busy week, he works 48 hours. Here's the calculation:

$2,500 × 12 (months) = $30,000.00 yearly salary
$30,000 ÷ 52 (weeks) = $576.92 weekly salary
$576.92 ÷ 40 (hours) = $14.42 is the standard hourly wage

Now let's calculate this person's overtime rate:

$14.42 × 1.5 ("time and a half") = $21.63
$21.63 × 8 (overtime hours) = $173.04 is the overtime pay for this week

Monthly gross pay would combine the regular monthly pay with the overtime pay:

$2,500 (regular) + $173.04 (overtime) = $2,673.04

The Salaried Weekly Employee Working Fewer Than 40 Hours a Week.

The regular rate is computed by dividing salary by hours regularly worked. The employee is paid this hourly rate up to 40 hours and 1.5 times this rate thereafter. In this example we'll say this employee also earns $2,500 per month, but works regularly only 35 hours per week. In a recent busy week, she worked 45 hours, calculated as:

$2,500 × 12 (months) = $30,000 yearly salary
$30,000 ÷ 52 (weeks) = $576.92 weekly salary
$576.92 ÷ 35 (hours) = $16.48 is the standard hourly wage

In calculating this person's overtime rate, remember that the regular hours worked are only 35. So the first 5 hours of "extra" time are used to satisfy the basic workweek requirement of 40 hours. This worker will receive only 5 hours of overtime pay.

$16.48 × 1.5 ("time and a half") = $24.72 is the hourly overtime rate
$24.72 × 5 (overtime hours) = $123.60 is the overtime pay for this week

Monthly gross pay would combine the regular monthly pay with the overtime pay:

$2,500 (regular) + $123.60 (overtime) = $2,623.60

The Employee Paid a Fixed Salary for Varying Hours per Week.

For this employee, the regular rate for computing overtime will vary with total hours worked, hence must be computed for each workweek. Since the straight salary applies by definition to all hours worked, only the overtime premium (of 0.5 times the regular rate) is added. In this example we'll say an employee is paid a straight salary of $400 a week. In a month, he worked

42 hours the first week, 50 the next, 45 the third, and 38 the fourth. Here are the four calculations:

Week 1

$$\$400 \div 42 \text{ (hours)} = \$9.52 \text{ regular rate}$$
$$\$9.52 \times 0.5 = \$4.76 \text{ overtime rate}$$
$$\$4.76 \times 2 \text{ hours overtime} = \$ 9.52$$
$$\text{Gross weekly pay: } \$400 + 9.52 = \$409.52$$

Week 2

$$\$400.00 \div 50 \text{ (hours)} = \$8.00 \text{ regular rate}$$
$$\$8.00 \times 0.5 = \$4.00 \text{ overtime rate}$$
$$\$4.00 \times 10 \text{ hours overtime} = \$40$$
$$\text{Gross weekly pay: } \$400 + 40 = \$440.00$$

Week 3

$$\$400.00 \div 45 = \$8.89 \text{ regular rate}$$
$$\$8.89 \times 0.5 = \$ 4.45 \text{ overtime rate}$$
$$\$4.45 \times 5 \text{ hours overtime} = \$22.25$$
$$\text{Gross weekly pay} = \$400 + 22.25 = \$422.25$$

For week 4 his pay is $400 because the hours he worked did not exceed 40, the amount covered by his fixed weekly salary.

The Minimum Wage Employee with Tip Credit and Extra Pay.
For computing the regular rate, the hourly wage is figured at minimum wage, since the employee will receive it either in tips or from the employer. This wage is multiplied by the hours regularly worked. To this figure, extra pay during the week is added. (This will include such things as bonuses or commissions, but not the balance of tips earned.) This total is then divided by the number of regular hours to arrive at the regular rate, after computing overtime for that week.

For example, a tipped employee whose base pay is minimum wage ($5.15 per hour) less the $3.02 tip credit, actually makes $2.13 per hour, which is paid by her employer. She is on the job 45 hours in one workweek and makes $150 in tips. In that same week, she earns a commission of $40 on wine sales along with a $70 bonus for having the highest overall sales for the week. First let's figure her standard weekly earnings under the minimum wage law:

$$\$5.15 \times 40 \text{ (hours)} = \$206.00 + \$40 + \$70 \text{ (bonuses)} = \$316.00$$
$$\$316.00 \div 40 \text{ (hours)} = \$7.90 \text{ regular hourly rate}$$

Now let's figure her overtime pay rate:

$$\$7.90 \times 1.5 \text{ (``time and a half'')} = \$11.85 \text{ overtime rate}$$
$$\$11.85 \times 5 \text{ hours overtime} = \$59.25 \text{ overtime pay}$$

So, altogether, this waitress earned:

$316 (wages and bonuses) + $59.25 (overtime) = $ 375.25

However, now we've got to deduct the tip credit, which is:

$3.02 (hourly tip credit) × 40 (hours) = $120.80

So her total weekly pay is her earnings, minus the tip credit:

$375.25 − 120.80 = $ 254.45 (Gross weekly pay)

Here's an even simpler computation for minimum wage employees with tip credits. The first 40 hours an employee works, you pay them at the minimum wage rate. To determine the overtime rate, just multiply the minimum wage rate by 1.5, then subtract the hourly tip credit. For instance:

$5.15 (minimum wage) × 1.5 ("time and a half") = $7.73 overtime rate
$7.73 (overtime rate) − $3.02 (tip credit) = $4.71 net overtime rate

As an example, we'll say an employee receives customer tips works 49 hours in a workweek and makes $170 that week in tips. For the first 40 hours, you pay him the tipped employee rate, which is:

$5.15 (minimum wage) − $3.02 (tip credit) = $2.13 per hour
$2.13 × 40 (hours) = $85.20

Now, add the overtime:

$4.71 (overtime rate, less tip credit) × 9 (overtime hours) = $42.39
Gross weekly pay: $85.20 + 42.39 = $127.59

(Also note: To check whether the amount of reported tips is sufficient to cover the tip credit requirements, divide the tip amount by the total number of hours the employee worked. In this case, the result is $3.46 per hour, which is more than the statutory $3.02 tip credit.)

Hourly employees must be paid from the time they report to work until the time they go off duty, whether they are working or not. Even if they go on working voluntarily beyond their normal hours, they must be paid for the extra time.

Contract Labor. Sometimes, people are hired seasonally, on a part-time basis, or as consultants to help with a particular project. They may be paid hourly, monthly or by flat fee, but with the special agreement that they won't be covered by the standard employee benefits and that no taxes or Social Security will be deducted from their paychecks. These people may refer to themselves as contract labor, freelancers, consultants, or independent contractors.

No matter what you call them, contract laborers are exempt from the minimum wage regulations. However, it is important to examine the relationship between the worker and the business, because the Internal Revenue Service certainly will! Some companies have been reprimanded in recent years for firing standard, full-time employees, then rehiring them as "contractors" to avoid having to pay employment-related taxes.

The IRS looks at the employee/business relationship with these three criteria in mind:

- **Behavioral control.** If the employer has control over where, when, and how the work is to be done, the worker is an employee, not a contractor.
- **Financial control.** If the worker is reimbursed for all business expenses, and has fixed costs—either profits or losses—then he or she can be considered a contract laborer.
- **Type of relationship.** This includes a number of things, like whether there is a written contract that describes the relationship; whether the services are a key aspect of the business; and whether the relationship is permanent. It is smart to document these types of "freelance" working relationships in writing, to protect both parties.

Payroll Taxes, Benefits, and Perquisites

In addition to wages and salaries, two other forms of compensation add to labor costs: payroll taxes and fringe benefits. Payroll taxes fund Social Security and unemployment programs. To employees, these are both forms of deferred compensation, but to the employer they are real and present labor costs. At this time, the employer's share of federal employment taxes includes:

Social Security taxes, also known as FICA (the Federal Insurance Contribution Act): This requires employers to pay 6.2 percent of each employee's wages and tips, for workers who make $76,200 or less per year. You are also required to withhold another 6.2 percent from the employee's gross pay, as his or her contribution to Social Security.

Federal Unemployment taxes, also known as FUTA: The employer pays this tax, which is 6.2 percent of the first $7,000 of all employees' wages and tips per year. However, most states give businesses a credit for this tax, which can effectively drop the rate to less than 1 percent. States also have unemployment taxes, which vary depending on the rate of unemployment claims against the employer.

Medicare is a tax of 1.45 percent of each employee's wages and tips that is paid by the employer; another 1.45 percent is withheld from the employee's paycheck: All wages and tips are subject to Medicare taxes—there is no upper income limit.

Tax deductions from paychecks cause a lot of employee grumbling because of the wide disparity between their gross pay and the much-reduced "take-home" pay. Every time an income-tax rate or a Social Security rate increases, the take-home pay drops accordingly. Yet at the same time, the payroll expense to the employer reaches considerably beyond the base pay.

What are those benefits that don't show up in the paycheck? The term **fringe benefits** refers to all tangible or significant compensation other than wages. The most common benefits are free meals and paid vacations.

If you let employees eat meals at your business because it's convenient for you, the value of these meals cannot be charged to them as taxable income. It is not subject to income tax withholding or any of the federal taxes listed above—that is, as long as the meals are provided free, and are consumed on your premises.

Many employers also offer group medical insurance and group life insurance. These costs are also not considered part of their wages, and are not subject to any federal taxes.

The majority of hospitality industry employers grant their workers, including bar personnel, paid vacations. As with other industries, the number of weeks of vacation time increases as years of service increase.

Some enterprises reimburse their management employees for job-related educational expenses and pay professional dues. Benefits that are related to specific jobs or job levels are known as **perquisites,** or "perks" for short. A car or car expenses for use on the job or a company credit card for business-related meals or travel are common perquisites. Sometimes interest-free loans are provided to top-level personnel.

Benefits and perquisites are part of an employer's labor cost, while for the employee, except for paid vacations and other cash benefits, they are tax-free additions to income.

Records and Reports

As soon as you become an employer, you must fill out the form to obtain an Employer Identification Number (EIN) from the Internal Revenue Service. It is the nine-digit number that you use as you report and pay federal taxes.

When hiring a new employee, each one must also fill out an IRS W-4 form (and/or an I-9 form, which was discussed earlier in this chapter). Use the W-4 information to determine the amount of income tax to withhold from each employee's wages and tips.

You must keep these forms on file and maintain records for each employee from his or her first day on the job. For workers who are subject to the minimum wage laws, the FLSA says the following information must be kept:

- Personal information: the worker's name, gender, home address, occupation, and birthdate (if under age 19). (You might as well keep their Social Security number on file, too.)
- The hour and day when their workweek begins.
- The total hours each person worked, by day and by workweek.
- Total daily or weekly "straight time" (regular pay) earnings.
- Their regular hourly pay rate for any week when overtime was worked.
- The overtime pay they received, by workweek.
- Any deductions from, or additions to, wages.

- The total wages paid to them for each pay period.
- The dates of pay days and the dates included in each pay period.

You must file monthly, quarterly, and annual reports with the IRS, and pay your share of federal taxes, as well as passing on the amounts you withheld from employees' paychecks. To keep abreast of federal rate and regulation changes, be sure you have a copy of the current year's IRS Circular E, the "Employer's Tax Guide." It will also contain the latest details on reporting taxable tips.

Wage Complaints by Employees. The other good reason to implement thorough, accurate record-keeping procedures is in case of a challenge by employees who complain they have not been paid or paid fairly. The U.S. Department of Labor's Wage and Hour Division can conduct investigations into these claims, or employees can hire a private attorney and file a civil lawsuit.

If the Labor Department audit of your records finds the claims are valid, you can be liable for payment of back wages and penalties. It might be two years of back pay or, if the violation has been determined to be "willful," it could be three years of back pay. "Willful" violations also carry a fine of up to $10,000 or even a prison term. And you cannot intimidate or fire an employee who has brought such a claim during the investigation. That's a violation of the FLSA.

Reporting Tip Income. You should encourage service employees to keep careful daily track of their tips. Employees who are tipped directly, either by cash or credit card, must report their tips to the IRS as income, less the amount they give up for tip pooling. As their employer, you must also know how much they make in tips, because you have to count tips as part of the employee's income when you deduct things like income tax and Social Security amounts, and when you pay the company's part of Social Security or unemployment taxes.

It is also your responsibility to report tips, which are figured as a percentage of gross sales, to the IRS. The current percentage figure required from the employer and expected from the employee is not less than 8 percent of gross sales. The employer must report tips of more than $20 per person per month, whether or not the employees report them.

What if your employees underreport the tip amounts they receive? The IRS is supersensitive to this very common problem; therefore, they require you to "allocate" tips. Here's how it works: Let's say that the combined food and beverage sales amount for your bar is $30,000, and you have 10 employees who receive tips. Each employee is allocated $3,000 of your total sales, and it is assumed (by the IRS) that each one made 8 percent of the total sales figure (or $2,400) as tips, on which he or she must pay taxes.

It may not seem like much for a waitress or bartender to pocket a few bucks tax-free. But tip income totals more than $7 billion annually, and the

IRS wants its share, just like any other type of income. Hiding or underreporting tip money has been such a problem that the IRS now has a voluntary program called the Tip Reporting Alternative Commitment, or TRAC. It gives employers protection from IRS audits if they keep proper records and instruct employees about their tip-reporting obligations. Be forewarned, though: both businesses and employees *will* be audited if the IRS suspects them of underreporting.

Other Types of Records. You must also keep information and withholding records for state insurance and tax programs, and you must file state returns and make the required payments.

Each employee must be given a year-end statement (called a W-2 form) of the total wages or salary paid, deductions for the year, and tips reported. Copies of this form must also be sent to the IRS and the Social Security Administration.

Record-keeping can be enormously simplified by computerized accounting programs. Virtually all payroll functions can now be handled electronically.

SUMMING UP

After reading this chapter, perhaps you have a whole new appreciation for your own employers, past and present. Did you have any idea there were so many laws, rules, and potential pitfalls when it comes to hiring, scheduling. and paying employees?

There are many reasons to proceed carefully in the bar business and to document as much as possible. This includes writing detailed job descriptions, training manuals, alcohol awareness and emergency procedures; taking notes in staff meetings and after confrontations with employees or guests; keeping written schedules and time logs; and keeping state and federal paperwork up to date. Be aware of the state and federal laws that govern hiring, alcohol service, and minimum wages, since these occasionally change.

Advertise for workers in the kinds of places and publications you'd expect them to look for jobs, and ask your current employees for recommendations. Both a written application and in-person interview are essential.

A training procedure should be set up from the first day on the job for a new hire, and then be an ongoing priority. Short, regularly scheduled training meetings not only will get your rules and messages across, but will also serve the important function of motivating employees and keeping them "in the loop." Beyond that, the employer who is fair, who takes care to communicate clearly, who respects employees as individuals while demanding their best work at all times, who succeeds in building a team of loyal workers, will be the one whose employees, in turn, help him or her to build the business. Wages, benefits, and incentives; laws, rules, and paperwork are also important, but not as crucial as the positive spirit conveyed from the top down.

POINTS TO PONDER

1. List and briefly explain three reasons why it is important to hire good bartenders.

2. List three things a sommelier should be able to do for his or her employer, other than recommend and open bottles of wine for customers.

3. What are the two things you must do to put together a good job description to hire someone? (Hint: They are both types of lists.) Name and briefly define each of them.

4. Where would you look for good potential employees for your bar? List places.

5. If you are a bar manager, what can you discuss in a job interview with a prospective employee?

6. What are the three kinds of training you should provide for employees? List them and write a sentence about the importance of each.

7. What are the basic ideas on which beverage laws are based?

8. Of all the workplace liability topics you read about in this chapter, are there any that surprised you? Explain why.

9. What is a tip credit, and how do bar or restaurant owners use it?

10. A bartender earns a weekly salary of $600, but someone called in sick one shift, so he volunteered to work 7 extra hours. During the week, he received $180 in tips. Figure his total pay for the week.

TERMS OF THE TRADE

barback	job analysis	tastevin
bartender	job specifications	tip credit
beverage steward	nonexempt employees	tip out
bouncer	perquisites	tip pooling
cover charge	regular rate (for overtime)	wine steward (cellarmaster)
exempt employees	sommelier	workweek
fringe benefits	subminimum wage	
I-9 form	task analysis	

CHAPTER 13

Purchasing, Receiving, Storage, and Inventory

Our focus shifts now from the front of the house to what goes on behind the scenes. The next two chapters will deal with managing the business side of the bar. This begins with providing the beverages to be sold to the customers: maintaining a steady supply and keeping track of the supply to ensure that what is bought produces sales. Managing the storeroom is a third priority, including physical care to maintain quality of the products, and watchdogging to maintain quantity.

This chapter examines purchasing policies and decisions; the routines of purchasing, receiving, and issuing; the inventory records and procedures commonly used; and the use of inventory figures to measure bar cost and purchasing efficiency.

This chapter should help you . . .

- Decide what, when, where, and how much liquor, beer, and wine to buy.
- Decide what to look for in selecting suppliers and examining their prices and discounts.
- Establish par stock for each bar and minimum and maximum storeroom stock levels.
- Know the functions and relationships of purchase orders, invoices, and credit memos.
- Set up routines for ordering and receiving.
- Store each type of beverage properly, efficiently, and safely.
- Establish inventory procedures and conduct physical inventories.
- Figure inventory value, bar cost, and inventory-turnover rate.

You may wonder how a straightforward subject like buying liquor and supplying it to the bar could take up so many book pages. Part of the answer is that alcoholic beverages are an investment in income-producing stock, and there are many facets to making the best investment for the least money. Another part of the answer is that the purchasing and the record-keeping processes are of critical importance to other aspects of the business. Still another part is that alcohol has an irresistible attraction for many people, and if you don't keep track of it, it will "evaporate," so to speak.

The goal of beverage purchasing is to provide a steady supply of ingredients for the drinks you sell at costs that will maximize profits. The purchasing function moves in a continuous cycle with several distinct phases:

- **Planning and ordering.** Selecting what you need at the most advantageous prices.
- **Receiving.** Taking delivery of exactly what you have ordered—brands, sizes, and quantities—at specified prices, in good condition.
- **Storing.** Keeping your beverage supplies until needed in a place that is secure against theft and deterioration.
- **Issuing.** Transferring your beverages from storeroom to bar, where they will be used to make drinks for your customers.

The sale of these drinks keeps the cycle revolving, since you must constantly replenish the supplies consumed. But it doesn't revolve by itself; it has to be managed. The process must be responsive to needs (sales volume and customer tastes), to the market (supply and price), to cash flow (money available for investment), and to indicators of change in any of these factors. The beverage manager must know what is going on at all times.

In a small operation, purchasing may be the responsibility of the owner or the head bartender. Large operations usually have a full-time beverage manager, while hotel and restaurant chains often have an entire department devoted to purchasing and other aspects of beverage management. But the principles and problems are much the same, no matter how large or small the enterprise.

PLANNING THE PURCHASING

The term **purchasing,** as it applies to food and beverage operations, is usually a two-step process. The first step is the **selection process,** making the decisions about what is to be served, what brands and sizes and quantities to buy, what to make from scratch or purchase premade. Selection also includes the amounts, styles, and sizes of glassware to be used.

Step 2 is the **procurement process,** the method used for purchasing items. This involves choosing and working with vendors, using a standard system of ordering, deciding on a budget and sticking to it, and determining how often to replenish stock.

Many factors go into the making of purchasing decisions. Some are management policies that, once established, should be followed to the letter. Others are day-to-day decisions based on current situations. They all boil down to: what to buy, where to buy it, how much to buy, when to buy, and what to pay.

What to Buy

Deciding what to buy involves two basic policy decisions: the quality of the beverages you will pour and the variety of items you will have available.

To meet customers' needs and avoid overstocked bars and storerooms, today's bar managers use a policy commonly known as **category management.** This involves tracking what sells and what doesn't and using that information to create a beverage program that delivers the best product mix to customers and the maximum profit for the bar. Today's sophisticated point-of-sale (POS) system can be an invaluable tool in accomplishing this.

The POS is very much like a personal computer. Its touch-screen technology and easy programmability give the user the ability to track multiple types of data: the brands of alcohol used in a drink and the server who sold it. (Finding out who isn't selling as much is also valuable as an indicator of who needs additional training.)

In a large operation, the POS terminals are "workstations," linked to a central computer (which is, ironically, also called a "server"). Another feature of these systems is the capability to keep a running inventory, automatically "deleting" the standard amount of each liquor that is used to mix each cocktail. Theoretically, this should give a bar manager almost instant usage numbers, which can later be compared with actual physical inventory. Some systems can even be programmed to draft purchase orders and e-mail them to a wholesaler when inventory hits certain levels.

In a large chain, computerization and category management are tremendously helpful. A company that operates several units can compare brand movement between locations and refine the menus, inventories, and promotional strategies accordingly. At Ruth's Chris Steak Houses, a popular southern fine-dining chain based in Louisiana, it was noted that one bar hardly sold any cognac. The reason? It was located in a seldom-seen portion of the backbar.

Market Watch magazine is an additional source that can be used to track beverage trends and desirable brands. According to the research firm *Impact Databank,* a "hot" brand is one that is:

- An established brand with a minimum 20 percent annual growth rate.
- A brand that has experienced double-digit growth rates for the past three years.
- A product that is new but "significant" in some way.

"Hot brands" must also meet annual volume requirements:

- For spirits, depletion of 200,000 9-liter cases
- For major domestic beer brands, 3.4 million 2.25-gallon cases
- For other, specialty beer brands, 1.1 million 2.25-gallon cases
- For imported beers, 1 million 2.25-gallon cases
- For domestic wines, 250,000 cases
- For imported wines, 200,000 cases

These findings are published regularly in *Market Watch*. Computers and technology give bars and restaurants access to more specific brand information than ever before. This negates the old "shotgun marketing" approach, whereby the bar would try one idea, then another, and another, in hopes of "hitting" on something successful. With research, the decisions are better informed and more likely to reap rewards.

Quality and Variety. Take quality first, since it will depend on your clientele and the quality they expect and are willing to pay for. It would be foolish to buy premium brands or fine French wines for a low-budget clientele, and equally foolish not to offer such items in a luxury restaurant. As in everything else, you must know your customers.

Beyond this, there is the quality of your **well brands** to consider, the liquors you pour in mixed drinks when the customer does not call for a specific brand. Also known as your **house brands** or **house liquors,** these represent about half of the liquor used in an average bar. Choose a set of well brands and stick to them, for the sake of consistency in your drinks. Many bars use inexpensive brands in the well on the theory that customers can't tell the difference in a mixed drink. Others use familiar, advertised brands in the middle price range. Still others use premium brands—this is sometimes called a **premium well** or **super well**—which they feature with pride in their merchandising.

By carrying premium brands in the well, in addition to making an impression, you eliminate having to carry well brands. This means less inventory and less cost. Premium brands are a good choice for bars where the clientele is value-conscious—that is, willing to spend a little extra to receive a higher-quality drink. Superpremium brands have the advantages of strong name recognition and customer loyalty, but they won't be worth your extra expenditure if you don't do a good job of letting your customers know they are being used.

Avoid using cheap liquors in the well, but charging higher prices. If you think you are fooling your customers, you are fooling yourself. Taste your own drinks and you will notice the difference, just as your customers will. You may save a few pennies per drink but you will never know how many customers never came back and how many others they told about your "cheap, high-priced drinks!" Besides, you don't save all that much. Take, for example, a liter of scotch costing $15 and one costing $9. If the portion is 1 ounce, the $15 scotch costs 44 cents per drink and the $9 scotch costs 26 cents, a difference of 18 cents per drink. Is the savings worth it when you may lose customers?

Since the drinks made using well brands are typically sold at all the same price, you can calculate the overall cost of your well by averaging it. Take the wholesale cost of the six standard well products (gin, bourbon, scotch, rum, vodka, and tequila), then divide by 6 to arrive at an average cost-per-liter. Divide that figure by 33.8 (and subtract any spillage allowance) to determine the cost per ounce of your well brands.

As further waste control, arrange the sequence of well brands in your speed rail (that bottle-width rack in the underbar) in this fashion:

GIN   BOURBON   VODKA   SCOTCH   RUM   TEQUILA

Light and dark liquors are interspersed, so they are less likely to be used accidentally by a bartender in a hurry.

The second major decision is the variety of items you will stock. The average bar in the United States may carry as many as 130 liquors and liqueurs on the backbar, and a showy backbar lined with bottles is the hallmark of many operations. Some bars take pride in never having to tell a customer, "I'm sorry but we don't have that." Such a policy, while it can be good merchandising for some types of clientele, has the potential of expanding inventory indefinitely with items that do not move. Liquor that does not sell does not earn a penny of profit, except to the degree that it contributes to atmosphere and image on that great-looking backbar.

Many bars prefer to limit their offerings to popular and well-advertised brands of each item, with the number of brands varying with the type and size of the operation. If a customer calls for a brand you don't carry, you probably won't lose either the sale or the customer if you can offer a well-known brand of comparable quality. But offer it—don't try to substitute another brand without the customer's knowledge. That is a very bad practice that will only create an image of mistrust for your place and your bartenders.

Still another approach is to deliberately limit the number of brands and items stocked by developing a printed drink menu based on a small number of beverages, as discussed in Chapter 11. Most customers will respond to such a menu by ordering from the drinks listed, and questions of call brands and unusual drinks seldom come up.

Where you draw the line on brands and items to be stocked will depend on your clientele, your type of enterprise, your volume of business, and the money available for such investment. But it is wise to draw the line somewhere and then hold it. A common mistake is to let inventory grow, over time, to unmanageable levels. Products do fall out of fashion, as in any industry. One way to avoid this proliferation of brands and bottles is never to add a new item of unpredictable demand without eliminating a slow-moving item from your list. In this case, "slow-moving" means a product that takes nine months or longer to use up a single bottle.

You also need to keep up with new products and to anticipate changes in customer tastes. One way to do this is to consult frequently with the salespeople for the wholesale buyers you deal with. They know who is launching a huge advertising campaign or coming out with a new light beer, and what new liqueur or imported beer is big in California or New York and coming your way. Many beverage managers have a regular time for sales personnel to call. In this way, the manager is not interrupted while immersed in some other task, and the salesperson has a receptive audience.

Do not, however, let anyone tell you what you should buy. Consider suggestions, but measure them against your own ground rules and current needs. Sales representatives will push their own products; that is their job. Compare what they say with what their competitors say and make up your own mind.

Another way to keep up with trends is to read sales and market surveys in trade magazines, such as *Market Watch,* for their survey results of those hot new brands. For local trends, remember to read the liquor-store ads in your local newspapers.

Beverage buyers can also peruse CD-ROMs to find what they need. In many cases, these have eliminated bulky product catalogs you used to obtain from suppliers. If a beverage is available somewhere in the world, and is distributed by someone, it is very likely you can locate it on a CD-ROM catalog. The next logical step is to link your own computer to the vendor's, so you can access current price lists, availability, and delivery information, and place orders by e-mail. On some systems, you can specify a replacement product you would consider acceptable if your first choice is not available. Some of the most sophisticated systems enable you to access historical data—such as how frequently you've ordered a certain product—or are set up to "cost" drink recipes.

If all this sounds less quaint than the neighborhood pub you've dreamed of owning, consider this: A 2000 survey in *Restaurants and Institutions* magazine says 29 percent of all restaurants and bars in the United States already use the Internet on a daily basis.

No matter how sophisticated the ordering process, buying individual products is still mostly a matter of brand selection and common sense. Where the liquor or beer brand concerns the customer, buy the brands your customers will buy. For your well, select the brands that make the quality of drinks you want to pour. This goes for your vermouths and liqueurs as well. It is a good idea to taste your own mixed drinks with different brands of spirits and liqueurs. Generic liqueurs in particular can taste quite different from one brand to another, and the expensive imported brands are not necessarily the best.

Buying wines is somewhat more complicated than buying beers and spirits. For one thing, customer demand is less clear-cut. For house wines, more and more enterprises are replacing generic wines with inexpensive varietal wines in 1-liter and 1.5-liter bottles. Some restaurants pour house wines by the glass from 750-ml bottles, and have the same wine available for sale by the bottle. An alert waiter can often convert orders for two or three individual glasses to a bottle of wine for the table.

Wines for your wine list need a different approach. Because they vary from one winemaker to another, one vintage to another, and one year of age to another, you must either rely on an expert or know a good deal about wines yourself. You can safely buy most young whites, rosés, and some of the simpler reds and sell them right away. The older the vintage date, the more skeptical you should be.

Fine whites and reds require special purchasing decisions. They should not be sold to customers before they are ready to drink. This means you must tie up your money in the wine cellar while they mature, or take a chance on purchasing them later at higher prices—if they are still available.

Keep supplies of the wines on your list in line with demand without overbuying. If you run out, you lose sales and disappoint customers; but if you overbuy, you have money tied up unproductively and may run the risk of having a wine outlive its life span in storage.

You should have regular sessions with salespeople who can advise you on current availability of the wines on your list as well as closeouts and bargain specials. But beware of a discounted price for a wine that may be approaching deterioration. Taste wines before you buy, then choose according to what you know of your customers' tastes, and get as much expert advice as you can. You may find it helpful to reread Chapter 5 on developing a wine list.

Where to Buy

The beverage buyer does not always have a great deal of choice about where to buy. State laws govern the purchase and sale of alcoholic beverages, and these laws vary from one state to another. Local laws also come into play. The first thing a buyer should do is to study the laws of the state, county, city, and even precinct as they apply to liquor purchase.

In 19 states or jurisdictions, the retailer (the seller of alcoholic beverages to the consumer) must buy from state stores. These states are known as **control states** or **monopoly states.** In the remaining states—known as **license states**—and the District of Columbia, the buyer is typically allowed to purchase from any wholesaler licensed by the state and, in some states, from licensed distributors and manufacturers as well. Table 13.1 lists the current status of each state. There may be local restrictions, however. For example, a county may have a law against buying in another county. To further complicate matters, the requirements and limitations are usually not the same for beers and wines as they are for spirits.

Table 13.1

Control States and License States

Control States	License States	
Alabama	Alaska	Mississippi (retail only)
Idaho	Arizona	Missouri
Iowa[a]	Arkansas	Nebraska
Maine	California	Nevada
Michigan	Colorado	New Jersey
Mississippi (wholesale only)	Connecticut	New Mexico
Montana	Delaware	New York
New Hampshire	Florida	North Dakota
North Carolina	Georgia	Oklahoma
Ohio	Hawaii	Rhode Island
Oregon	Illinois	South Carolina
Pennsylvania	Indiana	South Dakota
Utah	Kansas	Tennessee
Vermont	Kentucky	Texas
Virginia	Louisiana	Wisconsin
Washington	Maryland	Wyoming (retail only)
West Virginia	Massachusetts	District of Columbia
Wyoming (wholesale only)	Minnesota	

[a] Iowa has no state stores; its control board, as sole wholesaler, sells to privately owned outlets it licenses to sell to retail consumers.

In license states, alcoholic beverages are sold to retailers by a number of wholesale liquor distributors. Each of these will offer a wide variety of brands, and will probably pride themselves in offering a few "exclusives"—that is, products or brand names not available from other distributors in that market.

Depending on your state's laws, the makers of the products (or the importers, if it comes from another country) may sell to distributors; and the distributors sell to the retailers. Almost always, you will have to deal with several suppliers, who carry different items and brands. In some areas, the healthy competition between suppliers works to your advantage, since each one tries hard to come up with ways to please or impress you, their customer. However, in many states, there are now only a few major distributors. That same competitive nature, along with the advent of e-commerce, has forced smaller distributors to sell out to bigger ones.

For the individually owned bar, this has some important implications. First, product choice may be limited, especially for less well-known or unusual items. Second, the fewer the vendors, the less likely it is that a buyer can negotiate for more "personalized" service—specific delivery times, for instance. The monopolistic trend forces the smaller bar to conform to the dictates of the vendor, like it or not.

In most license states, a master list is published monthly (by the state's liquor control authority) containing the names of all the wholesalers in the state, the lines they carry, and the prices they charge. Monthly beverage journals list discount and "post-off" (sales) schedules. Individual wholesalers also have product catalogs and price sheets, quantity discounts, special sales, and promotional materials. As you learned earlier in this chapter, at least some of this information is available on CD-ROM. Control states publish lists of all brands available and their prices, along with the addresses of state stores.

Dealing with sales representatives is often easier than working with lists. Though you may not be able to buy from them directly, they can tell you where you can buy their products. They can also keep you posted on special sales and promotions.

Supplier Relations. Where you have a choice, price is certainly one reason for buying from one supplier rather than another; and you should always get competitive bids for large orders from different suppliers. But consider also what services the supplier offers—or doesn't offer. For instance:

- How often does a given supplier deliver? The more frequently, the better; and daily is best, even though you do not order daily. You do not have to stock as much and can get something quickly in an emergency.
- Does the supplier alter quality, quantity, and/or delivery time standards? You don't want to deal with someone who has basic organizational problems.
- Where is the supplier located? Suppose you are in a small country town and your suppliers must travel 50 to 100 miles to reach you. Does distance affect the delivery schedule? What about the weather? Will your wine or beer travel for hours in the hot sun? Will snow and ice interrupt service?
- What resources does the supplier have? A large and varied inventory kept well stocked, or a small stock that is constantly being depleted? Temperature-controlled warehouse facilities? Refrigerated trucks?
- Does the supplier give proper and systematic care to goods in storage or in transit? Are wines kept at proper temperatures, bottles on their sides or upside down? Are draft beer and unpasteurized package beer kept refrigerated? It is a good idea to pay a visit to the warehouse to see how things are cared for.
- Must you buy a certain minimum per order? Is there a maximum? Can you adjust your orders to meet these requirements? Is it worth it?
- Does the supplier extend credit, and what are the terms? (This is not often a negotiable point because of government restrictions.)
- Can you buy mixes and accessories from the supplier at advantageous prices and quantities?
- What is the supplier's **lead time,** the time between ordering and delivery? You must estimate consumption and order far enough ahead to compensate for the gap. The shorter lead time, the better.

- How much consultation, and training of your staff members, is the supplier willing to give?
- What other services does the supplier offer: blank order forms, promotional materials, 24-hour telephone service?

The number of suppliers a bar deals with usually depends on the variety of products it wishes to carry. Consider more than one supplier for each category (beer, wine, spirits) because brands play such a strong role in your needs and because one vendor may be out of stock on one of your critical items. Not all suppliers carry all brands, by any means.

The explosion of electronic commerce (e-commerce) has opened some new doors for purchase, and with them, created some new controversy. Today, alcoholic beverages no longer have to move from producer to distributor to retailer. The business-to-business movement is still in its infancy with alcohol, because it is more strictly regulated than most other types of products and because every state seems to have a tangle of different laws about selling it. At the time of this writing, these legal concerns are still being addressed.

Distributors stand to lose an estimated $25 billion in product markups if retailers can purchase directly from producers—distilleries, wineries, brewers, and importers. But some forward-thinking merchants say the cyber-marketplace just makes it easier to do business with distributors. When price lists and orders can be e-mailed, instant or short-term specials can be offered by computer, and catalogs of items can be viewed and updated online, the bar manager or purchasing agent is the ultimate beneficiary.

How Much to Buy

This is a central question for the beverage buyer. The answer is enough but not too much—enough to serve your customers what they want but not so much that numbers of bottles stand idle on shelves for long periods tying up money you could put to better use. If you overorder, things sit around too long; if you underorder, you may find yourself short of popular brands and unable to get more on short notice. Your goal is to never run out of your well brands, your house wines, your draft beers, the popular bottled beers, and call brands of spirits. But you might not reorder a slow-moving item until your last bottle is half gone.

Establish a **par stock** for each bar in your facility, using a form similar to the one in Figure 13.1. You can determine par stock needs from your detailed sales records. (If you are still in the planning stage, you can guesstimate your rate of sale.) A general rule is to have enough of each type and brand to meet one and one-half times the needs of your busiest day of the week. For a small restaurant bar averaging $500 in daily sales, this might work out to be the open bottle plus two full ones for each fast-moving brand, and the open bottle plus one extra for each slower-moving brand.

Bar Par Stock Form
Bar Name
Address

Effective as of (date): _____   Bar Outlet: _____

Page _____ of _____ (total pages)

Item Number	Item Name	Size	Bar	Par	Item Number	Item Name	Size	Bar	Par

Figure 13.1 Bar par stock form.

From par stock needs for each bar, you can figure what you should have in the storeroom to back them up. This then becomes your par stock for the storeroom, your normal storeroom inventory (that is, merchandise on hand).

You can also use par stock to measure your daily consumption. The bottles it takes to bring the bar stock to par represent roughly the consumption of the day before. Over a week's time, these bottles will yield an accurate figure of average daily consumption. This can guide your rate of purchase. Par stock is also a way of keeping up with customer tastes. You know which brands are moving quickly because you have par stock as a measure of their popularity. Thus it tells you what to buy as well as how much you are using.

Whatever your buying interval, it is a good idea to set minimum and maximum stock levels for each item, to maintain your storeroom inventory. The minimum level may be supplemented by a reorder point that gives you lead time, so that the stock does not drop below the minimum level before you receive delivery. Your maximum level represents the dividing line between enough and too much. Like the par stock level at the bar, it should represent one and one-half times what you expect to need before you replenish your supply.

Why be concerned about having too much? There are several arguments for keeping a small inventory geared closely to your sales volume. The major point is that beverages are expensive, even at discount rates, and they tie up money that is not earning anything and may be needed elsewhere. When you do finally use a bottle of liquor you bought months ago at a discount, it may have cost you far more in lost use of the money you paid than the money you saved in buying it.

There are other problems with large inventories. One is security: the more liquor you have, the more tempting it is, the harder it is to keep track of, and the easier it is to steal. The larger the inventory, the more space and staff are needed and the greater the burden of record-keeping and taking physical inventory. Perishable items, such as beers, should never be overstocked; some wines also deteriorate quickly. Customer tastes may change suddenly, leaving you with items you will never use.

On the other hand, some wines should be bought in quantity because they are scarce and will quickly disappear from the market. You will want to buy enough of them to last as long as your printed wine list does.

Beverage wholesalers sell mostly in case lots, sometimes offering discounts for a certain number of cases. You can buy cases of spirits and wines in the bottle sizes shown in Table 13.2. The size bottles you buy will depend on the type and size of your establishment and even more on the way you serve your beverages.

Some suppliers will sell a *broken case* or *mixed case* (a case of 12 bottles made up of several brands or items of your specification) and some will sell certain items by the single bottle or, for wines, a minimum of three bottles. The cost per bottle is higher for items in a broken case or by the bottle; the cost per bottle is lowest when purchased by the case or in multiple-case lots.

Certainly you should buy by the case anything you use a lot of—your well brands, house wines, domestic beers, and popular brands—to take advantage of cost savings as well as ensure an adequate supply. From there on, it becomes a matter of calculating your rate of use for each item and matching it with your purchasing intervals.

As you decide what and how much to stock, consider two more things: **carrying costs** and **capital risk.** Your carrying costs are the total combined dollar value of the liquor, wine, beer, mixes, and supplies at the bar. This figure should not vary widely, month to month. Capital risk is the risk you take when a bottle of liquor leaves the storeroom and goes to the bar—where it can be wasted, spilled, given away, consumed by employees, or otherwise not sold for profit. The way to control capital risks is to maintain a tight inventory, store as little as possible, and consistently enforce your inventory policies.

When to Buy

When and how often you place an order will depend on the volume of your business, the size inventory you are willing to stock, the requirements and schedules of the suppliers, the scheduling of your receiving people, the specials you want to take advantage of, and such variables as holidays and conventions and special events or a run of bad weather. Some enterprises order daily, some once per accounting period, others somewhere in between. Some might buy wine once a year, spirits weekly, and beer every day.

The more frequently you buy, the less inventory you have to cope with. On the other hand, every order initiates the whole purchasing-receiving-storing routine, which may not always be labor-efficient.

Other factors affecting the timing of purchases are your cash position and the payment or credit requirements imposed by state regulations or by the purveyor. Some states allow no credit at all; all sales must be cash. Other states require payment monthly or semimonthly or within some other interval, such as 10 days after the week of sale or the second Monday after delivery. Fines and publicity may accompany late payments or nonpayment. These requirements make it very important to integrate your purchasing times with your cash flow so that you are not caught short on the due date.

Table 13.2
Bottle and Case Sizes

Bottle Size[a]	Fluid Ounces	Units per Case
Distilled spirits		
50 milliliters	1.7	120
100 milliliters	3.4	60
200 milliliters	6.8	48
375 milliliters	12.7	24
750 milliliters	25.4	12
1 liter	33.8	12
1.75 liters	59.2	6
Wine		
50 milliliters	1.7	120
100 milliliters	3.4	60
187 milliliters	6.3	48
375 milliliters	12.7	24
750 milliliters	25.4	12
1 liter	33.8	12
1.5 liters	50.7	6
3 liters	101	4
Beer[b]		
6 ounces	6	
7 ounces	7	24
8 ounces	8	or
10 ounces	10	32
12 ounces	12	

[a] Not all sizes are legal in all states.

[b] For draft-beer container sizes see Table 13.4.

What to Pay

In control states, price markups are typically fixed by law and prices will be the same in all state stores. The only price decision the buyer must make is whether to take advantage of an occasional special or quantity discount.

In license states, it is often worth shopping around to find the best deal on the brands you want to buy. There are seldom large price differences because state laws are typically designed to avoid price wars. Manufacturers and distributors must give the same deals to everyone they sell to, so the price structure is fairly homogeneous. Nevertheless, in some areas, suppliers are free to set their own markups, grant their own discounts, and run their own specials—and they do. So, it is worthwhile to study price lists and talk to sales contacts and look at the ads in the trade journals.

There are several typical types of discounts found in the wholesale liquor industry. In general, they are: basic discounts, post-off discounts, size variations, and assorted discount structures.

A basic discount is usually volume-related, to entice buyers to purchase larger quantities. Let's say, for instance, the list price of Brand Z Vodka is $100 per case (there are 12 bottles in a case). But with a minimum 5-case order, the price drops to $92 per case; for 10 cases, you'll pay $88 per case; and for 15 cases, the price per case may be $84. Analyze this by cost per bottle, and you'll see in a small order (4 cases or less), you're paying $8.30 per bottle; while in the largest order (15 or more cases), the price per bottle drops to $7.

There are no "standards" for basic discounts; they'll vary tremendously between brands. But often, the liquors with the highest prices will also have the deepest discounts.

A **post-off discount** occurs when the distributor reduces the price of a particular brand to stimulate demand for it—either by the bottle or by the case. For example, Brand A Scotch has a $175 per-case list price. When a $9 post-off is announced for purchases of five or more, this drops the price to $166 per case.

Size variations also affect liquor's all-important cost per-ounce numbers. You want to be familiar with this, particularly the spirits, because you pour and price them by the ounce. The cost per ounce is highest when the bottle size is smallest and decreases as the bottle size increases. The cost per ounce is higher for items purchased by the bottle or in a broken case than when purchased by the case. Table 13.3 provides a price comparison for different bottle sizes.

Just by changing your purchasing from "750s" to liter bottles, the savings per ounce ($0.665 minus $0.608) equals $0.057—a little more than half a cent. The savings per liter ($0.057 multiplied by 33.8 ounces) is $1.92—almost $2 per bottle! That works out ($1.92 multiplied by 12 bottles) to a few pennies over $23, for the same Brand A Scotch.

In considering the larger, 1.75-liter bottle prices, remember that the number of ounces in a case of liters is greater than the number of ounces in a

Table 13.3

Price Comparison for Different Bottle Sizes

Bottles/Case	Bottle Size	Fluid Ounce	Cost/Bottle	Cost/Ounce
12	750 ml.	25.4	$16.90	$0.665
12	1 liter	33.8	20.40	0.603
6	1.75	59.2	27.90	0.471

case of 1.75 liters—the difference between 12 bottles and 6, respectively. The case of liters contains 405.6 ounces; the case of 1.75 liters contains 355.2 ounces.

Other than cost, another very important consideration is convenience of pouring. What is your pouring station and backbar set up to handle? With an automatic dispensing system, the use of the largest possible bottle is no problem; in other situations, these bottles may be unwieldy.

The fourth popular discount option is a simple variation of the basic discount structure, called the **multiple brands** or **assorted discount.** An importer or distiller offers this discount to encourage the bar owner to buy a wider range of its products. The total number of cases purchased is what the discount is based on. It's a "buy five cases of anything, and get 10 percent off" kind of deal, but it varies greatly. Since some of the cases are already discounted when you buy five or more of them, this additional discount can offer the conscientious buyer substantial savings, especially when buying in large quantities.

Let's look at how a typical assorted discount purchase might work. Our bar gets this price list from ABC Importers, its wholesale distributor:

Item	Size	List Price/ Case	5-Case Discount	10-Case Discount	15-Case Discount
Vodka	liter	$144	$ 9.00	$16.00	$20.00
Scotch	liter	$235	$14.00	$22.00	$30.00
Gin	liter	$165	$ 9.00	$17.00	$21.00

The bar places an order for two cases of vodka, one case of scotch, and one case of gin. The total ($288 for vodka + $235 for scotch + $165 for gin) comes to $688. However, if the bar would order *one* or more cases— bringing the total to five—the discount really "kicks in." Let's order one more case of vodka and see what happens:

For vodka: List price $144 per case, minus $9 per case discount = $135 per case

For scotch: List price $235 per case, minus $14 discount = $221 per case

For gin: List price $165 per case, minus $9 discount = $156 per case

When you total it up, the price for these five cases is:

Vodka (3 cases)	$405
Scotch (1 case)	221
Gin (1 case)	166
TOTAL	$792

And this, of course, is for a sale that would have cost $688 with only four cases purchased. The "extra" case of vodka ended up costing only $104.

When you do find good buys, you must weigh the money you save against your inventory size, rate of use, and what else you could do with the money. Sometimes the best price is not the best buy. Be wary, too, of the motives behind supplier specials. Sometimes these are intended to get rid of wines or beers approaching their limits. Fortunately you do not have to worry about this in spirits, which do not deteriorate.

PLACING THE LIQUOR ORDER

Earlier in this chapter, we discussed the idea of developing par stock levels. Once you know what you'll need, you can use the **periodic order method;** that is, select a fixed calendar of ordering dates, then calculate what your bar will use (and therefore, what will be needed) for each time period between order dates. A person in charge of the bar—the manager or bartender—then selects the best time of day for the beverages to be delivered, and the supplier should be able to comply.

An alternative system is the **perpetual order method.** In this system, the order dates are variable; the amounts are preset. Inventory cards list purchases and issues, along with other information, such as par stock, and the lowest amount to which the item must drop in inventory before reordering it. Someone checks the cards regularly, notes what is "running low," and orders it accordingly.

You must also develop a standard procedure for placing your orders. These procedures will be influenced by size and sales volume. At one extreme is the multicopy purchase order typically used by the large organization. At the other extreme is the informal verbal order given by phone or in person to a visiting sales representative. But even the verbal order should have a complete paper record to back it up. Every record, formal or informal, should contain the following information:

- Date of the order
- Name of the purveyor (seller)
- Name of the salesperson
- Purveyor's phone number

Purchase Order
Name of Bar
Address

Date _____   Purchase Order No. _____

Purveyor _____   Salesperson _____

Phone _____   Date Needed _____

Address _____   Hour of Delivery _____

Item #	Quantity	Unit	Brand	Unit Price	Total

P.O. Total _____

Ordered by _____

Figure 13.2 Purchase order.

- Anticipated date and time of delivery
- Items, brands, and vintages ordered
- Sizes of containers (bottle and case)
- Numbers of bottles or cases
- Unit prices (price per bottle for each item)
- Name of person placing order

There are four good reasons for keeping a written record of each order:

- It gives the person receiving the delivery the data needed to check it.
- It gives the person paying the bills data needed for checking the bill.
- It gives everyone concerned with the order—whether buyer, receiving agent, storeroom staff, accountant, bar manager, banquet manager, or bartender—access to exact data.
- It minimizes uncertainty, misunderstanding, and argument.

In a small operation, the record may simply be a memo of a phone order written on a form devised by the house, or it may be an order handwritten by a visiting salesperson. The only one concerned may be the owner/ manager who buys, receives, and stores the merchandise, stocks and tends the bar, and pays the bills. In a large organization, where responsibilities are divided among many departments, a formal, multicopy **purchase order** may be used (Figure 13.2) with the original going to the purveyor and copies sent to all concerned. Every purchase order has an order number (**P.O. number**), which is a key element in a network of paper records. It will be referenced on the purveyor's invoice, thus becoming the link between the two.

The **invoice** is the purveyor's response to the buyer's order. It reflects the information on the buyer's order sheet from the seller's point of view. It accompanies the delivery and must be signed by the buyer or the buyer's agent when delivery is received—which brings us to the second phase of the purchasing cycle.

RECEIVING THE LIQUOR ORDER

The primary goal of the receiving process is to be sure that the delivery conforms exactly to what was ordered. The signing of the invoice by the purchaser has legal significance: it is the point at which the buyer, at least technically, becomes the "owner" of the merchandise. Therefore, the delivery must be carefully checked before the invoice is signed. The person you give this responsibility to must be someone you trust, who has a good head for detail, and has been trained well for this assignment. There is no substitute for knowledgeable receiving personnel.

The first step is to check the invoice against the purchase order or memo. This must be an item-for-item check to see that the quantities, unit and case sizes, brands, vintages, and so on are listed as ordered and that the unit and case prices are quoted correctly. Then the math must be checked—the total costs per item (called **extensions**—the number of units multiplied by the unit cost) and the invoice total.

The second step is to check the delivery itself to see that it matches what is listed on the invoice. Each item must be checked as to quantity, unit, brand, vintage, and any other specification. Open cases should be verified bottle by bottle and examined for breakage, missing or broken stamps, and loose corks. Sealed cases should be examined for evidence of leaking bottles or weighed. The weight should agree with the weight printed on the case; a broken bottle will give a short weight. Beer should be checked for freshness, by reading the pull dates on the containers, and for temperature by feeling the bottle or the keg. Kegs should be examined for signs of leakage. Their contents can be checked by weighing the keg, writing the weight on the invoice, and subtracting the **tare weight** (weight of the empty keg) later. Table 13.4 gives the correct net weights for draft beer. It may seem like a hassle, but how would you know if a beer keg was full or empty simply by looking at it?

The third step is to request a **credit memo** for any discrepancies between the order memo and the invoice or the delivery itself. This will include items invoiced but not delivered, items invoiced and delivered that were not ordered, wrong merchandise (sizes, brands), items refused (overage beer, broken bottles, missing stamps, swollen beer cans), wrong prices, math errors. The credit memo at this point is usually a notation right on the invoice showing the item, problem, and amount, or it may be a separate credit slip on which the invoice date and number are written. In either case, it must be initialed or signed by the delivery person, and it too must be checked for accuracy. Only when everything has been checked, settled, and initialed does the receiving agent accept delivery by signing two copies of the invoice, one for you and one for the purveyor.

The purveyor will follow up the credit notation or memo with a confirming memo carrying the invoice date and number (Figure 13.3). This is, in

Table 13.4

Barrel and Keg Sizes

Container	Gallons	Liters	Net wt/lb	Net wt/kg	Fluid Ounces
Barrel	31	111.33	248	112.48	3968
½ barrel (keg)	15.5	58.67	124	56.24	1968
¼ barrel (½ keg)	7.75	29.33	62	25.12	992
⅛ barrel (¼ keg)	3.88	14.67	31	14.06	496

Credit Memo

Customer:

Credit Memo No. _____ Invoice No. _____ Date _____

No	Item Description	Quantity	Unit Price	Total
1				
2				
3				
4				
5				

Amount of credit _____

Reason for credit _____

_____

_____

_____

Purveyor Signature _____

Receiving Bar Signature _____

Figure 13.3 Confirming credit memo form.

effect, an amendment to the invoice and must be coupled with the invoice when the bill is paid. If not, or if you pay an unsigned invoice, you may end up paying for merchandise you never received.

The receiving routine must proceed as quickly as possible and with undivided attention. Then, just as rapidly, the delivery must be taken to the storeroom and signed in by the person in charge there. Liquor being received and transported is very vulnerable to pilferage and there is no point in increasing temptation.

A large organization may require the storeroom manager to repeat the check of merchandise using another invoice copy. When the storeroom manager signs for the beverages, he or she accepts responsibility for them from the receiving agent. There it rests until they are requisitioned for bar use.

The careful checking of deliveries has a double purpose: it is one-part protection against the purveyor's errors and one-part security against pilferage. Receiving a verified delivery is the first checkpoint along the system of controls that should follow your beverages from the time they enter your doors until they are poured at your bar and paid for by your customers.

STORAGE

The storeroom is the setting for the third phase of the purchasing cycle. It performs three functions: security from theft, physical care to maintain quality, and inventory maintenance and record-keeping.

The first essential step to achieving effective storeroom security is to limit access. This room is off limits to all but authorized personnel. Anyone withdrawing beverages does not enter the room, but must request what is needed from the storeroom staff or whoever has responsibility in a small operation. When open, the room must never be left unattended. If the person in charge must leave, even briefly, the door must be locked. This should be a substantial door with a deadbolt lock and only two sets of keys, one for the storeroom manager and one for emergencies, to be kept in the safe. Or it might have a combination lock that can be reset frequently, with only two people knowing the combination. If keys are used, locks should be changed often, in case someone makes duplicate keys. Locks should always be changed when someone who has had keys leaves your employment.

Windows should be barred or covered with barbed wire. Alarm systems are frequently used to protect against off-hour break-ins. Some of these systems depend on light or noise to scare away intruders or summon help; some alert police or a private security system directly.

An orderly storeroom is a security measure as well as a necessity for efficient operation. It should be divided into areas, each designed to stock a particular type of liquor. Each of these areas should be subdivided and clearly labeled, so that each brand has a specially marked place. This also holds true for ancillary items, from cocktail napkins to Champagne. A sample layout is pictured in Figure 13.4. When everything is systematically in place, anything amiss is soon noticed. Opened cases should be emptied immediately and their contents shelved, rotating the stock to put the older bottles in front. Never leave a case half empty; flatten empty cases and remove them promptly. It could be easy to steal away hidden bottles along with the trash.

Shelving should be made of wire, heavy and well braced, because liquor is heavy. Select shelf units that are easy to assemble and add to, and that can

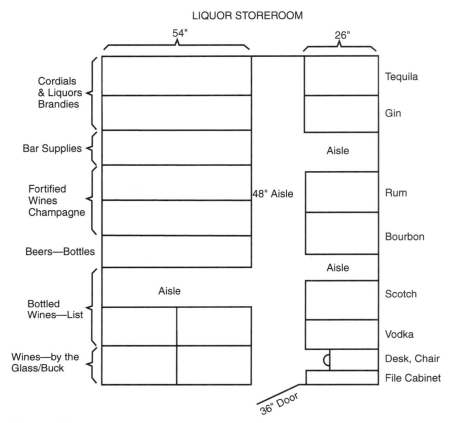

Figure 13.4 Layout of a liquor storeroom.

be fitted with casters so they can roll. Sealed cases can be stacked on low platforms until you need their contents.

Wine storage takes special care, since wines are perishable and must be protected from temperatures (too high, too low, or fluctuations), vibration, sunlight, and excessive humidity (which causes mold to form around the foil cap). Wines survive best in a cool, dark environment between 50° and 70° Fahrenheit (0° to 21° Celsius), with the ideal temperature being a constant 55° to 60° Fahrenheit, known as **cellar temperature.** Wines that get too warm can leak through their corks, and the seepage can stain or ruin the label. While high humidity is a problem, low humidity (below 55 percent) can dry the cork and allow air in.

Move wines as little as possible and, when you do, handle them gently. Agitating a wine may upset both its chemistry and its sediment, making it unservable until the sediment settles again. For this reason, newly imported wines should rest for 30 to 45 days before being served. However, since wines have limited life spans, rotating the stock becomes particularly important.

Wine racks are the best places to store wine, but not everyone has the room or money to purchase them. You can store wines on their sides or upside down in their sealed cases, but be careful not to stack them too high. More than five cases stacked atop each other causes too much pressure on the necks of the upside-down bottles, and can prompt them to break. Also, the sediment collects inside the bottle's neck, sticking to the cork and making it difficult to extract when the wine is finally opened. Places *not* to store wine? Near loading docks, the dishroom, the kitchen, air conditioning or heating exhaust ducts, and never under stairways.

Beer has the most limited shelf life of all. Canned and bottled beers should be stored below 70° Fahrenheit (21° Celsius) in a dark place, and their pull dates should be checked periodically. Draft beers and some nonpasteurized canned or bottled beers should be kept refrigerated; ask your supplier about optimum storage conditions for these. Draft beer must be kept at an even 36° to 38° Fahrenheit (2.2° to 3.3° Celsius) and should be used within 30 to 45 days. The best system of rotation has a handy acronym—FIFO—"first in, first out." For beer storage, consider keg or dunnage racks, as shown in Figure 13.5.

As custodian of the storeroom contents, the storeroom manager has responsibility for keeping track of the stock of each item at all times. This is an important part of any system for minimizing pilferage. Some storerooms use a system of individual *bin cards* to log stock in and out. A card for each item is attached to the shelf where the item is stored. A typical bin card shows

Figure 13.5 Keg and dunnage rack for beer storage. Photo provided by Kelmax Equipment ©1999.

the brand name, bottle size, quantity on hand, and sometimes a bin number or code number. The amount of stock delivered is immediately added to the quantity on hand, and the amount of stock issued for use is immediately subtracted. The number of bottles shown on the bin card should always agree with the actual number of bottles of that item. Spot-checking stock against bin cards helps to keep track of inventory. The minimum and maximum stock levels may also be recorded on the bin cards, making it easy to be aware of purchasing needs. The cards are also a quick index to rate of use.

ISSUING LIQUOR

Consider that the inventory levels at the bar change every time a bartender mixes a drink, and you have an idea of how difficult it is to keep track of what you have, where it is, and when you sold it. Like the other key points in the purchasing cycle, the issue of stock as it passes from storeroom to bar must be correctly carried out and duly recorded, with a series of overlapping internal tracking systems. The idea itself is not complicated, and neither are the systems. What's hard is getting everyone to use them correctly, fill out the necessary paperwork, and turn it in promptly.

The document used to record the transfer of inventory from the storeroom to a specific bar or outlet is a **requisition form** or **issue slip,** such as the one in Figure 13.6. You might think of it as a sort of in-house purchase order, with the bar as the "buyer" and the storeroom as the "supplier." The bar lists the brand, size, and number of bottles for each item required, with the date and the signature of the person requesting the issue. The storeroom adds the cost and value information to complete the record, and the person issuing also signs. The person receiving the stock at the bar adds his or her signature to complete the transfer of responsibility. Note, that means at least two or three signatures—an important way of tracking who is handling the stock.

Many bars require the bottles emptied the previous day to be turned in with the requisition. This is known as the *one-empty-for-one-full* system. The empties are collected and the requisition is made out at closing time, as noted in Chapter 9. The manager double-checks the requisition and the bartender's bottle count to be sure they agree. Both are turned in to the storeroom the following day by the opening bartender, and replacement stock is issued. In this way, the supply is automatically maintained at par stock level. As an additional benefit, the empty-bottle system enables management to check the par stock at any time against the par stock list to see if anything has disappeared. There should be a bottle for every bottle on the list, whether that bottle is empty or full.

Some enterprises mark each bottle with an identifying stamp when it is issued. Then, if an empty comes back without a stamp, you know somebody is up to something.

Requisition Form
Liquor, Beer, Wine, etc.
Bar Name
Address

Date: _____

Issued from: _____ (Store Room)

Issued to: _____ (Bar Outlet)

Item Number	Item Name	Size	Amount Ordered	Amount Issued	Perceptual Inventory Marked	Unit Cost	Extension
						Total	_____

Requested by: _____   Received by: _____

Date: _____   Date: _____

Issued by: _____

Date: _____

Figure 13.6 Requisition form.

In multiple-bar operations each bar has its own par stock, which is requisitioned and issued separately. For public bars and service bars, the one-empty-for-one-full system works well, but a different system must be used in supplying liquor for one-time events, such as banquets and conventions, a common situation in hotels. In this case, there are no empty bottles to replace and there is no one par stock. The brands and amounts are estimated in advance for each event based on anticipated consumption, past experience, and a safety allowance, and are issued to the person in charge of the event, using a special requisition form. The person in charge has the responsibility for returning all bottles, empty or full, to the storeroom when the event is over. The liquor used, represented by the empties, is charged to the cost of the event and the remaining stock is integrated into the storeroom inventory.

Sometimes the supply system breaks down during an unexpected rush or an emergency. If the storeroom is closed, liquor is likely to be borrowed by one bar from another so as not to lose sales, and no one thinks to keep track. Eventually empties end up in the wrong place, the records are scrambled, and sooner or later something disappears. It is the manager's responsibility to avoid such emergencies and keep the supply and record system on track.

INVENTORY

The beverage **inventory**—that is, the amount on hand at any given time—is of central importance to the purchasing function. The buyer must be able to determine exactly what is immediately available and the rate at which it is being used, in order to make intelligent purchasing decisions. In addition to storeroom records, other means of keeping track of total inventory are needed.

There are two reasons for keeping a constant check on inventory. One is to pinpoint losses quickly in order to put a stop to them. This has to do with controls, a subject discussed more fully in Chapter 14. The other reason has to do with purchasing. If you have lost stock due to theft, breakage, error, or whatever, you must buy stock to replace it, so that you can serve your customers. Therefore, you need to know what you really have on hand in order to plan each purchase.

Physical Inventory

The only accurate way to know what you have on hand is to take a complete **physical inventory,** that is, to count each bottle and keg on a regular basis. Ideally, you will do it weekly and again at the end of the accounting period. If possible, the inventory should be taken by persons who do not

Figure 13.7 A storeroom with everything well labeled and neatly organized. Courtesy of The Culinary Institute of America.

buy liquor or handle it on the job. As a double-check, it is best to have two people working together—one counting and the other writing down the count. Both people initial each page as it is completed. The inventory record should follow the arrangement of the storeroom, grouping items by category, and within categories by brand, and within brand by size. Figure 13.8 is a sample inventory form.

The liquor at the bar is also part of inventory until it is sold, and it, too, is counted in an end-of-the-month physical inventory. It is done in the same manner as the storeroom inventory except that there are opened bottles to be counted.

The simplest way to measure the contents of opened bottles is to estimate each bottle by sight and count the contents in tenths. Thus, a full bottle is 10/10, a half bottle is 5/10, while an empty bottle is 0/10. This gives you an approximate amount, of course, but it is close enough.

If you have a metered pouring system, you have a very accurate way of counting. The system counts the drinks it pours. You multiply the count by

Physical Inventory Form
Bar Name
Address

Location: 1. Bar # _____ .   3. Bar # _____ .
2. Bar # _____ .   4. Store Room _____ .

Date: _____

Inventory by: _____

Category (Circle One)   Beer   Wine   Liquor

Item #	Item Name	Size	1	2	3	4	Unit Cost	Extension
							Total	_____

Figure 13.8 Physical inventory form.

the size of the drink and compare this with what is left in the partly used bottle. You have to count the liquor in each line from bottle to dispensing head as part of the inventory. The manufacturer's representative should give you this capacity at the time the equipment is installed.

A bar owner or manager should conduct frequent audits of the actual inventory at the bar (not including the storeroom) at different times during the week or on different shifts. How often? This depends on sales volume: the higher the volume, the shorter time periods between audits. As you'll learn in Chapter 14, there are many ways for employees to be tempted, and security is a very real concern. The most powerful control tool you have is effective supervision.

One tool to speed the inventory process is the **bar code scanner.** Since practically every item is labeled today with a **Universal Product Code (UPC),** a hand-held model scanner can be used to scan each UPC label and download its identity to a computer instantly. A compatible scale can be used that is also able to read the UPC label, compute its total weight, subtract the tare weight (weight of the identical bottle when empty), and the weight of the pourer, if one is used on this bottle. Automatically, it calculates the net weight and converts it to ounces. This method is precise enough to provide real cost controls for a manager. It is a computerized way to compare the volume of beverages the POS system says *should* have been used (based on sales), and compare it to *actual* usage (based on the bar code scanner's readings).

No matter which method is used, inventory must be taken all at once, start to finish; and it must be done when the bar is closed, so that nothing changes while the count is being taken. Weekly inventories of individual bars or the storeroom may supplement the overall end-of-the-month count.

A **depletion allowance form** (Figure 13.9) should also be kept handy at the bar each day, to record any of the inventory that has been broken, spilled, transferred from one location to another (in large facilities), or given away as complementary beverages. Every bottle must be accounted for on a daily basis.

Perpetual Inventory

Another way of providing inventory information is to compile ongoing daily records from invoices and requisitions, adding each day's purchases and subtracting each day's issues for every item in stock. This task is typically performed by the accounting department, and the results are known as a **perpetual inventory.** It is kept by hand on forms (like the one in Figure 13.10) or bin cards—a separate card for each item—or by computer, which can report the stock record at any given moment with pushbutton ease.

At any point in time, the perpetual inventory is a paper record that should indicate exact quantities of every item you have on hand. It does not tell you

Depletion Allowance Form

(Circle one) Transfers, Spills, Comps, Broken

Bar Name

Address

Date: _____

Extended by: _____

Date	Item	Size/Quantity	Purpose/Outlet	Liquor Cost	Wine Cost	Beer Cost	Manager's Signature
Totals							

Figure 13.9 Depletion allowance form.

Perpetual Inventory Form
Bar Name
Address

Item Name: _____   Size: _____
Distributor: _____   Case Cost: _____
Item #: _____   Bottle Cost: _____

Date	Requisitioned/ Inventory/ Size	On-Hand Inventory/Size	Comments	Manager's Signature

Figure 13.10 Perpetual inventory form.

what you really have; only a physical inventory can do that. Its primary function is to provide a standard against which a physical count can be measured, item for item, at any given time. If everything is in order, the two inventories should agree. If separate records are kept on bin cards, they should also agree—they, too, are a form of perpetual inventory.

The more inventory you have, the more important it is that a perpetual inventory be kept. Since it should also clearly reveal a product's depletion rate, it has the added benefit of making the ordering process more accurate. It also greatly assists in detecting employee theft. And, finally, it assists you in meeting your state's licensing requirements to maintain accurate records of the bar's alcohol purchases.

If the actual count and the perpetual inventory record don't agree, you are faced with determining whether there are errors in the records or the count, or the items themselves have disappeared. You can trace errors in the record by going back to the invoices and requisitions; and errors in the count by recounting. If you can't find any mistakes, you may as well assume theft, and adjust your perpetual inventory record accordingly.

There are other ways of measuring discrepancies that are accurate enough for everyday use, and these will be examined in Chapter 14. Overall, the most critical reason for a good inventory management system is this: If you don't have a way of knowing where you ought to be, you can't measure where you are now.

Determining Inventory Value, Bar Cost, and Inventory Turnover Rate

When you have completed a physical inventory for an accounting period, you must determine the dollar value of the total stock. To do this, begin by entering the unit cost of each item on the inventory sheet on which you have recorded the count (refer to Figure 13.8).

The next step is to multiply the unit cost by the number of units to find the dollar value of the stock for each item. Enter each total on the form in the last column. Totaling the values of all the items then gives you the value of your entire inventory. This number is known as the **ending (closing) inventory** for the accounting period. The same number becomes the **beginning (opening) inventory** for the next accounting period.

Now you can use this figure to determine the value of all the liquor used to produce your sales for the period, in other words, your **beverage cost.** Here is the way to do it:

To: Value of beginning inventory *(BI)*
Add: Value of all purchases made during period *(P)*

Equals: Value of total liquor available during period
Subtract: Value of ending inventory *(EI)*
Equals: Value of total liquor used during period, or cost *(C)*

Or, to put this calculation in equation form:

$$BI + P - EI = C$$

For example:

BI	$1,245.16
+ *P*	5,015.16
	6,260.32
− *EI*	1,010.00
= *C*	$5,250.32

The dollar cost for liquor used in a given period is usually expressed as a percentage of the sales for the same period. To determine this percentage, you divide cost by sales:

$$\frac{C}{S} = C\%$$

For example:

$$\frac{\text{Cost } (C) \ \$5,250.32}{\text{Sales } (S) \ \$28,720.50} = .182 \text{ or } 18.2\%$$

This percentage is often referred to simply as **bar cost.** We will discuss some uses of this figure in the following chapter.

You can also use the values for ending inventory and purchases for the period to determine your **inventory turnover rate.** This rate will help you decide whether you are keeping too much or too little in inventory. To calculate this rate, you must first determine the average inventory. To do this, add the beginning and ending inventories for the period, then divide that sum by 2:

$$\frac{\text{Beginning Inventory} + \text{Ending Inventory}}{2} = \text{Average Inventory}$$

Then you divide costs for the accounting period by the average inventory number:

$$\frac{\text{Costs for the Period}}{\text{Average Inventory}} = \text{Turnover Rate}$$

For example, if purchases were $1,500 and closing inventory $1,500, the turnover rate would be 1; you have turned over your inventory once during the period. If purchases were $1,500 and closing inventory $2,000, your turnover rate would be 0.75, while if closing inventory were $1,000 with $1,500 in purchases, the turnover rate would be 1.5.

What is the significance of the turnover rate? Generally speaking, if your turnover rate is consistently below 1, you are probably stocking more than you need. If it runs above 2, you probably often run out of things you need and you might increase your sales if you increased your rate of purchase.

However, each type of business has its own optimum purchase rate, which may vary from industry norms. You really should calculate the turnover rates for beer, wine, and liquor separately, because they are not necessarily the same. There are several other ways to calculate inventory turnover, but this is the simplest, though not the most precise.

PURCHASING BAR SUPPLIES

Purchasing supplies for the bar follows the same cycle as beverage buying: purchasing, receiving, storing, and issuing. However, buying supplies is a good deal simpler because these are products not regulated by state or federal laws.

You can buy grocery items from grocery wholesalers and cocktail napkins from wholesalers of paper goods. But if you find beverage wholesalers who carry drink-related items, check them out. (Some state codes do not allow liquor dealers to sell anything but liquor.) The prices may be better, since the liquor dealer may get better quantity discounts on bar items, such as maraschino cherries and cocktail onions, than the grocery dealer does. Service may be better, too. The food wholesaler may pay little attention to your small order, whereas the liquor purveyor wants to keep your beverage business. The liquor dealer may also sell in smaller quantities than the grocery wholesaler, and if you have a small enterprise, it may take forever to use up a case of olives or a gross of napkins.

But liquor purveyors don't handle such items as lemons, limes, oranges, celery, eggs, milk, cream, or ice cream. You will buy your produce from a produce dealer and your dairy supplies and ice cream from a wholesale dairy. Such items must be refrigerated in the storeroom or go straight to the bar. Ice cream must go straight into a freezer.

In working out your orders, you will have a choice of can or bottle sizes in many items. The cost per olive or per ounce is nearly always cheaper in the larger container sizes. However, consider deterioration once the container is opened. If you use only half a can of something and have to throw out the rest, you haven't saved any money.

Receiving, storing, and issuing follow the same procedures used for alcoholic beverages. Like items must be stored together, and the stock must be rotated at each delivery. All types of bar supplies are counted on the regular physical inventory. However, once a container is opened, it is considered used and is not counted.

SUMMING UP

A good purchasing manager provides an adequate supply of beverages at all times without overinvesting in idle inventory. Purchasing involves both the selection and procurement of everything needed to run the bar.

The modern bar manager uses a category management system, tracking what sells well and what does not (most often by computer) and using the information to adapt the drink menu to deliver a beverage program that meets customers' needs and is profitable for the business.

It is important to maintain good relationships with suppliers, and to understand their pricing systems so you can evaluate the true "worth" of the sales and discounts they may offer. You can get a lot of product information online or on CD-ROM to help you make buying decisions; you may even be linked by computer to suppliers so you can order by e-mail. But it is still important to maintain some human contact with your salespeople. If you operate in a control state, you must purchase your liquor from state-run stores or warehouses; relationships are just as important in these cases.

A careful system of records is maintained at all phases of the purchasing cycle. You start by determining the par stock necessary to outfit your bar to be ready for a business day, and track the path of every bottle and its contents, from the time it is received to the time the empty is turned in. Through such records, management can keep track of supply and can pinpoint responsibility at any stage along the way from purchase to sale.

Physical inventory at regular intervals provides the basis for figuring needs, costs, and losses. Written or computerized perpetual inventory records provide standards against which physical inventory can be measured. Storeroom areas should include strict security precautions and limited access.

The system should include a series of forms for recording in writing sales, discrepancies, par stock, and other standards. A well-organized, well-managed purchasing system can contribute to profits by keeping costs down, efficiency up, and supplies flowing.

POINTS TO PONDER

1. What would your policy be on (a) quality of well brands and (b) variety of brands offered? Give reasons for your decisions.

2. Do you live in a control state or a license state? How does this affect purchasing?

3. Explain the relationship between the purchase order, the invoice, and the credit memo.

4. List and briefly discuss three qualities you would look for in a liquor supplier. Explain why they are important to you.

5. When buying wholesale liquor, what is the difference between a post-off discount and an assorted discount?

6. Discuss the advantages and disadvantages of a perpetual inventory record. What would computerization contribute?

7. What kind of information should be listed on a bin card, and what is its function?

8. What does your inventory turnover rate tell you about your purchasing management?

9. Why should physical inventory be taken by people who do not work at the bar or in the storeroom?

10. What numbers do you have to know in a bar business to arrive at its beverage cost or bar cost?

TERMS OF THE TRADE

assorted discount

bar code scanner

bar cost

beginning (opening) inventory

beverage cost

capital risk

carrying costs

category management

cellar temperature

control state, monopoly state

credit memo

depletion allowance form

ending (closing) inventory

extensions

inventory

inventory turnover rate

invoice

issue slip

lead time

license state

multiple brands discount

one-empty-for-one-full

P.O. number

par stock

periodic order method

perpetual inventory

perpetual order method

physical inventory

post-off discount

premium well, super well

procurement process

purchase order

purchasing

requisition form

selection process

tare weight

Universal Product Code (UPC)

well brands, house brands

SHARON GOLDMAN
Director of Marketing, Luxury Division
Beringer Blass Wine Estates

Sharon Goldman is the Director of Marketing for Beringer Blass Wine Estates' Luxury Division, which includes Beringer, Chateau St. Jean, and Chateau Souverain wine products. Her responsibilities include profit and loss metrics; designing wine packaging and labels; pricing the wines; deciding where they are sold and how they are publicized; and creating wine education programs for trade customers.

Sharon's résumé is an impressive list of marketing and management positions, from Lawry's Foods to Universal Studios. She took her marketing skills to the wine industry in 1990, first with Fetzer Vineyards, then as marketing manager for Kendall-Jackson Vineyards and Winery. In 1997, she was hired by Beringer. Today, the company produces wines at six California wineries, and imports wines from Australia, Italy, and Chile, with annual sales of $100 million.

Sharon received her bachelor's degree at University of California, Los Angeles, and did graduate work at University of California, Berkeley.

Q: What is the most important type of background to have to succeed in your industry, and what kinds of classes should you take to get it?

A: A diverse background is probably one of the strongest things you can have, and it is actually far preferable to coming into this business with a single area of focus. It is important to understand that the nature of the jobs will vary depending upon the size of the winery. There is a fairly small handful of large wineries that have more specialized jobs, versus the smaller wineries, where you can expect to wear multiple hats—one day you may be doing PR, one day you may be marketing, and the next day you may be in charge of sales—and that's all in the same position!

If your goal is to be in the restaurant side of the wine business, it helps to have experience outside of it, too. Numbers-crunching courses can be a real asset. Art classes will help with the more artistic and creative side of the business. In marketing,

we design labels and packaging, brochures, and other elements that use aesthetics. Naturally, learning about the hospitality industry will be an asset. And the fact that the wine business is also an agricultural enterprise gives you another course of study. As you can see, it just helps to be well rounded!

Q: What are the growth and consumption trends for wine, and how do they impact you?

A: The overall size of the business has not changed significantly, but people are paying considerably more for wine now than they were 10 years ago. One issue about wine that needs to be understood is that whether you're dealing with a coffee-shop style establishment or a high-end hotel bar, you're still dealing with price points that exclude a lot of people who are just not willing to spend the money on wine. They don't see that as where they should be spending their disposable dollars. So, there is a finite population that is interested in your product, and as the price goes up, the group becomes even more finite. It is also a relatively sophisticated audience, even at lower price points like White Zinfandel, which actually constitutes a good portion of the wine-drinking population. Wine is also a product that is very confusing because of the huge variety of wines that are out there—not just the grapes, but also the proliferation of labels.

Q: How much of an impact do nature's "curve balls," like rain or hail or diseases, really have on the price of wine?

A: Well, you're already talking about a considerable investment under the best of circumstances. To develop a vineyard in Napa (presuming you could buy a raw piece of land there), you need to figure on anywhere from $30,000 to $100,000 an acre to get it ready to produce grapes, and that's not including the purchase price of the land itself! It then takes three to five years to grow grapes that you can actually make into wine. Once you add the effects of Mother Nature, there is even more impact. A big heat wave may cause the grapes to be ready to be picked a month or so earlier than normal. It doesn't mean the grapes have full flavor, but it will mean they have to be picked. You get one crop a year and that's it. If Mother Nature is not nice to you, or if you're not nice to the grape, you're in big trouble. And that, eventually, can impact the price.

Q: How can a bar, restaurant, or store manager help educate the public to assist them in making the right wine choices—and ideally increase sales by doing so?

A: It is up to the store or bar manager to educate the public, whether it's by providing good descriptions on the shelf tag or on the menu or by ensuring that the staff is well informed and make patrons feel comfortable when they ask questions.

There are three primary reasons why someone will choose a wine: 1) someone has recommended it (usually a family member or a friend), 2) the server or store clerk recommends it and explains why they like it, and 3) price—in that order. If someone you trust suggests that you try the wine and says you're likely to enjoy it, most people follow through on that recommendation. Wine by its very nature is somewhat experimental. At the same time, it is often bought for a party or as a gift, so consumers or patrons want some assurance that they've made a good selection.

If you start developing a trust relationship with your clientele, your sales will grow. Remember that most people are too embarrassed to ask questions, so if your menu provides additional descriptive information or you have an informed staff person willing to assist, you are likely to get additional, incremental sales.

Q: What are some of the elements that go into making wine selections for a bar or restaurant wine list?

A: Just knowing that the *Wine Spectator* has rated a wine highly at a 90 or above is helpful, but it is often not sufficient to make a buying decision. Some wine buyers, bar managers, or restaurant managers say they create their wine lists because of their own palates (what they like and don't like). You also hear some say they won't put anything on the list that is readily available at retail down the street. On the other hand, if a wine is hugely popular and is widely available, it also may mean that people will look to order it, as they know it will be good.

A good range of wines by the glass is an easy and relatively affordable way for people to sample. I would suggest the wine list be balanced with some "safe" wines, and some lesser-known wines that you think are terrific. That can make it fun for you and the customer, if you can "hand-sell" it. This entails you getting to know your customers or ensuring that your waitstaff is sufficiently trained to describe each bottle of wine.

If you offer wine dinners or wine tastings, the actual winemaker doesn't have to be there. You can run the dinner yourself, or ask the local sales rep, who truly knows the product, to show up, and it can be a good experience that increases sales.

Q: What kinds of distribution issues do you face that might impact a bar or restaurant?

A: There are certain states that make it difficult for smaller wineries to get their wines into that market. In some states, you just can't ship directly from a winery to a restaurant; the wine must go through a distributor, such as Florida, Kentucky, New York, Texas, or Connecticut. Each state creates its own rules. If you have a restaurant in Florida and you want to buy a wine that was highly rated [99 in *The Wine Spectator*], unless you hook up with a distributor who takes its margin off the top, the wine can't get to you—it's illegal.

Q: How can a bar manager become more effective at dealing with distributors?

A: By making lots of noise! Seriously, if you are small and there are certain wines that you want, you may need to work a little harder at relationships with distributors. If you are small, you may not be called on by that distributor salesperson regularly and you're just not "on the radar screen." If you can't make an impact with your buying power, you are immediately at a disadvantage and you have to do it instead by personal contact. You need to let it be known that you want the "good stuff," but also let it be known that you're not going to be a "cherry picker." If you are knowledgeable and are willing to buy multiple products, they are more likely to want to assist you and supply you when the supply is tight. So you need to be somewhat of a partner with your vendors, and understand what sales mix they need to maintain. They can always sell the high-demand items.

Q: Is it important to have a mentor in this industry?

A: I actually think your network of connections within your peer group is more important than having a mentor, although I don't wish to discount the importance of having a knowledgeable person who knows the ropes. But when it's time to get a job or change jobs, it is your network that can help you. Many of the best positions are filled before the general public hears about them, and having an inside track will help you.

One good technique for learning about the wineries is to request "information interviews," where you make it clear that you are just trying to learn rather than "hit on them" for a job. Always close those interviews with a query about who to talk with next. Your contacts are very likely to assist you in getting where you want to go later on. If they have a job available or they know of one, they are likely to mention that. If you ask for a reference for someone else to talk to, they will know you're looking for a job anyway–it's just a softer approach.

CHAPTER 14

Planning for Profit

In a way, profit is what is left over after all expenses are paid. But that's a rather pessimistic way to look at it, and probably won't achieve the best results for you. If you look at profit as a goal to be achieved instead of as a "residue" of operation, you can chart your course and control the process.

This chapter shows how the principle of planning for profit works to structure the financial side of an operation toward reaching a profit goal. It discusses the budget as a profit plan and its use in measuring achievement of the profit goal. It explores the systematic pricing of drinks to maximize profits. Finally, it examines how to set up controls to assure that the beverages go into drinks, the money goes into the cash register, and the profit becomes a natural offspring of your successful business plan.

This chapter should help you . . .

- Establish a profit goal for your bar business.
- Prepare a budget that is aimed at a profit goal and measure progress toward that goal.
- Price each drink on the basis of beverage cost.
- Coordinate drink prices for maximum dollar sales.
- Use an income statement to measure achievement.
- Forecast cash flow.
- Calculate break-even point. Standardize drink size, recipes, and glassware.
- Establish a control system for detecting and measuring losses.
- Use par stock as a tool of control.
- Establish a system of sales records and cash control.

How often have you been shocked to hear that a popular bar or restaurant was going out of business? If you ask what went wrong, the usual reply is something like, "Poor management," or, "They didn't know what they were doing."

These criticisms could mean almost anything, but most likely money management was involved, and more than likely the failure also involved poor planning. A great many enterprises, especially small ones, operate with more enthusiasm than foresight, and count on advertising, or a particular trend, or entertainment, or somebody else's successful formula to generate profits. The accountant is expected to take care of the financial end of things.

But the shrewd entrepreneur knows that profit can and should be systematically planned for, budgeted for, and watched over like a hawk from one day to the next. Let us begin with the budget as a profit plan.

BUDGETING FOR PROFIT

Profit is the primary goal of a beverage enterprise, whether that goal is a hope or a dream or a very specific target. But profit, by itself, does not indicate the degree of business efficiency. Indeed, profit figures are not significant until they are expressed in relation to other factors—like sales or return on investment. A budget provides a closer look at what these figures mean, a strategy for reaching a target, and a tool for measuring progress along the way.

What Is a Budget?

A **budget** is a financial plan for a given period of time that coordinates anticipated income and expenditures to ensure solvency and yield a profit. The budget is a document with a dual personality. In the beginning, it is a plan detailing in dollar terms the *anticipated performance* of the bar during the period to come—the expected sales, the expenses that will be incurred in order to achieve the sales, and the desired profit. As the budget period arrives, the budget ceases to be a plan for the future and becomes a tool of control for the present. It now provides a basis for measuring *actual performance* and results against the performance goals of the plan.

Perhaps it is more accurate to think of the budget as a continuing two-phase process or system, rather than a static or inflexible set of figures. The planning phase requires the manager to project the financial future in detail and make realistic forecasts of income and outgo in relation to the ultimate profit goal. This very process of thinking ahead, gathering data for forecasting, figuring one's way through the facts and numbers, and applying them to a future that may change before it arrives may suggest operating adjustments that will help to achieve the profit goal.

In the second, or control, phase, the frequent measuring of actual results against a budget plan can signal threats to profits and indicate the areas of trouble. Quick action may put the business back on course. On the other hand, sometimes the original plan is unrealistic or circumstances change. Then, the budget can be modified to bring it into line with present reality. In this sense, the planning process continues during the operating period.

For the sake of simplicity, in discussing the budgeting process, we have ignored the fact that the majority of enterprises combine some form of food service with beverage service. Wherever this is true, most fixed expenses and some others are shared with the food service side of the enterprise. It is customary in this case to lump fixed expenses and relate them only to total sales and to figure the bar's share of the remaining expenses as a proportion of total sales. Thus, if beverage sales are projected at 25 percent of a restaurant's total sales, you would budget the remaining shared expenses at 25 percent of the total projection for those expenses.

The Planning Process

The first step in developing a budget is setting your profit goal, a specific, realistic goal, not just "as much profit as possible." How do you do this? Think of it in terms of return on money invested. Let's say that you have $100,000 invested in a going business or that you are going to invest that amount in a new project. What would this $100,000 bring you in a year if you put it in a savings certificate or mutual fund or invested it in real estate or some other not-too-risky venture? Let's say it would bring you $10,000 a year. Now, double this figure (a rule-of-thumb safety margin because of the risks you are taking) for a total of $20,000. This is your projected *return on investment*—your ROI—and your profit goal for the year.

Profit is the difference between income and expenses. Since your income comes from sales, your next step is to forecast your sales for the budget period. The accuracy of this forecast will determine how realistic the rest of your budget is and whether or not you will reach your profit goal or, indeed, make a profit at all.

Understanding the relationship between profit, volume, and costs is key to successfully budgeting by the month and forecasting for the future.

To forecast your sales, you must estimate the number of drinks you expect to sell in each period of each day, week, and month of the year. Figure 14.1 is a useful form for such a forecast. If you are already in business, draw on your past sales data. Break the data down in terms of number of drinks sold on the noon shift, the afternoon shift, and the evening shift, and by day of the week. Note the effect of price changes for special events or

Sales Forecast Form

Period: *From* _____   *To* _____

Date	Mon	Tue	Wed	Thu	Fri	Sat	Sun	Total Average
Shift 11–3								
Week ending ____								
Week ending ____								
Week ending ____								
Week ending ____								
4-week totals ____								
Shift 3–7								
Week ending ____								
Week ending ____								
Week ending ____								
Week ending ____								
4-week totals ____								
Shift 7–closing								
Week ending ____								
Week ending ____								
Week ending ____								
Week ending ____								
4-week totals ____								

Figure 14.1 Sales forecast form.

special drinks, as well as general price changes and the influence of holidays, conventions, and sports events. Make notes on high and low sales periods and seasonal variations. Then use this data to decide whether the upcoming year will be a rerun of the last, or whether you want to make it different and whether there will be external factors that will affect the forecast.

For example, has your competitive position changed? A new bar opened across the street, maybe? Is the general economy affecting your business? Are you going to make changes, such as renovating your facility or adding live entertainment and dancing? Do you have plans for special promotions? Adapt your historical figures to accommodate all the changes you foresee.

If you are just starting out in the bar business, make the same estimates on the basis of what you have found out about your chosen clientele, your market area, your competition, and your capacity—all discussed in greater detail in Chapter 3. And estimate conservatively!

Finally, multiply the number of drinks you forecast by the prices you plan to charge in the upcoming year. This is your sales forecast and your anticipated income. For the sake of argument, let's place this figure at $100,000 for the year (see Figure 14.2). The figures in this example are low for today's realities, but they make things easier to follow.

Your next step is to estimate all your expenses for the same period. You have two sources of information for these: the past year's history and any commitments you have made for the period ahead, such as a lease or a loan from the bank. Again, gather your data and make your estimated expense figures as precise as possible.

Expenses are usually grouped into two categories: fixed and variable. **Fixed expenses** are those that are not related in any way to sales volume but are fixed by contract or simply by being in business; that is, you could not operate without them, yet they go on whether or not you sell a single drink. Your rent, for instance, remains the same whether your sales are zero or a million dollars, and any increase in rent comes from your landlord and not from your volume of business. For the most part, payroll, insurance, licenses and fees, taxes (except sales taxes), interest on loans, depreciation, and so on are fixed expenses. They all continue independently of sales volume.

The good news is, fixed expenses are easily predictable. Write them down in dollar figures as in the sample budget (Figure 14.2); for example, fixed payroll at $750 a month or $9,000 a year, rent at $500 a month or $6,000 a year, and so on for taxes, fees, interest, insurance, depreciation, and amortization. Then add them all up for a total for the year.

Variable expenses are those that move up and down with sales volume. Chief among these are beverage and remaining payroll costs. Itemize these, too, in dollars for the coming year, going back to your drinks-per-day figures to estimate the beverages and staff you will need to produce these drinks.

Notice that a certain portion of the payroll is considered a fixed cost. Salaried employees—a manager, for example—must be paid whether you sell

Tentative Budget

	Dollars	Percent of sales
Projected Sales	$100,000	100%
Variable Expenses		
Beverage costs	$ 24,000	24.0%
Payroll costs, variable portion	$ 13,500	13.5%
Administrative expenses	$ 4,000	4.0%
Laundry and supplies	$ 3,600	3.6%
Utilities	$ 3,000	3.0%
Advertising and promotion	$ 3,500	3.5%
Repairs	$ 1,500	1.5%
Maintenance	$ 2,000	2.0%
Miscellaneous operating expenses	$ 700	0.7%
Fixed Expenses		
Payroll costs, fixed portion	$ 9,000	9.0%
Rent	$ 6,000	6.0%
Taxes	$ 1,160	1.16%
Insurance	$ 2,400	2.4%
Interest	$ 800	0.8%
Licenses and fees	$ 2,200	2.2%
Depreciation	$ 1,800	1.8%
Amortization	$ 840	0.84%
Profit Goal	$ 20,000	20.0%
	$100,000	100.0%

Figure 14.2 Tentative budget.

one drink or a thousand. A certain number of hourly employees also represent fixed costs because they must be there when the doors open for business. Some enterprises, in budgeting, divide payroll costs between fixed and variable expenses (as in Figure 14.2), identifying the cost of a skeleton crew as a fixed expense and the cost of additional staff needed for the estimated sales volume as a variable expense. This produces a more finely tuned budget than lumping payroll all together.

A third category of expenses, **unallocable expenses,** is sometimes listed separately because it consists of general expenses that are neither fixed nor directly tied to sales. They include promotion and advertising, but for simplicity's sake we include them under variable expenses. These dollar figures depend on your plans, which in turn depend on how much you think such expenditures will influence sales. A certain amount of advertising and promotion is often necessary just to keep your enterprise in the public consciousness and to maintain a certain sales level. Enter your planned dollar figures on your budget.

When you have estimated all your expenses for the year, add them all up. Then go back and figure each individual expense item as a percentage of your expected sales for the year, as shown in Figure 14.2.

The percent-of-sales figure is a precise way of expressing the relationship of a given expense to the sales it will help produce. This is a critical relationship, one that is watched closely in operation as a measure of performance against plan. The percent-of-sales figure is referred to in the industry as **percentage cost, cost percentage,** or **cost/sales ratio.**

When you have completed all of your percentage figures, enter your profit goal in dollar figures and again as a percentage of sales. Add the dollar profit goal to the total expenses, and compare this sum with your sales forecast. Next, add up all the percent-of-sales figures for expenses and profit.

If the dollar figure for expenses-plus-profit is the same as or less than the sales forecast, and the percent-of-sales figure is 100 percent or less, you are in good shape. If expenses-plus-profit dollars are more than the dollar sales forecast and the percentage figure is more than 100 percent, you have some readjusting to do. To reach your profit goal, you have two choices: to cut costs or to increase sales (raise volume or prices or both volume and prices). Whatever you do, you must reach a balance. If all else fails, you must reduce your profit goal. Your percentage figures can be very helpful in establishing a profit-yielding budget. You can see at a glance if any one category of expense is out of line. The percentages in Figure 14.2 are generally accepted industry norms, give or take a few points. However, don't look at them as hard-and-fast goals for your budget. Your plan must reflect your own realities.

Longer-Term Planning. Figure 14.3 is a more sophisticated budget form. This type of form enables you to base your projections for the coming year on what has actually happened during the current year—that is, the year just ending.

You start with actual historical figures for the current year. These are year-to-date figures taken from your last income statement, showing the cumulative totals in each budget category (Figure 14.3). Enter the figures in the two columns headed Actual, both in dollars and in percent of sales.

The next section, headed Change, is the key to your budgeting for the coming year. In this section, for each change you anticipate, enter either a dollar figure (usually for a fixed expense) or a percent of last year's figure representing the anticipated change (usually for a variable expense). For categories you expect to remain the same, do not enter anything.

Budget
Comparative format

Actual (*Current year*)		Change		Planned (*Next year*)		
Dollars	*Percent*	*Dollars*	*Percent*	*Dollars*	*Percent*	
						Sales
						Variable Expenses
						Beverage costs
						Payroll, variable portion
						Administrative expenses
						Laundry and supplies
						Utilities
						Advertising/Promotion
						Repairs
						Maintenance
						Misc. operating expenses
						Total Variable Expenses
						Fixed Expenses
						Payroll, fixed portion
						Rent
						Taxes
						Insurance
						Interest
						Licenses and fees
						Depreciation
						Amortization
						Total Fixed Expenses
						Profit Before Taxes

Figure 14.3 Budget: a comparative format.

The section headed Planned combines the figures for the current year with the anticipated changes to give the figures for your new budget, which you enter in the Planned columns. If a change is expressed as a percentage, convert it into dollars, add it to the dollar amount from the Actual column, and enter the total figure in the Planned column. If a change is expressed in dollars, combine it with the dollar figures from the Actual column and enter this total in the Planned column. All the dollar figures are then compared to calculate percent-of-sales figures for the total budget.

Financial statements that depict future period activity are called **pro forma statements** or reports. They represent what the bar is *supposed* to look like financially, based on a set of assumptions about the economy, market growth, location, and myriad other factors that affect that particular unit. You don't need a crystal ball to make these predictions. They won't be 100-percent accurate, but by using your own experience and common sense and by paying attention to industry trends as well as what's happening in your own town and neighborhood, you can do a good job. Even when you've made the predictions, there's nothing sacred about them. Industry experts suggest that if they are "off" more than 20 percent in a three-month period, redo them. If they are off less than 20 percent, wait another three months and see what happens; but don't change them more than three months at a time, unless you find you've omitted a major expense item or discovered a new source of revenue.

Why make predictions at all? They are really just summaries of your business forecasts. The idea is not to impress anyone, but to organize data and let it guide you. For one, your lender(s) and investors will be interested, so it is important to be methodical and thorough. You might err on the side of caution, slightly overstating expenses and understating sales figures. It is much better to exceed a conservative budget than to fall below an optimistic one. Second, over time you will notice that most expenses and income are fairly predictable, which should make it easier to continue planning and budgeting. Suggested pro forma statements are found in the "Uniform System of Accounts for Restaurants," a useful guide published by the National Restaurant Association. (The most current version, seventh edition, was published in 1996.)

Two other kinds of forecasts are of great value, especially if you are opening a brand-new enterprise. One is your break-even point. The other is a cash-flow forecast. These are refinements of the budgeting process that many managers overlook. They are also useful as the year goes on, as you track your progress and analyze your performance.

Break-Even Point. A **break-even point** is the level of operation at which total costs equal total sales, meaning there is no profit and no loss. Oddly enough, this is the level a new bar must reach fairly quickly if it is to survive. In a food and beverage operation, break-even figures may be expressed in dollars or in "units," which means number of guests served. But for bars, it is generally expressed in dollars.

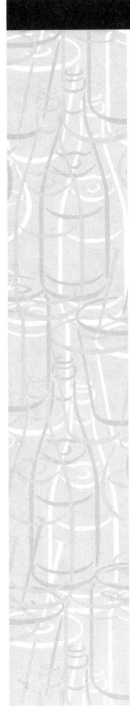

Sidebar 14.1

HOW TO CALCULATE A BREAK-EVEN POINT

Let's determine a break-even point using the sample budget figures that appear in Figure 14.2.

1. **Determine projected monthly sales.** In this example, we know that figure is $100,000.
2. Separate and list the monthly fixed and variable costs, as follows:

Fixed Costs		*Variable Costs*	
Fixed Payroll	$9,000	Beverage Costs	$24,000
Administrative	4,000	Variable Payroll	13,500
Laundry and Supplies	3,600		
Utilities	3,000		
Advertising	3,500		
Repairs	1,500		
Maintenance	2,000		
Miscellaneous	700		
Rent	6,000		
Taxes	1,160		
Insurance	2,400		
Interest	800		
Licenses and Fees	2,200		
Depreciation	1,800		
Amortization	840		
TOTALS	$42,500		$37,500

3. Divide total variable costs by total sales.

($37,500 ÷ by $100,000 = .375, or 37.5%)

4. Subtract the variable costs (as a percentage) from 1.000.

(1.000 − .375 = .625, or 62.5%)

5. To determine break-even point, divide the step 4 results into the total fixed costs.

($42,500 ÷ by .625 = $68,000)

This is the level of sales for this particular bar, at which there is no profit or loss. It means that, in this case, the bar has to make $68,000 per month just to "break even."

Further, we can factor in the $20,000 profit that has been budgeted by the hopeful owner, and use the formula to come up with a new figure:

$$\frac{\text{Total Fixed Costs} + \text{Profit}}{1.000 - \text{Percent of Variable Costs}} = \text{Desired Sales}$$

Using our sample figures, it would look like this:

$$\frac{\$42,500 + \$20,000}{0.625} = \frac{\$62,500}{0.625} = \$100,000$$

As stressful as it may sound, it is often useful to have a daily break-even point—a sort-of quota, so you'll know how much business you should be generating. First, you decide how many days per year the bar will be open—let's say 350 days. Then, you divide your yearly break-even sales by the number of days you plan to be open. For our fictitious bar, we can figure it two ways: a true break-even that includes no profit at all; and one that builds in a $20,000 profit goal. Here's how those look:

True Break-Even

$$\frac{\$68,000}{350} = \$194.28 \text{ needed per day}$$

$20,000 Profit Goal

$$\frac{\$100,000}{350} = \$285.71 \text{ needed per day}$$

To figure your daily break-even point, start with all fixed costs for one month. Add a month's wages and salaries for a skeleton crew, the fewest number of workers you can have to open your doors for business. Divide this total by the number of days in the month you will be open. This is your basic daily labor cost. Now add the cost of a day's liquor supply and any extra staff needed to serve it. This will give you the dollars you need in the register each day to break even.

A daily break-even point is useful at any time. When you use it over a period of days, it can show you when you might cut back on staff and what days it doesn't pay to open at all. Or it may indicate that you need to do something to raise your general sales level.

Forecasting Cash Flow. A bar can do a high-volume business, yet still run into trouble if there is not enough cash in the bank to meet payroll and pay bills. This can happen because, as anyone who's ever received a paycheck will attest, money does not come in and go out at the same daily rate.

Cash-Flow Forecast

+ = Money coming in
− = Money going out

		Jan	Feb	Mar	Apr	May	Jun
+	1 Cash sales						
+	2 Accounts receivable collections						
+	3 Other cash receipts						
	4 TOTAL CASH AVAILABLE						
−	5 Purchase payments						
−	6 Operating expenses						
−	7 Other cash expenses						
	8 TOTAL CASH PAYOUT						
	9 NET CASH FROM OPERATIONS						
+	10 Short-term financing						
+	11 Long-term financing						
+	12 Additional equity						
−	13 Repayment of short-term debt						
−	14 Capital expenditure						
−	15 Repayment of long-term debt						
−	16 Cash withdrawals						
	17 NET MONTHLY CASH POSITION						
	18 BEGINNING CASH						
	19 CUMULATIVE CASH POSITION						

Figure 14.4 Cash-flow forecast.

You may have lump-sum payments due at certain times. Customers may pay by credit card. You may spend a large sum to buy a special wine that is hard to get. Forecasting cash flow can help you avoid a crunch.

A **cash-flow forecast,** or *cash budget,* as it is sometimes called, is a short-term forecast of cash flowing into the bank and cash flowing out, week by week or month by month. It requires predicting each item that will put money in your bank account or take it out. If you are already an established business, you can use your monthly income statements from previous years and other records to help you estimate variables accurately. Fixed expenses such as rent, license fees, taxes, insurance, and loan payments are typically due on fixed dates in fixed amounts. Figure 14.4 is a detailed guide for setting up a cash-flow forecast. It is organized for a monthly forecast but can be made to work for any interval. The following list details each of the steps in the process.

1. **Cash sales:** Enter your estimated monthly sales based on last year's records, allowing for seasonal influences, inflation, and growth of decline in your business during the past year.
2. **Accounts receivable collections:** Enter receivables you expect to be paid during the month.
3. **Other cash receipts:** Enter anticipated cash income not directly related to sales.
4. **TOTAL CASH AVAILABLE:** Add items 1–3. This is the sum of all projected inflows of cash for the month.
5. **Purchase payments:** Enter amount to be paid out for beverages. Estimate this from last year's records, using the cost/sales ratio for the corresponding month.
6. **Operating expenses:** Enter anticipated operating expenses estimated from last year's income statement for the same month and last month's figures.
7. **Other cash expenses:** Enter all other anticipated cash expenses.
8. **TOTAL CASH PAYOUT:** Add items 4–7. This is the sum of all projected outflows of cash for the month.
9. **NET CASH FROM OPERATIONS:** Subtract item 8 from item 4.
10. **Short-term financing:** Enter cash you expect to come in from short-term loans during this month.
11. **Long-term financing:** Enter cash you expect to come in from long-term loans during this month.
12. **Additional equity:** Enter additional cash to be invested in the business by owners during this month.
13. **Repayment of short-term debt:** Enter payments on principal and interest on short-term loans due during the month.
14. **Capital expenditure:** Enter payments on permanent business investment, such as real estate mortgages, or equipment purchases due during the month.

15. **Repayment of long-term debt:** Enter payments on long-term principal and interest due during the month.
16. **Cash withdrawals:** Enter owners' cash withdrawals anticipated during the month.
17. **NET MONTHLY CASH POSITION:** Add items 9–12, then subtract items 13–16.
18. **BEGINNING CASH:** Enter previous month's cumulative cash (item 19 of previous month's forecast or actual cash position at first of month).
19. **CUMULATIVE CASH POSITION:** Add beginning cash (item 18) to net monthly cash position (item 17).

Industry Comparisons. On an annual basis, the National Restaurant Association and the accounting firm Deloitte and Touche team up to compile and publish a "Restaurant Industry Operations (RIO) Report." In this very helpful document, there are numerous tables and exhibits that should enable you to compare your bar operation with the national averages.

The example offered here (as Figure 14.5) is from the "RIO Report" for 2000. It is a table of expenses and sales for full-service restaurants, with average check (per person) under $15. The table shows three levels of sales costs: upper, median, and lower. It is best to use the median range when planning the budget for a new bar business.

You'll also notice these ratios are based on total sales, except for food and beverage cost ratios, which are based on their respective sales. And this is only a small portion of the total information available in the annual "RIO Report." There are also more detailed statistics with breakdowns based on:

• Metropolitan and nonmetropolitan restaurants
• Menu themes
• Average check
• Single-unit and multiunit franchises
• Types of ownership: sole proprietors, corporations, partnerships
• Sales volume
• Leased space and owned space

Further, the study offers several reports broken down by state, for the following states: California, Colorado, Florida, Illinois, Michigan, New York, Ohio, Pennsylvania, Texas, Washington, and Wisconsin.

THE CONTROL PHASE

On paper, your budget plan is a numerical blueprint for your operations during the coming year. To turn this "paper plan" into reality, you make whatever operating changes you have decided on to reduce costs and/or increase

Full-Service Restaurants (Average Check Per Person Under $15)
Statement of Income and Expenses—Ratio to Total Sales*

| | Type of Establishment | | | | | |
| | Food Only | | | Food and Beverage | | |
	Lower Quartile	Median	Upper Quartile	Lower Quartile	Median	Upper Quartile
Sales						
Food	100.0%	100.0%	100.0%	72.9%	84.2%	94.8%
Beverage	N/A	N/A	N/A	5.2	15.8	27.1
Total Sales	100.0	100.0	100.0	100.0	100.0	100.0
Cost of Sales						
Food	27.8	31.0	36.6	29.3	33.9	39.4
Beverage	N/A	N/A	N/A	23.3	27.9	34.2
Total Cost of Sales	27.8	31.0	36.6	28.6	32.3	37.1
Gross Profit	65.5	70.3	72.6	63.0	67.7	71.5
Operating Expenses						
Salaries and Wages	28.8	32.6	38.4	25.8	30.0	35.5
Employee Benefits	**	3.5	**	**	4.4	**
Direct Operating Expenses	3.6	4.7	8.0	3.7	5.0	7.5
Music and Entertainment	0.0	0.0	0.1	0.0	0.0	0.3
Marketing	0.7	1.2	3.0	0.9	2.0	3.7
Utility Services	2.1	3.1	4.0	2.1	2.8	3.7
Restaurant Occupancy Costs	3.2	5.6	8.1	2.9	5.1	7.6
Repairs and Maintenance	0.9	1.6	2.4	1.1	1.5	2.3
Depreciation	0.6	1.2	2.3	0.6	1.6	2.9
Other Expense/(Income)	0.0	0.1	0.9	0.0	0.1	1.8
General & Administrative Expenses	0.7	2.4	6.7	1.1	2.9	6.1
Corporate Overhead	0.0	0.2	3.6	0.0	0.0	4.7
Total Operating Expenses	54.2	60.9	66.4	53.6	60.7	66.7
Interest Expense	0.0	0.3	1.7	0.0	0.1	1.1
Other Expenses	**	**	**	**	**	**
Income (Loss) Before Income Taxes	1.2%	6.3%	10.3%	0.8%	5.2%	11.4%

Note Computations include respondents that provided zeros and numerical amounts.

*All ratios are based as a percentage of total sales except food and beverage costs, which are based on their respective sales.

**Insufficient data.

N/A Not applicable.

Figure 14.5 Expenses and sales for a full-service restaurant. Excerpted from *Restaurant Industry Operations Report 2000,* with permission of the National Restaurant Association, www.restaurant.org.

sales to match the numbers on the plan. From this point on, you monitor the actual performance of the bar, using the budget as a standard of measurement, a tool of control.

The control process consists of the following three steps:

1. Compare performance with plan to discover variations.
2. Analyze operations to track the causes of the variations.
3. Act promptly to solve problems.

These three steps are the links that connect the plan with the profit.

Naturally, the budget and the actual results are not going to correlate number for number every day or even every week or month. For example, you may put out a lot of money to buy liquor to cover the American Legion convention and the sales won't show up until the next monitoring period. So, in one period, both your dollar costs and your percentage costs rise, and then in the next period your dollar costs are back to normal but your percentage cost drops because your sales went up during the convention. So, how do you judge when a variation is significant?

A **budget deviation analysis** (BDA) should be part of your monthly budgeting process. It's like taking a second look at the newly completed month's budget, to see where—and how much—actual figures deviated from what you'd expected. A sample BDA form is shown as Figure 14.6. To compare your business' performance with other, national figures, the National Restaurant Association's Industry Operations Reports come in handy.

To some extent, the significance of any variation depends on what it is— a sales, labor or beverage cost, or something else. It also makes a difference how large it is and how persistent. You can set an acceptable variation percentage based on past history for several periods. There are also a few basic rules. Generally, a variation is significant if it shows up in both dollars and percent of sales. Less significant is a dollar variation by itself. Least significant is a percentage variation by itself. However, you ought to look into any persistent variation or one that is over your permissible plan.

The Income Statement

The most useful tool you have for comparing performance with plan is the periodic **income statement** prepared by your accountant. It is part of control because you measure results by it. It is part of planning because it is the basis for future decisions.

An income statement shows the kinds and amounts of revenue, the kinds and amounts of expenses, and the resulting profit or loss over a given period of time (Figure 14.7). It is routinely prepared at the end of each month or each accounting period. When you compare it with your budget and with the statements of preceding periods, it tells you how you are doing. It also gives you the dollar data you need to figure the cost percentages you use

Budget Deviation Analysis

From Income Statement for Month _____

	A ACTUAL	B BUDGET	C DEVIATION (B – A)	D % OF DEVIATION (C/B × 100)
TOTAL SALES				
Liquor				
Beer				
Wine				
TOTAL				
Less COST OF BEVERAGE SOLD				
Beginning inventory				
+ Purchases				
− Ending inventory				
TOTAL COST				
GROSS PROFIT				
Less OPERATING (VARIABLE/CONTROLLABLE)				
EXPENSES				
Payroll Cost				
Administrative expenses				
Laundry and supplies				
Utilities				
Advertising and promotion				
Repairs				
Maintenance				
Miscellaneous operating expenses				
TOTAL VARIABLE EXPENSES				
GROSS OPERATING PROFIT				
Less FIXED OVERHEAD (NONCONTROLLABLE)				
EXPENSES				
Rent				
Taxes				
Insurance				
Interest				
Licenses and fees				
Depreciation				
Amortization				
TOTAL FIXED EXPENSES				
NET PROFIT BEFORE INCOME TAXES				

Figure 14.6 Budget deviation analysis form.

INCOME STATEMENT: September 2001

	Liquor	Beer	Wine	September 2001		Year to Date	
TOTAL SALES							
Liquor $22,550.30						$67,230.20	
Beer 7,129.45						20,048.45	
Wine 13,743.85						37,965.00	
				$43,423.60	100.00%	$125,243.65	100.00%
Less COST OF BEVERAGE SOLD							
Beginning inventory	$2692.70	$1620.10	$2179.45				
+ Purchases	5101.35	2130.00	3603.10				
	$7794.05	$3750.10	$5782.55				
− Ending inventory	3622.24	902.10	1530.20				
TOTAL COST	$4171.81	$2848.00	$4252.35	$11,272.16	25.96%	$30,935.18	24.69%
GROSS PROFIT				$32,151.44		$94,308.47	
Less OPERATING (CONTROLLABLE) EXPENSES							
Payroll costs				$13,620.70		$40,075.90	
Administrative expenses				1,328.78		3,040.00	
Laundry and supplies				1,101.20		2,804.20	
Utilities				385.26		1,125.60	
Advertising and promotion				275.00		690.00	
Repairs				510.00		1,038.26	
Maintenance				874.00		2,196.00	
Miscellaneous operating expenses				162.00		250.35	
TOTAL VARIABLE EXPENSES				$18,256.94	42.04%	$51,220.31	40.89%
GROSS OPERATING PROFIT				$13,894.50		$43,088.16	
Less FIXED OVERHEAD (NONCONTROLLABLE) EXPENSES							
Rent				$850.00		$2,550.00	
Taxes				440.00		1,320.00	
Insurance				357.00		1,071.00	
Interest				818.00		2,454.00	
Licenses and fees				907.00		2,721.00	
Depreciation				774.00		2,322.00	
Amortization				320.00		960.00	
TOTAL FIXED EXPENSES				$4,466.00	10.29%	$13,397.00	10.69%
NET PROFIT BEFORE INCOME TAXES				$9,428.50	21.71%	$29,691.16	23.70%

Figure 14.7 A monthly income statement.

for analysis and control. The income statement is management's most important accounting tool.

The income statement is compiled from the various revenue and expense accounts for the period. It shows a summary figure for each account—the account balance. The way in which the income statement groups and presents these summary figures has a lot to do with its usefulness to the manager of the bar.

Figure 14.7 shows an income statement structured for maximum usefulness. There are two principles behind this arrangement:

- **Responsibility.** Revenues and expenses are grouped according to the responsibilities involved. Thus, for each grouping, the performance of the person responsible can be measured and evaluated.
- **Controllability.** Expenses are classified and grouped according to the extent to which they can be controlled. This income statement shows three levels of controllability: beverage expenses (directly related to sales and fully controllable), operating expenses (related to sales to some extent and controllable in some degree), and fixed expenses (noncontrollable overhead expense).

According to these two principles, this income statement is separated into three successive profit levels. Its structure is shown in Figure 14.8.

- The first level is **gross profit (contribution margin),** or profit from beverage sales less beverage costs. The responsibility includes sales volume, beverage supply, and beverage cost control. This level of profit is the responsibility of the manager.
- The second level is **gross operating profit,** or gross profit less operating expenses. This responsibility, also the manager's, includes supplying items of sales-related expense (labor, supplies, laundry, utilities, maintenance, promotion, and so on) in amounts that support and increase beverage sales, while controlling the costs of these items.

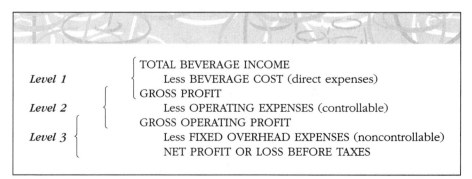

Figure 14.8 Structure of Figure 14.7.

- The third level is **net income** (*net profit before taxes*), or operating profit less fixed overhead expenses, such as rent, taxes, licenses and fees, insurance, interest, depreciation, and amortization. The responsibility here, to the extent that these expenses can be altered, involves finance and investment policy, contracts, and high-level decision-making. Those responsible for this segment of expenses and for the net-profit level are the owners of small businesses or top management in a large corporation.

Note, though responsibility for net profit remains at the top, as a practical matter, profitability depends on the extent to which the gross operating profit (Level 2) exceeds the fixed expenses. Since the manager is responsible for this level of profit, profitability is in his or her hands.

Thus, the goal should be to maximize gross operating profit, and the strategy should be to relate specific costs to the sales they produce, rather than simply thinking in general terms of maximizing sales and holding down costs. It's okay to spend money to make money. If increasing a cost increases sales by a more than proportionate amount, it is profitable to increase that cost.

Each monthly income statement tells you how you are doing when you compare it with your budget and the statements of preceding periods. It also gives you the dollar data you need to figure the cost percentages you need for analysis and control.

Data Analysis

The income statement is a form of data analysis. It arranges data in ways that show measurable relationships. If you carry the process further by translating cost and sales into percentage terms for specific budget items, you can see and measure relationships in significant ways. Then you can make changes that will decrease costs or increase sales. You will use your income statement in this way. In addition, if daily data are gathered and organized by computer, you can study what is happening almost as it happens.

Two areas of analysis are especially important: sales and operating expenses as they relate to sales. A third area, overhead expenses as they relate to sales, is also important, but since these expenses are fixed, there is less you can do about them.

All profits come from sales; therefore, increasing sales is one road to maximizing profits. To do this, you need all kinds of information about sales, such as volume per drink, per price, per shift, per day, per week, per month, and per season. If you gather the data and calculate the **cost/sales ratio,** you can see where the profit is being made and where to put your marketing emphasis. You can also measure the effects of any changes you make.

The other piece of the profit equation is cost: profit equals sales less cost. A bar's operating expenses are the manager's responsibility. They are tied in varying degrees to the rise and fall of sales, and they are always examined in relation to the sales they help produce. Keeping close track of this relationship can tell you a great deal about what is happening to profit day by day.

The two major categories of operating expenses—beverage cost and payroll expense—are called **prime costs** because they are the largest and most necessary items for which you spend your money. Beverage cost is the cost of the alcoholic beverages sold. Since the cost of these is dictated largely by customer taste, the manager's major focus is on controlling losses. Here, data analysis in the form of cost/sales ratios is a common way of detecting and measuring losses.

Payroll expense, the other prime cost, basically represents the cost of preparing and serving the products sold. Payroll costs should be correlated with sales for the same period in a cost percentage figure and measured against the budget goal and percentages for previous periods. If your cost/sales ratio is high, look for ways to avoid overtime or cut staff or hours worked.

Other operating expenses, as well as overhead expenses, should also be closely watched in terms of cost/sales ratios and compared with budget goals and past history. The higher the percentage for costs, the lower the percentage for profits. A decline in the cost/sales ratio might indicate action to step up promotion or to stay open longer or to think about renovating your facility.

Assessing the Achievement

The control phase of any budget plan should conclude with several comparisons:

- **With past performance.** How did you do this year compared with last year?
- **With industry performance.** How did you do compared to your competitors and to the industry at large?
- **With your own goals.** How close did you come to reaching your profit goal?

The final and most important question you should ask yourself is: How can you use your experience with the past year's budget in structuring next year's budget to meet your profit goal?

PRICING FOR PROFIT

Profit is the difference been total sales and total costs. For a bar, total sales are the number of drinks sold multiplied by the selling prices. The essence of profitable pricing is to set the individual prices to produce the maximum difference between total sales and total costs. Several factors are involved: the cost of each drink, the effect of price on demand for the drink, the contribution of each drink to total sales, and the effect of the sales mix on profits. There are many different ways of pricing in the bar business, used consciously or unconsciously, sometimes simultaneously, often inconsistently. Some managers set prices by a strict cost/price formula. Some set them by trial and error. Some charge what the traffic will bear. Many price according to neighborhood competition. Some copy the bar with the biggest business. Some set prices low, hoping to undercut their competitors; others set prices high to limit their clientele to a certain income level. A few lucky ones, in command of a unique facility such as a revolving skyscraper lounge, set skyscraper prices because they assume the customer expects them. Some use an impressive price/value combination as a basic merchandising strategy.

Whatever the pricing policy, the goal should be to set prices that will maximize the **gross profit** or **contribution margin** (sales less product cost). Each of the many drinks of the bar should be priced to achieve this total outcome.

The Cost/Price Relationship

Any sound method of pricing a drink should start with its cost. You can establish a percentage relationship between cost and price that will give you a simple pricing formula to work with. The cost percentage of the price pays for the ingredients in the drink, and the remaining percentage of the price (gross margin) goes to pay that drink's share of all your other costs and your profit. The cost percentage will be in the neighborhood of the beverage-cost percentage of your budget (refer again to Figure 14.2), though it will not correspond exactly since the latter represents the combined percentages of liquor, wine, and beer. Generally, your liquor-cost percentage will be 20 to 25 percent, while wine and beer will run higher—33 to 50 percent. Each enterprise must determine its own cost percentage to produce the profit needed.

To find the price, divide the cost of the ingredients by the cost percentage:

$$\frac{\text{Cost}}{\text{Cost Percentage}} = \text{Sales Price}$$

For example:

$$\frac{\$0.55 \text{ Cost of } 1\frac{1}{4} \text{ oz scotch}}{0.25 \text{ Cost Percentage}} = \$2.20 \text{ price for Scotch Mist}$$

You can turn this formula around and convert the cost percentage into a multiplier by dividing it into 100 percent, which represents the sales price. For example:

$$\frac{100\% \text{ (Sales Price)}}{0.25 \text{ (Cost Percentage)}} = 4 \text{ (Multiplier)}$$

$$4 \times \$0.55 \text{ (Cost)} = \$2.20 \text{ (Sales Price)}$$

In pricing mixed drinks, the simplest version of this cost/price formula is to use the cost of the beverage alone. This is known as the **beverage-cost method.** In the Scotch Mist example just given, this cost figure is very accurate, since scotch is the only ingredient. However, most drinks have more than one ingredient, many of them nonalcoholic, such as mixers, garnishes, and cream. A truly accurate cost/price relationship must be based on the cost of all the ingredients. The technique of determining total cost is based on the drink's recipe and is known as **costing** the recipe.

Here is a simple method of costing as an example:

1. We start with the standard house recipe.

1. Recipe: 2 oz gin
         ½ oz dry vermouth
         1 pitted olive

2. We determine the cost of the gin. To do this, we find:
   (a) The size bottle poured and its ounce
   (b) Bottle cost (from invoice)
   (c) Cost per ounce (divide bottle cost by ounce per bottle)
   (d) Recipe cost of gin (multiply ounce cost by number of ounces in recipe

2. Cost of gin:
   (a) Liter = 33.8 oz
   (b) $11.95
   (c) $\dfrac{\$11.95 \text{ bottle cost}}{33.8 \text{ oz per bottle}} =$
           $0.35 per oz
   (d) $0.35 cost per oz
       × 2 oz in recipe
       $0.70 recipe cost of gin

3. We determine the cost of the vermouth in the same way:
   (a) Size bottle and ounce capacity
   (b) Bottle cost (from invoice)
   (c) Cost per ounce
   (d) Recipe cost of vermouth (ounce cost × ounces)

3. Cost of vermouth:
   (a) 750 ml = 25.4 oz
   (b) $4.15
   (c) $\dfrac{\$4.15 \text{ bottle cost}}{25.4 \text{ oz per bottle}}$
           = $0.163 per oz
   (d) $0.163 cost per oz
       × 0.5 oz in recipe
       $0.081 recipe cost of vermouth

4. Then we determine the cost of the olive:
   (a) Jar size and olive count (from invoice or
   (b) Cost of jar (from invoice)
   (c) Cost per olive
   (d) Recipe cost of olive

4. Cost of olive:
   (a) Quart = 80 olives
   (b) $2.20
   (c) $\dfrac{\$2.20 \text{ container cost}}{80}$
           = $0.027 per olive
   (d) 1 olive = $0.027 recipe cost

5. Now we total the costs. This gives us our standard recipe cost as of the date of costing.

5. Total costs:
   $0.700 cost of gin
    0.081 cost of vermouth
    0.027 cost of olive
   $0.808 standard recipe cost

To arrive at the selling price of the drink, we divide the cost by the cost percentage. This gives us our sales price:

$$\frac{\$0.808 \text{ Recipe Cost}}{0.25 \text{ Cost Percentage}} = \$3.232 \text{ (Sales Price, which we round off to \$3.25)}$$

A quicker, though less accurate, way to arrive at a selling price is to base the price on the cost of the **prime ingredient**—that is, the base liquor—instead of the actual recipe cost, adding a certain percentage for the extra ingredients. This is a refinement of the beverage-cost method. Using our Martini as an example, it works like this:

$0.700	Prime Ingredient Cost
+ 0.070	10% allowance for additional ingredients
$0.770	Cost Base
× 4	Multiplier
$3.080	Sales Price (rounded off to $3.10)

Pricing mixed drinks on the basis of prime ingredient cost is a quick, easy, and widely used method. It is typically used to establish a base price for all drinks having the same amount of the same prime ingredient; then the percentage is added for drinks having extra ingredients. Obviously, the method is not as accurate as costing the recipe; you can see that the added percentage in the example does not reflect true cost. A single percentage figure will never be accurate for a whole spectrum of drinks.

A third method, the **gross profit method,** is used to express the amount of gross profit realized on the sale of one drink. It is determined by dividing the amount of gross profit by the sales price of the drink. Here's how it works: First, you subtract the cost of the drink from its selling price, then you divide the result (the gross profit) by the selling price. This gives you the gross profit margin as a percent. For example:

Selling price is $4.50
Cost of drink is $0.75
Gross profit: $4.50 − $0.75 = $3.75
Profit margin: $\dfrac{\$3.75}{4.50} = 0.833$, or 83.3%

You can, of course, "reverse" this method to set the prices of drinks. But first, you must use the gross margin percent to get a reciprocal figure (a percentage of 1.000) then divide this reciprocal figure into the cost of the drink. Let's look closer:

1.000 − 0.833 = 0.167, or 16.7%
(The "reciprocal" of the 83.3% gross margin is 16.7%)
Now, divide the cost of the drink by the reciprocal amount:
$\dfrac{\$0.75}{0.167} = \$4.491$ (round up to $4.50)

As you can tell, costing and pricing takes a great deal of time. But to arrive at a sound price structure you have to establish the cost of each drink, one way or another. Only if you look at each drink by itself can you establish sound cost/price relationships and build a coherent overall price structure.

The Demand/Price Relationship

Costs and percentages are not the whole answer to pricing. Price is only one of two factors in total sales. The other, as you likely know, is the number of drinks sold. And the price affects the number. It is the effect of prices on numbers that is the elusive secret of successful pricing—elusive because no one ever knows precisely what effect a change of price will have on demand in any given situation.

If you increase the price of a given drink, you increase the margin per drink sold, since cost remains the same. But sales volume is typically sensitive to changes in prices. In a normal situation (whatever that is), there is a seesaw relationship: when the price goes up, the margin per drink goes up but the number of drinks sold goes down (demand falls). When the price goes down, the margin per drink goes down but the number sold goes up (demand rises).

That said, one seldom has a totally "normal" situation. In any given bar, more than price is influencing demand—drink quality, ambience, food, entertainment, individual capacity, other drinks, other bars. How much of a price increase for a given drink will cause a customer to order fewer drinks or switch to a lower-priced drink? At what lower overall price level will customers choose you over your competitors? At what higher price levels will they start to patronize the bar next door instead? Where does the seesaw balance?

Most bars operate in a competitive environment in which demand is fairly responsive to price changes. The trick is to know your competition and especially your customers, make shrewd guesses on demand/price sensitivity, and watch your sales to see how they respond. Your objective is to balance the seesaw for all the drinks taken together in a way that will bring the largest overall margin for the enterprise.

Coordinating Prices to Maximize Profits. When you have the whole detailed picture of cost-based prices, you can round off and finalize drink prices with your eye on the seesaw of demand. The first modification of cost/price ratios is to simplify the picture by establishing several broad categories of drinks and setting uniform prices within each category. This makes it easier for everybody and enables bartenders and servers to complete sales transactions efficiently.

The following price categories may be useful; they should at least give you a point of departure for your own scheme:

- **Highballs.** Two prices, one for drinks poured with well brands and one for call-brand drinks. Generally, highballs make up the lowest price category.

PRICE LIST
Restaurant Bar

Glass/Size	Drink Category	Drink Size	Drink Price
9 oz.	**HIGHBALLS**		
	Well	1.5 oz.	$3.50
	Call	1.5	4.00
	Premium	1.5	4.24
	Superpremium	1.5	4.50
7 oz.	**ROCKS**		
	Well	1.5	3.50
	Call	1.5	4.50
	Premium/Superpremium	1.5	4.75
1.5 jigger/lined	**SHOTS**		
	Well	1.0 oz.	3.50
	Call	1.0	3.75
	Premium/Superpremium	1.0	4.00
7 oz. Rocks *or*	**MARTINI/MANHATTAN**		
4 oz. Cocktail	Well	2 oz./.25 oz.	4.25
	Call	2 oz./.25 oz	4.50
	Premium/Superpremium	2 oz./.25 oz	5.00
12 oz. Stemmed	**JUICE DRINKS**: Mary/Driver/Collins/Sling		
or	Well	1.5 oz.	4.00
12 oz. Tumbler	Call	1.5	4.50
	Premium/Superpremium	1.5	5.00
12 oz. Stemmed	**DAIQUIRI/MARGARITA/SOUR**		
or	Well	1.5 oz.	4.00
12 oz. Tumbler	Call	1.5	4.50
or	Premium	1.5	5.00
Specialty Glass			
12 oz. Snifter	**BRANDIES and LIQUEURS**		
	Well	1.5 oz.	4.00
	Call	1.5	5.00
	Premium/Superpremium	1.5	5.50
7 oz Rocks *or*	**CREAM and TWO-LIQUOR DRINKS**		
Specialty Glass	Well	1 oz. Plus 1 oz	4.00
	Call	1 oz Plus 1 oz	4.50
	Premium/Superpremium	1 oz Plus 1 oz	5.00

Figure 14.9 A comprehensive price list.

10 oz Coffee	**COFFEE DRINKS**		
Glass	Well/one-liquor	1.5 oz	$4.50
	Well/two-liquor	1 oz each	5.00
	Call/one-liquor	1.5 oz	5.00
	Call/two-liquor	1 oz each	5.50
10 oz Glass	**WINES**		
	House Wine	6 oz	4.00
		Bottle	14.00
	Premium Wine	6 oz	5.00
		Bottle	See wine list
6 oz Flute	**CHAMPAGNE**		
	Bottle	187 ml	8.50
	Bottle	750 ml	See wine list
12 oz Mug/	**BEERS**		
16 oz Pint/	Premium Draft	12 oz	2.75
32 oz Pitcher		16 oz	3.75
		32 oz Pitcher	5.50
	Superpremium Draft	12 oz	3.25
		16 oz	4.00
		32 oz Pitcher	6.00
	Premium Bottled Beer	12 oz	3.50
	Super/Premium Bottled Beer	12 oz	4.00
12 oz Wine	Bottled Water	Various	2.50
12 oz Mug	Soft Drinks	No Liquor	2.00
12 oz Wine	Nonalcoholic Drinks	No Liquor	2.50
12 oz wine	Fruit Juices	No Liquor	2.50

Figure 14.9 *(Continued)*

- **Cocktails.** Two prices, one for cocktails made with well brands and one for those made with call brands.
- **Frozen drinks and ice cream drinks.** Two prices, for well and call brands.
- **After-dinner liqueurs and brandies.** Two prices, one for ordinary liqueurs and one for premium liqueurs and French brandies.
- **Specialty Drinks.** Two prices, for well and call brands.

All pricing decisions involve interdependent relationships among drinks and drink prices. The price you charge for one kind of drink can affect the demand for others. For example, if you raise your cocktail prices, you may sell fewer cocktails and more highballs for fewer total dollars. On the other hand, if you introduce a high-priced frozen drink with customer appeal, you may sell more of them and fewer of your lower-priced highballs and cocktails. A high-profit coffee specialty at a premium price may not affect demand for predinner drinks at all. You have to keep potential interrelationships in mind in order to arrive at a combination that maximizes the sum total of all drink profits. This is known as **total business pricing.**

Some drinks always have a lower margin because demand drops sharply as the price goes up. Among these are beer and wines by the bottle. In most places, few bottles of wine are sold when they are priced at three or four times the cost. On the other hand, it is usually easy to get a high margin for specialty drinks and house wine by the glass.

You can use a lower-margin price as a way to increase volume by bringing in new customers. You can also reduce prices selectively to create a mood for buying other drinks. You might, for example, have a special low price on frozen Strawberry Daiquiris on a hot day and sell many other frozen drinks at their regular price just by planting the frozen-drink idea. Or you can reduce your standard prices on higher-priced drinks and raise them on lower-priced drinks and you may come out ahead.

All these price relationships must be worked out for your own enterprise. Some work well in some places and others don't. Whatever combination of prices gives you the best overall price-times-numbers-less-cost is the best set of prices for you . . . for the moment, at least. Things change, and you have to watch sales closely. It is a fascinating game.

It is a good idea to provide a list of standard prices, both for the customer and for service personnel. You can post prices at the bar (see Figure 14.9) or print them on a menu. They will eliminate arguments between employees and customers, and they will make it harder for unscrupulous employees to overcharge and pocket the difference.

The Pour-Cost Analysis

Yet another way to assess a bar's financial performance is to analyze its **pouring costs.** This is a way to compare the different cost percentages of wine, beer, and distilled spirits. Since each of these broad categories sell at substantially different cost percentages, you should calculate each category separately.

Pouring costs are figured by dividing the cost of the depleted inventory ("cost of goods sold") by the gross sales earned over a given time period—say, one month. The owner or manager decides the time period, but the shorter time it encompasses, the more information you have about the bar's true financial state.

Here are sample calculations for a pour-cost analysis:

Opening Inventory Value	$12,720	
plus (+) Liquor Purchases		28,340
TOTAL Amount Available for Sale	$41,060	

Closing Inventory Value	$12,135	
plus (+) Cost of Spillage		103
plus (+) Cost of Complimentary Drinks		427
plus (+) Transfers Out from the Bar		268
Adjusted Closing Inventory	$12,933	
Total Available for Sale		$41,060
minus (−) Adjusted Closing Inventory	12,933	
Liquor Cost		$28,127

$$\frac{\$28,127 \text{ Liquor Cost (Cost of Goods Sold)}}{\$172,820 \text{ (Gross Liquor Sales)}} = 0.162, \text{ or } 16.2\%$$

Industry Standards for Pouring Costs

Category	Cost Percentage Range
Liquor	
Well Liquor	9%–10%
Call Liquor	12%–14%
Premium Liquor	16%–18%
Superpremium	18%–20%
Top-Shelf Liquor	20%–24%
Overall Liquor Pour Cost	16%–20%
Beer	
American Bottled Beer	17%–33%
Imported Bottled Beer	20%–37%
Microbrews Bottled	25%–35%
Overall Bottled Beer Pour Cost	18%–28%
American Draft Beer	10%–20%
Imported Draft Beer	14%–35%
Microbrews Draft	22%–33%
Overall Draft Beer Pour Cost	16%–28%
Wine	
House Wine by the Glass	12%–18%
Varietals by the Glass	20%–25%
Varietal Bottled Wine (750ml)	33%–60%
Overall Wine Pour Cost	16%–33%

Figure 14.10 Industry standards for pouring costs. *Source: Successful Beverage Management,* Robert Plotkin and Steve Goumus (*Bar Media,* 2001).

Table 14.1

Bar Sales/Cost Mix

Category	Monthly Sales	Monthly Costs	Percentage Cost/Month	Monthly Mix
Liquor	$35,248	$ 7,627	21.6%	45.8%
Beer	22,730	6,913	30.4%	29.6%
Wine	18,970	7,016	36.9%	24.6%
TOTALS	$76,948	$24,679	32.0%	100.0%

(**NOTE:** In the Totals row, the 32 percent figure is obtained by dividing the monthly costs by the monthly sales.)

This calculation may be further analyzed with the following operating factors in mind:

- The quality and cost of the well liquors. If the bar is pouring the more expensive brands, the well liquor will yield very favorable pouring cost percentages for this category.
- There is a wide disparity in beer quality and price between domestic, imported, and microbrewed brands. The pouring cost percentages here will be greatly affected by the beer sales mix percentages—what, and how much, you pour. If your customers drink more of the lower-cost bottled beers, the pouring costs for beer will be lower overall.
- When you calculate pouring costs of wines by the glass, two factors are critical: the cost per ounce for the wine and the portion size served.

The industry standards for pouring costs, shown as Figure 14.10, come from *Successful Beverage Management* by Robert Plotkin and Steve Goumas (Bar Media, 2001.)

The sales mix at the bar will also affect pouring cost. By "sales mix," we mean the percentages of total bar sales that are beer, wine, and spirits. Table 14.1 shows a breakdown of bar sales and cost mix. For this table to be helpful, you need to compare the Monthly Sales Mix column between reporting periods. As the sales mix increases in a category that has a high monthly cost percent (the third column), pouring costs will also increase. Therefore, for the most favorable pouring costs, look for high sales mix percentages in categories with low monthly cost percentages.

ESTABLISHING PRODUCT CONTROLS

In Chapters 10 and 11 on mixology, you learned what makes a successful mixed drink and how to develop recipes for your drinks so that each drink served from your bar will taste the way you want it to. But how can you be sure the recipes you have carefully developed will be faithfully followed by each bartender, keeping in mind that each has his or her personal ways of pouring, and that bartenders come and go from your employ at the normal rate for the species?

Not only do you want the drinks served at your bar to be your recipes, you want them to be prepared the same every time they are ordered. Product consistency is very important in building a clientele. New customers expect your Bloody Mary to taste the way a Bloody Mary should, and repeat customers expect your Bloody Mary to taste the way it did the last time. Meeting customer expectations may be even more important to profit than setting your drink prices correctly. It is sales price multiplied by sales volume that produces the profit your budget stipulates, and you can't build volume on the basis of drinks that don't consistently meet customer needs and desires.

To achieve this consistency, you need to establish standards for all drinks; that is, standard ingredients, quantities, portion sizes, and procedures for making them. When these standards are put into practice, and everyone is required to follow them, the customer will get the same drink every time no matter who makes it.

In addition to producing consistent drinks, these standards give you ways of controlling the quantities of liquor used. If you can control the quantities, you also control the costs. And if you control the beverage costs, you can maintain your protected cost/sales ratio and protect your profit. To achieve all this, you must standardize three major elements for each drink: size, recipe, and glass.

Standard Drink Size

In the vocabulary of the bar, the term **drink size** refers to the *amount of the prime ingredient* used per drink poured, *not* the size of the finished drink. In each bar, this amount is the same for most spirit-based drinks, with different standard amounts for a few drink types and special drinks. Thus, if your drink size is 1½ ounces, you pour 1½ ounces of the base liquor in each drink, whether it is a gin drink or vodka or scotch or whatever. This is your **standard drink size.**

Each bar has its own standard drink size. Most bars pour a 1-ounce or 1¼-ounce standard drink, but it varies across the industry from ¾ ounce to 2 ounces, depending on the nature of the enterprise and the clientele. In each bar, special drink types that vary from the standard will have its own standard drink size. You can see how this works in one bar by studying the Drink Size column in Figure 14.9, shown earlier.

To pour a standard drink, the bartender must have an accurate means of measuring the liquor. As discussed at length in Chapter 10, there are several ways of measuring: hand measuring, metered or automated pouring, and free-pouring.

In a bar concerned with consistency and tight liquor controls, free-pouring is out of the question, no matter how skilled the bartender. There is too much potential for variation. The most common way of measuring is to use a shot glass and stainless-steel jiggers of various sizes. All shot glasses should be the standard drink size. They will function as the jigger for the base liquor. Different sizes of stainless-steel jiggers will provide the means of measuring the smaller amounts called for in drinks containing more than one liquor as well as larger amounts for brandies and oversize drinks. If the bartender is well trained, skillful, and honest, measuring with these hand measures will produce controlled, consistent drinks.

Even so, overpouring and underpouring are hazards of the hand method, whether intentional or caused by the rush of business. In a bar with annual sales of $100,000, a steady overpouring of $\frac{1}{4}$ ounce per drink could add $2,000 to $3,000 a year to your costs. Many enterprises, large and small, are using some method of controlled pour, either pourers that measure or an automated pouring system.

Several types of automated pouring systems were described in Chapter 4. Preset to pour the standard-size drink and to record each drink poured, they eliminate overpouring, underpouring and spillage, and help to provide a consistent drink. Most systems pour only the major liquors, however, so there is still more for error, inconsistency, and loss.

Whatever the measuring method, a list of drink sizes should be posted at the bar showing mixed drinks, wine, beer, and special drinks. Again, refer back to Figure 14.9, which is a comprehensive list of drink sizes, glass sizes, and prices.

Standard Drink Recipe

The mixology chapters emphasized the importance of proportions in making a good drink and the wisdom of writing them down in recipe form. A recipe that specifies exactly how a given drink is made at a given bar is known as a **standardized recipe** (Figure 14.11). It specifies the exact quantity of each ingredient, the size glass to be used, and the exact procedure for preparing the drink. The garnish is included, as is anything else that is necessary to the drink. If there is a picture of the finished drink in its assigned glass, so much the better.

You should have a standardized recipe for every drink you serve. Keep the recipes together in a loose-leaf notebook with plastic page covers or, better yet, enter them in your computer. Use copies or printouts to train new bartenders, and see that every bartender, old and new, follows the house recipes to the letter. If you can make this happen, you will really have achieved control of quality and quantity.

The standardized recipe is the basis for the costing and pricing described earlier. Every recipe should be costed periodically, and the cost of each ingredient should be recorded on the recipe card, along with the date of costing. It is a good idea to review the whole recipe at this time, to be sure you

INGREDIENTS

2 oz gin
1/2 oz dry vermouth
1 olive

DRINK: Martini

GLASS: 4-oz cocktail
7-oz rocks

PROCEDURE

Stir gin/vermouth with 1/3 mixing glass cube ice.

Strain into prechilled cocktail glass or over cube ice in rocks glass.

Garnish with olive.

INGREDIENTS		BOTTLE	BOTTLE COST				DRINK	DRINK COST			
	DATE:					DATE:					
Gin											
Vermouth											
Olive											
			DRINK TOTALS								

DATE	
COST	
PRICE	
COST%	

Figure 14.11 Standardized recipe card with cost and price data.

haven't changed a garnish or a glass, or changed Cointreau to triple sec in your Sidecar without recording the change.

Standard Glassware

Each standard drink should be served in a **standard glass,** a glass of specified size and shape that is used every time that drink is poured. The size is the most important, since it controls the quantity of the ingredients that must fill it as well as the taste, as explained in Chapter 10. But a standard, distinctive shape is important, too. It makes a drink look the same every time, as well as taste the same, and it reduces the possibility of using the wrong-size glass. If you have two glasses of different sizes with the same shape, it is easy to get them mixed up, and if you use the wrong one it will alter the drink considerably. (A word to the wise: Order replacements by both size and catalog number. It is difficult to judge capacity by appearance.)

Some people equate glass size with portion size, and this has a superficial validity. But the real portion size is the drink size—the base liquor—controlled by the shot glass or jigger. In most cases, the drink glass has more to do with proportion than portion.

In standardizing your glassware, choose whatever size and shape will give each drink the most appeal. This doesn't mean the glassware itself has to be special; it means that the drink in the glass should look appealing. For example, a drink on the rocks looks skimpy if the glass is either too big or too small. A straight-up cocktail looks undersized in too large a glass. Shapes can make a big difference. A footed glass can make a drink look bigger than it does in a tumbler of the same capacity. Rounded shapes make a difference in the way the ice fits in, and that changes the way the liquid fills in around the ice. You really have to experiment. You must also allow for what the garnish will do to the drink. No glass should be so small that the measured drink fills it to the brim.

You can manage nicely with very few styles and sizes of glass if you wish: one glass for cocktails and Champagne, one for rocks drinks, one for highballs, one for tall drinks and beer, one for wine, and one for brandy and after-dinner liqueurs. The fewer the glass types, the fewer the mistakes in service. Your choices depend on your clientele, your drinks, and your image.

The glass for each drink should be specified on its standardized recipe record. It should also be on your drink list posted at the bar.

ESTABLISHING BEVERAGE CONTROLS

Ideally, all beverages "used" or "consumed" should be used to make drinks for which payment is collected and which are consumed by the paying customer. But not all liquor is so used or consumed. It may be overpoured, spilled, improperly mixed, or otherwise wasted. It may cling to the sides of empty bottles. It may be rung up incorrectly. Customers may refuse the drink, avoid paying for it, or pay too little. It may be pilfered by your own employees. One way or another, it is no longer available for sale. This kind of use, unchecked, can quickly deplete your profit margin.

If you have standardized your cost percentages, drink sizes, recipes, prices, inventory procedures, and par stock, you have already minimized certain kinds of losses. You have also provided tools for measuring loss. If measuring reveals that losses are indeed threatening profits, you can track down the causes and plug the leaks.

Three techniques of measuring are commonly used. One is based on cost percentage, a second compares ounces used with ounces sold, and the third measures potential sales value against actual sales. Each, in its own way, measures what you have to sell against what you do sell.

The Cost-Percentage Method

The first technique of measurement compares the cost of liquor used during a given period to the sales of the same period. The resulting percentage figure is then compared to the standard-cost percentage. This method requires a physical inventory of storeroom and bar at the beginning and end of the period, plus purchase and sales figures for the period. With this information in hand, make the following calculations:

1. To find the value of the liquor available for sale during the period, add the beginning inventory value to the value of the purchases:

$$\frac{\begin{array}{l}\text{Value of beginning inventory}\\ \text{plus (+) Value of liquor purchases}\end{array}}{\text{Value of liquor available for sales}}$$

2. To find the cost of the liquor used during the period, subtract the value of the ending inventory from the value of the liquor available:

$$\frac{\begin{array}{l}\text{Value of liquor available}\\ \text{minus (−) Value of ending inventory}\end{array}}{\text{Cost (value) of liquor used}}$$

3. To find the bar cost percentage, divide the cost of liquor used by the total sales for the period:

$$\frac{\text{Cost of liquor used}}{\text{Total dollar sales}} = \text{Bar-cost percentage}$$

The percentages for beer, wine, and spirits must be figured separately because they are all different.

The percentage figure can now be compared to the planned, or standard, bar-cost percentage (your budget figure) as well as to the percentages of previous periods. If your bar cost for the current period is more than 1½ percentage points higher than your planned bar cost or the average bar cost of several periods, you should start looking for the reasons.

You probably recognize this procedure as part of the end-of-the-month inventory routine described in Chapter 13. But if you wait until the end of the month, the damage is done and you may not be able to trace the cause. It is better to take weekly or even daily inventories to keep track of your bar costs. Where only beverage is concerned, physical inventories are usually not major undertakings.

The Ounce Method

The second technique of measurement compares the ounces of liquor used with the ounces of liquor sold. In this method, beginning and ending inventories at the bar each day reveal the number of ounces sold. You take the beginning inventory before the bar opens but after the par stock has been replenished, and the ending inventory after the bar closes. Then, you use your data as follows:

1. Subtract the ounces of each liquor in the ending inventory from the ounces of liquor in the beginning inventory. This gives you ounces used.
2. From your guest checks, tally the drinks sold by numbers of each type. For each type, multiply the ounces of liquor in one drink by the number of drinks sold, giving you the number of ounces per drink type. Then add them all up to find the number of ounces sold.
3. Subtract the number of ounces sold from the number of ounces used.

This is a daily measure, and it measures only what is happening at the bar, but it is accurate and it pinpoints this area of loss. Unfortunately, it takes time, unless you have a computerized register that can replace the guest check and the hand tally. (We'll discuss the uses of computers at the bar in just a moment.)

The Potential Sales-Value Method

The third method of measurement compares actual dollar sales with potential sales value. Each bottle you buy represents potential dollars in the register. We can determine its potential sales value by using standard drink sizes, standard drink selling prices, and the number of drinks that can be served from each bottle. For example, if you pour 1-ounce drinks, sell each drink for $1.00, and use only liter bottles, you should have $33.80 in the register for each bottle you use.

In real life, things are more complex. Most bars have more than one drink size and more than one drink price. Therefore, the potential sales value of each bottle must be adjusted for these variations. One method of doing this, the **weighted-average method,** is based on averages of drink sizes and prices for drinks actually sold over a period of time.

For the sake of illustration, let us telescope our time period into one typical day:

1. Find the average drink size for all the drinks made with one kind of liquor—gin, for instance:

Drink	Drinks Sold	Ounces Sold
Gimlet (1.5 oz.)	10	15
Martini (2 oz.)	40	80
Gin and Tonic (1.5 oz.)	12	18
	62	113

To complete this step, divide the total ounces sold (113) by total drinks sold (62) to obtain an average drink size:

$$\frac{113 \text{ oz.}}{62 \text{ oz.}} = 1.82 \text{ oz. Average gin drink size}$$

2. Find the number of drinks per bottle. If we divide our liter of gin (33.8 oz.) by our average drink size (1.82 oz.), we obtain the number of drinks per liter:

$$\frac{33.8 \text{ oz.}}{1.82 \text{ oz.}} = 18.57 \text{ Average drinks per liter of gin}$$

3. Next, find the average selling price of these drinks:

Drink	Number Sold	Total Sales
Gimlet @ $3.25	10	$ 32.50
Martini @ $3.25	40	130.00
Gin and Tonic @ $2.75	12	33.00
	62	$195.50

To complete this step, we divide total sales ($195.50) by the total drinks sold (62) to obtain the average drink-selling price:

$$\frac{\$195.50}{62} = \$3.15 \text{ Average selling price}$$

4. Finally, find the potential sales value of each liter of gin by multiplying the average drinks per liter (18.57) by the average selling price ($3.15):

$$\begin{array}{r} 18.57 \\ \times\ \$3.15 \\ \hline \$58.49 \end{array} \text{ (Potential sales value of 1 liter of gin)}$$

In the same way, we can figure the potential sales value of every bottle of liquor used in a given period. We can then compare the actual sales dollars with the potential sales value of the bottles to measure discrepancies. Ideally, the actual sales should equal the potential sales value.

The weighted-average method assumes that the sales mix, liquor costs, and sales prices remain constant; when anything changes, everything must be refigured. Moreover, this method consumes many hours with a calculator in hand in order to approximate accuracy, and it requires further refinements to take into account drinks having more than one liquor.

There is another, simpler method of approximating potential sales value. It requires a test period of 45 to 60 days during which you enforce all standards to the letter and observe all bar operations continuously. At the end of the period, you carefully determine bottle consumption from purchases, issues, and inventories, and translate it into potential sales value as though all liquor had been sold by the straight drink. Then you compare this value with actual sales during the period. The difference represents the varying amounts of liquor in your drinks, plus an inescapable minimum of waste and inefficiency. You convert this difference into a percentage figure and accept it as your **standard difference.** You can use it from then on to compare potential sales with actual sales. Any time the percentage of difference is higher than the standard difference, investigation is in order.

If costs and sales prices change, the percentage figure is still applicable. If the sales mix changes, a new test period is needed to determine a new standard difference.

The Role of Par Stock

In earlier chapters, we talked about par stock as a means of assuring a full supply of liquor at the bar and as an inventory tool. Now we can see par stock in still another role: as a key tool of control at the bar, where it is a standard against which consumption can be measured at any time.

With the one-empty-for-one-full system of requisitioning, a manager has only to count the bottles at the bar and compare the number with the par-stock form to determine whether anything is missing. This can be done as part of a full-bar inventory or the manager can spot-check any given brand at any time. And it is a wise manager who does so from time to time. Frequent checking is sometimes enough to prevent pilferage entirely. The more often you check, the more closely you can pinpoint the possible culprits, and the less likely they will be tempted. Even if you are not actually preventing losses, you will have a measure of what is missing, how serious it is, and who is most likely responsible.

Par stock is the last step in the series of controls over the liquor itself. In Chapter 13, we followed the liquor controls in a large operation from receiving to sale. Liquor was counted by the receiving agent, who assumed responsibility by signing the invoice. It then moved to the storeroom, where it was again counted and responsibility was transferred to the storeroom supervisor. The requisition, signed by the storeroom supervisor and the receiver, transferred the responsibility to the receiver, usually the bartender, who again counted the bottles. There the responsibility lies until it is sold.

This chain of responsibility resting in the hands of a single person at all times is a system every manager would do well to follow. It does not guarantee security, but it discourages theft and it facilitates finding the leaks and plugging them. In a small enterprise, of course, the owner/manager carries all the responsibilities that are divided among several people in the large establishment.

ESTABLISHING CASH CONTROLS

When a customer buys a drink, there has to be a way of making sure that the sale is recorded and that the money finds its way into the cash register. There are many systems of paying for drinks. The simplest procedure, and the riskiest, is for the bartender to pick up the cash laid out on the bar and ring it up on the register without the benefit of a guest check. The most complicated—and probably the safest though most expensive—is a computerized system that prerecords the sale, pours the liquor, and rings up the sale on both register and guest check, with a receipt for the customer. In between are many different systems. Some bars may run on a pay-as-you-go system; others may use a running-tab system in which drinks are entered on the guest check but not paid for until the customer is ready to leave. In some places, the customer pays the bartender. In others, he or she pays the server, who pays the bartender or a cashier. In still others, the customer pays the cashier directly. In busy bars, the server may carry a "bank," paying the bartender for the drinks when they are ordered and collecting and making change on the spot as each round of drinks is served.

Whatever the system, you need standard procedures for handling cash and some form of guest check for the record. You need the record. You want the cash. There may be others among your personnel and your customers who want the cash, too.

When payment is routed through several persons, it is usually intended as a system of checks and balances, but sometimes it works the other way. More people are exposed to temptation and opportunity, and losses are more complicated to track to the source. On the other hand, at the bar you have one person taking the order, filling the order, recording the sale, and collecting the cash, uninhibited by the controls a division of responsibility might provide, and surrounded by opportunity. For you it is a catch-22 situation, magnified by the large number (let's hope) of fast-paced individual transactions and an environment permeated with liquid gold and money changing hands.

Here are some common practices that make cash disappear. Most are at your expense, but sometimes it is the customer who is out of pocket, and that can hurt your business, too.

The Bartender
- Fails to ring up sales and pockets money
- Overcharges and pockets the difference
- Shortchanges customer and keeps change
- Brings in own liquor and sells it (using house mixes and garnishes)
- Brings in empty bottle, turns it in to storeroom, then sells from bottle that replaces it and pockets money
- Short-pours a series of drinks, then sells others from same bottle, keeping money
- Sells liquor from one bottle without ringing up, then waters remaining booze to cover theft
- Substitutes well liquor for call brand, collects for call brand but rings up well price, keeps change
- Smuggles out full bottles

The Server
- "Loses" guest check after collecting and pockets money
- Reuses a check and keeps money for own use
- Overcharges for drinks and pockets difference
- Makes intentional mistakes in totaling check and keeps overage
- Intentionally omits items from check to increase tip
- Changes items and prices on check after customer pays
- Gives too little change and pockets balance

The Cashier
- Gives too little change and pockets balance
- Fails to ring up check, pockets money, and "loses" check (blame falls on server)

The Customer
- Walks out without paying
- Sends back drink after half-emptying glass
- Uses expired credit card
- Pays with hot check

The cash-control system you devise to forestall all these little tricks should both reduce opportunity and pinpoint responsibility. You need a system that you can enforce that also leaves a trail behind when it is evaded. Then you must keep after it. Wherever it is not foolproof, you must keep checking up. If your employees know you are policing the system, they are likely to remain honest. Lax enforcement invites pilferage and, sadly, almost seems to condone it. Here is a suggested system:

1. To start with, use numbered guest checks with your bar's name or logo. Each bartender or server signs out a sequence of numbers for the shift and turns in the unused checks at the end of the shift. You keep the master list and check the used and unused checks. A missing check is a serious breach of work rules that justifies a severe penalty. Make this penalty very clear.

2. Direct staff to write all guest checks clearly and in ink. Prohibit alterations unless they are initialed by a responsible person. Drinks should be machine-priced.

3. If possible, use a precheck method of registering drinks. In this system, the order is rung up before the drinks are poured. When payment is made, another register or another section of the same register is used to ring up the same sale on the same check but a different record. The totals on the two records should be the same.

4. Ring up, total on the register, or add on an adding machine all items on the check before presenting the check to the customer for payment. Do not rely on the server's mathematics.

5. Instruct the server to print the amount received from the customer on the bottom of the check. A box for this purpose is useful.

6. Ring up each check individually when paid, and close the register drawer after each transaction. File the paid check in an assigned place, even in a locked box.

7. Give receipts to customers along with their change.

8. Allow only one person at a time to operate the cash register and to be responsible for the cash in the drawer. Train that person thoroughly in the register function and in your opening and closing routines, as mentioned in Chapter 9.

Some other suggestions: Post prices for all drinks so that both customers and servers are informed. Position the register so that the customer can see the amount being rung up. Make access to the bar interior difficult, and lock up the liquor when the bar is closed. Check credit cards against lists of invalid cards provided by the card companies.

Computers at the Bar

A register that provides sales breakdown by drink categories, sales periods, salespersons, and departments can help you to pinpoint discrepancies quickly and determine their origin. But, today, technology is on your side; you can purchase entire information systems that can track sales by product, by employee, by price point, by time of day. Historically, bars have used two types of sales-capture and cash-control devices: the computerized **point-of-sale (POS) system,** and the electronic cash register (ECR). Until recently, POS systems were used mostly in large chains and hotel-based operations—they were just too expensive for most small, independent bars. Their owners opted instead for an ECR that, although it has its merits, does not provide detailed information necessary to track productivity or product movement or to detect employee theft.

Since the introduction of Microsoft Windows, which is affordable and easy to use, many bars are now computerizing their POS systems and even developing their own software. Microsoft Office is one widely used suite of programs. However, because it was originally designed for an office environment, not a bar and beverage operation, failures are more frequent than with an industry-specific system, and on a busy night, a terminal or printer or system failure can be a disaster. Industry experts say the major cause of computer system failures is electrical power fluctuations. Other than using surge suppressors, not much can be done to avoid them.

To implement, maintain, and support a computerized system, Robert Plotkin and Steve Goumas share these tips in their book, *Successful Beverage Management* (Bar Media, 1996):

- Know the vendor and dealers' reputations.
- Know the vendor's experience, particularly with bar operations.
- Know the features and requirements of the system. Ask about its performance and reliability.
- Know the true costs: cabling, data communications, high-speed phone line capability, electrical requirements.
- Examine the vendor's proposal carefully, and negotiate all contract terms.
- Test the system, if possible, and visit sites or talk with other customers who are already using it.
- Get specifics about the installation and training plan.
- Demand ongoing support for both hardware and software. You'll want seven-day availability (at least 6:00 A.M. to 2:00 A.M.) for hardware; on-site maintenance with a response time of less than 30 minutes. Be sure your agreement includes routine software upgrades.

A computerized POS system can cost $10,000 or more, so before you buy, have a clear understanding of what you expect it to accomplish and what you can afford to spend. Among the common benefits of such a system:

- Increased accuracy in handling of guest checks and cash.
- Easier tracking of each server's credit card and cash sales, and elimination of lost checks.
- Speed of service and less confusion behind the bar.
- Improvement in making and controlling price changes.
- Reduced employee theft.
- Ability to track server productivity.
- Ability to generate reports of sales by category: type of drink, type of beverage, dollars of profit.
- Ability to place orders, record deliveries, and keep inventory records.

The bar and beverage business is like any other: it's being increasingly revolutionized by computers and other technology. In a May 2001 survey of bar operators by the International Foodservice Equipment Manufacturers Association, 6 out of 10 respondents said they already use the Internet to obtain industry news, research recipes, and gather information from manufacturers. Nearly 87 percent regularly use e-mail, and 47 percent have Web sites.

Two additional points to end this chapter: No matter how your data is recorded—with a pen and legal pad or a top-of-the-line computer system—it is only useful if it is both accurate and timely. It takes a commitment of time and personnel to learn your system and maintain it. Second, remember that no records of any kind actually control costs: they only pinpoint losses. The flip side of controls—the effective side—is taking steps to stop the losses.

SUMMING UP

A budget is the financial plan for your business for a given period of time; it's a way to measure your actual performance and forecast your anticipated performance. Your first goals in a new business should be to set up a specific, realistic profit goal and prepare a financial plan for reaching it. This also allows you to continuously measure the degree of success the bar is achieving in its operations. Your budget should work for you by allowing you to pinpoint variations, figure out why they are occurring, and correct any problems. One important figure to calculate is your break-even point, an amount you must make in a business day to "break even" with costs and expenses.

Statistics are available from trade groups, like the National Restaurant Association, that allow you to compare your own expenses and sales figures with those of other restaurants. Within this chapter are all the basic forms you'd need to create a restaurant budget and profit plan.

Since profit is the margin of sales over costs, the profit plan sets up a two-pronged effort: to maximize sales and minimize costs. On the sales side, pricing is of strategic importance in maximizing profit per drink without inhibiting demand and reducing volume. In this chapter, you learned three different ways to "cost" (determine what to charge for) a cocktail. On the cost side, while every expense must be watched, the primary focus is on controlling beverage losses. There are two major ways to do this: minimize the opportunities for pilferage, and set up control systems for measuring and pinpointing losses and take prompt action to stop them.

No matter what kind of system is used, owners and managers must commit time, personnel, and resources to keeping accurate records and updating them on a regular basis.

POINTS TO PONDER

1. In what ways does making a budget depend on past history? On present conditions? On future hopes? On specific plans for change? Which elements do you see as most important and why?

2. How do you treat fixed costs in making a budget based on performance in the preceding year? Do you treat variable costs differently? If so, how?

3. What is a break-even point and why do you need to know it for your bar?

4. How does competition affect price structure? Which pricing techniques can be used to gain a competitive edge, short of wholesale price-cutting?

5. What are the advantages of using standard drink sizes, standardized recipes, and standard glassware?

6. Where do you think liquor losses are most likely to occur? What can be done to stop them?

7. To what extent does an automatic (metered) pouring system control losses?

8. How would you evaluate the following methods of figuring losses (give pros and cons): The cost-percentage method? The ounce method? The potential sales-value method?

9. How does a system of sales records and cash controls operate to minimize losses? In your view, what two control measures would be the most effective?

10. How would you decide what to price a Tequila Sunrise? Use one of the three different costing formulas explained in this chapter and the recipe given in Chapter 10.

TERMS OF THE TRADE

beverage-cost method

break-even point

budget

budget deviation analysis

cash-flow forecast

cost percentage (or percentage cost)

cost/sales ratio

costing

cost-percentage method

drink size

fixed expenses

gross operating profit

gross profit (or contribution margin)

gross profit method

income statement

net income (net profit)

ounce method

point of sale (POS)

potential sales-value method

pouring costs

prime costs

prime ingredient method

pro forma statement

standard (glass, drink, etc.)

total business pricing

unallocable expenses

variable expenses

weighted-average method

CHAPTER 15

Marketing Your Business

"**M**ake a better mousetrap and the world will beat a path to your door" may have been true when Emerson said it, but it's not true today. You can't create a product—even a better one—and then wait for people to come and buy it. They may not want it; and even if they do, they may not know they want it or even know that it exists. Selling something people want and getting them to buy it from you is what marketing is all about.

Marketing should begin while your enterprise is still only a gleam in your eye, and your marketing efforts should go on as long as the enterprise does. In Chapter 3, we explored those critical first steps: studying the market, choosing a particular customer group, analyzing the competition, and determining that there is room in your chosen area to make your enterprise financially feasible. In this chapter, we use what you have learned, to shape your products and services to fill your chosen customers' needs and desires. The right types of marketing will attract them to your enterprise, sell them your wares, and make them want to come back.

This chapter should help you . . .

- Focus on the needs and desires of a chosen clientele, and plan products and services to please them.
- Position your enterprise favorably in relation to your competition.
- Create an atmosphere appropriate to the chosen clientele.
- Attract customers through word of mouth, publicity, and personal contact.
- Select appropriate forms of advertising.
- Plan on-premise promotions and train personnel in successful sales techniques.
- Use pricing as a merchandising tool.

Marketing is often thought of as selling, but it is both more and less than that. It is more in the sense that it deals with all the things that will bring the buyer to the seller. It is less in the sense that it does not deal with the actual sale of a product to a buyer. The buyer (Patron) needs or wants something (Product). The seller wants to sell the same kind of something the buyer needs or wants. **Marketing** is developing a Product people (Patrons) want, and Promoting it so they will buy it from you at a Profit. Its focus is on four Ps: Patron, Product, Promotion, and Profit.

Marketing deals in intangibles, especially in the bar-restaurant field. Patrons' needs and wants are feelings that only they experience. The products and services of bars and restaurants are bought and consumed simultaneously in a brief period of time and there is nothing to take home but feelings and memories—intangibles. The goals of marketing and the methods used concern the intangibles of needs and desires, expectations, perceptions, enjoyment, satisfaction, and image.

In marketing, you don't sell your products and services; rather, you arouse positive responses from your real or potential customers. If they haven't visited your establishment yet, you create the desire to visit. While they are buying your products/services, you create satisfaction with the experience by meeting or exceeding their expectations. If you have done that, you have created a happy memory and, ideally, the desire to return. You have used intangibles to enable you to sell your product.

CREATING A BUSINESS PLAN

Before you embark on a marketing plan, you must create an overall business plan. This is the "résumé" of your business, an instrument that shows a seasoned consideration for all aspects of running it. Your business plan will help determine what kinds of marketing you will need and how much money you can afford to spend on it. A good business plan should accomplish three things:

- It should serve as your basic operating tool.
- It should be useful to communicate exactly who and what you are.
- It should be useful in obtaining financing.

The process itself—writing the business plan—is useful. It requires objective thinking about the operation, so that you can effectively set long-term goals for growth and income. In fact, it is the opinion of some management experts that the owner of the business should *never* write a business plan alone, that it should be the group effort of a trusted team of managers, investors and/or advisers, along with the owner.

As an operating tool, here are the questions a business plan should answer: Where are we now? Where do we want to be next year? What about two or three years from now? How are we going to get there?

Putting all this in writing, so it can be referred to regularly, is a constant reminder of the original concept of the bar, and helps the owners and managers stay on course. It can be used as a benchmark to measure actual performance versus expectations; and it can be used to guide management in making day-to-day decisions.

As a communications tool, many operations use their business plan to explain the bar's concept to others—whether it's the staff, the public, or prospective investors. It is important that your employees know your goals and how you plan to achieve them, so why not let them read the business plan? And a written plan is a must if you are trying to obtain outside financing—from bankers, venture capitalists, or even family members.

So what, exactly, should be in the business plan? The National Restaurant Association's Business Plan Checklist is a good start (Figure 15.1). Once you answer the questions and assemble the related documents (tax returns, sample menus, etc.), if you're not much of a writer, you can hire a freelancer to spend a few hours organizing, editing, and making the whole thing fit together.

The National Restaurant Association also recommends three broad aspects of research that should be included in your business plan. These topics should be revisited periodically, as long as you're in business. They are:

- **Location analysis.** This requires a detailed description of the physical structure (your building) and its neighborhood location. Factors worth including are traffic in the area (car and foot), zoning, accessibility, parking, and crime.
- **Competitor analysis.** This is a comparison of your operation's actual (or anticipated) performance against similar types of businesses. This forces you to figure out the activities, strategies, and strengths of your competition, and to decide how effective they are. We'll discuss in just a moment ways to thoroughly research your competition.
- **SWOT analysis.** SWOT is an acronym for "strengths, weaknesses, opportunities, and threats." The first two items are internal—things that are controlled by you. The next two are external—things you can notice and react to. The real objective of this analysis is to identify the weaknesses and turn them into strengths, and identify threats in order to turn them into opportunities. You might also notice that your weaknesses are your competitors' strengths, and vice versa.

PLANNING YOUR MARKETING APPROACH

In a beverage-service operation, you are the seller of products (alcoholic beverages) and services (the dispensing of these beverages in a congenial environment). Potential customers are out there somewhere in the area in which you have chosen to operate. Since you cannot move your products/services to them, you must induce them to come to you and, once there, to buy your products/services and come back to buy again.

Business Plan Checklist

___ **Cover Sheet**

___ **Executive Summary**

___ **Statement of Purpose**

___ **Description of the Organization**
___ Management summary
___ Type of organization

___ **Description of the Concept** (Mission statement)
Note: It is not necessary to include the five questions (Who am I? What makes me unique?, etc.) in the business plan.

Market Analysis and Marketing Strategy
Description of Target Market
___ Demographics/psychographics/lifestyle
___ Market potential (size, rate of growth)
___ Market share

___ *Pricing Strategy*

Location Analysis
___ Description of area
___ Commercial/residential profile
___ Traffic
___ Accessibility

Competitive Analysis
___ Number of competitors
___ Location
___ Sales and market share
___ Nature of competition
___ New competitors

Advertising and Promotional Campaign
___ Objectives
___ Techniques
___ Target audience/means of communication
___ Schedule

Other Information
___ Schedule of growth
___ Financing schedule
___ Schedule of return on investment

Financial Data

PROPOSED RESTAURANT
Balance Sheet
___ Pro-forma

Income Statement (pro-forma)
___ 1st year-detail by month
___ 2nd year-detail by quarter
___ 3rd year-detail by quarter

Cash Flow Statement (pro-forma)
___ 1st year-detail by month
___ 2nd year-detail by quarter
___ 3rd year-detail by quarter

EXISTING RESTAURANT
Balance Sheet
___ Previous three (3) years

Income Statement
___ Previous three (3) years

Cash Flow Statement
___ Previous three (3) years

Tax Returns
___ Previous three (3) years

Appendices
___ Sales projections
___ Organizational chart
___ Job descriptions
___ Résumés of management team
___ Legal documents
___ Leases
___ Licenses
___ Firm price quotations
___ Insurance contracts
___ Sample menu
___ Furniture, fixtures, and equipment (FF&E)
___ Floor plan
___ Letters of intent
___ Anything else that is relevant

Figure 15.1 Business plan checklist. Excerpted from *A Guide to Preparing a Restaurant Business Plan*, with permission of the National Restaurant Association, www.restaurant.org.

To be successful in this, you must understand your potential patrons' needs and wants and offer them the goods and services that will satisfy these needs. If you don't offer what they want, or they don't want what you offer, they will not come.

There are three major steps in shaping your marketing plan:

1. Define your market. This is your chosen customer group or market segment. A **market segment** is a more or less homogeneous subgroup of the total consumer market; its members have similar needs and wants, attitudes, lifestyles, income levels, purchasing patterns, and so on.
2. Determine what products and services this market segment wants to buy.
3. Only after you have defined these two essentials can you take the third step: Shape everything about your enterprise to attract the customers and sell the product at a profit. In the process, you can *position* your enterprise in relation to the competition by creating an **image** that will set you apart from the rest.

Positioning Your Business

In a competitive marketplace, it is not enough simply to choose your customers and the products and services they want. You must position your enterprise in relation to all the others who are competing for the same market segment. Positioning involves two elements, customers and competitors. Let's discuss them both in greater detail.

The Patron. The success of your bar will depend to a large degree on your ability to know your customers—and that doesn't always mean calling them by their first name or remembering what they drink, although those are certainly handy skills. What we refer to is keeping a watchful eye on the types of people who visit your establishment. How do they dress? What times of day are your rush hours, and how do you think your business hours impact the types of people you attract? How often do people use credit cards to pay? Do they arrive in groups or as couples? What seem to be the favorite cocktails—and does that change from month to month? Do customers order more domestic, or imported, beer and wine? More premium or superpremium brands? How do they react to drink specials, price increases, new products? Your service personnel and bartenders will be key players in helping you keep up with these small but important details, but *you* are the "most key" player. Walk around, introduce yourself, and talk to guests. Ask them to taste a new product you're considering serving. Put comment cards on the tables, and have a place for guests to turn them in as they leave. (Not many guests actually fill out these cards, and those who do tend to be the ones who've had a problem. But it is one way to receive feedback.)

Guests are not statistics or concepts. They are people, and good bar owners make the study of people—their needs, their wants, their characteristics—a priority. If you want to call them "VIPs," use the term to stand for "very individual people." And at your bar, they will have very individual experiences. The overall **guest experience** is always impacted by how the customer felt walking into the bar in the first place. A person who is happy about meeting up with friends for an after-work drink will have distinctly different needs from one who is walking into the same bar hoping he or she doesn't run into the same coworkers, since he or she just got fired.

The other components of guest experience are:

- The **service encounter,** the "moment of truth" in which the guest and server first converse and strike up a relationship, however temporary. In this moment, the server represents the entire bar, and can make or break a customer's experience. The **delivery system,** in getting the drink ordered, produced, and delivered to the customer, is part of the service encounter.
- The **service scape,** also called *landscape*, refers to the environment in which the service encounter takes place. Some bars make catchy service scapes their specialty: Hard Rock Café, Planet Hollywood, Rain Forest Café, among others.
- The product itself. Let's assume that the guest wouldn't be in a bar if he or she didn't want an alcoholic beverage. But the experience includes whether the bar carries (or the bartender can make) what the guest wants; the presentation, portion size and price of the product; and whether it is attractive and a fair value. The average bar stocks 125 to 140 liquors and liqueurs, and there are no clear-cut guidelines about what, or how much, to stock.

The Competitors. We have already stressed the importance of studying your competition—not just other bars and restaurants in the area, but others anywhere in your town that might attract similar types of customers. This should give you much important information. It will show you who else is competing for the entertainment dollars in your area (which will help you gauge the demand for your bar's services); allow a more objective and informed assessment of your planned location; and give you ideas (that you can adapt!) about why other bars have been successful.

Primary competitors are those bars with concepts similar to yours. **Secondary competitors** are those that could be considered competition simply because they are located near your proposed site. Try to include up to a total of 10 competitors in your market survey within a 15-minute drive from your site. In fact, if there are more than 10 bars there to begin with, you should immediately question whether there is sufficient demand in the area to support your concept.

Try to visit each place during busy periods, to see how efficiently the staff handles a crowd, and take notes. Here's what you are looking for:

Physical Attributes

Location: How close or far is it from your proposed site? Is it in a mall? A hotel or office building? Is it part of a restaurant? What are the traffic patterns? Is it close to anything—a movie theater, other merchants—that helps generate business?

Accessibility: The ease with which a guest can drive or walk to the bar is extremely important to its overall success. Look for physical barriers: lack of parking, one-way streets, entrances that are hard to locate.

Visibility: What kinds of signage are apparent from the street? Can you read them, and make your decision to turn in, within 400 feet?

Appearance: The business' exterior should be inviting and well-maintained. Its interior should be attractive and clean, free from clutter and trash. Both should reflect the overall concept.

A combination of factors give a bar its unique "feel" or ambience. These include:

Ambiance Attributes

Menus and drink lists: How do you know what is served? Are there house specialties, signature drinks, wines by the glass? How are these presented to customers? How extensive are the food offerings?

Prices: Make careful note of what the drinks cost. Are there specials, happy hours, senior discounts, and so on?

Food service: Is food available in the bar? What kinds and what portion sizes? Are there complementary appetizers, mixed nuts, pretzels, or other "munchies"?

Service style: How are beverages delivered to guests? Are there separate servers for food and beverages? Who buses the tables? Do servers use trays? Is there silverware, linen napkins, nice wine glasses, or plasticware, paper napkins, and less expensive glassware? How are the servers dressed?

Atmosphere: Estimate the numbers of barstools, cocktail tables, booths, and so on. Notice the layout of the space. Are the tables too close together or too far apart? Can you readily discern what the theme or concept is? Does the place look clean? Does the bar seem well organized or chaotic? Look at floor coverings, walls and ceilings, lighting and decorations, fans and vents. What type of music is played, and is it live, on CDs, from a jukebox? Overall, how would you describe this bar in a couple of words: quiet, loud, romantic, businesslike, exotic, boring, lively, colorful?

Special characteristics: Make note of any special promotions or events that are being advertised, or any special design features—a sunken floor or dance floor, an elevated bar, an outdoor patio, or private party room available for rent.

No, your guests will never look at your operation in this much depth. But this is exactly the kind of detail you will need to make your own place better in the long run. And that's the whole reason you're doing research.
There is one other question to be answered, by local bankers, the restaurant or merchant's association, or suppliers: Have bars gone out of business in this area, and why? Their answers may be revealing. Put all of your market research in writing, and share it with your team as you create the marketing plan.

ATMOSPHERE AS MARKETING

Your position in the market will be a positive *image* in the minds of customers that sets your enterprise apart. An image is, by definition, a subjective impression based on something unique or memorable about your place. It may come from a single feature, or it may be the customer's total experience. Image is the element that you will emphasize in promotions, advertising, and on-site merchandising.

By this time, you probably have a pretty good idea of the overall impression you want to create—the atmosphere, or *ambience,* of your place. These words are hard to define, but you know what they mean. They have to do with what is seen, heard, touched, and tasted—the total of sensory impressions, to which the customer adds a psychological ingredient of response. Ambience may well be the most influential part of the customer's experience, and it is likely to make its impact immediately.

One glimpse of the front of the building, one step inside the door, and the reaction is immediately one of pleasure or disappointment. If you have done your job well, this reaction will depend on the type of customer that comes to the door. What pleases those you are after may well disappoint the others. Consider the groups of customers identified in Chapter 3.

Diners are likely to be mature men and women, alone, together, or with children in tow. They want to enjoy their drinks and meals in comfort and relative quiet. They want to be able to read the menu without a flashlight, converse without shouting, watch other people like themselves, and feel well taken care of. They don't like loud music and noisy talk, and don't come for fancy décor, although they don't object to it. For this group, you might choose a fresh, friendly, low-key atmosphere, conservative but definitely not dull. You should certainly offer a change of pace from eating and drinking at home.

Leisure-time customers in search of entertainment or a partner for the evening are likely to want just the opposite type of atmosphere. They enjoy noise, action, crowds, and loud music. They respond to the newest in décor, the latest in drinks, gimmicks, activity—the sense that something fun is going on here.

A subgroup of these two groups is a more serious group of diners who are really leisure-time customers, for whom the entertainment *is* eating and drinking. The atmosphere takes its cue accordingly.

Drop-in customers are typically less involved with a special ambience. They want prompt service and good drinks; they like to have things move along briskly, and they usually enjoy a crowded, friendly bar.

Neighborhood bar customers want familiar, relaxed, comfortable surroundings and an atmosphere of good fellowship. Never mind the hype and entertainment; they will provide their own.

There are many, many exceptions to and variations of these scenarios, but you get the idea: one person's meat can easily be another's poison.

As you plan the atmosphere of your bar, look at it through the eyes of the group you want to serve. Your awareness of their view of the world is very important. Plan a décor they respond to. Offer services they are looking for. Train a staff that knows how to deal with them and is sensitive to their ways of perceiving things. If you can really get into their outlook on life and create an atmosphere that expresses it, you can make them feel "this is my kind of place." You are building an image.

There are two major components to work with in creating atmosphere: physical factors and human factors. Among the physical factors, appearance and comfort are most important. Appearance has the most immediate impact, from the entrance and the interior as a whole to the lesser details of uniforms, restrooms, tabletops, glassware, and matchbook covers. Restrooms deserve special attention; they can cancel out a previously favorable impression.

Décor and Customer Comfort

Using décor to create atmosphere was discussed at length in Chapter 3. You might want to reread that discussion in light of all you have learned since. Think in terms of your total concept, your individuality, and your image. The look of your place is one of your most potent marketing tools—it's the packaging of your product.

Décor creates the first impression; comfort has a slower but no less significant impact. Furnishings—part décor, part comfort—can be chosen to fill both needs. Lighting is also both décor and comfort, and there is sometimes a fine line of compromise to be drawn here. Temperature is not important to the customer until it is too hot or too cold; then it becomes very important—too cold in front of the air-conditioning vent, too hot without it. A ventilation system that draws smoke away and keeps the air fresh is an essential element of a comfortable bar environment. Noise level is still another comfort factor that you can control according to customer tastes.

Sight and sound provide the first impression, but human encounter provides the second and most lasting. Remember the "service encounter"? Customers of every group respond to the way you and your people greet them, treat them, and deliver your products and services. They like to be cordially welcomed, to be served promptly and efficiently; and to feel their needs are getting personal attention. This single element of your atmosphere is the one most likely to bring satisfied customers back and to cause them to spread the word about your place to friends.

Achieving customer satisfaction doesn't happen by itself. It depends on selecting friendly, people-oriented staff and training them thoroughly in your products, serving routines, customer relations, and philosophy of service. It also depends on your own performance with people, both for your own personal impact and as the model you set for your employees. It depends, too, on whether your employees are happy in their jobs and in your enterprise—in the working atmosphere you create for them. An employee at odds with the management is likely to carry an edge of frustration and anger into customer relationships.

Another human ingredient of atmosphere is the customer. If you focus your marketing efforts on attracting a certain clientele, you will have a compatible mix, and people will feel comfortable from the beginning, ready to enjoy their experience. And enjoyment itself is contagious. Yesterday's bar, a dark, mysterious place where people drank in isolated corners and dark booths, and could not see or be seen, is a thing of the past. In today's bar, everybody is visible; people-watching and shared experiences are part of the fun. If you can foster a sense of belonging—if people feel that your bar or club is their own special place—you will encourage them to come for sociability, as the British enjoy their local pubs, the Germans their beer gardens, the French their bistros. Building a regular following is much cheaper than looking for new customers all the time.

Using atmosphere to attract customers is not just for the new enterprise; it can also revive one whose business is falling off. A certain amount of customer turnover is in the nature of things: job transfers to other cities, marriages, babies, inflation, shifts in buying habits, sickness, and death can eat away at your customer count at the rate of about 15 percent a year. Of course, there are plenty of potential new customers: young people reach legal drinking age, new families move into the homes of those who moved away, new offices and shops move into the area, and customers bring in friends. But not many of these people will become patrons unless you do something to attract them. Examine your premises with a critical eye and think about giving a new look and feel to your place when it needs it.

Successful bar operators make frequent physical improvements, ranging from painting and papering to buying new furniture, opening up a patio, or renovating a facility completely. Customers are quick to spot neglect. Peeling paint, stained carpets, weeds in the shrubbery, and potholes in the parking lot raise doubts about whether you wash your glasses carefully and keep the roaches away. A spic-and-span look, on the other hand, invites the customer in and promises a shipshape operation with careful attention to product and service. Upkeep is something that should be budgeted as part of the profit plan on a regular basis. In the process, you can subtly modify and update your whole concept.

Bar Food and Snacks

What you serve says as much about your bar as how the room looks. More and more bars are replacing chips, popcorn, and pretzels with "real food," and charging for it. The simple addition of a "bar menu" can create a completely different atmosphere. Raising the quality of the food you offer, even if the menu is limited, does a number of important things: It adds to the enjoyment of the drink; it prompts people to spend a bit more time and money; and it slows the absorption of alcohol into the guest's system, making the cocktail-drinking experience a safer one.

Menus that are well thought-out and meet customer expectations should also make money for you. Remember, people "use" bars differently today than they did 10 or 15 years ago. Instead of stopping at a bar to have a cocktail on the way to dinner someplace else, today's customer is far more likely to go to a bar for drinks and appetizers in lieu of a big meal. So the bar menu can be positioned as a "lighter," less filling, and less costly alternative to full-sized portions. Whether you call them tapas, hors d'oeuvres, appetizers, starters, small plates, or shareables, you have a whole new way of eating. The choices can be simple (hot wings and potato skins) or sophisticated (baked brie and oysters on the half-shell), and nobody really expects a bar menu to be extensive. Interestingly, the smaller portion size often prompts guests to order more and to share them.

No matter what else you decide to serve in the way of food, a good snack mix is still a bar staple and a hungry customer's best friend—something crunchy and tasty that's worth munching while they decide on the rest of their order. It doesn't take much to make your own bar mix, and it is a low-cost endeavor. Just be sure it is absolutely fresh and a bit distinctive: Add vegetable chips, or raisins, or nuts to the mix. Season it with thyme, rosemary or oregano, not just salt. Make it unique—just like your bar.

ATTRACTING CUSTOMERS

Let us assume you have targeted a customer group, decided on your products and services, and created an atmosphere that will favorably impress your chosen clientele. But they won't be impressed unless they come through your doors. How do you get them in?

You must send them messages that will make them want to come. The goal is to get the messages through to the people you want to reach in a way you can afford. You should plan this in advance and in detail and prepare an ongoing budget. As a ballpark figure, many enterprises use 1 to 5 percent of sales.

There are numerous ways to send messages. Those that are more or less free are word of mouth, news releases, dining or entertainment reviews, feature stories, personal contact, and participation in community affairs. Those that cost money are various forms of advertising—direct mail, newspaper, magazine, radio, TV, Internet or Web site marketing, and outdoor advertising. Let us look first at the cheapest, the most effective, and perhaps the least controllable.

Word of Mouth

By far the most effective marketing vehicle is one the eager entrepreneur can approach only indirectly: **word of mouth;** that is, people telling other people about your place. If you have satisfied customers' needs and desires, their comments will be favorable and should encourage others to come.

To initiate effective word-of-mouth promotion, give customers something they'd really like to talk about. Be different. Be better. Be special. Offer something unusual. One way to stimulate talk is to have the most of something that is image-building, like the world's largest collection of bourbons or the world's longest wine list. In Washington, DC, the Brickskeller Bar has a nine-page beer list, with some 500 different brands from all over the world, and a display of antique bottles and cans. A few miles away, Bullfeathers restaurant-bar has a collection of more than 50 single-malt scotches. Such collections are not cheap and will move slowly, but your customers will certainly talk about them; they will pay for themselves if they project an image, generate word of mouth, and bring in customers.

On a smaller scale, unusual decorative items or artwork on display, chosen especially with your clientele in mind, are things your customers will want to tell their friends about. You can make deals with a local gallery to exhibit its wares and change them periodically. On an even smaller scale, you can encourage such business-generating talk by providing take-home items with your name and logo. You can also personalize matchbooks, coasters, menus, and placemats, or print out recipes for special drinks. Anything that goes home with a customer becomes a conversation piece and an ad for your place. Make sure it reflects your image.

You can have glassware marked with your logo and invite the customer to take it home; you include the cost of the glass in the price of the drink. In the bar, it promotes the sale of the drink; at home, it becomes a word-of-mouth promotion piece.

Specialty drinks are good for starting word-of-mouth promotions. If you invent a new one and dress it up in a special glass, you may be lucky enough to catch customer fancy and become the talk of the town. Two historic examples are the Buena Vista's Irish Coffee and the Cock 'N Bull's Moscow

Mule, drinks invented more than 50 years ago that are still bringing people into the bars where they were created.

The classic example of using specialty drinks as a marketing technique is Victor Bergeron's drinks for Trader Vic's restaurants. In the 1970s, he concocted a whole menuful of drinks with a Polynesian aura—many of them oversized—designed a special glass for each one, and charged a price that made you know you were getting something really special.

But you don't really need the kind of word of mouth that makes a place famous. The best kind is simply spread by satisfied customers telling their friends that yours is the place to go. It helps if you can provide your own special twists that linger in the memory—your Café Diablo made with a flourish at tableside, your ocean view, your fabulous hors d'oeuvres, and your jukebox with everything from Bach to the Rolling Stones. Such things extend the conversation, and the detail sticks in the listener's mind far better than the vague general recommendation, "It was nice." If you meet the customer expectations outlined earlier, and your guests go home wanting to come back, they will tell their friends.

One of the major ingredients of such satisfaction is a feeling of having been well served with person-to-person attention. Personal service is a facet of marketing in which the owner/manager has a golden opportunity. The proprietor who welcomes each guest personally is a refreshing holdover from the past. In today's impersonal world of machines, numbers, computers, self-service, and canned entertainment, people are hungry for conversation and personal attention. The owner/manager, as one of the last of the species of individual entrepreneurs, has a unique chance to fill this need and to sell personality along with refreshment. The warmth of the boss, reflected in the equally warm personal attention of the staff, will give customers something really special to tell their friends about. Don't underestimate its impact. People love it!

The downside of word of mouth is that you have no direct control over it. Unfortunately, unfavorable word of mouth is also easily triggered—like a tale told by someone who was turned off on a bad night at your place when the bartender made an Old-Fashioned with gin; or filled up a short-poured drink with water from the rinse sink. In fact, one of the most important ingredients of generating favorable word of mouth is to have well-trained, high-performing personnel as part of your image. Satisfied customers enthusiastically telling their friends about your establishment is the most solid kind of image-building word of mouth that you can have.

News, Reviews, and Feature Stories

You needn't depend solely on your patrons' word of mouth to attract the numbers of new customers you want. A story in the paper or on radio or TV can reach new people, as well as increase the awareness of those who have already heard about you, and its only cost is time and effort or what you might pay someone else to write a news release.

In order to get a news story published or aired, it must be considered newsworthy by the person to whom you submit it—a newspaper editor or columnist, the assignment editor or feature reporter at a local television station, or the producer or host of a radio program. These people make their judgments on the basis of what will be of interest to their readers, viewers, or listeners. An entertainment editor might be glad to cover your grand opening or first anniversary party, or the band that will play at your place on a certain Saturday night. Newspapers don't just do articles; they feature many small (one- or two-paragraph) "mentions" of local happenings. Details of your upcoming wine tasting, for instance, might run in the food or lifestyle section of the newspaper or in the dining critic's column. If you have regular entertainment—live music, comedians, and so on—be sure the entertainment editor receives a regular list of "who's playing when."

Most local radio stations allow their deejays to read informative tidbits about "what's going on," and they would be happy to include your events— if they know about them far enough in advance. If you sponsor or host an event for a local charity, or give some of one day's profits (for instance) to a charity, you're assured of at least some publicity. But, again, the amount and quality of the publicity depends on how effectively *you* get the word out. Think about "maximizing your mentions." If you need to, hire a local freelance writer to get you started and to familiarize you with what editors need and expect.

The standard vehicle for getting a news story published is a news release sent to the appropriate editor. The writer can help you with this, too. The news release consists of a few short paragraphs providing the pertinent details about an upcoming event. It should be written simply, accurately, and well. Write it as though it will be published word for word (as it may well be, by a smaller newspaper). Angle it to arouse the reader's interest immediately, and include the five Ws: who, what, where, when, and why—in the first two sentences. Include all the other essential facts in the first two paragraphs, too. Less-important facts and additional interesting detail can follow. If the editor decides to shorten the story, he or she can simply drop the last paragraph or two without eliminating anything essential.

Type the story double- or triple-spaced on one side of the page only. It should be only one or two pages long. In a news release, less is more. If it is more than one page, type "—More—" centered at the bottom of the page. At the end of the story, type "—30—" or "###" centered below the last line (this, in journalism jargon, indicates the end of the item).

Give the story a short, catchy headline to identify it for the editor. In the upper-right comer, type the release date; for example: "FOR RELEASE JANUARY 22, 2002," or "FOR IMMEDIATE RELEASE." Check and double-check your spelling and grammar! Check and double-check your facts! Errors can be disastrous.

Type the story on your letterhead if you have one. If you don't, be sure the release carries the name and address of your enterprise and the name and phone number of a person to contact for more information. And be sure to send it well in advance, that is, at least two weeks prior to its release date.

One important type of publicity is the review written by a columnist for a local paper or magazine. Many such publications systematically review the restaurants in town and publish lists with assessments of the product, atmosphere, and service, along with price-range information. This is a form of publicity over which you have no control. Usually, you do not know when a reviewer is coming, and most of them try hard to be anonymous anyway, so there is nothing you can do to influence the outcome of a particular visit. If you're newly open for business—or if you've changed menus, concepts, locations, whatever—and you feel you're truly ready for a review, the best way to get on the list is to send a copy of your menu with a nice note to the reviewer.

If you have a shipshape operation and have trained your staff well both in skills and in customer service, chances are you will get a favorable review. If the column carries a recommendation, you have one of the best kinds of word of mouth going for you: the word of a specialist. You can enlarge the review and display it on your front door or even quote it in paid ads. If you continue to serve your clientele well, you may get into the guidebooks of *Places to Go,* and then you've got it made—at least for a while.

On the other hand, a critical review may hurt you. The day your place was reviewed may have been the day a substitute bartender mistook the vodka bottle for gin and a new server spilled the wine. Or the reviewer did not see things through the eyes of your special clientele, did not share their values, and did not feel comfortable in your setting. In any case, there is little you can do about a negative review except to learn from it. Think about it as "free customer feedback." You can analyze the criticisms objectively, correct those that are legitimate, and invite the reviewer for another visit. But if you are pretty sure the problem was a mismatch between the reviewer and your carefully created ambience and image, then you may as well forget it. You really don't need customers who, like the reviewer, wouldn't feel comfortable in your place.

Feature stories are still another publicity vehicle. They are written by someone else at your suggestion, and they must fill the writer's journalistic needs—to help fill the weekly food section or Sunday magazine, for example, with interesting reading. You do not control what is said, but if you and the writer develop the idea together, the story is likely to be favorable.

The starting point is an interesting or unusual angle to intrigue first the writer and then the reader. If, say, you have renovated a historic house, that's a good story idea for the Sunday magazine. You may have an employee with an unusual background and talent. Your head bartender and what she goes through on a busy Saturday night might make a good profile story or radio interview. Your interior design—that unique artwork you display—is worth a story somewhere. Such stories keep your image in the public eye and can increase your patronage.

Once you start thinking of story possibilities, you will probably have many ideas. You might have a brainstorming session with your staff; it can be interesting for them and it will encourage their involvement and their spirit of teamwork.

MARKETING THROUGH PERSONAL CONTACT

Word of mouth and publicity stories are great when they work for you, but they are always in someone else's hands. There are ways to approach your market more directly. One is to work through personal contact. You can broaden your own contacts and you can get people you know to bring in people they know.

One way to expand your contacts is to work for popular community causes—youth groups, church activities, fundraising for charities, and the like—perhaps even assuming a leadership role. This can establish you as a respected working member of the community and broaden your acquaintanceship with other community leaders. Community goodwill is an important and continuing asset in any business, and this is especially true in the bar business. If, in the process, you offer your bar as a convenient place for meetings at quiet hours, this may also contribute directly to your business. But be careful that your involvement is not simply for personal gain. This motive quickly becomes apparent, people resent it, and it backfires.

Another way of using personal contact is to encourage your customers to bring in other customers. One way to do this is to give a party and ask your present customers to invite their friends. Print up invitations to a celebration of St. Patrick's Day or Greek Independence Day or Halloween and ask your customers give them to their friends. This is likely to produce a congenial group at the party. For future use, each invitation should have a place for the guest's name and address. This gives you the nucleus of a mailing list.

One restaurant works through its customers by offering an "Angel's Check" to reward anyone who brings in a group of six customers. The Angel's reward is a gift certificate for $5 to be used on the next visit.

Still another idea for building clientele through your customers is to organize games or contests centered around their interests. You might even form a club and give members membership cards to pass out to their friends. Such games as darts, shuffleboard, pool, and videogame contests are fun both to play and to watch. Interest builds if you form teams or set up tournaments— a good idea for slow evenings. Players may bring in friends to watch and cheer them on. A good crowd attracts additional business as passersby stop in to see what is going on. You do a good business that night, and some of the new people will probably come back. This sort of thing is particularly appropriate for neighborhood bars and other enterprises catering to a clientele seeking entertainment and relaxation.

Another version of the game/contest idea is to sponsor an athletic team that plays in a league of teams sponsored by other establishments. Bowling leagues are a common type; you may also find interested baseball, softball, touch football, and soccer leagues. A team of your own not only builds business (everybody adjourns to the bar after the game), but sports contests of any kind are usually good word-of-mouth generators.

PROMOTING THROUGH PAID ADVERTISING

There will always be potential customers who cannot be reached by word of mouth, publicity stories, or personal contact. Sooner or later, you will want to try advertising. It costs money, but if it is successful, it will pay its own way.

Planning an Overall Program

Planning a total program of repeat advertising over a period of time is likely to give the best results. Before you do anything, however, find out what your state and local regulations allow you to do. Some areas have very specific requirements and prohibitions for advertising liquor and places that sell it.

Your advertising should be planned with several objectives in mind. First, you want to plant a clear, distinctive, and favorable image in the minds of potential customers (this is often referred to as **institutional advertising**). Second, you want to make them continuously or repeatedly aware of your enterprise. This involves a series of ads over a period of time, and is called **reminder advertising.** Third, you want your advertising to make your target customers choose you in preference to others (**competitive advertising**). Finally, you want them to visit your place as soon as possible. If there is an incentive to visit immediately, say for example, a grand opening or a special entertainer, this kind of ad is known in the trade as a **presell.**

It takes skill and experience to turn out finely tuned advertising that accomplishes your objectives. A skilled professional who is sensitive to your message is well worth the fee charged. In terms of the added business, the fee is minimal.

And speaking of added business, be ready for it. You don't want the competitive advantage you have gained to be frittered away in frantic efforts to cope with a crowd you weren't prepared for. You must fulfill their expectations. If you do, you have a splendid chance of turning them into loyal customers.

The two advertising methods most frequently used are:

- **Direct mail.** Reaching potential customers individually, in a letter, brochure, or flier.

- **Media advertising.** Sending out your message to a mass of people by radio, newspaper, or other medium of general communication and hoping your potential customers will single it out.

Let's look at these methods in turn.

Direct-Mail Advertising. When you advertise by direct mail, you can reach potential customers directly. You can send your messages selectively to people who live or work in a certain area by zip code, or who belong in a certain income group or have certain interests compatible with your type of place. So the first thing you need is a selective mailing list.

The core of a good list consists of names and addresses you have collected through your own contacts, such as people who have come to your parties or have signed your guest book. You can have your servers ask customers if they would like to be on your mailing list. You can add to this nucleus by clipping the names from newspapers of people who seem to be your kind of customer. Other sources are membership lists of clubs, business or social groups, lodges, fraternal orders, and so on. You can sometimes get such lists from customers who are members. Many such groups do not have their own meeting places or bar facilities and might even be interested in using your place for meetings.

You can also buy lists from other organizations. Choose them on the basis of how well they match your clientele and your geographical area. Your local phone company will rent you a directory of subscribers arranged by street address. Credit-card companies are other sources of lists. American Express, for example, can sell you lists according to zip code, giving you a specific geographic area and a certain degree of income-level selectivity. For a modest price, your local motor-vehicle bureau can supply a list of every car owner in your city. For a higher price, you can get a more selective list, such as owners of specific late-model cars. You can also find mailing-list specialists in the Yellow Pages under Advertising-Direct Mail, or on Internet web directories.

Consider next the purpose of your mailing. You can cover your objectives with a series of short and simple messages. Image will be conveyed by your logo, the look of your piece (paper, color, and arrangement on the page), and the way you send it (postcard, first-class letter, or hand-delivered flier). Take care that the envelope doesn't look like junk mail. The "reminder" function should be carried out through regular mailings—at least quarterly—because continuity is important. To get the recipient to visit soon, offer a reason for coming: a special attraction on a specific date (see a sample in Figure 15.2), or a discount good for a limited time. Such specifics can also help you measure the success of your mailing.

If you send a letter, make it short, informal, and personal in tone. Say something interesting about your place—"In June, we'll open our second-floor balcony. You can enjoy the city lights amid cool, night breezes . . ."

4TH ANNUAL
CLASSIC ITALIAN
CAR & MOTORCYCLE
SHOW
SATURDAY OCT 6TH
STARTS
AT 2:00 PM

AT
DAVINCI'S
190 E. STATE ST.
939-2500

Figure 15.2 Direct mail advertising pieces such as this one often remind customers of special events taking place. Courtesy of da Vinci's, Eagle, Idaho.

and end with a specific suggestion: "Join us on the 30th—we're having a beer-tasting party!"

Direct mail has many advantages. You can handpick your audience and speak to them personally. You can measure response by including a discount coupon to be redeemed by a certain date. And don't be discouraged by the results; you may be surprised to learn that, statistically, a 1 to 2 percent response is generally considered good; any more is very good. An unknown percentage will read and register your message without responding this time around, but maybe they will next time. Another advantage is a somewhat flexible schedule: there is no press deadline to meet and you can vary the timing of your mailings according to your calendar of events. The main thing is to keep your mailings coming: at least four times a year is what experts recommend.

There are also certain drawbacks to using direct mail: It is more expensive than you might think, what with the costs of printing, postage, and the labor costs of assembling, addressing, stamping, and mailing each piece. Another problem is that you're competing with the deluge of mail everyone is subjected to these days, much of which they throw out unopened or set aside to read later and never do. Thus you should make every effort to distinguish yourself from the junk, not only to ensure that your piece is read, but for the sake of image. By all means, send it first class, hand-stamped and, if possible, hand-addressed rather than machine-printing and pasting on the address labels. If you staple anything, position the staple so that it doesn't tear into the message, spoiling both appearance and readability.

For certain types of customers, a brochure may be useful. For example, you may want to tell business organizations about your meeting facilities and services, and perhaps include the menu. Usually, a letter addressed by name to the person in charge should go along with the brochure. If it suits your customer mix, you can also place a supply of brochures with hotels, convention centers, trade shows, and chambers of commerce.

A brochure is more formal than the usual direct-mail piece. It is considered institutional advertising, a reference piece rather than a call to action. It should be designed and prepared by a professional to convey both your image and the essential facts about your place: your services, facilities, address, phone number, days and hours of service, and the person to call to make specific arrangements. It should be professionally printed on paper sturdy enough to withstand repeated handling.

Fliers or handbills delivered by hand are sometimes substituted for direct mail. They are often effective if they are eye-catching, brief, and make an offer of some kind. They are an inexpensive and useful way to blanket a certain neighborhood or office building. If you add the message "Bring in the coupon," for example, you can more accurately measure the flier's effectiveness.

Direct mail should be coordinated with the rest of your advertising plan. The style, message, and frequency should reinforce your media ads while taking advantage of the direct and selective approach. And all of it, of course, should be focused on the needs and desires of your chosen clientele.

Advertising Media. You have several choices of media in which to advertise your enterprise: radio, newspapers, magazines, television, Internet, and outdoor (billboard) advertising. All these expose your message to masses of people, in contrast to the selectivity of direct mail. Hence, you must take care to place your message in a medium that your target customers are likely to see or hear, and your message must be designed to catch their specific attention.

In choosing a medium, consider all these elements:

- Audience or readership: size and appropriateness
- Media availability in relation to your needs for coverage and frequency
- Price, discounts, and cost-effectiveness of each medium
- Your ad budget

In considering cost and budget, cost-effectiveness must be related to the cost per impression. How many readers does a given newspaper have? How many people listen to a given radio station at a given time of day? A prime-time radio spot, though it costs the most dollars, may reach the most people. This is your **cost per impression.** However, in any advertising medium, keep in mind that you are paying for many readers, listeners, and viewers who are *not* potential customers, a fact that makes cost per impression meaningless unless you know how many were "impressed," so to speak. The only way to measure this is a resulting increase in your business—tied, if possible, to a specific offer on your part.

Radio is a medium often chosen by bars and restaurants. Its cost is fairly reasonable, though the dollar cost of prime time—commuting time, 5:00 to 7:00 P.M.—is high. You would schedule your advertising to appear on the kinds of stations and during the kinds of programs your target clientele might listen to and at times of day they are likely to listen. You would run your "spots" (the commonly used slang for "commercials") regularly for a certain period of time, to take advantage of the value of reminder advertising. To spur immediate action and measure response, you can invite the listener to a special event or offer a discount for a limited time.

Radio spots have many advantages. In addition to reasonable cost, there is the personal quality of a voice speaking directly to the listener. Most stations make their staff of deejays available to do ads; and often, if the ad runs on that particular station, there is no extra charge for the voice talent. You might have a snatch of musical theme that could become a signature for your name and message.

On the other hand, there are certain disadvantages to radio. One is that people listening to the radio are usually doing something else at the same time, such as driving to or from work, getting the kids off to school, or working at the office. In short, their attention is divided, the ad is over in 30 seconds, and there is nothing to refer to later. Consequently, you should make your name very prominent, keep your message very simple, and suggest immediate action of some kind before the image "vanishes" in the busy, cluttered mind of the listener.

Newspapers are probably the most popular medium for bar and restaurant ads. A newspaper ad has visual impact, providing another dimension to your message; it is always timely and not outrageously expensive. You may have a choice of morning and afternoon papers; some people use both, so as not to risk missing half their audience. In large cities, you can sometimes reach specialized audiences through foreign-language papers. Newspapers have known circulation, and by using coupons you can measure your ad's effectiveness.

The timing of your ad and its position in the paper are critical. The best day of the week is probably Friday, when the weekend is coming and people are thinking of relaxation and entertainment. Most papers have special entertainment pages, and this is where most bar and restaurant ads are placed. In fact, these pages are often so crowded with ads that readers don't even look at any of them. Would people be more likely to see your ad in the sports section ("Drop in after the game and bring this coupon")? What about the midweek food and wine pages? (If you learn that the paper is planning an article on California wines, you may be able to tie in an ad on the same page, mentioning the California wines you serve.) What about the Sunday magazine? People browse through it more slowly. Would your ad stand out there, or would it not even be noticed? Should you place it on the pages adjacent to the restaurant reviews?

There are no surefire answers to these questions. Some people in the business feel that direct mail, though far more expensive, is cheaper in the long run simply because it is direct. Wherever you decide to place it, your ad must position you in terms of your special clientele, projecting your image in both the graphics and the printed message. Graphics include your logo, headline lettering, style of type, borders, and any other artwork. Your message should be clear and simple. It should also project your image, and it should issue an invitation the reader cannot resist! Repetition is important: You should place an ad in the same paper at least once a month.

Local magazines are a promising medium. Each has a known circulation and a predictable market, and some have columns on restaurants and nightclubs. Such pages might be logical spots for your ads, if you are on a columnist's "recommended" list. Theater programs are another ad medium worth exploring. Big-city and resort hotels often have giveaway magazines for their guests. In fast-growing areas, real estate firms sometimes offer giveaway magazines to their customers, which are also good spots for your ads.

If you opt for either radio or print advertising, you should definitely work with a professional copywriter and/or designer. You don't necessarily need to hire an ad agency—any station or paper has its own salespeople who are happy to help you craft your ad and discuss its proper placement. Not only must your ad look professional to convey your image, but an advertising specialist knows all the ins and outs of what is and isn't possible in terms of scheduling, placement, positioning, and procedures. If yours is a small or medium-sized operation, come up with your own ideas and a budget, then shop around and talk with salespeople, as well as freelance writers or designers. Find someone you are comfortable working with and whose terms fit your needs. Assess the ad's "pulling power" periodically through coupons and increased volume of business.

Television would be a splendid medium if it weren't so expensive. It is typically out of reach for all but major hotels and chains. Outdoor advertising is very expensive, too, and is forbidden by law in many states for selling liquor. Even the sign in front of your premises may be restricted. Check out this form of advertising with care.

More and more bars and restaurants are creating their own Web sites to promote business. You've already got the basics to convey: address (perhaps with a map), a clever description of your concept, and a menu and/or drink list. Add some nice color photos. It doesn't have to be complicated, and it should always include opportunities for customers to contact you with ideas and comments. The most important thing about adding a Web site to your marketing mix is that you incorporate its Internet address into all your other advertising, from printing it on bar napkins to placing it in newspaper ads. Otherwise, how will people know to look for it? Having a Web site gives you the added advantage of offering it as a "link" from (or to) other sites. Your local merchants' association, for instance, or chamber of commerce, could direct people to your site—and others—with a link on their sites. Web site designers can help you with the "look" and the content of your own Internet site. Sidebar 15.1 suggests some popular brewpub Web sites as examples of

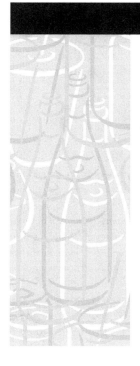

Sidebar 15.1

VIRTUAL PUBS

Here's a list of just a few of the local brewpub Web sites around the United States. There are plenty more, but this gives you an idea of what some bar owners are doing to promote their businesses.

Pyramidbrew.com: This Seattle ale house features games and prizes on its Web site.

Toronado.com: This is a San Francisco-based pub that gives customers a chance to suggest new brews on its Web site.

Maproom.com: The Map Room in Chicago includes an interest-ing "beer journal" on its site, plus a look at its menu.

Horsebrass.com: A Portland, Oregon, pub that has a curious history. Its Web site is personal, yet educational.

Mcmenaminspubs.com: This chain of Pacific Northwest pubs talks about its beers, bed and breakfasts, artwork, theaters, and more.

Drinkgoodstuff.com: You can find out when each of the kegs was tapped on this Web site for a New York City brewpub.

what can be done online. Your site should be regularly updated, too, every 30 to 45 days, so customers will have reasons to return to it.

And, finally, don't forget about the telephone book and its traditional Yellow Pages. Few customers will shop here for a drink, but it is one way out-of-towners choose their destinations; and it is still the best place for making your address and phone number easy to find.

As for the cost of marketing, the crucial judgment is always the relationship between the outgo and the added business, the familiar cost/sales percentage. A more expensive medium may pay for itself several times over if it brings in a flood of new customers, while a low-cost ad in the wrong form and place may bring in no business at all and, therefore, prove to be very expensive.

ON-PREMISE PROMOTION

Inside your doors, your marketing effort continues. It has several goals: You want your guests to be favorably impressed, you want them to come back, and you want them to tell their friends about you. Most of all, at this point, you want them to buy your wares.

The guest's impression is a series of impacts on the mind and senses. There is the initial impression of sight and sound, followed by the impression of staff and guests. There is another impact as the order is taken, still another as the drink is served, and yet another with the first sip. These points of impact offer possibilities for merchandising and salesmanship as unlimited as the imagination and skills of you and your staff.

Promotional Materials

You can make almost anything into a promotion piece if it is (1) eye-catching and (2) informative. Again, imagination is the key. Here are some ideas that have proven successful.

Displays catch the eye, inform the viewer, and often awaken thirst. A wine rack in your lobby shows the arriving guest the variety and quality of your offerings and sets the mind spinning about which one to order. Prominently displayed labels of your pouring brands of spirits look like little coats of arms proclaiming your pedigree. Backbar displays of your call brands and reserves are the classic way of impressing guests.

Drink menus and wine lists are extremely important as merchandisers. They should attract and inform, especially if your offerings are new to the guest. People will seldom buy a drink or a wine they know nothing about—so tell them about it. Menus can also be intriguing, amusing, and appetite provoking. Wineglasses as part of the table setting suggest wine with the meal. Sparkling clean glassware and nicely garnished drinks cannot help but be noticed by guests—even as they are on their way to be delivered at another customer's table.

"Specials" spark interest and can often focus a drink order. Single them out for special attention on a blackboard in your entryway or at the bar, or highlight them on a table tent or a menu clip-on (Figure 15.3). Suppliers may help you pay for the printing of these items. In fact, many kinds of promotional materials are offered by manufacturers, distributors, and sales personnel, provided state laws allow such giveaways. Posters, backbar signs, neon logos or signage, ashtrays, coasters, table tents, T-shirts, lapel buttons for servers, and recipe booklets are some typical items.

Personal Selling

The final step on the path to profit takes place at the bar or tableside. Here the marketing effort is in the hands of your staff. You have carefully selected people who are friendly, outgoing, upbeat, alert, articulate, creative, flexible, confident, service-oriented, and sensitive to customers' needs, and adept at relating to them—in short, perfect in every way. You have trained them in your routines and taught them everything you know about wines, drinks, and people. Now, you are going to teach them how to sell.

Figure 15.3 This image folded creates a table tent for a bar table. Courtesy of Fish Tale Ales and Mary Sue Wilson.

Staff sell in two ways: (1) they sell your beverages and (2) they sell your place by the way they promote and serve your drinks. Their approach must be customer-oriented: it begins with understanding the customer's needs and desires, then filling those needs and desires in a way that maximizes both the guest's satisfaction and the profit to the enterprise. The profit goal is both short term and long term: a fat check average (plus a big tip) and repeat customers (plus future tips).

Today, in the shadow of the tragedies of drunk-driving accidents and the risk of third-party liability, and influenced by neotemperance and the perceptible decline in overall alcohol consumption, serving personnel must have an entirely new emphasis when selling drinks. Though the goal is still profit—the fat check average plus the big tip—the long-term goal is more important: satisfied customers who get home safely and want to come back as regulars.

The sales training you provide should be directed toward this overall goal rather than the size of the check, and servers should be interested in both. Training should focus on relating to the customer, knowing the products, increasing the check average without overselling, avoiding intoxication and handling it properly if it happens, and making the customer want to come back again. Among customers who do not return, by far the most frequent reason is a complaint about the server or the service.

The importance of the server-customer relationship cannot be overemphasized. The first contact can set the tone of the guest's entire experience. It must be genuinely cordial. Guests will usually be pleased to be recognized from a previous visit and offered their favorite drink; it makes them feel they belong.

A friendly, helpful approach is the best possible salesmanship, if it is not overdone. Some customers know what they want and don't appreciate suggestions. The most successful servers develop sensitivity to people—they recognize the person who is uncertain, the one who is suggestible, and the one who resents suggestion. They have learned that seeing things through the customers' eyes is the first principle of good marketing.

Servers should be thoroughly trained in product knowledge so that they can explain clearly the ingredients in mixed drinks, the house specialties, the tastes and pedigrees of wines. Servers should stick to the facts and present them objectively. Predictions are risky: "Try it, you'll like it" puts you out on a limb. If the customer doesn't like it, you've lost your credibility and probably another sale. "It's one of our most popular drinks," is factual and makes the same point.

Servers should also be carefully trained in the rituals of service—the presentation of a wine list, the opening of a bottle, the correct service of a beer or a glass of mineral water. It is all part of personal selling; it sells your image.

Your servers must also be well trained in recognizing the effects of alcohol on customer behavior. (It is not enough to count the drinks served; the guest may have been drinking somewhere else.) Now is a good time to review the training programs described in Chapter 2 and the course of action to be taken if, in spite of all precautions, a customer becomes intoxicated.

There are many ways to increase the check average without overselling alcohol. Servers can promote specialty drinks that are made with fruit juices and liqueurs, served in tall glasses or balloon glasses, and beautifully garnished. These encourage sipping instead of gulping and are deliberately lower in alcohol, which is just what some of those "drinking-less-but-drinking-better" people are looking for. Frozen drinks are another such choice, again dressed up, to be sipped slowly through straws from an oversized Margarita glass. Bonaventure's hotel/restaurant in Los Angeles developed 10 12- to 14-ounce specialty drinks, served them in its own special take-home containers, priced them at $7.50 to $10 each, and sold a million dollars' worth in one year.

Today, many bars are experimenting with their own concoctions or are borrowing recipes from little booklets put out by liqueur manufacturers. If you really dress them up—serve them in oversized glasses, garnish them lavishly, flame them, anything to call attention—the specialty drinks will often sell themselves just by carrying them through the room. It is easier to get an extra dollar or two for a specialty drink than it is to raise the price of beer by a nickel.

Many bars are maintaining or fattening the check average by adding menu items, as mentioned earlier. Another successful combination is a cheese-and-fruit tray to accompany a bottle of wine. This is a popular item at wine bars. Such food items have customer appeal, and they slow down the rate at which alcohol reaches the bloodstream. A useful idea is to offer a fancy mocktail on the house for the designated driver. This is good public relations. It shows customers you care about them. Some suggestions: Virgin Mary, a Bloody

Mary without the vodka, also called Bloody Shame; Virgin Colada, a Pina Colada without the rum; and the Sunrise Special, orange juice and grenadine. Make them beautiful—garnish them lavishly. There is also a choice of non-alcoholic beers.

The taking of an order and the serving of the drink are the culmination of this final phase of marketing. The sum of all these individual encounters adds up to the success of your enterprise. Only if each sale is a mutually beneficial experience will the success be lasting. The talents and skills of your staff are the final critical link in your marketing.

Good sales personnel are also good sources of ideas for specialty drinks, promotions, and selling techniques. They can tell you about trends in customer tastes and perhaps what your competition is doing. A good staff is an invaluable resource, deserving praise, encouragement, and even occasional pampering.

PRICING AS A PROMOTION TOOL

The role of pricing in promotion used to be viewed in terms of a simple formula: reduce a price and you increase demand. Now, most of us look at this idea more soberly (pun intended). Not too long ago, the universal means of applying the formula was the *happy hour*, a period of time in the late afternoon or early evening when drinks were all reduced in price, or two drinks were offered for the price of one. Now, the happy hour is against the law in many states. Many managers sighed with relief, since they generally only broke even during happy hours, and went along with them only to remain competitive. Besides, in today's climate, few managers want to flirt with the risks of the intoxicated customer.

But lowering a price has other, subtler uses than increasing the demand by each person for more drinks. One of these is to make a certain high-profit drink a "special of the day" by cutting its profit margin in half. Many people are bargain hunters by nature, and the very idea of getting something for less excites them. In this way, you reinforce their enjoyment of your place, yet you are not stuck with a lower price tomorrow.

Another use of specials is to associate them in the minds of your customers with a special period of service you are trying to promote, such as Sunday brunch. A specially priced Mimosa not only merchandises the drink, but also promotes the whole idea of Sunday brunch.

Still another way to use a special is to reduce the price of something expensive that your customer might not ordinarily buy at all—a good wine or a good brandy, for example. You may create a taste for it that will benefit you the next time the customer comes to your place.

Since prices are directly related to image, the overall level of prices should be kept stable. When increased costs force you to raise prices, set them high enough so that you won't have to raise them again soon. Customers can take an occasional change in stride, but several raises in a row can raise eyebrows and temperatures as well.

Above all else, customers must feel that the value they receive from you is equal to or greater than the prices they pay—perceived value, a fair deal, their money's worth. It does not matter what the actual costs and money values are. If they think they are paying too much for what they are getting, you have set your prices too high because they won't be back.

The marketing role of pricing must not interfere with its financial role. The two must continue together in a coordinated relationship; both are important to profitability.

SUMMING UP

Creation of a business plan is the first step in deciding what types of marketing you need to do and how much you can afford to spend on it. This involves visiting at least 10 local competitors to see what they are doing and how well their concepts are working (or not working). Only after this research is done can you position your business within that marketplace.

Once you have identified a clientele you know is out there, your entire enterprise should be shaped to meeting their needs, desires, and expectations. Create an ambience these customers respond to; serve drinks to their liking, from servers who care about them; add a menu of appropriate foods or snacks; and make their total experience memorable so they'll come back and bring their friends.

You can depend on word of mouth for a certain amount of customer loyalty, but advertising and promotion are the more serious and ongoing parts of marketing. An overall plan, with the media and the message directed to your chosen clientele, should project your distinctive image and create a desire to visit your place. You can focus on direct mail marketing to a specific audience, and offer them something on the piece, which prompts them to read it or keep it instead of tossing it out as "junk mail." Or you can focus on media placement—in newspapers, magazines, on radio or television. You can buy ads, or send news releases and keep in touch with reporters, editors, and producers in hopes of getting "feature story" publicity, or perhaps a review from a local columnist. You can also create a Web site for your business.

On-premise, the marketing focus shifts to sales. Displays, special drinks, and special prices are good promotional tools, but the real sellers are your serving staff, with personal attention and interpersonal communication as their highest priorities on the job. To sell the product, serve the customer!

POINTS TO PONDER

1. Explain why marketing should begin with the customer rather than the product.

2. Why is it important for a bar to have a business plan? Give two reasons.

3. What are the three types of analysis you should do in creating your business and marketing plans? Describe each in one or two sentences.

4. What is a market segment?

5. Think of two groups of customers who are very different in their tastes and values. Make a list of three or four things you might find in a bar that would attract one group but completely turn another one off.

6. What makes up a guest experience at a bar?

7. List 10 things you should know about the customers in any market segment. How will you use this information to create your marketing plan?

8. What are three ways to keep your name circulating in public without spending a lot of money on advertising? Write a few of sentences about each, and how well you think they might work.

9. What would be the benefit of having a Web site for your bar or restaurant business? How would people know to look for it?

10. Suggest three ways for a server to increase his or her check average without overselling alcohol.

TERMS OF THE TRADE

advertising: institutional, competitive, reminder

cost per impression

delivery system

guest experience

image

marketing

market segment

presell

primary competitors

secondary competitors

service encounter

service scape

SWOT analysis

word of mouth

JULIE HANSEN

Regional Manager
Oregon Liquor Control Commission

Pregnancy & Alcohol
DO NOT MIX
Drinking alcoholic beverages, including wine, coolers and beer during pregnancy can cause birth defects.

Oregon is one of the control states, with a governor-appointed commission that regulates the sale and distribution of alcoholic beverages, issues licenses to vendors, and enforces the state liquor laws.

Julie Hansen got her first job with the Oregon Liquor Control Commission in 1981, as a secretary. She took advantage of an Upward Mobility Program within the organization, and took additional college courses in business and law enforcement to become an inspector and license investigator before moving into management positions. Today, Julie is a Regional Manager. She supervises five license investigators and five district inspectors whose territory is the Portland, Oregon, metropolitan area.

Q: Do you have any particular insight into the bar and restaurant business now that you've dealt with it as a regulator?

A: I have a certain amount of respect for the people who work in it; I know that it's a really tough business. I see lots of businesspeople who don't cause trouble, who obey the laws, but who still don't make it in business. They have not done their advance research or they don't have the financing to stay afloat for those first few months while they are building a clientele.

I'd like to encourage new bar or restaurant owners to become a part of the community where they're opening their business. Join the neighborhood association. Work with local law enforcement. It's understandable that neighbors may be worried about a bar that will be staying open till 2:30 in the morning. The customers who leave may be loud, get in fights,

park in the wrong places. There is cause for concern, and it's important to be able to work through any problems with your neighbors. We ask prospective licensees to get local government endorsement of their application, to make sure neighbors get a chance to have input to the local government before the license is even issued.

Q: What are license investigators and what are inspectors?

A: A license investigator goes through the application process with people who are trying to get a liquor license. They gather all the documentation they need to make a recommendation about their qualifications for the license—lease documents, proof of financial fitness, the individual's background or history. In Oregon, a liquor license is a personal privilege, like a driver's license. So each person or corporation applies for their own new license, even if they're buying a business with an existing license.

An inspector is responsible for compliance with liquor laws for the licensees within their district. They have separate geographical areas, with up to 300 licensees in each area. Every inspector is required to make premises visits; they visit each of their licensees at least once every two years.

Q: What kinds of things do the inspectors look for?

A: We have a checklist they take with them: whether the license certificate is displayed; whether the servers have a service permit; if the appropriate signs are posted about minors not being served; whether food is being served according to the state guidelines for food and alcohol service. In Oregon, if you sell distilled spirits, there are foodservice requirements. You have to have a cook on duty for a minimum of three hours during your meal periods, and you have to have at least five distinctly different menu items—sandwiches, burgers, entrées with side dishes. Even outside of meal periods, you have to offer what we call "minimum food service," with at least five food items available at all times that distilled spirits are being served.

Q: What are some of the differences in requirements if you want to sell beer and wine, not distilled spirits?

A: If you have a license that allows you to sell beer and wine, there isn't any requirement that you also have food available. If you qualify, you can sell beer between 7:00 A.M. and 2:30 A.M., and sell beer up to 14 percent alcohol, and sell wine up to 21 percent alcohol, for consumption on the premises. You don't have to have any food available, but a lot of places do. There is more paperwork for a distilled spirits license than for a beer and wine license, because you have to submit your menu and a floorplan showing what seats are used for dining and what hours the dining will take place; and you have to document the hours that your cook is on duty, and so on.

Q: What are the most common problems you see with people, either accidentally or intentionally, breaking the law?

A: Both the OLCC and police departments around the state have minor decoy missions, where someone underage attempts to purchase alcohol, and that's where we see the most violations. Licensees need to be so careful about checking identification and not selling to minors, and the computer age has made teenagers very creative about making fake IDs. I got called to a bar downtown Portland recently where the security person had detained a boy from Australia. He had made his own "Australian" ID cards, in three different names, all with his picture on them! We see more and more very sophisticated IDs that look valid. And the trouble is, it sometimes *is* valid, but they have obtained it fraudulently!

Another priority is overservice, and we do undercover observations in bars to make sure they're not overserving alcohol. Our law talks about visible intoxication, and we give lots of training to licensees to show them what they need to be looking for. The licensees attend Law Orientation, a half-day training session before they even get their license. A bartender or cocktail waitress also attends a half-day training to get their service permit. They take a test and have to pass it, and they get a service permit card good for five years. To renew, they have to take the class again.

Q: How do you work in conjunction with the Federal Bureau of Alcohol, Tobacco and Firearms?

A: We do work closely together at times, but BATF has its own process and permits and fees that are completely separate from ours. It also has its own people who inspect all wineries, breweries, distillers—they focus on manufacturers of alcoholic beverages.

Q: Control states are, and probably always will be, controversial. So speak from your vantage point about the value of the system.

A: One of the concerns about privatizing alcohol and allowing it to be sold in supermarkets is that it would give minors so much easier access. And if, in Oregon, there were not a liquor commission, there wouldn't be as much focus on service to minors and overservice, because law enforcement would have to do it all. They have to prioritize, and this might not end up on the top, despite its very serious consequences.

The OLCC raised $540 million this biennium from license fees, fines, taxes, and liquor sales; $100 million of that goes into the state's General Fund.

Q: What about advice for students who are interested in this type of career?

A: I would highly recommend that they job-shadow an inspector or investigator, to find out if they'd really like this kind of work. It's not police work, but it is regulatory work and we do work closely with licensees. We try to help them in lots of ways—education, training—we're not out there just to 'nail' people. We try to work with them and teach them to do the right thing.

Q: What kind of personality traits would make a really good field person?

A: Somebody who is comfortable talking with people, a good communicator, in situations where you have to think on your feet. You've got to use good judgment and be fair in your dealings with people. And you've got to like working on your own. Every day is different; you not only deal with licensees, but with law enforcement, with parties or "keggers" involving minors, in schools doing outreach and education—those sorts of things. You work with quite a variety of people. I've liked every job that I've had here! I love this agency. I like regulation. It's really a challenge.

CHAPTER 16

Regulations

There are many federal, state, and local laws that apply to the sale of alcoholic beverages to be consumed "on-premise," that is, at the same site where they are purchased. Some of these laws you are surely aware of, but others may never have crossed your mind. Many can have serious consequences—for you, or your employer—if you break them, so it is crucial for you to know and observe all laws that apply to you.

The purpose of this chapter is to inform you of federal regulations and to make you aware of typical state and local beverage laws. Since these vary greatly, it is up to you to find out what laws are in force in your locale.

This chapter should help you . . .

- Research your state and local regulations before you buy or lease a property.
- Meet licensing, registration, and code requirements.
- Observe legal hours of sale and sell only beverages you are licensed to sell.
- Avoid selling to underage or intoxicated persons.
- Buy your beverages from licensed suppliers.
- Avoid illegal relationships with suppliers.
- Observe laws about record-keeping, bottle closures, empty bottles, and official inspections.
- Avoid illegal advertising.
- Train your employees to be aware of and observant of beverage laws.

It is often pointed out that the alcoholic beverage industry is the most highly regulated industry in the United States. Regulations of one sort or another can affect where you locate, what you serve, whom you serve, how many you serve, the days and hours you stay open, where you buy your supplies, what records you keep, when you pay your bills, your advertising, your reputation, what you do with your empty bottles, and your ability to do any business whatsoever.

Why? There are two blanket reasons: public revenues and public interest. There is nothing new about either of these reasons. Riotous drinking was the subject of legislation in Babylonia 4000 years ago, and it was the tavernkeeper who was punished for allowing it by losing a limb or even his life. In colonial America, laws restricted hours of sale and prohibited selling to minors, drunks, Indians, servants, and slaves. The tavernkeeper was selected and approved by the town fathers, and the tavern was hemmed in with rules for keeping it as respectable a part of the community as possible.

As for revenue, licensing fees brought income to early colonial towns and cities. British taxes on Dutch rum helped to spark the American Revolution. A tax on whiskey caused the Whiskey Rebellion in 1794. When George Washington crushed the rebellion, he established firmly the right and tradition of the federal government to tax liquor for general revenue. You'll learn more about current alcohol taxes in a moment.

Today, the mishmash of alcohol-related laws is truly fascinating. Some of them are unusual, impractical, and even downright comical. For instance, at the time of this writing:

- In Arkansas, you cannot buy liquor using a credit card.
- In Alabama, you cannot purchase alcohol by telephone, fax, or e-mail.
- In Minnesota, the only grocery stores that can sell wine are in the state's three largest cities.
- In Utah, a server cannot offer a wine list to a guest; the guest must ask for it.
- In Florida, wine cannot be sold in containers larger than 1 gallon.
- Colorado requires that only miniature bottles be sold in hotel minibars, not regular cans of beer or half-bottles of wine.
- You can purchase beer in grocery stores in New York State, but not wine.

And the list goes on.

REGULATIONS: AN OVERVIEW

Today's regulations, many in the name of public interest, date from the repeal of Prohibition, and they still reflect the earnest desire of citizens and governments to prevent both the excesses of the pre-Prohibition era and the abuses by the illegal industry during the Prohibition years. Far outweighing the concerns of the past, however, are those of the present—the continuing toll of drunk-driving accidents, the effects of alcohol on unborn and nursing babies, and the problem of alcoholics—that address the 10 percent of drinkers who cannot seem to control their drinking. No matter how you feel about whose responsibility these real and present dangers are, you are urgently advised to know and observe every regulation—federal, state, and local—that applies to you.

Control States

How did the laws become so different in different areas? Following the repeal of Prohibition, the federal government established the broad outlines of alcoholic beverage control and turned over most aspects of administration to the states—where, many were convinced, it had always belonged. The popular thinking was that the United States was too vast, and its traditions and values too diverse, to suit any specific standards of sobriety.

Today, each of the 50 states still formulates its own laws and has its own administrative agency. The states, in turn, may authorize counties and municipalities to pass more stringent regulations. The resulting network of laws, as our few examples attest, can be complex and bewildering. But from a practical standpoint, the nation does at least accommodate the zeal of the "drys," the thirst of the "wets," and the obvious special interests of the liquor industry.

Today, 18 states operate as **control states,** where alcoholic beverages are sold through stores run by the state, not by private industry. Bars that operate in control states also buy their wares from the state—sometimes only liquor; sometimes beer and wine as well. Canada, and some Scandinavian countries, exercise similar controls. The control states are as follows:

Alabama	Montana	Utah
Idaho	New Hampshire	Vermont
Iowa	North Carolina	Virginia
Maine	Ohio	Washington
Michigan	Oregon	West Virginia
Mississippi	Pennsylvania	Wyoming

and Montgomery County, Maryland

The sales of distilled spirits in control states have consistently accounted for about 25 percent of the U.S. market, according to the National Alcohol Beverage Control Association, a trade group to which all the jurisdictions belong.

In a control state, the government creates an agency, department, or commission that acts, in a sense, as a wholesale liquor distributor. Spirits (and sometimes, beer and wine) are ordered and delivered to the agency's warehouses or central distribution points, then sold through a system of state-owned stores to consumers, bars, and restaurants. Or, in some states, the liquor stores are privately owned, but they have to buy their wares from the state. Again, the setup and rules that govern each state vary widely, so check with your own state authority for specifics.

Some control states require a mark or stamp on bottles, indicating taxes have been paid or that the bottle was purchased legally and in salable condition by the state.

Taxes and Revenue

Officials in control states walk a fine line between strictly regulating alcohol sales and trying to market the products in their warehouses and state-owned stores. It's a battle that plays itself out in many state legislatures from year to year. Interestingly, these states benefit most from the trend toward drinking high-end spirits. There are usually laws against—or at least, rules that minimize—the advertisement of alcohol by the state. But even without promoting it, a few states have managed to make astonishing profits. The list of the most profitable control states has included the same five, in varying order, since the early 1990s:

Michigan
Pennsylvania
Ohio
North Carolina
Washington

As with private industry, flexibility and innovative operation have made them top performers.

Taxes on alcoholic beverage are owed by anyone who sells or provides them, on or off their premises. There are a few *limited retail dealers* who are exempt from the tax. These include fraternal, civic, church, labor, veterans' or other organization, for specific situations: entertainment, picnics, festivals, and so on. But these groups are still required to pay for permits to serve alcohol. Depending on the event, it may be a single-use permit with a one-time fee paid to the city or county.

The taxes paid depend on the type of beverage. For beer, each 31-gallon barrel produced includes $18 in federal taxes, and another 5 cents for each 12-ounce can. Producing a wine of 14 percent alcohol or less, the winery pays $1.07 per gallon in federal tax, and another 21 cents for each 750-milliliter bottle. Distilled spirits are taxed at $13.50 per "proof gallon," with credit given for any percentage of that gallon that is strictly wine or flavoring, not alcohol, and another $2.14 per 750-milliliter bottle. Bars pay these taxes when they purchase the alcohol for their mixed drinks, draft kegs, and wine lists, then pass them on to customers.

These taxes bring billions of dollars into the U.S. Treasury. Today, the retail price of a typical bottle of spirits is more than 50 percent taxes and fees paid into federal, state, and local treasuries. Alaska tops the states, with the highest state-imposed taxes on alcoholic beverages. At this writing, Florida was debating a law to reduce state taxes on alcohol served in restaurant settings.

WHAT YOU MUST DO BEFORE OPENING YOUR DOORS

If you own a bar or restaurant serving alcoholic beverages, you are defined in legal terms as an **on-premise retail dealer.** In this role, you are subject to federal laws, state laws, and local laws. You must also meet requirements of local zoning ordinances, building codes, health codes, and fire codes. State and local laws vary widely and there is no way in the world this book can cover them all. But we can indicate the kinds of restrictions that are typical and what you ought to check out before you take action.

Both you and your premises must meet several requirements in order to open at all. Some of them involve a good deal of time and legwork. You may have to attend a city council meeting, go before a judge, post a notice in a newspaper, be fingerprinted—whatever the state and local laws require. The first thing to do, even before you sign a lease or buy a property, is to familiarize yourself with all the state and local regulations. Your local licensing agency will be able to provide them.

Regulations That Impact Your Choice of Location

State laws generally allow the sale of mixed drinks in hotels, restaurants, and private clubs, though a few set limits and conditions, such as a related percentage of food sales. Several states limit the alcohol content of beer and other malt liquors; this might discourage you from opening a brewpub in one of these states.

Most states have **local option** laws; that is, the state allows the people of local communities to choose whether or not they will allow the sale of alcoholic beverages, and if so, how. Thus, although state law may allow liquor to be sold by the drink, some communities, or even voting precincts, may not, even in different parts of the same city or county. The popular term for this mixture is *wet* and *dry* areas, "wet" meaning alcohol is sold and "dry" meaning it is not—or, in some cases, not without the purchase of a special "membership." If your city or county is one of these, it behooves you to check carefully where the lines of demarcation are drawn. You must also find out which beverages are permitted in your locale, because there are often different regulations for spirits, beers, and wines.

Even in areas that allow liquor by the drink, there may be zoning laws that prohibit operating a bar in your chosen location. For example, if you want to remodel an old house, the area may turn out to be zoned only for residential use. In other instances, an area zoned for commercial use may specifically prohibit retail sale of liquor.

Many city ordinances have parking lot requirements, for example, one parking space for a certain number of square feet of customer floor space. Is there room on your chosen premises to abide by the parking rules?

In many areas, you cannot locate a bar within a certain distance of a church, school, or hospital—300 feet, 1,000 feet, or a city block. The way the distance is measured—from lot line to lot line, or from door to door—may be enough to disqualify the premises you are planning to use.

Some local authorities limit the number of licenses they will grant. Some areas restrict hours of sale more than others. In some places, sales of drinks must have a certain percentage relationship to sales of food. Many communities require that you sell food if you're going to sell alcohol. In short, some areas' regulations may be so restrictive that you will decide to do business elsewhere.

Licensing and Registration Requirements

Once you have determined that your chosen location meets both your requirements and the law's, you must secure the required state and local licenses and permits and register your place of business with the federal government before you open your doors.

A **license** and a **permit** for on-premise retail sales are essentially the same thing: a document granting permission to sell specific beverage types at a specific location by a specific business entity, provided certain conditions are carried out. In some jurisdictions, the two terms are used to distinguish between various types of permission: for instance, a permit to sell wholesale and a license to sell retail, or a permit to sell mixed beverages and a license to sell beer (or vice versa).

The federal government does not issue licenses or permits for retail sales. Jurisdiction over retail sales is reserved for the state. The state may pass on the right to local bodies. The intricacies of state and local laws are so complex and vary so widely, there is no way to indicate here what licenses and permits you will need in any given location in order to sell what you plan to sell. The licenses vary, as do the requirements you must meet, the procedures you must go through, and the fees you must pay.

In some places, you must obtain a state license, in others a local license, and in still others both. In some states, a state license must have local approval; in other states, it is the other way around. In some areas, you must have separate licenses or permits for spirits, beers, wine, and mixed drinks.

In some areas, you can get a license to sell spirits only if you operate a private club. In a few places, you must sell your drinks by the miniature bottle.

Licenses and permits typically run for a year, requiring annual renewal and payment of an annual fee. Such fees vary greatly. Some are flat fees. Others may be tied to sales volume or number of rooms in a hotel or seats in a restaurant. Amounts vary from as little as, say, $50 for a beer license in Indiana to $3,000 for a mixed-beverage permit in Texas, while Honolulu County, using a percent-of-sales system, sets its ceiling for hotels at $18,000.

In some areas, a separate operator's license may be required in addition to the license for the business or premises. This may have such requirements as age (over 21), character ("good moral character"), U.S. citizenship, or residency of a certain length of time in the city or state. The penalties for selling alcoholic beverages without a license are severe. In fact, you could put yourself out of the bar business forever.

When you have your state and local permits and licenses in hand or are sure you are going to receive them, it is time to turn your attention to some federal requirements. Federal law requires a retail dealer in alcoholic beverages to register each place of business owned and to pay a **special occupational tax** for each place of business each year. In return, the government issues a special **tax stamp** for each place of business. Your tax for each location is an annual $250, whether you are serving wine, or spirits, or beer, or any combination thereof. If your business is a circus, a carnival, or some other enterprise traveling from place to place across interstate borders, you are considered a **dealer at large** and your stamp and tax ($250) cover all your activities throughout the United States.

The vehicle for registering, paying the special taxes, and receiving your stamps is ATF Form 5630.5, which you may get from any office of the federal **Bureau of Alcohol, Tobacco, and Firearms (BATF).** You must file this form and pay your tax before you begin selling any drinks, and each year thereafter. You must keep your special tax stamp, which is your tax receipt, available for inspection by BATF officers. If you deliberately sell alcoholic beverages without paying the special tax, you may be fined up to $5000, or imprisoned for up to two years, or both.

If you move your place of business, you must file an amended return (another Form 5630.5) within 30 days, and send in your tax stamp to be amended accordingly. You cannot transfer your registration or tax stamp to anyone. If you sell your business, the new owner must start over with the BATF and new stamps. If you buy someone else's business, you must start fresh. State and local license regulations have similar provisions for change of ownership. It is government's way of providing accountability.

The federal registration and tax payment do not permit you to sell liquor; they just prohibit you from selling liquor without them. Registration is mainly a mechanism for keeping track of retail liquor dealers in order to enforce some of the public-interest laws concerning the liquor itself. We will discuss that topic a little later.

Other Local Regulations

Your premises must meet the standards required by various other local codes. If you build or renovate a structure, the finished work must pass the building code inspection. Electrical work and plumbing must meet electrical and plumbing codes. The entire facility must meet the code of the fire district. This will include the requisite number and placement of exits, lighted exit signs, fire extinguishers, fire doors with panic bars that must open outward and be kept unlocked during business hours, smoke alarms, sprinkler systems in kitchens and high-rise buildings. There is also usually an occupancy requirement limiting the number of persons allowed inside the premises at one time. There will also be specifications about employee training and fire drills.

When you are all set up and ready to open, your facility and personnel must pass inspection by the local health department. Usually, you must have certain specified equipment such as a triple or quadruple sink for dishwashing, or a mechanical dishwasher and handsink. All equipment must be approved by the National Sanitation Foundation International (NSFI) and must be installed according to health department rules. For example, your ice machine and other equipment with drains must have a minimum of 6 inches of space below allowing for adequate cleaning. Other requirements pertain to floors (tile or concrete), counters, general cleanliness, proper food storage, proper temperatures for refrigerators and freezers, freedom from pests (rodents and roaches), sanitary practices such as keeping everything but ice out of the ice bin, air-drying glasses, keeping bathrooms clean and stocked with soap, towels, and tissue. You may not open for business until you have a Certificate of Occupancy.

Health departments sometimes require that employees pass a health examination and that you keep their health certificates available for inspection. This practice is becoming less and less prevalent. They also look for personal cleanliness, and may require things like signs posted in bathrooms reminding employees to wash their hands. Generally, smoking behind the bar is a violation of the health code; some states allow bartenders to have a drink on the job, but many do not. Health inspectors usually make periodic, unannounced visits to make sure that you comply with their requirements.

WHAT, WHEN, AND TO WHOM YOU MAY SELL

Generally, the regulations governing drinks, hours, and customers are state or local, and you've already learned there is considerable variation among them. The only federal requirement is that you may not sell any type of beverage for which you have not paid the special occupational tax, nor any spirit not carrying a portion of a strip stamp or other approved seal on the bottle.

What You May Sell

What you may sell is governed everywhere by the type of licenses you hold (mixed drinks, wine, beer) and special restrictions such as mini-bottles in place of custom-mixed drinks or beers of no more than a certain strength. Local laws may further limit what you may sell. The information you are given when you receive your local license will specify the rules.

When You May Sell

Nearly all states have regulations governing the hours an on-premise retail dealer may be open. These hours are usually fairly generous. Most states require closing for at least a few early-morning hours, and many forbid the sale of liquor on Sunday for part or all of the day. Many states prohibit the sale of liquor on Election Day, at least while the polls are open, and many specify closing on certain national holidays, Christmas being most commonly mentioned. Many states allow local bodies to further curtail hours and days of service.

To Whom You May Sell

All 50 states and the District of Columbia prohibit the sale of alcoholic beverages of any kind to persons under the age of 21. This raising of the **drinking age** was brought about by the federal government, which denied federal highway funds to states unless they set the drinking age at 21. The thrust of the law has been to curb the excess drinking that was typical on college campuses, and especially to reduce the number of drunk-driving accidents caused by the 18- to 21-year age group.

You and your servers are part of the law enforcement team. Chapter 2 discussed the importance of checking the age of anyone in doubt, as well as the consequences of serving alcohol to someone underage. We suggest you review this material now in the light of all you have learned since.

The other category of persons you may not sell to is the person who is **clearly intoxicated.** Many, if not most, states and communities have this law on their books. This subject is also discussed in depth in Chapter 2. We suggest you also review this material and look into the various server training programs available. Now is also the time to reread the sections in Chapter 2 on the physiology of alcohol and third-party liability. In terms of the law, these are the most important issues you face.

It is, of course, against the law to refuse to serve a customer on the basis of race, religion, skin color, sex, national origin, or disability. If you are dealing with an intoxicated person who happens to be the subject of such laws, you will be wise to make sure you have witnesses to the intoxication in case the person concerned charges discrimination.

There are other types of incidents related to drunken customers for which you may be liable under various laws. Among them are allowing injuries to take place on your premises, even when inflicted by other customers (stop the fight), allowing an intoxicated customer to drive away from your place (call a cab), and using more than "reasonable" force in dealing with an intoxicated person. In at least one state, the law requires you to remove an intoxicated person from your premises entirely, including your parking lot. But one way or another, you had better keep that person from driving even though the drinking wasn't done at your place—calling a friend, a taxi, the police if necessary.

Now that your eyes are open, review your liability insurance carefully, just in case. And train your bar personnel in handling troublesome customers as well as in avoiding them.

REGULATIONS THAT AFFECT PURCHASING

Federal, state, and local regulations may affect your purchasing both directly and indirectly.

Where You Can Buy

As you've learned, in 18 states, the sale of distilled spirits is a state monopoly, and bar operators must buy from state-owned stores or from stores authorized by the state to sell to your particular type of operation. Prices are the same in all state stores, since there is a markup formula mandated by the state. The markup plus state taxes varies from one state to another. Thus, although manufacturers' prices may be the same everywhere, the price to the bar operator varies from one state to another. Nevertheless, you must buy within the state.

In the remaining states, bar operators can buy only from suppliers that have the required licenses and permits—state, local, and federal. The federal document is known as a **wholesaler's basic permit** and is free; the wholesaler must also pay a federal special occupational tax. In some states, you can also buy directly from state-licensed manufacturers or distributors. In Texas, you can buy only from retail package stores that also hold a federal wholesaler's permit. This came about because the package stores opposed legalizing liquor-by-the-drink because it would cut heavily into their business; before that, the customer took a bottle of liquor in a brown bag and the bar host provided the setups and ice.

In most license states, the state does not control prices or markups. Prices may vary from one supplier to another, though the manufacturer or distributor price must be the same to all wholesalers. Most license states require manufacturers and wholesalers to file brand and price information with the state beverage-control agency and to post prices and discounts. Publication of suppliers' prices is usually required. The overall objective is to avoid price wars and monopoly-building of the kind that caused the beverage industry to degenerate in the years before Prohibition. Many state laws specify that manufacturers' prices must be "no higher than the lowest price" offered outside the state. This gives the producers' price structure a certain national homogeneity, varied somewhat by the amount of state and local taxes and fees.

Credit Restrictions

Nearly all states restrict credit given by the supplier to the on-premise retailer, requiring either cash or payment within a specific time period, usually 30 days or less. Extensions of credit are prohibited in many states, and federal laws prohibit extensions of credit beyond 30 days on goods figuring in interstate commerce.

Relationships with Suppliers

State laws regulate or prohibit certain interrelationships between on-premise dealers on the one hand, and wholesalers, manufacturers, importers, and distributors on the other. The purpose of these laws is to maintain fair competition and prevent retailers from being controlled by other segments of the industry, as the saloons were controlled by brewers in the old days.

Here are some of the most important prohibitions typically found in state beverage codes:

- No **tied-house** relationships. No supplier may have a financial or legal interest in your business, premises, or equipment.
- Suppliers may not furnish equipment or fixtures.
- A supplier may not pay your debts or guarantee their payment.
- A supplier may not sell to you on consignment, that is, postpone payment until goods are sold, with return privileges for goods unsold. This is also a federal law.
- Suppliers may not give you special discounts that are not available to all on-premise dealers.
- Suppliers may not give you gifts, premiums, prizes, or anything of value except specified items of limited dollar value for advertising or promotional purposes, such as table tents or a beer sign for your window, or consumer giveaways, such as matches, recipe booklets, napkins, coasters.
- A supplier may not induce you to purchase all or a certain quota of your beverage supplies from his or her enterprise.
- Bribery for control of your purchasing carries severe penalties.

In sum, suppliers may not own a piece of your business nor induce you to give them your trade. You too may be breaking the law if you accept such inducements. On the other hand, there is no law against giving most or all of your business to one supplier if you make the choice without inducement.

If you are tempted to accept deals and favors—and who doesn't love to get something for less or for nothing?—check out your state and local laws to be sure the deal or the favor is legal and has no strings attached. Laws that maintain a competitive beverage market, though framed primarily in the public interest, protect you as an entrepreneur as well.

Internet Sales and Purchases

Currently, the whole alcoholic beverage industry is divided over the direct shipment of products from producers to consumers via online Internet orders. This bypasses the middleman, of course, pitting suppliers against wholesalers, wholesalers against retailers, and consumers against the entire three-tiered system designed to make all three tiers profitable and to ensure payment of liquor-related taxes.

The controversy all started with the advent of Web sites for wineries and "wine clubs" that offer bottle and case sales directly to the public. They've agreed to pay the taxes to states where sales are made, so what's the problem? Well, some states allow shipment of alcohol across state lines, but others do not. There are state laws that prevent the shipment of alcohol except by licensed transport; laws that say you're not supposed to mail alcohol; and strict interpretations of interstate commerce laws. (Technically, shipments that arrive from another state are interstate commerce.) Already, these laws have been challenged in seven states and, at this time, experts feel the issue will eventually end up in the U.S. Supreme Court for resolution.

In the meantime, direct sales by Internet continue to grow. In 1999, they totaled $1 billion, with wine sales accounting for $750 million of that figure. By 2005, direct wine shipments alone are expected to reach almost $3 billion—a full 10 percent of the retail wine market!

Much will depend on the court's interpretation of the continued need for the three-tiered system. After all, it was created back in the 1930s to keep gangsters out of the liquor business. For that purpose, it worked well. But times have changed radically, and the Internet has created a new business dynamic that no one fully anticipated. It will be interesting to see what transpires in the next decade to allow liquor merchants to do commerce in new ways.

REGULATIONS THAT AFFECT OPERATIONS

In addition to regulating your buying and selling, other regulations—both federal and state—touch some of the smallest details of your beverage operation.

Policing the Product

During Prohibition, the illegal production and sale of alcoholic beverages was widespread, and much of the stuff was harmful and even deadly, two major reasons why Prohibition was finally repealed. It had proven impossible to control illicit production. The only answer was for the government to work hand in hand with a legal beverage industry and to set up controls to protect the public from unscrupulous producers and bad products.

Accordingly, the federal government established Standards of Identity for each product, plus systems of inspection and control at licensed distilleries, breweries, and wineries to see that the standards were met. Today, federal regulations assure you, the customer, that the product inside the bottle is exactly what the label says. Labels must correctly state the product class and type as defined in the Standards of Identity, its alcoholic content (except for beer), the net contents of the bottle, and the name of the manufacturer, bottler, or importer. Periodic on-premise inspections by federal agents of the BATF assure that contents and label agree (Figure 16.1). Bonded warehouses under lock and key are further controls against substandard merchandise. Imports are controlled in similar fashion through customs regulation, inspection, and labeling requirements.

Federal control of the product extends right into your storeroom, speed rack, and backbar, via the closure on the bottle and certain regulations concerning the bottle itself. The **strip stamp,** that red or green stamp that used to span the top of each bottle of distilled spirits, has generally been replaced by a **tamper-evident** type of closure, such as certain pull tabs or a screw top that leaves a thin metal ring around the bottle neck when opened. The closure (whether stamp or otherwise) is a key control in three federal government activities:

- Collecting revenue from distillers.
- Maintaining product quality.
- Preventing the sale of illegal spirits.

Figure 16.1 BATF inspectors checking box markings at a distillery warehouse. Photo courtesy of the Bureau of Alcohol, Tobacco and Firearms.

The closure goes on the bottle at the time of bottling, when taxes are paid, and the bottle, its contents approved, leaves the warehouse. The closure is affixed in such a way that the bottle cannot be opened without breaking the closure. That closure must remain attached and unbroken until you open the bottle at your bar. It is your assurance that no one has tampered with its contents, that they are exactly as they were when they left the distillery.

If a delivery from a supplier includes one or more bottles with broken or mutilated closures, you should not accept such bottles. It may be an accident, but it can also mean that the original contents have been altered and you are not getting what you ordered. Besides, possession of bottles without proper closure is against federal law. Substitute closures are available, but let your supplier cope with getting new closures. Send the bottle back.

When you open a bottle you must leave a portion of the closure attached to the bottle. You must leave the liquor in that bottle and not transfer it to any other bottle. Make this very clear to all your personnel. If you have liquors without portions of closures on your premises, you are subject to a fine of up to $10,000 and/or imprisonment for up to five years! Again, a bottle without a portion of its closure may be an accident, but if an inspecting federal agent should find it, it puts you under suspicion of having bought illicit goods.

For you, a broken or missing closure on a full bottle may be a clue that someone having access to your liquor supply has substituted something else and has gone off with your good liquor. So the stamp or other closure can work for you as well as for the government.

It is also against federal law for you, or anyone, to reuse an empty spirits bottle for any purpose whatsoever. The primary thrust of this law is to prevent illegal distillers from refilling such bottles with their product and passing them off as the real thing. But it is just as illegal for you to use an empty liquor bottle for your simple syrup or your sweet-sour mix, even if you label it as such.

Federal law does allow you to return empties to a bottler or importer that has federal permission to reuse them, or to destroy them on your premises, or to send them elsewhere for destruction. But many state or local laws require spirits bottles to be broken as soon as they are empty. Moonshining and bootlegging are far from dead, and both federal and state beverage-control authorities are actively engaged in rooting it out.

There is also a federal law against adding anything—other spirits, water, any substance—to the original contents in a bottle. Oddly enough, this forbidden practice is known as **marrying.** You may not even combine the contents of two nearly used bottles of an identical product, partly for sanitation reasons and partly as a precaution against illegal refilling. This is one reason why you should inquire first about making your own *infusions*, a process described in Chapter 5, by steeping fruits or herbs in alcohol. In some states, your liquor bottles may carry an additional state stamp. It may show that state taxes have been paid, or it may have some other identification purpose. These state stamps should also always be left on the bottles.

Labels and Labeling Laws

The BATF has specific labeling requirements for alcohol—in fact, there's an Alcohol Labeling and Formulation Division of the agency responsible for issuing certificates of label approval. It's a busy place, issuing more than 50,000 certificates a year.

One legal requirement for all alcoholic beverage containers is the Health Warning Statement. Whether the spirit is produced domestically or elsewhere, this wording must be present—and presented separately from any other information on the label. It reads as follows:

GOVERNMENT WARNING
(1) According to the Surgeon General, women should not drink alcoholic beverages during pregnancy because of the risk of birth defects.
(2) Consumption of alcoholic beverages impairs your ability to drive a car or operate machinery, and may cause health problems.

Other label requirements (alcohol content, proof, etc.) are spelled out depending on the specific type of beverage and the laws and rules in its country of origin.

In recent years, there has been a campaign by winemakers to include educational labels on wine bottles. These include statements like the following, which was approved by the BATF in 1999: "The proud people who made this wine encourage you to consult your family doctor about the health effects of wine consumption."

This created quite an uproar in the industry, since it is not really a "warning," and, in fact, refers to some of the health benefits associated with drinking moderate amounts of wine, an issue that was discussed briefly in Chapter 2.

Another controversy arose when winemakers began putting statements on labels to the effect that certain wines were "made from organically grown grapes." The U.S. Department of Agriculture (USDA) wants to put a stop to this practice, not because it's an untrue statement, but because it may be misleading. A small percentage of people have allergic reactions to *sulfites*, antibacterial and antioxidant agents that are routinely added to many wines to stabilize them during the winemaking process. These are added even if the grapes are organically grown, and, in fact, some sulfites are found naturally on the grapes themselves. The USDA contends this makes wine a "manufactured" product, not "organic." At the time of this writing, the debate continues.

Records and Inspections

The federal government requires you to keep records of all spirits, wines, and beers received: quantities, names of sellers, and dates received. You may keep this in book form or in the form of all your invoices and bills. State and local governments may require you to keep daily records of gross sales, especially if you must pay sales taxes or collect them from the customer. You must keep all your records for at least three years.

Your place of business, your stock of liquors, your records, and your special tax stamp and receipt are subject to inspection at any time by BATF officers (Figure 16.2). This is not likely to happen unless they think you might have some evidence that would help them in tracing someone who has bro-

Figure 16.2 A BATF inspector checks the labels on alcoholic beverages to ensure compliance with federal labeling requirements. Photo courtesy of the Bureau of Alcohol, Tobacco and Firearms.

ken the law. Your licenses and permits, your records, and your entire operation are also subject to inspection by state and local officials if your state and local codes so state-and they probably do. All such officials carry identification that they must show to you. Once you have verified their identity, you must show them anything they want to see.

Other State/Local Regulations

If there are state or local sales taxes, you will undoubtedly be required to collect them from your customers. For this, you must keep daily records of sales of taxable items, with separate records for each category of taxables (beer, wine, spirits, mixed drinks) if the tax rates distinguish between them. The simplest way to keep these records is the point-of-sale cash register with a separate key for each category. Each category will be totaled separately, and you will have a printed record on the tape.

You will be required to make sales tax reports and payments at regular intervals, and your records will be subject to audit. You must keep your daily records for however long state/local laws specify.

Another frequent provision of state beverage codes concerns the credit you may extend to customers. Some states forbid it entirely, requiring that all drinks be paid for in cash. Others permit customers to charge drinks to their hotel bills or club membership accounts or to pay by credit card. Still others have no credit restrictions.

Nearly all codes set limits on advertising involving alcoholic beverages. The federal government has stringent regulations designed to prevent false, misleading, or offensive product advertising. Most states follow suit. Code provisions that might affect a beverage-service enterprise concern billboards advertising your bar or restaurant, the content of your magazine and newspaper ads, signs identifying your place or your products, window displays. Many beverage codes forbid ads associating your products with provocative women, biblical characters, or Santa Claus.

A final category of regulation has to do with keeping your enterprise an acceptable member of your community. Here are some kinds of things for which, under some state or local laws, you may be liable for fines, imprisonment, or loss of license:

- Possessing or selling an illicit beverage.
- Permitting lewd, immoral, or indecent conduct or entertainment on your premises (exposure of person, obscene language, disturbing display of a deadly weapon, prostitution, narcotics possession or use).
- Disturbing the peace.

New Political Issues

Bars and restaurants should expect heated activity on several fronts, in Congress and perhaps in their own state legislatures. As this textbook is being written, here are some of the hot-button issues:

- **Minimum wage.** An increase of up to $1 per hour is a top issue, which will definitely impact your bottom line. The current prediction is that the $1 raise will be phased in over a number of years.
- **Business meal deductibility.** Legislation is being actively promoted to allow businesspeople to write off 80 percent of the cost of their meals on their income taxes, instead of the current 50 percent. This would be a boon to small businesses and self-employed persons, and might well mean a boost in your business.
- **Immigration.** In light of the terrorist acts of September 11, 2001, labor shortage issues and the problems of undocumented foreign workers in the United States are being addressed with new vigor and multiple approaches. It may mean changes to the amnesty program passed by Congress in 1996.

- **Health care.** Health insurance for people who don't make much money is a big concern in Congress. There are proposals to allow self-employed persons to write off more of their health insurance costs; to allow small businesses to get lower-cost insurance through trade associations instead of having to buy higher-cost individual or small-group policies for employees; and to expand the amount a person can put into his or her Medical Savings Account.

As you can see, there is nothing static about your industry if you are a bar owner or restaurateur. Keep up with all of it by reading the trade journals. It can be frustrating that there seems to be no aspect of manufacturing, importing, selling, or advertising that escapes the scrutiny of at least one level of government. But that side of the story is beyond the scope of this book.

If you find the laws bewildering, contradictory, and time-consuming, you are not alone. It helps to see them in the perspective of history and to realize that the seeming chaos simply grew that way in response to differing local needs and desires, with a good bit of emotion and politics thrown in to keep things interesting. It also helps to realize that frustration and contradiction are not forever but can be amended through education, the political lobby, and the voting machine.

It helps, too, to recognize that many of the regulations benefit and protect you. Thanks to regulations, you have a product of guaranteed consistency and an environment of free and fair competition. Within the framework of regulation, the beverage industry is an essential and respected element in the economic and social fabric of America. When it comes to profitability, that is worth a lot in goodwill.

So inform yourself of your local laws, pay your beverage taxes (budgeting them firmly into your profit plan), and comfort yourself with the thought that beverage laws are necessary precisely because the demand for your product is inexhaustible.

SUMMING UP

The sale of alcoholic beverages is heavily regulated in many places, and the beverages themselves are heavily taxed. There might be even more regulation if alcohol wasn't such a good source of revenue for governments on all levels.

In some states, alcohol is sold in stores like any other product. In other states, its sale is carefully regulated by "liquor control" or alcoholic beverage commissions, and sold only through state-run stores or authorized retailers who must purchase their inventory from the state system. Everyone who sells alcohol must have some sort of license or permit to do so; for a bar or restaurant, you are licensed as an *on-premise retail dealer.* On-premise means people consume the alcohol on your premises; off-premise means a store situation, where they buy the liquor and consume it elsewhere. There is also federal registration required (and a fee due) with the U.S. Bureau of Alcohol, Tobacco and Firearms (BATF), plus local health and safety standards and building codes to comply with.

The observance of existing laws, however absurd some of them may seem, is important for two reasons. One is for your own immediate good; the other is for the good of the industry as a whole. If the industry is to maintain a respected place in American life, we must all be good, law-abiding citizens.

You can only buy alcohol from licensed wholesale distributors (or from the state, in a control state) and there are rules about what kinds of "extras" or "special deals" you can accept from your wholesalers. A wholesaler cannot, for instance, have a financial or legal interest in your business, premises, or equipment; or make special payment arrangements for you that are not offered to others. The issue of selling alcohol (especially wine) over the Internet is a hot one that is now challenging the traditional ways of doing business, and at this time, it is far from being resolved.

The bottles themselves must be sealed in such a way that you know they have not been tampered with when you receive them; empty bottles cannot be reused; and the contents of two partial bottles cannot be combined—all requirements of federal law.

The laws—and all the paperwork you must keep current to prove you are abiding by them—are reminders that the dual nature of alcohol is always with us and that we operate within the shadow of its dark side. It is important for anyone in the industry to keep up to date on legal issues and changes.

POINTS TO PONDER

1. In what ways does the bar operator benefit from government regulations applying to alcoholic beverages?

2. Banning bars avoids what kinds of problems in a community? What problems does it create?

3. What is a local option law?

4. Why shouldn't a supplier be allowed to own a bar or restaurant?

5. How would you go about refusing an intoxicated person a drink?

6. In your community, what are the procedures for obtaining the required licenses to operate a full bar?

7. Why should age be a barrier to buying a drink?

8. In your state, are you allowed to buy alcohol from merchants on the Internet?

9. What is the purpose of the tamper-evident stamp on liquor bottles?

10. What kinds of records should you keep to be able to pay the proper amount of taxes for selling alcohol?

TERMS OF THE TRADE

Bureau of Alcohol, Tobacco & Firearms (BATF)

clearly or visibly intoxicated

control (monopoly) states, license states

credit restrictions

legal drinking age

license, permit

local option

marrying

on-premise retail dealer

special occupational tax, tax stamp, dealer at large

tamper-evident closure, strip stamp

tied-house, inducements to purchase

wholesaler's basic permit

Glossary

Absinthe. An herbal liqueur from France that is strictly regulated for containing a small amount of nerve-damaging ingredient called *alpha thujone*. Absinthe is illegal to purchase in the United States.

Adjunct. Any cereal grain added to malted barley in making beer. Also called a *malt adjunct* or *grain adjunct*.

Aging. Storing wine or spirits in wooden casks for a period of time to improve flavor.

Aguardiente (ah-GWAHR-dee-EN-tay). The Mexican name for rum made with more than 50 percent sugar cane-based spirits.

Ah-so. A wine-opening device that consists of two prongs, wedged into the neck of the bottle between cork and glass and twisted.

Alcoholic. A person who is addicted to alcoholic beverages.

Alcoholic beverage. Potable liquid containing .5 percent or more of ethyl alcohol (by definition under federal law).

Alcoholism. Addiction to alcoholic beverages.

Ale. Malt beverage (beer) made by top fermentation at lukewarm temperatures.

Alembic, alambic. Copper pot still used in distilling Cognac.

Amaretto. An almond-flavored liqueur.

Ambience. Another term for *atmosphere*; the overall sensory and psychological impact of surroundings.

Amphora. Airtight clay containers used by the ancient Greeks for wine storage. (See *pitching*.)

Anejo Tequila. Tequila that has been aged in wood for at least one year. The word "anejo" means "aged" in Spanish.

Angostura (ANN-goh-STIR-ra). Condiment bitters from Trinidad.

Anisette. A generic name for a sweet liqueur made with anise seed, fruit peels, and other herbs.

Annealing. The slow cooling process used to harden melted glass; part of the process of making glassware.

Aperitif (a-PAIR-ih-TEEF). 1) Fortified wine flavored with herbs and spices. 2) Wine served as an appetizer before a meal.

Appellation controlee (ah-pel-la-SEE-awn kawn-tro-LAY). Phrase on a French wine label indicating the wine comes from the controlled area named and meets its strict legal standards.

Applejack. American brandy distilled from apple cider and aged in wood.

Apricot brandy. On an American bottle, brandy made from apricots. On an imported bottle, an apricot-flavored liqueur made from brandy.

Aquavit (ah-kwa-VEET). Danish spirit; a neutral spirit flavored with caraway.

Aqua vitae (OCK-wah VY-tah). Literally, "water of life," an early term for a distilled spirit.

Arak, arrack. Brandylike rum from Indonesia, aged in The Netherlands.

Armagnac (AR-man-yak). Brandy made in the Armagnac district of France.

Aroma. Fruity or flowery scent of a wine.

Aromatized wine. Fortified wine to which aromatic herbs and spices have been added, such as vermouth.

Assorted discount. A price reduction based on quantity purchases: "Buy five cases and get a 20 percent discount." Also called a *multiple brands* discount.

Astringent. Wine-tasting term referring to an aspect of the wine that makes the mouth pucker.

Auslese (AUSCH-lay-za). German wine made from particularly ripe grapes picked very selectively in bunches.

AVA. Acronym for Approved Viticultural Appellation. U.S. counterpart of the European appellation system; the phrase is applied to a unique vineyard area officially defined and controlled.

Bacchus. The god of wine in Greek and Roman mythology; still used as a popular symbol of wines and drinking.

Backbar. Rear structure of bar behind bartender, including storage, equipment, glassware, and liquor displays.

Balance. A term in wine tasting that describes how the components in a wine relate to each other to form a "good" or harmonious overall taste.

Bank. The amount of starting cash 1) in the register, for making change; or 2) in some payment systems, the cash carried by each server.

Bank count slip. A paper (like a deposit slip) on which a list of all bills and coins is made for the start and/or end of a business day, or work shift.

Barback. A bartender's helper, usually an apprentice bartender.

Barbera (bar-BAHR-uh). An Italian red grape, also grown extensively in California, and used primarily for blending with other reds.

Bar code scanner. A handheld device that reads the UPC "bar codes" commonly affixed to most items sold today. See *Universal Product Code*.

Bar cost. See *beverage cost percentage*.

Bar die. The vertical structure that supports the front portion of the bar and shields the underbar from public view.

Bar knife. A small to medium-size stainless-steel knife, such as a paring or utility knife.

Bar manager. Person in charge of all aspects of operation in a bar, or all aspects of beverage operation in a restaurant.

Bar mixer. A blender used strictly for making mixed or frozen drinks.

Barrel. 1) In beer-making, a 31-gallon glass- or stainless-steel-lined tank. Breweries' output is measured in barrels. 2) In making distilled spirits or wines, the wooden casks in which the liquid is stored to age and mature it.

Barrel house. The storage area for barrels at a bourbon-making distillery.

Barspoon. Shallow, long-handled spoon for mixing drinks, equal to 1 teaspoon.

Bar strainer. A round wire coil on a handle, used with mixing glass or shaker to strain a freshly mixed drink into a glass.

Bar sugar. Superfine sugar.

Bartender. Person who mixes and serves drinks to bar customers and fills drink orders for servers.

Base. The primary liquor in a mixed drink; usually at least a jigger.

BATF. Bureau of Alcohol, Tobacco and Firearms, the federal department that regulates those items.

Beer. 1) Fermented beverage made from malted grain (usually barley), water, hops, and yeast. 2) Fermented grain mixture, or wort, from which whiskey or grain neutral spirits are distilled; distiller's beer.

Beer belly. Weight gain manifested around the stomach, at least partly due to beer (or other high-caloric) intake and not enough exercise.

Beer box. Refrigerator specially designed for a draft-beer system; also called a *tap box.*

"Beer-clean" glass. A glass that is free of grease, soap, and lint.

Beerenauslese (BAHR-un-OUSCH-lay-zah). German wine made from individually picked, perfectly ripened grapes.

Beer system. Draft-beer supply system, consisting of keg of beer, beer box, tap, lines, and CO_2 cylinder.

Beginning inventory. Dollar value of physical inventory at beginning of an accounting period (which should be equal to the ending inventory of previous accounting period).

Benedictine. A prestigious French liqueur made by Benedictine monks from a secret recipe of herbs.

Beverage cost. Cost of spirits, wine, and beer for a given time period, determined by subtracting your beginning inventory from ending inventory for that period.

Beverage-cost method. A formula for pricing mixed drinks based on the costs of their individual ingredients.

Beverage cost percentage. Beverage cost expressed as a percentage of sales (C/S = C%); often called simply *bar cost.*

Beverage director, beverage manager. Person in charge of all phases of beverage operation in a large organization. May also be called *beverage steward.*

Bin card. Storeroom card for each beverage item showing bin number and amount of stock on hand.

Bin number. A number assigned to each wine on a wine list, which makes it easier to organize and inventory, and easy for customers to refer to it by number if they can't pronounce the name.

Binge drinking. Consuming four or more alcoholic beverages (for women; five or more for men) in rapid succession, usually in a party setting.

Bitter. British-style ale, high in flavor and low in alcohol.

Bitters. Spirits flavored with herbs, bark, fruits, and so on without addition of sugar. *Flavoring bitters* are used in minute quantities as condiments; *beverage bitters* are potable beverages.

Blanc de blancs (blawn da BLAWN). White wine made entirely from white grapes, usually a Champagne made from the Chardonnay grape.

Blanc de noirs (blawn deh n'WAHR). White wine made from red grapes, usually a Champagne made from the Pinot Noir grape.

Blend. 1) To mix, or *marry,* wines or spirits of different ages, character, or origin before bottling. 2) To mix a drink in a blender.

Blended American whiskey. Whiskey containing at least 20 percent straight whiskey plus neutral spirits, with no aging requirement.

Blonde beer. An ale or lager with a very light color and medium-bodied flavor.

Blood alcohol content. The percentage of alcohol in an individual's blood, used as a measure of degree of intoxication. Abbreviated BAC.

Blue Agave. The type of desert plant used to make Tequila, grown in five specific government-authorized regions of Mexico. Agave plants are also called *maguey* in some parts of Mexico.

Blush wine. "White" or rosé wine made from red grapes, having the pale color of the original grape.

Bock beer. Rich, heavy, dark, malty beer, high in alcohol, made seasonally in Germany; also made in various styles in the United States.

Body. 1) Of a wine, the feel of a wine in the mouth, the result of its alcohol, sugar, and glycerin content. 2) Of a spirit, the amount of flavor and aroma.

Bonded warehouse. Warehouse in which liquor is stored under government supervision.

Botanicals. Herbs and spices used as flavorings in spirits, especially liqueurs, and fortified wines.

Botrytis cinerea (bo-TRY-das sin-AIR-ee-a). "Noble rot," a mould that dries ripened grapes, concentrating their sugar and flavor (French *pourriture noble*, German *Edelfaule*). These grapes are used to make supersweet dessert wines of high quality.

Bottled in Bond. Phrase on a bottle's label indicating the spirit inside is straight, distilled at 160 proof or less at one plant by one distiller, aged at least four years, and bottled at 100 proof in a bonded warehouse.

Bottom fermentation. Method of making lager beers, in which yeasts act from the bottom of a fermenting tank at low temperatures.

Bouncer. A security person for a bar whose job is to be on the lookout for unruly behavior and be able to deal with it firmly but gracefully.

Bouquet. Complex and interesting odor of a mature wine.

Bourbon. Whiskey made with 51 percent or more corn plus other grains, aged at least two years in charred new oak containers.

Brandy. Distilled spirit made from wine or other fermented fruit juice.

Break-even point. The point in operating a business at which no profit is made and no loss is incurred. Handy to know so you can track the minimum number of dollars that should be made each day to show a profit.

Breathe. A term for wine being exposed to air when it is first opened; also called *aeration.*

Brewer's yeast. Special types of yeast used in beer-making; ale yeast or lager yeast.

Brewing. The process of boiling *wort* with *hops* to make beer.

Brewpub. Bar-restaurant combination in which at least some of the beer served is brewed on-site.

Broken case. Case of 12 bottles made up of different items. Also called a *mixed case.*

Brown goods. A nickname for whiskies, brandies—spirits dark in color and with hearty flavors.

Bruised beer. Beer that has been warmed and cooled again, which may suffer in quality as a result.

Brut (BROOT or brutt). On a Champagne label, *dry* (meaning the grapes used to make it contained little or no sugar). Brut is the driest style of Champagne.

Budget. Financial plan for a given period that coordinates anticipated income and expenditures to ensure solvency and yield a profit.

Build. To mix a drink in its glass.

Bundling. Offering more than one item (for example, a bottle of wine with two dinner entrées) as a combination, often for a single or special price.

Cabernet Franc (CAB-ur-NAY fronk). A relative of the Cabernet Sauvignon grape, often used for blending.

Cabernet Sauvignon (CAB-ur-NAY so-vin-YON). One of the world's most important grape varietals, it is used to make red wines of Bordeaux in France, also in California, Australia, and other reds.

Cachaca (cah-CHOK-ah). A Brazilian-made type of rum.

Call brand. Brand of liquor specified by customer ordering drink; brands frequently requested ("called for") by name.

Cage. The wire hood that encases a Champagne bottle cork, holding it in firmly.

Calvados (KAL-vah-dose). French apple brandy.

Campari. Bitter Italian spirit, 48 proof, the most popular of the beverage bitters.

Canadian whiskey. Blended whiskey imported from Canada, light in flavor and body, aged at least three years.

Capital risk. Financial risks that, through a number of ways, may be preventable, such as waste, breakage, and spillage.

Capsule. Foil or plastic cap covering the top of a wine bottle.

Carafe (kah-RAFF). A glass container used to serve house wines, that holds two to four glasses.

Carrying costs. The total dollar value of your inventory; items for which you have already paid but have not yet been sold or used.

Cash flow. The cash that comes into and goes out of a business. Tracked as a *cash-flow forecast* or *cash budget*.

Cash register. Machine for recording and totaling sales. Also see *POS*.

Cask-conditioned beer. A secondary fermentation of beer, done by adding yeast and priming wort to a wooden cask, called a *firkin*. The beer is served directly from the firkin.

Cask Strength. A term used on a whiskey label that means no water was added to the whiskey to dilute it before bottling.

Category management. Tracking specific sales to see what sells well and what does not, then using that information to make more profitable business decisions.

Cava. Spanish-made sparkling wine.

Cellarmaster. See *sommelier* or *wine steward*.

Cellar temperature. For the wine storeroom, 55° to 60° Fahrenheit.

Chambord. A French liqueur flavored with raspberries.

Champagne process. French process of making Champagne, in which yeast and sugar are added to a bottle of still wine, which undergoes a second fermentation in the bottle.

Chapitalization. In winemaking, extra sugar added before fermentation when grapes do not contain enough natural sugar of their own.

Chardonnay. One of the world's top white wine grapes, or the wine of the same name. It is also the grape used to make French Chablis and White Burgundies.

Charmat (shar-MAH) **process.** Method of making a sparkling wine in a large closed container under pressure rather than in individual bottles. Also called *bulk process* or *charmat bulk process*.

Chartreuse. A brightly colored herbal liqueur, very expensive and made in a single monastery from a secret recipe since the seventeenth century.

Chaser. An additional liquid, like beer or water, drunk immediately after gulping a *shot* of alcohol.

Chateau (shah-TOE). Vineyard in France. Some American vineyards have picked up the term in naming their wineries.

Chateau-bottled. Wine bottled at the vineyard by its owner, made exclusively from grapes grown at that vineyard.

Chenin Blanc (SHEN-in BLONK). A popular white grape used to make wines of the same name, and the Vouvray wines (in France) and Steen wines (in South Africa).

Claret. The British term for a red Bordeaux wine.

Classified growth. Wines from the chateaux of France that have been recognized for their high quality. The classification began in 1855 and lists the wineries (chateaux) by "first growth" (best and most prestigious) to "fifth growth" (also excellent). As you might imagine, the classifications are subjective, and a lot has changed since 1855.

Clientele. The people served by an enterprise, usually having certain needs, tastes, and values in common.

Coarse salt. Salt that is larger than table salt, used for *rimming* glasses. Also called *kosher salt* or *Margarita salt*.

Cobra gun. The dispensing head of an automatic beverage dispensing system, for soft drink or liquor pouring. So named because of the lines that "snake" toward its head; the head itself has buttons on it that are pushed to dispense each beverage. Nicknamed a *handgun* or *six-shooter*.

Cocktail. A mixed drink.

Cocktail glass. Stemmed glass with flared bowl, usually holding 3 to 5 ounces.

Cognac (CONE-yak). Brandy made in the Cognac district of France.

Cointreau (KWON-trow). A brand-name liqueur that is a blend of several citrus fruits.

Collins glass. Tumbler of 10 to 12 ounces.

Collins mix. A sweet-sour combination of lemon juice, sugar, and Club soda, used in making Collins drinks.

Competitive advertising. Ads that prompt your customers specifically to choose your business over other similar ones.

Compound gin. Gin made or flavored by mixing high-proof spirits with the extracts of juniper berries or other botanicals.

Concept bar. A bar in which the décor transforms the space into an exotic place or another time period. Rainforest Cafés are examples of popular concept restaurant/bars.

Condiment. 1) Pungent or spicy product used to flavor drinks, as bitters,

Tabasco. 2) Garnish, used in this sense largely by manufacturers of condiment trays.

Condiment tray. The multicompartment tray in which garnishes (cherries, lemon wedges, etc.) are stored at the serving station.

Congeners (CON-jun-ers, or cun-JEEN-ers). Products present in minute amounts in fermented and distilled beverages, providing the beverages' distinctive flavors and aromas and certain features of a hangover.

Consultant. Specialist in design, market survey, feasibility, facilities design, or other aspect of bar development or operation who works on a fee or retainer basis.

Continuous still. Continuously operating pair or series of interacting columns in which spirits are vaporized by steam. Also called a *column still,* a *patent still,* or a *Coffey still.*

Contract brewer. A brewery hired to make, label, and market private label brands for brewpubs, under contract. (Also see *regional specialty brewery.*)

Contribution margin. Sales less product cost; another term for *gross profit.*

Control. Means of preventing, detecting, measuring, or eliminating waste, error, and pilferage.

Control state. A state in which all alcoholic beverages are sold from state-run stores; also called a *monopoly state.* Compare *license state.*

Cooler. 1) Bucket for wine service, in which wine is surrounded by crushed ice; wine chiller. 2) Kitchen jargon for refrigerator. 3) A glass tumbler with a capacity of 15 to 16 ounces. 4) Tall iced drink.

Cordial. Brandy or other spirit sweetened and flavored with natural flavorers; also called *liqueur.*

Cordial glass. Stem glass of 1 to 3 ounces.

Corked. A wine with an unpleasant taste, usually due to chemicals on the cork that have come into contact with the wine.

Cork retriever. Long wires on a handle, used to grab a cork that has been pushed into a wine bottle and turned upright to remove it.

Corkscrew. A device with a spiral screw, used to open a corked bottle. See *worm.*

Corn whiskey. Whiskey made with 80 percent or more of corn, aged in uncharred or used charred oak barrels. Not common as a bar whiskey.

Costing. Establishing the exact cost of a drink by figuring the cost of each ingredient in its recipe.

Cost percentage. 1) Cost expressed as a percent of sales. 2) As a control method, measurement of actual bar cost percentage (based on physical inventory) against standard bar cost percentages and past performance.

Cost per impression. An advertising industry term that refers to how much money a business spends for each time an individual hears or sees an ad (making an "impression").

Count. Number of items to the container.

Cover charge. A small entry fee charged at the door of a bar, usually when there is live entertainment, that is often used to pay the band.

CPU. Abbreviation for central processing unit, of a computerized register system (POS).

Craft brewery. Another term for *microbrewery.*

Credit memo. Seller's document crediting buyer for short, broken, or otherwise unsatisfactory merchandise or mistakes on invoice.

Crus classes. Another term for *classified growths,* the formal quality ranking of chateaux wines in Bordeaux and certain other French wine districts.

Cruvinet (KROO-vin-AY). The brand name of a popular wine cabinet.

Cryptosporidium. A common waterborne parasite that causes illness.

Cullet. Reused bits of broken glass, melted with soda, lime, and fine sand to make glass.

Curacao (KYOOR-a-sau). A liqueur made from the peel of a Caribbean fruit called the bitter orange.

Cup. 1) An 8-ounce liquid measure. 2) Metal can of shaker or blender. 3) Wine punch.

Dash. $\frac{1}{6}$ teaspoonful, or about 10 drops of a liquid.

Dasher. A dispenser built into the neck of a bottle from which no more than a *dash* is usually dispensed (like Tabasco or bitters).

Dealer at large. A liquor retailer who travels and makes sales in more than one state, like a circus or carnival.

Decant (dee-KANT). To carefully pour wine from a bottle to a carafe (a *decanter*) so that the sediment remains in the bottle.

Delivery system. The process for ordering, producing, and delivering food and drinks to customers.

Demeraran rum. Rum made in Guyana; when specified in a drink recipe, it often means 151-proof rum.

Demi-sec. On a Champagne label, the literal translation is "half dry," but, actually, this is one of the sweetest styles of Champagne.

Demographics. Statistical data on population of a given area, such as age, income, dine-out habits, lifestyle.

Denominazione di Origine Controllata (de-nom-ee-NATZ-ee-OH-na dee OR-ih-JEEN-ah KON-troh-LAT-ta). Phrase on an Italian wine label indicating the wine comes from the controlled district named and meets its strict legal standards. Abbreviated *D.O.C.*

Depletion allowance form. A paper on which any problem with inventory is recorded: breakage, spills, transfers from one bar or site to another, or any beverage given away for any reason.

Dessert wine. 1) A class of fortified wines, often sweet, that includes port, sherry, Madeira, marsala, angelica, muscatel. 2) Any sweet wine served at the end of a meal.

Detail tape. The paper tape made by a POS system or cash register as a way of documenting sales.

Diastase. The enzyme in *malt* (sprouted grain) that changes starches to sugars.

Die. Vertical structure supporting top of front bar and dividing customer's side from bartender's side.

Distillation. Separation of alcohol from a fermented liquid by heating to vaporize the alcohol and then condensing the vapors.

Distilled spirit. Alcoholic beverage made by distilling a fermented liquid.

D.O.C.G. In Italy, this label designation indicates the wine meets even higher standards than the normal *D.O.C.* The "G" stands for "garantita," or guaranteed.

Doppelbock. German for "double bock," this especially rich, strong bock beer is made as high in alcohol content as possible. (See *bock beer.*)

Doux. A seldom-seen designation on a Champagne label, indicating extreme sweetness.

Draft beer. Unpasteurized beer drawn from keg to glass. The British spelling is *draught.*

Drambuie (dram-BOO-ee). A brand-name liqueur made from scotch and honey.

Dramshop laws. State laws dictating (among other things) that the seller of alcohol to an intoxicated person may be held liable for damages caused by that person.

Drink size. Amount of base ingredient used per drink.

Dry. 1) Lacking in sweetness. 2) Person favoring prohibition of alcoholic beverage sale. 3) Term used for an area in which sale of alcoholic beverages is forbidden.

Dry beer. Beer with less sweetness and little or no aftertaste; light and lively.

Dry gin. English-style gin, as opposed to Dutch gin.

Dutch gin. Full-bodied, malt-flavored gin imported from Holland; also called Hollands, Genever, Schiedam. Not a bar gin.

Eau de vie (oh da vee). French translation of Latin aqua vitae, water of life; general term for a spirit.

ECR. Abbreviation for electronic cash register; a computerized cash register.

Edelfaule (ay-dul-foy-la). Botrytis cinerea, "noble rot."

Eighty-six. 1) Signal to stop serving liquor to someone who has had too much to drink. 2) Sign that a supply of a product has run out.

Eisbock. A concentrated, highly alcoholic beer made by freezing the beer, then removing the ice crystals from it.

Eiswein. Rare wine (usually German) made from grapes that have frozen on the vine before harvesting, concentrating their richness and sweetness.

Ending inventory. Dollar value of physical inventory at end of accounting period.

Enology. The science of winemaking; a college degree in winemaking.

Estate-bottled. Term for wine bottled at the vineyard by the vineyard owner and made exclusively from grapes grown at that vineyard.

Ethanol. Type of alcohol found in spirits, beer, and wine.

Exempt employee. Employee who is exempt from federal overtime pay requirements because of managerial or supervisory duties.

Extensions. On an invoice, multiples of the same item at the same price.

Extra. On a Cognac label, means aged at least 5½ years.

Extra sec. On a Champagne label, the translation is "Extra Dry," but it means the wine contains a small amount of added sugar.

Falernum. Sweet syrup with almond-ginger-lime flavor, 6 percent alcohol.

Feasibility study. Detailed analysis of whether a planned enterprise can make a profit on a given site.

Fermentation. Action of a yeast upon a sugar in solution, which breaks down the sugar into carbon dioxide and alcohol.

Fetal alcohol syndrome. Pattern of birth defects in a child whose mother drank alcohol during pregnancy. Abbreviated FAS; also known as *fetal alcohol effects* (FAE).

FICA. Federal Insurance Contributions Act, or Social Security.

Filler cap. The rubber or vinyl top to a blender.

Financial statement. Statement showing the assets, debts, and net worth of an individual or enterprise.

Fine Champagne. On a Cognac label, means made from at least 50 percent of grapes from the Grande Champagne section of the Cognac district and the balance from the Petite Champagne section.

Finish. 1) Aging of wine in the bottle, bottle finish. 2) Aftertaste of a wine.

Firkin. The wooden cask used to store a certain type of beer. See *cask-conditioned beer.*

Fixed expenses. Expenses that remain the same regardless of sales volume.

Flag. Garnish of sliced orange or other citrus fruit on a pick, usually with a cherry.

Flaker. A machine that produces soft, snowlike ice used primarily to keep things cold, such as on a salad bar or in a wine bucket. Also called a *flake-ice machine.*

Flexhose. Flexible metal hose on which a *cobra gun* is mounted.

Flight. Several samples of different beers or wines purchased together, in lieu of a single glass or beer or wine, to encourage experimentation.

Float. To pour a liqueur or cream on the surface of a drink without mixing.

Flute glass. Champagne glass, footed or stemmed, having a narrow, slightly flaring bowl.

Folio. A folder for enclosing the guest check for presentation to the customer.

Food and Beverage Director. A management position in a restaurant, bar, or hotel that involves ordering products, menu development, and hiring staff members. Nicknamed "F-and-B."

Footed glass or footed ware. Glasses with a bowl that sits on a base or foot.

Foreseeability. The legal premise that a person can reasonably anticipate that a particular course of action (such as serving one more drink to an intoxicated person) could result in harm or injury, to that person or a third party.

Fortified wine. Wine to which brandy or other spirits have been added.

Frangelico (fran-JEL-ih-koh). The brand name for an Italian liqueur flavored with herbs and hazelnuts.

Free-pour. To pour liquor for a drink without using a measure, estimating the amounts.

Fringe benefits. Compensation other than wages, such as free meals or paid vacations.

Frizzante (free-ZAHN-tay). An Italian term for slightly sparkling wine, such as Lambrusco.

Front bar. That part of a bar structure used by customers.

Frozen drink dispenser. A machine that produces frozen, premixed drinks in large quantities.

Fruit juice drink. A highball made with liquor and fruit juice instead of a carbonated mixer. A Screwdriver or a Salty Dog are examples of fruit juice drinks.

Fruit squeezer. A hand-operated gadget used to squeeze half a lemon or lime for fresh juice for a single drink without pits or pulp getting into the drink.

Funnel. A cylinder with a sharply tapered end, for pouring from large containers into smaller ones.

Galliano (GAL-ee-AH-noh). Brand name of an Italian liqueur that is yellow in color and made with herbs.

Gamay Beaujolais (gam-AY BO-zha-lay). A light, fresh and fruity red wine made from gamay grapes. The first wines of each vintage are released as *Nouveau Beaujolais* in an annual French celebration that has been adopted in other countries.

Gay-Lussac system. The percentage of alcohol in a spirit, by volume; the label designation (instead of *proof*) commonly used in Europe.

Generic wine. An American wine of a general style or type whose name is borrowed from a famous European wine, as burgundy, Chablis. U.S. law refers to them as *semi-generic*.

Geneva, genever (jeh-NEE-vur). Dutch gin.

Gewurztraminer (gah-VURTZ-tra-mee-ner). A pinkish-colored grape from Germany and the Alsace region of France; used to make spicy, fruity white wines of the same name. Nicknamed "Gewurz (gah-VURTZ)," it is also used to make late harvest whites.

Giardia Lamblia. A common waterborne parasite that causes flulike symptoms when ingested.

Gin. Neutral spirit flavored with juniper berries.

Glass brush. A sturdy type of brush used specifically for cleaning glassware. There are glass brushes for use by hand, and motorized models.

Glass froster. A small, top-opening freezer to put glasses or beer mugs in for chilling before use.

Glasswasher. A small, mechanical dishwasher made for cleaning and drying glassware that fits in an underbar or backbar area.

Glycerin. An odorless, colorless liquid found in wine as a by-product of fermentation; you can see it on the inside of a wine glass after swirling it, clinging to the sides of the glass. These streams of glycerin are called *legs*.

Grain neutral spirits. Spirits distilled from a grain mash at 190 proof or above.

Grand Cru (gron KRU). The highest classification of Burgundy wines that means "great growth" in French. Beneath Grand Cru is *Premier Cru* (PREM-ee-yay KRU).

Grand Marnier (GRAN marn-YAY). A French brand name mixture of *Cognac* and *Curacao*.

Grande Champagne. On a Cognac label, made from grapes grown in the Grande Champagne section of the Cognac district.

Grappa (GROPP-ah). A highly alcoholic liqueur (most are from Italy) made by distilling the leftover skins, stems, and seeds from winemaking.

Grenache (gren-OSH). A red grape that makes a fairly sweet, light red wine, such as France's Tavel Rosé; also used in blending.

Grenadine. Sweet red syrup flavored with pomegranates.

Gross operating profit. Sales less product costs and controllable operating expenses.

Gross profit. Sales less product cost; also known as the *contribution margin*.

Gross profit method. A formula for determining the percentage of profitability of a particular drink. The same method can be reversed to help correctly price that drink.

Guest experience. A guest's total impression of your establishment, from their mood as they walk in, to how they are treated and whether they enjoy what they've ordered.

Handgun. Dispensing head for an automatic soda or liquor system.

Hangover. The chemical imbalance experienced after overindulging in alcohol; common symptoms include headache, queasiness, stomach cramps, dizziness, and dehydration.

Happy hour. Limited period of the day, often early evening, during which drink prices are reduced.

Head. 1) Collar of foam at the top of a glass of beer. 2) In distilling, the top section of a pot still, where alcohol vapors are collected.

Highball. A drink made by mixing a spirit and carbonated water (or other mixer) and serving it with ice in a highball glass. Gin and Tonic or Scotch and Soda are examples of highballs.

Hollands. Dutch gin.

Hops. Blossoms of the female hop vine, an essential flavor ingredient of beer.

Hourglass. Common term for an all-around beer serving glass of 10-16 ounces.

House brand. Another name for *well brands*; those liquors commonly poured when customers don't specify a specific brand. Also called *pouring brands*.

House wine. A specific wine a restaurant sells by the glass or carafe.

Hydrochlorofluorocarbons. Chemical refrigerants used in icemakers and other refrigeration systems. These are newer-style chemicals that don't do as much damage to the atmosphere as their predecessors, *chlorofluorocarbons*. Abbreviated HCFCs.

Hydrofluorocarbons. Chemical refrigerants used in icemakers and other refrigeration systems. Abbreviated HFCs. (See *hydrochlorofluorocarbons*.)

I-9 Form. Government form for establishing a person's proof of identity and eligibility to work in the United States.

Ice bin. The container in which ice is stored.

Ice crusher. A machine that crushes cubed ice into smaller pieces.

Ice machine. A machine that freezes water to make ice cubes. Also called an *icemaker*.

Ice scoop. A plastic implement for getting ice out of an ice bin; for bars, a 6- or 8-ounce capacity works best.

Ice tongs. Tongs used for handling one cube of ice at a time, so that hands don't touch the ice.

Image. Customer concept of the unique identity of an enterprise.

Income statement. Financial report showing kinds and amounts of revenue, kinds and amounts of expenses, and resulting profit or loss for a specific period.

Infusion. Flavoring a spirit by immersing fruit or spices in it and letting it marinate at room temperature.

Inlet chiller. A unit that can be added to an ice-making system that collects cold water as it drains away from the icemaker and recirculates it, chilling incoming water while saving energy.

Institutional advertising. Ads that build a distinctive and favorable image for a business, focusing on its attributes instead of denigrating the competition.

Inventory. 1) The amount of stock on hand at any given time. 2) The process of "taking inventory," by counting each bottle on hand.

Inventory turnover rate. The speed at which you use up existing inventory; a figure used to decide if you're keeping too much, or too little, in inventory.

Invoice. Seller's document that specifies what goods were delivered in an order.

Irish whiskey. Whiskey made in Ireland from several grains by a triple-distillation process.

Jamaican rum. Dark, full-flavored rum distilled from molasses, used in certain tropical drinks.

Jigger. Glass or metal measure for liquor, sized in ounces or fractions of ounces.

Job analysis. The process of creating a *job description* by listing individual tasks and the equipment and skills required to do them.

Job description. A written list of duties and responsibilities for a worker.

Job specifications. A list of knowledge, skills, or abilities a worker must have to perform specific jobs or tasks.

Jockey box. See *pouring station.*

Jug wine. Inexpensive wine available in bottles, or boxes, larger than liters.

Kabinett (KAB-ih-net). German quality wine made from grapes ripe enough to ferment without added sugar; or a German quality designation for top-quality unsugared wines, one of five categories.

Kahlua (kuh-LOO-uh). Brand name of a Mexican-made liqueur that contains sugar cane-based spirits flavored with coffee and vanilla.

Keg. Half-barrel of beer, containing 15½ gallons.

Kilning. The process of drying barley or other grain in a kiln.

Kirsch (keersh), **Kirschwasser** (KEER-SCH-voss-er). Wild-cherry brandy, usually from the Rhine River valley of Germany, colorless and unaged.

Krausening (KROY-zun-ing). In making beer, the addition of a small amount of newly fermenting wort to beer during the lagering stage, to induce additional fermentation and carbonation.

Lager (LAW-gur) **beer.** Beer made by bottom fermentation at cool temperatures.

Lagering. Storing beer to mellow or condition it.

Lambic beer. A well-known style of wheat beer, often used as the base for adding fruits.

Lambrusco (lam-BROOS-koe). Red grape grown primarily in Northern Italy and used to make a sweet, fruity red wine of the same name, with some natural "fizz" or carbonation.

Lay down. To store wine in the bottle; aging wine until it is ready to drink.

Layout. Arrangement of furniture, fixtures, traffic patterns in a room.

Lead time. The time between when you order items and their actual delivery to you.

Ledger. Book(s) of individual accounts for each category of assets, liabilities, and equity.

Lees. In winemaking, the stems, skins, pulp, and seeds left over after grapes have been pressed and their juices removed. In other countries, lees are known as *vinaccia* or *pomace.*

Legs. See *glycerin.*

Liabilities. The money owed by a person or business to others; debts.

License state. A state in which retail dealers may buy from any supplier licensed to sell to them rather than from state stores. Compare *control state.*

Light beer. Beer having less alcohol and fewer calories than regular or Pilsner-style beers.

Light whiskey. American whiskey distilled at 160 to 190 proof, light in flavor and body but not in alcohol.

Limited retail dealer. An organization, usually charitable or nonprofit, exempted from paying state liquor taxes for special events—church festivals, benefit concerts, and so on—as long as they pay for a permit for the event.

Liqueur. Brandy or other spirit sweetened and flavored with natural flavorers; also called cordial.

Local option. The state's right to allow a county, city, or voting precinct the right to choose whether to sell alcoholic beverages in that jurisdiction.

London dry gin. Gin in the English style, made with high-proof spirits redistilled with juniper berries or mixed with extracts.

Long. A slang term for a drink that totals more than five measures of fluid.

Maceration. Steeping or soaking herbs or other flavor sources in a spirit to make a liqueur.

Macrobrewery. A large national or international beer-making business, with multiple locations and an annual output of more than 500,000 barrels.

Maderized. Term used to describe a wine that smells overly sweet (like a Madeira or port) when it is not supposed to. Usually means the wine has been improperly stored and may be bad.

Malt. Grain, usually barley that is sprouted to about 3/4 inch, then dried.

Malt beverage. Term used by U.S. Standard of Identity in place of *beer* for a beverage made by fermenting malted barley with hops in water.

Malt liquor. Lager beer with a higher alcohol content than Pilsner, 5.5 to 6 percent or more.

Malt scotch. Unblended whiskey made in Scotland entirely from malted barley.

Marketing. Developing a product patrons want, and promoting it so they will buy it from you at a profit.

Market segment. Subgroup of the total customer market having similar needs, attitudes, lifestyles.

Marry. 1) To blend wines or spirits. 2) To add something to the liquor in a bottle.

Mash. In making beer or spirits, to cook malt, with or without other grains, to convert starches to sugars; the resulting product is a mash.

Mash tun. The container in which the *mash* is cooked.

Mega-tap bar. A beer bar that offers hundreds of different beer brands on tap.

Merlot. A red grape or the mellow, uncomplicated red wine made from it, grown primarily in Bordeaux, Italy, and California.

Mescal. A white, Tequila-like spirit made from agave plants that are not blue agave or not located in one of Mexico's specific Tequila-producing regions. Also spelled *mezcal*.

Metaxa (meh-TAX-ah). Greek brandy, slightly sweetened.

Metered pour. Liquor dispensing system that measures and controls drink size.

Meyers's Rum. Brand name of a heavy, dark rum from Jamaica.

Microbrewery. A small, independent brewery that produces fewer than 15,000 barrels of beer annually. Also called a *craft brewery*.

Micron rating. The measure of how effective a water filter is at removing dangerous parasites and particles; the lower the micron rating number, the greater the filtration capabilities.

Minimum wage. The lowest amount that can be paid by federal law to most hourly employees. (See *subminimum wage*.)

Mise en bouteille au chateau (MEEZ on bou-TAY oh shah-TOW). Chateau-bottled, estate-bottled. Also seen as *mise au chateau* or *mise du chateau* on French wine labels.

Mise en place (MEEZ ohn PLASS). A French phrase meaning "Everything in its place"; in bartending, mise en place means the bar is correctly set up, looks good, and is ready for business.

Mix can, mixing cup, mixing steel. Metal cup portion of a shaker or shake mixer.

Mixed case. See *broken case*.

Mixed pint. Blending one beer with another (or with another type of alcohol) in a single glass.

Mixing glass. Heavy glass container in which drink ingredients are stirred with ice.

Mixology. Art or skill of mixing drinks containing alcohol.

Mocktail. A cocktail, made without the liquor.

Monopole (MONN-oh-POLE). In France, a brand name or wine name that belongs exclusively to a particular wine producer or shipper.

Monopoly state. See *control state.*

Moonshine. The nickname for liquor brewed secretly in illegal stills.

Muddler. Wooden implement for crushing fruit and cube sugar and cracking ice.

Muller-Thurgau (MYOOL-ur TUR-gau). A popular white grape grown in Germany and used to make a variety of styles of table wine.

Multiple brands discount. See *assorted discount.*

Multiple facings. Three or four bottles of the same liquor brand, displayed together on the backbar.

Muscat. A popular grape—there are both red and white varieties—used to make sweet, fruity wines, such as Italy's sparkling Asti Spumante.

Must. Juice from crushed grapes before fermenting.

Napoleon Cognac. Cognac aged at least five and a half years. (No brandy actually dates from Napoleon's day.)

Nature (nah-TOUR). On a Champagne label, dry (little or no sugar); *brut.*

Nebbiolo (neb-ee-OH-loh). The red Italian grape used to make Barbaresco and Barolo wines.

Negociant (neh-GO-see-ahn). French wine merchant, shipper, sometimes blender and bottler as well.

Neoprohibitionism. Modern-day movement to outlaw sale of alcoholic beverages.

Neotemperance. Modern-day movement to control alcohol abuse through legislation while allowing use of alcohol in moderation.

Net profit. Sales less all expenses.

Neutral spirits. Spirits distilled at 190 proof or above; almost pure alcohol, with no distinct flavor or odor characteristics. Used in blending to make other types of spirits.

Nitrogenated beer. A smooth, creamy beer style made by forcing nitrogen out of beer just before pouring, using a special flow restrictor in the *tap.*

Noisette (nwah-SET). A French brand-named, hazelnut-flavored liqueur.

Nonalcoholic beer. A malt beverage with the flavor of beer containing less than 0.5 percent alcohol.

Nonexempt employee. An employee who must be paid the federal minimum wage for hourly work.

151° rum. Rum that is 151 proof, used especially for flaming and as a float on mixed drinks.

Off-premise sales. Selling alcoholic beverages to be consumed at a different place from where the sale takes place. A supermarket would be an off-premise retailer. Compare *on-premise sales.*

One-empty-for-one-full. System for controlling losses by requiring an empty liquor bottle to be turned in to the storeroom for each full bottle issued.

On-premise sales. Selling alcoholic beverages to be consumed at that site, on the same premises where the sale takes place. Bars and restaurants are examples of on-premise retailers. Compare *off-premise sales.*

On the rocks. Served over ice cubes.

Orange flower water. Flavoring extract used in mixed drinks.

Orgeat (oar-ZHAY). Sweet almond-flavored syrup.

Ounce method. A liquor measurement and control technique that compares total number of ounces of liquor used (based on physical inventory) with the number of ounces sold (based on drink sales).

Ouzo (OO-zoe). Greek anise-flavored liqueur.

Overhead expenses. Fixed expenses not related to sales volume or hours of operation.

Overproof. A spirit (usually rum) that has a higher than normal proof, or alcohol content.

Overrun. The percentage of air forced into the liquid drink mix by the pump in a frozen drink machine. The overrun increases the overall volume of the mix, making the drinks light and slushy.

Overtime. Time worked in excess of 40 hours in a workweek.

Oxidized. A wine that has gone bad because oxygen has gotten into the bottle, with a dull or rust color and vinegary or musty flavor.

Par stock. The amount of each liquor, beer, and wine to be kept at the bar at all times.

Participatory bar. A bar business that includes customers as part of the entertainment, like playing pool or singing karaoke.

Pasteurization. In making beer, heating briefly in the can or bottle to kill bacteria and remaining yeast cells.

Pear William. American translation of *Poire Williams*, a colorless, unaged brandy made in France or Switzerland that usually has a whole pear encased in its bottle.

Peat. Decomposed vegetation that is harvested and burned for drying barley in making scotch, giving the liquor a smoky favor.

Perceived value. Value of product/ service in customer's eyes, whatever its actual worth.

Percolation. In making liqueurs, adding herbs other flavors by pumping the spirit through them over and over.

Periodic order method. A system of reordering merchandise on certain dates every month.

Perpetual inventory. Ongoing daily record of purchase and issue for each inventory item, compiled from invoices and issue slips.

Perpetual order method. A system of reordering merchandise when existing inventory drops below a certain number.

Perquisites. Fringe benefits related to specific jobs or job levels. Abbreviated "perks."

Per se law. A law (in this case, a drunk driving law) that says police can use a single piece of evidence (such as a breath test or a driver's refusal to take the test) to determine guilt.

Peychaud's (PAY-shows). A brand of strong bitters from New Orleans.

pH. The abbreviation used to describe the amount of acidity in water, expressed on a scale of 1 to 14; an important component of the beer-brewing process.

Phenolic compounds. Natural antioxidants found in red grapes that give them their red coloring and the acidity known as *tannins*.

Physical inventory. Counting inventory in stock, bottle by bottle.

Pickup station. Section of front bar where serving personnel turn in and receive drink orders and return empty glasses.

Pilsner. Mild, dry style of beer, usually 3.2 to 4.5 percent alcohol by weight (4 to 5 percent by volume). Sometimes spelled "Pilsener."

Pinot Blanc (PEE-noh BLONK). A white grape used primarily for making sparkling wines, in California, Italy, and France.

Pisco (PEES-ko). Peruvian brandy.

Pitching. The ancient process of coating the insides of clay containers (amphora) with tar to keep them watertight.

P.O. number. Abbreviation of purchase order number.

Pony. Slang term for 1 ounce.

Portable bar. A rolling bar unit, popular in hotel use, that can be positioned at a meeting, banquet, or reception for beverage service.

Porter. Dark, bittersweet specialty ale, about 5 to 7.5 percent alcohol by volume.

POS. Abbreviation of point-of-sale cash register.

Positioning. Establishing an enterprise favorably in customers' eyes in relation to its competition.

POS system. A system in which a point-of-sale register functions as an input terminal for a central processing unit (*CPU*).

Postmix system. System of dispensing carbonated beverages from a handgun by mixing carbon dioxide, water, and concentrated syrup from bulk supplies.

Post-off discount. Dropping the price of an item, usually if it is bought in quantity, to increase sales.

Potential sales value. Sales dollars a given bottle of liquor would earn if all contents were sold; a control tool for measuring losses when compared with actual sales.

Pot still. Pot-shaped still in which spirits are distilled by using direct heat from below.

Pouilly Fuissé (POO-ee fweh-SAY). A well-known French white wine from the Macon region.

Pouilly Fumé (POO-ee foo-MAY). A well-known French white wine made from Sauvignon Blanc grapes from the Loire Valley; not to be confused with *Pouilly Fuisse*.

Pour. In a drink recipe, to add an ingredient as is, without straining it.

Pourer. Device that fits into the neck of a liquor bottle to reduce the flow of liquor to a controllable speed or to a preset amount.

Pouring costs. A comparison of what it costs to offer beer, wine, and mixed drinks. Each category is figured by dividing the cost of goods sold by the gross sales for a given time period, to arrive at a percentage.

Pouring station. The area of the bar where each bartender works, with his or her own supply of liquor, mixes, ice, glasses, and so on. In busy or large establishments, there are multiple pouring stations. Also called a *cocktail station, cocktail unit, beverage center,* or *jockey box*.

Pousse-café (POOS-kaf-FAY). After-dinner drink consisting of liqueurs floated in layers, one atop another, in multiple colors and densities.

Precheck. To ring up a drink order before the drinks are poured.

Premier Cru (PREM-ee-ay CROO). The secondary quality designation for Burgundy wines. See also *Grand Cru*.

Premium well. A well stocked with upscale, more expensive name-brand liquors. Also called a *super-well*.

Premix system. System of carbonating beverages from bulk supplies as they are dispensed from a handgun.

Preset. Key on a computerized cash register that is set to figure and record extensive information on a specific item sold.

Press release. Announcement about a newsworthy upcoming event sent to a newspaper editor. In today's world of electronic journalism, more accurately known as a "news release."

Pressware. Inexpensive, commonly used glassware made by being pressed into a mold.

Primary competitor. A bar that vies for the same market segment because it has a concept similar to yours. See also *secondary competitor.*

Prime costs. The largest and most necessary expenses to do business; in bars, beverage and payroll costs.

Prime ingredient cost. Cost of the major ingredient in a drink (its base liquor), used as a basis for pricing the drink.

Product/service mix. The combination of products and services offered to customers by a given enterprise.

Pro forma statement. A financial report that shows what a business should be making and spending, based on a set of assumptions about the industry, local economy, and other market factors.

Prohibition. The period of time in U.S. history (1920 to 1933) when manufacture, sale, and transportation of most alcoholic beverages was illegal.

Proof. A measure of the alcoholic content of a spirit, each degree of proof being .5 percent alcohol by volume.

Proof gallon. In the United States, 128 fluid ounces of 100-proof liquor.

Proprietary name. Brand name belonging to a wine producer or shipper.

Pub. Short for "public house," the British slang term for a casual, neighborhood bar.

Pull date. The date a product should no longer be sold, after which it begins to deteriorate; typically pull dates are marked on cans, bottles or other packaging.

Purchase order. Buyer's document specifying merchandise ordered.

Purchasing. The process of deciding what is to be served, what supplies are needed to produce these items, and procuring (ordering and buying) them.

Qualitatswein (KVAHL-ee-tots-VINE). German wine quality category; middle-quality wine from a designated region. Abbreviated QbA.

Qualitatswein mit Pradikat (KVAHL-ih-tots-VINE met PRAD-dih-kut). In Germany, a superior quality rating for wines having special attributes based on ripeness of the grape. Abbreviated QmP.

Racking. In winemaking, the process of draining the juice off of the lees (skins and stems) and into a fresh cask.

Rail. 1) Recessed portion of bar top closest to bartender, where drinks are poured. This part of the bar is also called the *glass rail, drip rail,* or *spill trough.* 2) On antique bars, the brass footrest at the bottom front of the bar.

Reasonable care. The legal term for what an ordinary, prudent person would do to prevent harm or injury.

Rectification. Alteration of a distilled spirit by blending, adding flavors or color, or redistilling to purify or concentrate.

Refrigeration circuit. The system of equipment that chills and circulates air and correctly humidifies refrigerated space.

Refrigeration cycle. The process of removing heat from a refrigerated space.

Regional brewery. By output, a brewing facility that produces from 15,000 to 500,000 barrels of beer annually.

Regional specialty brewery. A brewery whose main or largest-selling product is a microbrew or specialty beer.

Regular rate. The hourly rate for determining overtime pay.

Relish fork. Long, thin two-tined fork for spearing olives, cocktail onions, and so on.

Reminder advertising. A type of institutional advertising that uses a series of ads, placed over time, to "remind" customers about a business.

Reorder point. Point at which supplies must be ordered to maintain minimum stock.

Reposado Tequila. Mexican Tequila that has been aged 2 to 11 months by law. "Reposado" means "resting" in Spanish.

Requisition. 1) To request stock from storeroom to be released for use at the bar. 2) Form for requesting issue of stock and record of such issue. This form is sometimes called an *issue slip*.

Resveratol. An antioxidant that is found naturally in the skins of red grapes.

Retailer. Enterprise selling beverages to the consumer; this may be a package store selling by the bottle or a bar selling by the drink.

Riesling (REES-ling). A fruity white grape used to make many German white wines, including (when it is picked overripe) late harvest and dessert wines.

Rim (or Rimming). To coat the rim of a glass with salt, sugar, or celery salt.

Rimmer. Device for rimming a glass evenly.

Rioja (ree-OH-hah). Spanish wine district producing mostly red wines in the Bordeaux style; or the red wine that comes from this district.

ROI. Abbreviation for return on investment; share of profit expressed as a percentage of amount invested.

Rosé (roe-ZAY). Wine made from dark-skinned grapes whose juice is allowed to ferment with the skins only 12 to 24 hours, resulting in a light peach or pink color.

Rotate stock. Put new supplies behind existing stock so oldest will be used first.

Router. See *zester*.

Rum. Spirit distilled from molasses or sugarcane.

Rye. 1) Whiskey made with 51 percent or more of rye plus other grains, aged at least two years in charred new oak containers. 2) In the East, popular term for blended whiskey.

Sake (sah-kee). A Japanese wine made from rice.

Sambuca (sam-BOO-kah). The generic name for a clear liqueur with a licorice flavor.

Sangiovese (SAN-gee-oh-VAY-zee). The red Italian grape used to make Chianti.

Sanitize. To destroy bacteria with a chemical solution.

Sauvignon Blanc (SO-vin-yon-BLONK). The adaptable white grape used to make many French wines, including white Bordeaux, Graves, Sancerre, Sauternes, and Pouilly Fumé. In the United States. and elsewhere, used to make the white wines known as Fumé Blanc and Sauvignon Blanc.

Schnapps. In the United States, a sweet liqueur, usually fruit- or mint-flavored.

Scotch. Whiskey made in Scotland, typically a blend of malt whiskies and grain neutral spirits.

Screw-pull. A type of corkscrew that twists into a wine bottle cork and extracts it. Also called a *lever-pull*.

Seasonal ale. A specialty ale made for spring or fall release, with hints of spices.

Sec. French for "dry." On a Champagne label, though the word means "dry" the wine itself is slightly sweet.

Secondary competitor. A bar that is competition to yours simply because it is located in the same area.

Sekt (zekt). A German term for sparkling wine.

Semillon (SEM-ee-YON). A white grape that used to be used primarily for blending but is now bottled as its own varietal, a rich, fruity white wine.

Server. A waiter or waitress.

Service bar. Bar pouring drinks for table service only, often out of public view.

Service encounter. The server's first contact and subsequent "relationship" with a guest.

Service napkin. A clean, white towel or napkin carried by a wine server; used to wipe condensation off the bottle, and to wipe the lip of the bottle before pouring. Also referred to by the French word for "napkin," *serviette*.

Service scape. The environment in which the service encounter takes place; also called a *landscape*. Service scape includes décor, lighting, music and anything else that impacts the *guest experience*.

Shake. To mix a drink by shaking it in a shaker or using a shake mixer.

Shake mixer. Top-shaft mechanical drink mixer; also called a *spindle blender*.

Shaker. Combination of mixing glass and stainless-steel container fitting over glass, in which drink ingredients, plus ice, are hand-shaken.

Shelf life. Length of time a beverage can be stored without loss of quality.

Sherry butt. A wooden cask in which sherry is aged.

Shooter. Small, straight-up drink served in a shot glass, typically consumed all at once as in drinking a toast.

Short. A slang term for a drink that totals less than five measures of liquid.

Shot. Portion of liquor served straight in a shot glass with a glass of icewater or other liquid on the side.

Shot glass. The small glass in which a *shot* is served.

Silica. The fine sand used in making glass.

Simple syrup. Sweetener for mixed drinks made of 1 part sugar and 1 part water.

Singani. A Bolivian-made brandy from grapes, a type of *pisco*.

Single-cask. Unblended scotch from a single cask in a single distillery; usually the most exclusive (and expensive) type of scotch.

Single-malt scotch. An unblended malt scotch, from a single distillery.

Slivovitz (SHLIV-uh-vits). Plum brandy made in central Europe.

Snifter. Footed glass with large rounded bowl in which brandy is typically served.

Sommelier (SUM-el-yay or SOHM-ee-yay). Person who handles ordering and serving of wines in a restaurant, typically having considerable wine knowledge. Also called a *wine steward, cellarmaster, winemaster,* or *wine waiter.*

Sour. A family of mixed drinks made with lemon juice, served in a sour glass and garnished with cherry and orange. A Whiskey Sour and a Daquiri are examples.

Sour mash. In whiskey making, a distilling method in which a portion of fermented mash from a previous fermentation is added to fresh mash.

Sparkling wine. Wine containing carbon dioxide in solution which bubbles when poured.

Spatlese (SHPAYT-lay-zah). German wine from fully ripened grapes, late-picked after the official harvest date.

Special occupational tax. Annual federal tax each liquor retailer is required to pay for each place of business.

Speed bar. A very busy, high-volume bar that requires experienced bartenders who can work under pressure.

Speed rail, speed rack. Bottle-width rack for liquor bottles attached to the apron of underbar equipment.

Splash. Slang term for $1/4$ of an ounce.

Sports bar. A bar with a sports theme that attracts customers by showing a variety of sporting events, usually on big-screen television sets.

Spumante (spoo-MON-tee). An Italian sparkling wine.

Standard. Another term for the *tap* or faucet of a keg-beer dispensing system.

Standard cost percentage. Cost/sales ratio based on standardized drinks, providing a standard for measuring actual cost/sales ratio.

Standard drink size. Standard amount of prime ingredient used per drink.

Standard glass. Glass of specified size and shape for a given drink.

Standardized drink. Drink having standard ingredients in standard quantities, a standard portion size, a standard glass size, and standard preparation procedures. See *standard*.

Standardized recipe. Recipe listing specific ingredients and amounts that all bartenders in the business must follow. See *standardized drink*.

Standards of Identity. The U.S. government's definitions of the various classes of spirits, wines, and malt beverages, including how it is made, what it is made of, its alcohol content, and the type of container it is aged in.

Station. Area of a bar set up for a certain part of the drink service process—a pouring station, or a serving station.

Steam beer. Beer made by combining bottom fermentation with higher temperatures of ale fermentation. The name refers to the steam that is released when the barrels are tapped. (In Germany, known as *dampfbier*.)

Stemmed glass or stemware. Glass having a foot, stem, and bowl.

Still wine. Wine without bubbles; nonsparkling.

Stir. To mix a drink by stirring its ingredients with ice in a mixing glass.

Stout. Full-flavored dark ale, usually imported, having an alcohol content ranging from 4 percent by volume to as high as 10.5 percent.

Straight. A liquor served "as is," without mixing in other ingredients.

Straight up. A drink served in a chilled glass without ice.

Straight whiskey. Unblended whiskey containing 51 percent or more of a single grain type, usually corn or rye.

Strainer, bar strainer. Wire spring with a handle and ears that fit over the rim of a measuring glass or cup.

Stripper. Hand tool used for cutting twists of fruit peel.

Strip stamp. Federal stamp placed over the top of a sealed liquor bottle; now most often a tamper-evident closure of metal or plastic.

Structure. 1) The term for a combination of attributes of a wine: its sweetness, acidity, and the amounts of tannins and alcohol in the wine. 2) For a cocktail, the components that are mixed together to make it: base spirit, complementary ingredients to modify or enhance flavors and garnish.

Submicron filter. A water filter that removes most types of dangerous parasites from water systems.

Subminimum wage. A lower wage (lower than the federal *minimum wage*) allowed to be paid only to workers under age 20 and only during their first 90 days on the job. Sometimes referred to as a "training wage."

Suggestive selling. The technique of offering or recommending additional items to customers.

Sulfites. Chemicals found naturally in many wines; a small percentage of people have allergic reactions to them.

Sweet-sour mix. Bar substitute for sugar and lemon or lime in mixed drinks.

Swizzle stick. Stir stick used to mix a drink in the glass.

SWOT analysis. An appraisal of four common business factors: strengths, weaknesses, opportunities, and threats.

Syrah. An adaptable red grape that makes a tannic, full-bodied red wine, used often in blending. Called *Shiraz* in Australia.

Table tent. Card folded into a triangle that stands on a table top, to advertise specialty drinks or a short wine list.

Table wine. Grape wine—red, white, or rosé—having an alcohol content of up to 14 percent by volume.

Tafelwein (TOF-el-vine). Lowest-quality category of German wines; literally, table wine.

Tall drink. Drink served in a large glass—Collins or larger—in which there is a high proportion of mix and ice to spirit.

Tamper-evident closure. Closure on a liquor bottle, part of which remains on the bottle when the bottle is opened.

Tap. 1) Beer faucet. 2) To set up a keg of beer for bar use by connecting one line to a carbon dioxide tank and one line to the tap.

Tare weight. The weight of an empty container, which is used to calculate the weight or volume of its contents.

Tastevin (TAT-vin or TASS-tah-van). A wine-tasting cup that hangs from a cord or ribbon from the neck of a sommelier; a traditional part of his or her uniform.

Tax stamp. Proof given by the BATF to a retailer when he or she pays the *special occupational tax.*

Temperance. A word meaning moderation, self-restraint, and sobriety, and used to label people or groups who believe in very stringent legal limits on drinking, or forbidding it altogether; the "Temperance Movement" historically had a powerful voice in the United States.

Tempering. In the glassmaking process, the step in which cooled glass is reheated to high temperatures to "shock" it and make it more temperature-resistant. When the entire glass is tempered, it's called *fully tempered*; when only the rim receives this treatment it is called *rim tempered.*

Tempranillo (TEMP-rah-NEE-yo). The primary red wine grape grown in Spain and used to make Rioja wines.

Tennessee whiskey. A whiskey made in Tennessee, filtered through maple charcoal; similar to bourbon and often considered a bourbon by its devotees.

Tequila (teh-KEE-lah). Distinctively flavored spirit from Tequila district of Mexico, distilled at low proof from the fermented juices of the blue agave plant.

Tequila Puro. Mexican Tequila made from 100 percent agave sugars.

Tequillaria. (tah-KEE-lah-REE-ah) An upscale restaurant with a menu of Tequila-based foods and drinks.

Tequiza. A brand name beverage that combines beer, Tequila and lime.

Third-party liability. Legal concept holding that the seller of alcohol to an intoxicated person may be held liable for damages caused by that person to a third party.

Throw sediment. A wine that has been chilled, or chilled too quickly, causing solid crystals to precipitate on the cork or at the bottom of the bottle. The crystals (calcium carbonate) are harmless, but off-putting to some consumers.

Tia Maria. Brand name of a Jamaican-made, coffee-flavored liqueur.

Tied house. Financial or legal interest in a retail enterprise held by a brewer, distiller, or wholesaler—a violation of the law in most states.

Tip credit. Percent of minimum wage that an employer may subtract from wages of tipped employees.

Tip out. The practice of servers sharing tips with busboys, barbacks, and other service people who are not commonly tipped as part of the service team.

Tipped employee. An employee who receives at least $30 per month in tips.

Tip pooling. The practice of servers combining all or a percentage of their tips and dividing the total amount among the staff.

Top fermentation. Method of making malt beverages in which the yeasts act from the top of the fermenting beverage.

Total business pricing. The concept that your menu items must work together (some expensive to make but popular; others inexpensive and very profitable) to maximize your total profit.

t-PA antigen. A beneficial enzyme in ethanol (alcohol) that helps prevent blood clots.

Training wage. For new employees under 20, 85 percent of minimum wage, allowable for first 90 days on job.

Trebbiano (treb-ee-AH-no). An Italian white grape used to make Soave wines and some sparkling wines.

Triple sec. The generic name for *Curacao* liqueur that is clear (colorless).

Trockenbeerenauslese (TROCK-un-BAHR-un-OWSCH-lay-za). Rich, sweet German wine made from individually selected overripe grapes shriveled with Edelfaule ("noble rot").

Tulip glass. Stem glass with a tulip-shaped bowl, used for Champagne.

Tumbler. Flat-bottom glass without stem or foot.

Twist. Strip of citrus fruit peel used as a garnish.

Ugni blanc. A type of white grape used primarily in making Cognac.

Unallocable expenses. Expenses that are neither fixed nor directly tied to sales.

Underbar. Equipment installed behind and under the front bar.

Universal Product Code. A series of vertical bars of varying widths printed on the packaging of most consumer products, which can be read by a computerized scanner for inventory purposes. Abbreviated *UPC*.

Upsell. To suggest that a customer have his or her drink made with a more prestigious or expensive liquor than the *well brand*.

Variable expenses. Expenses that fluctuate, depending on sales volume.

Varietal (va-RY-ah-tul). A wine named for its predominant grape.

Vatted Malt Scotch. Scotch that is a blend of 100 percent malt whiskies from more than one distillery. Also called *Pure Malt Scotch*.

Vieille reserve. On a Cognac label, aged at least five and a half years. French for "old reserve."

Vini da tavola. Italian table wine produced outside the DOC framework but not necessarily of lesser quality. See *DOC*.

Vintage. On a wine label, the year the grapes were crushed and the winemaking process began for that bottle.

Vintage-dated. A wine that has its year printed on the label, indicating all the grapes used to make it were harvested in that year.

Vodka. Neutral spirit treated to remove distinctive character, aroma, and taste.

VS. On a Cognac label, stands for Very Superior, aged at least one and a half years.

VSOP. On a Cognac label, stands for Very Superior Old Pale, aged at least four and a half years.

Waiter's corkscrew. A combination *worm* (the screw itself), small knife, and lever for extracting a cork from a wine bottle at tableside. It folds up, much like a pocketknife. Also called a *waiter's friend*.

Weighted average. Method of figuring potential sales value of a bottle of liquor.

Well. 1) The supply of most-used liquors at a pouring station. 2) The area of the underbar in which these liquors are stored together; the *bottle well*.

Well brand. Brand of liquor poured when customer does not specify a brand.

Wet area. Area (county, voting precinct, etc.) in which the sale of alcoholic beverages is legal.

Wheat beer. A top-fermented beer made with wheat as well as barley malt; fruity in flavor and aroma. Also known as *white beer*.

Wheel. A round slice of lemon, lime, or orange used as a garnish.

Whiskey. Spirit distilled from grain. Alternate spelling: whisky.

White goods. An industry nickname for the colorless spirits: for example, vodka, gin, rum, Tequila.

Wholesaler's basic permit. Federal permit that allows a liquor or wine wholesaler to sell to retailers.

Wine. Fermented juices of grapes and occasionally of other fruits.

Wine bar. A bar with a theme of wine appreciation and featuring a wine list that encourages sampling and learning about different types of wines.

Wine basket. Wicker basket for carrying a bottle of wine horizontally from cellar to table to avoid agitation.

Wine cabinet. A storage unit for wines in which partially full bottles are filled with inert gas to keep the remaining wine fresh. A popular brand name is Cruvinet.

Wine chiller. A bucket or container into which ice and water is placed to surround a wine bottle and chill it quickly.

Wine gallon. In the United States, 128 fluid ounces of alcoholic beverage of unspecified alcoholic content.

Wine spritzer. A drink made by combining wine and sparkling water over ice.

Wine steward. Person who handles customers' wine orders and service; a *sommelier*.

Wing corkscrew. A rather bulky style of corkscrew with handles (known as "wings") that rise as the screw or *worm* is twisted into the cork; the cork is extracted when the wings are pushed downward.

Word of mouth. Publicity generated by customer recommendations, for example, of a place of business.

Workweek. Fixed and regularly recurring period of 168 hours—7 consecutive 24-hour periods.

Worm. 1) In a still, a coil in which the hot alcoholic vapors are cooled and condensed. 2) Spiral part of a corkscrew, also called the *screw* or *augur*.

Wort. In making beer and whiskey, the liquid in which starches have been converted to sugar.

Yeast. Ingredient responsible for fermentation in making alcoholic beverages by breaking down sugar into alcohol and carbon dioxide.

Zest. Thin outer skin of a lemon or orange containing flavorful oils.

Zester. Tool that cuts a narrow strip of zest; also called a *router*.

Zinfandel (ZIN-fun-DELL). An adaptable red grape that is used to make light, fruity *White Zinfandel* wines and the dark, full-flavored regular Zinfandels. Grown primarily in California.

Appendix A

RESPONSIBLE BEVERAGE ALCOHOL SERVICE GENERAL AUDIT

This general audit includes questions on issues that are relevant to many beverage alcohol-serving establishments.

As you inspect your establishment(s), mark the following questions **yes** or **no.** Any **no** answer should be carefully evaluated. If necessary, correct your procedures.

Blank lines follow each section for you to take notes or customize the audit form.

Make copies of this form to use at multiple locations.

Name of Operation: _____

Location of Operation: _____

General Manager: _____

Person Conducting Inspection: _____

Date of Inspection: _____

Date of Last Inspection: _____

Establishing a Responsible Beverage Alcohol Service Program

Do you regularly review past records of beverage
alcohol-related incidents? ❏ yes ❏ no

Are written policies in place and regularly evaluated
and updated? ❏ yes ❏ no

Does your attorney review your policies for legal
compliance?   ❏ yes   ❏ no

Does your insurance agent review your policies for
adequate protection from legal liabilities and
business interruptions?   ❏ yes   ❏ no

Have you developed good working relationships with:

- Local hospitality associations?   ❏ yes   ❏ no
- Citizen groups concerned with beverage
  alcohol service?   ❏ yes   ❏ no
- Government agencies regulating beverage
  alcohol service?   ❏ yes   ❏ no
- Law enforcement agencies?   ❏ yes   ❏ no

Comments: _____
_____
_____
_____

Complying with the Law

Do you only purchase beverage alcohol containing the
amount of alcohol allowed by the law?   ❏ yes   ❏ no

Do you obtain proof from your employees that they are
of legal age to serve beverage alcohol?   ❏ yes   ❏ no

Are guests lawfully allowed to transport beverage alcohol
on and off your premises?   ❏ yes   ❏ no

Does the amount and type of food you serve comply
with your liquor license?   ❏ yes   ❏ no

Do you avoid mentioning the alcohol content of
beverages in your advertising?   ❏ yes   ❏ no

Do you legally post all signs concerning serving
beverage alcohol to minors and pregnant women
(the effects of alcohol on the fetus)?   ❏ yes   ❏ no

Do you observe local laws concerning the days and
hours of operation?   ❏ yes   ❏ no

Comments: _____
_____
_____
_____

Training Employees

Are your hiring policies and procedures designed to identify potential employees who have the experience, skills, and attitudes necessary to responsibly serve beverage alcohol? ❐ yes ❐ no

Do you check the applicant's references and work history? ❐ yes ❐ no

Do new managers, bartenders, servers, and doorstaff receive training in responsible beverage alcohol service? ❐ yes ❐ no

Are seasonal, special event, and temporary servers trained in responsible beverage alcohol service? ❐ yes ❐ no

Are managers and servers trained in:

- The criminal and civil laws governing your establishment's service of beverage alcohol? ❐ yes ❐ no
- Your state's BAC defining intoxication? ❐ yes ❐ no
- How alcohol affects the body? ❐ yes ❐ no
- The proof and percentage of alcohol in the liquor you serve? ❐ yes ❐ no
- The amount of alcohol in the drinks your establishment serves? ❐ yes ❐ no
- Alcohol equivalents of different drinks? ❐ yes ❐ no
- The signs of intoxication? ❐ yes ❐ no
- Handling intoxicated individuals? ❐ yes ❐ no
- Recognizing false IDs? ❐ yes ❐ no
- Handling suspected illegal drug activity? ❐ yes ❐ no

Are employees introduced to your policies, required to read them, and then required to sign a document stating that they understand and agree to follow the policies? ❐ yes ❐ no

Are employees required to pass a test to prove their knowledge of establishment procedures? ❐ yes ❐ no

Are employees paid for training time? ❐ yes ❐ no

Are servers and managers evaluated on total sales rather than on beverage alcohol sales alone? ❐ yes ❐ no

Are employees reprimanded or dismissed for policy infractions? ❐ yes ❐ no

Are managers trained in the following areas:

- Using staff meetings to keep employees alert to beverage alcohol service policies and to review past beverage alcohol-related incidents? ❐ yes ❐ no
- Using positive reinforcement to reward and encourage employee efforts? ❐ yes ❐ no

■ Tactfully using disciplinary measures?   ❐ yes   ❐ no

■ Supporting staff decisions, such as not overriding
a server's decision to discontinue beverage
alcohol service?   ❐ yes   ❐ no

Are training programs continuously updated to respond
to changes in the laws, your employees, your clientele,
your neighborhood, and your menu?   ❐ yes   ❐ no

Comments: _____

_____

_____

_____

Standardizing Alcohol Beverages and Service

Have you standardized the recipe and alcohol content
of every drink your establishment serves?   ❐ yes   ❐ no

Do you use standardized pouring devices or measuring
jiggers to be sure the correct amount of beverage
alcohol is served?   ❐ yes   ❐ no

Are beverage alcohol and non-alcohol beverages consistently
served in different and easy-to-recognize glasses?   ❐ yes   ❐ no

Do you avoid serving double- and triple-strength
alcohol beverages?   ❐ yes   ❐ no

Do you avoid selling mixed drinks by the pitcher?   ❐ yes   ❐ no

Do you wait until a guest has completely finished
one alcohol beverage before serving him or her another?   ❐ yes   ❐ no

Do you make sure that guests receiving complimentary
beverage alcohol drinks want them?   ❐ yes   ❐ no

Do you keep track of the beverage alcohol a guest
has consumed?   ❐ yes   ❐ no

Do you slow or stop beverage alcohol service to keep
guests from becoming intoxicated?   ❐ yes   ❐ no

Do you promote the sale of high-protein food?   ❐ yes   ❐ no

Do you provide complimentary, non-salty table snacks?   ❐ yes   ❐ no

Do you stock, competitively price, and promote
non-alcohol beverages?   ❐ yes   ❐ no

Do you upsell to more expensive, call and premium
brands of beer, wine, and spirits?   ❐ yes   ❐ no

Do you use table tents, menus, napkins, and coasters to inform guests that servers are trained in responsible beverage alcohol service?　　❐ yes　❐ no

Comments: _____
_____
_____
_____

Monitoring the Door

To prevent overcrowding, do you limit the number of guests admitted into your establishment?　　❐ yes　❐ no

Is there adequate lighting for checking age identification?　　❐ yes　❐ no

Do you provide enough doorstaff to handle large crowds?　　❐ yes　❐ no

Are guests' IDs checked every time they enter the establishment?　　❐ yes　❐ no

Is the manager always contacted when the police arrive?　　❐ yes　❐ no

Are the police allowed free access into your establishment?　　❐ yes　❐ no

Comments: _____
_____
_____
_____

Establishing Last Call Procedures

Do you stop serving drinks with two or more kinds of beverage alcohol at least an hour before last call?　　❐ yes　❐ no

Is last call scheduled well before closing? (An hour before closing is recommended.)　　❐ yes　❐ no

Is last call clearly announced to all guests?　　❐ yes　❐ no

Do you offer high-protein food and reduced-priced non-alcohol beverages at last call?　　❐ yes　❐ no

Do you make sure that all guests leave at closing?　　❐ yes　❐ no

Comments: _____
_____
_____
_____

Serving Minors

Do you know what IDs are valid in your area?	❏ yes ❏ no
Do you know the correct procedures for checking IDs?	❏ yes ❏ no
Do you check IDs for everyone who appears younger than 30?	❏ yes ❏ no
Do you require a manager be notified when a minor attempts to use a false ID?	❏ yes ❏ no
Do you contact the police when a minor attempts to use a false ID?	❏ yes ❏ no
If lawful, do you confiscate false IDs?	❏ yes ❏ no
Do you restrict minors from entering areas of your establishment where beverage alcohol is served?	❏ yes ❏ no
If lawful, do you prohibit the sale of beverage alcohol to adults who give beverage alcohol to minors?	❏ yes ❏ no

Comments: _____

_____

_____

_____

Serving Intoxicated Individuals

Are your procedures set up to prevent guests from becoming intoxicated?	❏ yes ❏ no
Do you slow or stop beverage alcohol service if and when guests show signs of intoxication or consume considerable amounts of beverage alcohol?	❏ yes ❏ no
Are intoxicated guests handled in a discreet and tactful manner?	❏ yes ❏ no
Is reasonable care exercised with guests who arrive intoxicated, or guests who become intoxicated and attempt to drive away from your premises?	❏ yes ❏ no
Do you warn the intoxicated guest that the police will be called if he or she drives away?	❏ yes ❏ no
Do you write down a physical description of the guest's car, including its license plate number, make, and model, and a physical description of the driver?	❏ yes ❏ no
Do you have an arrangement with a reliable cab company to provide rides for intoxicated guests?	❏ yes ❏ no
Do you inform guests about your cab arrangements and prominently post the cab company's telephone number?	❏ yes ❏ no

Do you support a designated driver program by:

- Identifying a group's designated driver with an arm band, button, or other form of identification? ❐ yes ❐ no
- Ensuring that the designated driver is not served beverage alcohol? ❐ yes ❐ no
- Recording the designated driver's name in a log? ❐ yes ❐ no
- Keeping each shift of servers informed of the designated driver's identity? ❐ yes ❐ no
- Serving free or low-priced non-alcohol beverages to the designated driver? ❐ yes ❐ no
- Not allowing other members of the group to become intoxicated? ❐ yes ❐ no

Comments: _____
_____
_____
_____

Assessing Equipment and Facilities

Are external areas, such as driveways, parking lots, walkways, alleys, and doorways kept clean and well-lit? ❐ yes ❐ no

Are first-aid kits stocked and easily accessible? ❐ yes ❐ no

Are there areas for discreetly dealing with intoxicated guests? ❐ yes ❐ no

Are tables arranged so bartenders and servers can easily monitor their areas? ❐ yes ❐ no

Have you met the health and fire regulations in your area that apply to establishments that serve beverage alcohol? ❐ yes ❐ no

Comments: _____
_____
_____
_____

Managing a Crisis

Is a manager always on duty during hours when beverage alcohol is served? ❐ yes ❐ no

Can a manager always be contacted? ❐ yes ❐ no

Are managers contacted and incident reports filled out when the following situations occur:

- A minor attempts to use a false ID? ❐ yes ❐ no

■ An intoxicated individual attempts to enter the
establishment and then attempts to drive away?   ❏ yes   ❏ no

■ A guest shows signs of intoxication or has consumed
a considerable amount of beverage alcohol?   ❏ yes   ❏ no

■ Servers need to slow or stop beverage alcohol service?   ❏ yes   ❏ no

■ An intoxicated guest is kept from driving away
from the establishment?   ❏ yes   ❏ no

■ Regulatory or law enforcement agents arrive to
investigate a beverage alcohol-related incident?   ❏ yes   ❏ no

■ A guest has a beverage alcohol-related accident
or becomes ill?   ❏ yes   ❏ no

Are incident reports kept on file for at least as long
as the law requires?   ❏ yes   ❏ no

Does your crisis management plan for beverage alcohol-
related incidents include procedures for the following:

■ Contacting a manager?   ❏ yes   ❏ no

■ Dealing with guests while an incident is being
resolved?   ❏ yes   ❏ no

■ Contacting police, emergency services, ambulances,
and hospitals?   ❏ yes   ❏ no

■ Gathering information about an incident?   ❏ yes   ❏ no

■ Contacting your establishment's attorney and
insurance agent?   ❏ yes   ❏ no

■ Assigning a spokesperson to handle requests for
information from the media and regulatory and
law enforcement agencies?   ❏ yes   ❏ no

■ Safeguarding guests and employees by cleaning up
spills and breakage caused by an incident?   ❏ yes   ❏ no

■ Assessing damages to property, employees' wages,
and the flow of business?   ❏ yes   ❏ no

■ Repairing damaged facilities?   ❏ yes   ❏ no

■ Adapting marketing efforts to offset bad publicity?   ❏ yes   ❏ no

■ Returning to normal working operations?   ❏ yes   ❏ no

■ Identifying the rewarding employees who
reacted quickly?   ❏ yes   ❏ no

■ Implementing policy changes and training to
prevent the incident from reoccurring?   ❏ yes   ❏ no

Comments: _____

_____

_____

_____

Exhibit 1
Sample Proof of Training
and Policy Acknowledgment Form

PROOF OF TRAINING

_____ is committed to the safety and well-being of
(Name of establishment)
its guests and employees. To provide responsible beverage alcohol service, management has established an ongoing training program for all
employees.

I verify that _____ has been trained in responsible
(Name of employee)
beverage alcohol service in the following areas:

     How Alcohol Affects the Body
     The Law and Your Responsibility
     Techniques for Responsible Beverage Alcohol Service
     Service in Difficult Situations

_____
Name of Manager/Supervisor/Trainer   Date

POLICY ACKNOWLEDGMENT FORM

I, the undersigned, have read and understand the responsible beverage
alcohol service policies set forth by _____ .
(Name of your establishment)
I agree to abide by these policies.

I realize that I may be terminated if I violate these policies and/or participate in illegal activities on the premises at any time and/or during
working hours at any other location where I represent this company.

_____
Employee   Date

_____
Witnessed by Manager/Supervisor/Trainer   Date

Appendix B

COCKTAIL LOUNGE DESIGN QUESTIONNAIRE

A well-designed cocktail lounge requires a good understanding between the designer and the client. Please identify your operation by completing this questionnaire.

1.0 GENERAL

1.1 Theme/Concept

_____ Restaurant and Cocktail Lounge

_____ Cocktail Lounge only

_____ Describe décor and/or theme: _____

_____

1.2 Space

_____ Size of building lot = _____

_____ Square footage of building = _____

_____ Space allocations

Dining Room(s)	= ____ %	Cocktail Lounge	= ____ %
Kitchen	= ____ %	Common Area(s)	= ____ %
Office	= ____ %	Restrooms	= ____ %
General Storage	= ____ %	Bar Storage	= ____ %
Other: _____	= ____ %	Other: _____	= ____ %

_____ Is a floor plan attached?

     _____ Yes _____ No

     _____ To be provided on _____

1.3 Sales Analysis

_____ Projected gross sales:
Food = ____ %   Beverage = ____ %   Bar Snacks = ____ %

_____ Projected beverage sales:
Liquor = ____ %   Beer = ____ %   Wine = ____ %
Non-Alcoholic = ____ %

_____ Projected liquor sales:
Highballs and traditional cocktails = ____ %
Specialty drinks = ____ %

_____ Projected beer sales:
Bottles/cans = ____ %   Draft = ____ %

_____ Projected wine sales:
Bottle = ____ %   Glass = ____ %   Carafe = ____ %

_____ Projected non-alcoholic sales:
Soft drinks = ____ % Bottled water = ____ % Other = ____ %

1.4 Peak Volume

_____ Please complete for the peak *hour:*

Number Customers		Drinks Consumed Per Hour		Production Requirements
_____	×	1	=	_____
_____	×	2	=	_____
_____	×	3	=	_____
_____	×	4	=	_____
_____	×	____	=	_____
			TOTAL	══════════════
				Drinks Per Hour

1.5 Budget

_____ What is your budget for:

	$	%
Total Project	$_____	_____%
General Construction	_____	_____
Kitchen Equipment	_____	_____
Cocktail Lounge Equipment	_____	_____

1.6 Planning

_____ This is a single use design? _____

_____ This is a prototype for more projects? _____

_____ Project number of units for:
next 12 months = _____ next two to five years = _____

2.0 OPERATIONS

2.1 *Products Served:*

Category	Total Number of Brands	Total Number of Bottles in "Par Stock"	Number of Brands Bottle Poured	Machine Poured
Liquors	_____	_____	_____	_____
Liqueurs, Cordials, Aperitifs	_____	_____	_____	_____
Bottle & can beer— returnable	_____	cases = _____	_____	_____
Bottle & can beer— nonreturnable	_____	cases = _____	_____	_____
Draft Beer	_____	kegs = _____	_____	_____
Bottle Wine— Room temperature	_____	_____	_____	_____
Bulk Wine— Refrigerated	_____	Gal. = _____	_____	_____
Perishables, juices	_____	_____	_____	_____
Soft drinks	_____	_____	_____	_____
Bottled water— Room temperature	_____	_____	_____	_____
Bottled water— Refrigerated	_____	_____	_____	_____
Coffee	_____	Check if ___ warmer, or ___ maker		
Hot water	_____			
Iced tea	_____	Check if ___ dispenser		
Cappuccino, Expresso	_____	Check if ___ machine		
Other _____	_____	_____	_____	_____

2.2 **Specialty Drinks**

_____ Will specialty drinks require _____ soft ice cream or _____ hard ice cream?

_____ Will frozen cocktails be served?

_____ Will specialty drinks require any unusual condiment, garnish, or preparation tool?
If so, please list: _____
_____

_____ Attach your drink menu and recipes.

2.3 **Condiments**

_____ Please list your condiments: _____

_____   _____   _____

_____   _____   _____

_____   _____   _____

2.4 *Glassware*

Please list your glassware:

Type	Manufacturer	(1) Model No.	Capacity	(2) Model No.	Capacity
Shot Glass	_____	_____	_____	_____	_____
Old Fashion/Rocks	_____	_____	_____	_____	_____
Highball	_____	_____	_____	_____	_____
Chimney/Hurricane	_____	_____	_____	_____	_____
Cordial	_____	_____	_____	_____	_____
Snifter	_____	_____	_____	_____	_____
Cocktail	_____	_____	_____	_____	_____
Champagne	_____	_____	_____	_____	_____
Sour	_____	_____	_____	_____	_____
Port	_____	_____	_____	_____	_____
Wine	_____	_____	_____	_____	_____
Wine Carafe	_____	_____	_____	_____	_____
Beer	_____	_____	_____	_____	_____
Beer Pitcher	_____	_____	_____	_____	_____
Specialty #1	_____	_____	_____	_____	_____
Specialty #2	_____	_____	_____	_____	_____

2.5 *Ice*

_____ Please describe your type of ice:
Manufacturer _____ Cube size _____
_____ Is shaved or crushed ice required? _____
_____ Projected ice capacity required: _____ pounds

2.6 *Cash Control*

_____ Cash management: (check all that apply)
_____ by bartender behind bar
_____ by cashier in separate cashier station
_____ cocktail servers will carry "banks"
_____ hard checks for all sales
_____ tabs are allowed
_____ pre-check registers for cocktail servers
_____ other: _____
_____ List the name of your cash register: _____
_____ Number of cash drawers: _____
_____ stacked or _____ side-by-side

2.7 *Personnel*

_____ Projected number of cocktail stations: _____
_____ Projected number of bartender shifts: _____
_____ Projected number of cocktail server shifts: _____

2.8 Miscellaneous

_____ Do you plan off-sale beer, wine, or liquor? _____

_____ Do you serve bar snacks? _____

Please identify: _____

_____ Are dinner menus kept behind the bar? _____

_____ Do you promote drinks or food with table tents?

3.0 FACILITY

3.1 List name of liquid dispensing equipment: _____

Number of portion sizes = _____   Number of brands = _____

Number of stations = _____

3.2 Open liquor stock

_____ Is a lighted bottle display required? _____

_____ Do you use a "We proudly pour" sign or bottle display?

If so, what are the dimensions: _____

_____ Should bottle displays have night security covers
and locks? _____

_____ If not, how will you secure open stock? _____

_____

3.3 Bottle and Can Beer

_____ Type of refrigeration:

_____ Back bar with rear feed walk-in

_____ Back bar with __ remote or __ self-contained compressor

_____ Top open or __ door open cooler under the bar

_____ List manufacturer: _____

_____ Does refrigeration require:

_____ Lights? _____

_____ Locks? _____

_____ Is back-up supply under refrigeration? _____

_____ Are hanging bottle openers required? _____

3.4 Draft Beer

_____ Where are kegs stored?:

_____ In bar refrigeration

_____ Walk-in behind bar

_____ Remote location

_____ List name of draft beer equipment: _____

Model number: _____

3.5 *List name of wine dispensing equipment:* _____

_____ flexhose, or _____ tower

3.6 *Type of soft drink equipment:*

_____ Pre-mix

_____ Post-mix

_____ Name of manufacturer: _____

Model Number: _____

_____ Is the soda water chilled by _____ cold plate, or _____
mechanical system?

_____ Is the dispenser a _____ flexhose, or _____ tower?

_____ Are tanks stored _____ in bar, or _____ remote?

3.7 *Other dispensers or beverage machines:*

_____ List types and/or names of other dispensers/machines:

_____ Juice: _____

_____ Coffee: _____

_____ Iced tea: _____

_____ Cappuccino, Expresso: _____

_____ Other: _____

3.8 *Specialty Drink Equipment*

_____ Name of blenders: #1 _____ #2 _____

Model Numbers: #1 _____ #2 _____

_____ Name of soft service machine or ice cream freezer: _____

Model Number: _____ Capacity: _____

_____ Other specialty drink equipment: _____

_____

3.9 *Condiments*

_____ Where are condiments stored over night? _____

_____ Type of condiment containers:

_____ Tray with removable inserts and hinged lid—size = ____

_____ Underbar drawer type—size = _____

_____ Pans built into ice bin sneeze guard—
size and number of pans = _____

3.10 *Type of mug chiller or froster*

_____ Manufacturer: _____

_____ Model Number: _____

3.11 *Glassware*

_____ Do you require overhead hangers for stemware? _____

_____ Estimated number of glasses in the cocktail lounge
when fully stocked: _____

3.12 Glass Washing

_____ Glass washing will be performed: (please check)
  _____ With the kitchen dishwasher
  _____ By hand by the bartender with a three- or four-compartment sink
  _____ By an undercounter, rack-type glasswasher
  _____ By an automatic, conveyor glasswasher
_____ The glasswasher will be loaded and unloaded by: (please check)
  _____ The bartender only
  _____ The bartender and/or the cocktail server
  _____ Other: _____

3.13 Where is the ice maker located?

_____ In the cocktail lounge area
_____ In the kitchen
_____ In a separate storage room
_____ Other: _____
_____ How much ice storage is required for the cocktail lounge?
  _____ pounds

3.14 Cash Register

_____ The dimensions of the cash register = _____
_____ The dimensions of the cash drawer = _____

3.15 Is a drawer or cabinet required for dry storage? _____

_____ Locked
_____ Unlocked

3.16 The following instruments are behind the bar: (Please check all that apply)

_____ Telephone
_____ Light switches and dimmers
_____ Intercom system
_____ Background music controls
_____ Stereo system
_____ Television set
_____ Other: _____

3.17 Seating

_____ Number of seats at bar _____   Diameter of Cocktail table _____
_____ Number of seats in lounge _____   Height of Cocktail table _____
_____ Square feet per lounge seat _____

3.18 *Construction*

_____ Bar Height:
    _____ Stool seating (42")
    _____ Stand Up (44")
    _____ Sit Down (30")

_____ Type of bar stool required: (Please check)
    _____ With back
    _____ Without back
    _____ With swivel
    _____ Without swivel

_____ Are standup tables required? _____

_____ Type of foot rest required: (Please check)
    _____ Finished step
    _____ Unfinished step
    _____ Brass foot rail

_____ Type of arm rest required: (Please check all that apply)
    _____ Flush to bar top
    _____ Extended from bar top
    _____ Padded
    _____ Laminated
    _____ Wooden rail
    _____ Other: _____

3.19 *Miscellaneous*

_____ Is underbar lighting required? _____

_____ Describe the floor coverings: _____
_____

_____ Is there a facility to wash ashtrays behind the bar? _____

_____ Where is the timeclock located? _____

_____ Is there a remote service bar? _____

_____ What is the most direct, largest opening to get equipment into the building? _____
_____
_____

4.0 MISCELLANEOUS

4.1 Are National Sanitation Foundation International (NSFI) and Underwriter's Laboratories (UL) regulations strictly enforced in the area? _____

4.2 Is a storage area and/or dressing room required for entertainers? _____

4.3 Are sealed cold plates required? _____

4.4 List any other unusual regulations which may affect the cocktail lounge design: _____

_____

5.0 PERSONAL

This form was completed by:

_____
Name

_____
Title

_____
Company Name

_____
Street Address

_____
City, State, Zip Code

_____
Phone Number

_____
Date

Index